This book presents the techni[...] theory in a manner operation[...] ness problems. In contrast to most texts, the authors emphasize the processes of theorizing and model building as tools of economic reasoning. The early chapters provide the organizational structure for the entire book on decision-making for the firm. These and others build in new flexibility in economic analysis. The authors view the firm in a "linear programming" context rather than the traditional marginal context. They show how governments impose limitations on the firm, and how firms can reconcile conflicting goals. Different parts of economic reasoning are presented as parts of a few broad models, and thus economic theory is more thoroughly integrated than has been done in the past.

Irvin M. Grossack is presently a professor at Indiana University where he teaches business economics and public policy in the Graduate School of Business. He is co-editor of *Regional Perspective of Industrial and Urban Growth,* and author of articles appearing in the *Journal of Political Economy* and the *Review of Economics and Statistics.* Formerly he was program economist for USAID in New Delhi.

David D. Martin, professor of business economics and public policy in the Graduate School of Business, Indiana University, is currently serving as Chief Economist of the Senate Subcommittee on Antitrust and Monopoly. He is author of *Mergers and the Clayton Act,* and of numerous articles in such publications as the *American Economic Review* and the *Southern Economic Journal.*

Managerial Economics

LITTLE, BROWN SERIES IN ECONOMICS

Richard E. Caves, CONSULTING EDITOR

Managerial Economics
Microtheory and the Firm's Decisions

IRVIN MILLMAN GROSSACK

Indiana University

DAVID DALE MARTIN

*Indiana University and Chief Economist
United States Senate Subcommittee
on Antitrust and Monopoly*

Little, Brown and Company

Boston

This book is dedicated to

G_w, G_s, G_{d1}, G_{d2}, M_w, M_{d1}, M_s, M_{d2},

less abstractly known as
Maryann, Marshall, Victoria, and Mara Grossack
Nancy, Carol, David, and Melinda Martin

Preface

If our own experience and the experience of others whom we know
is a guide, the teaching of managerial economics has presented a
dilemma to many economists engaged in that activity. On the one
hand, they want their students to obtain a solid grounding in microeconomic theory. On the other hand, they would like their version of
microeconomic theory to be less abstract and more applied and realistic than the traditional approaches to this subject, to focus upon the
firm rather than the market as the central economic institution, to be
flexible enough to deal with a wide variety of business and economic
problems, and to be reasonably compatible with what is taught in
other business fields. Our aim in this book is to restructure microeconomic theory so that all these objectives can be obtained.

The key to the approach we have chosen is to build the theory of the
firm on a programming (both linear and non-linear) foundation, in
contrast to the more traditional approach of focusing on the cost and
revenue functions, and their marginal derivatives, as the basis for
the firm's decisions. Linear and non-linear programming are, of
course, no longer novel. However, what has not been fully recognized,
we believe, is that programming is much more than a specialized
technique with which to solve optimization problems. Rather, programming can be a new type of mathematics that – in contrast to the
calculus that has provided the foundation for more traditional microeconomic theory – enables a much more flexible and realistic analysis
of the firm and its decision-making problems. We still present the
traditional microeconomics, for which we maintain a good deal of
respect. But instead of the programming models being the special
cases of an economics built on the calculus, the traditional marginal

models become part of a broader and more flexible framework constructed on programming.

The programming format has the major advantage, in our opinion, of enabling an emphasis upon the constraints facing the firm rather than upon optimization techniques. Optimization, after all, is only a mathematical procedure. The understanding and estimation of the constraints, in contrast, are truly the problems in economic analysis facing any decision-making organization. Most of this book, therefore, is concerned with identifying the different types of constraints, estimating the constraint parameters, learning how these parameters change and might be altered, and combining and manipulating the constraints, together with objectives, to yield optimal solutions. The constraint parameters are shown to be the keys to the important distinction between short-run and long-run decisions. In the short run, the firm does the best it can under a given set of constraints; in long-run decision-making, the firm is concerned with the costs and benefits of changing the constraints. The constraint parameters are also the basis for all uncertainty: it is because decision makers are not sure of all the constraint parameters that problems in uncertainty arise. Finally, this emphasis upon the constraints enables one to understand clearly the bases for the types of functions used in traditional microeconomic theory.

We have been using this book, while writing it, for the last five years. We have used it with, we like to believe, considerable success in both undergraduate and MBA-level courses in managerial economics in a major business school. Although written primarily for business students, we think the book is also suitable for intermediate microeconomic theory courses in a liberal arts college. Although we have by no means tried to avoid mathematics, we have endeavored to keep the mathematics simple and, in almost all cases, illustrated with graphs.

We feel compelled to say a few words on the length of this book since it has become so fashionable to write short, so-called "rigorous" books in managerial economics and microeconomic theory. Much of this shortness and rigor, we are afraid, are obtained only by considering a small number of models and ignoring much of the complexity and variety in the real world. Our experience shows that the student learns best, and all of us gain insights, only when a large number of flexible models, with many variations, are analyzed. Insights into the working of the real world come mainly from the comparisions of models built on different facts and assumptions.

The traditional theory of the firm is based on a specific set of assumptions—particularly assumptions about the mathematical properties of the production function. Throughout the text we have been careful to include wherever possible the "classical case" among the variations on the basic model. Departures from those classical (more accurately, neoclassical) assumptions, we feel, add greatly to the student's understanding of the traditional theory as well as to his ability to apply microeconomic theory to business decision problems. To aid the reader in finding the more familiar topics scattered throughout much of the book, however, we have gathered a number of entries under the heading "Classical Theory of the Firm" in the index. Throughout the index an attempt is made to identify topics with terms recognizable to a reader familiar with the terminology of more traditional texts even though different terms sometimes appear in our table of contents.

A number of individuals deserve our thanks for their help. Professor Richard Caves of Harvard, the consulting editor, reviewed the manuscript in detail, and made a number of important suggestions. Professor Robert Dorfman, also of Harvard, had much to do with the organization and approach we have adopted, although he may not be aware of this fact: he reviewed an earlier incarnation of parts of this book, and his criticisms and suggestions led us to the tack we have subsequently taken. Basil Dandison of Little, Brown served admirably as the entrepreneur who combined the different type of resources needed to produce a book like this. Pat Herbst, David Lynch, Deborah Otaguro, and Jane Richardson, all members of the Little, Brown editorial staff, made the writing considerably smoother than it would otherwise have been, and did yeoman work in paring down a manuscript that was threatening to become unwieldy. Most important, we would like to thank our students at Indiana University, too many to name here, who worked with our manuscripts at different stages and in unfinished form. Many of our students responded to our requests to comment upon the manuscripts, and pointed out portions that were not clear to them. We learned a great deal from our students' criticism.

Work on this book was essentially completed before one of the authors took leave from his academic post to join the staff of the United States Senate Subcommittee on Antitrust and Monopoly of the Committeee on the Judiciary. No views expressed in this book should in any way be attributed to any person or organization other than the authors.

Irvin Millman Grossack
David Dale Martin

Contents

5 Short-Run Decision Models: The Firm as Producer 137

6 Long-Run Decision Models: The Firm as Owner 189

7 The Firm's Supply of Output to the Market and Its Demand for Inputs 219

8 Consumer Demand and Market Demand Curves 255

9 Market Models and the Firm's Demand Constraint 311

Managerial Economics

1 Scope and Models

DEFINITIONS AND SCOPE OF
MANAGERIAL ECONOMICS

The boundaries and scope of managerial economics are not firmly established. To some, managerial economics is coterminous with microeconomics, which is the study of individual units such as firms and households, and their interactions on markets. To others, managerial economics is a mathematical approach to specific business problems and merges into operations research and management science. Still others see managerial economics as the study of business cases, with little of the theoretical underpinnings of microeconomics. And, finally, there are those who view managerial economics as an amalgam of economics, marketing, finance, production, and the other functional areas of business.

In our view managerial economics is primarily a set of tools and methods of reasoning, based upon microeconomics, that can help solve and provide insights into some, but not all, of the problems faced by firms operating in a market system. The tools and methods derive from theory designed to help economists predict and understand the behavior of firms under alternative circumstances. Managerial economics, however, diverges from microeconomic theory. Microeconomics focuses on the operations of markets and the economic system; managerial economics focuses on the firm. Managerial economics, instead of being concerned with a body of economic theory per se, is concerned with the processes of economic reasoning and the application of theory to a wide range of problems.

Of course, managerial economics is not the only branch of a major discipline to contribute to the art of analyzing and solving business problems. However, its contributions are unique. One is the application of the tools of abstract reasoning to the firm and the development

1

of a consistent model, or theory, of the firm. To a considerable extent, of course, the tools of abstract reasoning are now used in the various applied fields of business; this is partly attributable to the influence of economic theory. Perhaps the main contribution of the economist is his view of the firm as an integral component of an economic system; his primary concern is the firm's interaction with other components of the economic system. In other words, the economist has been most interested in firms as purchasers and sellers of goods and services.

Being economists, we emphasize firms' problems in buying and selling. We treat lightly the scheduling of operations, control, accounting, organization, motivation, personnel policy, and other business problems, not because they are unimportant but because we must put into operation a time-honored maxim of economics, the division of labor. We feel compelled, however, to present our material in a way that is consistent with what is taught in other business fields.

In assessing the contributions of economic analysis to business decisions, we should be aware that economists have not been interested in the firm for its own sake. Their primary interests have been the organization of economic activity and the role of public policy in economic affairs. The main organizer of economic activity, at least to Western economists, is the market. Although the role of government has recently increased, economic theory still focuses upon the interactions of buyers and sellers in the market to explain prices, the composition of output, wage rates, investment, and other economic phenomena. The entities that interact in the market—firms and households—are participants that more or less react to the dictates of an impersonal market. Clearly, the market has been, and still is to most economists, the central economic institution.

To understand the behavior of markets, economists had to develop theories to explain and predict the behavior of the participants in the market, namely firms and households. They had to be able to predict the quantities of goods and services that firms and households would buy and sell under various circumstances. The theory of the firm developed for this purpose has become the basis of managerial economics and has proved useful in some other business fields.

The theory of the firm and the household originates from the utilitarian view of man as a hedonist—that is, as a seeker of pleasure and avoider of pain. Because many of man's activities produce both pleasure and pain, the "rational" hedonist tries to maximize the difference between them. The hedonistic behavior of the individual was assumed to carry over into the activities of the firm, which was completely identified with an entrepreneur who both owns and manages it. Consider the firm's problem of deciding how much to produce of a given item. The revenue obtained from the output is the pleasure and varies with the level of output. The costs or expenditures and other sacrifices made by the firm in its production effort are the pain, which also varies with the output. The difference between revenues and costs is the profit. Just as the rational hedonist maximizes the difference (net happiness) between pleasure and pain, the rational entrepreneur seeks the level of output at which the difference (the profit) between revenues and costs is maximized.

Until the 1930s, the economist's model of the firm was quite simple. Economists generally assumed that the firm could buy and sell only at prices determined by the market. Thus the theory of the firm dealt only with forces determining the firm's level of output and its purchases of inputs. The model assumed that the firm usually produced one product and viewed the organization only from the perspective of the entrepreneur.

In the last forty years or so, largely because of the development and dominance of large corporations, economists have had to pay greater attention to the firm and revise their models to explain the workings of the economic system. When there are many small firms in a market, they can react only to the prices established by the market. But conditions change when there are few firms in a market and we allow for the possibility of firms' influencing the demand for their products: The firms, acting either independently or in concert, can to a degree control the markets for both their inputs and their outputs.

Because large firms can influence or control the behavior of markets, we can no longer maintain that the workings of markets should be the focus of attention of those who want to predict or understand prices, outputs, wages, and employment. If we wish to predict, say, the price and output of potatoes, only a very simple model of the potato producer is required. We should instead concentrate on the workings of the potato market. But if we wish to predict and understand the pricing and output of automobiles, we must have a detailed and sometimes complex model of how companies such as General Motors, Ford, and Chrysler make their decisions. In many industries, surely, the firm has replaced the market as the most important institution in the organization of economic activity.

For reasons other than market power the advent of large corporations has stimulated interest and work on the theory of the firm. A problem not present in the "entrepreneurial" firm is the complexity of the large corporation and its goals. We could reasonably assume that an individual entrepreneur would try to maximize his profits, but many economists are not prepared to assume that the short-run goal of a large corporation is profit maximization. The actions of large firms substantially affect the markets for their inputs and outputs, and so the immediate maximization of profits may not always be consistent with the maximization of profits in the future. Another factor in the reexamination of goals is the separation of management and owners in a large corporation. Many economists would argue that managers find goals other than maximization of the corporation's profit to be most compatible with their interests.

The large firm has increased the demand for new tools of analysis and decision-making. Because decisions of large firms frequently involve millions of dollars, managers find it worthwhile to seek the advice of management consultants, economists, statisticians, psychologists, and other specialists able to utilize new analytical tools such as linear programming. These developments have enriched the economist's model of the firm and have enhanced the value of managerial economics.

As we embark on a study of managerial economics, we must be aware of, and be a little awed by, the diversity of the individual firms and markets. No two firms are exactly alike; all are products of their history and the personalities that shaped them. Similarly, all markets have their peculiar quirks. The salesman's saying "you've got to know the territory" has the ring of reality. Nevertheless, despite the individuality and diversity of firms and markets, all have features in common. All firms buy inputs, transform inputs into outputs, and sell outputs. All markets have buyers and sellers who compare offers to buy and sell and make decisions on the basis of these comparisons. The task of theory is to abstract the common features, necessarily ignoring some of the particular characteristics. A successful theory would produce a unified framework within which all decision-making problems could be analyzed.

In a book on managerial economics, it is well to distinguish between economic theory as an established body of thought and the processes of economic theorizing and model-building. Every student of economics knows *the* theory of the firm and *the* theory of the household, both of which are part of *the* theory of price. Such well-defined and widely accepted theories are useful. They have given a common language to economists; they provide a body of doctrine; they have proved useful to economists, enabling them to make tolerably accurate predictions of behavior. Yet we should always be a little wary of well-established theories. They are consistent, elegant, all-encompassing; this is especially true of microeconomic theory. But any theory is potentially a trap, for its logic can too often close our minds to new developments in the real world. Sophisticated theorists know that the proper use for theory is its application to a variety of conditions in a changing world. Theory should not be mistaken for the real world.

We present traditional theories of the firm, markets, and households in this book, but we stress the processes of model-building and theorizing. Instead of describing one model of the firm, we set forth many models so that through comparisons readers will understand the processes of economic reasoning. Yet, we cannot present all combinations of the theoretical concepts and can only hope that the reader learns enough to confidently apply the theories to real-world circumstances. Only when we understand the processes of economic analysis can we deal with the diversity of the real world.

MODELS AND THEIR USES

The real world, especially the part of the real world consisting of mankind, is exceedingly complex. It consists of thousands of physical objects and occurrences of "events" that continually bombard our senses. The scientist's job is to bring some order to our ways of viewing this seemingly chaotic reality so that we can determine the relations between the various objects and events and separate the important from the unimportant as we try to explain why certain events occur.

Models are the means whereby we use the mind to view the real world in an organized, orderly manner. In its most elementary sense, a model may be defined as a representation of some portion of the real world. The ways in which a model approximates reality vary. Sometimes every feature of the real world is "mapped" into the model, which then has a one-to-one correspondence with the reality it represents. More often, only some features of the real world are represented, and models do not have perfect correspondence with the real world. When the correspondence is imperfect, we say the model abstracts from reality. Models can be considered realistic if their correspondence to the real world is great. Realism is a virtue, but other aspects of models may be important enough to warrant sacrificing some realism.

A theory may be viewed as a special subset of models. A model may merely represent reality without saying anything about relationships in the real world. A theoretical model purports to define relationships and to establish causes and effects.

Models are sometimes divided into three groups: scale models, analogues, and symbolic models. A scale model is a reduced or enlarged version of the reality it represents and has a strong visual resemblance to it, although not necessarily a one-to-one correspondence. Model airplanes, ships, and buildings are common scale models. So is any kind of sample, such as a consumer panel or one drawn by a pollster.

Analogues have no close physical resemblance to the reality they represent. A map is perhaps the most common analogue, although we have become so accustomed to thinking of geographic areas in terms of maps that the map itself is easily thought of as the reality. A guinea pig, often used to represent man, is another. A wind tunnel, used by aeronautical engineers, is an analogue of the atmosphere.

Symbolic models use words and other written symbols to represent and describe reality. The most common symbolic language is of course ordinary speech. When we describe something, we are constructing a symbolic model. It is abstract to the extent that not every feature of the reality is actually described. Diagrams are another symbolic model. A football coach, for example, uses circles and crosses to represent players and directed lines to represent the movement of the players. Mathematics, another symbolic language, is especially efficient for representing relationships. Symbolic models are more removed from reality than scale and analogue models, but they have a greater power to describe relationships. We will be using symbolic models almost exclusively in our work.

Perhaps the major reason for building models, at least in the social sciences, is the necessity to simplify. The real world is too complex and diverse for anybody to fully comprehend. If we want to understand reality, we have to focus on its most salient aspects; that is, in order to build models we have to abstract from the real world the most relevant features. Abstraction involves classifying objects and events by their common properties and often neglecting specificities. Paradoxically, we learn most about the real world by ignoring part of it; it is actually realistic to be a little unrealistic.[1]

Another reason for model-building is to relate objects and events to each other. Our senses tell us that a student is walking toward a building at a certain time and that a class is to meet in that building, but only the human mind can connect these two events. Similarly, only a theoretical model can show that there is a relationship between the rainfall in Idaho and the price of potatoes in New York.

Theoretical models are useful in prediction. In a complex social system, all things are somehow interrelated — especially in the economy. Yet when predicting anything, we cannot possibly take everything into account. Instead, we have to establish what is of primary importance in influencing the occurrence of events. Models usually cannot take everything into account, so we expect our predictions to be subject to error.

Models are often used for experimentation. Ideally, we should experiment in the real world, but such experimentation is often too difficult, expensive, or perhaps impossible. We would rather see the aeronautical engineer test various wing structures in his wind tunnel instead of sending planes out to see what happens. We would also rather test the effect of a cancer-inducing chemical on guinea pigs instead of on people. In experimentation we use a model to simulate occurrences under various conditions.

The decision model is a special class of models that makes use of both the predictive and the experimental capabilities of models. Some of the events or objects represented by the decision model are subject to control or manipulation by the decision-maker, who uses the model to test the consequences of alternative manipulations or choices as a prelude to taking action. In the economist's model of the firm, choices are mainly about quantities to buy or produce and prices to charge or offer for various inputs and outputs. The consequences of these decisions affect profits, costs, cash flows, and asset values.

[1]For more on this topic, see Kenneth Boulding, *Economics as a Science* (New York: McGraw-Hill, 1970).

Theoretical models also serve as guides to the gathering of information. They tell us the facts that are needed and the kinds of relationships that must be established if we are to understand the determinants of happenings in the real world. When we can quantify relationships, theoretical models become empirical models. But even without numerical estimates, models can reveal much about the direction of change in one component and that in another component.

Theory does more than point out needed information. It is needed to interpret and make sense of data and facts. Justice Holmes once made clear how theory (or a model) brings significance to observations. A man whistling in front of a bank may be doing nothing wrong. But if his whistling is linked by a model as a warning to cohorts who are robbing the bank, it becomes illegal. Facts (observations or data) alone do not prove anything. Rather, they lend support to theories or models. When Perry Mason proves his client's innocence, he presents an explanation of the crime that differs from the model constructed by the district attorncy. The facts both men gathered are used to support their respective models of the crime. All the facts are not needed; the model is supposed to provide the complete picture, and sometimes only a few facts validate it.

A model gives us something that is manageable; it can be readily handled and manipulated to provide various types of insights. To keep models tractable, we abstract only the most relevant features of the real world. All model-builders have to determine an optimal level of abstraction. We may say that in abstraction there is a trade-off between tractability and reality. We want models to be as realistic and tractable as possible. However, too much reality can make a model so complex that we cannot manipulate it to provide insights and answers, and too much tractability and too little reality can produce a model without relevance.

Abstraction involves classification. When we call an apple a piece of fruit, a type of food, or a product, we are abstracting. By using higher levels of abstraction (calling the apple a product), we ignore some of the reality and specificity of an apple, but we may see the similarity of, say, the demand for apples and the demand for other products. By using higher levels of abstraction, we can devise models that have a wide degree of applicability.

How do we know which features of the real world to abstract for a model? Much depends on what we wish to investigate and study. An aeronautical engineer does not need a model airplane with a one-to-one correspondence with reality. He tests only the stability of the airplane under various conditions and is unconcerned about the lighting and design of the interior. The interior designer, on the other hand, does not care if his model has no wings. Consider the different kinds of maps made by geologists, political scientists, transportation experts, and economic geographers. All abstract different features. The sciences dealing with man abstract different features for their models. The sociologist abstracts features relevant to man's behavior as part of a group. The industrial engineer is interested in man's relation to machines. The economist (alas!) abstracts characteristics that make man akin to a self-serving calculating machine.

How do we know if a model is good? Much depends on its purpose. Many would argue that the final test of a model designed to predict is the accuracy of its predictions. Not all models, however, are designed to predict. Often they are used to experiment, to simulate various conditions, and to provide insights into complex phenomena. The final test of models that are not designed to predict is the usefulness of the understanding and insights they provide. Usefulness, however, is not always easily measured and agreed upon, so we must also assess the reasonableness of the model's assumptions, its formal construction, and its plausibility. A model could be in error—perhaps useless is a better term—if it abstracts the wrong features of the real world or if the relationships are not put together properly. A model can be appropriate for one use but not for another. The difference between the models we use every day and scientific models is that the latter are supposed to be continuously tested for logical construction and for whether they are relevant and useful for the purposes for which they are designed.

Virtually all models and theories use assumptions. In its broadest sense, an assumption is something we agree to consider true for a given purpose, even though it may not be literally true or there is not sufficient evidence to ascertain its truth. Assumptions are not correct or incorrect, or even bad or good. Rather we should ask whether an assumption is reasonable when judged not just by its correspondence to reality but also by its effect on tractability and relevance.

Even though assumptions may turn out to be incorrect, we have to make them if we are to take any actions or make any plans or predictions. Consider the act of walking into a building. We would not do this if we thought the building was going to collapse. Most of the time we assume the building will remain standing and enter it. Yet it might collapse; our assumption might be incorrect. Consider the football coach designing his offensive strategy. He has to assume that the defensive players will do certain things. He does not really know whether their behavior will match his assumptions, and his strategy may not work. Yet he must make assumptions if he is to design the play.

Consider next the economist's assumption that a firm seeks to maximize profit. With such an assumption, he can predict the behavior of a firm under a given set of circumstances. A critic of the assumption may point out instances in which a businessman does not seek to maximize profits but perhaps behaves in response to any of hundreds of things—a headache, a fight with his wife. The economist's response to the critic should not be to abandon the profit-maximizing assumption but to ask for a better assumption. Without an assumption, we can predict nothing about the firm's behavior. It is clearly preferable to make an assumption, predict behavior, and see how often we predict correctly than to figuratively throw up our hands in despair.

Sometimes we make assumptions to simplify our models even though we know the assumptions are literally untrue in the real world. In many of the models we construct, we assume that prices, inputs, and outputs can be varied by infinitely small amounts. In the real world such variations may not be possible, but the assumption is generally reasonable and allows us to draw smooth curves and use mathematical functions. Sometimes economists devise an economic system consisting of two people using two inputs and producing two outputs. Of course there is no such simple economy in the real world. Yet such assumptions simplify our investigation of complex phenomena and may provide useful insights about the real world.

How reasonable and realistic should assumptions be, and how much latitude should the model-builder have in choosing them? Much depends on whether the model is to be used to predict or provide the basis for serious decisions or whether it is to be used to explore, experiment, and obtain insights. When used for the former purposes, the assumptions should be reasonable, rooted in reality, and, when possible, tested independently of their use in the model. However, when the model is to be used to explore and give insights, less realistic assumptions should be permitted. There is nothing wrong with making unrealistic assumptions for such uses, although the model-builder should make clear to the reader which of his assumptions are unrealistic or unreasonable.

Some scholars, such as economist Milton Friedman, maintain that models do not have to be based on realistic assumptions.[2] The argument for this position is that the purpose of models is to predict and that if the predictions are successful, we should not care about the validity or reasonableness of the assumptions. Accordingly, the usefulness of a model, and by implication its assumptions, lies in its predictive power. When a model fails to predict adequately, it should be discarded and replaced. This position presents some problems. Many models are not devised for prediction purposes, and many models built to predict are never tested. Also there is the question of who decides what constitutes an adequate record of prediction for a model.

Assumptions, then, are what the model-builder asks the reader or user to accept as true for the purposes of that model. Good scientific

[2]See Milton Friedman, "The Methodology of Positive Economics," in Friedman, *Essays in Positive Economics* (Chicago: University of Chicago Press, 1953). For other views on the role of assumptions, see the discussion on this topic in *American Economic Review* (May 1963).

practice requires the model-builder to make his assumptions as explicit as possible, and it is always fair for a critic to point out implicit assumptions and to question the reasonableness of all the assumptions. Those who want to tinker with a model, and perhaps improve it, are free to vary the assumptions. When a person wishes to use a model for predictive or decision-making purposes, he must judge how close the assumptions correspond to the real world. Even abstraction is often based upon assumptions because the model-builder may not always be sure which features of the real world are relevant and which are of second-order importance.

Models and assumptions are crucial to orderly thinking and good decision-making. But we should always be a little skeptical of them. Models sometimes cannot embody all the relevant features of the real world, especially those that cannot be quantified. Even for the features of the real world that can be adequately expressed in models, obtaining sufficient data to accurately determine relationships is usually quite difficult. Good data on the past may be available, but decisions are made with regard to the future. The sophisticated decision-maker should not make his decisions solely on the basis of a model. He should use the model and the "answers" it provides as a starting point from which to exercise his own judgment.

We should not be overly impressed with the validity and usefulness of models because they use mathematical symbols. Mathematics is a wonderful language and tool with which to construct models and, to the initiated, can make clear the underlying assumptions and logic of a model. But mathematical models can be incorrect or useless despite their veneer of elegance.

Models can close our eyes to the necessity to observe the real world. Because of their logic and internal consistency, they can easily give a false impression that everything is understood. Gaining knowledge and understanding the real world are more difficult than constructing a model. A little modesty and skepticism toward models are, we think, useful attitudes.

To many, models are much more than a tool. Through models we tend to view much of the real world, and it is tempting and easy to think a model is the real world. Models often also become the basis of doctrine, ideology, and orthodoxy. They become implanted in people's minds as the way the world should be. Sometimes model-builders allow their judgments of what the world should be like to creep into the construction of their models.[3]

[3]For a critical evaluation of economic theory from this viewpoint, see Gunnar Myrdal, *The Political Element in the Development of Economic Theory* (Cambridge, Mass.: Harvard University Press, 1954).

Discussion Questions

1. In discussing the utilitarian view of man and the firm, we have asserted that the rational entrepreneur seeks to maximize profits. Is this goal inherently rational, or is profit maximization rational only because it is consistent with the view that men seek to maximize their net happiness? Are actions rational or irrational only because they are consistent or inconsistent with goals?

2. Economists generally consider profit maximization to be in the public interest when firms are small and unable to influence prices in any way. When viewed from the public interest, how does profit maximization appear when firms are large and powerful and can control prices for their products? Is there a connection between the power of firms and the current writing on the "social responsibility" of businessmen?

3. Are stereotypes of people kinds of models? Is it sometimes necessary to use such stereotypes to make judgments and decisions? Are they scientific? What dangers must we be aware of when using them?

4. How might novelists and moralists criticize the use of abstract models to study human behavior?

5. To what extent could case studies be alternatives to theoretical models? Could generalizations from case studies be drawn without such models? What might be some of the difficulties in doing this?

6. What do you think of the model known as economic man? Is he a nice fellow? Might he be a hero? Would you trust him? Would you want him to work for you? Is he an individualist?

7. Could we play bridge or chess without making assumptions? Give some examples of the types of assumptions made. Might they turn out to be incorrect?

8. Discuss some of the ways that assumptions and models can be tested. Is it possible that some theories can never be tested?

9. Is a blueprint of a utopian society, such as that developed by Plato or Thomas More, a model? In what sense is or isn't it?

10. Does the use of models for decision-making preclude the use of judgment and common sense?

11. Philosophers have debated the question of reality for many centuries. In what sense could a model actually become reality?

2 An Overview of the Firm and Its Decisions

No business firm is typical of all business firms. Yet most real-world firms have some characteristics in common. In constructing models and submodels of business firms, we need to include common characteristics and ignore many traits that give particular firms their individuality. We also must ignore characteristics that overly complicate our model, making it difficult to reason our way from assumptions to conclusions. In the following pages we begin to identify the characteristics that will be included in our models of firms. We shall also describe in this chapter some of the complications a firm must face in the real world.

THE FIRM AS PRODUCER AND OWNER

Most business firms can be viewed as having two semi-distinct roles — producer of goods and services, acquirer and owner of assets. As producer, a model firm may be considered an input-output mechanism that converts input services into various types of outputs. Its activities are acquiring appropriate input services, physically transforming them into outputs, and disposing of the outputs. As owner, however, a firm is not directly concerned with production but rather with the control of assets. A firm is the holder of legal claims to things that usually can be bought and sold and that yield productive services and incomes. Such assets may be liquid or fixed. In addition to obvious assets such as inventories, machinery, and cash, there are trademarks, patent holdings, and contracts. As owner, the firm's main activities are buying and selling assets — or, perhaps more nearly accurate, exchanging some types of assets for other types, for example, cash for a machine, or the right to share future profits for cash.

The firm's two roles are not distinct. We may assume that the firm as owner will rent assets or sell services to the firm as producer. Consequently, the firm as owner, in acquiring its assets, will attend to the needs of the firm as producer. Yet, important as the interconnection of roles usually is for real-world firms, in many activities there is little or no correspondence between them. The firm as producer may acquire most of its input services not from the firm as owner but from individuals and organizations that are not part of the firm. The firm as owner does not have to sell the services of all or even any of its assets to the firm as producer. Loans of money, use of patents, and rental of buildings, equipment, and land are services of assets that can be sold to other firms. Therefore, firms as producers acquire input services from themselves as owners and from outside sources; firms as owners rent assets or sell their services, to themselves as producers and to outsiders. The firm in each of its roles transacts business with outsiders; these transactions take place on terms determined by arm's-length bargaining. The terms for transfers within the firm are determined by administrative discretion.

The point at which the two roles of the firm most obviously differ is the recording of activities. The activities of the firm as producer are recorded in the accountant's income statement; those of the firm as owner are recorded in the balance sheet. The only link between these accounting statements is in the transfer of the net revenues of the firm as producer via the balance sheet to the firm as owner. This transfer is, in effect, the payment of the firm as producer to the firm as owner for the use of the latter's assets.

The activities of the firm as producer may be conceptualized as a "flow"; inputs and outputs are defined as quantities per unit of time. The ownership of assets, on the other hand, is a "stock" concept, with quantities defined at a point in time. The most obvious, though often overlooked, distinction between the two roles is in the criteria by which the firm is judged. We usually judge a firm as producer by its profits; in its role as owner, the firm is judged by returns on, and the value of, its assets. This conceptual distinction between the two roles of the firm will enable us to more clearly analyze different types of problems and to distinguish short-run from long-run decision-making.

THE FIRM AS PRODUCER:
THE ECONOMIST'S MODEL

The activities of the firm as producer can be divided conveniently into three categories: (1) obtaining the inputs of productive services necessary for the production process, (2) transforming various inputs into outputs, and (3) disposing of the outputs to other economic units. Economists have traditionally been interested primarily in transactions between economic units, such as the firm and the family, and only to a secondary extent in production processes within the firm.

The traditional interests are reflected in the detail and emphasis given to the firm's transactions with others "outside" the firm — the first and third categories. The second category, activities that take place within the firm, is more abstract and consists mainly of "production functions" that summarize technological relationships between inputs and outputs.

Acquiring Inputs. In order to understand the whole process of obtaining inputs, we must maintain a sharp and sometimes subtle distinction between a productive service and the agent rendering the service. The *service* of a worker performing a task is an input to the production process. The worker himself is not the input; he is the agent that renders the service. When a warehouse is used to store materials, the input service is not the warehouse but the use of floor space. The warehouse is the agent. When a lathe is used, the lathe is the agent; the things the lathe does are the productive services. The distinction between the service and the agent is fairly obvious for labor and capital assets. It is somewhat subtle for things that are used up in the production process, such as materials. Consider the use of steel sheets in the manufacture of a product. The input *service* is not the steel sheet itself but rather the services of the steel in imparting to the product a certain structure, durability, and strength. The steel sheet is the agent that provides these services to the product.

In its role as producer, the firm is directly concerned with obtaining productive services and is interested in agents of production only as a means of obtaining them. It is well to conceptually separate the service from the agent rendering the service. This conceptual distinction enables us to see clearly all production possibilities. Thus, if instead of thinking of steel sheets as the input, we think of the input as the services of imparting structure, durability, and strength to the product, then we are prepared to consider alternative agents to steel such as aluminum and plastic.

Various groups of productive agents can be distinguished upon a number of different bases. One of the most important is the durability of the agent, how long it can provide its service. Materials, fuels, and components are all nondurable agents; that is, in providing their services, they are completely exhausted as productive agents. Steel sheets, for example, in imparting their services to a product, are no longer available to the firm for any other purposes. Although in a way the sheets do not actually physically disappear by their transformation into part of a product, they can no longer yield the same productive service to the firm. Once such materials are no longer serviceable, they are sold as part of the output, dumped on the environment as waste, or recycled into other uses.

Workers and capital assets, unlike materials, are durable agents because with use they can continue their productive services, often over substantial periods of time. However, the durability of durable agents varies, and to differing extents their productive powers are altered as they provide their services. For capital assets, the alteration is usually for the worse and leads to the notions of wear and tear and depreciation. The use of human labor, because of learning processes, often leads to improvements in productive powers.[1]

Ideally, productive services should be identified and classified on the basis of the service itself, without reference to the agents providing it. Productive services, for example, could be identified as the ability to move something, the ability or capacity to transmit heat or electricity, the ability to form or shape, the ability to cut, the ability to smooth. We are so accustomed, however, to merging the concept of productive agents with that of productive services, that we usually identify the service by the name of the agent or sometimes identify the agent by the name of the service—for example, management services, legal services, money services, labor services, lathe services, stamping machine services, steel services, transport services. In common language the service is much more often clearly identified as a separate entity for the durable agents than for the nondurables. Thus banking services and warehouse services have a familiar ring that is usually not present in phrases such as steel services and textile services. In many of our examples, we identify the service by its agent rather than by the more abstract identification of the service independently of the agent, although the latter is technically more nearly accurate.

MEASUREMENT OF INPUT QUANTITIES. All inputs have quantitative dimensions, although at times quantification requires some ingenuity. Usually input services are discrete and easily measurable quantities—hours of a particular type of labor service, tons of steel, lathe-hours, kilowatt hours of electricity, calories of heat, square feet of space. But sometimes the input service uses some kind of "capacity"—the capacity of a pipe to carry liquids, the use of certain types of know-how, the use of a public waterway. In such cases, the input services are often measured not in discrete quantities but as percentages of available capacity.

All inputs should have quantitative dimensions. They also should have time dimensions, because production is a "flow" that takes place over time. Inputs enter the production process not only as quantities but also as rates per time period. Examples of the full input dimension are man-hours of labor services per week, tons of steel per week (month, year), calories of heat per month (day, hour, week).

ARRANGEMENTS FOR INPUT ACQUISITION. Three sorts of agents provide productive services: (1) nondurable agents (materials, fuels, components), (2) durable human agents (all types of labor, including management and professional), (3) durable nonhuman agents (land,

---

[1]A notable exception to labor-improving is in organized sports. Owners of professional teams are allowed to "depreciate" their players for tax purposes.

machinery, buildings, transport facilities, patented processes, trademarks). In the real world, input services are obtained in various ways. A few come from free agents such as rain, air, and sunlight. Some are provided by public agencies and paid for indirectly through taxes. Some are obtained from the owners of the agents under complex contractual arrangements. Still others are obtained by purchasing the agents or by purchasing exclusive rights to use the services for a specific period of time. Purchase of some services or agents may be tied in various ways to each other or to future purchases. As a first approximation in developing a model of a firm, however, we can consider all inputs to come from one or the other of two basic arrangements: (1) purchase of the agent, (2) purchase of a specific quantity of service.

How productive services are obtained depends on the nature of the service-rendering agent. The law prohibits slavery, so human agents are not purchasable. Labor services, therefore, can be obtained only by purchasing the service. The law discourages long-term contracts, and all labor sales agreements can be easily dissolved, although sometimes not without payment of damages. There are no such legal restrictions on obtaining the nondurable agents, but, because nondurable agents are consumed in rendering their service, for all practical purposes their services can be obtained only through purchase of the agent. The services of nonhuman durables can be purchased directly or obtained by purchase of the agent. Machinery, land, transport equipment, money, patents, and buildings could all be owned or their services bought directly by renting them.

The durable agents a firm owns are among its assets. A consideration of the firm as owner is concerned primarily with the buying and selling of these assets, although contractual rights to purchase services directly are also assets that may be bought and sold. In its role of producer, the firm purchases some services from other enterprises and some from itself as owner of agents. In this sense, the firm as producer buys only services.

Whether a firm buys productive services or the agents that render services, it must play a role as buyer. Real-world buying arrangements can be reduced to two categories: (1) purchase in open markets and (2) purchase from identified sources. When the firm obtains productive services or agents in the open market, it is free to choose from among all willing suppliers. But often firms make contractual arrangements with identified suppliers in which the supplier agrees to provide specified quantities of specified productive agents or services over a period of time. These contracts usually set forth various terms of future transactions such as prices and performance. Although purchase contracts are also reached in open market transactions, these are one-shot affairs, and we will reserve the expression "contractual agreements" for cases in which the firm has contracts with identified sources that bind the parties over a number of sales. Unless a firm has an exclusive contract with an identified supplier and has agreed to buy all its requirements of a particular type from that supplier, the firm could simultaneously obtain its supply of that productive service or agent under a number of contracts and in the open market.

TERMS OF ACQUISITION. The last dimension of input acquisition has to do with the terms by which the productive agents or productive services are alienated from their suppliers. By far the most important term is the nominal price. Other terms, however, may be important: credit, guarantees of quality, and performance. It is often useful to include in the nominal price not only the money paid to the seller, but also the delivery and other costs necessary to bring the production agent to the site where production takes place.

Special price problems arise when the firm as producer "buys" the productive services of assets owned by the firm. Should the firm as producer use these assets as if they were free? Should prices be based on estimates of the degrees by which the assets depreciate? Should the prices be what the firm as owner could obtain by renting the assets to other enterprises? Or should the prices for these assets exhaust all the money that remains to the firm as producer after it pays off all its outside suppliers? These difficult questions have not been resolved to everybody's satisfaction. There can be no meaningful price for these asset services if price is defined as the rate of exchange arrived at by a buyer and seller bargaining at arm's length. The "prices" between the firm as owner and producer are, it would therefore seem, set by administrative discretion, although administrators may try to fix the price on the basis of what the price would have been if there were arm's-length bargaining.

Disposing of Outputs. We shall conceive of the model firm as a producer of valuable (scarce) economic goods and services. In reality outputs are of many different types and are disposed of under a variety of institutional arrangements. The identification and measurement of a firm's outputs may be difficult. One output might be distinguished from another on the basis of (1) whether it is a service or an agent that renders a service; (2) whether it is used in production or consumption; (3) the extent to which it is used in conjunction with other services or products; (4) if it is an agent, whether it is used up concomitantly with rendering its service or is durable; (5) the specific uses to which it is put; (6) the geographical area of use; or (7) any physical characteristics of the product and its users that might differentiate it from other outputs. In building models of firms, we will speak of their outputs without always specifying all the characteristics of each. In the real world, defining and distinguishing particular products or services present considerable difficulty.

When viewed in the context of the firm as producer, all outputs have both quantitative and time dimensions and thus can be measured as rates—for example, number of automobiles per week, tons of steel per month, number of patients seen per day, number of students educated per semester. Of course, in many instances defining and measuring the output require considerable imagination and ingenuity.[2] Often whether the output rate refers to production or to sales needs to be made clear. These can, of course, vary if the product is storable, in which case the firm can hold inventories. "Output," according to the context, will refer either to production or to sales, and, unless otherwise stated, we will by-pass inventory problems by assuming that the firm's output is immediately sold.

There are many institutional arrangements for disposing of output, some of which mirror arrangements for acquiring inputs. The outputs of goods can be sold outright, their services can be sold, or both can occur. A firm may, as owner, retain the goods it produces and sell their services. In such a case the outputs become assets of the firm, and their services become outputs. Whether agents or services are sold, sales may be made in an open market, in which anyone willing to pay the asked price can buy, or sales may be made to specific customers with whom the firm has contractual relationships. These contracts can be in a variety of forms, such as a franchise, tie-in sales, and long-term requirements arrangements.

It is sometimes possible and usually profitable for a firm to break the total market for a product into market segments. Segmentation can be made on many different bases—geographic areas; category of dealer, such as wholesaler, jobber, retailer; differentiating the product to appeal to different age groups, income classes, education levels. When a market can be successfully segmented and separated so that buyers are not able to arbitrage by buying in one market and selling in another, the firm can set a different price in each market to take advantage of the special characteristics of that market. Market segmentation has become an important phenomenon.

The conditions on which the different outputs are alienated from the firm include many terms. The most important is the nominal price. Others are delivery dates, credit terms, penalties for nonfulfillment of contract, and guarantees of quality. There does not necessarily have to be a single price for a given output; there can be as many separate prices as there are separate market segments.

Input-Output Transformation. The input-output transformations can be thought of as the internal operations of the firm. These operations begin at the separation of the input services from their agents (labor and assets) and the separation of the nondurable agents from

---

[2]Measurement of output is usually most difficult when the output is a service rather than a product. The outputs of "nonprofit" institutions such as universities, police departments, and hospitals are particularly difficult to define and measure.

their owners. They end at the point at which the output is to be alien-ated from the firm as producer and either dumped on the environment or transferred to others—consumers, government agencies, other business organizations, the firm as owner of assets.

Except for the activities dealing with assets (the firm as owner), and the dealing with suppliers on the one hand and customers on the other hand, all other activities of the firm are concerned with this input-output transformation. Included in these activities is not only the actual physical act of production—the conversion of inputs to outputs—but also the transport of the outputs to points where they be-come the property of customers, the scheduling of operations, the con-trol and monitoring of production, the development of organization and procedures.

The economist generally sums up these internal operations as pro-duction functions, which usually are mathematical expressions relating the quantities of outputs to the quantities of inputs. Produc-tion functions may be compared to chemical reactions in which differ-ent elements or compounds (inputs) are combined to yield new elements in compounds (outputs).

THE FIRM AS PRODUCER: THE ROLE OF PROFIT

The firm as producer, like all input-output mechanisms, can be evalu-ated in terms of its efficiency. A common measure of efficiency is the ratio of output to input. We evaluate automobiles, for example, on the basis of the number of miles they travel per gallon of gas consumed. In general, the greater the ratio of output (miles) to input (gasoline), the greater is the efficiency.

There are, however, problems in measuring efficiency when there is more than one input or output. Say we consider oil as an input in addition to gasoline. If one automobile gets 20 miles per gallon of gas and 1,000 miles per quart of oil and a second automobile gets 25 miles per gallon of gas but only 500 miles per quart of oil, which is more efficient? We cannot answer this question by forming the ratio miles/gallons of gas + quarts of oil, because we cannot add together the two terms in the denominator. The problem is even more difficult if we consider the possibility that one car is more comfortable or safer than the other. Then we would have to evaluate the following ratios for each car: miles + degree of comfort + degree of safety/gallons of gas + quarts of oil.

Although we cannot add gallons of gas to quarts of oil, we can add the *values* of these two items. If we multiply the price per gallon by the number of gallons, the unit "gallons" cancels out, so that we get the dollar value of the gasoline. Similarly we can calculate the dollar value of the oil. The two dollar values can now be added together to get dollars in the denominator. The numerator in this case presents greater difficulties, for the different outputs may not have prices.

However, it may be possible to express each of the outputs in terms of psychological satisfaction, or psychological "value in use," although these satisfactions may vary from one car-owner to the next. When this can be done — we do it all the time — the outputs in the numerator too can be added together to get total satisfaction. We could then calculate the ratio of satisfaction per dollar for each car to compare their efficiencies.

The efficiency of the firm can also be evaluated by expressing the outputs and inputs in terms of values. This is much easier to do for the firm than for the automobile because the outputs of the firm are for sale. We can objectively value the outputs by their prices instead of having to depend on subjective measures of psychological satisfaction, as was necessary for the car. Thus we can evaluate the firm by comparing the values of the outputs with the values of the inputs. Although the firm physically transforms inputs into outputs, the creation of value that accompanies this transformation — the difference between the values of the outputs and inputs — is of greater importance.

Likewise, evaluation of the efficiency of a firm with one or more outputs and two or more inputs requires a comparison of the *value* of outputs and the *value* of inputs rather than a comparison of the physical quantities. More important than the physical transformation of inputs to outputs is the creation of value that accompanies the transformation. The value created is the value of the physical outputs minus the value of the physical inputs.

Profit and Efficiency. The value of inputs may be measured by the price per unit paid for them, if inputs are obtained by a simple market transaction. The value of outputs may be measured by the price per unit charged for them, if the outputs are disposed of by a simple sales transaction. If we have such prices, we can treat the price per unit multiplied by the number of units used during a particular time period as the value of a particular input. Thus, if the wage rate is W dollars per man-hour for a particular type of worker, and the number of man-hours of input per week is L, then the product of the two will be the value of that input measured in dollars per week. Man-hours "cancels out," so we have the value of that input measured in units that can be added to the value of other inputs. The addition of physical quantities of gas and oil or labor time and machine time is meaningless, but the monetary value of labor input can be added to the monetary value of machine services or material inputs over some time period to get the firm's costs of inputs for the period. Let us denote costs C of inputs over period of time t as C_t.

If outputs also have prices attached and we can obtain the total value per period for each output by multiplying its price per unit by the number of units produced per period, and if we add up these total values for period t, we obtain the firm's revenues R for that period, R_t.

Given the total values of the outputs per period t, R_t, and the total values of the inputs for that same period, C_t, various measures of the firm's efficiency can be devised. One possibility that an engineer might favor would be the ratio of the revenues to the costs. If we designate E_t as this measure of efficiency, E_t would be found from the equation $E_t = R_t/C_t$. E_t measures the amount of output value per unit of input value.

In addition to the ratio of R_t to C_t, we can use the difference between R_t and C_t. This difference is known as profit, which we designate by the symbol π_t and define as $\pi_t = R_t - C_t$.

Which of these two measures of efficiency, E_t or π_t, is preferable? As a pure measure of efficiency, E_t is perhaps better, and an outside observer might prefer it for analyzing various aspects of the firm's activities. But the firm itself is almost surely more interested in profit as an object of pursuit and therefore judges itself by the profit criterion. A firm may find efficiency in the engineering sense profitable, but it may not too. The profits belong to the firm and provide income to the firm's owners.

Profit Maximization as a Goal. Economists have traditionally assumed profit maximization to be the goal of their model firms for several different reasons. From the "positive" view, profit maximization is assumed to be the goal because it helps the economist to understand and predict how the firm behaves under different circumstances. Each firm does not have to consciously have profit maximization as a goal; it generally suits the economist's purpose if the firm behaves as if it approximately maximizes profits. From the normative viewpoint, firms *should* maximize profits. This advice has traditionally been given by economists who argue that, with the presence of certain conditions of competition, profit maximization is socially desirable. We will for the most part consider profit maximization the primary goal of the firm as a producer, partly because it is a desirable goal in its own right and partly because it enables us to organize facts and concepts and evaluate results.

However, mainly because of the advent of giant corporations with immense economic power, many students of business and economics question whether profit maximization is, or should be, the main goal of the firm. Many distinguished business leaders stress the importance of social service, good or "fair" wages, and taking the interests of suppliers and customers into account in making decisions. They usually see managers not as agents only of stockholders but as individuals who are supposed to balance the conflicting claims of various groups who are part of, or deal with, the firm. Some economists argue that the behavior of the firm can best be understood if decisions are assumed to maximize the interests of management rather than those of stockholders.[3] In some instances political leaders ask, and pressure,

---

[3]This has been an important theme in economic literature in the past decade. See for example Robin Marris, *The Economics of the Managerial Firm* (New York: Basic Books, 1964).

business firms to sacrifice some of their profits in order to help achieve social goals such as noninflationary growth of the whole economy, a more nearly equal distribution of income, and training for socially disadvantaged groups.[4]

Even when profits are accepted as the primary goal of a firm, the profit goal may not always provide an unambiguous guide for the firm's action, because actions taken to affect profits in an immediate period may hamper profits in later periods. A very high price charged by the firm during a period of shortage, for example, may lead to high immediate profits but may also alienate customers to the extent that the firm's profits will suffer in future periods.

The profit goal may not be as important as the way it is achieved, the rules of behavior that are followed. The maximization of profits through vigorous competition, production of superior products, and increased productive efficiency is desirable both to the firm and to society in general. But the pursuit of profit maximization through product adulteration, price-fixing agreements, or bribing government officials is certainly not desirable. In the last three instances, the goal of profit maximization is not at fault; there is a failure to specify, follow, or enforce appropriate rules of business behavior. As long as suitable rules of behavior are followed, the profit-maximization goal becomes little more than "doing the best possible under the circumstances." What is possible and what the circumstances are are more important than the goal itself.

Profit Notation. Let us assume that our model firm sells all its output produced in period t (or, alternatively, assigns a price for all unsold output placed in inventory, which is equivalent to income). The total revenue is the sum of all the outputs multiplied by their prices. If P_i is the price of the ith product, and Q_i is the quantity of that product produced and sold, the revenue from that product during period t is

$$R_{it} = P_{it}Q_{it}. \tag{2.1}$$

If there are n different products, numbered $1,2,3, \ldots, i, \ldots, n$, then the total revenue in period t is the aggregate of the individual output revenues, or

$$R_t = P_{1t}Q_{1t} + P_{2t}Q_{2t} + \ldots + P_{it}Q_{it} + \ldots + P_{nt}Q_{nt}. \tag{2.2}$$

In the conventional summation notation, equation 2.2 can be more compactly written as

$$R_t = \sum_{i=1}^{i=n} P_{it}Q_{it}. \tag{2.3}$$

---

[4]The responsibilities of business have received a great deal of attention in the last few years. See for example John Larson, *The Responsible Businessman* (New York: Holt, Rinehart and Winston, 1966).

In turning to the cost function, we must remind ourselves once more to maintain a sharp distinction between input services and the agents that render these services—especially when the agents are durable. If we emply 1,2, . . . , j, . . . , m, to designate the m input services, p_j to designate the price of the jth input service, and x_j to designate the quantity of that service, all in period t, the cost function in extended form is

$$C_t = p_{1t}x_{1t} + p_{2t}x_{2t} + \ldots + p_{jt}x_{jt} + \ldots + p_{mt}x_{mt} \qquad (2.4)$$

which, in compact notation, becomes

$$C_t = \sum_{j=1}^{j=m} p_{jt}x_{jt}. \qquad (2.5)$$

With revenue and cost denoted by equation 2.3 and 2.5, profits can be defined:

$$\pi_t = R_t - C_t = \sum_{i=1}^{i=n} P_{it}Q_{it} - \sum_{j=1}^{j=m} p_{jt}x_{jt}. \qquad (2.6)$$

We may wish to relax the assumption that a particular output or input is sold or bought at a single price. If an output or input is sold or bought in different market segments or from different sources, we can incorporate the different prices for these inputs or outputs. Thus, if output 1 is sold in market segments 1 and 2, we would replace $P_{1t}Q_{1t}$ by $P_{11t}Q_{11t} + P_{12t}Q_{12t}$, in which the second subscript refers to the particular market segment.

The Central Decision Problem. Profit in a given period depends on the inputs and outputs that are obtained and sold and their quantities and prices. The Ps, Qs, ps, and xs, with subscripts identifying the input or output, are the decision variables. They alone define profit. With the goal of our model firm as producer taken to be the maximization of π_t, the decision problem for the firm as producer is to select the inputs and outputs, and values for their prices and quantities, that maximize π_t. But before optimal values can be selected, we must know which inputs, outputs, and the values of their prices and quantities are possible. And, going one step further, we must be able to consider whether it is possible to change the range of values these decision variables can take. The last step is part of the activity of the firm in its role as owner.

In any given period of time, the firm may have no choice about expending money for some input services because they must be paid for whether they are used or not. These fixed input services can be divided into two categories: (1) services from assets owned by the firm that cannot be used elsewhere and (2) services that the firm has agreed to purchase in contracts that cannot be changed. The payment for fixed input services is a fixed cost, which must be paid regardless of output decisions. Fixed costs result from decisions made by the firm as owner about assets (we are considering contracts to be assets). Payments for the other input services are known as variable costs. Because fixed costs do not vary with changes in output, the firm can maximize profit by maximizing the difference between revenue and the variable (controllable) costs. This difference, the cash flow to the firm as producer from its choice of outputs and controllable inputs, is denoted here by Z. A maximization of Z_t is completely consistent with a maximization of π_t and will be used here extensively.

If we divide costs into two categories, V_t and F_t (variable and fixed), then $\pi_t = R_t - V_t - F_t$, and $Z_t = R_t - V_t$. Since F_t cannot be changed, choices of outputs and variable inputs that maximize Z_t also maximize π_t. Cash flow is an especially useful concept when the firm produces two or more products, for ignoring F_t spares us from unnecessary problems in allocating F_t to the different products. There is also the subtle distinction that fixed costs arise from investment decisions, and variable costs arise from current short-run production decisions. The cash flow, Z_t, legally belongs to the firm as owner. We must make clear that Z_t is the cash flow only from current productive activities. Later, we discuss other categories of cash flows.

THE FIRM AS OWNER

The role of the firm as owner includes not only the rendering of input services to the firm as producer but also the management of change through time in the composition of the firm's assets and liabilities.

Cooperating Inputs. The firm as producer can divide the input services it uses during a time period into three groups: (1) variable services purchased from outsiders, of which the firm can purchase any quantity; (2) inputs of purchased and nonvariable services that the firm must pay for, whether they are used or not, usually under some contractual arrangement: (3) inputs from firm-owned productive agents. For the first two groups, the firm usually makes cash payments to outsiders at negotiated prices. The price "paid" for input services in the third group is what is left over from revenues after the owners of the first two groups have been paid.

The firm-owned productive agents are, of course, the firm's assets, to which it holds legal title. Among these assets could be machinery, buildings, land, money, and patents. The status of inventories is rather ambiguous. They are assets to the firm but from many points of view could be considered "buffers," providing the firm with materials and outputs easily at hand. The second group of inputs — those obtained from outsiders under contractual arrangements and paid for whether or not they are used — are also assets. They are not quite assets such as those owned by the firm, being of an obviously different nature, but, having been paid for, it is well to think of them as among the firm's assets.

Activities. The firm as owner is concerned mainly with the third group of input services—from assets it owns. The firm as owner engages in a limited number of activities. It acquires and disposes of assets; it transfers the services of assets to itself as producer; it sells the services of assets to other entities. We might also include the maintenance of assets as one of the "ownership" activities. The acquiring and disposing of assets show up on the balance sheet only on "capital account." The transfer of services of the assets provides the link between the income statement and the balance sheet, as the transference of payment for the use of these assets from the income statement to the balance sheet.

There are many ways of acquiring a specific asset. The simplest and most obvious is through an outright purchase for cash—which can be viewed as an exchange of one asset for another, cash also being an asset. The acquired asset could be a building, a patent, a mine, a machine, even a whole firm. A second method of acquiring assets is through an exchange of stock by two firms. The acquiring firm's payment in the merger is the right given to the stockholders of the acquired firm to share in the acquiring firm's profit. A third method of acquiring assets is for the firm to build them. Some firms have the capacity to build machines or structures. Perhaps a more interesting variant is the development of assets through research or advertising—resulting in patents, know-how, trademarks, brand acceptance. The assets so developed, though intangible, are as valuable as tangible items. A fourth method of acquiring assets is by issuing new corporate securities. Such granting of a claim to profits is most frequently done in acquiring the asset "money" in exchange for stock. When, however, a firm acquires money by issuing bonds, it does not own the money but is only renting it.

There are no intrinsic reasons why firms must be sole owners of assets. Joint ventures, with joint ownership, have become fairly common in a number of fields. Of course, when assets are owned jointly, the individual owners lose some flexibility to determine how the services of the joint venture are sold to the firms as producers. Joint ventures usually involve long-term contractual arrangements for the sale of services of the jointly owned agents.

The firm could dispose of its assets in a number of ways, the most common being for cash, or, sometimes, by selling itself for stock in an acquiring company. The firm can also rent its assets to others under varying contractual arrangements. Renting can include purchase of another company's stock, when the purchase does not lead to control. Income received from the renting of assets is known as nonoperating income.

We can also consider fixed contractual payments for the use of assets and for productive services as part of the activities of the firm as owner. Such fixed commitments will lead to fixed cash outflows that are not directly related to the level of output of the firm as producer.

Motivations for Holding Assets. Because the firm as producer can, if it wishes, usually rent assets from other firms or buy materials from other firms, what accounts for its desire to own assets? One reason is that often acquiring certain types of assets on a rental basis or buying the services of someone else's assets on a nonexclusive basis is difficult. Assets are frequently "bolted down" and inseparable from other assets with which they are used. A second reason is that often the expenditure to acquire productive services through ownership of assets is smaller than the expenditures that would be incurred from buying the services of similar assets from outside. A third reason for acquiring assets, mainly in integrating vertically backward, is for the firm to assure itself of sources of supply. (Backward vertical integration is the acquisition of sources of supply, as when a steel-making company acquires a coal mine.) A fourth reason—in forward vertical integration—is to assure itself of outlets. Fifth, the acquiring of some assets, especially those connected with know-how or specifically designed equipment, may enable the firm to become a more efficient producer. A sixth motive is capital appreciation. Certain assets may be expected to be worth more in the future, either because their purchase prices will rise or because the assets will become more valuable with better management. Finally, the motivation for acquiring some types of assets—usually through merger—may be either to obtain a better bargaining position vis-à-vis customers or suppliers or to deny sources of supply, or outlets, to competitors. (If motivated in the last way, the acquiring of the assets may be illegal.) Other motives for acquiring assets are probably of secondary importance.

What Belongs to the Firm as Owner? Let us consider once more the firm as producer, with its three types of inputs—two being all the inputs obtained from individuals and organizations outside the firm; the other type being asset services provided by the firm as owner. Consider now the division of the revenue received over a period of time. Two portions of the revenue received by the firm as producer go to the contributors of productive services "outside" the firm for nonvariable and variable input services. The third portion, the remainder of the revenues, belongs to the firm as owner. It can be divided into several components. One part, which the firm calls depreciation, is placed in a special account. The firm is free to use these funds in any way it sees fit and may use them to replace existing assets. What remains after depreciation is deducted is profit, which is usually divided by a corporation into taxes, dividends, and retained earnings.

Profits legally belong to the owners of the assets. If, however, depreciation covers the costs of using the assets—the physical wear and tear—we may question the justifiability of the owners of the assets receiving all the profits; after all, labor, other suppliers of asset-services, suppliers of materials, and management contribute to the production process. There have been many justifications for profits: The owners of the assets take risks by acquiring something not easily convertible into cash; they have to wait, after they have invested their cash in the assets, to receive their profits; they have taken on the burden of organization and entrepreneurship.[5]

There are elements of truth in these justifications. But the notion and defense of profits going to the owners of the assets can best be understood by realizing that the owners are residual claimants. All other contributors to the production process are paid at predetermined negotiated prices arrived at by arm's-length bargaining. The "prices" the owners receive, in contrast, are completely variable, being whatever remains after paying the contributors to production whose prices are negotiated. The owners can be said to have a claim on the profits because they have agreed to accept the residual funds: They take the risks of not knowing what they will receive and agreeing to make up any shortfalls out of the value of their assets.

Arrangements could exist in which groups other than the asset-owners could be the residual claimant to profits. Consider a group of workers who go into business and, instead of buying assets, rent everything they need at negotiated prices. These workers, having paid for all inputs at predetermined prices, will receive the residual. Or consider a group of suppliers who sell through a single cooperative organization. If all the expenses of the cooperative, including those for the use of assets, are paid at predetermined prices, the suppliers of the materials (usually) receive the profit. The most important notion about profit is that it is the residual or surplus or "whatever is left."

The Rate of Return on Investment. The firm as producer measures how well it has performed by its total profits. The firm as owner evaluates its past performance in terms of rate of return on investment. This rate is the ratio of net income to the book value of the assets required to generate the income. The net income includes operating income and nonoperating income.

Operating income is derived from the activities of the firm as producer. In any particular accounting period, this operating income is the difference between revenues from production and all expenditures on inputs. With R_t the revenues in this period, V_t the expenditures on variable or controllable inputs, and F_t the fixed payments, operating income is defined as $(R_t - V_t - F_t)$. Because we have defined Z_t, the cash flow due to current activities, as $(R_t - V_t)$, operating income can also be defined as $(Z_t - F_t)$.

The definition of F_t could be ambiguous and requires some elaboration. The fixed payments could be regarded as all payments the firm must pay in a current accounting period because of fixed commit-

[5]Karl Marx made the major attack on the legitimacy of profits.

ments to outsiders. Included would be interest, contractual payments for materials and the use of assets owned by others, and even salaries of personnel that are on an annual basis. What about depreciation of the assets owned by the firm? Even though depreciation is allowed as an expense for tax purposes in much the same way as payments to outsiders, it does not involve an outflow of cash. Thus, F_t is defined here only as cash outflows due to fixed commitments and does not include depreciation.

If we designate D_t the accounting depreciation for this current period, we can define profits as $\pi_t = Z_t - F_t - D_t$, where Z_t is revenue minus variable (noncontractual or controllable) expenditures. This equation can also be written $\pi_t + D_t = Z_t - F_t$. Thus the definition of operating income as $(Z_t - F_t)$ is equivalent to profits in the traditional accounting sense plus depreciation.

Nonoperating income is usually obtained from investments in other firms or by renting assets, including cash, to other organizations. We represent this income by Y. Although nonoperating income is generally small in comparison to operating income, it is well to emphasize that the firm as owner could earn income on its assets by renting them to others as an alternative to allowing their use by the firm as producer.

The net worth of the firm is generally taken to be the value of the firm's assets minus its liabilities. The concept of rate of return is frequently employed, however, with income compared to some other definition of asset value such as gross assets, fixed assets, fixed assets plus inventory, or assets devoted to a particular use.

We can define rate of return on investment symbolically; $\rho_t = (Z_t - F_t + Y)/A_t$. In this equation ρ_t stands for rate of return on investment in period t; Z_t is cash flow, defined as revenue from sales minus expenditure for variable inputs bought from others; and F_t is expenditure for nonvariable input services bought from outside owners. The payments included in F_t would arise from past contracts that bind the firm to pay in this period for input services or assets whether or not they are used. Y_t designates nonoperating income. A_t stands for the book value of the firm's assets in period t.

The decision problems of the firm as owner have to do with future rather than past performance. The firm as owner, therefore, must make decisions that affect the future values of assets, operating income, and nonoperating income. In building models of firms, several alternative assumptions might be made about the goals of the firm as owner. One is to assume that the firm as owner attempts to maximize ρ_t in *each* future time period. But the firm may have opportunities to do things that reduce rate of return in some periods and raise it in others. To take into account such interdependencies among time periods, we must develop concepts with which to compare revenues or expenditures received or made at different points in time.

The Present Value of Future Cash Flows. Any firm or individual is concerned with the timing as well as the magnitude of money receipts and payments. Given a choice between receiving a dollar today or receiving a dollar a year from today, under most circumstances most persons would choose to receive the dollar today, because opportunities exist for earning interest on the dollar by allowing someone else to use it. If the price of using money owned by others is expressed as the amount paid for its use per year, then the price is called the annual rate of interest. If the annual rate of interest is 0.06, or 6 percent, then one dollar can be "rented out" for a year and its owner will receive $1.06 at the end of a year. Therefore, a dollar received today is worth the same as one dollar and six cents to be received a year from today. The *present value* of $1.06 to be received a year from today is one dollar, if 0.06 is the relevant discount rate.

When money is "rented out" by its owner, the interest will earn interest if it is not paid as it accrues. In this event, we say that the interest is compounded. If we let M_0 stand for the amount of money owned by a firm but "rented out" to someone else, and if we let r stand for the annual rate of interest, then the value of the firm's money after one year would be $M_0 + rM_0$, which is equal to $M_0(1 + r)$. After a second year, during which the borrower is paying for the use of the original amount of money plus the previous year's interest, the value of the asset money would be $M_0(1 + r) + r[M_0(1 + r)]$, which is equal to $M_0(1 + r)(1 + r)$, or $M_0(1 + r)^2$. Thus, if a firm rents out an amount M_0 for t years at annual interest rate r compounded once each year, then the value of this money at the end of t years would be: $M_t = M_0(1 + r)^t$.

It is possible, of course, to negotiate a rental agreement for cash assets under which the compounding takes place more than one a year. If the interest is compounded n times a year instead of once, then two changes must be made in the formula: Annual rate r must be divided by n, and the number of $(1 + r)$ terms must be multiplied by n, so that the general relationship is $M_t = M_0(1 + r/n)^{nt}$.

This relationship provides a basis for comparing magnitudes of money receipts (or payments) at different points in time.[6] If an amount M_0 presently available could be increased in value to M_t by being put

---

[6]For the special case in which $M_0 = 1$, $r = 1.00$, and $t = 1$, as n increases without limit, M_t approaches the limit e, where e is the familiar mathematical constant approximately equal to 2.718. That is,

$$e = \lim_{n \to \infty} \left(1 + \frac{1}{n}\right)^n.$$

Furthermore, for values of M_0, r, and t other than 1,

$$M_t = M_0 e^{rt} = \lim_{n \to \infty} M_0 \left(1 + \frac{r}{n}\right)^{nt}$$

therefore, $M_0 = M_t e^{-rt}$ and $M_t = M_0 e^{rt}$.

out at annual interest rate r compounded n times a year, then an amount M_t to be received t years hence is equivalent to M_0 presently available. Therefore, we can say:

$$M_0 = \frac{M_t}{\left(1 + \dfrac{r}{n}\right)^{nt}}.$$

If money is to be received at different periods in the future, leading to a "stream" of money, the present value of this stream is obtained by adding the discounted values. Thus, if various amounts of money are to be received in periods 0, 1, 2, . . ., t, . . .,∞, the present value of this stream, V_0, is

$$V_0 = \frac{M_0}{\left(1 + \dfrac{r}{n}\right)^0} + \frac{M_1}{\left(1 + \dfrac{r}{n}\right)^n} + \frac{M_2}{\left(1 + \dfrac{r}{n}\right)^{2n}} + \cdots + \frac{M_t}{\left(1 + \dfrac{r}{n}\right)^{tn}}$$

$$+ \cdots + \frac{M_\infty}{\left(1 + \dfrac{r}{n}\right)^\infty}$$

$$= \sum_{t=1}^{t=\infty} \frac{M_t}{\left(1 + \dfrac{r}{n}\right)^{tn}}.$$

The Goal of the Firm as Owner. Selecting the goal of the firm as owner is not a simple matter. Some time ago, the firm as owner seemed to aim at selecting a structure of assets and liabilities that would maximize the present value of future dividends and other cash payments to the owners of the common stock. However, with capital gains taxes and with active markets for a firm's stock, stockholders may be better served if management tries to maximize the market value of the stock or, better still, the market value of a share of stock. What determines the value of a firm's stock? This question cannot be answered with certainty. In all probability the market value is determined mainly by the "going concern" value of the firm, which in turn is defined as the present value of all the expected cash inflows minus the expected cash outflows. Two other factors can influence stock prices. One is dividends. The second is the liquidity value of the firm's assets – that is, what the firm's assets could bring if they were sold for cash.

The present value of the expected cash inflows and outflows in all future time periods can be taken as the going concern value. These cash inflows and outflows can be grouped into four categories. One of the inflows is Z_t, the difference between revenues of the firm as producer minus its payments for variable inputs in period t. These inflows have expected values for all accounting periods in the future. A second inflow is nonoperating income, Y_t. One outflow is the payment to outsiders the firm makes for all nonvariable inputs in a particular period t for which it has made commitments, which we call F_t. Cash outflow could also result from purchases made to increase the firm's noncash assets. We can call such cash flows ΔA_t. If the firm sells assets, ΔA_t would be positive—that is, it could be a cash inflow. If the firm buys assets, ΔA_t is negative. There are other inflows and outflows, due to borrowing, purchase or sale of equities, and taxes, that we defer to Chapter 6.

Because inflows and outflows are "streams" that take place in the future, in a number of time periods, their present value should be discounted by r, the rate at which the firm could loan out its money.[7] The value of the firm as a going concern can then be defined as:

$$V_0 = \sum_{t=0}^{t=\infty} \frac{Z_t + Y_t - F_t + \Delta A_t}{\left(1 + \dfrac{r}{n}\right)^{nt}}. \qquad (2.7)$$

As a first approximation, the firm as owner can be assumed to structure its assets and liabilities to maximize V_0, the present value of the firm. However, various factors could temper its decisions. First, the market value of stock is determined not only by the value of the firm as a going concern but by its dividend payments. Thus, it may be necessary to pay dividends even though those funds could be used to increase the value of V_0. Second, the firm must be concerned with avoiding liquidity problems and possibly bankruptcy. It must keep its assets in a form that will allow creditors to be paid from assets in the event that cash flows are negative in any future period. In other words, the firm must be concerned with the liquid value of its assets. Third, the stockholders who control the firm presumably want to maintain control. Thus, the firm may not wish to issue new stock, or debt securities, that would jeopardize control.[8] Subject to these limitations, the maximization of the present value of the firm will be considered the goal of the firm as owner. Because the firm as owner controls the firm as producer, this can be considered the overall goal of the firm.

SIMPLIFYING DECISION MODELS

Although it is useful to consider the firm an entity that maximizes the discounted present value of future cash flows, the problem of ascertaining the effect on present value of each particular decision may be impossible to solve. Difficulties in applying the model to the

---

[7]There is considerable controversy over the "appropriate" discount rate. Many think it should be the firm's "cost of capital." We think analysis would be simpler and more nearly correct if the discount rate is taken as the rate at which the firm could loan out money.

[8]We will go into these objectives in greater detail in Chapter 6.

decision problems of real-world businesses require the development of simpler models for particular decisions. Insofar as possible such simpler models should be consistent with the general present value model. For example, we can say that anything a firm can do to raise Z in any period is desirable if it has no negative effect on Z in any other period or on the other variables in the present value function (equation 2.7). Therefore, our earlier model of the firm as producer may be quite consistent with the more general model of the firm as owner.

The model of the firm as producer is too complex to use without simplifying assumptions. Profit from operations in a particular time period is determined by only four types of variables — output prices, output quantities, input service prices, and input service quantities — as shown in equation 2.6. Yet there are thousands of different outputs and input services. In addition, there are innumerable types of assets from which the firm as owner may choose. Even with computers, the job of simultaneously considering all the various outputs, input services, and assets from which the firm can choose is an immense task, still beyond our capabilities. We therefore have to devise ways to reduce the number of outputs, input services, assets, and prices to manageable proportions. In this section, we consider as ways of limiting the numbers of variables affecting Z_t and V_0, the use of subsystems, and aggregation of variables, as well as a distinction between short-run and long-run models.

Subsystems and Suboptimization. In complex organizations, decentralization enables each of several subsystems to deal with a limited and, hopefully, manageable portion of the "system" decision-making. Thus, universities are divided into colleges, which are further divided into departments; and governments are divided into bureaus, which are further divided into offices. Each subsystem can then be delegated the task of making the best possible decisions within the constraints imposed on it from above. A skillful organizer structures and constrains the subsystems so that suboptimization in each part is consistent with optimization for the whole organization. The subsystems are structured, and therefore coordinated, by higher management, which sets targets, delegates authority, and provides budgets.

The firm can be divided into subsystems on such bases as product, function, plant, and geographic area. Of these different types of division, the product is both common and useful. When the production and marketing of a product are essentially independent of the production and marketing of other products, then it makes particularly good sense to view that product — decisions about its output level, its price, and the inputs to use in its production — as a subsystem. When this can be done, the selection of profit-maximizing values for the product's decision variables is completely consistent with the maximization of profits for the whole firm. The ability to view a single product in this way can greatly simplify our models as it does decision-making in the real world. Much of our analysis will therefore be concerned with single-product subsystems of multi-product firms or, sometimes, with simple single-product firms.

If a product is not independent of other products, it would be an error to view that product as a separate subsystem, to be separately suboptimized by, for example, maximizing profits attributable to that product. Such lack of independence frequently arises when some input that is in limited supply is necessary to the production of that and other products. If this were the case for products 1 and 2, a selection of values for the decision variables that would maximize the profit attributable to product 1 would probably interfere with the profits that could be made from product 2 and may therefore not be consistent with the maximization of profits for the whole firm. In this event the interdependent products should be part of the same subsystem, and we would normally want to maximize the joint profit from both products. But even when each product cannot be viewed as a subsystem, decisions are still greatly simplified by grouping inter-dependent products into separate subsystems.

There are other useful ways to structure the subsystems. We have already presented one – the division of the activities of the firm into those of producer and owner. In our choice of the maximization of the present value of future cash flows (rather than maximization of profits in any period) as the main goal of the firm, we have in effect relegated the firm as producer to the role of a subsystem of the firm as owner. By dividing the activities of the firm as producer into an acquirer of productive inputs, a seller of outputs, and a transformer of inputs into outputs, we have subdivided a subsystem into sub-subsystems.

Aggregation. A second method for simplifying decision problems is to combine physically distinctive inputs and outputs into input and output "packages." Such procedures obviously reduce the number of decision variables and could give the single-product subsystem greater applicability. In many real-world circumstances, it is obvious that such aggregation is desirable. Consider, for example, a garment manufacturer who cuts different sizes from the same basic pattern or who produces his product in a range of colors. It would often be an unnecessary complication to treat each size and color as a separate product. Many types of inputs in the real world have to be used together in reasonably fixed proportions and can therefore be aggregated into packages, or "bundles" of inputs.

These packages can be handled in two basic ways. Perhaps the most obvious way is to view them as packages, as we have been doing. A package of inputs or outputs has a package price, which depends on the prices and quantities of the individual inputs or outputs that constitute the package. A less obvious way to view a package is to define the product so abstractly that it could be thought to encompass a combination of the elements in the package. Thus, the garment manufacturer refers to a model number as the product, with an understanding it comes in a variety of sizes and colors. This abstraction enables us to use the average, or representative, price of the combination of inputs or outputs as the price.

There is one important common-sense rule to follow for aggregating inputs and outputs: The inputs or outputs being aggregated should be in reasonably fixed proportion to each other. If it is feasible and perhaps desirable to vary the proportion of the elements constituting the product, then any aggregation only obscures the problem of finding the best mix. If the garment manufacturer has to make a choice between different proportions of red dresses and blue dresses, then red dresses and blue dresses should be considered different products. But if he knows on the basis of market studies or past experience that three blue dresses can be expected to be sold for every red dress sold, then the different colors can be combined into a package.

The Short Run and the Long Run. Economics has made much use of the concepts of the short run and the long run, and these terms have passed into general usage in many fields. They are important in our development of decision models; indeed, we will organize much of our discussion by dividing the firm's decisions into short-run and long-run categories. Because of the widespread usage and the importance of these terms and because we will use them somewhat differently than is traditionally done, some background information to provide perspective may be useful.

The economist generally given credit for systematically introducing the terms was Alfred Marshall.[9] In distinguishing between temporary and normal market prices, Marshall argued that prices and profits could be temporarily high for short periods but that in competitive markets prices and profits tend to become normal — that is, approach the cost of production, given time for reactions to take place. The difference between the temporary price and the normal price ultimately depends on the ability of firms to expand, or contract, the supply.

Let us say that there is an unforeseen rise in demand for a particular product. For the immediate period following that rise, supply will not increase commensurately because firms need time to acquire new capital assets or to enter the market and supply the demand. Thus the increase in supply will be limited to the additional quantities that firms can produce by using more labor and other variable inputs with the fixed quantity of capital assets. The immediate effect of this comparative shortage of supply will be a higher price and higher profits. If the increased demand is expected to continue, high profits

[9]Marshall's *Principles of Economics*, originally published in 1890, is considered a landmark of economic reasoning.

will induce firms to expand their capital assets and new firms to enter the market. Eventually the new assets will be put into production, and there will be an increase in supply, which will have the effect of lowering the price and profits. Additional capital assets will continue to be brought into production as long as there are above-normal profits. At some point profits will drop to "normal," and no more capital assets for this industry will be acquired (except to replace those that wear out). The price at this "equilibrium" point should approximate the cost of production, plus a normal profit. There are, then, a short-run or temporary price and a long-run or normal price. The length of time that the temporary price will hold depends on the speed with which capital assets are put into production. Marshall was aware that normal prices and profits may never actually be observed, because short-run conditions could change frequently; thus the long-run, normal price would be simply the direction toward which the temporary price would move until some new development altered demand conditions.

As economics became more mathematical, it became necessary to define the short run and the long run more precisely. In the traditional theory of the firm, the definition depended on the ability of the firm to expand or contract the fixed assets used in production. The short run therefore is generally defined as the period of time during which the firm cannot expand or decrease its fixed assets and can therefore increase or decrease its output only by varying the "variable" inputs, such as labor and materials. The long run is the period of time beginning after the firm has had a chance to expand or decrease its (no longer) "fixed" assets. The direct effect of the inability to expand capital assets is upon the available choices of input services to the firm; the indirect effect is upon cost and output.

These traditional definitions rest mainly on the view that capital assets cannot be immediately expanded because constructing them generally takes considerable time. A firm cannot decrease its capital assets readily because they are specialized and therefore not easily sold. But what could be said about the short run and long run if the firm could obtain assets within a short period of time by buying them from other firms or could sell them easily? What if manufacturers of some capital assets keep an inventory of finished goods? These conditions may be increasingly true for many types of physical assets. What about important intangible assets, such as patents, trademarks, and the contractual right to buy at an advantageous price? These can often be acquired immediately. Is the concept of the short run meaningless under such conditions?

The short run and the long run can be most useful concepts if emphasis is on the willingness of the firm to acquire capital assets rather than on the time it takes to construct these assets. Consider a steel producer who expects an upsurge in business in the upcoming month. If it wishes, the firm could buy a steel mill from another company and have it operating in a short period of time. The firm must choose how to expand output: It could use its existing mill more intensively, or it could buy the new mill. Common sense tells us that with business expected to improve only for the upcoming month, the firm should opt for more intensive use of existing plant. Why not buy the new mill? Because it could cost a great deal of money, financing may be difficult, business may not be good in future periods, the firm may not be able to sell the mill after the month is over. However, suppose the firm makes a long-range forecast and is persuaded that business will improve for the next twenty years. In this situation the purchase of the mill seems quite sensible and should certainly be explored. What has changed? The firm, by looking into the distant future, may now be willing to make a more or less irreversible commitment that it would not even consider on the basis of expected events in the immediate future.

We can now offer more useful definitions of the short run and the long run than those traditionally given. First, we should state what may not be too obvious: Decisions must always be made in the present. The firm is willing to make some decisions in response to its view of a short period of time into the future; others are made only in response to its view of the distant future. Decisions could, therefore, be divided into short-run and long-run decisions. Consider now a period of time, starting from the present, during which the firm is unwilling to make new long-run commitments or if the firm makes long-run commitments, they cannot be completed. This would be the short-run period. Beyond that period is the long run.

The short run and long run correspond to our concepts of the firm as producer and owner. The firm as owner is largely concerned with acquiring fixed and expensive assets. Thus it "operates" in the long run. The firm as producer operates with the assets at hand, in the short run. The firm as owner, however, through its acquisition and disposal of capital assets, influences the choices available to the firm as producer.

We ask the reader to accept these views and definitions of the short and long run as first approximations. In the four chapters that follow, these important concepts will be developed with greater precision.

Discussion Questions

1. What is to be gained by viewing the firm as producer and as owner?

2. What are some of the advantages of distinguishing an input service from the agent that renders the service?

3. Could an engineer determine the efficiency of an input-output mechanism if there is more than one input or usable output? How can the difficulties be overcome by "valuing" the inputs and outputs? What kinds of problems

could arise in the valuation process? What if there were no markets on which prices are determined? Can we see why it is easier to evaluate the performance of a firm than the performance, say, of a government?

4. Many are currently debating whether profit maximization is a socially desirable goal for the firm. How might the "rules of the game" enter into the debate?

5. What are some of the problems of determining the values of input services from assets that have been acquired in the past?

6. Does anything inherent in our theology, folklore, or legal system require that profits belong to those who legally own the firm's assets? Can you think of alternative institutional arrangements by which profits could go to customers, workers, managers, lenders, suppliers, society in general? What can you say about the real distribution of profits if the firm pays more than it has to for workers or managers or if the firm sells at lower prices than it could obtain?

7. In what sense is a firm doing a better job by increasing the rate of return on its assets? Does society benefit in any way from a higher rate of return? How might differences in capital intensity among different industries give a false picture of how well a firm is using its assets?

8. How do we value assets in general? What is meant by "capitalizing" an income stream? It is commonly observed that stock market prices tend to rise when interest rates fall and fall when interest rates rise. How might such phenomena be explained? What do we really purchase when we buy a share of stock?

9. What are the relationships between subsystems, suboptimization, organization, and decision-making? What kind of problems can arise when an organization is divided into subsystems for decision-making purposes?

10. Give some examples of short-run and long-run decisions from everyday life. How does the degree of reversibility of a decision influence how far ahead we must look when evaluating a decision?

3 The Elements of Short-Run Decision Models

In our model of the firm as producer, we showed that the decision problem was to select the values of the output levels, the input levels, and the prices of outputs and inputs that would maximize either π_t, the profit per period, or Z_t, the cash flow per period from productive activity. In this chapter the elements that are necessary for these decision problems are defined and discussed. Four types of elements can be distinguished in the decision process: (1) the decision variables, the values of which must be selected; (2) a preference criterion, or objective function, that relates the values chosen for the decision variables to a goal; (3) the constraints, which limit the possible choices of values of the decision variables; (4) an optimization process, which ascertains the best values for the decision variables, given the preference criterion and the constraints.

Even with only four types of decision variables – the quantities of outputs and inputs and their prices – the decision models can be quite complicated if there are large numbers of inputs and outputs. Therefore, to keep our models reasonably simple, we shall assume that the firm produces only one or a small number of outputs and that it uses only a small number of inputs. We should, of course, bear in mind that more complex models are often needed in the real world.

The constraints in particular will receive most of our attention. Indeed, in much of this book we shall be concerned with understanding and estimating the constraints and learning how they can be changed. We shall show that the key distinction between the short run and long run, or between the firm as producer and as owner, depends on whether the firm is willing and able to change the constraints. The firm as producer operates under a given set of constraints. The firm as owner seeks to change the constraints.

THE BASIC ELEMENTS

We can illustrate the basic ingredients in a short-run decision model by assuming that the firm, or a unit of a firm, produces only one product and uses inputs of only two productive services. Thus, there are only six decision variables: the quantity (Q) of output to produce per day (or other unit of time), the price (P) per unit to ask for that output, the quantities per day to purchase and use of each of the two input services $(x_1$ and $x_2)$, and the prices per unit to offer for each input $(p_1$ and $p_2)$.

If we assume that the goal of the firm is to maximize profit (π), defined simply as the difference between revenue and expenditures per time period, then the objective function can be expressed:

$$\pi = PQ - p_1x_1 - p_2x_2. \tag{3.1}$$

For each set of values of the six decision variables, there exists a unique value of the criterion or goal variable, π. The set of values of the prices and quantities that gives the highest profit is, of course, the best set. If the firm operated with no constraints on its freedom to pick values for the decision variables, it could earn an infinitely high profit simply by choosing an infinitely high value for P and Q and a zero value for p_1, p_2, x_1, x_2. Real-world firms, however, cannot make profits of infinity squared because their freedom to choose values for the decision variables is constrained — for example, by the freedom of others to not buy and not sell. Although the firm is free to ask an infinitely high price for its output, it seems reasonable to assume that if it did so, it would sell a zero quantity. Likewise, if it offers zero prices for inputs, it could buy only zero quantities and not be able to produce any output. Such interdependencies can be stated in the form of constraint equations and inequations.

For example, the assumption that the quantity sold cannot be determined independently of the asking price can be stated as $Q \le f(P)$, which implies that there is some maximum quantity of output that could be sold at each asking price. Similarly, the fact that the output quantity depends upon the input quantities can be expressed as $Q \le f(x_1, x_2)$, which implies that the maximum output depends on combinations of the inputs. Even for so simple a problem as we are considering, there could be a larger number of additional constraints. For example, the quantity used of input 1 may not be independent of the price of input 1. Thus, we would also have this constraint, $x_1 \le f(p_1)$, which means that the amount of productive service 1 that we can purchase can be no more than some maximum amount that depends on the price we offer.

When all constraints are known and listed, they together determine the "opportunity set," which is the set of values for the six decision variables from which the firm can choose. The constraints determine which values are possible. The preference criterion and objective function indicate preferability among alternative combinations of these values. The optimization process consists of selecting the best possible combination of values from among all those contained in the opportunity set. Optimization is essentially a mathematical operation. Not all problems of this type are solvable. The analyst may have to manipulate the constraints and objective function by simplifying or combining them in various ways to make optimal solutions both possible and readily obtainable. Therefore, although a decision-maker might be able to take a well-defined objective function and a set of precisely stated constraints to a mathematician and get him to select the set of values for the decision variables that maximizes the objective function, subject to the set of constraints on those values, in practice the economist or decision-maker would have to participate in the optimization process.

Variables, preference criteria, and constraints are our conceptual model-building tools, but they do not come neatly labeled as such in the real world. They can, in fact, differ in classification from one problem to the next. That is, a variable, an objective function, or a constraint can change as we change the context. For example, to the firm as a whole the Q in equation 3.1 is a decision variable. When the value of Q has been determined, however, Q becomes a target or goal. The production department, in particular, takes Q as a target; *its* decision variables are the inputs to use. Furthermore, Q should not be seen strictly as the goal of the production department; it is more nearly accurately described as producing the targeted output at the least possible cost. Together with the input-output relationship, as in $Q \leq f(x_1, x_2)$, the targeted output becomes a constraint on the possible choices of inputs. Often, constraints and objective functions can be meaningfully classified only in the context of a specific problem.

PREFERENCE CRITERIA

A decision model must include some statement of the criterion on the basis of which choices are to be made. Usually the criterion is assumed to be the goal of making a variable — profit, revenue, cost — as large or as small as possible. The preference criterion must consist of the goal variable expressed in terms of the decision variables, plus a statement to maximize or minimize the goal variable, although sometimes this statement may be to achieve some fixed target value for the goal variable. The relation between the goal variable and the decision variables is often called the objective function.

In the manipulation of objective functions and constraints, it is frequently possible to incorporate one or more constraints into the objective function as a step in the optimization process. We can, therefore, have two classes of objective functions — without and with an incorporation of the constraints.

Objective Functions with No Incorporation of Constraints. Maximization of profits is the most widely assumed goal of the firm as producer. For the one-product two-input case, the objective function is

$$\pi = PQ - p_1 x_1 - p_2 x_2, \tag{3.2}$$

and the goal is to select the values for the decision variable that maximize the goal variable, π. Possible values of these decision variables will be limited by the constraints. In more general form, for multiple outputs and inputs, the objective function is

$$\pi = P_1 Q_1 + P_2 Q_2 + \ldots - p_1 x_1 - p_2 x_2 - \ldots$$

When some of the inputs are fixed and paid for whether or not they have been used—most commonly the services of the firm's fixed assets—these input terms could be left out of the profit function. When this is done, the profit function is converted into a cash-flow function, which consists of the revenues from the outputs minus the expenditures on the variable, or controllable, inputs. Thus, in the one-product case, if x_2 is the fixed input, the profit function (equation 3.2) becomes the cash-flow function, $Z = PQ - p_1 x_1$.

For the one-product case, it usually does not make much difference whether we use the profit equation or the cash-flow equation as the objective function in optimization problems. But for multiple-product cases in which the same fixed input(s) is required for a number of different outputs, our optimization techniques are easier to use when the objective function is specified in terms of the cash flow. Thus, if we have a two-product case with three inputs, where input 3 is fixed and must be paid for, the cash-flow objective is

$$Z = P_1 Q_1 + P_2 Q_2 - p_1 x_1 - p_2 x_2. \tag{3.3}$$

A little algebraic manipulation of equation 3.3 enables us to express Z in terms of the cash flow associated with each output. Let us assume for this purpose that input 1 is used only in output 1, while input 2 is used only in output 2. Now, we first multiply and divide each of the expenditure terms by Q_1 and Q_2 respectively. This gives

$$Z = P_1 Q_1 + P_2 Q_2 - \left(\frac{p_1 x_1}{Q_1}\right) Q_1 - \left(\frac{p_2 x_2}{Q_2}\right) Q_2.$$

The terms in parentheses are now the variable expenditures per unit of the designated outputs. Next we add the first and third terms, and the second and fourth, to obtain

$$Z = \left(P_1 - \frac{p_1 x_1}{Q_1}\right) Q_1 + \left(P_2 - \frac{p_2 x_2}{Q_2}\right) Q_2.$$

The terms in brackets are the cash flows per unit of each of the outputs. For the first output, for example, P_1 is the revenue per unit of product 1, $p_1 x_1 / Q_1$ is the variable cost per unit of product 1, and the difference is the cash flow per unit of product 1.

Another important goal, generally a subgoal rather than the main goal, is the minimization of cost. If C is the cost goal, then the decision variables are the input quantities and prices. In a two-input case, the objective function is $C = p_1 x_1 + p_2 x_2$. We would usually want to select the values for the decision variables that minimize C, almost always subject to producing some level of output.

Sometimes revenue is the goal variable, in which case the objective function for a multi-product firm is expressed in terms of the output prices and quantities:

$$R = P_1 Q_1 + P_2 Q_2 + \ldots$$

Occasionally, output may be the goal variable as well as a decision variable. Then the objective function is to maximize $Q_1 = Q_1$.

Objective Functions with Constraints Incorporated. Incorporation of one or more constraints into the preference criterion may help in the solution of the optimization problem. Such a "compound" preference criterion is obtained by starting with a "pure" preference criterion and substituting for one or more of the decision variables in the objective function from the constraints.

To see how this may work, let us consider our one-product two-input case. If we assume that the firm wants to maximize profit, π, the objective function, is

$$\pi = PQ - p_1 x_1 - p_2 x_2. \tag{3.4}$$

Even in this simple case, there are six decision variables — not a convenient number to work with.

Let us now say that one of the constraints shows the maximum price that could be obtained for any quantity of output and that it is

$$P \le 100 - 0.5Q. \tag{3.5}$$

Clearly, the goal is best served if the firm asks the maximum price for any given level of output. Therefore, inequation 3.5 can be changed into a simple equation:

$$P = 100 - 0.5Q. \tag{3.6}$$

It is now possible to use equation 3.6 to substitute the term $(100 - 0.5Q)$ for P in equation 3.4, which yields

$$\pi = (100 - 0.5Q)Q - p_1 x_1 - p_2 x_2. \tag{3.7}$$

This simple mathematical manipulation has accomplished a number of things. First, it has reduced the number of decision variables in the objective function from six to five — a step in the right direction. In the optimization process, there will be one less constraint to deal with. Notice that the process of substituting for P in equation 3.4 does not eliminate the constraint or the necessity of eventually deciding on a value for P. The constraint — which can be thought of as the statement that P is not able to be varied independently of Q – is still operative, although it is now part of the objective function. The disappearance of P simply means that, in the optimization process, only Q would be determined. That optimal value of Q, however, could be inserted in equation 3.6 to obtain the optimal value for P.

In some models, it may be possible to incorporate all the constraints into the objective function, thereby reducing the objective function to just one decision variable. When this can be done, the optimization problem becomes a simple problem of finding the maximum (or minimum) value of a function of one variable. In the one-product model in particular, we can often incorporate constraints in such a way that the expenditures on inputs are expressed in terms only of Q. When this can be done, the expenditure terms in equation 3.7 would be replaced by an output cost function, and profit is then a function only of Q. However, certain conditions must be met when a constraint is incorporated into an objective function, which will be discussed later.

Open-ended, Fixed Target, and Minimum Target Goals. To assess alternative sets of values for the decision variables, an analyst must have not only an objective function but also a statement regarding the value desired for the goal variable. The maximization and minimization goals just discussed are open-ended. We call them open-ended because literally no figure for the criterion (goal) variable is too high if we wish to maximize (or too low if we wish to minimize). Instead of maximization or minimization, however, a firm may seek to achieve some fixed value for the criterion variable or some minimum target.

Examples of fixed target goals could be $4 profit per share this year, revenues that are 5 percent higher than last year's, an output level that gives the firm 30 percent of the market. We must be careful to distinguish between true fixed target goals and the use of a target to spur on the efforts of an organization – for example, "Let's see if we can hit $4 per share earnings this year." In a true fixed target goal, overfulfillment of the goal – making $5 per share – would be less preferable than the target of $4.

A third type of goal is one in which there is a minimum target for the criterion variable. Examples are at least $4 profit per share this year, revenues that are at least 5 percent higher than last year's, an output level that gives the firm at least 30 percent of the market. Minimum target goals do not imply any undesirability of overfulfillment of the targets and thus are probably much more widely used than fixed target goals.

Graphic Representation of Preference Criteria. A preference criterion with no more than two decision variables can be represented on a two-dimensional graph. Consider, for example, a simple revenue

criterion for a one-product firm. The objective function can be written
$R = PQ$.

This equation would actually be three dimensional, with its three
variables defining space. It would appear as a cone as in Figure 3.1.

This three-dimensional figure could be shown on a two-dimensional
graph in the same way that the contours of a hill are portrayed on
maps. First, we could measure some distance along the R-axis — say
to where R equals 100 — and then take a cross-section of the three-
dimensional graph. The intersection of the cone with a plane that goes
through the point ($R = 100$) and that is parallel to the P,Q plane can
be projected down to the P,Q plane. The shape of such an intersection, or contour line, will appear as in Figure 3.2. Because the plane
was sliced at the point where R equals 100, the P,Q combinations
shown in the diagram — that is, the cross-section — all yield revenues
of \$100. For this reason, the curve is known as an isorevenue curve
("iso" is the Greek equivalent of "same").

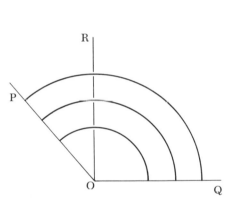

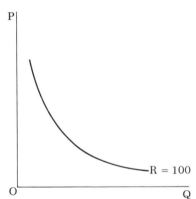

FIGURE 3.1   Three-dimensional
representation of a revenue function

FIGURE 3.2   Isorevenue curve

When the same procedure is followed for different values of R, an
isorevenue map is generated, as in Figure 3.3. Each isorevenue curve
shows all the P,Q combinations that would yield the specified value
of R. Although we show only a few curves on this map, notice that
an infinite number of isorevenue curves could be drawn — one for each
possible value of R.

The substitution of the fixed value, 100 for R, in $R = PQ$ is the
algebraic equivalent of slicing a plane through the R-axis at $R = 100$.
Each contour line in Figure 3.3 is simply the graph of the two-variable
function that results from treating the third variable as a constant.

Since higher values of R have isorevenue curves farther to the
right, we can readily say whether any point representing a combination of the decision variables P and Q is better than, as good as, or

worse than, any other point. Thus, it is clear that, from the viewpoint of revenue maximization, point A in Figure 3.3 is preferable to any of the other labeled points and that point B is preferable to all others except point A. Points C and D are equally preferable because both of these combinations of P and Q yield the same value of R. The decision-maker is therefore indifferent between C and D. For this reason such maps are often called indifference maps.

Points C and D are both clearly preferable to E and F. It is not immediately clear whether point E is better than, as good as, or worse than, point F. The doubt, however, can easily be dispelled by the simple expediency of drawing in more isorevenue curves, such as the dashed curve in Figure 3.4. Because of our ability to draw as many isorevenue curves as we wish, it is always possible to evaluate the relative preferability of any two P,Q combinations.

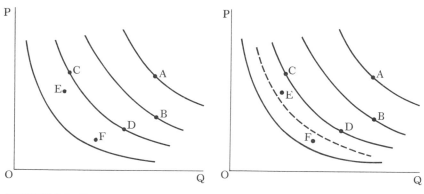

FIGURE 3.3   Isorevenue map   FIGURE 3.4   Isorevenue map

Maximization of revenue is not a meaningful goal unless constraints involving profits or costs are included in the model. We have used a revenue-maximization criterion here not because of its inherent importance but because of the ease with which it can be illustrated graphically. Another example that is both important in analysis and amenable to graphic illustration is the preference criterion of minimization of cost, subject to constraints on input prices.

Let us consider the objective function $C = p_1 x_1 + p_2 x_2$. If we limit the number of inputs to two and assume that their prices are constant amounts, $\bar{p}_1$, and $\bar{p}_2$, then these price constraints can be incorporated into the objective function. We have, then, the goal of minimizing

$$C = \bar{p}_1 x_1 + \bar{p}_2 x_2.$$

This objective function can be depicted in three dimensions as in Figure 3.5. The cost surface appears as a plane that goes through the origin. The degree of "tilt" in each direction is determined by the magnitude of the two prices.

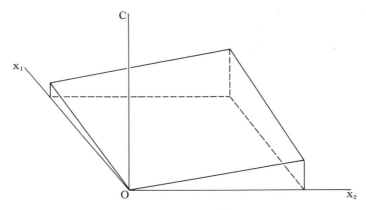

FIGURE 3.5   Input cost function

We can show this input cost function in two dimensions with contour lines, each of which is the locus of x_1, x_2 combinations having the same cost. The lines are called isocost lines because each line represents input combinations all having the same expenditure. They appear as straight lines in Figure 3.6 because the surface they map is a plane. The isocost map readily shows preferability for input combinations. Because lower costs are more desirable, input combinations closer to the origin are more desirable than input combinations further from the origin. Thus, the input combination designated by A is preferable to input combinations B, C, D; B is preferable to C and D; C and D are equally preferable.

These preference maps are most useful when an objective function is expressed in terms of two decision variables. There are many other preference functions where such maps can show preferability of combinations of decision variables.

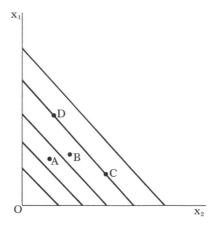

FIGURE 3.6   Isocost map

How do we represent graphically a profit objective function such as equation 3.4? We can consider isoprofit curves analogous to iso-revenue curves. In the sense that we can determine all the combinations of the six decision variables that yield the same profit such curves might be defined, but they cannot be graphically presented in two- or three-dimensional space. If, however, some of the constraints are incorporated into the objective function, the number of decision variables might be reduced enough to permit graphic representation of the objective function.

Goal Reconciliation. Business firms, like other forms of organizations and individuals, may have many goals, some of which may be difficult to clearly define. A firm may want to maximize short-run profit, long-run cash flows, and sales, and minimize costs. In addition it may want to maintain a viable organization, avoid "too large" risks, and maintain good relations with competitors, governments, customers, and communities. These goals can often conflict because the attempt to advance one of them can often be accomplished only at the expense of one or more of the others.

Problems of goal conflict arise even in traditional models of the firm, which assume profit maximization is the firm's only goal. The conflict concerns future and present profit maximization. The maximization of short-run profits would be completely consistent with the maximization of the stream of future profits and cash flows only if the firm's short-run choices of decision variables have no effect on its long-run prospects. Such consistency is generally not present for a large firm whose activities in the short run can influence its constraints and choices in future periods. Consider the firm whose profit-maximizing price in the short run is high enough to make likely the entry of new competitors. Should it not take into account in its short-run decisions the possibility that what it does may affect its future profits?[1]

The goal of profit maximization may also conflict with the goal of preserving the viability of the firm. In a dynamic economy, various opportunities and threats can be expected to arrive in the future, but the future can generally be foreseen only dimly. Should not the firm maintain an organization that can take advantage of the opportunities and cope with the threats? What if the development of such viability requires that some short-run profits be sacrificed?

Often problems of goal reconciliation arise because different units in the firm, and different individuals, have, and should have, different goals. The marketing department might have revenue maximization as a goal; the cost accountant could have cost minimization; public relations men may worry about the firm's image; antitrust lawyers are concerned about marketing practices. Obviously there has to be

[1]In economics, we call a price set low enough to deter new entrants a limit price.

some means of coordinating the different units of a firm by reconciling their goals.

The discussion of open-ended, fixed target, and minimum target
goals, provides us with some of the conceptual tools with which to
reconcile goals. First, we may state categorically that it is impossible
to work simultaneously toward two or more open-ended goals that depend on at least one of the same decision variables. An attempt to
simultaneously maximize sales volume, profit, and revenues cannot
be even logically approached. About all we might do with two or more
such "irreconcilable" goals is to construct a "utility" function in
terms of these three goals. For example, we may say that

$$U = f(\pi, R, Q)$$

and devise a weighting system to measure how important π, R, and
Q are as goals giving "utility" to the firm. We could determine the
values of the decision variable that would maximize U, but this does
not mean that π, R, and Q are maximized.

Although we cannot entertain two or more open-ended goals, it is
possible to have one open-ended goal and any number of target goals
(especially minimum target goals), as long as the target goals are not
inconsistent with each other. Consider, for example, the open-ended
goal that profits be maximized, and the target goals that output be
at least 1,000 units and revenues at least $10,000. It is perfectly pos-
sible to pursue these three goals if the two target goals are consistent—that is, if there are in the opportunity set a set of P,Q values
that can make Q greater than or equal to 1,000 and PQ greater than
or equal to $10,000.

Consider next the goals of the production department. It is not
possible to have simultaneously the goals of cost minimization and
output maximization. But it is possible to have the goals of cost minimization and an output target of 1,000 units. Or alternatively the
goals may be output maximization and expenditure on inputs of
$7000. We should be able to see that that allocation of target and
open-ended goals among units of the firms is the way to coordinate
activities while letting each unit pursue its individual goal.

If we view the open-ended goal as *the* goal—thinking of it in this
way is useful—then the target goals can be thought of as constraints
upon the choice of values for the decision variables that limit the
pursuit of the open-ended goal. An open-ended goal of profit maximization and a minimum target goal of revenues of $10,000 will, after
all, mean that the minimum target goal will foreclose, or limit, some
of the P,Q combinations that could be selected in an attempt to
maximize profit.[2] Or an output target will mean that the input com-

---

[2]Economists who argue that large firms are run primarily for the managers
usually take sales revenue as the "open-ended" goal and some amount of
profit as the minimum target goal. See, for example, William J. Baumol, *Economic Theory and Operations Analysis*, 2nd ed. (Englewood Cliffs, N.J.:
Prentice-Hall, 1965), p. 301.

binations the production department could choose in its attempt to minimize cost will be limited. These target goals are evidently constraints in much the same way as other constraints, except for the fact that they are "self-imposed."

Why are we so certain that the firm (or any organization or individual) can simultaneously have one open-ended goal and any number of consistent target goals? Because in the implicit sequencing of decision-making the open-ended goal is what might be called the residual claimant. Thus when we say we will maximize profits subject to the self-imposed constraint (or minimum target goal) that revenues be at least $10,000, we are really saying the following: First make sure that revenues are at least $10,000; then, try to make the highest possible profits. Which goal is more important, the goal we wish to safeguard or the goal that will occupy all our energies after the first goal has been safeguarded? There does not seem to be any immediate answer to this question. But we can say that one goal becomes relatively more or less important with a change in the target. If, for example, the revenue target is lowered from $10,000 to $5000, are we not downgrading the revenue goal vis-à-vis the profit goal? A major management problem is the ordering of the firm's priorities implicit in such goal-setting.

CONSTRAINTS

Several types of constraint limit the firm's short-run choice of values for its decision variables. One type has as its source the freedom of outsiders to deal, refuse to deal, or limit their dealings with the firm. This freedom limits a firm's choice of price-quantity combinations for individual outputs and inputs. A second limitation on the firm's choices are technological necessities, which prevent the firm from selecting output quantities independently of input quantities. The "fixities" of certain types of productive services are another constraint. Acquiring the assets needed to yield certain services may take a great deal of time, or it may not be economically feasible; thus the availability of these services is limited in the short run.

"Indivisibilities" arise when the firm is unable to divide output, input, or prices into reasonably small units. As a result, the field of choice cannot be defined as consisting of all real and positive numbers, and the assumption of infinitely small changes is unreasonable. Indivisibility typically occurs when the output is a big unit, such as an aircraft carrier, or when an input comes in big chunks, such as a whole bridge or tunnel or some particular machine.

A fifth constraint is legal. The legal authority to which the firm is subject is generally some branch of government but may be a non-government authority to which the firm has agreed to submit, such as a commissioner of an industry or a labor arbitrator. Self-imposed limitations are another constraint. They generally arise because of the need to reconcile conflicting goals. Knowledge and access to market, or more accurately, lack of knowledge and barriers to access, also limit the firm's choice of values in the short run. Unawareness or lack of the possibilities of producing certain outputs or using certain inputs is an effective limitation on choice.

Constraints may be divided into two categories—simple and compound. A simple constraint is one in which only one of the seven sources of constraint plays a part. Compound constraints arise principally because we have considerable flexibility to combine simple constraints. We shall see that combining constraints eliminates some variables, simplifies the optimization problem, and permits portraying the constraint on a two-dimensional diagram. In the analysis that follows, in order to make maximum use of graphs, we have picked constraints that have only two variables. In the real world, however, we frequently work in more than two dimensions.

Outsiders' Freedom. A firm can sell or buy either from identified sources under contract or on the open market. Those under contract are not free to not deal with the firm. In open market deals any potential buyer or seller can choose to deal or not deal with our model firm. A law-abiding firm selling to buyers free not to buy can sell some maximum quantity at each alternative asking price. If we assume that only one asking price will be chosen in a given time period, a unique maximum quantity demanded constrains the quantity the firm can sell at that price. The whole range of alternative asking prices and maximum quantities that can be sold is known as a demand curve. Although the presence of this constraint is independent of the firm's knowledge of it, prior knowledge of the maximum quantity that can be sold at each potential price enables the firm to know the combinations of asking price and sales quantity that are available.

We represent the limitation the asking price places on the quantity that could be sold by the inequation $Q \leq f(P)$. Represented graphically, with asking price on the vertical axis and quantity on the horizontal axis, the constrained set of alternatives is the shaded area of Figure 3.7. The demand curve can be viewed as the outer boundary of the price and quantity combinations from among which the firm may choose. Although many demand curves appear as in Figure 3.7, they could have a variety of shapes and are not necessarily always smooth curves.

Rather than setting an asking price, the firm may choose a quantity to throw on the market at whatever price it will bring. Again the freedom of buyers will assert itself—this time in the maximum price that buyers *in toto* are willing to pay for a particular quantity. Once more the combinations of quantity offered and maximum price define a demand curve, which again can be viewed as the boundary of a set of possible price and quantity combinations from which the firm may pick. In general, this set could be symbolically represented as $P \leq f(Q)$. Sometimes, however, there is a "ruling market price" for

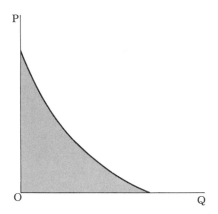

FIGURE 3.7   Demand curve constraint

the firm's output, and the firm can sell any quantity at that price or at any lower price. With $\bar{P}$ designating that price, the constraint becomes $P \le \bar{P}$.

Why is the freedom of buyers the basis for the constraint on the P, Q choices available to the firm? If there is no direct regulation, the firm is legally free to set any price it wishes and to place any amount of output on the market. But, because there are two sides to the market, the firm cannot independently select the price *and* the actual sales volume, or the sales volume *and* the price. Freedom of buyers not to deal enters the picture because if the firm were allowed to coerce buyers, it could dictate both the price and the actual sales volume. It should be noted that, although a demand curve exists because of the freedom of buyers, its position and shape depends mainly on the alternatives available to the buyers.

Why do we show these constraints as inequalities rather than as equalities — that is, in Figure 3.7, the whole shaded area rather than just the boundary (the demand curve)? Would not businessmen always select a point on the boundary? For two main reasons we show the constraints as inequalities and, therefore, the choice set as an area. First, we want to maintain a sharp distinction between a preference and a constraint. If we showed only the boundary, we would have implicitly introduced either the businessman's or the analyst's preference. Second, we want our tools to be applicable to as wide a variety of problems as possible. A firm's goal and other constraints may sometimes induce the firm to limit output and price more than this constraint dictates.

Whereas the freedom of the firm's customers restricts the P, Q combinations, the freedom of the firm's suppliers restricts its choices of the price and quantity of the particular inputs. We can think of a firm offering alternative prices, with various maximum quantities suppliers will supply to the firm. Thus, in general symbols, we could write these constraints as $x \le f(p)$. Alternatively, we can think of the firm as offering to purchase various quantities, agreeing to pay whatever price is necessary for any quantity. With this view, the constraint would be written $p \ge f(x)$.

Very often, a ruling market price for an input is unrelated to the quantity purchased by our model firm. If we designate this market price as $\bar{p}$, the constraint becomes $p \ge \bar{p}$. Whereas in $P \le \bar{P}$ the ruling market price for output provides the upper boundary to the firm's asking price, in $p \ge \bar{p}$ the market price provides the lower boundary to offering prices.

The outer boundaries of

$$x \le f(p), \qquad p \ge f(x), \qquad p \ge \bar{p}$$

can be thought of as supply curves facing the firm. They show the best terms on which the firm can buy various quantities of the input. Figure 3.8 displays the set and boundary for a constraint such as $p \ge \bar{p}$.

Before turning from the constraints arising from the freedom of others, we should make clear that these demand and supply curves reflect a whole system of political and economic freedom. They are present only when buyers and sellers are free not to deal with an organization and are found in their strongest form in free market systems. In fact, they are the main characteristic of the free market system. If the firm were allowed to use compulsion, there would not be such limitations on its choices.[3] We can say that one man's political and economic freedom is another man's constraint.

Technology. Perhaps the most obvious of all the constraints are those having technologically determined input-output relationships as their source. Such constraints reflect the fact that the firm is not free to choose its output levels independently of its input levels. For any level of input, there will be a maximum level of output that the firm can choose. Or, in other words, for any level of output, there must be minimum levels of input. Restricting ourselves for purposes of simplicity to a one-output two-input case, this statement can be expressed symbolically, $Q \le f(x_1, x_2)$. The boundary of this inequation is known as the production function.

Inputs can have various relations to each other and to the output. One important class of relationships is that in which there are possibilities of continuous substitution among the inputs, so that a large variety of alternative input combinations could produce the same

---

[3]The government can, of course, use compulsion. This is why it is able to obtain "inputs" for the armed forces, through the draft, below the supply price. Similarly, organized crime is often able to select a P,Q combination outside the P,Q opportunity set that faces a law-abiding seller.

level of output. A commonly used mathematical form showing these substitution possibilities is known as the Cobb-Douglas function:

$$Q \leq a x_1^{\alpha} x_2^{\beta} \tag{3.8}$$

where a, α, and β are the parameters. The parameters α and β can take on any positive real values, but when they add to 1 we have a production function that is homogeneous to degree 1; that is, a doubling (or tripling, etc.) of all inputs will lead to the same multiple change of output. Production functions that are homogeneous to degree 1 — Cobb-Douglas and other types — are perhaps the best representation of most real-world input-output relationships.

Graphically, inequation 3.8 would have to be shown in three dimensions. We can, however, display cross-sections of it by selecting a constant for one of the variables and then showing the relationship between the other two variables. For example, if production of fixed quantity $\bar{Q}$ is desired, we can substitute $\bar{Q}$ for Q in inequation 3.8 and then solve for x_1, to obtain

$$x_1 \geq \left(\frac{\bar{Q}}{a x_2^{\beta}}\right)^{1/\alpha}.$$

When this inequation is plotted, it might look like Figure 3.9; the boundary graphically shows the minimum quantity of x_1 that can be used with any amount of x_2 to produce $\bar{Q}$ units of output. The boundary is obtained by treating the inequation as an equation.

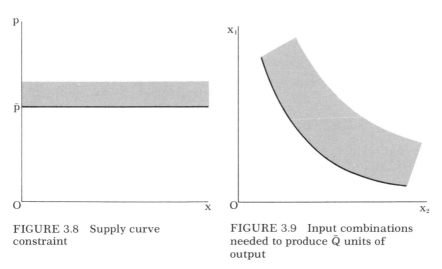

FIGURE 3.8   Supply curve constraint

FIGURE 3.9   Input combinations needed to produce $\bar{Q}$ units of output

In Figure 3.9 the boundary is known as an isoquant because it shows all the x_1, x_2 combinations that yield the same quantity of output, $\bar{Q}$. The shaded area of the diagram, the interior of the opportunity set, contains possible combinations, although not efficient ones. From the viewpoint of cost minimization, for any point in the interior of the opportunity set there is a better point on the boundary. All points outside this set are input combinations that cannot yield the quantity, $\bar{Q}$.

We could also show the set of combinations for one of the inputs and the output, for example, x_1 and Q, on a two-dimensional graph. If x_2 is some fixed amount, $\bar{x}_2$, this amount can be substituted for x_2 in inequation 3.8, yielding $Q \leq a x_1^\alpha \bar{x}_2^\beta$, graphed as Figure 3.10, which shows the combinations of x_1 and Q available to the firm, given some particular value for $\bar{x}_2$.

In many production processes in the real world, inputs cannot be substituted for each other, but instead there is some minimum required quantity of each input for every level of output. With k representing the minimum requirement of an input per unit of the output, the two-input case would have the following inequations as the constraint:

$$x_1 \geq k_1 Q, \qquad x_1 \geq k_2 Q.$$

If we specify some level of output, $\bar{Q}$, we can graphically show the possible x_1, x_2 combinations as in Figure 3.11. Although all points within the set are possible, there is always a point on the boundary that is preferable from the cost viewpoint to a point in the interior of the opportunity set. Furthermore, the single point determined by the intersection of the constraints is preferable to any other point because it is the only point on both boundaries. Either the whole boundary or the corner point (the intersection) could be called an isoquant.

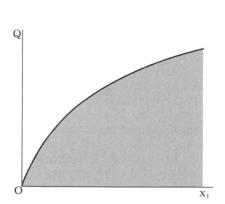

FIGURE 3.10 One-input/one-output opportunity set with other input constant

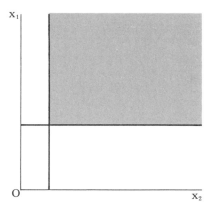

FIGURE 3.11 Input combination opportunity set to produce a given level of output when inputs are in fixed proportion to output

Fixities. Upper limitations on one or more of the input services occur for inputs obtained from assets owned by the firm as well as for services obtained from others. Such "fixities" are likely to exist during a short period of time. The upper limitations on input services exist particularly in cases in which more input could be obtained only by acquiring the assets that yield the services. It is often either impossible or not economically feasible to acquire such assets in, or for, a short period of time. Even in the case of purchase of services from others, moreover, supply arrangements may include complicated contracts with other firms that cannot be readily changed. When an input can be obtained from only one source, a contract may limit the maximum that can be obtained. On the other hand, contracts may specify the purchase of a minimum quantity.

The upper limitations on particular inputs are handled quite simply. An upper limitation on the input x_1, designated $\bar{x}_1$, would be $x_1 \leq \bar{x}_1$. In words, this says only that the amount of x_1 used cannot be greater than the amount available. Figure 3.12 employs this constraint together with the input-output constraint graphed in Figure 3.9 to show how both constraints together can define the opportunity set of x_1 and x_2 for $\bar{Q}$ units of output.

Sometimes the fixity may not be of a particular type of input service but instead stems from a limitation on the amount of money available. We call such a limitation on money a budget constraint. It does not limit any particular input; rather, it limits the combinations of inputs that can be purchased. A budget constraint involves a number of simple constraints; so we defer its discussion to the section on compound constraints.

Indivisibilities. In general, it is desirable to define the field of choice for the decision variables as all real and positive numbers. This definition enables us to assume that prices and quantities can be varied by very small amounts, to use continuous curves as boundaries of opportunity sets, and to consider the whole area of such a set to be subject to choice. In many cases, however, perfect divisibility cannot be reasonably assumed; that is, some inputs or outputs are "lumpy." They may be varied, but only by addition or subtraction of relatively large units. Occasionally, prices also may take on only discrete values and not be continuously variable.

Consider input x_1, limited in quantity to $\bar{x}_1$. Suppose that $\bar{x}_1$ represents the services of one boiler that must be used to capacity or not at all. The whole amount of $\bar{x}_1$ must be used if used at all. Expressed symbolically, this constraint is $x_1 = \bar{x}_1$, rather than the $x_1 \leq \bar{x}_1$ it would be if there were divisibility. The opportunity set for obtaining as much as $\bar{Q}$ output under this additional constraint would become the horizontal "fixity" line alone to the right of the isoquant rather than the whole shaded area in Figure 3.12. The line labeled "fixity" should be relabeled "fixity and indivisibility."

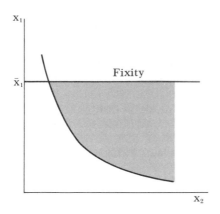

FIGURE 3.12   Input opportunity
set as constrained by technology
and fixity of one input

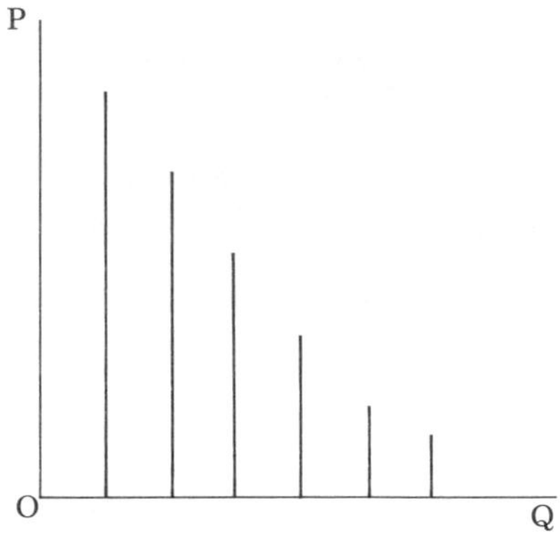

FIGURE 3.13 P,Q opportunity set
with indivisible output

As another example, consider the price and quantity combinations in the opportunity set if the output unit cannot reasonably be assumed to be divisible but the price can take on continuous values within a range. Instead of the continuous boundary and opportunity set in Figure 3.7, the opportunity set includes only the points on the vertical lines in Figure 3.13.

Legally Imposed Constraints. Governments at all levels place various constraints on the choices available to business firms. Sometimes the controls are direct, as when an upper or lower limit is placed on a price, an output quantity, or an input quantity. At other times, the controls are indirect, as when certain kinds of activity are prohibited if they tend to undermine competitive markets. With increasing frequency, regulations are influencing input mixes of firms, as the government attempts to assure certain levels of quality or safety or to diminish pollution.

Regulated industries such as public utilities and railroads are, of course, subject to direct controls on prices and output. Indeed, when we say an industry is regulated, we generally mean that direct controls are imposed. In the supposedly unregulated industries, there are many controls — minimum wage laws, output or input restrictions in agricultural industries, rent ceilings, and import quotas. Patent protection is also a form of control, for it constrains firms from producing certain outputs or using certain inputs. Direct controls are sometimes viewed as a substitute for the "competitive market system," which is supposed to automatically regulate prices, inputs, and outputs. When the market system does not work well — for example, during a war or when firms and labor unions have a great deal of monopoly power — there is a tendency to impose a variety of controls.

A large number of indirect controls arise from the public policy of maintaining competitive markets and prohibiting unfair business practices. The antitrust enforcement agencies and the courts may think a price is too low if the intent and effect of that price is to drive competitors out of business. Or a firm may not be allowed to charge different prices to different buyers for the same goods if the effect is to give some buyers unfair competitive advantages over other buyers. Sometimes a firm may not be able to "tie" the sales of one product to the sales of another.

An increasing number of limitations on the firm's choices arise from the application of safety and pollution standards to protect consumers and lessen the ecological disturbances of production and consumption. The United States Department of Agriculture and the Pure Food and Drug Administration specify that different foods, drugs, and cosmetics must or must not have certain ingredients. Labeling laws, especially in textiles and textile products, require that relevant facts be given to potential buyers. Building codes specify the kinds of materials that may be used. Safety laws constrain the input choices of automobile, tire, and appliance manufacturers.

Laws that place upper or lower limits on prices and quantities are generally easy to portray as constraints. Consider the effect on the price and quantity choices of a firm already faced with a demand curve, when the government specifies a maximum price and a minimum output level. Then in addition to the constraint imposed on the firm by the freedom of buyers, there would also be the following constraints: $P \leq \bar{P}_{max}$ and $Q \geq \bar{Q}_{min}$. The opportunity set for the P, Q's then appears as in Figure 3.14.

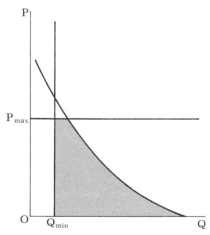

FIGURE 3.14 *P,Q* opportunity set as constrained by demand curve and government regulation

Next, let us consider a regulation whose effect is to specify that some input, x_1, must be at least as great as some function of x_2. Suppose the constraint takes the form $x_1 \geq hx_2$. This constraint, portrayed by the line through the origin in Figure 3.15, would mean that x_1, x_2 combinations cannot be to the right of that line. Starting with Figure 3.12, we can see in Figure 3.15 how the combination of technology, a fixity, indivisibility, and this legally imposed constraint together determine the opportunity set of x_1, x_2 combinations from which the firm may choose in order to get an output as great as $\bar{Q}$. This combination of constraints limits the opportunity set to the points on the line between A and B. If the indivisibility constraint were not operative, the whole area enclosed by the three curves would define the opportunity set.

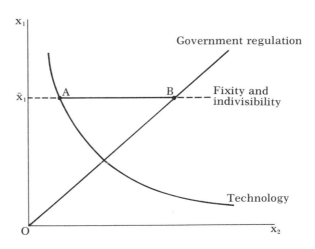

FIGURE 3.15   Input combination opportunity set for some output level as constrained by technology, fixity, indivisibility, and government regulation

Self-imposed Constraints. Self-imposed constraints often arise because of the conversion of some goals into targets. They can also arise out of desires to keep the firm viable. Constraints are imposed by one unit of the firm on another unit as part of the management process in complex organizations.[4] Examples are output targets, limitations on the use of an input, and limitations on the amount of money that can be used. Contracts too may be self-imposed; such constraints are compound.

There are many examples of self-imposed constraints. A desire to avoid the possibilities of new entries to the industry or some kind of

[4]For more information, see Herbert Simon, *Administrative Behavior* (New York: Macmillan, 1958).

action by government may induce the firm to place an upper limit on its selling prices. Concern over the reactions of rivals may produce minimum price levels that the firm imposes on itself. To maintain its reputation for quality, the firm may limit the use of some inputs. To keep the firm growing to attract competent managers, the firm may impose minimum constraints on total output or revenues. To maintain its position in different markets and to be in a position to move rapidly when opportunities arise, the firm may place minimum targets for particular outputs or inputs.

Suppose that the firm places on itself both maximum and minimum prices in order to avoid entry and price-cutting reactions of rivals. Let us also say that the firm specifies a revenue target of at least $\bar{R}$ dollars. These self-imposed constraints can be symbolically shown:

$$P \leq P_{max}$$
$$P \geq P_{min}$$
$$PQ \geq \bar{R}.$$

Together with the constraint imposed by freedom of buyers, $Q \leq f(P)$, the choice set of P, Q combinations might appear as in Figure 3.16. If $\bar{R}$ were set too high, of course, the opportunity set would contain no price and quantity combinations.

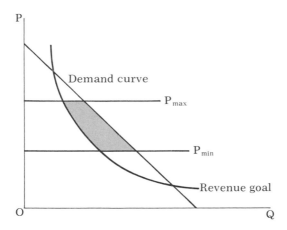

FIGURE 3.16 P, Q opportunity set as constrained by freedom of buyers and self-imposed limitations

Lack of Knowledge and Barriers to Markets. Firms in the short run usually limit themselves to the use and production of certain inputs and outputs. This limitation is also a constraint generally arising from two principal sources: (1) lack of detailed knowledge about production techniques and markets and (2) lack of access to outlets for outputs and supplies of inputs. Ignorance of production techniques and market conditions can be overcome, but only by use of costly resources. Barriers to entry to markets as seller or buyer may arise from government action and legal contraints and from the power of other firms to make entry unprofitable to a newcomer.

COMPOUND CONSTRAINTS

It is often possible and desirable to combine "simple" constraints into a compound constraint. Three categories of compound constraints are of special interest: the production possibility frontier, the budget constraint, and contracts. With ingenuity and mathematical tools, an almost unlimited number of compound constraints can be devised from the simple constraints.

Production Possibility Frontier. The production possibility constraint appears when some inputs are limited in quantity and needed in the production of two or more outputs. It is constructed by combining constraints arising from technology with constraints with fixities as their source.

Let us say that input x_1 must be used in the production of products 1 and 2. If k_1 represents the quantity of x_1 required per unit of product 1, and if we designate x_{11} as the quantity of x_1 devoted to product 1, we have the technological constraint $x_{11} \geq k_1 Q_1$. Similarly, if k_2 units of x_1 are needed per unit of product 2, and if x_{12} represents the amount of x_1 used in the production of product 2, another technological constraint is shown as $x_{12} \geq k_2 Q_2$.

Let us now say that the total amount of x_1 employed is limited by the amount, $\bar{x}_1$, available. We then have the fixity constraint $x_1 \leq \bar{x}_1$. That is, we cannot use more x_1 than the amount available. If x_1 is used only in these two products, we also have $x_{11} + x_{12} \leq \bar{x}_1$.

We can now use the technological constraints to substitute for x_{11} and x_{12}: this yields $k_1 Q_1 + k_2 Q_2 \leq \bar{x}_1$. This inequation shows how the Q_1, Q_2 combinations are limited by the availability of x_1. Figure 3.17 shows this compound constraint graphically. Notice that we treat the

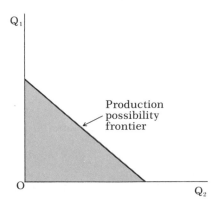

FIGURE 3.17 Q_1, Q_2 opportunity set

two technological constraints as equations when substituting for x_{11} and x_{12}. This assumes that the minimum required quantity of this input will be used for both products; that is, there is no waste.

The non-axis boundary of this opportunity set is known as the production possibility frontier. Its slope and intercepts are determined by the technologically determined values of k_1 and k_2 as well as by the level at which x_1 is fixed. The combination of the two simple constraints into the compound constraint lets us conveniently show how the limitations of an input make it necessary to trade-off the two outputs. That is, if we assume Q_1, Q_2 combinations will be selected on the frontier, an expansion of one output must result in a contraction of the other.

Budget Constraint. The budget constraint is a combination of a fixity on the "liquid" input—money that can be spent—and the freedom of suppliers. If two inputs are purchased by the unit constrained, which is limited to spending no more than $\bar{B}$ dollars, then the expenditure *in toto* cannot be greater than $\bar{B}$ dollars. That is, $p_1 x_1 + p_2 x_2 \le \bar{B}$.

Now let us say that sellers of x_1 will not sell to the firm if it pays less than $\bar{p}_1$ per unit and sellers of x_2 will not sell if the offering price is less than $\bar{p}_2$ per unit. This freedom of suppliers is shown symbolically as $p_1 \ge \bar{p}_1$ and $p_2 \ge \bar{p}_2$. If we now assume that the firm will not pay more than it has to, we can view $p_1 \ge \bar{p}_1$ and $p_2 \ge \bar{p}_2$ as equalities and substitute for p_1 and p_2 to obtain $\bar{p}_1 x_1 + \bar{p}_2 x_2 \le \bar{B}$.

With $\bar{p}_1$, $\bar{p}_2$, and $\bar{B}$ now numbers, or parameters, rather than variables, we can see that the budget constraint limits the firm's (or unit's) choice of inputs. Graphically, this compound constraint is shown in Figure 3.18. The amount of the budget as well as the magnitude of the prices determines the trade-off possibilities between the two inputs and the quantities that can be purchased.

Contracts. Usually, the terms of a contract are not determined by one party. The model firm must bargain, or negotiate, because of the

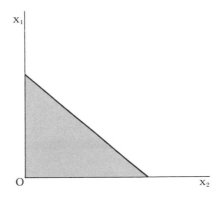

FIGURE 3.18   Input choices as constrained by budget

freedom of the other party. A contract reflects self-imposed limitations: The model firm, in agreeing to a contract, generally finds that
some of its choices have been restricted. To the extent that a contract is
enforceable by law, there is an element of a legally imposed constraint.

Let us say that the model firm makes a contract with a specific buyer.
The model firm agrees to deliver some minimum amount of output.
The buyer agrees that if the model firm wishes to provide more, some
maximum must be taken, and the model firm agrees upon a maximum
specified price. If P and Q are the decision variables, then the contract
imposes the following constraints on our firm and its sales to the
buyer: $Q \geq Q_{min}$, $Q \leq Q_{max}$, and $P \leq P_{max}$. The opportunity set for the
selling firm appears as in Figure 3.19.

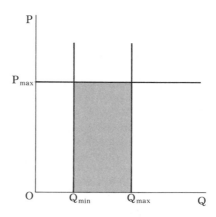

FIGURE 3.19   P,Q choices as constrained by a contract

CHARACTERISTICS OF OPPORTUNITY SETS

Before examining the optimization process, let us consider several
characteristics of the opportunity sets defined by the constraints
placed on the firm's freedom to choose values for its decision variables.
Particularly important in the optimization problem are (1) whether
the opportunity set can be represented geometrically or algebraically,
(2) whether the constraints leave any possible values for the decision
variables, (3) whether any of the constraints are noneffective, and
(4) the nature of the parameters that give specific content to the
constraints.

Mathematical Representation. Geometrical or graphic representation of the opportunity set is easy for models with only two decision
variables. Within the domain defined by the two variables depicted
with ordinary Cartesian coordinates, the constraint boundaries can
be graphed. The opportunity set consists of the subset of combinations
of values that "satisfy" all the constraints. Figure 3.15 illustrates
such representation in a case with two decision variables and three

constraints. In that example, however, output is assumed to be fixed by a target goal at the level corresponding to the isoquant. If we treat output as a third decision variable, we would have a three-dimensional volume as the opportunity set. Such three-dimensional graphs are difficult to use on a two-dimensional printed page, but such geometrical analogies are conceivable in the mind.

If we add to the model decision variables such as those involving prices of outputs and inputs, we must abandon direct geometrical representation of the opportunity set. Three alternatives remain, however. We can depict "cross-sections" of the set in two or three dimensions. We can incorporate some of the constraints into the objective function and depict the remaining constraints geometrically, if that process reduces the number of variables sufficiently. Or we can use algebraic rather than geometric representation.

Null Sets. It is possible to define a group of constraints so that no points—or combinations of decision variables—will satisfy all the constraints. We call them null sets. They are especially likely to arise because of unrealistic targets for the self-imposed constraints. As a simple graphic example of a null set, consider Figure 3.20, in which a revenue target is set so high that no P, Q combinations limited by the demand curve could meet this target. The appearance of such null sets is usually evidence that some of the self-imposed targets are inconsistent with each other or with the other constraints.

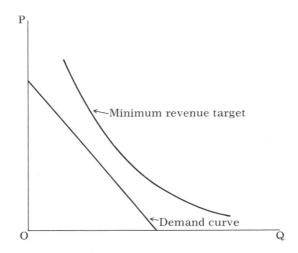

FIGURE 3.20   A null opportunity set: inconsistent constraints

Noneffective Constraints. Constraints can be placed into two classes, effective and noneffective, depending on whether the constraint effectively limits the opportunity set. All the constraints portrayed so far have been effective. But consider a case in which the government

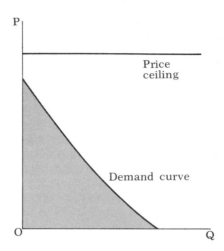

FIGURE 3.21   A noneffective constraint

places a price ceiling on a product higher than the price any buyer
would be willing to pay. Then the two constraints and the P,Q opportunity set might appear as in Figure 3.21, which clearly shows that
the price ceiling is not an effective constraint; its imposition or removal does not alter the opportunity set, which is here determined
solely by the demand curve. However, whether a constraint is effective depends on the configuration of the other constraints. If, for example, the demand curve in Figure 3.21 were to shift to the right, the
price ceiling could become an effective constraint.

The Crucial Role of the Constraint Parameters. A constraint can be
considered to be composed of three elements: the variables, the
"forms" of the relations among the variables, and the parameters
that make the relations specific. The forms of the constraints previously used have included straight lines, exponential curves, hyperbolas, cones, and planes. The parameters have been shown by letters
meant to represent specific numbers. The form can be thought of as
being determined by a subset of the parameters, for the form of an
equation depends on whether certain parameters take on the value
of zero. For example, the equation $P = aQ^k + bQ + cQ^2$ is a straight line
if k and c are both zero. We can thus couch our discussion in terms of
the "parameters," which is meant to include form.

   The determination of, or assumptions about, these parameters
has always played an important role in economic measurement and
theory. When an economist wants to know or to anticipate what a firm
will do, he generally manipulates the constraints of his model and
"tests" behavior under various constraint parameters.

   For real-world firms, the parameters are determined by past decisions and steps taken consciously by the firm to influence the parameters as well as by a combination of forces over which the firm has no control. The degree of influence the firm is able or willing to exercise over these parameters is an important feature that distinguishes short-run from long-run decisions. We can think of short-run decisions as choices of values of decision variables subject to a given set of constraints. The firm accepts the constraints for the time being and does the best it can. Simultaneously, however, the firm may take steps to change one or more of the constraint parameters. Decisions to do so are long-run decisions. The degree of acceptance of the constraint parameters is the key concept in distinguishing between short-run and long-run decisions.

For some types of constraint, real-world firms can know parameters with a high degree of certainty. For others, especially the demand curve, it is difficult to know the parameters with certainty, especially in the future. If we assume the firm can define its goals, all questions of risk and uncertainty arise because of difficulties in estimating the constraint parameters. Much of this book will concern problems of estimating the constraint parameters.

OPTIMIZATION TECHNIQUES

The optimization problem consists of finding a combination of values for the decision variables that is both feasible and also better than all other feasible combinations of values. Economic theory makes use of several interrelated maximization techniques such as marginal analysis, programming, and the LaGrangian multiplier.

Marginal Analysis: Complete Incorporation of Constraints. Any short-run decision problem can be posed in this way: Select the decision variables from the opportunity set, as determined by the constraints, that maximize (or minimize) the criterion variable. If, for example, the objective function is

$$\pi = PQ - p_1 x_1 - p_2 x_2 \tag{3.9}$$

and if we have the following constraints:

$P \leq f(Q)$	Demand curve	(3.10)
$p_1 \geq \bar{p}_1$	Supply curve of x_1	(3.11)
$p_2 \geq \bar{p}_2$	Supply curve of x_2	(3.12)
$Q \leq f(x_1, x_2)$	Production function	(3.13)
$x_2 \leq \bar{x}_2$	Fixity	(3.14)

we would select that set of values for the six decision variables from the opportunity set, as determined by the five constraints, that maximizes π.

To simplify the optimization process, we can "incorporate" the constraints into the objective function to reduce the number of variables, although we may not always be able to do this for all the constraints. The ultimate in this incorporation process is to bring all the constraints into the objective function so that π can be expressed in terms of a single decision variable. If we use the demand curve of inequation 3.10 to substitute for P in equation 3.9, we see that the revenue term, PQ, can be expressed in terms only of Q (and parameters). A much more difficult task is to express all the expenditure terms— that is, $p_1 x_1 + p_2 x_2$—in terms of Q. That is, we express the expenditures on the inputs in terms of Q, the level of output. This means incorporating four constraints into the expenditure portion of the objective function.

With $R(Q)$ the revenue in terms of Q, and $C(Q)$ the expenditures in terms of Q, the profit function can be expressed

$$\pi = R(Q) - C(Q). \tag{3.15}$$

A number of techniques can be used to select the value of Q that maximizes π. One is to graph the revenue function, the relation between Q and revenue, the cost function, the relation between Q and expenditure (or costs), and find the level of Q where the difference between these two functions, which is profit, is maximized. This is done in Figure 3.22. The profit-maximization output level is where the slopes of $R(Q)$ and $C(Q)$ are the same.

A second, quite related, technique makes use of what could be called marginal reasoning. Let us assume that we are considering whether to produce the first unit of output. That output would lead to an increase in revenue, which we call marginal revenue (MR). It will also lead to an increase in cost, which we call marginal cost (MC).

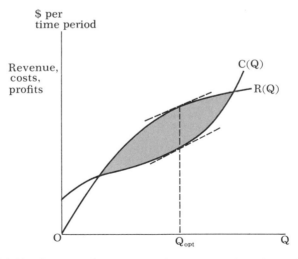

FIGURE 3.22   Optimization using total revenue and total cost functions

This unit should be produced if MR is greater than MC, because profit is increased. Consider the second unit of output. It too would lead to an increase in revenue (MR of the second unit) and cost (MC of the second unit). This too should be produced if the associated MR is greater than MC. Extending this line of reasoning, we would continue to expand output so long as MR is greater than MC for each unit. When would we stop? At the output level at which MR equals MC, which would exist if we assume infinitely small change in Q, and $R(Q)$ and $C(Q)$ have shapes as in Figure 3.22. (In Chapter 5 we shall show that under some conditions there will be no value of Q at which MR equals MC, but the marginal reasoning discussed here will still be applicable.)

The incorporation of the constraints into the objective function as in

$$\pi = R(Q) - C(Q) \qquad (3.16)$$

enables us to use the differential calculus to find the value of Q that maximizes π. This is done by taking the first derivative of π with respect to Q, setting this equal to zero, and then solving for Q:

$$\frac{d\pi}{dQ} = \frac{dR(Q)}{dQ} - \frac{dC(Q)}{dQ}$$

$$\frac{dR(Q)}{dQ} - \frac{dC(Q)}{dQ} = 0$$

$$\frac{dR(Q)}{dQ} = \frac{dC(Q)}{dQ}.$$

The first derivative of $R(Q)$ is nothing more than marginal revenue, and the first derivative of $C(Q)$ is marginal cost, so that optimization by the calculus tells us what we had deduced earlier—namely, that MR equal to MC is a necessary condition for an optimum value of Q. The second derivative must be negative to assure that we have the Q that maximizes rather than minimizes the value of π. Again, we point out there may be cases in which there is no value of Q for which MC is equal to MR.

After the optimum value of Q has been determined, we can go on to find the optimum values for the other decision variables. By substituting the optimum value of Q in inequation 3.10, the demand curve, we can find the optimum value of P. Also, once we have established the relation between Q and the best x_1, x_2 combinations, which would have to be done in the construction of the $C(Q)$ function, we can determine the optimum values for p_1, p_2, x_1, x_2.

In general, the incorporation of the constraints into the objective function is convenient only when two assumptions are met. The first is that the firm would want to select a point on the boundary of a constraint. The demand curve of inequation 3.10 is originally stated as an inequality because it is possible for a firm to ask less than the maximum possible price. In order to substitute $f(Q)$ from inequation

3.10 for P in $\pi = PQ - p_1x_1 - p_2x_2$, it is necessary to view inequation 3.10 as an equation rather than as an inequation; by doing this we assume that the firm would want to be on the boundary of $P \leq f(Q)$ — that is, that it would ask the maximum price for any value of Q. Generally, such an assumption is reasonable because it is consistent with profit maximization. But for some types of problems this assumption may not be reasonable, in which event we cannot easily incorporate the constraint into the objective function.

The second assumption necessary to easily incorporate a constraint into an objective function is that the relationship between the variables of the constraint be continuous. Consider the demand curve of inequation 3.10 once more. Let us say that as the result of a legally imposed constraint there is a maximum price, $P_{\max}$, that the firm can charge. Then the demand curve does not hold for all values of P and Q but only in the range below the legally imposed value of $P_{\max}$. This was shown in Figure 3.14. Now if we incorporate $P \leq f(Q)$ into $\pi = PQ - p_1x_1 - p_2x_2$ by substituting for P, we would have to attach the "side condition" that because P cannot take on all values (because of the legally imposed maximum), Q cannot take on all values. We can still incorporate the demand curve into the objective function, but with this side condition this function is awkward to work with.

Programming: Incomplete Incorporation of Constraints. It may not always be possible or desirable to incorporate all the constraints into the objective function. We may want to incorporate only some of the constraints, generally those that are continuous and in situations in which it is reasonable to assume that a solution will be on the boundary. The objective function with the incorporated constraints then becomes the preference criterion. The constraints that have *not* been incorporated into the objective function then determine the opportunity set. By not having to incorporate all the constraints into the objective function, we have the basis for a powerful and flexible technique that can handle problems in which constraints are discontinuous or are treated as inequations rather than as equations.

The programming technique itself can be thought of as the superimposing of a preference map on an opportunity set, after which the preference map is used to select the best combination of values for the decision variables from the opportunity set. To be able to do this, the axes of the opportunity set and the preference map must always be the same decision variables.

As one example, consider the objective function $\pi = PQ - C(Q)$. In this equation the expenditures for inputs have been expressed in terms of output by incorporation of the constraints

$$p_1 \geq \bar{p}_1$$
$$p_2 \geq \bar{p}_2$$
$$Q \leq f(x_1, x_2)$$
$$x_2 \leq \bar{x}_2.$$

But we have *not* substituted for P in $\pi = PQ - p_1 x_1 - p_2 x_2$ by incorporating $P \le f(Q)$ into it. Thus the profit is expressed as a function of both P and Q. The graph of this function takes the form of a preference map in which the contour lines each represent a specific profit level, as in Figure 3.23. These contour lines are known as isoprofit curves. Preference for P,Q combinations is shown by the arrow.

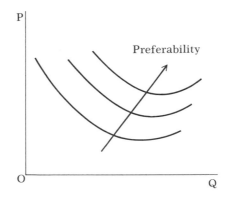

FIGURE 3.23   Isoprofit map in terms of P and Q

Because the demand curve, $P \le f(Q)$, has not been incorporated into the objective function, it becomes the basis for the opportunity set of P,Q combinations. The objective function and the opportunity set are both in terms of the P,Q decision variables. Normally, there would be no reason, given the problem as stated, not to incorporate the demand curve into the objective function. But if we added another constraint — a price maximum imposed by the government, for example — the demand curve would be discontinuous and could not be incorporated into the objective function. The demand curve and the price ceiling set by the government would together determine the P,Q opportunity set as shown in Figure 3.24.

For the optimization procedure, we first superimpose the isoprofit map, Figure 3.23 upon the opportunity set, Figure 3.24. This is shown in Figure 3.25. We want to pick a P,Q point that is possible, yet lies on the highest isoprofit line. In Figure 3.25 point A is preferable to the other points but does not lie in the feasible, or opportunity, set. Point C is possible but is not so desirable as point B, which is also possible. Point D is as desirable as point B but is not possible. Obviously the optimal combination of price and quantity is at point B.

The optimization process is apparently quite simple as long as the problem is limited to just two decision variables so that graphs can be used. If it is not possible to use this graphic method, then a quite similar arithmetical or analytical technique may be used. We first set up the objective function $\pi = PQ - C(Q)$ and then place different P,Q value combinations from the opportunity set into the objective

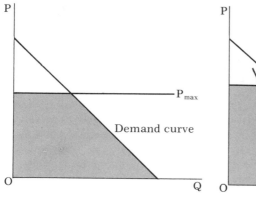

FIGURE 3.24 P,Q opportunity set   FIGURE 3.25 Optimization by
                                       programming method

function. For each P,Q point, an associated value of π can be calculated. The P,Q point that gives the highest value for π is then the optimal solution.

The LaGrangian Multiplier.[5] A third optimization technique, known
as the LaGrangian multiplier, can be used with constraints that are
too complicated to be solved and substituted for one of the decision
variables in the objective function. The technique is based on a bit of
algebraic trickery, which will be illustrated without proof.

Suppose that we wish to find the P,Q combination that will give us
maximum profit subject to a set of constraints. Suppose we have
managed to incorporate some of the constraints into the objective
function and can express the cost portion of the objective function
in terms of output. Let the objective function be, for example,

$$\pi = PQ - 100 - 5Q - 0.01Q^2. \tag{3.17}$$

Suppose the demand curve is something complicated that cannot be
readily solved for P, such as

$$0.3Q^{1.7} - P^{0.6}Q - 100 = 0. \tag{3.18}$$

The problem is to find the combination of price and output that satisfies equation 3.18 and makes π as large as possible.

---

[5]The use of the LaGrange multiplier requires expertise in a higher level of
mathematics than we have assumed our readers possess. It will be used in
only one more section of this book. In general, the LaGrange multiplier has
been used by economists only in highly theoretical work.

LaGrange ingeniously thought of adding an extra variable to the problem to simplify it. The constraint function is multiplied by the new variable, λ, and incorporated into the objective function by addition:

$$\pi' = PQ - 100 - 5Q - 0.01Q^2 + \lambda(0.3Q^{1.7} - P^{0.6}Q - 100). \quad (3.19)$$

If the demand constraint is satisfied – that is, equal to zero – the added term will be equal to zero, and the value of π' will be equal to the value of π at its maximum value. We have a problem of finding the combination of values of P, Q and λ that yield the largest π'. If the function has appropriate mathematical properties, the answer can be found by using partial derivatives. That is, we take the derivative of the new objective function first with respect to P, treating Q and λ as if they were constant parameters, and then do the same for Q and for λ. The three resulting "derived" functions are set equal to zero, because the maximum π' will be at the top of the hill where the slope is zero with respect to moves in any direction. These three "conditions for maximization" are

$$\frac{\partial \pi'}{\partial P} = Q - 0.6\lambda Q P^{-0.4} = 0 \qquad (3.20)$$

$$\frac{\partial \pi'}{\partial Q} = P - 5 - 0.02Q + 0.51\lambda Q^{0.7} - P^{0.6} = 0 \qquad (3.21)$$

$$\frac{\partial \pi'}{\partial \lambda} = 0.3Q^{1.7} - P^{0.6}Q - 100 = 0. \qquad (3.22)$$

We now have three equations involving the three variables. The solution of three such simultaneous equations will provide the combination of P, Q and λ that makes π' a maximum or minimum. "Second order conditions" can be found with second derivatives to assure that the solution values are for a maximum. The question still remains whether the values of P and Q that give a maximum value of π' will also give a maximum for π. The answer is yes, because if equation 3.22 is satisfied, the added term in equation 3.19 is zero and π is equal to π'. Furthermore, since equation 3.22 turned out to be the same as equation 3.18, the demand constraint has been satisfied.

The use of the LaGrangian multiplier technique requires that (1) the constraints can be expressed as functions equal to zero, (2) all functions are continuous and possess first and second partial derivatives, and (3) the "first order conditions" are a set of simultaneous equations for which a solution can be found.

The LaGrangian multiplier is especially useful in abstract reasoning, in which the functions are not specified. Let us say that we do not know the cost function in terms of output and express it abstractly as $C = C(Q)$ and that we do not know the demand function, and express it as $P = P(Q)$. Then, the LaGrange equation could be

$$\pi' = PQ - C(Q) + \lambda[P - P(Q)]. \qquad (3.23)$$

Getting partial derivations of π' with respect to P and Q and setting them equal to zero yield

$$\frac{\partial \pi'}{\partial P} = Q + \lambda = 0 \tag{3.24}$$

$$\frac{\partial \pi'}{\partial Q} = P - \frac{\partial C(Q)}{\partial Q} - \lambda \frac{\partial P(Q)}{\partial Q} = 0. \tag{3.25}$$

We do not bother to get the partial derivative with respect to λ. Now if we solve equations 3.24 and 3.25 for λ and equate the results, we get

$$P - \frac{\partial C(Q)}{\partial Q} = Q \frac{\partial P(Q)}{\partial Q}. \tag{3.26}$$

This gives us an optimization condition. The price minus marginal cost (which is $\partial C(Q)/\partial Q$) must be equal to output times the change in price with a change in output. Such results are sometimes useful in abstract work.

Fixed-Target Optimization. Figure 3.26 is like Figure 3.25 except that only one isoprofit curve is shown—the one corresponding to a fixed-target profit goal. All points on the isoprofit curve are equally desirable. But only the segment of the curve lying within the opportunity set contains possible points. All points on the segment are optimum. In this instance, as is frequently the case with fixed targets, the firm has considerable discretion on values to select for the decision variables. There is no unique optimum.

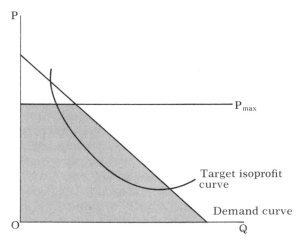

FIGURE 3.26   Optimization with fixed target

Discussion Questions

1. A one-product firm uses two inputs, labor and machinery. Each unit of output requires two units of labor and one unit of machinery. The firm owns 100 units of machinery and cannot obtain any more in the short run. The cost of the machinery is estimated at $5 per unit. The firm can obtain as much labor as it wants at $3 per unit (man-hours). The demand curve is estimated as $P = 100 - 0.5Q$, where P is the asking price and Q is the quantity the firm can sell.

   Assigning symbols, formulate the objective function on the assumption that profit maximization is the goal. Formulate the constraints. Incorporate all the constraints into the objective function, making the necessary assumptions. What alternatives might there be to incorporating all the constraints into the objective function? What would the objective function look like if all constraints other than the demand curve were incorporated? How could this objective function be depicted on a two-dimensional diagram? What would the opportunity set look like under this condition? How would this opportunity set change if the government imposed a price ceiling of $25?

2. Let us say that a firm has a number of objectives. It wants to make high profits; it wants an "adequate" level of revenues; it does not want to charge "too high" a price; it does not want to charge "too low" a price; it needs some minimum amount of output to maintain its organization and stake in the market. Assume its profit function is $\pi = PQ - 1,000 - 5Q - 0.01Q^2$, where some of the constraints have already been incorporated, and that the demand curve is $P = 100 - 0.5Q$. How could these various goals be reconciled, made consistent, and be brought into the analysis? What kinds of questions would have to be faced in reconciling these goals?

3. In what way is political and economic freedom the basis for the firm's demand curve constraint? If somehow the options of buyers in buying from other firms were restricted, what would happen to the demand curve facing the firm? What would happen if the firm, perhaps because of lack of knowledge, selected a price-quantity combination that lies outside the opportunity set determined by the demand curve?

4. A manufacturer of one-pound candy bars uses three inputs—chocolate, caramel, and nuts. The manufacturer promises on the wrapper that at least 25 percent of the weight will be nuts and that there is at least as much caramel as chocolate. At least 20 percent of the weight, for technological reasons, must be chocolate. Show algebraically the production function—that is, all the alternative combinations of the three ingredients that can produce the one-pound candy bar.

5. Consider the enclosure of a rectangular area (the output) by fencing (the inputs). Two parallel sides must be made of steel fencing, and the other two parallel sides use wood fencing. What is the production function? If the output is to be 100 square yards to be enclosed, determine the opportunity set of possible combinations of wood and steel fencing. What would the opportunity set be if no more than 20 linear yards of steel fencing are available? What would the relation between wood fencing and output be if the 20 linear yards of the steel fencing available were all used? What would this last relation be if there were 30 yards of steel fencing, all of which was used?

6. Determine the opportunity set in question 5 if 100 square yards are to be enclosed, only 20 yards of steel fencing are available, and the firm has to use the full 20 yards of steel fencing or not use it at all? What would the opportunity set be if both inputs were unlimited but the steel fencing has to be used in multiples of 10 (that is, 10, 20, 30, etc.). Assume that 100 square yards are to be enclosed.

7. How would the opportunity sets in questions 5 and 6 change if the government passed a law that at least 50 percent of the fencing used must be made of wood?

8. The fence encloser has only $100 to spend on the wood and steel fencing in question 5. If the price of a yard of wood fencing is $3 and the price of a yard of steel fencing is $5, to what combinations of inputs is he constrained?

9. A firm produces two products, both of which require the same machinery plus labor. Product 1 requires one hour of the machine per unit of output; product 2 requires four hours of the machine per unit of output. If the amount of the machine is limited to 100 hours per day, and if the firm can obtain as much labor as it wants, what is the production possibility frontier for the two products? What is the opportunity set?

10. Identify the constraint parameters in our various exercises. In what way are the constraint parameters crucial to our distinction between short-run and long-run decision-making?

11. In what ways do "complete" and "incomplete" incorporation of constraints into the objective function affect our optimization techniques?

12. Is it more or less difficult to predict the behavior of a firm with a fixed target profit goal than the behavior of a firm that maximizes profit? Which firm might you expect to complain more about government-imposed price controls? Why?

4 Production Theory and the Output Cost Function

In Chapter 3 we suggested that the optimization problem could be simplified if the objective criterion, either profit or cash flow, could be expressed in terms of a small number of decision variables. We saw that the number of decision variables could be reduced if some, or possibly all, of the constraints could be incorporated into the objective function.

One way to reduce the number of variables in the objective function is to replace the expenditure terms with a function in terms only of output. Thus, if the profit function for the one-product two-input firm is

$$\pi = PQ - p_1 x_1 - p_2 x_2,$$

we can simplify our optimization procedures if we can express the expenditures, $p_1 x_1$ and $p_2 x_2$, in terms only of output, which we would call the output cost function. The expenditures can be expressed in terms of output by incorporating the input-output technological constraint, the supply constraints on the inputs, fixity constraints on one or more of the inputs, and possibly indivisibility and self-imposed and government-imposed constraints into the single output cost function. We should point out that the output cost function — that is, the relation between output and costs — is of considerable interest aside from its use in optimization.

The incorporation of all these constraints into the objective function (replacing the expenditure terms with the output cost function) is not a simple task. As a first step, we have to understand the theory of production — that is, the various relations between the inputs and the outputs and between the inputs themselves. The second step is to derive the output cost function.

THE ELEMENTS OF PRODUCTION THEORY

Production Processes and Production Functions. Production processes are the building blocks of production functions. A production process may be defined as one way that two or more inputs can be combined to produce an output. In a production process, all the inputs are in fixed proportion to the output; any level of output will require some proportional amount of each input.[1] Let us say, for example, that one unit of output requires two units of input x_1 and three units of x_2. Then the inequation $x_1 \geq 2Q$ represents the minimum amount of x_1 that is required for any level of output, and inequation $x_2 \geq 3Q$ represents the minimum amount of x_2 required for any level of Q.

These two inequations allow for the possibility that more x_1 or x_2 than is needed might be used. But using too much of either input is wasteful, and if we assume that no input will be wasted, the inequations can be converted into equations:

$$x_1 = 2Q \qquad x_2 = 3Q.$$

These two equations together define this production process.

Because x_1 and x_2 are in fixed proportion to the output, they are also in fixed proportion to each other. If we solve $x_2 = 3Q$ for Q, which is $x_2/3$ and substitute this value for Q in $x_1 = 2Q$, we obtain $x_1 = (2/3)x_2$. This equation shows the fixed relation between the inputs: For any amount of x_2 there must be 2/3 of that amount of x_1.

Let us generalize this simple illustration by using symbols. Let k_1 be the technological coefficient that relates x_1 to Q, and let k_2 be the same type of coefficient that relates x_2 to Q. Then $x_1 = 2Q$ and $x_2 = 3Q$ in generalized form are

$$x_1 = k_1Q \qquad x_2 = k_2Q$$

and the relation between the inputs—as in $x_1 = (2/3)x_2$—is

$$x_1 = (k_1/k_2)x_2.$$

Although we have shown these relations as equations, there may be models in which they should be treated as inequations.[2]

[1]It is possible to define a production process in which the proportion between the inputs and the output varies. We believe such production processes to be rare in the real world and thus think of a production process as having fixed proportions between the output and inputs—fixed under the assumption that no inputs are wasted.

[2]Although, for simplicity, we limit ourselves to two-input cases, a production process could have a large number of inputs, all in fixed proportion to the output. If we have n inputs, then the production process would be depicted in n equations as follows:

$$x_1 \geq k_1Q$$
$$x_2 \geq k_2Q$$
$$x_3 \geq k_3Q$$
$$\vdots$$
$$x_n \geq k_nQ,$$

where the $k_1, k_2, \ldots, k_n$ are the technological coefficients that give the minimum number of units of the designated input required per unit of output.

There may be more than one process for producing a given output. For example, another production technique may allow the firm to use two units of x_1 per unit of Q and four units of x_2. In this event, the process would be expressed in the following equations:

$$x_1 = 2Q \qquad x_2 = 4Q.$$

Following $x_1 = (k_1 k_2) x_2$, x_1 and x_2 would be in fixed proportion to each other as

$$x_1 = (1/2) x_2.$$

There is no reason why there must be only two production processes. There can be three, four, five, ten. There can even be so many that we can view them as infinite in number. A farmer, for example, can use an infinite number of combinations of seed, water, labor, fertilizer, pesticides, and land to produce a given level of output. Each combination of these inputs is a different process, so there is virtually an infinite number of processes. There are many examples of infinite processes outside agriculture as well. Consider the pumping of gas through a pipe, where the output is gas delivered per unit of time. A vast variety of pipe diameters and pump pressures would deliver the gas, and each pipe and pump combination can be considered a separate production process.

A production process can be said to be inefficient if it uses more of both (or all) inputs than an alternative process uses, or if it uses more of one of the inputs without any saving in the use of the other input than an alternative process. Let us say, for example, that the following process is available: $x_1 = 1Q$, $x_2 = 2Q$. A process such as $x_1 = 2Q$, $x_2 = 5Q$ is inefficient in comparison to the first because for any level of Q, it requires more of both inputs. A process $x_1 = 1Q$, $x_2 = 3Q$ is also inefficient in comparison to the first process; it uses more of input 2 per unit of Q without any saving of input 1. A process such as $x_1 = 5Q$, $x_2 = 1Q$, however, is not in this sense inefficient in comparison to the first process. It uses more of input 1 than the first but less of input 2 and, depending on the relative prices of the two inputs, might allow production at a lower cost.

Generally, we can disregard inefficient processes. However, if one of the inputs is indivisible – that is, if it must all be used – the firm may have to select inefficient production processes. Let us say, for example, that there are two alternative processes. Process 1 is $x_1 = 2Q$, $x_2 = 1Q$; process 2 is $x_1 = 5Q$, $x_2 = 2Q$. Process 1 is evidently more efficient than process 2. Let us say now that two units of x_2 cannot be divided and that we want to produce only one unit of output. We may have to use process 2 to produce this unit. The only other conceivable instance in which a firm might use an inefficient process is when the price of an input is negative; that is, when the firm is *paid* for using an input. Given the possibility of payments by governments to avoid pollution, such negative prices may not be too far-fetched.

A production function is defined as all the possible efficient production processes. As one exception, however, we define it to include inefficient processes if, because of the indivisibility of an input, efficient processes are not available to the firm. The production function can consist of a single process, two processes, ten processes, or any number, including an infinite number of processes.[3] In our discussions of production functions we will include only efficient production processes, except when indivisibility of an input might preclude the use of efficient processes.

Production Functions. Production functions can be categorized by the number of processes. Thus, we can have single-process, two-process, ten-process, and infinite-process production functions. There are two widely used infinite-process production functions, the Cobb-Douglas and the "classical." The former is named after two economists, while the "classical" production function is so designated because of its importance in the development of economic theory. We will depict some of these production functions, using both graphs and algebraic notation.

SINGLE PROCESS. For a two-input process that is the only efficient process, the whole production function can be presented algebraically:

$$x_1 \geq k_1 Q \qquad x_2 \geq k_2 Q,$$

where the ks are the technological coefficients. When graphed in three dimensions, the surface of that production function appears as in Figure 4.1. When no x_1 or x_2 is wasted, the production function is the straight line OR', which rises above the x_1, x_2 plane with more of

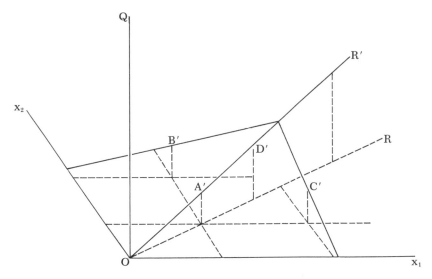

FIGURE 4.1   Single-process production function

[3] We are indebted to Vivian Walsh for viewing the production function as a set of processes. Vivian Walsh, *Introduction to Contemporary Economics* (New York: McGraw-Hill), 1970.

these inputs and is in three dimensions. The line OR' is known as a process ray. If we allow for the possibility of waste of inputs, then the production surface—which gives the maximum amount that can be produced with any combination of inputs—consists of two planes, x_2, O, R', and x_1, O, R', that intersect at the process ray. A', B', C' are all drawn to be the same level of Q. But B' requires more x_2 than is necessary, and C' requires more x_1 than is necessary. Point D' represents a higher level of output than does point A'. The line OR is the projection of the process ray on to the x_1, x_2 plane.

TWO PROCESS. Algebraically, we can represent the production function that consists of two processes with two sets of inequations, one for each process. Thus, we have

$$x_{11} \geq k_{11}Q \qquad x_{21} \geq k_{21}Q,$$

where we designate the process, here process 1, by the second subscript. Similarly, the second process is algebraically shown as

$$x_{12} \geq k_{12}Q \qquad x_{22} \geq k_{22}Q.$$

When there is no wastage of inputs, these two sets of (now) equations graph as process rays R_1' and R_2' in Figure 4.2, which are projected on the x_1, x_2 plane as OR_1 and OR_2. The points A' and B' represent the same level of output with each process. Allowing for wastage, the planes x_1, O, R_1' and x_2, O, R_2' are part of the production surface. The plane R_1', O, R_2' is also part of the production surface. Output levels on this last plane can be achieved by using *combinations* of the two processes, a point that will receive considerable attention.

FOUR PROCESS. We now consider the production surface when there are four efficient production processes. Each production process can be algebraically represented by a pair of inequations. Each process,

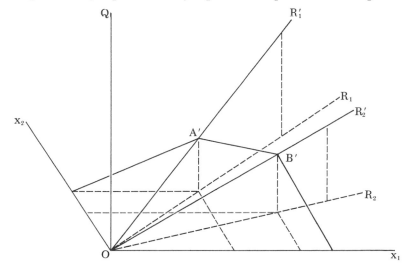

FIGURE 4.2 Two-process production function

when there is no wastage, becomes a process ray as in Figure 4.3. The production surface consists here of five planes: x_2, O, R_1'; R_1', O, R_2'; R_2', O, R_3'; R_3', O, R_4'; R_4', O, x_1.

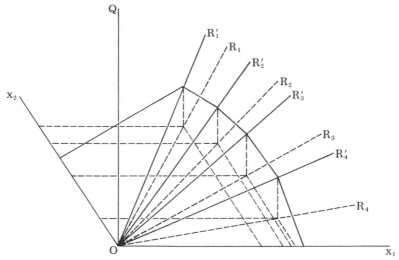

FIGURE 4.3   Four-process production function

COBB-DOUGLAS. The Cobb-Douglas production function consists of an infinite number of process rays, none of which is inefficient. These are depicted in the three-dimensional diagram, Figure 4.4, although with just a sample of the rays. Because there are an infinite number of rays, the production surface is not a series of flat planes,

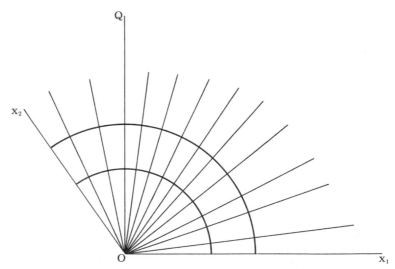

FIGURE 4.4   Surface of the Cobb-Douglas production function

as it was for the previous production functions, but is instead a smooth, continuously curved surface. It can be thought of as a part of a cone.

With an infinite number of processes, it is possible to continuously substitute one input for the other, in contrast to the previous cases where discrete processes must be used. As a result, the Cobb-Douglas production function can be represented by a single continuous equation, $Q = ax_1^\alpha x_2^\beta$, in which a, α, and β are parameters that reflect technology. The Cobb-Douglas production function is particularly useful because it can be expressed in a single, fairly simple equation and is therefore "mathematically tractable."

CLASSICAL. The classical production function is difficult to graph in three dimensions and to express algebraically. The essence of the classical production function is that there are extreme processes — that is, those that combine a great deal of one input with a small amount of the other input — that are so inefficient that production can be *raised* if there is less of the abundant input. For example, consider the use of labor, fertilizer, or water on a farm of fixed acreage. It is conceivable that so much labor, fertilizer, or water could be used that production would be *increased* if less labor, fertilizer, or water were used. Or consider five workers trying to operate a huge blast furnace. Very possibly, they would be able to produce nothing or little. But if the blast furnace were smaller, they might be more successful.

The production surface for such a function is shown in Figure 4.5. It looks very much like the Cobb-Douglas, except that in the classical case there are sharp drops in output for the extreme process rays. The nature of this production surface is difficult to show in three dimensions but will become clearer when we take various cross-sections of the three-dimensional picture.

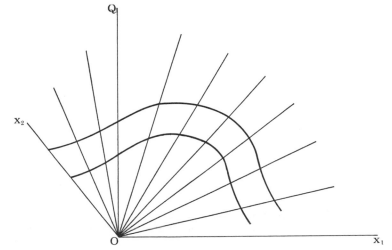

FIGURE 4.5 Surface of the classical production function

Isoquants and Input Substitution Possibilities for Different Production Functions. Given a three-dimensional production surface, or the equation(s) representing the production function, it is interesting and useful to determine the isoquants – that is, the input combinations that yield particular levels of output. The isoquants show us the substitutability of the inputs in the production function. When we have a number of isoquants, with different isoquants for different output levels, we generate a two-dimensional map that is easier to work with than three-dimensional figures.

SINGLE PROCESS. Consider first the single-process production function, depicted as Figure 4.1. If we select some output level, say $Q = 10$, and pass a plane perpendicular to the Q-axis at that output level, this plane will give a cross-section of all the x_1, x_2 combinations that could produce 10 units of output. More generally, if we pass such a plane at any level of Q, the cross-section gives all the x_1, x_2 combinations for that level of output. When these cross-sections are "projected" down to the x_1, x_2 plane, they give us an isoquant map. Figure 4.6 portrays a sample of these projected isoquants, together with the projection of the process ray.

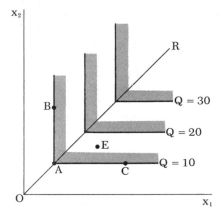

FIGURE 4.6   Isoquant map: single-process production function

We can see that all efficient production must take place at the "corners" of the isoquants, through which the projection of the process ray passes. The input combinations represented by points B and C yield the same output as point A, but the A combination enables the use of less x_2 than the B combination with x_1 the same, or less x_1 than the C combination with x_2 the same. Thus point A is most efficient in the sense that it uses the fewest inputs. Notice that an isoquant is a "boundary" of an area of possible input combinations. Thus, 10 units of Q *could* be produced with units of x_1 and x_2 represented by point E. But point E obviously uses a less efficient combination of inputs than point A.

An isoquant – or, more accurately, the boundary of the x_1, x_2 set that can produce some level of Q – enables us to determine whether one input can be substituted for the other and still give the same output level. In the single-process case, there are no substitution possibilities, a very important attribute of this production function. Consider points A or B. If we take away some x_1 at these points, there is no amount of additional x_2 that can be used that still gives 10 units of Q.

The isoquants can also be obtained from our algebraic formulation of this production function. Say the process is depicted as

$$x_1 \geq 2Q \qquad x_2 \geq 3Q.$$

To find the isoquant for $Q = 10$, we simply substitute 10 for Q to get

$$x_1 \geq 20 \qquad x_2 \geq 30.$$

These two inequations plot as an area as in Figure 4.7. It should be noted that substituting 10 for Q in $x_1 \geq 2Q$ and $x_2 \geq 3Q$ is the algebraic equivalent of passing a plane perpendicular to the Q-axis in Figure 4.1 at $Q = 10$. In both cases we hold Q constant at 10, so that we get the relation between x_1 and x_2 at that value of Q.

TWO PROCESS. Consider now the two-process production function graphically shown in Figure 4.2. If we pass planes perpendicular to the Q-axis at $Q = 10$ and $Q = 20$, and project the cross-sections down to the x_1, x_2 plane together with the two process rays, we obtain Figure 4.8.

We can select combinations of inputs such as point C that, even though they do not lie on either process ray, are nevertheless possible. Such points are possible because we have the option of using the two processes in combination. Let us say that we produce 10 units with process 2, giving the input combination designated by point B, and

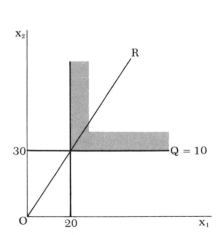

FIGURE 4.7 Isoquant as a boundary of an x_1, x_2 opportunity set

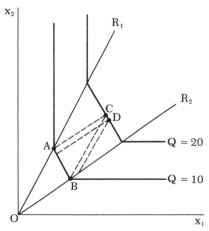

FIGURE 4.8 Isoquant map: two-process production function

10 units with process 1, with the input combination designated by point *A*. If we add the inputs required by these two processes, we get point *C*, which should lie on the *Q* = 20 isoquant. Similarly, if we produce 11 units by process 2 and 9 units by process 1, we get the combined input combination at point *D*, which also lies on the *Q* = 20 isoquant. When we combine processes, the sloped lines between the process rays become part of the isoquants.

For the input combinations lying between the process rays, it is now possible to substitute one input for another and still remain at the same output level. Let us say we are at point *B*, which uses only process 2. If we take some x_1 away and use more x_2, it is possible to continue to produce 10 units of *Q* by using process 2 in combination with process 1. However, if we start at point *B* and take away some x_2 there is no amount of x_1 that enables a production of *Q* = 10. Substitution between x_1 and x_2 is therefore possible only on the portions of the isoquants lying between the process rays. The degree to which one input can be substituted for the other is known as the marginal rate of technical substitution (MRTS). In this case, the MRTS is constant between the two process rays in the sense that the same amount of x_2 can be substituted for each unit of x_1, or vice versa.

FOUR PROCESS. By slicing planes perpendicular to the *Q*-axis at different values of *Q* in Figure 4.3, we once more obtain cross-sections of the possible x_1, x_2 combinations for any value of *Q*. Projecting a sample of those cross-sections to the x_1, x_2 plane, together with the process rays, we obtain the isoquant map as in Figure 4.9.

Again we see that input combinations that do not lie on one of the process rays are possible. This is so, once more, because combinations of processes can be used. Thus, point *E* is an input combination that can produce 20 units of *Q* with combinations of processes 3 and 4, and 20 units of *Q* can be produced with input combination *D* by using the appropriate combination of processes 2 and 3.

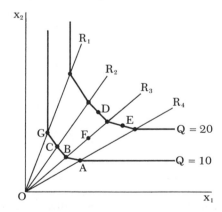

FIGURE 4.9   Isoquant map: four-process production function

Although the isoquants still consist of straight-line segments, they are beginning to approach smooth curves. We can see that in the portions of the isoquants lying between the process rays, it is possible to substitute one input for another and still have the same level of output. But the marginal rate of substitution changes from one segment to the next. Suppose we start at input combination A, which uses only process 4. As we move from A to B, we give up x_1, use more x_2, and change our process mix from process 4 to more and more of process 3. At B we only use process 3. Between these points the marginal rate of technical substitution is constant. Now, as we move from B to C, we continue to use more x_2 and less x_1 and change our process mix gradually from 3 to 2. When we get to C, we use only process 2. Notice that the marginal rate of technical substitution of x_2 for x_1 is greater in the BC segment compared to the AB segment. (It is, however, constant *within* the segment.) Similarly, the MRTS is greater in segment CG than in BC. Why should this be so? Essentially because of the implicit assumption that production tends to be greatest when the inputs are approximately in equal proportion. When we move away from R_4, which has a high proportion of x_1, we do not need as much x_2 to compensate for x_1, for we are moving toward processes with more nearly equal proportions. But when we move toward R_1, which uses a high proportion of x_2, we are moving *away* from equal proportion processes and thus need more x_2 to compensate for the loss of x_1. This characteristic need not be present in all production functions.

Let us ask one more question of this model. Let us say that process 3 is so inefficient that the input combination designated by point F is needed to produce 10 units. Would the isoquant for $Q = 10$ go from A to F to C? The answer is no, because combinations of processes 4 and 2 can always produce 10 units of output with fewer inputs than process 3. Process 3 would then be considered inefficient with respect to the process 4 and process 2 combinations and would therefore normally not be used. Part of the isoquant would then be a straight line from A to C. The nonuse of such inefficient processes assures us that the isoquants will be convex to the origin.

COBB-DOUGLAS. From Figure 4.4, representing the Cobb-Douglas production function, we can obtain the isoquant map in the usual way, by slicing planes perpendicular to the Q-axis at different values of Q and projecting the cross-sections down to the x_1, x_2 plane. The general form this isoquant map will take is shown in Figure 4.10. It should be noticed that, in contrast to the production functions with a small number of processes, the isoquants are now smooth and continuous curves. These curves are hyperbolas. Because the marginal rate of technical substitution gives the rate at which one input can be substituted for the other, which is geometrically the slope of the isoquant, we can see that the MRTS continuously changes as we move along the isoquant.

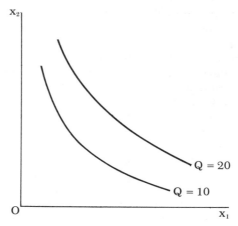

FIGURE 4.10   Isoquant map: Cobb-Douglas production function

The Cobb-Douglas production function is readily represented by a simple function,

$$Q = ax_1^\alpha x_2^\beta. \tag{4.1}$$

Thus we can calculate the isoquants and MRTS algebraically. To calculate the isoquant at $Q = \bar{Q}$, we simply substitute $\bar{Q}$ for Q in equation 4.1 to get

$$\bar{Q} = ax_1^\alpha x_2^\beta. \tag{4.2}$$

Solving for x_2 gives

$$x_2 = \left(\frac{\bar{Q}}{ax_1^\alpha}\right)^{1/\beta}. \tag{4.3}$$

When the parameters are known, equation 4.3 is readily graphed.

The MRTS is the change of x_2 with respect to x_1 or the change of x_1 with respect to x_2. Thus, when we use the slope of x_2 with respect to x_1, the MRTS can be calculated with the calculus:

$$MRTS = \frac{dx_2}{dx_1} = -\frac{\alpha}{\beta}\left(\frac{\bar{Q}}{a}\right)^{1/\beta}\left(\frac{1}{x_1^{\alpha/\beta+1}}\right).$$

To illustrate with numbers, let $a = 2$, $\alpha = 0.5$, $\beta = 0.5$, and $\bar{Q} = 100$. Then the MRTS is

$$MRTS = -\left(\frac{0.5}{0.5}\right)\left(\frac{100}{2}\right)^2\left(\frac{1}{x_1^2}\right)$$

$$= -\frac{50^2}{x_1^2}.$$

When x_1 is, say, 60, the MRTS is $-50^2/60^2$, or about -0.7. Thus at *this* value of x_1, a decrease of x_1 by one unit could be compensated by an increase in x_2 by 0.7 units. When x_1 is smaller, say 20, the MRTS is

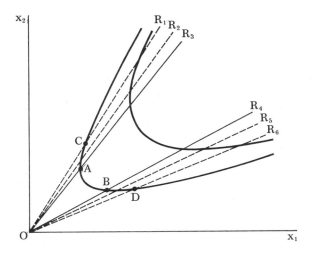

FIGURE 4.11 Isoquants: classical production function

$-50^2/20^2$, or about $-6\,1/6$. Thus, at $x_1 = 20$, a decrease in x_1 by one unit requires an increase in x_2 by $6\,1/6$ units for Q to remain at 100.[4]

CLASSICAL. The classical production function contains processes in which there is too much of one of the inputs. This shows up in iso-quants that "curve back" for the inefficient processes.

Figure 4.11 displays two isoquants and a number of process rays. The process rays shown by dashed lines — R_1, R_2, R_5, R_6 — are inefficient — that is, any level of output requires more of both inputs than do efficient processes. Rays R_3 and R_4 are the "last" efficient process rays and therefore define the boundaries of the set of efficient processes. Consider the different input combinations that can produce the quantity represented by the lower isoquant. The segment of that isoquant from A to B represents efficient processes. Notice that in this segment, x_1 can be substituted for x_2, and vice versa. Now consider point C on inefficient process ray R_1. The same quantity is produced but requires more of *both* x_1 and x_2 than does A. Similarly, point D, which also lies on an inefficient process ray, requires more of both inputs than does point B, which lies on an efficient process ray. Notice also that in the "uneconomic regions" the isoquants are positively sloped. This means that an expansion of one of the inputs

---

[4]We do not have to use the calculus to calculate the MRTS. Say we have $a = 2$, $\alpha = 0.5$, $\beta = 0.5$, and $\bar{Q} = 100$. Then equation 4.3 becomes

$$x_2 = \frac{100^2}{2\sqrt{x_1}} = \frac{10,000}{4x_1}.$$

Now, say we want to find the MRTS at $x_1 = 50$. When $x_1 = 50$, then $x_2 = 10,000/200 = 50$. If we reduce x_1 by 1, so that x_1 is 49, we need $x_2 = 10,000/4(49) \approx 51$. Thus, about one unit of x_2 is needed to compensate for a loss of one unit of x_1 at $x_1 = 50$, so that $MRTS = -1/1 = -1$.

requires an *expansion* of the other input as well to maintain the same level of output. In the economic region, in contrast, one input could be substituted for the other input.

Returns to Scale. A concept of great importance in production theory is the relationship between a percentage change in *all* the inputs and a percentage change in the output. When a production function is such that a given percentage change in all the inputs leads to the same percentage change in the output, we say there are constant returns to scale. When a given percentage change in all the inputs leads to a larger percentage change in the output, we say there are increasing returns to scale. Finally, when the given percentage increase in all the inputs leads to a smaller percentage increase in output, we say there are diminishing returns to scale.

As we have seen, production functions do not have to be expressed in the form where quantity of output is a function of the inputs, as in the Cobb-Douglas production function. In the single-process production function, we expressed the function in a number of equations where inputs were a function of outputs. Recall, for example, the single-process production function expressed as $x_1 = k_1 Q$ and $x_2 = k_2 Q$. Our concepts of economies of scale still hold in this case, but in somewhat different form. The production function has constant returns to scale if a given percentage increase in the output requires the same percentage increase in all the inputs. If a given percentage change in output requires a smaller percentage increase in all the inputs, there are increasing returns to scale. And if that percentage increase in output requires a greater percentage increase in all the inputs, there are diminishing returns to scale.

Throughout this chapter we have assumed and will continue to assume that the production functions show constant returns to scale. Such an assumption accords strongly with common sense. Do constant returns to scale imply that large firms cannot be more efficient than small firms? Not necessarily. If the prices of input services are lower to the large firms, they may be able to produce for less cost than the small firm, even though the production functions of both firms are the same and have constant returns to scale. Also, the large firm may be able to use a different production function embodying different technologies. Thus constant return production functions are not necessarily inconsistent with what we call economies of size. We elaborate on these ideas in Chapter 11.

Mathematical functions that are known as homogeneous to degree 1 are useful as production functions because they give constant returns to scale. In general, a function of several variables is homogeneous to degree m if, after we multiply each independent variable by some constant, λ, it is possible to factor out λ raised to the m power. Consider, for example, the function

$$z = x^2 + xy - y^2. \tag{4.4}$$

Multiplying the independent variables by the constant λ gives

$$z = (\lambda x)^2 + \lambda x \lambda y - (\lambda y)^2, \qquad (4.5)$$

which can be factored as

$$z = \lambda^2 (x^2 + xy - y^2). \qquad (4.6)$$

Thus, equation 4.4 is homogeneous to degree 2. This implies that a doubling of x and y quadruples z. The function

$$z = a + bx \qquad (4.7)$$

is not homogeneous because λ cannot be factored out, unless $a = 0$. But the function

$$z = ax + by \qquad (4.8)$$

is homogeneous to degree 1. Notice that

$$z = a\lambda x + b\lambda y = \lambda^1 (ax + by). \qquad (4.9)$$

A function such as equation 4.8, however, is generally not useful as a production function, for it implies that it is possible to produce with only one of the inputs, which is seldom the case.

The Cobb-Douglas function is homogeneous to degree 1 if and only if the exponents of the inputs add to 1. Thus

$$Q = ax_1^{0.4} x_2^{0.6} \qquad (4.10)$$

gives

$$Q = a(\lambda x_1)^{0.4} (\lambda x_2)^{0.6} = \lambda^1 (ax_1^{0.4} x_2^{0.6}). \qquad (4.11)$$

But if the function is

$$Q = ax_1^{0.5} x_2^{0.8}, \qquad (4.12)$$

we get

$$Q = a(\lambda x_1)^{0.5} (\lambda x_2)^{0.8} = \lambda^{1.3} (ax_1^{0.5} x_2^{0.8}). \qquad (4.13)$$

Thus equation 4.12 is homogeneous to 1.3. Cobb-Douglas functions that are homogeneous to degree 1 — that is, where the exponents of the inputs add to 1 — give constant returns to scale. They give increasing returns to scale, however, when the exponents add to more than 1 and decreasing returns to scale when the exponents add to less than 1.

When a production function is homogeneous to degree 1 or, alternatively, has constant returns to scale, all the process rays are straight lines in three-dimensional space. All the functions that we have been using have this property.

Returns to a Single Input:The Total Product Curve. In the preceding section we were interested in the increases in output that take place when all inputs are increased. But in the short run the firm often is subject to a fixity constraint on one input while it can obtain as much as it wants of the other (variable) input. We are particularly interested in the relation between output and the use of the variable input, which is known as the total product curve, when the fixed input is limited to some maximum amount. Sometimes the relation between the variable input and the output depends on whether the fixed input is divisible – that is, whether the services of that input can be divided into small units.

When the fixed input is indivisible (let us use x_2 as the fixed input), the relation between Q and x_1 can be obtained by passing a plane perpendicular to the x_2-axis in the three-dimensional production surfaces at the fixed value of x_2, which we label $\bar{x}_2$. (See Figures 4.1 through 4.5.) The cross-section obtained provides the Q, x_1 relationship at that particular value of x_2, when *all* the x_2 is used. However, when x_2 is divisible, it may at times not be completely used, and expansion of output would take place by using more of x_1 and x_2. The use of x_1 and x_2 together implies a movement along a process ray. But we can *project* this process ray on the plane perpendicular to the x_2-axis to get the Q, x_1 relation.

SINGLE PROCESS. We can illustrate this rather difficult concept with Figure 4.12, where we have a single-process production function. OR' is the process ray in three-dimensional space, and OR is the projection of that ray onto the x_1, x_2 plane. Let us say now that x_2 is limited to $\bar{x}_2$ and that we want to find the relation between x_1 and Q. First we pass a plane perpendicular to the x_2-axis at $\bar{x}_2$, which is designated by B, $\bar{x}_2$, and D. Notice that this plane is parallel to the Q, O, x_1 plane. If x_2 is divisible, increasing amounts of x_1 will allow the expansion of production along the OR' ray. However, at point A we cannot continue along the OR' ray because we are now using all the available x_2. The distance between the x_1, x_2 plane and A represents

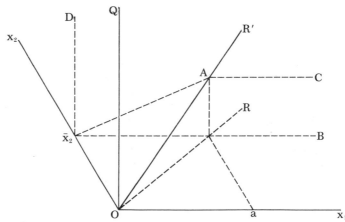

FIGURE 4.12   Relation between variable input and output: single-process production function

the maximum attainable production. What if we use still greater amounts of x_1? Then, with x_2 limited to $\bar{x}_2$, we move along the plane through $\bar{x}_2$ from A toward C. More x_1 is used, but because of the limitation on x_2, no more output can be produced. Hence, all points on the AC segment are the same levels of output.

If we now project the OA segment of the process ray, which is in three dimensions, onto the plane passing through $\bar{x}_2$, we obtain the two-dimensional relationship between x_1 and Q at that level of x_2. This projection is the line segment $\bar{x}_2 A$. Thus $\bar{x}_2 A$ gives the relation between x_1 and Q on this plane. The segment AC, which also relates x_1 and Q, is already on this plane, because for this segment all $\bar{x}_2$ is being used.

If we now place the $B, \bar{x}_2, D$ plane onto this page, we see the relation between x_1 and Q, as in Figure 4.13. This relation between x_1 and Q holds only for the particular value for x_2, namely $\bar{x}_2$. There are constant returns to x_1 up to output Q_a; that is, every additional unit of x_1 produces the same additional amount of Q. However, at output Q_a, all $\bar{x}_2$ is used up and if more x_1 is used there will be no additional output. That is, when more than a units of x_1 are used, there are zero returns to x_1. This relation between x_1 and Q is an important property of the single-process production function.

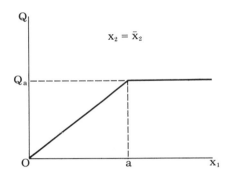

FIGURE 4.13   Relation between variable input and output: single-process production function

What we have just done graphically can be illustrated algebraically. Consider the single-process production function in this way:

$$x_1 = 2Q$$
$$x_2 = 3Q$$

which can also be written as

$$Q = (1/2)x_1 \qquad\qquad (4.14)$$
$$Q = (1/3)x_2. \qquad\qquad (4.15)$$

(We are assuming, as we shall for the rest of this section, that no inputs are wasted.) We also have the relation between x_1 and x_2 as

$$x_1 = (2/3)x_2. \tag{4.16}$$

Let us say now that x_2 is fixed at 60 units. Then equation 4.15 tells us that the maximum output is $Q = 20$. Say we start with $x_1 = 0$ and begin using x_1 with the appropriate amount of x_2. Then, from equation 4.14 we see that each additional unit of x_1 yields 1/2 unit of output, when x_1 and x_2 are used in the proportions designated in equation 4.16. When, however, the full amount of $x_2 = 60$ is used, at which amount $x_1 = 40$, there can be no additional output no matter how much x_1 is used.

TWO PROCESS. Let us now apply these techniques to find the relation between x_1 and Q, with x_2 fixed at $\bar{x}_2$, when there are two production processes. Figure 4.14 shows two process rays, designated by OR_1' and OR_2'. Notice that process 1 uses a higher proportion of x_2 and process 2 uses a smaller proportion of x_2. We have passed a plane E, x_2, F perpendicular to the x_2-axis at $\bar{x}_2$ upon which we have projected the two process rays. The portion of the OR_1' ray, OA, is projected on this plane as $\bar{x}_2 A$, while the portion of the OR_2' ray, OB, is projected as $\bar{x}_2 B$. At the output level using process 1 designated by A, all the available $\bar{x}_2$ is used in process 1; at the output level designated by B, all the available $\bar{x}_2$ is used in process 2.

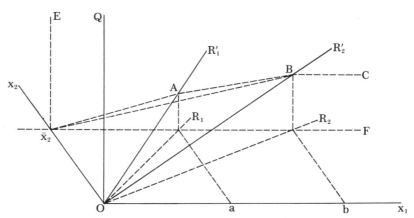

FIGURE 4.14   Relation between variable input and output: two-process production function

Let us say now that we start at $x_1 = 0$ and want to start producing.[5] Which production process should we use at low levels of x_1? Figure

[5] We ask the reader not to introduce the concept of time into the analysis. When we say we start at $x_1 = 0$ and then expand x_1, we do *not* mean this is a sequence of possible activities at different points in time. Rather we are just examining all the alternative relationships of the variables. Generations of students have been confused by implicitly introducing time into the analysis.

4.14 shows that of the projections of the two process rays on the plane through $\bar{x}_2$, Q rises faster if process 1 is used. Why should this be so? Because process 1 uses a higher proportion of x_2 than does process 2. Consequently, a unit of x_1 produces more output with process 1 than with process 2. Process 1 should be used exclusively up to the point where the output designated by A is reached, for process 1 always gives higher outputs for any level of x_1 than does process 2.

Figure 4.14 shows, however, that A is not the maximum output that can be reached, because the output designated by B is higher. Why should process 2 eventually yield the higher output? The answer lies in process 2 using a smaller proportion of x_2, the limited input. Let us say, for example, that process 1 is

$$x_1 = 2Q \qquad\qquad (4.17)$$
$$x_2 = 3Q \qquad\qquad (4.18)$$

and that process 2 consists of

$$x_1 = 3Q \qquad\qquad (4.19)$$
$$x_2 = 2Q. \qquad\qquad (4.20)$$

If x_2 is now fixed at 60, we can see that the maximum attainable output is 20 with process 1, but 30 with process 2.

Should we then switch completely to process 2 when output A is reached? The answer is in the negative. If we are using process 1, where $x_2 = 60$, then with full use of x_2, we would produce 20 units, and according to equation 4.17 we would use 40 units of x_1. This is point A. Let us say now that we suddenly switch to process 2.[6] With these inputs ($x_1 = 40$ and $x_2 = 60$), only 13 1/3 units of output could be produced. Even if we expanded x_1 slightly, output would still not be 20.

Thus, the expansion after A should not take place by using only process 2. Rather, output is best expanded by the use of *combinations* of the two processes. As we continue to increase x_1, we could use increasing amounts of process 2 and less of process 1. These process combinations, as we increase x_1, result in output rising along segment AB in Figure 4.14. When we reach B, only process 2 is used. If we try to continue expanding x_1 beyond B, output will not rise. Hence, the line segments $\bar{x}_2A$, AB, and BC represent the projection of the best possible relation between x_1 and Q on the plane sliced through $\bar{x}_2$. This relation is shown in Figure 4.15.

Over the input range O to a, it can be seen that the output return to x_1 is constant in the sense that each additional unit of x_1 produces the same additional amount of Q. The return is also constant in the input range from a to b. But an increment in this second range yields a smaller increment in output than does an increment of x_1 in the O to

[6]Reread footnote 5.

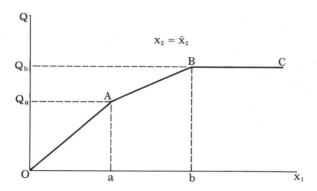

FIGURE 4.15   Relation between variable input and output: two-process production function

a range. Why should this be so? Because in the *O* to *a* range, we use only process 1, which uses a high proportion of x_2. Hence, an increase in x_1 yields a "high" increase in output. But in the *a* to *b* range, we mix in process 2, which uses a lower proportion of x_2. Hence, the increase per unit of x_1 is smaller. We can say there are diminishing returns to x_1 in the *a* to *b* segment in comparison to those in the *O* to *a* segment.

A little example might clarify these none-too-simple concepts. First let us write the production processes:

$$Q = \frac{1}{2}x_1 \left.\right\} \qquad\qquad\qquad (4.21)$$
$$\left. \text{Process 1} \right.$$
$$Q = \frac{1}{3}x_2 \left.\right\} \qquad\qquad\qquad (4.22)$$

$$Q = \frac{1}{3}x_1 \left.\right\} \qquad\qquad\qquad (4.23)$$
$$\left. \text{Process 2} \right.$$
$$Q = \frac{1}{2}x_2 \left.\right\} \qquad\qquad\qquad (4.24)$$

If we expand x_1 by one unit, we see that we get an increase in Q by 1/2 unit if we use process 1 but only by 1/3 unit if we use process 2. Clearly, then, we should at first use only process 1.

When $x_2 = 60$ is used with process 1, we see that output can be only 20 units. Can we expand output further? Let us say we take a unit of x_2 away from process 1 and use it in process 2, always using the corresponding amounts of x_1. Then, according to equation 4.22 we produce 1/3 less unit of output by process 1. But, with the switch of this unit of x_2 to process 2, we see from equation 4.24 that we produce 1/2 unit of Q with process 2. Thus, the switch of one unit of x_2 from process 1 to process 2 gives a net increase in output of 1/2 minus 1/3, or 1/6 unit of Q. Every time we switch another unit of x_2 from process 1 to process 2 we increase output by 1/6 unit. When we switch all 60 units of x_2 to process 2, therefore, output goes up by 60(1/6), or 10 units, from the 20 units of output we could get if we used only process 1.

Let us now view the switch of x_2 from process 1 to process 2 in terms of the increment in output with respect to x_1. Equations 4.21 and 4.22 can be combined as

$$x_1 = \frac{2}{3}x_2 \qquad \text{Process 1 proportions}$$

while equations 4.23 and 4.24 can be combined as

$$x_1 = \frac{3}{2}x_2 \qquad \text{Process 2 proportions.}$$

Now, assuming we are producing the maximum with process 1, let us say we switch one unit of x_2 from process 1 to process 2. We saw that this increased Q by 1/6 unit. From the process 1 proportions we see that we need 2/3 unit less of x_1 in process 1, but from the process 2 proportions we see that we need 3/2 units more of x_1 in process 2. Thus the switch of one unit of x_2 from process 1 to process 2 requires $3/2 - 2/3$, or 5/6, additional units of x_1. Since Q rises by 1/6 unit with the switch of one unit of x_2 from process 1 to process 2, and x_1 rises by 5/6 of a unit, the ratio of the increase in Q to the increase in x_1 is $1/6 \div 5/6$, which is 1/5. We can therefore say that when combining the processes, an increase of one unit of x_1 leads to an increase of 1/5 of a unit of Q. Contrast this with the use of x_1 when process 1 is used alone: In that case an increase in x_1 by one unit increases Q by 1/2 unit. (See equation 4.21.) This is why Q rises at a higher rate in segment *OA* of Figure 4.15 than in segment *AB*. Thus, the returns of Q per unit of x_1 are higher in the *OA* segment than in the *AB* segment of Figure 4.15.

FOUR PROCESS. The same procedure developed for the two-process case can be applied to production functions with any number of processes. We get diminishing returns per unit of x_1, in segment *AB* compared to segment *OA*, then, because in segment *AB* we switch from a process using a high proportion of x_2 to x_1 to a process using a low proportion of x_2 to x_1. For the four-process case the relation between the variable input and the output for some fixed value of $\bar{x}_2$ will have the general shape shown in Figure 4.16. Within any segment of the curve, an increase in input x_1 leads to the same increase in Q. But there are diminishing returns in each segment in comparison to those in the segment before it. That is, increases in x_1 over the *a* to *b* range yield smaller increases in output than do increases in x_1 in the *O* to *a* range; increases of x_1 in the *b* to *c* range yield smaller increases in output than do increases of x_1 in the *a* to *b* range; etc. We are beginning to see the famous "law" of diminishing returns: When one or more inputs are fixed in availability, an expansion of the input in unlimited supply yields smaller and smaller increases in output per unit of the unlimited (or variable) input. These diminishing returns to x_1 occur

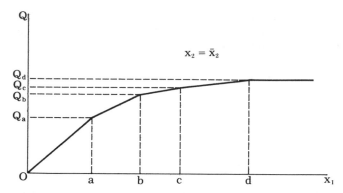

FIGURE 4.16   Relation between variable input and output: four-process production function

because, in order to increase output when x_2 is limited, it is necessary to switch to production processes using smaller and smaller proportions of x_2 to x_1.

COBB-DOUGLAS. From our analyses of the one-, two-, and four-process production functions, we may surmise that the curve relating x_1 and Q becomes smoother as we increase the number of processes. (There can be other types of functions that have an infinite number of efficient processes, but they are not widely used and will not be considered here.) With an infinite number of *efficient* processes (all having to use at least some of both inputs), we have the Cobb-Douglas production function.

With an infinite number of processes, some process can always use any proportions between the inputs. As a consequence, except for the trivial case where $x_1 = 0$, all the fixed amount of x_2—that is, $\bar{x}_2$—will be used. (This is true, we should add, only when the x_2 is already paid for, and cannot be used in any other way. Then, it would always pay the firm to use all of the x_2 for any level of output.) That is, at low levels of x_1 we will use processes with very high proportions of x_2. An expansion of x_1 enables a *continuous* shifting from one process to the next, where each process uses more of x_1 in proportion to x_2. Because we keep shifting to processes that employ smaller and smaller proportions of x_2 to x_1, we expect continuous diminishing returns in output to x_1, the variable input. Thus, the relation between x_1 and Q has the general shape depicted in Figure 4.17. In the Cobb-Douglas, there will always be some increment in output with an increase in x_1, but we can think of these increments in output approaching zero with very high levels of x_1.

Because we can readily express Cobb-Douglas as a relatively simple function, we can algebraically derive the relation between x_1 and Q. Let us say the function is

$$Q = 2x_1^{0.5} x_2^{0.5}. \tag{4.25}$$

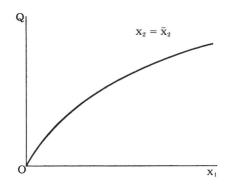

FIGURE 4.17   Relation between variable input and output: Cobb-Douglas production function

Now, if x_2 is limited, say, to 100 and is all used, this equation becomes

$$Q = (2x_1^{0.5})(100^{0.5}) = 20x_1^{0.5}. \tag{4.26}$$

Equation 4.26 directly gives the relation between x_1 and Q, which would have the same form, when graphed, as in Figure 4.17. If x_2 were higher, say at 200, any level of input x_1 would yield a higher output than if x_2 were smaller. The exponent of an input tells us the percentage increase in output that would take place with some percentage increase of that input when the other input is held constant. Thus, in equation 4.26, where the exponent of x_1 is 0.5, a 1 percent increase in x_1 leads to a 0.5 percent increase in Q.

CLASSICAL. We have, finally, the classical production function, with its inefficient extreme processes. In traditional literature, the assumption is made that the fixed input, here x_2, is indivisible. This implies that when only a small amount of x_1 is used, the inefficient production processes—those with a very high proportion of x_2 to x_1—must be employed. As x_1 is expanded, the processes used become less and less *in*efficient, which implies that output should increase at an increasing rate with an expansion of x_1. In this range of increasing returns to x_1, there are negative returns to x_2—that is, more Q could be produced if there were less x_2. At some level of x_1, which should occur *before* the first efficient process is reached, there will be increasing returns to x_2 and decreasing returns to x_1. Put another way, the *rate* at which the processes become less efficient with expansion of x_1 becomes smaller before the first efficient process is reached. Beyond this value of x_1, and extending through the range of efficient processes, the increase in output per unit of x_1 decreases as switches are made to processes that use less and less x_2 per unit of x_1. With continued expansion of x_1 beyond the last efficient process, we again reach inefficient processes—this time because of too much x_1 per unit of x_2—and output should actually fall.

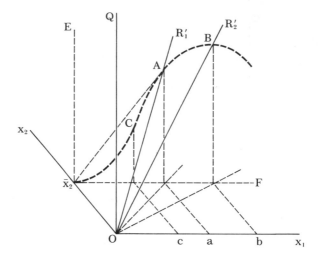

FIGURE 4.18   Relation between variable input and output: classical
production function, x_2 divisible and indivisible

Figure 4.18 shows the general nature of the relation between x_1 and
Q when a plane $E, \bar{x}_2, F$ is sliced through the production surface at $\bar{x}_2$.
The process ray OR_1' represents the first efficient process that is
reached when x_1 is expanded, and OR_2' represents the last of the
efficient production processes. As the curve shows, output increases
at an increasing rate as x_1 expands from O to c. This is along the
curved portion of $\bar{x}_2$ to A. When x_1 is expanded from c to b, output
increases, but at a diminishing rate. With expansion of x_1 beyond b,
output falls. Point C on the curve is known as an inflexion point, for
it is here that the rate of output changes from a rise at an increasing
rate to a rise at a decreasing rate. Output is at a maximum at point B.
    What if we drop the assumption that $\bar{x}_2$ is indivisible, so that we do
not have to use all the $\bar{x}_2$? With $\bar{x}_2$ divisible, the firm would use only
some of its x_2 with small amounts of x_1, so that the inefficient processes can be avoided. It would then at first expand along the process
ray OR_1', which is efficient. This can be done when x_2 can be subdivided.
After it reaches point A (using a units of x_1), all the $\bar{x}_2$ is employed,
and output can only be expanded by switching to processes using a
higher proportion of x_1 to $\bar{x}_2$. The OR_1' process ray is projected onto the
plane through $\bar{x}_2$ as $\bar{x}_2 A$, which is a straight line. Thus, the relation
between x_1 and Q is along the straight line $\bar{x}_2 A$, instead of along the
curve from $\bar{x}_2$ to A. The projection shows that for any level of x_1, expansion along the OR_1' ray yields higher output than when inefficient
processes must be used. Beyond A, the divisibility of $\bar{x}_2$ has no effect,
because all the $\bar{x}_2$ is used. The relation between x_1 and Q is shown in
Figure 4.19 for $\bar{x}_2$ divisible and indivisible.

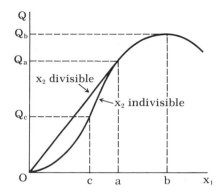

FIGURE 4.19 Relation between variable input and output: classical production function

Marginal and Average Products. Two other relations between the output level and the variable input are of considerable use. One is the marginal product; the other is the average product.

The marginal product of an input is the ratio of the change in output with respect to a change in that input, when all other inputs are held constant. Thus, if we have the unspecified production function

$$Q = f(x_1, x_2),\qquad(4.27)$$

then the marginal product of x_1, with x_2 held constant, is defined as

$$MP_{x_1} = \frac{\Delta Q}{\Delta x_1} = \frac{\Delta f(x_1, x_2)}{\Delta x_1}.$$

If we use the differential calculus, the marginal product of x_1 is defined as

$$MP_{x_1} = \frac{\partial Q}{\partial x_1} = \frac{\partial f(x_1, x_2)}{\partial x_1}.$$

The marginal product tells us the rate at which Q changes as we change x_1 while holding x_2 constant, and it may vary for different levels of x_1.

The average product of an input is defined as the total output divided by the quantity of that input. With the unspecified production function of equation 4.27, the average product of x_1 is

$$AP_{x_1} = \frac{Q}{x_1} = \frac{f(x_1, x_2)}{x_1}.$$

The average product of the variable input, which is Q/x_1, the number of units of output produced per unit of x_1, can also change for different levels of x_1.

Given the relation between total product and the variable input on

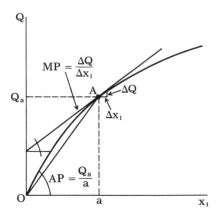

FIGURE 4.20   Derivation of marginal and average products

a graph, the marginal and average products can be deduced from the graph as in Figure 4.20. Let us say that we want to know the marginal and average products at point A on the total product curve, where Q_a units are produced and a units of x_1 are used. The marginal product can be determined as the slope of a straight line drawn tangent to point A. The slope of this line measures the change in Q with respect to a change in x_1 at that particular value of x_1. The average product at point A is Q_a/a. Notice the right triangle O,a,A. The segment aA is Q_a; the segment Oa is a, the number of units of x_1, and the angle of the hypotenuse OA to the x_1-axis represents the ratio Q_a/a.

Wherever the slope of OA is greater than the slope of the tangent line at point A, the average product is greater than the marginal product.[7] On the other hand, if the slope of the tangent is greater than the slope of OA, the marginal product is greater. Usually the slope of the tangent will be greater if the total product curve at some particular value of x_1 increases at an increasing rate. For the part of a total product curve that is a straight line through the origin, if such a line exists, the slopes are the same, and, therefore, marginal product equals average product. The average product is constant—that is, it does not change for different values of x_1—only if the total product curve is a straight line through the origin.

Figures 4.21–25 show the total product (*TP*), marginal product (*MP*), and average product (*AP*) relations for the one-process, two-process, Cobb-Douglas, and classical production functions. Two versions of the classical case are shown—one in which the fixed input is divisible, one in which it is indivisible.

---

[7]The slope of the tangent represents the ratio of the *change* in Q to the *change* in x_1. The slope of the line through the origin represents the ratio of the *total* amount of Q to the *total* amount of x_1.

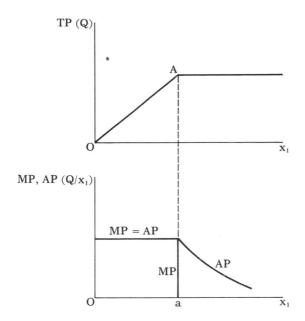

FIGURE 4.21 Total, marginal, and average product curves: single-process production function

In the single-process case (see Figure 4.21) both *MP* and *AP* are the same up to point *A*, the maximum possible output. Notice that the slope of a tangent to the segment *OA* is the same as the *OA* segment. They are both also constant for all values of x_1 up to *a*. At point *A*, however, *MP* drops to zero, for more x_1 will result in zero increases in output. The *AP* curve drops too, but only gradually, as beyond *A* the constant output is divided by increasingly larger values of x_1.

In the two-process case (see Figure 4.22), *MP* and *AP* are the same and constant up to point *A*; over this range only one process is used. *MP* then drops immediately at point *A* to a lower level, where it is constant over the *AB* range. This drop occurs because the firm is shifting to the second process, in which a smaller proportion of x_2 is used with x_1; hence increases in x_1 yield smaller increments in output. The *AP* curve, however, drops only gradually. Notice that the slope of a line drawn through the origin to any point on the *AB* segment as say *OD* – whose angle represents Average Product – is always greater than the slope of the *AB* segment, which represents Marginal Product. At point *B*, where the output cannot be increased, *MP* drops to zero. The *AP* curve, however, only gradually falls.

For the Cobb-Douglas production function, output always increases at a decreasing rate. Hence the slope of the total product curve always falls and, consequently, *MP* always declines (see Figure 4.23). If we draw lines from the origin to different points on the *TP* curve, we find that with more x_1, the angles always become smaller. Hence *AP* also

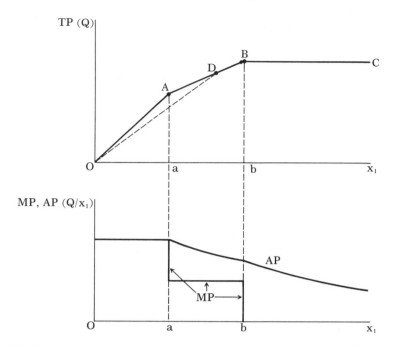

FIGURE 4.22   Total, marginal, and average product curves: two-process production function

always falls. However, *AP* is always greater than *MP*. Notice that a straight line drawn through the origin to any point on the *TP* curve always has a greater slope than the tangent drawn at that point.

The classical case (see Figure 4.24) with indivisibility of the fixed input is the only case in which *MP* is sometimes greater than *AP*. From *O* to *C*, the inflexion point, *TP* increases at an increasing rate. Hence, *MP* rises. Along this part of the total product curve, the slope of the curve at any point, represented by a tangent at that point, is always greater than the slope of a line through the origin to this same point. Hence *AP* always is less than *MP*. At point *C*, the *TP* curve increases at a decreasing rate. Hence *MP* reaches its maximum at point *C* and then begins to fall. However, *AP* continues to rise after point *C* and reaches its maximum at point *A*. Notice that the line through the origin to point *A* has the largest angle for any similar line drawn to any other point on the *TP* curve. A tangent drawn at point *A* has the same slope as this line, so that *MP* is equal to *AP* at point *A*. Both *MP* and *AP* fall beyond point *A*, but *MP* falls at a more rapid rate. At point *B*, the maximum possible output, a further increase in x_1 leads to a decrease in output. Hence *MP* is zero at point *B* and becomes negative beyond *B*. The *AP* curve continues to fall beyond *B*, and if so much x_1 were used that *TP* becomes zero, *AP* would become zero.

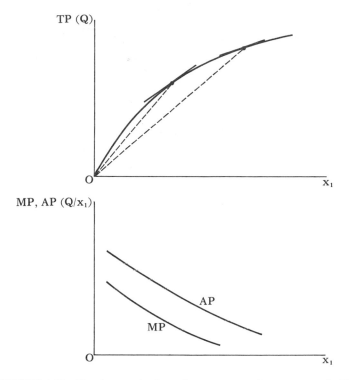

FIGURE 4.23 Total, marginal, and average product curves: Cobb-Douglas production function

When, in the classical case, the fixed input is divisible, *AP* and *MP* are the same and are constant (that is, the same for all values of x_1) up to point *A* (see Figure 4.25). In this range, output expansion takes place along a process ray. Beyond point *A*, the *AP* and *MP* curves take the same shape as in the indivisible case.

AP and *MP* are the same when expansion of output takes place along a process ray. This occurs only in the single-process case and parts of the two-process and classical divisibilities cases. This is because x_1 and x_2 are being expanded together in fixed proportions. At all other times we shift from one to another process, and *AP* and *MP* differ.

The mathematically tractable Cobb-Douglas function enables us to calculate the *MP* and *AP* curves algebraically. Let us say that the function is

$$Q = ax_1^\alpha x_2^\beta.$$

Then the marginal product of x_1 is

$$MP_{x_1} = \frac{\delta Q}{\delta x_1} = a\alpha x_1^{\alpha-1} x_2^\beta, \qquad (4.28)$$

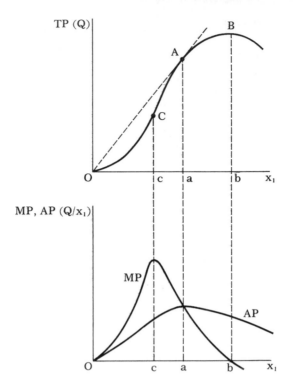

FIGURE 4.24   Total, marginal, and average product curves: classical case
with fixed input indivisible

and the average product is

$$AP_{x_1} = \frac{Q}{x_1} = \frac{ax_1^\alpha x_2^\beta}{x_1} = ax_1^{\alpha-1} x_2^\beta. \tag{4.29}$$

Notice that the only difference between equations 4.28 and 4.29 is α
(not the exponent) in equation 4.28. Because α is generally less than
1, we see that for any value of x_1, MP is less than AP.

OUTPUT COST FUNCTIONS

In Chapter 3 we saw that when the expenditures on inputs can be
expressed in terms of Q, the level of output, the optimization problem
is greatly simplified. This function can be obtained by "incorporating"
a number of constraints—namely, the production function, the freedom of sellers, fixity (or limitation on inputs), and the indivisibility
of an input—into the expenditure portion of the objective function.
In this section we derive the output cost function by using the relationship between a variable input and output, by algebraic manipulation, and by using least-cost expansion paths that show the relation

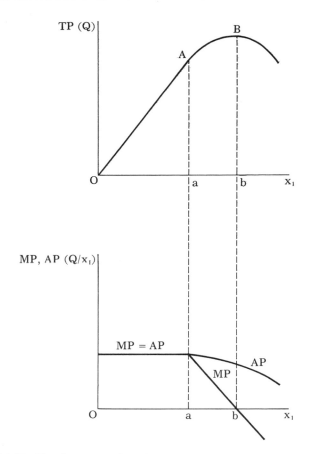

FIGURE 4.25 Total, marginal, and average product curves: classical case with fixed input divisible

between output and the use of inputs. We shall also discuss the marginal and average cost functions, which can be derived from the total output cost function. Throughout this section we treat x_1 as the variable input and x_2 as the input in limited supply that must be paid for whether or not it is used. The expenditures on x_2 are the fixed costs; the expenditures on x_1 are the bases for the variable costs. In a number of instances, however, we will relax the assumption that x_2 is in limited supply and must be paid for. It is important to bear in mind that all inputs, outputs, and costs must be thought of as rates per unit of time.

Derivation of the Output Cost Function from the Total Product Curve.

SINGLE PROCESS. Consider the single-process relation between x_1 and Q, which was shown in Figure 4.13 and is here given in Figure 4.26. If we multiply x_1 by $\bar{p}_1$, the market price of x_1, the x_1-axis becomes

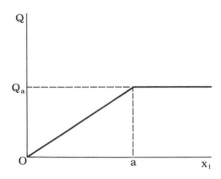

FIGURE 4.26 Relation between
variable input and output:
single-process production
function

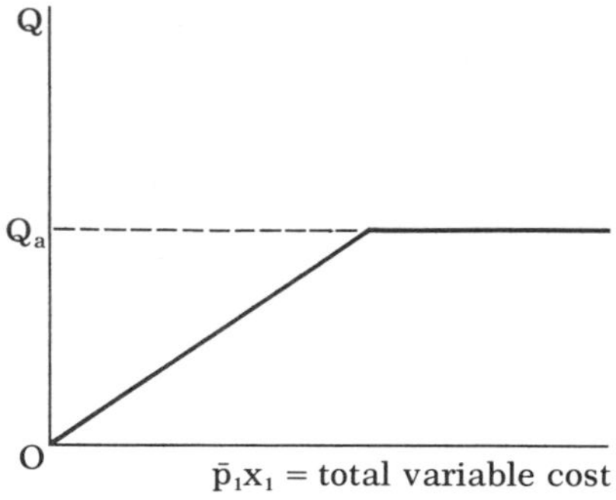

FIGURE 4.27 Relation between
total variable cost and output:
single-process production
function

$\bar{p}_1 x_1$, which is the variable costs. Then Figure 4.26 is transformed
into Figure 4.27, in which the abscissa is now $\bar{p}_1 x_1$, or variable costs.
The shape of the curve will not change: We have merely replaced
the quantity of x_1 in Figure 4.26 by the expenditure on that quantity.
(The curve would change, however, if $\bar{p}_1$ is not constant but somehow
varies with x_1.)

Because we want to express costs as a function of output—rather
than output as a function of cost—we simply flip Figure 4.27 around
so that Q is the abscissa and total variable cost (TVC) is the ordinate.
Thus, we have Figure 4.28. Notice that when we get to output Q_a,
which is the maximum possible output because of the limitation on
x_2, we cannot increase output though we can increase expenditures.

What about the fixed costs, which would be $\bar{p}_2 \bar{x}_2$, the expenditure
on the fixed input? We simply add these to the variable costs in Figure
4.28, noticing that they are a constant amount at all levels of Q. We
thus get the total cost curve as in Figure 4.29. It might be more convenient to think of the fixed cost as the costs at zero output and then
adding the variable cost curve. The total cost curve is the same. This
variation is shown in Figure 4.30.

We turn now to the marginal cost curve, which is defined as the
change in total cost with a change in output. Given the total cost curve
as in Figure 4.31, the marginal cost at a particular level of output,
here Q_b, is $\Delta TC / \Delta Q$, for a small increment in output. If we use the
differential calculus, the marginal cost is the slope, or first derivative,
of the total cost curve. We generally wish to know the marginal costs
of producing another unit of output at all levels of output.

In this single-process cost curve, because the cost curve up to Q_a is
a straight line, the marginal cost is the same at all levels of Q. Notice
that the fixed costs do not influence the marginal costs. If fixed costs
were raised or lowered, the total cost curve would be raised or lowered,
but $\Delta TC / \Delta Q$ would remain the same. When the firm tries to expand

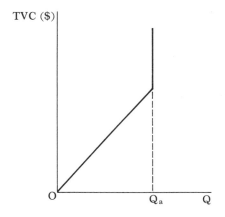

FIGURE 4.28   Total variable cost
as a function of Q: single-process
production function

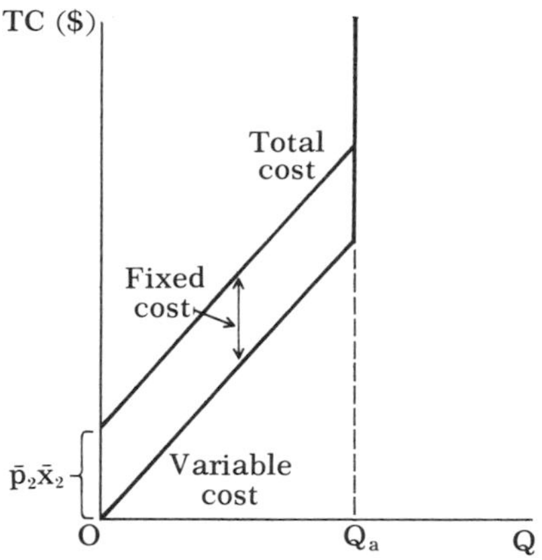

FIGURE 4.29   Derivation of total
cost curve: single-process
production function

output beyond Q_a, the marginal cost becomes infinite, although it is
more accurate to call it undefined beyond Q_a. With marginal cost constant at all levels of Q up to Q_a, but undefined beyond Q_a, the marginal
cost curve is a straight horizontal line for the single-process case as
in Figure 4.32, up to Q_a, after which it can be viewed as a straight
vertical line. (Marginal cost is constant for the single-process case
only when $\bar{p}_1$ is fixed; if p_1 varies with the firm's purchases, the *MC*
curve would not be constant.)

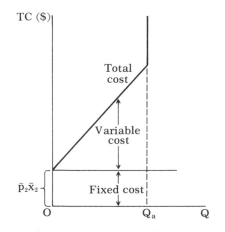

FIGURE 4.30   Alternative version
of total cost curve: single-process
production function

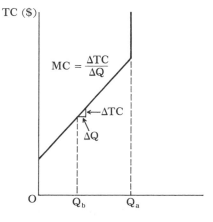

FIGURE 4.31   Basis of marginal
cost

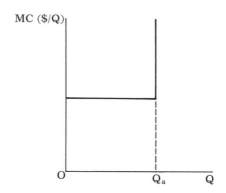

FIGURE 4.32   Marginal cost curve: single-process production function

The average total cost (*ATC*) curve is an important concept that tells us how the total costs per unit of output varies as we vary the level of output. The *ATC* for any level of output is calculated by simply dividing the total costs (*TC*) associated with that level of output by the number of units of output. When this process is repeated for all levels of output, we obtain the complete *ATC* curve.

Figure 4.33 illustrates the procedure. For output Q_b, the *ATC* is calculated as TC_b/Q_b. Similarly, for outputs Q_c and Q_a, the *ATC* would respectively be TC_c/Q_c and TC_a/Q_a. Geometrically, the slopes of lines drawn through the origin to different points on the *TC* curve tell us whether *ATC* is falling, remaining the same, or rising as Q is expanded. In this case, *ATC* continuously falls as Q is expanded, as shown in the bottom half of Figure 4.33.

We can gain additional insight into the *ATC* curve by dividing costs into their fixed and variable components. Figure 4.34 shows what happens to average fixed costs (*AFC*) when output is expanded. They continuously decrease, but at a decreasing rate. This should be expected: Fixed costs are $\bar{p}_2 \bar{x}_2$, and average fixed cost is simply $\bar{p}_2 \bar{x}_2/Q$. As Q is expanded, *AFC* always becomes smaller, but the change is much greater when Q goes from 1 to 2 (*AFC* falls by 50 percent) than when Q goes from 10 to 11 (*AFC* now falls by 10 percent).

Let us now look only at total variable cost (*TVC*) which was shown in Figure 4.28 and is given in Figure 4.35. The average variable cost (*AVC*) is defined as *TVC/Q*. We can see that this ratio is the same at output levels Q_b, Q_c, Q_a, and at any other level of output up to Q_a. Thus *AVC* is constant for all levels of Q up to Q_a (we disregard the vertical part of the *TVC* curve), and the *AVC* curve in this case is a horizontal line as in Figure 4.36.

The *AFC* and *AVC* functions could be placed on the same diagram because they are both in terms of dollars per unit of output. They can also be "added" vertically to get *ATC*. These curves are all shown in Figure 4.37.

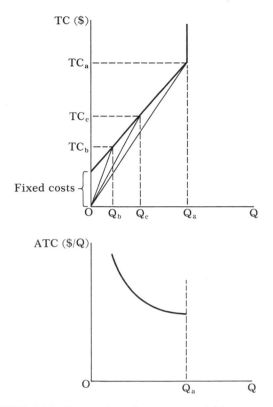

FIGURE 4.33   Derivation of average variable cost curve

Let us generalize our procedures. First, we start with the relation between the variable input and output. Second, we multiply the variable input by its price to get the cost of that input. This converts the relation between output and the variable input to a relation between output and the cost of the inputs. Third, we "flip" the axes over,

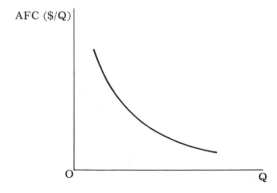

FIGURE 4.34   General shape of average fixed cost curve

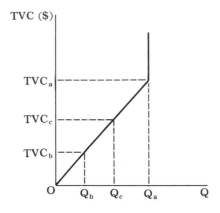

FIGURE 4.35   Total variable
cost curve: single-process
production function

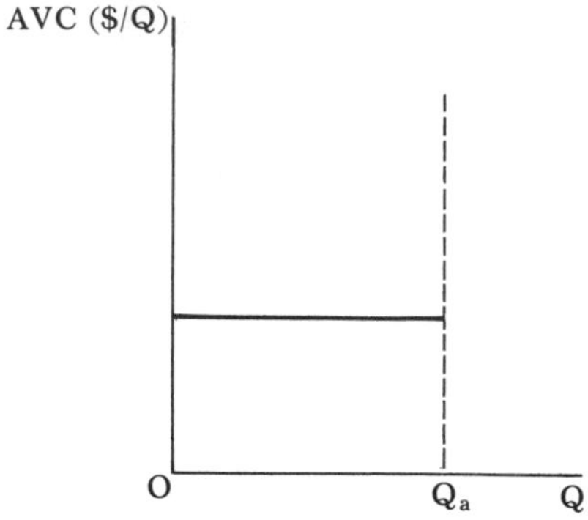

FIGURE 4.36   Average variable
cost curve: single-process
production function

which gives the relation between output and variable cost, which
we can call the total variable cost curve. Fourth, we "push up" the
total variable cost curve by the amount of the fixed costs, which gives
us the total cost curve. These four steps are shown in panels 1 through
4 in Figure 4.38.

The marginal cost is the change in total cost with a change in output. It could be obtained from panel 4. Or, because only the variable
costs change with output, the marginal cost could also be obtained
from panel 3. The average variable cost for any value of Q can be
obtained from panel 3 by dividing TVC by that value of Q. When we
do this for all values of Q, we get the AVC curve. The average fixed
cost can be obtained from panel 4 by dividing TFC by different values

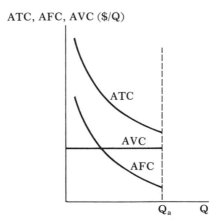

FIGURE 4.37   All average cost curves: single-process production
function

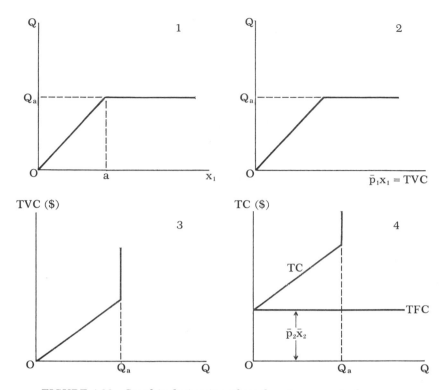

FIGURE 4.38 Graphic derivation of total cost curve: single-process production function

of Q, thereby getting a relation between average fixed cost and Q. Algebraically, the average fixed cost is $\bar{p}_2 \bar{x}_2$ divided by Q. The average total cost is the sum of *AVC* and *AFC* for each value of Q. The *ATC* curve can also be determined directly from the *TC* curve of panel 4. Because the marginal cost and the various average cost curves all have \$/Q as the ordinate, they can be placed on the same diagram, as in Figure 4.39.

TWO PROCESS. We now apply this procedure to the two-process production function. With the first panel of Figure 4.40 giving the relation between the variable input and output, we first derive the total cost function in the same steps as in Figure 4.38.

Looking at either panel 3 or at panel 4, we can see that from zero output to Q_a, total cost (or total variable cost) rises at a constant rate. Hence marginal cost is the same over this range of output values. However, from Q_a to Q_b, although cost rises at a constant rate over this range, the rate of increase is greater than in the first output range. Hence the marginal cost "jumps" up to a higher level. Notice that the jump in *MC* is nothing more than the other side of the coin to a fall

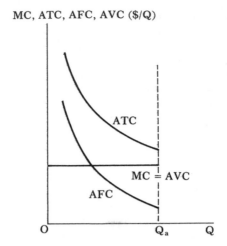

FIGURE 4.39   Marginal and average cost curves: single-process production
function

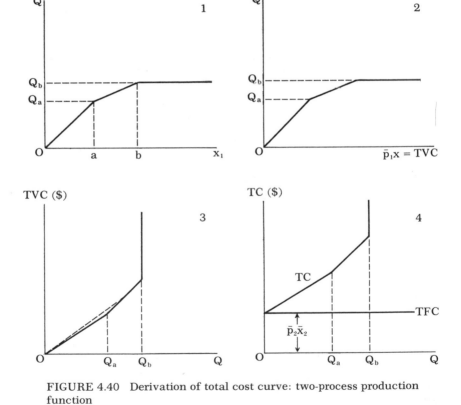

FIGURE 4.40   Derivation of total cost curve: two-process production
function

in the marginal product of x_1. A decrease in output per unit of x_1 is equivalent to an increase in x_1, and therefore costs, per unit of Q.

There is no problem with average fixed cost; it has the same shape as in the single-process case. The average variable cost curve, however, is more complicated. Notice panel 3, and recall that the slope of a line drawn through the origin to any point on the curve gives the average variable cost at that associated value of Q. In the first segment, up to Q_a, the slope of such a line is the same for all values of Q. Thus AVC is constant up to Q_a. (It is also the same as marginal cost.) As we increase output beyond Q_a, however, lines drawn through the origin to points on the curve have higher and higher slopes as we increase Q. Hence the AVC curve rises continuously as we move from Q_a to Q_b. It is never as high as MC, however, over the Q_a to Q_b range. Notice that any line drawn through the origin to a point on the Q_a,Q_b segment always has a smaller slope than the slope of the segment itself. This implies that for all output levels between Q_a and Q_b, the MC is greater than the AVC. The general shapes of all these curves are shown as Figure 4.41.

The ATC curve is especially interesting. Notice that over the range of output up to Q_a the ATC curve is a fixed amount above AFC. Two contrary forces are acting on the ATC curve beyond Q_a. As we expand output AFC continues to get smaller, so that it tends to lower ATC. However, the AVC curve is rising, so that it tends to increase ATC. With output expanding, however, ATC, after it reaches some minimum, will tend to rise. Why? Because AFC decreases at a decreasing rate, while AVC increases at an increasing rate. Hence AVC has the greater affect on ATC as output gets larger.

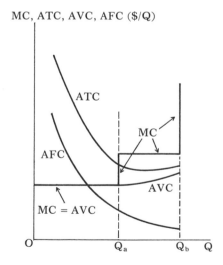

FIGURE 4.41   Marginal and average cost curves: two-process production function

COBB-DOUGLAS. Figure 4.42 gives the relation between the variable input and the output in panel 1, from which we can derive the total cost curve with our graphic techniques. Notice that decreasing returns to the variable input in panel 1 imply that *TVC* increases at an increasing rate in panel 3.

From either panel 3 or panel 4, we see that *TVC* or *TC* is always rising at an increasing rate. Thus the tangents to these curves, whose slopes give the marginal cost at any particular values of Q, are always rising as Q is expanded. Hence *MC* continuously rises. *AFC* is again no problem: It is the same as in the previous cases. The *AVC* curve, however, rises for all levels of Q. Notice that the slopes of lines drawn through the origin become greater at higher levels of output. Thus, it is higher at point *B* in panel 3 than at point *C*. Notice also that the slope of the tangent (giving *MC*) is always greater at any point than the slope of the line through the origin (the *AVC*). Thus, *MC* is always greater than *AVC* for any value of Q. The curves appear as in Figure 4.43.

One attribute of the Cobb-Douglas is that the *MC* curve intersects

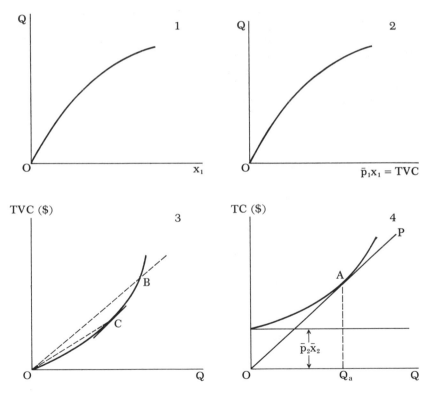

FIGURE 4.42   Derivation of total cost curve: Cobb-Douglas production function

MC, ATC, AVC, AFC ($/Q)

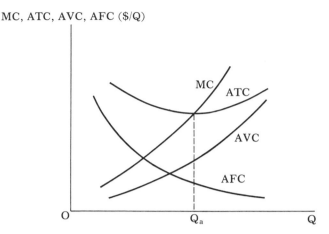

FIGURE 4.43 Marginal and average cost curves: Cobb-Douglas production function

the *ATC* curve at the minimum of the *ATC*. To see why this should be so, consider the line *OP* drawn in panel 4 of Figure 4.42. The slope of this line is smaller than a similar line through the origin drawn to any other point on the *TC* curve. Because the slopes of these lines from the origin represent the average total cost, the output level at which the line *OP* is tangent to the *TC* curve must be the output level at which *ATC* is a minimum. Now consider a tangent line to this same point on the *TC* curve, point *A*. The slope of this tangent represents the change in *TC* with a change in *Q*. Hence it is the marginal cost. But the tangent is the same as *OP*. As a consequence, *MC* equals *ATC* when *ATC* is at a minimum. There is no other point on this *TC* curve where the slope of a line through the origin is the same as the slope of a tangent.

CLASSICAL PRODUCTION FUNCTION: INDIVISIBILITY. Next, we have the classical production function with fixed input indivisible. Figure 4.19 provides the relation between the variable input and the output. Figure 4.44 shows how the total cost function is derived.

Panel 3 can best illustrate the marginal cost curve. Notice that up to Q_c, the inflexion point, costs increase at a decreasing rate and that the slopes of the tangents drawn to these parts of the curve become smaller as outputs is expanded over this range. Thus, we expect marginal cost to fall over this range. Beginning at the output level Q_c, *TVC* rises at an increasing rate; hence marginal cost begins to rise at Q_c. *MC* is undefined past output Q_b. Next we deduce the *AVC*, using panel 3 once more. If we visualize lines from the origin to different points on the curve, it can be seen that the slopes of these lines become smaller as output is expanded. At the output Q_a, however, the line through the origin, labeled *OP*, has the smallest possible slope. Beyond Q_a, lines drawn through the origin have increasingly steeper

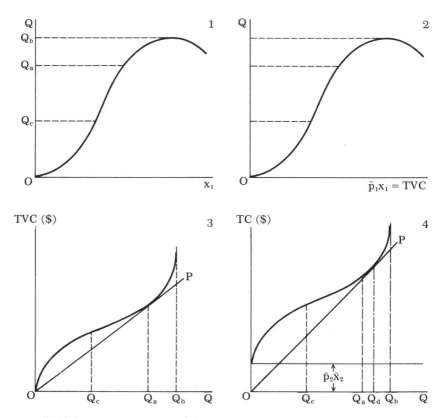

FIGURE 4.44   Derivation of total cost curve: classical production
function with divisibility

slopes. Because the slopes of these lines represent average variable
cost, it is evident that AVC falls until it reaches Q_c and then rises.
Notice that at output Q_c, the line through the origin has the same
slope as the tangent at that point. Hence AVC is equal to MC at output Q_c. Because AVC is a minimum at output Q_c, we see that AVC is
equal to MC at the minimum point on the AVC curve. In the same
vein, notice the line OP through the origin in panel 4. At output Q_d,
this line has the smallest possible slope to the ATC curve. Hence Q_d
is the output at which average total cost is a minimum. Notice that a
tangent drawn at the ATC line at output Q_d has the same slope as the
OP line. Thus, MC is equal to ATC at Q_d, where ATC is at a minimum.
These curves are all shown in Figure 4.45.

CLASSICAL PRODUCTION FUNCTION: DIVISIBILITY. As the final case,
we have the classical production function where the fixed input is
divisible. From Figure 4.19 we derive the total cost curve in four
panels, as shown in Figure 4.46.

Because the divisibility of the fixed input affects only the cost
curve up to Q_a, all the marginal and average cost curves will be the

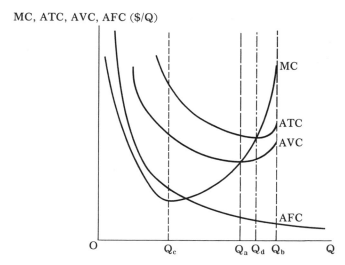

FIGURE 4.45   Marginal and average cost curves: classical production function with indivisibilities

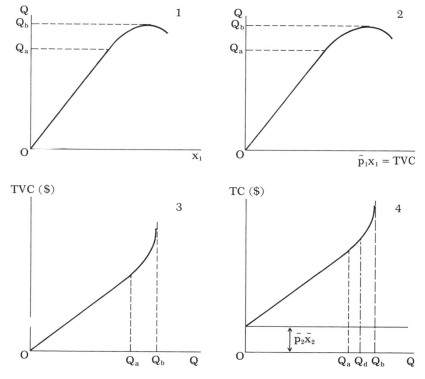

FIGURE 4.46   Derivation of total cost curve: classical production function with divisibility

same as in Figure 4.45 beginning at Q_a. However, as panel 3 in Figure 4.46 shows, *TVC* is a straight line through the origin up to Q_a. This implies that *MC* and *AVC* are the same up to Q_a. *AFC* does not change at all. Hence the marginal and average cost curves for this case are as shown in Figure 4.47.

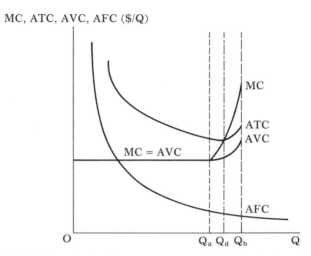

MC, ATC, AVC, AFC ($/Q)

FIGURE 4.47 Marginal and average cost curves: classical production function, divisible fixed input

Cost Curves Through Algebraic Manipulation. There is much to be learned by algebraically "incorporating" the constraints into the expenditure portion of the profit function, thereby expressing cost as a function of output. The main advantage of this procedure over graphic representation is that it lets us see more clearly how the various parameters influence the output cost function. We derive these functions for the Cobb-Douglas and single-process production functions but omit the classical production functions because they cannot be readily represented algebraically and the two-process function because the algebra is too involved.

COBB-DOUGLAS. Let us start with the input total cost function

$$TC = p_1 x_1 + p_2 x_2 \tag{4.30}$$

and set our task as that of expressing *TC* only in terms of *Q*. Let us say that we have the following constraints:

$$p_1 = \bar{p}_1$$
$$p_2 = \bar{p}_2$$
$$x_2 = \bar{x}_2$$
$$Q = a x_1^\alpha x_2^\beta. \tag{4.31}$$

These constraints, shown as equalities, are: Price p_1 is market price $\bar{p}_1$ for input 1; similarly for p_2; x_2 is the fixed input limited to $\bar{x}_2$; the last constraint is the production function. In writing the constraints as equalities, we assume that the firm will not pay more than it has to for inputs, that the firm will always use all the fixed input (this may not be a good assumption for other production functions), and that no inputs will be wasted.

We can immediately incorporate the price parameters, $\bar{p}_1$ and $\bar{p}_2$, into equation 4.30, obtaining

$$TC = \bar{p}_1 x_1 + \bar{p}_2 x_2. \tag{4.32}$$

Now solve the production function (equation 4.31) for x_1, which gives

$$x_1 = \left(\frac{Q}{ax_2^\beta}\right)^{1/\alpha}.$$

This equation can be used to substitute for x_1 in equation 4.32. Thus we have

$$TC = \bar{p}_1\left(\frac{Q}{ax_2^\beta}\right)^{1/\alpha} + \bar{p}_2 x_2. \tag{4.33}$$

Next we notice that x_2 is fixed at $\bar{x}_2$. Substituting $\bar{x}_2$ for x_2 in equation 4.33 yields:

$$TC = \bar{p}_1\left(\frac{Q}{a\bar{x}_2^\beta}\right)^{1/\alpha} + \bar{p}_2 \bar{x}_2. \tag{4.34}$$

Equation 4.34 now has total cost expressed in terms of only one variable, Q, and the various parameters. By incorporating the constraints, we have the output cost function. The first right-hand term is the variable costs, those that vary with Q; the second right-hand term, $\bar{p}_2\bar{x}_2$, is the fixed costs. The higher the value of $\bar{p}_1$, the higher is the cost at any level of Q; the higher the value of $\bar{x}_2$, the lower is the variable cost at any value of Q, but the higher the fixed costs; the higher the value of a, α, or β, the lower is the variable and total cost at any value of Q. Notice that the output cost function depends on: Q, the level of output; p_1 and p_2, the input prices; $\bar{x}_2$, the amount of the limited input; and a, α, and β, the "technology" coefficients.

From equation 4.34, we calculate the marginal cost by taking the first derivative of TC with respect to Q. Thus,

$$MC = \frac{dTC}{dQ} = \frac{\bar{p}_1}{\alpha}\left(\frac{1}{a\bar{x}_2^\beta}\right)^{1/\alpha}(Q^{1/\alpha-1}).$$

The average total cost curve is obtained by dividing equation 4.34 by Q. Thus, we have

$$ATC = \frac{TC}{Q} = \left[\bar{p}_1\left(\frac{1}{a\bar{x}_2^\beta}\right)^{1/\alpha}Q^{1/\alpha-1}\right] + \left(\frac{\bar{p}_2\bar{x}_2}{Q}\right). \tag{4.35}$$

The first right-hand term of equation 4.35 can be seen to be the *AVC* while the second term is the *AFC*.

Let us use some numbers to illustrate these cost functions. Say $\bar{p}_1 = \$3$, $\bar{p}_2 = \$5$, $\bar{x}_2 = 100$, and that the production function is

$$Q = 2x_1^{0.5} x_2^{0.5},$$

so that $a = 2$, $\alpha = 0.5$, $\beta = 0.5$. Then the total cost function is

$$TC = 3\left(\frac{Q}{2\sqrt{100}}\right)^2 + 500$$

$$TC = \frac{3}{400}Q^2 + 500.$$

The marginal cost function is

$$MC = \frac{dTC}{dQ} = \frac{6}{400}Q$$

and the average total cost function is

$$ATC = \frac{TC}{Q} = \frac{3}{400}Q + \frac{500}{Q}.$$

SINGLE PROCESS. We begin the derivation of the single-process production function output cost function with cost expressed in terms of the inputs:

$$TC = p_1 x_1 + p_2 x_2.$$

Again let the constraints be

$$p_1 = \bar{p}_1 \qquad\qquad\qquad (4.36)$$
$$p_2 = \bar{p}_2 \qquad\qquad\qquad (4.37)$$
$$x_2 = \bar{x}_2 \qquad\qquad\qquad (4.38)$$
$$x_1 = k_1 Q \qquad\qquad\qquad (4.39)$$
$$x_2 = k_2 Q \qquad\qquad\qquad (4.40)$$

where equations 4.39 and 4.40 together are the production function.

We now substitute from the constraints for p_1, p_2, x_2 (from equation 4.38) and x_1 (from equation 4.39), to get

$$TC = \bar{p}_1 k_1 Q + \bar{p}_2 \bar{x}_2. \qquad\qquad\qquad (4.41)$$

Notice that we do not use equation 4.40 to substitute for x_2 because the fixed costs do not depend on Q.

Equation 4.41 cannot stand by itself, because the limitation on $\bar{x}_2$ and the requirement that x_1 and x_2 be used together imply that there is an upper limit to Q. This upper limit is easily found from equation 4.40. If we substitute $\bar{x}_2$ for x_2 in equation 4.40 and solve for Q, we get the maximum quantity of Q that can be produced, which can be written as

$$Q \le \frac{1}{k_2}\bar{x}_2. \qquad\qquad\qquad (4.42)$$

We can then add equation 4.42 as a "side condition" to equation 4.41, which says that Q can vary only between zero and $1/k_2(\bar{x}_2)$. Thus, the output total cost function is

$$TC = \bar{p}_1 k_1 Q + \bar{p}_2 \bar{x}_2, \qquad 0 \leq Q \leq \frac{1}{k_2} \bar{x}_2. \qquad (4.43)$$

With the side condition in effect, we can readily obtain the marginal and average cost curves:

$$MC = \frac{dTC}{dQ} = \bar{p}_1 k_1 \qquad (4.44)$$

$$ATC = \frac{TC}{Q} = \bar{p}_1 k_1 + \frac{\bar{p}_2 \bar{x}_2}{Q}$$

$$AVC = \frac{\bar{p}_1 k_1 Q}{Q} = \bar{p}_1 k_1$$

$$AFC = \frac{\bar{p}_2 \bar{x}_2}{Q}.$$

We can immediately see that MC and AVC are the same and are constant values that depend on the price of input 1 and the quantity of x_1 required per unit of Q (the k_1). It can be seen that both ATC and AFC fall with output expansions because the fixed costs are spread over a larger amount of output.

It might be well to derive the total cost on the assumption that x_2 is unlimited. Then we substitute for x_1 and x_2 from equations 4.39 and 4.40 into the input cost function to get

$$TC = \bar{p}_1 k_1 Q + \bar{p}_2 k_2 Q = (\bar{p}_1 k_1 + \bar{p}_2 k_2)Q.$$

The output cost function is now a straight line with no limits on Q. The marginal cost is

$$MC = \frac{dTC}{dQ} = \bar{p}_1 k_1 + \bar{p}_2 k_2,$$

which is constant, but higher than in the case where x_2 is fixed at $\bar{x}_2$. (Now the cost of x_1 and x_2 both vary with Q.) The ATC curve, which is also the AVC curve, is

$$ATC = \frac{TC}{Q} = \bar{p}_1 k_1 + \bar{p}_2 k_2.$$

We see that ATC is now the same as MC. There are, of course, no fixed costs in this case.

Least-Cost Expansion Path and the Cost Curves. A third method of deriving the cost curves, one that yields additional insights, is by finding the least-cost expansion path — that is, the combination of inputs that, for any output, costs the least amount. To get the least-cost expansion path, we use an isoquant map in which an isoquant, together with other constraints that limit the possible combinations of inputs, determines the opportunity set of inputs for any particular level of output. An isocost map is also employed, which is the preference function that is used to select the least-cost input combination for any level of output. All these least-cost combinations generate what we call the least-cost expansion path. Because that least-cost expansion path tells us the inputs required for any output level, the least-cost expansion path can provide the basis for the output cost function. We proceed by studying the single-process, two-process, Cobb-Douglas, and classical (both versions) production functions.

SINGLE PROCESS. Earlier in this chapter we derived the isoquant map for the single-process production function, which is reproduced as Figure 4.48. Each isoquant is treated as the boundary of an opportunity set of the possible x_1, x_2 combinations that can produce the associated level of output. The possible combinations inside the boundary are shown as shaded areas. We show on this diagram the process ray. There are no limitations on either input.

To obtain the isocost preference map, we start with the input cost function

$$C = \bar{p}_1 x_1 + \bar{p}_2 x_2$$

where we assume the input prices are given by the market. Solving for x_2 yields

$$x_2 = \frac{C}{\bar{p}_2} - \frac{\bar{p}_1}{\bar{p}_2} x_1,$$

which enables us to easily graph the isocost lines. Notice that the isocost map is comprised of straight lines with a negative slope that depends on the ratio of $\bar{p}_1$ to $\bar{p}_2$. By selecting different values of C, we generate the isocost map, which would have the general form as in Figure 4.49.

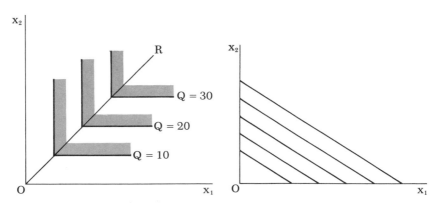

FIGURE 4.48   Single-process
isoquant map

FIGURE 4.49   Iso-cost map

To illustrate the construction of the isocost map with numbers, let us assume that $\bar{p}_1$ is \$3 and that $\bar{p}_2$ is \$5. Then the input cost function, when solved for x_2, is

$$x_2 = \frac{C}{5} - \frac{3}{5}x_1. \qquad (4.45)$$

A single line on the isocost map can be obtained by assuming a value for C — say 100. Then by substituting 100 for C in equation 4.45, we obtain the line

$$x_2 = \frac{100}{5} - \frac{3}{5}x_1, \qquad (4.46)$$

which represents all the x_1, x_2 combinations that can be purchased for \$100. If we plot equation 4.46, we have one isocost line. To obtain the whole map we substitute different values for C and plot the corresponding lines. We can have as many of these lines as we wish. All the lines taken together constitute the isocost map. Notice that the lower the value of C, the further to the SW direction is the isocost line. Thus, assuming we want to minimize costs of output, input combinations lying on isocost lines in the SW direction are preferable to input combinations in the NE direction.

By superimposing the isocost preference map on the isoquant opportunity sets, we can obtain the optimal least-cost combinations of inputs for each output level. The least-cost input combinations for all output levels constitute the least-cost expansion path. The procedure is shown in Figure 4.50. Notice that all the least-cost input combinations are at the "corners" of the isoquants and that these corners

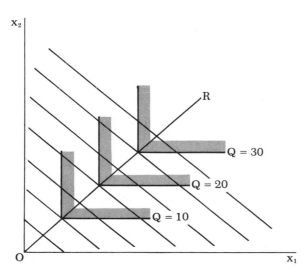

FIGURE 4.50   Least-cost expansion path: single-process production function, no fixity constraint

would be the least-cost input combinations for any positive values of $\bar{p}_1$ and $\bar{p}_2$. The process ray, *OR*, then, is clearly the least-cost expansion path.

We can derive the output cost function from the expansion path. For any value of Q, represented by an isoquant, we can tell the quantities of the inputs required to produce that level of Q. By multiplying these input quantities by the input prices, we get the cost of that level of Q. This procedure can then be repeated for all values of Q. The outputs and their associated costs can be plotted on a diagram, as in Figure 4.51, and the locus of these points is the output cost function.

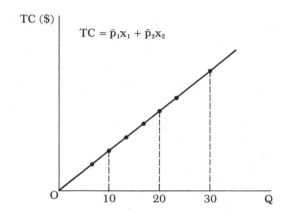

FIGURE 4.51   Output total cost function: single-process production function, no fixity constraint

We have derived the "long-run" expansion path and output cost function, for the long run is usually characterized as the case where both inputs are unlimited. Let us, however, say that x_2 is limited to $\bar{x}_2$ and that all the units of x_2 must be paid for whether or not they are used. The isoquant map would thus have the fixity constraint, so that the opportunity sets would now appear as in Figure 4.52.

The isocost map would change as the result of $\bar{x}_2$ having to be paid for. In the context of paying for the inputs used, the *use* of x_2 has a zero price because, having been paid for, it cost the firm nothing to use.[8] Thus, the input cost function is $C = \bar{p}_1 x_1$, which, with $\bar{p}_1$ given by the market, provides an isocost map as in Figure 4.53.

Superimposing this isocost map upon the opportunity set gives the least-cost expansion path as in Figure 4.54. Because an isocost line

---

[8] We should price the units of x_2 at zero only if there is no alternative use of x_2. Its opportunity cost—that is, the money that is lost by using x_2—is then nothing. But this may not always be the case. Say the firm could rent out the equipment that provides x_2 and can calculate the price of a unit of x_2 as, say, $2. Then there is an opportunity cost of $2 in using a unit of x_2, and it should be so priced.

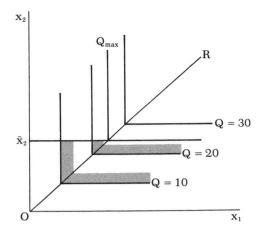

FIGURE 4.52 Input combination opportunity set, constrained by technology and fixity

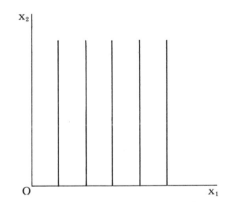

FIGURE 4.53 Iso-cost map when x_2 is "free" in use

does not give just a single best input combination corresponding to an output level, any expansion path lying between the lines OR and $\bar{x}_2$ (including these lines) is equally good. Thus the expansion path AB is as good as OR, although it seems to "waste" some x_2. All expansion paths must stop at the isoquant labeled Q_{max}, which, because of the limitation on x_2, is the maximum that can be produced. Notice that there are no points in the opportunity set for $Q = 30$; this quantity cannot be produced.

Assuming that we select OR as the expansion path, let us next derive the total cost curve. (It would make no difference if we took any other of the possible least-cost expansion paths.) Since $\bar{p}_2 \bar{x}_2$, the payment for the fixed input, must be made no matter what the output level is, the cost at zero output will be $\bar{p}_2 \bar{x}_2$. To this cost we can add the variable cost associated with each level of output. This cost is

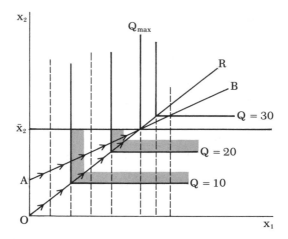

FIGURE 4.54   Least-cost expansion path: single-process production function, one input limited and paid for

obtained by finding, for a particular level of output, the quantity of x_1 that will be used. Then, by multiplying this value of x_1 by $\bar{p}_1$, we obtain the variable cost for that level of Q. We repeat this procedure for all levels of Q and add the variable costs to the fixed costs as in Figure 4.55.

What if both x_2 and x_1 were limited to $\bar{x}_2$ and $\bar{x}_1$ respectively and had to be paid for whether or not they were used? The isoquant map with the two fixity constraints would appear as in Figure 4.56. The maximum output will now be determined by the input in shortest supply, in this case $\bar{x}_1$.

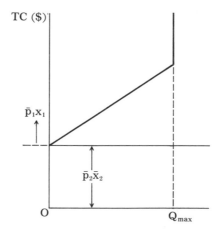

FIGURE 4.55   Total cost function: single-process production function, one input fixed and paid for

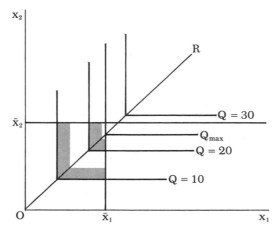

FIGURE 4.56 Input opportunity set with fixity constraints on both inputs

What will be the isocost map? With both inputs paid for, both p_1 and p_2 are zero in the use of the inputs, so that there is no isocost map. Any expansion path of possible x_1, x_2 combinations gives the same costs. In drawing the output cost function, there are only fixed costs, equal to $\bar{p}_1\bar{x}_1 + \bar{p}_2\bar{x}_2$, so that the output cost function is as in Figure 4.57. Notice that the marginal cost would be zero, because costs do not vary with output. The average total cost curve would be the same as the average fixed cost curve.

TWO PROCESS. Turning to the two-process production function, let us first examine the case where both inputs are unlimited and are paid for only when used. Figure 4.58 shows the isoquant map (and opportunity set) and two alternative isocost maps, one with solid lines, the other with dashed lines. If the isocost lines have the slope denoted by the solid lines, the least-cost points are all on the OR_1 process ray, which becomes the least-cost expansion path. If, however,

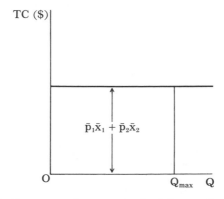

FIGURE 4.57 Output total cost curve, both inputs fixed and paid for

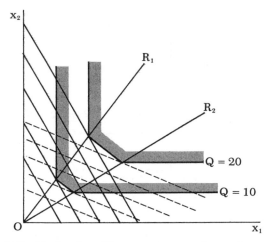

FIGURE 4.58   Derivation of least-cost expansion path: two-process production function, neither input limited

the slope of these isocost lines is the dashed lines, then the OR_2 process ray is the least-cost expansion path. Notice that, if the slope of the isocost lines is steeper than the portions of the isoquant lines between the process rays, the OR_1 ray is always the least-cost expansion path. But if the slope of the isocost lines is gentler than those portions of the isoquants, OR_2 is the least-cost expansion path. If the slope of the isocost lines is the same as the slope of these portions of the isoquants, OR_1 and OR_2 are equally good expansion paths. Expansion paths of combinations of the two processes are also as good.

Let us write the isocost lines as

$$x_2 = \frac{C}{\bar{p}_2} - \frac{\bar{p}_1}{\bar{p}_2} x_1.$$

If $\bar{p}_1$ is high relative to $\bar{p}_2$, the isocost lines are steep and process 1 would be used. Notice that process 1 uses a high amount of x_2 relative to x_1. Thus, we should expect this process to be used if x_1 is expensive relative to x_2; it "economizes" on the expensive variable. On the other hand, if $\bar{p}_1$ is low relative to $\bar{p}_2$, the isocost map has a gentler slope, and process 2 is used. Notice that process 2 uses a higher proportion of x_1 to x_2. Again the use of process 2 seems logical when $\bar{p}_1$ is low in comparison to $\bar{p}_2$.

Let us now say that x_2 is limited to $\bar{x}_2$ and must be paid for whether or not it is used. Then the use of x_2 is "free," and the isocost map is as in Figure 4.53. The isoquant map together with the fixity constraint gives the opportunity sets as in Figure 4.59. If the isocost map of Figure 4.53 were superimposed on the opportunity sets of Figure 4.59, the expansion path would be the line marked by the arrows. Expansions of output would first take place along OR_1, which uses a high proportion of the "free" x_2. Notice that in this expansion x_1 and x_2

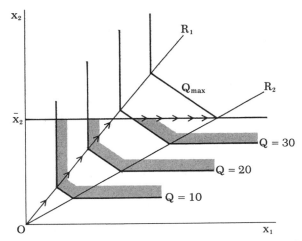

FIGURE 4.59 Least-cost expansion path: two-process production function, with x_2 constrained

are used in fixed proportions. After all the $\bar{x}_2$ is used, further output expansion can take place only along the horizontal line at $\bar{x}_2$. In this phase of the expansion, process 2 is combined with process 1. When only process 2 is used, output is at the maximum, denoted by the iso-quant Q_{max}. In this second phase of the expansion, we should expect a smaller increment in output per unit of x_1, because with the use of process 2, we use a process in which a smaller amount of x_2 is used per unit of x_1 – thus, getting diminishing returns to x_1 in the second phase compared to the expansion along the OR_1 process ray. These diminishing returns to x_1 imply increasing amounts of x_1, and there-fore variable costs, per unit of Q as was pointed out earlier.

We will not graph the total cost function in terms of output but only point out the procedure. The fixed costs would be $\bar{p}_2 \bar{x}_2$. To get the variable cost for any level of Q, we find the corresponding point on the expansion path, notice the amount of x_1 used, and multiply this amount of x_1 by $\bar{p}_1$. By taking many different values for Q, we can thereby generate the variable cost function, which, when added to the fixed costs, gives the total output cost function.

Let us try another variation on this model by assuming that x_2, although limited to $\bar{x}_2$, is not completely paid for but rather only the amount of x_2 used must be paid for. Then x_2 is no longer free in its use and has the price $\bar{p}_2$. The isocost map then would appear as in Figure 4.49 rather than Figure 4.53. If this isocost map is steeper than the portion of the isoquant map between the process rays in Figure 4.59, the expansion path will be as shown in this figure. But if the slope of the isocost map is gentler than those portions of the isoquants, the expansion path would be along the OR_2 process ray.

COBB-DOUGLAS EXPANSION PATHS. We now attack the Cobb-Douglas expansion path, assuming first that both inputs are unlimited and do

not have to be paid for unless used. Then, the isocost map of Figure
4.49 will be applicable because there are positive prices for both
inputs. Figure 4.60 shows the isoquant map, which gives the opportunity sets, together with two alternative isocost maps.

The isocost map with the solid lines is the steeper one, reflecting a
high value of $\bar{p}_1$ relative to $\bar{p}_2$. Notice that the least-cost combination
for any level of output is the point on the corresponding isoquant
where the slope of the isoquant — which is the marginal rate of technical substitution — is equal to the slope of the isocost lines. A little
example will show why these two slopes must be equal if there is
to be a least-cost combination. Let us say $\bar{p}_1$ is $2 and $\bar{p}_2$ is $1, so that
the slope of the isocost line is −2. Say now that a point has been selected on an isoquant where it is possible to substitute one unit of
an input for one unit of the other input and still have the same output
level. Then if one more unit of x_2 were used, and one unit of x_1 were
replaced, the expenditures on the inputs could be reduced by $1, be-
cause a unit of x_1 costs $2, while a unit of x_2 only costs $1. Obviously,
we should move along the isoquant line in the direction of more x_2 as
long as the cost of the additional x_2 is less than the cost of the x_1 that
is not used. When the MRTS is two units of x_2 for one unit of x_1, then,
at these prices, nothing would be gained, and something lost, if we
moved to a different point on the isoquant.

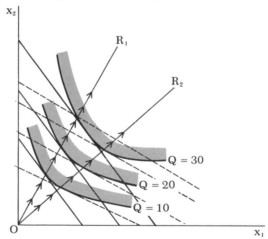

FIGURE 4.60   Alternative expansion paths: Cobb-Douglas production
function, both inputs unlimited

The isocost lines with the solid lines therefore lead to an expansion
path that would be a straight line, as OR_1 in Figure 4.60. This expansion path would consist of a single process. If, however, the isocost
lines were the dashed lines — $\bar{p}_1$ is now low relative to $\bar{p}_2$ — the expansion path would be along the process ray OR_2. Because the Cobb-Douglas production function consists of an infinite number of processes,

there can be an infinite number of expansion paths. Which one of these is the "least-cost" expansion path depends on the slope of the isocost lines, which in turn reflects the relative prices of the inputs.

Let us say now that x_2 is limited to $\bar{x}_2$ and that all $\bar{x}_2$ units must be paid for whether or not they are used. Then the technology constraint in conjunction with the fixity constraint will determine the opportunity sets for each level of output as in Figure 4.61. With x_2 already paid for, its *use* is free, so that Figure 4.53 is the relevant type of isocost map, which is shown in Figure 4.61 as the vertical dashed lines. It can be seen that for any output level, the part of the opportunity set determined by the intersection of the isoquant and the fixity constraint always lies on the lowest isocost line. As a consequence, the horizontal line at $\bar{x}_2$ is the least-cost expansion path. Notice that output is always expanded by using increasing amounts of x_1 with the fixed amount of $\bar{x}_2$.

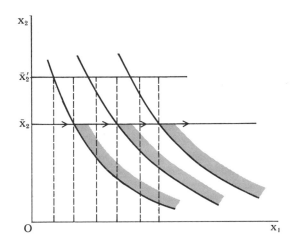

FIGURE 4.61   Expansion path: Cobb-Douglas production function with limited input

From the expansion path, we can derive the total cost curve as done previously: by finding for each level of output the input required, and then multiplying these inputs by their prices and adding these values to get the associated costs.

What would happen to the cost curve if there were more $\bar{x}_2$, say $\bar{x}_2'$? The expansion path would be higher, at $\bar{x}_2'$ in Figure 4.61. One effect of the increased amount of x_2 is that the fixed costs are higher. But the variable costs at any level of Q are lower with the higher amount of x_2. Notice that in Figure 4.61, for any output level, less x_1 is used when x_2 is fixed at $\bar{x}_2'$ than when it is fixed at $\bar{x}_2$. More of the fixed input therefore raises the fixed costs but reduces the variable costs — an important point indeed. The two alternative cost curves are given in Figure 4.62.

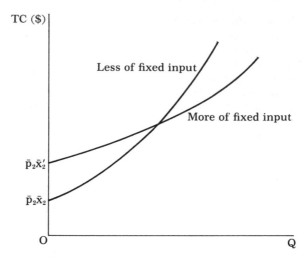

FIGURE 4.62   Total cost curves with two different levels of fixed input

CLASSICAL CASE: INDIVISIBILITY. Let us first examine the expansion paths of the classical production function when all inputs are unlimited. Figure 4.63 gives the isoquant map, which determines the opportunity sets, with one isocost map superimposed.

The process rays OR_1 and OR_2 represent the limits of the range of efficient processes. The process ray OR_3 is the least-cost expansion path. Notice that this expansion path is determined by the input com-

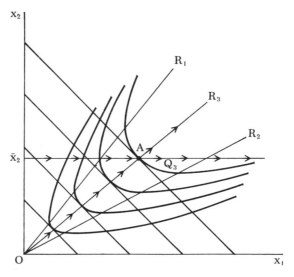

FIGURE 4.63   Long-run and short-run expansion paths: classical production function, indivisible fixed input

bination within an opportunity set that lies on the lowest possible iso-cost line. Also notice that at these least-cost input combinations, the marginal rate of technical substitution is the same as the slope of the isocost map.

We have also placed on Figure 4.63 the fixity constraint that arises from the limitation on input 2, which is the horizontal line at $\bar{x}_2$. If $\bar{x}_2$ is indivisible, then there is only one possible expansion path, which is the horizontal line at $\bar{x}_2$. Notice that part of this horizontal line lies in the area with inefficient processes. For contrast it should be noted that when there is no limitation on inputs, expansion takes place along a process ray by combining the inputs in fixed proportions. But when x_2 is limited and indivisible, expansion takes place by using more and more x_1 with the fixed amount of x_2.

It would be instructive to draw in the general shapes of the total cost curves for the cases when x_2 is limited and unlimited. Notice that at output Q_a, the two expansion paths intersect, so that only at that output level do we expect the total cost for both cases to be the same. For the no limit no fixed cost case, the total cost curve would be a straight line through the origin. For the fixed cost limited input case, the cost curve is as in Figure 4.44. Both cost curves are shown in Figure 4.64. Notice that except for the output Q_a, the "short-run" cost curve (x_2 limited and indivisible) is always higher than the "long-run" cost curve in which both inputs are variable. It should be noted that at output Q_a, the *ATC* short-run curve is at its minimum.

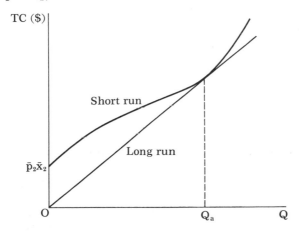

FIGURE 4.64 Long-run and short-run total cost curves: classical production function, fixed input indivisible

CLASSICAL CASE: FIXED INPUT DIVISIBLE. When neither input is limited, the expansion path for the divisible case is the same as for the indivisible case. But when a fixed input is divisible, the expansion path for the divisibility case differs from that for the indivisibility case.

Figure 4.65 derives the least-cost expansion path when x_2 is fixed at $\bar{x}_2$, is paid for whether or not used, and is divisible. The isoquants and the fixity constraint together determine the x_1, x_2 opportunity set for any level of output. With x_2 now paid for, its *use* can be considered free, so that Figure 4.53 depicts the nature of the isocost map. As the diagram shows, output is first expanded along the "first" efficient process ray, using x_1 and x_2 in fixed proportion. After all the available x_2 is being used, further output can take place only by using more and more x_1 with the fixed quantity of x_2. If x_1 is expanded beyond the OR_2 process ray, output would fall.

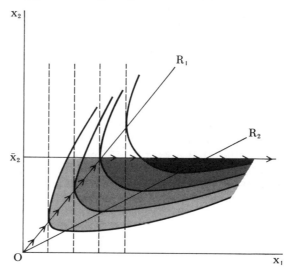

FIGURE 4.65 Expansion path: classical production function, x_2 limited but divisible

A Note on the Production Period and the Cost Functions. Production is a flow process in which both inputs and outputs are measured as rates per period of time, or rates per production period. What would happen to the cost curves if the production period were increased, say, from one day to two days?[9]

Assume that input is limited to some fixed amount per day. Expanding the production period from one to two days is equivalent to doubling the amount of x_2 available per production period (although not, of course, per day). For any given level of output per production period, it would now be possible to employ a process that uses a higher proportion of x_2 to x_1. As a result, the variable costs would be smaller

[9]This problem was considered by Armen Alchian, in "Costs and Output," in M. Abramovitz (ed.), *The Allocation of Economic Resources*, (Palo Alto: Stanford University Press, 1959).

for any level of output. But the fixed costs per production period would now be higher, because we are "paying" for these fixed inputs over two days rather than one. The "stretchout" in the production period is equivalent to obtaining more of the fixed input services, and the contrast between the total cost curves for the one- and two-day production periods would be much the same as those shown in Figure 4.62. Notice that the total costs would be higher, as a result of the stretchout, for low levels of output, but smaller for higher levels of output. The average variable, and marginal, cost curves, however, would be lower for all levels of output with the longer production period.

Two factors, however, tend to deter the firm from too long a stretchout. First, a given level of output spread over a two-day period gives the firm only half as much to sell per day. To compensate, the output level for the firm could be made twice as great for the two-day production period as for the one-day period by expanding the limited input. If such expansion made total cost smaller, the firm should certainly consider the longer production period. A second factor, however, may mitigate against the stretchout, even though costs are reduced. Customers may not be willing to wait for the longer delivery times implied by long stretchouts in the production period. It is interesting to notice, then, that the state of the market in which the firm sells its product may affect the firm's choice of production period and, as a consequence, its output cost curve.

Discussion Questions

1. Consider two firms—one whose production function consists of a small number of production processes and one whose production function consists of a large number of production processes. Which firm is more likely to change its input mix in response to small changes in the prices of inputs? Why? If you were a labor union leader who wants higher wages but fears the effect of higher wages on the employment of your members, with which firm are you more likely to attain your objectives?

2. Consider an area encloser who wants to enclose 100 square yards and must use wood fencing for one parallel pair of sides and steel fencing for the other pair of sides. Say he is considering the input combination of 20 yards of each type of fencing. If one yard less of steel fencing is used, how much more wood fencing would be required? Say now that he is considering the combination of 40 yards of steel fencing and 10 yards of wood fencing. If one yard less of steel fencing is used, how much more wood fencing would be required? Finally, let us say that he considers the combination of 10 yards of steel fencing and 40 yards of wood fencing. If he uses one yard less of steel fencing, how much more wood fencing would be required? What is the marginal rate of technical substitution at each of these three input combinations? How does the MRTS change as the area encloser considers production processes that use higher and higher proportions of one input to the other? Which input combination uses the least

amount of both types of fencing? Would the area encloser necessarily select that combination? Why or why not?

3. If there were increasing returns to scale for firms in a given industry, how many firms would we want in that industry?

4. Evaluate the validity of the following statement: If there were no diminishing returns to an input when the availability of other inputs is fixed, the world's food supply could be grown in a flower pot. Would we have to worry about Malthus' warnings against overpopulation?

5. A single-process production function for a firm is expressed as $x_1 = 1Q$, and $x_2 = 2Q$, where x_1 is labor and x_2 is machinery. What is the marginal product of a unit of labor? What must be assumed about the availability of machinery? What happens to the marginal product of labor if the firm acquires more machinery?

6. Assume a two-process production function whose process 1 is $x_1 = 1Q$, $x_2 = 2Q$, and process 2 is $x_1 = 2Q$, $x_1 = 1Q$, and where x_1 is labor and x_2 is machinery. Assume also that x_2 is limited to 100 units per time period. What process produces more per unit of labor? Which process is labor intensive, which machinery intensive? Which processes produce more per unit of machinery? Which process should be used at low levels of output if the machinery is paid for as well as limited? Why? Which process should be used to obtain the maximum possible output? Why? How should the firm change its process mix and input proportions as it expands from low to high levels of output? Why do we get diminishing returns to labor as a shift is made from process 1 to process 2? What happens to the returns per unit of machinery as output is expanded? What happens to the average product of labor as it is expanded? What happens to the average output per 100 units of machinery as output is expanded?

7. Consider the Cobb-Douglas production function $Q = 2x_1^{0.5}x_2^{0.5}$, where x_1 is labor and x_2 is machinery. With x_2 taken as constant, what happens to the marginal product of labor as labor is expanded? What would happen to the marginal product of labor if x_2 were a higher constant? What significance does the amount of x_2 have for labor productivity?

8. What special features of the classical production function and the divisibility of the fixed input account for the increasing marginal product of the variable input at low levels of that input?

9. Consider once more the fencing problem, where two parallel sides are made of steel and two sides of wood. Assume initially that the area encloser wants to enclose 100 square yards, that the price of wood fencing is $3 per yard and the price of steel fencing $5 per yard, and that both inputs could be obtained in any quantities. Using an isoquant and isocost map, determine the least-cost input combination. What is the least-cost expansion path?

Assume now that the maximum amount of steel fencing that can be obtained is 50 yards, with the wood fencing unlimited. If the firm has to pay the above-mentioned prices only for what it uses, determine the least-cost expansion path.

Assume further that the firm is not only limited to the 50 yards of steel fencing but has agreed to pay for the full 50 yards whether or not it is used. What is the least-cost expansion path now?

5 Short-Run Decision Models: The Firm as Producer

The elements of decision models can be combined in many ways to create many optimization models. We develop here a substantial number of models, but they are really only a subset of the very large set of models that could be developed from the different elements presented in Chapter 3. Attention is focused, therefore, on the techniques of model-building rather than on the models themselves. In the models presented here, we use the simplifications developed in Chapter 4. Some or all of the constraints are incorporated into the objective function in order to reduce the number of decision variables and to simplify the optimization problem.

All the decision models in this chapter can be characterized as short-run models. That is, the firm's role as producer of one or more products rather than its role as owner of assets is the focus of attention. The model firm is assumed to seek its goals within the framework of a set of constraints that it cannot change. It seeks to find the best set of values for its decision variables, given the constraints. We leave for the next chapter all questions of the worthwhileness to the firm of efforts and expenditures directed toward changing these constraints.

Insight into the management problems of business firms in the real world comes primarily from comparisons of models based upon alternative assumptions about the constraints. Although we assume the constraints are given to the firm in the short run, as analysts we can change these constraints in order to ascertain the sensitivity of the optimum solution to such changes. By developing many rather than only one or two models, we also learn how to apply the tools of economic theory to a wide range of business problems. By comparing alternative models, we can form beliefs about the causal relations in the real world. The appropriateness of such conclusions, of course, depends upon how well the models correspond to the real world. Because we choose our assumptions for tractability as well as for realism, the results should be viewed as insights rather than as discoveries of the laws of nature. Such insights, however, can be of great help to business managers in making decisions for real-world firms.

SINGLE-PRODUCT OPTIMIZATION MODELS: ALL PRICES DETERMINED BY THE MARKET

The General Approach. In Chapter 3 we visualized the firm's short-run decision problem as that of selecting values for the decision variables that would optimize the criterion variable of an objective function, subject to a set of constraints on those decision variables. We also suggested that the optimization problem could be simplified by incorporating the constraints into the objective function. Sometimes it is feasible to incorporate all the constraints into the objective function, in which event the criterion variable, such as profits, can be expressed in terms of only one variable, Q,[1] the output level. At other times incorporating all the constraints may not be feasible: They may be discontinuous, or it may not be desirable to assume the solution will lie on the boundary of a constraint.

COMPLETE INCORPORATION OF CONSTRAINTS: COST AND REVENUE FUNCTIONS. If we assume that the firm uses only two inputs, its profit function is defined as

$$\pi = PQ - p_1 x_1 - p_2 x_2.$$

Chapter 4 was devoted largely to constructing an output cost function, where cost (or expenditure on the inputs) is expressed in terms only of output.[2] This was done, in effect, by incorporating the constraints on the supply prices to the firm, the production function, the fixity of an input, and indivisibility of an input in use, into the part of the profit function that consisted of expenditures on inputs. If $C(Q)$ is used to represent the output cost function, we have in effect substituted $C(Q)$ for the expenditure terms in the profit function, so that this function becomes

$$\pi = PQ - C(Q).$$

---

[1]It is also possible to express the objective function in terms of a variable input. This is done in Chapter 7, when we investigate the firm's demand for a variable input.

[2]Output is the only decision variable in the output cost function. In addition, there are also the parameters that reflect the various constraints.

Profit is now expressed as revenue minus cost. The revenue portion of the profit function is simply price multiplied by the quantity of the output, because we are assuming that all the output is sold at the same price. Price, however, is also a variable. To express the profit function in terms only of Q, we can substitute for P from the demand curve. If, for example, the demand curve is $P = \bar{P}$, where $\bar{P}$ is the market price, the revenue portion of the profit function is $\bar{P}Q$, where $\bar{P}$ is some constant number. If the price the firm can sell at depends on the quantity it places on the market, such as $P = a - bQ$, we can still substitute for P in the PQ term to get $(a - bQ)Q$. In both cases revenue is expressed now only in terms of one variable, Q. If we designate $R(Q)$ as the revenue function, the profit function is now expressed in terms of only one variable, Q: $\pi = R(Q) - C(Q)$.

$R(Q)$ can be called the total revenue function; it tells us the total revenue the firm receives for any level of output. From the total revenue function, we can derive two useful relationships — the marginal revenue function and the average revenue function.

Marginal revenue is defined as the change in the total revenue corresponding to another unit of output. If we wanted to know the marginal revenue of the eleventh unit of output, this could be done by calculating the total revenue (TR) when $Q = 11$, calculating the total revenue when $Q = 10$, finding the difference between these two total revenues. We can define the marginal revenue as

$$MR = \frac{\Delta TR}{\Delta Q}.$$

It is important to realize that the marginal revenue always applies to some *particular* unit of output.

If we are willing to make the simplifying assumption that output can be divided into small fractions, we can view the marginal revenue curve as the increments in total revenue with very small increments in output. Then, MR can be defined as the first derivative of TR with respect to Q, or

$$MR = \frac{d(TR)}{dQ}.$$

Average revenue is defined as total revenue divided by Q, or

$$AR = \frac{TR}{Q}.$$

Because TR is PQ, it can be seen that average revenue is nothing more than P or, more generally, the demand curve. If the demand curve is $P = \bar{P}$, AR will be $\bar{P}$. If the demand curve is $P = a - bQ$, AR will be $(a - bQ)Q/Q = a - bQ$.

When the market price is a fixed number, $\bar{P}$, that cannot be influenced by the firm, the construction of the three revenue functions is quite simple. The total revenue function is

$$TR = \bar{P}Q;$$

the marginal revenue function is

$$MR = \frac{d(\bar{P}Q)}{dQ} = \bar{P};$$

and the average revenue function is

$$AR = \frac{\bar{P}Q}{Q} = \bar{P}.$$

It can be seen that the *TR* function would graph as a straight line through the origin, when *TR* is one axis and *Q* is the other axis. Obviously, *MR* and *AR* are the same when, as in this case, the price at which the firm can sell is not influenced by its output.

When profits are a function just of Q, there are a number of different methods for finding the optimal value for Q – that is, the value of output that maximizes profit. One simple method consists of plotting the total revenue and total cost curves on the same graph. For any value of Q, the difference between the total revenue and cost curves will be profit (or loss if the cost curve lies above the revenue curve) at that level of output. We then search for the value of Q that gives the maximum profit (or sometimes minimum loss). Figure 5.1 illustrates this simple procedure. At output level Q_{opt}, the vertical distance between the total revenue and total cost curves is greatest.

A second method for determining the optimal value of Q is through use of the calculus. In this method we take the first derivative of π with respect to Q, using the profit function $\pi = R(Q) - C(Q)$, set this first derivative equal to 0, and solve for Q. If the second derivative is negative, then this solution for Q is the one that maximizes profit.[3] In symbols, we do the following:

$$\pi = R(Q) - C(Q)$$
$$\frac{d\pi}{dQ} = \frac{dR(Q)}{dQ} - \frac{dC(Q)}{dQ} = 0. \tag{5.1}$$

Notice that if marginal profit – that is, $d\pi/dQ$ – is zero, it will also be true that marginal revenue will equal marginal cost. For the value of Q at which equation 5.1 holds, therefore:

$$\frac{dR(Q)}{dQ} = \frac{dC(Q)}{dQ}.$$

Notice that in the optimizing process we find that the first derivative of the revenue function (which is marginal revenue) is equal to the first derivative of the output cost function (which is marginal cost).

A simple illustration might be helpful. Let us say that the market

---

[3]This is known as the second-order condition. Symbolically, for a value of Q to maximize rather than minimize π, we must have $d^2\pi/dQ^2 < 0$ as well as $d\pi/dQ = 0$.

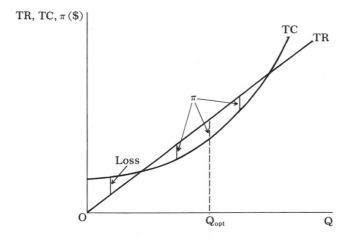

FIGURE 5.1 Profit maximization by comparing total revenue and total cost functions

price is $10, so that the total revenue function is 10Q. Say the total cost function is $100 + 2Q + 0.1Q^2$. Then the profit function is

$$\pi = (10Q) - (100 + 2Q + 0.1Q^2). \tag{5.2}$$

The first derivative of equation 5.2 is

$$\frac{d\pi}{dQ} = (10) - (2 + 0.2Q). \tag{5.3}$$

Notice that the 10 is *MR* and that the $2 + 0.2Q$ is *MC*. When we set equation 5.3 equal to zero and solve for Q, we get the profit-maximizing value of Q, which is 40. The second derivative of equation 5.3 is -0.2, which assures us that $Q = 40$ maximizes profit. When $Q = 40$, $MC = 2 + 0.2(40) = 10$, which is equal to *MR*. The fixed cost term, 100, does not in any way affect the optimal output. If, for example, the total cost curve was $TC = 200 + 2Q + 0.1Q^2$, the optimal solution would still be $Q = 40$.

Although generations of students have learned this method, together with its finding that π is maximized when *MR* is equal to *MC*, it may not always be applicable. It may not always be possible to express the revenue and cost functions as continuous curves. Continuous functions are necessary to the use of the calculus. When, in particular, the production function consists of only a small number of processes, the cost function may be such that there is no value of Q for which *MC* is equal to *MR*.

The third optimization technique makes explicit use of what could be called marginal reasoning. Marginal reasoning utilizes the fact that a change in output will result in a change in revenue (*MR*) and a change in cost (*MC*). Starting from zero output, we ask whether *MR* is greater than *MC* for the first unit of output. If it is, we would produce this unit and ask the same question of the second unit. This procedure would continue as long as any increment in output results in the MR for that unit being greater than the MC for that unit. The level at which MR is equal to MC is the optimal output level. We must not, however, apply marginal reasoning too mechanically. There may be instances in which MR is always greater than MC over the range of physically possible output levels. We would continue to produce up to physical capacity in such cases, but there would not be any output at which MR was equal to MC.

PARTIAL INCORPORATION OF CONSTRAINTS: PROGRAMMING. There may be cases in which it is impossible or awkward to incorporate all the constraints into an objective function. Sometimes cases like these arise because we cannot be sure that the solution will be on the boundary of a constraint, in which event we should treat such a constraint not as an equality but rather as an inequality. Let us say, for example, that there are two fixed inputs and that the production function calls for them to be used in a 1:1 ratio, but the firm has more of one of them. Then we cannot treat the fixity constraint on the surplus input as an equality, for this implies that all that input will be used. Another factor that mitigates against the incorporation of all the constraints into the objective function is that they may be discontinuous in some way so that they cannot be represented by a single equation. This may happen if one constraint limits the range of another constraint. In Chapter 3 we pointed out that the range of a demand curve may be limited by a price ceiling imposed by the government. We cannot then easily bring this demand curve into the objective function, by substituting for P, for P does not vary with Q over the complete range of Q.

For these and other reasons, it is well to learn how to optimize when some of the constraints are not incorporated into the objective function; it vastly increases our ability to handle a variety of problems. The constraints that are incorporated into the objective function become part of that function; the constraints that are not incorporated into the objective function define the opportunity set. The "programming" technique is then used to obtain the optimum values for the decision variables. This is done by converting the objective function into a preference map and superimposing this map on the opportunity set to obtain the optimal solution.

To demonstrate the method, let us say we have a one-product firm that uses two inputs, so that its profit function is

$$\pi = PQ - p_1 x_1 - p_2 x_2.$$

Say now that we have the following constraints:

$P \leq \bar{P}$	Demand curve	(5.4)
$p_1 \geq \bar{p}_1$	Supply curve of input 1	(5.5)
$p_2 \geq \bar{p}_2$	Supply curve of input 2	(5.6)
$x_2 \leq \bar{x}_2$	Fixity constraint	(5.7)
$Q \leq f(x_1, x_2)$	Production function	(5.8)

If we assume that the firm will not sell below the market price and that it will not pay above the market price for inputs, inequations 5.4, 5.5, and 5.6 become equalities. Also, if we assume the firm will use all the fixed input, inequation 5.7 becomes an equality. With these equalities, we can easily incorporate the constraints into the profit function, which now becomes

$$\pi = \bar{P}Q - \bar{p}_1 x_1 - \bar{p}_2 \bar{x}_2. \tag{5.9}$$

Notice that there are only two decision variables in equation 5.9, Q and x_1.

Let us say that for some reason it is awkward to incorporate the production function into the objective function. If we incorporate inequation 5.7 into 5.8, the production function becomes

$$Q \leq f(x_1, \bar{x}_2). \tag{5.10}$$

This production function has the same two decision variables as equation 5.9, namely Q and x_1. We then have the basis for the "programming" solution. Inequation 5.10 will define the opportunity set of all possible Q, x_1 combinations. Equation 5.9 provides the basis for a preference map for these two decision variables. By superimposing the preference map on the opportunity set, we can find the optimal Q, x_1 solution.

PROFITS AND CASH FLOW. One of the fundamental theorems of economic analysis is that fixed costs do not influence in any way the optimal values for the decision variables in the short run. It is therefore not really necessary to include the fixed costs in the objective function. Sometimes, it is much more convenient to leave the fixed costs out of the profit objective function, particularly when we use programming techniques to find optimal solutions. When the fixed costs are omitted, we obtain a cash-flow equation, which is the difference between revenues and variable costs. Thus, equation 5.9 is converted into a cash-flow equation: $Z = \bar{P}Q - \bar{p}_1 x_1$. The maximization of cash flow will always be completely consistent with the maximization of profits.

Optimization: Single-Process Production Functions.
OPTIMIZATION BY COMPARING TOTAL REVENUE WITH TOTAL COST. Figure 5.2 has on it the short-run total cost curve, where x_2, one of the inputs, is fixed at $\bar{x}_2$, so that there is some maximum possible output. Also shown on this graph are total revenue curves with three different prices, $\bar{P}_1$, $\bar{P}_2$, and $\bar{P}_3$. Since $TR = PQ$, it is evident that the higher the price, the greater will be the slope of the TR function. When the price is $\bar{P}_1$, the highest of the three prices, it is clear that profit is maximized when Q_{max} is produced. At this output, the difference between the TR and TC curves, which is π, is at a maximum. The intersection of the TR and TC curves, at point E, determines the "breakeven" level of output. Knowledge of this breakeven point is useful in planning new products, because it indicates the minimum rate of output that is necessary to at least recover the fixed cost.

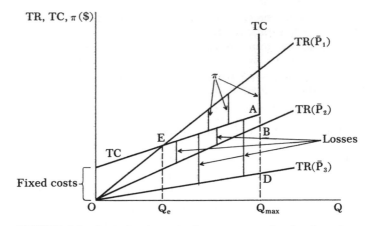

FIGURE 5.2   Optimization: single-process production function

The total revenue curve with price $\bar{P}_2$ is drawn so that it always lies below the *TC* curve. The vertical difference between these two curves is then the loss. What should the output be in this case? Notice that as output is raised, the loss always becomes smaller, so that here too output should be at Q_{max}. There will be a loss at that output of *AB*, but the loss is smaller than at any other level of output. When the price is $\bar{P}_3$, however, the loss becomes larger as output is expanded, and the firm should not produce anything. Its loss then would be limited to the fixed costs.

The reason price $\bar{P}_2$ leads to maximum output while $\bar{P}_3$ leads to zero output is best seen when we view the optimization process in terms of cash flow, thereby neglecting the fixed costs. If we look only at cash flows, we replace the *TC* curve with the total *variable* cost curve. This is done in Figure 5.3.

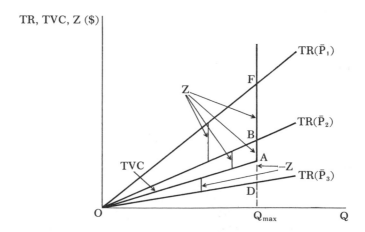

FIGURE 5.3   Optimization using cash flow

If our objective is to maximize cash flow—the difference between TR and TVC—it is clear that when the price is $\bar{P}_1$, the output level should be Q_{max}. The cash flow, measured here by AF, is higher at Q_{max} than at any other level of output. When price is $\bar{P}_2$, the cash flow is always positive from expanding output. We now see that Z is maximized at Q_{max} and is equal to AB, even though the firm sustains a loss because the cash flow is not great enough to cover fixed costs. When the price is $\bar{P}_3$, however, there is a *negative* cash flow as output is expanded, so that the firm should produce nothing.

Consider what would happen if *all* the input had to be paid for whether or not it was used. Then there would be only fixed costs, and the TVC curve would be zero for all levels of output. Now, if the price were $\bar{P}_3$, there would be a positive cash flow that would increase as Q is expanded, and the firm would produce Q_{max}. We could deduce that, with all costs fixed, the maximum output would be optimal at any positive price for the output.[4]

OPTIMIZATION BY COMPARING MARGINAL REVENUE AND MARGINAL COST. Let us now use marginal costs and marginal revenues. Figure 5.4 shows the MC curve and three MR curves, all corresponding to the curves in the two preceding diagrams. The cash flow is now Z/Q, or cash flow per unit of Q: This is equal, for any particular unit of Q, to the difference between MR and MC for that unit.[5]

A glance at Figure 5.3 will show why the marginal curves in Figure 5.4 have their shapes and positions. All four "total" curves are straight lines. Hence the marginal revenues and cost are constant at all levels of Q. For the revenue curves, the MRs are nothing more than their prices. The MC curve depends on the price of the variable input and the technological coefficient determining how much of the variable input is required per unit of Q.[6] The MR curves for $\bar{P}_1$ and $\bar{P}_2$ are higher than the MC curve because, as can be seen from Figure 5.3, $TR(\bar{P}_1)$ and $TR(\bar{P}_2)$ have steeper slopes than TVC for all values of Q—at least up to Q_{max}. $TR(\bar{P}_3)$, however, has a gentler slope, so that MR at $\bar{P}_3$ is smaller than MC for all values of Q.

When we invoke our marginal reasoning, we see that MR is greater than MC at all levels of output when the output price is either $\bar{P}_1$ or $\bar{P}_2$. Hence, Q_{max} should obviously be produced. Every additional unit of output, because it has a positive cash flow, adds to the total cash flow. Notice that MR is nowhere equal to MC, although they can be considered equal at Q_{max} if we think of MC becoming completely vertical at Q_{max}.[7] When the price is $\bar{P}_3$, MC is always greater than MR, and every unit of Q leads to a negative cash flow. Evidently, nothing should be produced.

[4]In general, the higher the degree of fixed costs to variable costs, the more the firm would produce at any price. This is an important proposition when we are trying to understand the effect of market prices on output.
[5]When we compare MC to MR, for any value of Q, the difference is the marginal cash flow attributable to *that* unit of output.
[6]See equations 4.43 and 4.44.
[7]More technically, MC is undefined at Q_{max}.

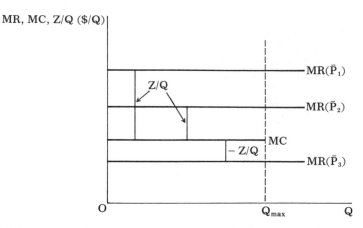

FIGURE 5.4   Optimization by comparing marginal revenue with marginal cost.

A PROGRAMMING SOLUTION. Let us now attack the solution problem without incorporating all the constraints into the objective function. We shall use cash flow as the objective function, so that it is expressed as

$$Z = PQ - p_1 x_1.$$

Let us say we have the following constraints, treating them as equations:

$$P = \bar{P} \tag{5.11}$$
$$p_1 = \bar{p}_1 \tag{5.12}$$
$$x_2 = \bar{x}_2 \tag{5.13}$$
$$x_1 = k_1 Q \tag{5.14}$$
$$x_2 = k_2 Q. \tag{5.15}$$

The last two equations are the single-process production function.

If we incorporate equations 5.11 and 5.12 into the objective function, it becomes

$$Z = \bar{P} Q - \bar{p}_1 x_1. \tag{5.16}$$

It is now in terms of only two decision variables. If we solve equation 5.16 for Q, we obtain

$$Q = \frac{Z}{\bar{P}} + \frac{\bar{p}_1}{\bar{P}} x_1. \tag{5.17}$$

This is an isocash-flow equation. If we put some value in for Z, we can obtain all the Q, x_1 combinations that yield that value of Z. By using different values of Z, we can generate an isocash-flow map, as in Figure 5.5, which is positively sloped, and where the more preferable Q, x_1 combinations are in the NW direction. From equation 5.17 we see that the slope of these isocash-flow lines is determined by the ratio of $\bar{p}_1$ to $\bar{P}$.

Let us turn now to the construction of the opportunity set. If we substitute the fixity constraint for x_2 in equation 5.15, we get

$$\bar{x}_2 = k_2 Q. \tag{5.18}$$

Solving equation 5.18 for Q now gives the maximum possible output, which is

$$Q_{max} = \frac{\bar{x}_2}{k_2}. \tag{5.19}$$

Now we solve equation 5.14 for Q, which gives the relation between output and x_1, the variable input:

$$Q = \frac{1}{k_1} x_1, \qquad 0 \le Q \le \frac{\bar{x}_2}{k_2}. \tag{5.20}$$

We have put the side condition along with this equation to denote that equation 5.20 holds true only up to the maximum possible output, which is limited by the fixity constraint on x_2. This equation is the boundary of the opportunity set of possible Q, x_1 combinations, which is shown as Figure 5.6. Notice that the slope of the boundary (below Q_{max}) is equal to $1/k_1$, which is also the marginal product of x_1.

We now superimpose the isocash-flow map upon the opportunity set to obtain the optimal solution of both Q and x_1, as in Figure 5.7. The Q, x_1 combination in the opportunity set that lies on the highest possible isocash-flow line is the optimum set of values for Q and x_1.

Optimization: Two-Process Production Function. We now show three methods for finding the optimum values for the decision variables when the production function consists of two processes.

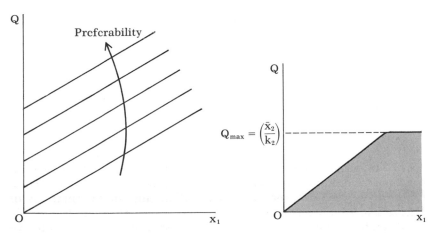

FIGURE 5.5   Q, x_1 isocash-flow map

FIGURE 5.6   Q,x_1 opportunity set

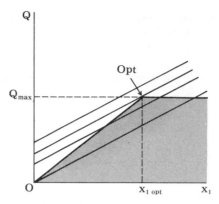

FIGURE 5.7   Optimal solution: programming method

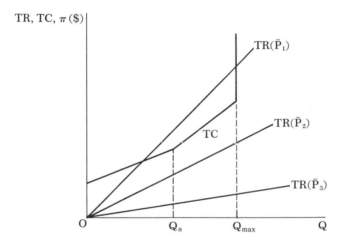

FIGURE 5.8   Optimal solution: two-process production function

COMPARING TOTAL REVENUE WITH TOTAL COST. Figure 5.8 displays the total cost function together with three TR curves that correspond to three different prices. When the price is $\bar{P}_1$, it should be clear that Q_{max}, the maximum possible output, should be produced. A little investigation would show that Q_{max} is optimal so long as the slope of the TR curve is greater than the slope of the second segment of the TC curve. When price is $\bar{P}_2$, it can be seen that there is a loss at every value of Q, but the loss is minimized at Q_a. If the fixed cost is left out of TC so that it becomes a TVC curve, it could be seen that there is a positive cash flow for all values of Q up to Q_a. When the price is $\bar{P}_3$, it can be seen that the firm's loss will be minimized when $Q = 0$. The loss will be the fixed costs. Again, if we used the TVC curve instead of TC, it would be seen that Z, the cash flow, would be negative. Figure 5.9 shows graphic solutions using cash flows.

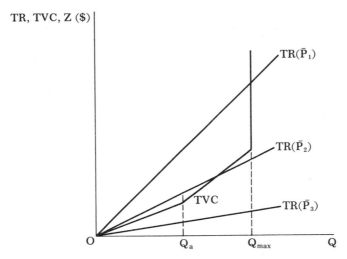

FIGURE 5.9   Optimal solution: two-process case, using cash flow

COMPARING MARGINAL REVENUE AND COST. In Figure 5.10, we have the MC curve for the two-process production function. It is constant up to Q_a, where one process is used, and then "jumps" up to a higher level, reflecting the output range over which output is produced by combining processes. At Q_{max}, the maximum possible output, MC becomes "infinite." Marginal reasoning clearly dictates that Q_{max} should be produced when the price is $\bar{P}_1$. The cash flow per unit of Q is always positive up to that output level. When the price is $\bar{P}_2$, cash flow is positive up to Q_a but negative beyond that quantity, so that Q_a is optimal. When the price is $\bar{P}_3$, the cash flow is negative for all values of Q, so that output should be zero.

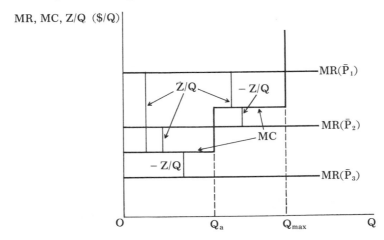

FIGURE 5.10   Optimal solution by comparing MC and MR

OPTIMIZATION BY PROGRAMMING. Optimization by programming is somewhat more complex in this instance than the other techniques, but it yields some insights that will be useful when we later turn to multi-product models. The essence of the programming technique is to *not* incorporate some of the constraints into the objective function. The constraints not incorporated provide the basis for the opportunity set.

Say that Q_1 is the output produced by process 1 and that Q_2 is the output produced by process 2. Let us say further that the output from either process is sold at the same price P. Let us also say that x_{11} is the quantity of input 1 devoted to process 1, while x_{12} is the quantity of input 1 used in process 2. Input 1 is the only variable input, whose price is p_1. The cash-flow equation is then the revenues from Q_1 and Q_2 minus the expenditures on the variable inputs, or

$$Z = PQ_1 + PQ_2 - p_1 x_{11} - p_1 x_{12}. \tag{5.21}$$

We turn now to the constraints. If the output price and the price of input 1 are determined by the market, we have the "freedom of others" constraints:

$$P \leq \bar{P} \tag{5.22}$$
$$p_1 \geq \bar{p}_1. \tag{5.23}$$

Let us say that the two processes are defined in this way:

$$\left. \begin{array}{l} x_{11} \geq k_{11} Q_1 \\ x_{21} \geq k_{21} Q_1 \end{array} \right\} \text{Process 1} \qquad \begin{array}{l} (5.24) \\ (5.25) \end{array}$$

$$\left. \begin{array}{l} x_{12} \geq k_{12} Q_2 \\ x_{22} \geq k_{22} Q_2 \end{array} \right\} \text{Process 2} \qquad \begin{array}{l} (5.26) \\ (5.27) \end{array}$$

In these process inequations x_{21} is the amount of x_2 used in process 1, and x_{22} is the amount of x_2 used in process 2. The ks are the technological coefficients: k_{11} is the amount of x_1 required per unit of Q_1; k_{21} is the amount of x_2 required per unit of Q_1; k_{12} is the amount of x_1 required per unit of Q_2; k_{22} is the amount of x_2 required per unit of Q_2. Finally, let x_2 be fixed at $\bar{x}_2$, so that we have the fixity constraint

$$x_2 \leq \bar{x}_2. \tag{5.28}$$

Which of these seven constraints can be incorporated into the objective function, equation 5.21? If we assume the firm will not sell below the market price, we can incorporate inequation 5.22 into equation 5.21 by substituting $\bar{P}$, the going market price, for P. Similarly, if we assume the firm will not pay above the market price for input 1, we can incorporate inequation 5.23 into equation 5.21 by substituting $\bar{p}_1$ for p_1. These two steps eliminate two of the six decision variables in inequation 5.22, so that Z is now in terms of the decision variables Q_1, Q_2, x_{11}, x_{12}.

Could we eliminate x_{11} and x_{12}? Consider inequation 5.24, which gives the production relation between x_{11}, the amount of input 1 devoted to Q_1, and Q_1. If we assume none of the x_{11} will be wasted, inequation 5.24 becomes an equation, and we can substitute $k_{11}Q_1$ for x_{11} in equation 5.21. This step eliminates x_{11} from equation 5.21. By similar reasoning, we can eliminate x_{12} by assuming no x_{12} will be wasted in the production of Q_2, thus enabling us to use inequation 5.26 to substitute $k_{12}Q_2$ for x_{12} in equation 5.21.

The result of "incorporating" the constraints (inequations 5.22, 5.23, 5.24, and 5.26) in the objective function is to give us the objective function as

$$Z = \bar{P}Q_1 + \bar{P}Q_2 - \bar{p}_1(k_{11}Q_1) - \bar{p}_1(k_{12}Q_2). \tag{5.29}$$

Notice that the objective function now only has two decision variables — Q_1, the quantity to produce with process 1; and Q_2, the quantity to produce with process 2. Everything else in the objective function is now parameters.

Three of the constraints, inequations 5.25, 5.27, and 5.28 — all of which involve the fixed input, x_2 — have not been incorporated into the objective function. Could they be? Because there is no x_2 in the objective function, we cannot readily incorporate the fixity constraint, inequation 5.28. If we assume no x_{21} is wasted in the production of Q_1, inequation 5.25 can be treated as an equation, and we could substitute x_{21}/k_{21} for Q_1 in equation 5.21. But such a substitution does not *eliminate* a decision variable in the objective function: We merely "trade" x_{21} for Q_1. Similarly, there is nothing to be gained by using inequation 5.27 to substitute x_{22}/k_{22} for Q_2 in equation 5.21. Thus, these three unincorporated constraints, inequations 5.25, 5.27, and 5.28, will provide the basis for our opportunity set.

Let us return to equation 5.29, the objective function with four of the constraints incorporated. If we collect terms, this equation can be written

$$Z = (\bar{P} - \bar{p}_1 k_{11})Q_1 + (\bar{P} - \bar{p}_1 k_{12})Q_2. \tag{5.30}$$

The first term in parentheses is the cash flow per unit of Q_1: $\bar{P}$ is the selling price; k_{11} tells how much x_1 is required per unit of Q_1; and $\bar{p}_1 k_{11}$ measures the expenditure on x_1 required per unit of Q_1. Similarly, $(\bar{P} - \bar{p}_1 k_{12})$ is the cash flow per unit of Q_2.

Let us solve equation 5.30 for Q_1, which gives us

$$Q_1 = \frac{Z}{(\bar{P} - \bar{p}_1 k_{11})} - \frac{(\bar{P} - \bar{p}_1 k_{12})}{(\bar{P} - \bar{p}_1 k_{11})}Q_2. \tag{5.31}$$

In this form, we can construct an isocash-flow map by assuming different values for Z. For any value of Z, equation 5.31 tells us the Q_1, Q_2 combinations that would produce that total cash flow. By varying the value of Z, we generate the isocash-flow map as in Figure 5.11. Notice that the slope of these lines is determined by the ratio

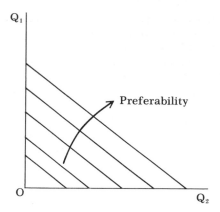

FIGURE 5.11   Isocash-flow preference map: two processes

$(\bar{P} - \bar{p}_1 k_{12})/(\bar{P} - \bar{p}_1 k_{11})$ in equation 5.31, which is the ratio of the cash flow per unit of Q_2 to the cash flow per unit of Q_1.

Let us now return to the three unincorporated constraints, inequations 5.25, 5.26, and 5.27, which we claimed can provide the basis for the opportunity set. First notice that x_{21}, the amount of x_2 used in Q_1, and x_{22}, the amount of x_2 used in Q_2, cannot together be greater than the amount of x_2 available, which is $\bar{x}_2$. We express this obvious condition as

$$x_{21} + x_{22} \le \bar{x}_2. \tag{5.32}$$

If we now assume that none of this input is wasted in production, inequalities 5.25 and 5.27 become equalities. Thus, we can use them to substitute for x_{21} and x_{22} in inequation 5.32 to get

$$k_{21} Q_1 + k_{22} Q_2 \le \bar{x}_2. \tag{5.33}$$

With k_{21}, k_{22}, and $\bar{x}_2$ parameters (or numbers), inequation 5.33 tells us all the Q_1, Q_2 combinations that can be produced. It is therefore the opportunity set of Q_1, Q_2 combinations. To find the boundary of this opportunity set, we treat inequation 5.33 as an equation (all $\bar{x}_2$ will be used), and solve for Q_1:

$$Q_1 = \frac{\bar{x}_2}{k_{21}} - \frac{k_{22}}{k_{21}} Q_2. \tag{5.34}$$

This opportunity set is shown in Figure 5.12. Note that the slope of the boundary of the opportunity set is determined by the ratio of the two technological coefficients.

Notice that the intersections of the boundary with the axes are labeled $\bar{x}_2/k_{21}$ and $\bar{x}_2/k_{22}$, which measure the maximum possible quantities of either Q_1 or Q_2. Look at equation 5.34. If Q_2 is zero, the maximum quantity of Q_1 is $\bar{x}_2/k_{21}$, which is the value of Q_1 where the boundary intersects the Q_1-axis. But if Q_1 is zero, a solution of equation

5.34 for Q_2 would show that $\bar{x}_2/k_{22}$ is the maximum Q_2 that can be produced. There should be no mystery here. If, for example, there were 300 units of x_2 available and 3 units of x_2 were required per unit of Q_1 (that is, $k_{21} = 3$), then a maximum of 100 units of Q_1 could be produced.

With the preferences for Q_1, Q_2 combinations shown in Figure 5.11 and the opportunity set of Q_1, Q_2 combinations shown in Figure 5.12, it is a relatively simple matter to superimpose the preference map on the opportunity set to obtain the optimal Q_1, Q_2 combination. This is done in Figure 5.13, where we see that only process 2 is used – that is, only Q_2 is produced. If the parameters were such that the isocash flow map had a gentler slope than the slope of the boundary of the opportunity set, only process 1 would be used.

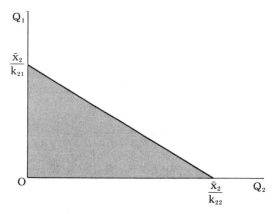

FIGURE 5.12 Q_1, Q_2 opportunity set

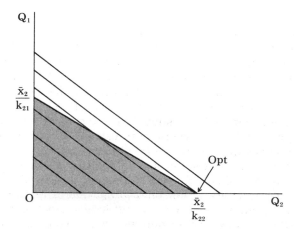

FIGURE 5.13   Programming solution: two-process production function

We can devise some interesting variations on this model. Let us say that from society's viewpoint process 2 is less desirable than process 1: perhaps it pollutes too much. If the government passes a law prohibiting the use of process 2, we would have the additional constraint that $Q_2 = 0$. Then the opportunity set is reduced to the Q_1 axis. Or the law may require the firm not to use process 2 more frequently than it uses process 1. This law would be expressed in the following constraint: $Q_1 \geq Q_2$. With this law, the opportunity set would be as in Figure 5.14. If the preference map remained as in Figure 5.11, the optimum solution would be at the intersection of the government-imposed constraint and the original boundary, which was determined by technology and the fixity of x_2. We can see why this programming approach permits a great deal of flexibility in economic analysis.

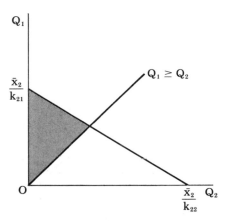

FIGURE 5.14 Q_1, Q_2 opportunity set with government-imposed constraint

Cobb-Douglas Production Function.

OPTIMIZATION BY COMPARING TOTAL REVENUE AND TOTAL VARIABLE COST. In Figure 5.15 we show two alternative total revenue functions and, instead of the total cost curve, we have the *TVC* curve. The difference between *TR* and *TVC* is the total cash flow, or Z. When the price is $\bar{P}_1$, the cash-flow maximizing output is Q_b; when price is $\bar{P}_2$, that optimum becomes Q_a. It should be ascertained that, in contrast to the single-process and two-process production functions, there is now a different optimal Q for every different price. It should also be noted that there would be some optimal output even at very low prices for the output. Why should this be so? Because it is possible to produce with processes that use a very high proportion of the fixed input to the variable input. Thus, at low output levels, when such processes are used, there is only a very small use of x_1, which is what leads to the variable costs. As a consequence, it is possible to have a positive cash flow even when the output price is very low.

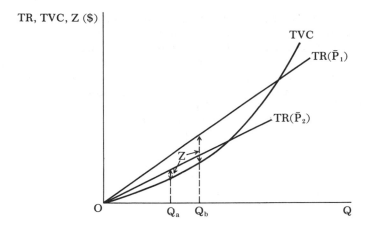

FIGURE 5.15   Optimization by comparing *TR* with *TVC*: Cobb-Douglas

OPTIMIZATION BY COMPARING MARGINAL REVENUE WITH MARGINAL COST. Figure 5.16 displays the *MR* lines at two alternative prices, plus the marginal cost curve and the three average cost curves. When the price is $\bar{P}_1$, the optimal output is Q_b; and when the price is $\bar{P}_2$, the optimal output is Q_a. It should be seen that the higher the output price, the higher is the optimal output.

From such a diagram, we can graphically determine both profits and cash flow. Consider the case in which the output price is $\bar{P}_1$. The difference between the output price and the average total costs, which is *BC* in the diagram, is the average profit per unit of output. When this profit per unit is multiplied by the output level, Q_b, we obtain total profit. This is measured by the area of the rectangle *ABCD*. The difference between the price and the *AVC* curve, which is *BE* on the

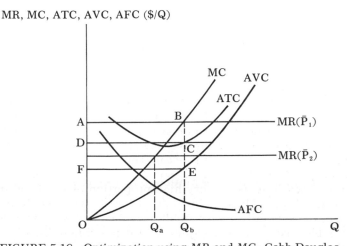

FIGURE 5.16   Optimization using *MR* and *MC*: Cobb-Douglas

diagram, is the average cash flow per unit of output. When it is multiplied by the output level, Q_b, we obtain total cash flow. This is measured by the area $ABEF$. The cash flow for any particular unit of output can be measured as the difference between MR and MC. When the cash flows for all units of output are added together, we get an alternative measure of total cash flow. Thus, the area enclosed by the MR and MC curves, or ABO in the diagram, is an alternative measure of the total cash flow. These geometric representations of profit and cash flow could be obtained for all cases in which optimization is done by comparing MC and MR.

ALGEBRAIC SOLUTION. When we have the Cobb-Douglas function, we can use algebra and calculus to find a solution for the optimal value of Q. This method is a little difficult but yields additional insights.

First define the cash-flow function as

$$Z = \bar{P}Q - \bar{p}_1 x_1, \tag{5.35}$$

where we have already incorporated the price constraints. The Cobb-Douglas function is

$$Q = a x_1^{\alpha} \bar{x}_2^{\beta}, \tag{5.36}$$

where we have already incorporated the fixity constraint on x_2. We can solve this equation for x_1, to get

$$x_1 = \left(\frac{Q}{a \bar{x}_2^{\beta}} \right)^{1/\alpha}. \tag{5.37}$$

Now we substitute for x_1 in equation 5.35 to obtain the cash flow in terms only of Q.

$$Z = \bar{P}Q - \bar{p}_1 \left(\frac{Q}{a \bar{x}_2^{\beta}} \right)^{1/\alpha}. \tag{5.38}$$

We can now use the calculus to find the value of Q that maximizes Z. The first derivative of equation 5.38 is

$$\frac{dZ}{dQ} = \bar{P} - \frac{\bar{p}_1}{\alpha} \left(\frac{1}{a \bar{x}_2^{\beta}} \right)^{1/\alpha} Q^{1/\alpha - 1}$$

When we set this expression equal to zero and solve it for Q, we get the optimal value of Q, which is

$$Q_{\text{opt}} = \left[\frac{\bar{P}}{\dfrac{\bar{p}_1}{\alpha} \left(\dfrac{1}{a \bar{x}_2^{\beta}} \right)^{1/\alpha}} \right]^{\frac{1}{1/\alpha - 1}} \tag{5.39}$$

This is a rather complex equation, but it enables us to see all the parameters that determine the optimal value of Q. Higher values of $\bar{P}$, a, α, β, and $\bar{x}_2$ all result in a higher value for the optimal Q. Conversely, lower values for these parameters would reduce the optimal value of Q. A higher value for $\bar{p}_1$, the price of the variable input, would lead to a lower value of the optimal Q.

To those of us who suffer from symbol shock, some numbers might be helpful. Let us say that the Cobb-Douglas is

$$Q = 2x_1^{0.5} \bar{x}_2^{0.5} \tag{5.40}$$

and that $\bar{x}_2 = 100$. Then a solution for x_1 is

$$x_1 = \left(\frac{Q}{20}\right)^2. \tag{5.41}$$

Assuming $\bar{P} = 10$, and $\bar{p}_1 = \$3$, and substituting for x_1 from equation 5.41, the cash-flow function (equation 5.35) becomes

$$Z = 10Q - 3\left(\frac{Q}{20}\right)^2. \tag{5.42}$$

The first derivative is

$$\frac{dZ}{dQ} = 10 - \frac{6}{400}Q. \tag{5.43}$$

Setting this equal to 0 and solving for Q gives the optimum value of Q as about 666. This works out fairly easily because we set both α and β at 0.5; generally, the solution would require much more arithmetic.

A PROGRAMMING SOLUTION. A programming solution is easy to explain if we build on the previous example. This time we will leave the demand curve "unincorporated." Starting with the cash-flow equation

$$Z = PQ - p_1 x_1, \tag{5.44}$$

let us say that we have all the numerical values for the parameters in the last example, but we do not incorporate the demand curve. Then, equation 5.42 becomes

$$Z = PQ - 3\left(\frac{Q}{20}\right)^2 \tag{5.45}$$

or

$$Z = PQ - \left(\frac{3}{400}\right)Q^2.$$

Solving equation 5.45 for P gives us

$$P = \frac{Z}{Q} + \frac{3}{400}Q. \tag{5.46}$$

From this equation we can construct an isocash flow map in terms of P and Q that would appear as in Figure 5.17.

The unincorporated constraint is the demand curve. If we assume a ruling market price of $\bar{P}$, this demand curve gives the constraint of $P \le \bar{P}$, which is shown as the shaded area in Figure 5.18. We have also superimposed the isocash-flow map on this P, Q opportunity set to get the optimal P, Q solution. This optimization method could be very useful if the constraints on the P, Q combinations were more complex than in our illustration.

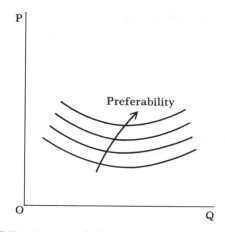

FIGURE 5.17   Isocash-flow map in terms of P and Q

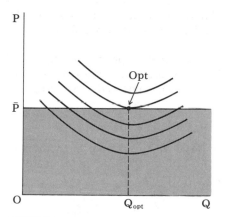

FIGURE 5.18   Programming solution

Classical Model: Indivisibility. Using the classical production function with the fixed input indivisible, we show the optimization techniques in only two ways—by comparing total revenue with total
variable cost and by comparing marginal revenue with marginal cost.
Our inability to express the classical production function algebraically makes the programming technique not feasible.

   COMPARING TOTAL REVENUE WITH TOTAL VARIABLE COST. Figure 5.19
depicts the total variable cost curve and total revenue curves that
correspond to three different prices. The difference between TVC and
TR is the cash flow, which is negative when the TVC curve lies above
the TR curve. When the price is $\bar{P}_1$, it can be seen that cash flow is
negative when output is below Q_c and becomes negative when out-

put is greater than Q_d. The output Q_b is that at which the positive cash flow is maximized; hence, this output level is the optimum. When the price is $\bar{P}_2$, cash flow is negative for all outputs except Q_a, at which point cash flow is zero. A line drawn through the origin tangent to the *TVC* curve gives the output at which *AVC* is at a minimum. Since $TR(\bar{P}_2)$ is equivalent to such a line, we can deduce that an output price equal to the minimum point on the *AVC* curve is the lowest price at which the firm would produce any output. This will be seen when we compare *MR* and *MC* to find the optimum output. When the price is $\bar{P}_3$, cash flow is negative at all output levels except zero, in which case cash flow is also zero. Clearly, the firm would not produce any output at price $\bar{P}_3$ or at any other price below $\bar{P}_2$.

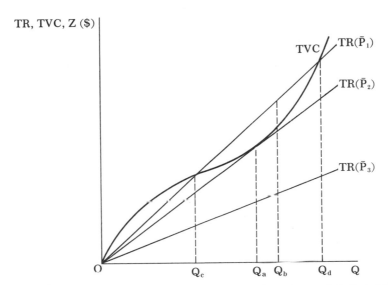

FIGURE 5.19 Optimization: classical production function with indivisibility

COMPARING MARGINAL REVENUE WITH MARGINAL COST. Figure 5.20 shows the marginal and average cost curves and three marginal revenue curves that correspond to three different output prices. When the price is $\bar{P}_1$, the optimal output by marginal reasoning is at Q_b, where *MC* is equal to *MR*. This diagram shows why we must be careful in applying marginal reasoning, for *MC* is also equal to *MR* at Q_e. We could deduce that the only part of the *MC* curve that should be used for this purpose is that lying above the *AVC* curve. When price is $\bar{P}_2$, output could be Q_a, although the firm is actually indifferent to whether it produces anything. The cash flow per unit is just zero. When price is below $\bar{P}_2$, cash flow per unit is negative at all output levels; hence, output should be zero. Notice that we could be led astray in this case if we equate *MR* and *MC* when the price is $\bar{P}_3$.

MR, MC, ATC, AVC, AFC ($/Q)

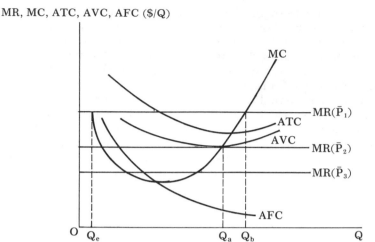

FIGURE 5.20   Optimization by comparing *MC* with *MR*: classical with indivisibility

Optimization Techniques: Classical Production Function with Fixed Input Divisible. Most of the special problems of comparing *MC* with *MR* disappear in the classical production function model when the fixed input is divisible. We here show the optimization procedures in two ways—by comparing total revenue with total cost and total variable cost and by comparing marginal revenue with marginal cost.

COMPARING TOTAL REVENUE WITH TOTAL COST. Figure 5.21 gives both the *TC* and the *TVC* curves for the classical case, with divisibility, and three different *TR* curves. The difference between *TR* and *TC* is profits, that between *TR* and *TVC* is cash flow. When the output price is $\bar{P}_1$, the output at which *both* profit and cash flow are maximized is Q_b. Notice that there is a loss when Q is less than Q_c but that cash flow is always positive for all outputs up to Q_d (although maximized only at Q_b). When the price is $\bar{P}_2$, the *TR* curve and *TVC* curve coincide up to Q_a. Thus, cash flow is zero over this range. Beyond Q_a, cash flow is negative. The firm is indifferent to any level of output between zero and Q_a. $\bar{P}_2$ should be viewed as the minimum price at which any output should be produced. When price is $\bar{P}_3$, it can be seen that cash flow is negative beyond output of zero and becomes a larger negative number as output is expanded. Consequently, the optimal output is zero, in which case the firm's loss will be restricted to its fixed costs.

COMPARING MARGINAL REVENUE WITH MARGINAL COST. Figure 5.22 depicts *MC*, *AVC*, *ATC*, and three *MR* curves. Notice that, up to Q_a, *MC* is equal to *AVC*. They are equal in this range of output because, with divisibility, output expansion takes place along a process ray. They differ after Q_a because beyond Q_a expansion of output takes

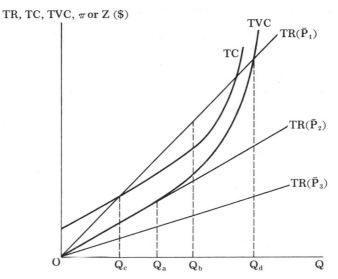

FIGURE 5.21   Optimization by comparing *TR* with *TC* or *TVC*: classical with divisibility

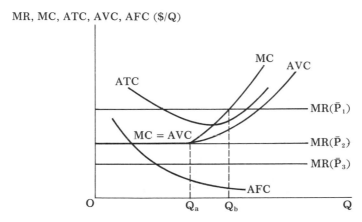

FIGURE 5.22   Optimization by comparing *MR* with *MC*: classical with divisibility

place by increasing the proportion of the variable to the fixed input.

If the price is $\bar{P}_1$, the optimal output is Q_b. There are no ambiguities in setting *MC* equal to *MR* in this case, because *MC* does not fall over any range of output. If price is $\bar{P}_2$, the firm is indifferent among all outputs from zero to Q_a. There is neither positive nor negative cash flow. If the price is below $\bar{P}_2$, as for $\bar{P}_3$, *MC* is always greater than *MR* and cash flow is always negative for all values of Q. The firm should not produce any output.

MULTI-PRODUCT DECISION MODELS

Most business firms in the real world produce more than one product. Sometimes, in such cases, the single-product decision models are completely applicable, specifically when the production of one product does not "interfere" with the production of another product. At other times, the production of one product does affect the ability to produce one or more other products. Such cases most commonly arise when different products use an input that is in limited supply. In this section we consider the conditions in which an allocation problem arises, the general approach to optimization when the production of one product interferes with the production of another, and multi-product optimization models.

Models with No Allocation Problems. Just because a firm produces two or more products does not necessarily mean that our single-product decision models are inapplicable. If the products use completely different input services, the production of one of the products has no effect on the ability to produce the other product. If these products are also not at all connected on the marketing side (this is implied in our assumption that the output prices are determined by the market), then the determination of the profit-, or cash-flow, maximizing output levels of the different products can each be approached separately with our single-product models. In effect, the independently determined profit-maximizing output level for each product will also maximize total profits for the firm.[8]

Even when an input is used in two or more products, the single-product optimization models may still be usable for each of the separate products, if this commonly used input can be obtained in any quantity. When there is no fixity constraint on the common input, then an increase in production of one of the products will not entail a reduction in the output level of the other product. We can go still further and say that even with a limitation on the commonly used input, a problem of choice among the products arises only when this limited commonly used input is fully utilized.

The single-product models are inapplicable only when all three of the following conditions are met: (1) at least one input service is common to at least two of the products, (2) the common input is limited in the quantity of the services available per time period, (3) the limited input is fully utilized. When these conditions occur, techniques for total profit maximization must be used that enable the joint choice of the optimum output mix of the two or more products.

[8]Sometimes, a product, such as safety razors, is necessary or helpful to the marketing of another product, such as blades. This would be reflected in the demand curve for one of the products, being partly dependent on the price and availability of the other product. Production of these products must then be jointly determined.

Production Possibility Frontier Approach. We first show why the techniques of optimization that compare revenues and output cost functions cannot be applied when a common fixed input is used in both (or more than two) outputs. Consider a profit function, with two outputs and three inputs:

$$\pi = \bar{P}_1 Q_1 + \bar{P}_2 Q_2 - \bar{p}_1 x_1 - \bar{p}_2 \bar{x}_2 - \bar{p}_3 x_3.$$

We have assumed here that all prices are determined by the markets. Hence, we have already incorporated the "freedom of others" constraints. Let us say that x_1 is the variable input used in product 1 and that x_3 is the variable input used in product 2. The input x_2, on the other hand, is limited at $\bar{x}_2$ and is used in the production of both products.

One approach to the problems of determining the output levels might be to set up cash-flow equations showing the cash flow from each output. Thus, we could have:

$$Z_1 = \bar{P}_1 Q_1 - \bar{p}_1 x_1$$
$$Z_2 = \bar{P}_2 Q_2 - \bar{p}_3 x_3.$$

Because the total cash flow is equal to $Z_1 + Z_2$, we could find the optimal output level of each product to maximize total cash flow. To do this, we can find the relation between x_1 and Q_1 and between x_3 and Q_2 and substitute for x_1 and x_3, thereby expressing each cash flow in terms only of output. Then we use the single-product optimization techniques to find the optimum values of Q_1 and Q_2.

There is, unfortunately, a major drawback to this technique. In all our production functions, the relation between the variable input and the output depended on the quantity of the fixed input. Thus, the only way we can solve this problem with the techniques just described is to assume some allocation of the fixed amount of x_2 to each of the outputs. We could then obtain a solution corresponding to any allocation of this input. But how would we know if we made the best allocation of x_2, for both the x_1, Q_1 and the x_3, Q_2 relations will change with any allocation of the x_2? With this technique the answer to this question can be obtained only by trying *all* the possible divisions of $\bar{x}_2$ among the two products and finding the optimal Q_1 and Q_2 – those that maximize $Z_1 + Z_2$. This is a difficult task, and fortunately we have other techniques.

The easier technique is based on an incomplete incorporation of the constraints into the objective function. The constraints that we omit from the objective functions are those that limit our capacity to produce the outputs. The nonincorporated constraints then jointly give the opportunity set of possible output combinations, whose boundary is the production possibility frontier. We can then use the programming optimization technique, where the cash-flow function gives a preference map with which to select an output combination from the output opportunity set. Usually, this output combination is on the production possibility frontier.

To illustrate this method, let us say that we have the profit function

$$\pi = \bar{P}_1 Q_1 + \bar{P}_2 Q_2 - \bar{p}_1 x_1 - \bar{p}_2 \bar{x}_2 - \bar{p}_3 x_3$$

where all the "price" constraints are already incorporated. If we omit the fixed cost term, $\bar{p}_2 \bar{x}_2$, we obtain this cash-flow equation:

$$Z = \bar{P}_1 Q_1 + \bar{P}_2 Q_2 - \bar{p}_1 x_1 - \bar{p}_3 x_3. \tag{5.47}$$

Say now that the remaining constraints are the fixity constraint

$$x_2 \leq \bar{x}_2 \tag{5.48}$$

and the production function for each of the products, which we assume to be single-process functions:

$$\left. \begin{matrix} x_1 \geq k_1 Q_1 \\ x_{21} \geq k_{21} Q_1 \end{matrix} \right\} \text{ Production function for product 1} \qquad \begin{matrix} (5.49) \\ (5.50) \end{matrix}$$

$$\left. \begin{matrix} x_3 \geq k_3 Q_2 \\ x_{22} \geq k_{22} Q_2 \end{matrix} \right\} \text{ Production function for product 2} \qquad \begin{matrix} (5.51) \\ (5.52) \end{matrix}$$

Because x_2 is used in both products, we have placed a second subscript to x_2 and the associated technological coefficients to denote the product to which that quantity of x_2 is assigned.

Because x_1 and x_3 are variable inputs and thus play no part in limiting the Q_1, Q_2 combinations, we can incorporate inequations 5.49 and 5.51 into the cash-flow equation, 5.47, by assuming none of these inputs will be wasted. Thus, we have

$$Z = \bar{P}_1 Q_1 + \bar{P}_2 Q_2 - \bar{p}_1 (k_1 Q_1) - \bar{p}_3 (k_3 Q_2), \tag{5.53}$$

which, when we combine terms, becomes

$$Z = (\bar{P}_1 - \bar{p}_1 k_1) Q_1 + (\bar{P}_2 - \bar{p}_3 k_3) Q_2, \tag{5.54}$$

which can also be written as

$$Q_1 = \frac{Z}{(\bar{P}_1 - \bar{p}_1 k_1)} - \frac{(\bar{P}_2 - \bar{p}_3 k_3)}{(\bar{P}_1 - \bar{p}_1 k_1)} Q_2.$$

We have our cash-flow equation expressed in terms of two decision variables, Q_1 and Q_2. Notice that the terms in parentheses give the cash flow per unit of each of the outputs.

The nonincorporated constraints – inequations 5.48, 5.50, and 5.52 – are those that limit the Q_1, Q_2 combinations and thereby define the opportunity set. Since the amount of x_2 that is assigned to each of the outputs cannot be greater than $\bar{x}_2$, the total amount of x_2 available, we have

$$x_{21} + x_{22} \leq \bar{x}_2. \tag{5.55}$$

If we assume that x_{21} and x_{22} will not be wasted in production, inequations 5.50 and 5.52 are treated as equalities, so that we can use these equations to substitute for x_{21} and x_{22} in equation 5.55:

$$k_{21} Q_1 + k_{22} Q_2 \le \bar{x}_2.$$

This inequation defines the Q_1, Q_2 opportunity set, and the boundary of this set is the production possibility frontier. Notice that it depends on the amount of $\bar{x}_2$ available and the technological coefficients that show how much x_2 is required per unit of each of the products. (This opportunity set is often called the "feasible set.")

This formulation should look familiar because it is the same as the "programming" solution to the two-process one-product case. In effect, each of the processes has now become a product.

We did not just happen to select a one-process production function for both products in our example. If the production functions were Cobb-Douglas or classical, the technique would not be applicable, unless we were able to make the generally unreasonable assumption that somehow the variable inputs are also limited to the firm, perhaps because it has a fixed sum of money that can be spent on the variable inputs. If such an assumption cannot be made, which would more closely reflect reality for the firm, problems arise because there is not a usable production possibility frontier. If the production functions are Cobb-Douglas, we can always use more of the variable input to produce more output. Hence, there is literally no outer boundary to the Q_1, Q_2 combinations that can be produced. If the production functions are classical, there will be a production possibility frontier because there are input combinations in which more of a variable input will reduce output. But there is no reason why the firm will want to select an output combination on such a frontier, for a firm will not use a variable input up to the point that its marginal product is zero. This section will therefore be devoted only to production functions consisting of one or a small number of processes. We will have to defer the more complex output mix problems where the production functions allow continuous substitutability between inputs to a later chapter. It must be deferred because other problems, not taken up until Chapter 7, must first be solved.

Optimization with One Fixity Constraint. We have already gone through the procedure for attacking the output mix problem when there is one fixity constraint using symbols for the prices, technological coefficients, etc., so that we will proceed by offering a numerical example.

Let us say that the firm produces two products, 1 and 2, that x_1 is the variable input used in product 1, that x_3 is the variable input used in product 2, and that x_2, which is fixed at $\bar{x}_2$, is used in both products. Then the cash-flow equation is

$$Z = P_1 Q_1 + P_2 Q_2 - p_1 x_1 - p_3 x_3.$$

Let us say that the constraints are:

$$P_1 \leq 10 \left.\vphantom{\begin{matrix}a\\a\\a\\a\end{matrix}}\right\}$$

$$\begin{aligned} P_1 &\leq 10 \\ P_2 &\leq 8 \\ p_1 &\geq 3 \\ p_3 &\geq 2 \end{aligned} \right\} \quad \text{Freedom of others}$$

(5.56)
(5.57)
(5.58)
(5.59)

$$x_2 \leq 100 \quad \text{Fixity}$$ (5.60)

$$\left.\begin{aligned} x_1 &\geq 2Q_1 \\ x_{21} &\geq 1.5Q_1 \end{aligned}\right\} \quad \text{Production function for product 1}$$

(5.61)
(5.62)

$$\left.\begin{aligned} x_3 &\geq 3Q_2 \\ x_{22} &\geq 0.5Q_2 \end{aligned}\right\} \quad \text{Production function for product 2}$$

(5.63)
(5.64)

We turn first to the construction of the cash-flow objective function. If we assume the firm will not sell for less than the market price, will not pay more than the market price, and will not waste any of the variable inputs, we can incorporate inequations 5.56, 5.57, 5.58, 5.59, 5.61, and 5.63 into the objective function. Thus, we have

$$Z = 10Q_1 + 8Q_2 - 3(2Q_1) - 2(3Q_2),$$ (5.65)

which, when we collect terms, becomes

$$Z = (10 - 6)Q_1 + (8 - 6)Q_2$$
$$Z = 4Q_1 + 2Q_2.$$ (5.66)

We see that the cash flow is \$4 per unit of Q_1 and \$2 per unit of Q_2.

Now, we solve equation 5.66 for Q_1:

$$Q_1 = \frac{Z}{4} - \frac{1}{2}Q_2.$$

Inserting different values for Z, we can generate an isocash-flow map as in Figure 5.23, noting that the slopes are all $-1/2$.

Notice that we did not incorporate inequations 5.60, 5.62, and 5.64 into the objective function. (Indeed, we cannot do this, because there

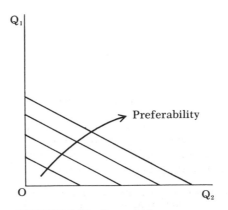

FIGURE 5.23   Isocash-flow map

is no x_2 term in the objective function.) Hence, they together will define the opportunity set of the Q_1, Q_2 combinations. Because the x_2 devoted to each of the two outputs cannot be greater than the amount of x_2 available, we have this constraint:

$$x_{21} + x_{22} \leq 100. \tag{5.67}$$

We use the inequality here because we may not use all the available x_2 — particularly if the cash flows from both products are negative.[9] If we assume that we do not waste any x_2 in any of the products, in-equations 5.62 and 5.64 become equalities. We can therefore substitute for x_{21} and x_{22} in inequation 5.67 to find the opportunity set in terms of Q_1 and Q_2:

$$1.5Q_1 + 0.5Q_2 \leq 100. \tag{5.68}$$

We find the boundary by treating equation 5.68 as an equality and solving for Q_1:

$$Q_1 = \frac{100}{1.5} - \frac{1}{3}Q_2.$$

The Q_1, Q_2 opportunity set is therefore as in Figure 5.24. Notice that the maximum Q_1 is determined by the amount of x_2 divided by the technological coefficient showing how much x_2 is required per unit of Q_1. With our assumed numbers, $Q_{1\,max}$ is $100/1.5$. Similarly, the maximum amount of Q_2 that can be produced is $100/0.5 = 200$.

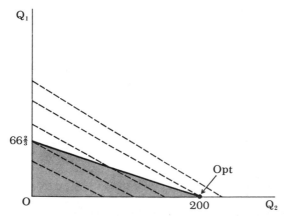

FIGURE 5.24 Q_1, Q_2 opportunity set with optimal solution

The optimization procedure is now quite simple. We superimpose the isocash-flow map upon the opportunity set. In this case, the solution is to produce 200 units of Q_2 and no Q_1. Should this be surprising in light of the fact that Q_1 gives a cash flow of $4 per unit while Q_2

[9] When we have a number of fixity constraints, we must treat them as inequalities because it is likely that some fixed inputs will not be completely utilized.

only gives a cash flow of \$2 per unit? Not necessarily. The slope of the production possibility frontier implies that we can get three additional units of Q_2 by giving up one unit of Q_1. Thus a "trade" of one unit of Q_1 for three units of Q_2 increases the cash flow from product 2 by \$6, and it decreases the cash flow from product 1 by only \$4. Consequently, we end up producing only Q_2.

Optimization with Two Fixity Constraints. Let us complicate our problem somewhat by assuming that the firm still produces two products but that each product uses two different variable inputs and that each product uses some of two different inputs that are in limited supply. Let x_1 and x_2 be the variable inputs used in product 1, x_3 and x_4 be the variable inputs used in product 2, and x_5 and x_6 be the fixed inputs, fixed at $\bar{x}_5$ and $\bar{x}_6$, that are used in both products.

With two outputs and four variable inputs, the cash-flow equation is

$$Z = P_1 Q_1 + P_2 Q_2 - p_1 x_1 - p_2 x_2 - p_3 x_3 - p_4 x_4.$$

Let us say the constraints are

$$
\left.
\begin{aligned}
P_1 &\le \bar{P}_1 \\
P_2 &\le \bar{P}_2 \\
p_1 &\ge \bar{p}_1 \\
p_2 &\ge \bar{p}_2 \\
p_3 &\ge \bar{p}_3 \\
p_4 &\ge \bar{p}_4
\end{aligned}
\right\} \text{Freedom of others}
$$

$$\begin{aligned}(5.69)\\(5.70)\\(5.71)\\(5.72)\\(5.73)\\(5.74)\end{aligned}$$

$$
\left.
\begin{aligned}
x_5 &\le \bar{x}_5 \\
x_6 &\le \bar{x}_6
\end{aligned}
\right\} \text{Fixity}
$$

$$\begin{aligned}(5.75)\\(5.76)\end{aligned}$$

$$
\left.
\begin{aligned}
x_1 &\ge k_1 Q_1 \\
x_2 &\ge k_2 Q_1 \\
x_{51} &\ge k_{51} Q_1 \\
x_{61} &\ge k_{61} Q_1
\end{aligned}
\right\} \begin{aligned}&\text{Single-process production function} \\ &\text{for product 1}\end{aligned}
$$

$$\begin{aligned}(5.77)\\(5.78)\\(5.79)\\(5.80)\end{aligned}$$

$$
\left.
\begin{aligned}
x_3 &\ge k_3 Q_2 \\
x_4 &\ge k_4 Q_2 \\
x_{52} &\ge k_{52} Q_2 \\
x_{62} &\ge k_{62} Q_2
\end{aligned}
\right\} \begin{aligned}&\text{Single-process production function} \\ &\text{for product 2}\end{aligned}
$$

$$\begin{aligned}(5.81)\\(5.82)\\(5.83)\\(5.84)\end{aligned}$$

As before, we designate the output to which a fixed input is assigned by the second subscript.

Let us assume that the firm will sell and buy at the market prices and will not waste any variable inputs. Thus, the following constraints can all be incorporated into the cash-flow function — inequations 5.69 through 5.74, 5.77, 5.78, 5.81, and 5.82. This gives us

$$Z = \bar{P}_1 Q_1 + \bar{P}_2 Q_2 - \bar{p}_1 k_1 Q_1 - \bar{p}_2 k_2 Q_1 - \bar{p}_3 k_3 Q_2 - \bar{p}_4 k_4 Q_2,$$

which, when we collect terms, becomes

$$Z = (\bar{P}_1 - \bar{p}_1 k_1 - \bar{p}_2 k_2) Q_1 + (\bar{P}_2 - \bar{p}_3 k_3 - \bar{p}_4 k_4) Q_2. \qquad (5.85)$$

Solving equation 5.85 for Q_1 gives us the isocash-flow lines for any value of Z:

$$Q_1 = \frac{Z}{(\bar{P}_1 - \bar{p}_1 k_1 - \bar{p}_2 k_2)} - \frac{(\bar{P}_2 - \bar{p}_3 k_3 - \bar{p}_4 k_4)}{(\bar{P}_1 - \bar{p}_1 k_1 - p_2 k_2)} Q_2 \qquad (5.86)$$

The terms in parentheses are still the cash flows attributable to a unit of either product 1 or product 2. Equation 5.86 would graph an isocash flow map as in Figure 5.23 if both cash flows are positive.

Six of the constraints have not been incorporated into the objective function. They can provide us with the Q_1, Q_2 opportunity set. These all deal with the limited inputs, x_5 and x_6. The procedure in forming this set is to determine how each of the fixed inputs limits the possible Q_1, Q_2 combinations. The Q_1, Q_2 combinations that are still possible, subject to *both* of the limited input constraints, then become the opportunity set.

First, let us consider the limitation on the outputs that arise because of the fixity constraint on x_5 (inequation 5.75), and the necessity to use x_5 in the production of both products – shown by inequations 5.79 and 5.83. The amount of input 5 assigned to the two products, x_{51} and x_{52}, cannot be greater than $\bar{x}_5$, so that we have

$$x_{51} + x_{52} \le \bar{x}_5. \qquad (5.87)$$

If no x_5 is wasted in either output, inequations 5.79 and 5.83 are equalities. We can therefore substitute from these constraints for x_{51} and x_{52} in inequation 5.87 to get

$$k_{51} Q_1 + k_{52} Q_2 \le \bar{x}_5. \qquad (5.88)$$

This gives us one limitation on the output combinations. Its boundary can be found by treating inequation 5.88 as an equality and solving for Q_1. Thus,

$$Q_1 = \frac{\bar{x}_5}{k_{51}} - \frac{k_{52}}{k_{51}} Q_2. \qquad (5.89)$$

Input 6 defines another constraint. Using the same procedure, we first have

$$x_{61} + x_{62} \le \bar{x}_6. \qquad (5.90)$$

Substituting from inequations 5.80 and 5.84 gives us

$$k_{61} Q_1 + k_{62} Q_2 \le \bar{x}_6. \qquad (5.91)$$

The boundary of this constraint is

$$Q_1 = \frac{\bar{x}_6}{k_{61}} - \frac{k_{62}}{k_{61}} Q_2. \qquad (5.92)$$

Equations 5.89 and 5.92 together determine the boundary of the opportunity set of Q_1, Q_2 combinations, which is often referred to as

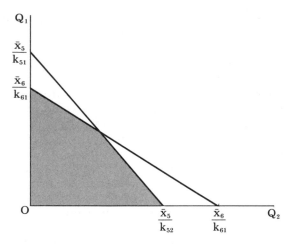

FIGURE 5.25 Q_1, Q_2 opportunity set: two fixity constraints

the feasible set. This set could appear as in Figure 5.25. Notice that
the intersection of the boundaries with each axis is determined by
the availability of the fixed inputs and the technological coefficients
that determine the quantity of the fixed input required per unit of the
output. These boundaries would be "pushed out" if there were more
of the fixed inputs or if fewer fixed inputs were required per unit of
output (the ks would become smaller). The non-axes boundary of the
opportunity set consists of two straight-line segments.

It is now a simple matter to superimpose the isocash-flow preference
map on the Q_1, Q_2 opportunity set to get the optimal output combination. In Figure 5.26, this optimal output combination is at the "corner"
point B, at which both outputs are produced. If the isocash-flow map

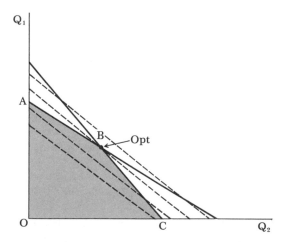

FIGURE 5.26   Linear programming optimization

were much steeper (reflecting high cash flow from product 2 relative to product 1), the optimal output would be at point C – that is, all Q_2. If the isocash-flow map had a very gentle slope (reflecting small cash flow from product 2 relative to product 1), the optimum would be at point A – that is, all Q_1. If the cash flows were negative from both products, the optimal output would be at zero – that is, neither output would be produced. (We shall show why this is so later in this section.)

It is important to see that in the case we have specified, one of the corner points O, A, B, and C of the feasible set will be the optimum solution *except* when the cash-flow lines are parallel either to the AB or to the BC segment. But in the latter exceptions, a corner solution is as good as a point on the segment. Thus, we can say that a corner point is *at least as good* as any other Q_1, Q_2 point in the opportunity set. This is an important mathematical proposition. It means in practice that we need only examine the corner points to find the optimum Q_1, Q_2 combination. This may not seem very important when we work with a simple problem that can be graphed. But when we have large numbers of outputs, the proposition that the solution must be at a corner provides the basis for the simplex method, which is designed to solve large problems of this type. However, one of these corner points is optimal only when the opportunity set is bound by straight-line segments and when the cash-flow map gives straight lines. These straight lines are the basis of linear programming. But when either the opportunity-set boundary or the cash-flow map consists of non-linear curves, a corner point may not be optimal and nonlinear programming methods must be used.

We urge the reader to experiment with this simple model. First, assume a set of values for the parameters and work through a solution. Then change some of the parameters and work through new solutions. By comparing the new solutions with the first, it is possible to ascertain the impact of changes in various parameters.

The General Solution. It may be helpful to generalize our procedure to handle any number of outputs and inputs. The first step is to form the cash-flow equation:

$$Z = \sum_{i=1}^{i=n} P_i Q_i - \sum_{h=1}^{h=m} p_h x_h,$$

where there are n products and m variable inputs. For x_h, it is often useful to add a second subscript designating the output to which a variable input is assigned. Thus, if x_3 is used in products 5 and 7, we would have two separate terms for this input, $p_3 x_{35}$ and $p_3 x_{37}$.

The next step is to list all the "freedom to deal" constraints that, for the model to be linear, must be the market prices, where price does not vary with the firm's output or input. Then all the fixity constraints should be listed. Finally, all the production functions should be listed, one for each output. A production function could consist of a large number of inputs, all in fixed proportions to output. They must all be single-process production functions.[10]

All the "freedom to deal" constraints and all those parts of the production functions that deal with variable inputs are incorporated into the cash-flow equation. When the terms are collected by output, this cash-flow function gives the cash flow for each output. Thus, if z_i is the cash flow for the ith output, the total cash flow equation is

$$Z = \sum_{i=1}^{i=n} z_i Q_i. \tag{5.93}$$

The constraints not incorporated into the objective function are the fixity constraints and the portions of the production functions concerning the limited inputs. Each fixity constraint becomes the basis of a constraint on the opportunity set of all the Qs. Let us say that the jth input is limited to $\bar{x}_j$ and is used only in products 1, 7, 8, and that the technical relations are $x_{j1} = k_{j1} Q_1$, $x_{j7} = k_{j7} Q_7$, $x_{j8} = k_{j8} Q_8$. (Obviously we have to learn how to keep the subscripts straight.) Then the constraint imposed by the jth limited input is

$$k_{j1} Q_1 + k_{j7} Q_7 + k_{j8} Q_8 \leq \bar{x}_j.$$

When this is done for each of the fixed inputs, we obtain all the constraints on the Qs, which together define the feasible set of all the possible Qs. If there are more than three Qs, the feasible set cannot be graphed.

Because computers do not know that outputs cannot be negative and are so extensively used in solving large linear programming problems, we must list the "non-negativity" constraints, so that the solution would not have negative values for any of the outputs. This is simply done by adding the constraints $Q_1 \geq 0$, $Q_2 \geq 0$, etc.

We would then take the objective function (equation 5.93) and these constraints to our favorite computer expert and tell him to find the values for the Qs that maximize Z subject to the constraints. Or, better still, we can learn the simplex technique and computer programming and find the solution ourselves.[11]

Linear Programming When Production Functions Have a Small Number of Processes. So far we have been working with only a single-process production function. However, the optimization model thus far developed can handle production functions that consist of a limited number of processes. To do this, we treat each process as if it were a separate product.

---

[10]In the next section we discuss an exception to the general rule that the production functions must be single-process types.

[11]For an elementary discussion of the simplex method, see William Baumol, *Economic Theory and Operations Analysis* (Englewood Cliffs, N.J.: Prentice-Hall, 1965).

To illustrate, let us assume that the firm produces two products, 1 and 2, but that product 1 can be produced by two different processes. Assume that x_1 is used in both processes as the variable input, with x_{11} the amount assigned to process 1 and x_{12} the amount assigned to process 2. Let x_3 be the only variable input used in product 2. Let x_2 be fixed at $\bar{x}_2$, and let x_2 be used in both processes producing product 1 and the single process producing product 2.

With all the prices incorporated, the Z function is

$$Z = \bar{P}_1 Q_{11} + \bar{P}_1 Q_{12} + \bar{P}_2 Q_2 - \bar{p}_1 x_{11} - \bar{p}_1 x_{12} - \bar{p}_3 x_3.$$

We have the following fixity constraint and production functions:

$$x_2 \leq \bar{x}_2 \qquad \text{Fixity} \tag{5.94}$$

$$\left. \begin{array}{l} x_{11} \geq k_{11} Q_{11} \\ x_{211} \geq k_{211} Q_{11}, \end{array} \right\} \text{Production of product 1 by process 1} \tag{5.95}$$

where the subscripts of the last x refer to the input designation, the product, and the process respectively. Similarly,

$$\left. \begin{array}{l} x_{12} \geq k_{12} Q_{12} \\ x_{212} \geq k_{212} Q_{12} \end{array} \right\} \text{Production of product 1 by process 2} \tag{5.96}$$

$$\left. \begin{array}{l} x_3 \geq k_3 Q_2 \\ x_{22} \geq k_{22} Q_2 \end{array} \right\} \text{Production function for product 2} \tag{5.97}$$

The parts of the production functions with variable inputs are incorporated into the Z function. Thus, we have

$$Z = \bar{P}_1 Q_{11} + \bar{P}_1 Q_{12} - \bar{p}_1 k_{11} Q_{11} - \bar{p}_1 k_{12} Q_{12} - \bar{p}_3 k_3 Q_2$$
$$Z = (\bar{P}_1 - \bar{p}_1 k_{11}) Q_{11} + (\bar{P}_1 - \bar{p}_1 k_{12}) Q_{12} + (\bar{P}_2 - \bar{p}_3 k_3) Q_2.$$

The terms in parentheses give the cash flow per unit from producing product 1 with process 1, the cash flow per unit from producing product 1 with process 2, the cash flow per unit of product 2.

The unincorporated constraints (inequation 5.94, and the fixed input portions of 5.95, 5.96, and 5.97) provide the basis for the opportunity set. The use of x_2 is constrained in this way:

$$x_{211} + x_{212} + x_{22} \leq \bar{x}_2.$$

Substituting for the left-hand xs from inequations 5.95, 5.96, and 5.97 gives us

$$k_{211} Q_{11} + k_{212} Q_{12} + k_{22} Q_2 \leq \bar{x}_2.$$

This last inequation defines the opportunity set of Q_{11}, Q_{12}, and Q_2. The solution technique is exactly as before, except that now we also determine how much Q_1 to produce with each of the alternative processes.

Negative Cash Flows. In all our examples, we have assumed that cash flows are positive for all products. Let us now investigate some

cases where one or more cash flows are negative. This can occur
whenever the value of the variable inputs used per unit of a particular product is greater than the output price of that product.

As our first case, let us say that the cash flow per unit of product 1
is \$4, and there is a negative cash flow of \$2 per unit of product 2.
Then the cash-flow equation is

$$Z = 4Q_1 - 2Q_2.$$

Solving for Q_1 gives us

$$Q_1 = \frac{Z}{4} + \frac{2}{4}Q_2.$$

Notice that the isocash-flow lines have positive slopes. If we assume
only positive values of Z, the cash-flow map appears as in Figure 5.27,
with preferability as shown by the arrow. It is evident that only Q_1
would be produced if we superimposed such an isocash-flow map on
a feasible set such as Figure 5.25.

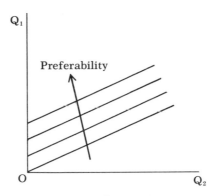

FIGURE 5.27   Cash-flow map when cash flow from Q_2 is negative

Consider next the case in which the cash flow from product 1 is
negative at \$2 per unit, while the cash flow from product 2 is a posi-
tive \$3 per unit. Then the cash-flow equation is

$$Z = -2Q_1 + 3Q_2,$$

which, when solved for Q_1, is

$$Q_1 = \frac{Z}{-2} + \frac{3}{2}Q_2.$$

Once more the isocash-flow lines have positive slopes. But now the
preferability is as shown in Figure 5.28, and for all positive values of
Z the cash-flow lines cannot intercept the Q_1 axis at positive values
for Q_1. Hence, it is obvious that only Q_2 will be produced.

As the final case, we consider negative cash flows from both prod-

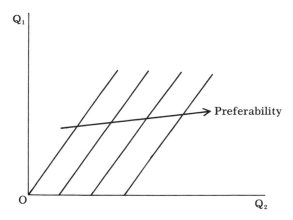

FIGURE 5.28   Cash-flow map when cash flow from Q_1 is negative

ucts. Let us assume the negative cash flows are \$2 for each of the products, so that the objective function is

$$Z = -2Q_1 - 2Q_2,$$

which, when solved for Q_1, is

$$Q_1 = \frac{Z}{-2} - Q_2. \tag{5.98}$$

The cash-flow line can be seen from equation 5.98 to have the "normal" negative slope. But for any positive value of Z, the cash-flow lines would not be in the positive Q_1, Q_2 quadrant and would appear as in Figure 5.29, with preferability shown by the arrow. If

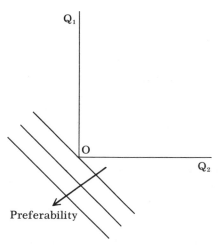

FIGURE 5.29   Cash-flow map when cash flow from both products are negative

possible, we would wish to produce negative amounts of both outputs. But of course this is not possible. The only point from the opportunity set that lies on an isocash-flow line is $Q_1 = 0_1$, $Q_2 = 0$. Thus, there should be no output when both cash flows are negative.

VARIATIONS ON THE BASIC MODELS

Our assumptions about the constraints in this chapter were made for tractability—that is, so that we could develop optimization models capable of solution with important elementary techniques. Thus, we assumed that the firm had no influence over either its selling or its buying prices and that it bought and sold at single prices. Except for one example, we also assumed an absence of legally imposed or self-imposed constraints. In this section we move toward greater realism and greater flexibility in our models by relaxing some of these assumptions.

Sloping Demand Curves for Outputs. Instead of assuming the price of the firm's product is some constant, $\bar{P}$, which is determined by the market, let us assume that buyers in the aggregate will take more at a lower price and less at a higher price. Symbolically, this "freedom of others" constraint becomes either $Q \le f(P)$ or $P \le f(Q)$, where the latter is more convenient for optimization purposes. We expect these relations to be inverse.

One consequence of assuming such a demand curve is that the total revenue curve will be nonlinear. If, for example, the demand curve is a downward-sloping straight line,

$$P = a - bQ, \tag{5.99}$$

the total revenue curve will be

$$TR = PQ = (a - bQ)Q = aQ - bQ^2. \tag{5.100}$$

This equation graphs as a parabola that increases at a decreasing rate.

The first derivative of the TR function is the marginal revenue curve; that is, it indicates the change in total revenue with a change in output. With equation 5.100 the TR function, MR is

$$MR = \frac{d(TR)}{dQ} = \frac{d(aQ - bQ^2)}{dQ} = a - 2bQ.$$

Notice that the slope of this MR curve is twice the slope of the demand curve of equation 5.99. The average revenue curve is

$$AR = \frac{TR}{Q} = \frac{aQ - bQ^2}{Q} = a - bQ,$$

which can be seen to be the same as the demand curve. Figure 5.30 shows the general shapes of these various revenue functions.

Let us demonstrate the effect of the sloping demand curve on the optimal output for a one-product firm. We use a single-process produc-

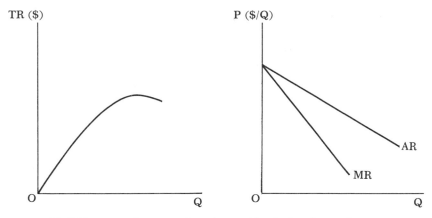

FIGURE 5.30 Revenue functions with sloping demand curve

tion function and optimization obtained by comparing total revenue with total cost. Figure 5.31 shows the total revenue and total cost curves. Notice that the optimum output is now at Q_a rather than at Q_{max}. Why should this be so? Because the firm, by increasing its output, reduces the price it receives on *all* its output; thus, it is very likely that optimal output would be smaller than it would be if its output did not affect the price.[12]

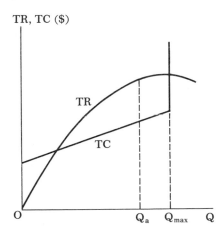

FIGURE 5.31 Optimization, sloping demand curve: single-process production function

Figure 5.32 shows the solution by comparing marginal revenue with marginal cost. Again the optimal output is Q_a, which is where *MR* is equal to *MC*. By finding the price, here P_a, that corresponds on the demand curve to Q_a, we also determine the optimal price.

[12]The optimal output is likely to be smaller only when we assume that the firm can charge only a single price for its output. But there may not be a reduction of output if the firm could charge *different* prices for its output.

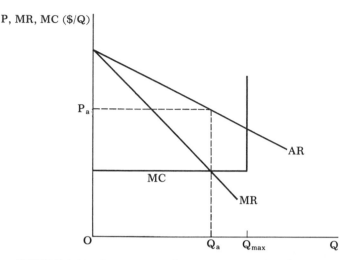

FIGURE 5.32   Optimization by comparing *MC* with *MR*

Let us next show the solution by comparing the *MR* and *MC* curves for the classical (indivisibilities) case. Figure 5.33 displays all the marginal and average revenue and cost curves. It can be seen that *MR* is equal to *MC* at Q_a; hence, Q_a is the optimal output and P_a is the optimal price.

We turn now to the effect of a sloping demand curve on the multi-product solutions. The prices of the outputs in our earlier illustrations were fixed amounts that entered into the objective function to determine the cash-flow lines. When the demand curve for a particular product slopes, however, the procedure is to substitute the demand curve in terms of Q for the corresponding price.

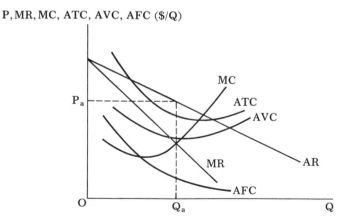

FIGURE 5.33   Optimization by comparing *MC* with *MR*: classical with sloping demand curve

Consider equation 5.65 (reproduced as equation 5.101), which, with all the constraints incorporated into the objective function, is

$$Z = 10Q_1 + 8Q_2 - 3(2Q_1) - 2(3Q_2). \tag{5.101}$$

Let us say now that the price, P_1, which, instead of being \$10, is a function of output,

$$P_1 = 20 - 0.2Q_1.$$

Then instead of the \$10 for P_1 we would use $(20 - 0.2Q_1)$. Equation 5.101 thus becomes

$$Z = (20 - 0.2Q_1)Q_1 + 8Q_2 - 3(2Q_1) - 2(3Q_2).$$

When we collect terms, this is

$$Z = 14Q_1 - 0.2Q_1^2 + 2Q_2.$$

The cash-flow objective function now has a squared term and is therefore no longer linear. The isocash-flow map would then appear as in Figure 5.34. When superimposed upon the Q_1, Q_2 opportunity set (see Figure 5.24), the optimal solution is now some combination of Q_1 and Q_2 rather than all of one or the other. When the isocash-flow map has this type of curvature, the corners of the opportunity set are no longer necessarily as good as any other point. Hence, nonlinear programming is much more difficult than linear programming.

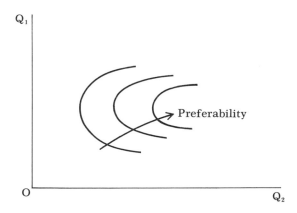

FIGURE 5.34   Nonlinear isocash-flow map

Sloping Supply Curves for Inputs. Let us now consider the consequences of assuming that the price of a variable input varies with the quantity purchased. In the real world increasing the quantity purchased sometimes yields lower prices when sellers give "discounts" for larger volumes. At other times a firm may be so large relative to the market in which it buys an input that its purchases push the price upward. If we assume the latter to be the case for x_1, then $p_1 = f(x_1)$, with $dp_1/dx_1 > 0$ — that is, an increase in the quantity of the input purchased and used raises its price. For illustrative purposes, let us assume this relation to be $p_1 = a + bx_1$.

In all the work that we have done thus far in this and the preceding chapter, the implications of having such a sloping supply curve — negative as well as positive — can be worked out by using $a + bx_1$ whenever there was a $\bar{p}_1$. This substitution will affect some expansion paths, all cost functions, all cash-flow and profit functions, and, usually, the optimum solutions. Not affected will be revenue functions, technological relationships, and the opportunity sets of our multi-product decision models. We cannot go through all the ways our models will be influenced but instead offer a few illustrations.

Let us consider the effect of a sloping supply curve on the short-run cost curve for a single-process production function. The input cost function is

$$C = p_1 x_1 + p_2 x_2.$$

Let us say that we have the following constraints:

$$\begin{array}{lll}
p_1 = 2 + 0.1x_1 & \text{Sloping supply curve} & (5.102) \\
p_2 = 3 & \text{Market-determined supply curve} & (5.103) \\
x_2 = 60 & \text{Fixity} & (5.104) \\
\left.\begin{array}{l} x_1 = 2Q \\ x_2 = 3Q \end{array}\right\} & \text{Production function} & \begin{array}{l}(5.105)\\(5.106)\end{array}
\end{array}$$

Because x_2 is limited at 60, from equation 5.106 we see that maximum output is 20 units. Let us first incorporate the constraints expressed in equations 5.102, 5.103, and 5.104 in the input cost function:

$$C = (2 + 0.1x_1)x_1 + 3(60)$$
$$C = 2x_1 + 0.1x_1^2 + 180.$$

Now we convert this function into an output cost function by incorporating equation 5.105 in the function. Thus,

$$C = 2(2Q) + 0.1(2Q)^2 + 180$$
$$C = 4Q + 0.4Q^2 + 180, \quad Q \le 20.$$

It is evident from this cost function that it is no longer a straight line up to the maximum output but instead increases at an increasing rate. The contrasts are shown in Figure 5.35.

Let us now investigate the effect of a sloping supply curve for x_1 on the two-product optimization model. The cash-flow function (equation 5.65) is shown as

$$Z = 10Q_1 + 8Q_2 - p_1 x_1 - 2(3Q_2),$$

where we leave p_1 and x_1 in their initial formulation. Say now that

$$p_1 = 2 + 0.1x_1.$$

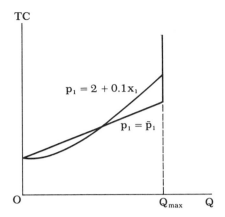

FIGURE 5.35   Effect of sloping supply curve on TC function: single-process production function

The cash-flow equation becomes

$$Z = 10Q_1 + 8Q_2 - (2 + 0.1x_1)x_1 - 6Q_2$$
$$Z = 10Q_1 + 8Q_2 - 2x_1 - 0.1x_1^2 - 6Q_2.$$

Recall that in inequation 5.61 the variable input x_1 was related in the production function to Q_1 as $x_1 \geq 2Q_1$. Then, the cash-flow equation becomes

$$Z = 10Q_1 + 8Q_2 - 2(2Q_1) - 0.1(2Q_1)^2 - 6Q_2$$

$$Z = 6Q_1 - 0.2_1Q_1^2 - 2Q_2.$$

It is clear from this equation that the cash-flow map will now consist of curves rather than straight lines. Once again, the optimal solution need no longer be at a corner, and we have a nonlinear programming problem.

Government-imposed Constraints: Price and Wage Controls. Business firms operate within a social system in which public policy constrains their freedom to do as they wish. Indeed, whether "what is good for the firm is good for the country and vice versa" depends on whether appropriate constraints are imposed on the firm to make its optimization consistent with a politically determined public interest. Some public policy constraints are implicit in the formulation of the models of the firms we have presented. For example, the treatment of the firm as an independent maximizing entity reflects a policy against agreements in restraint of trade. The assumptions that buyers are free not to buy and that inputs must be paid for reflect a limitation on the power of the firm to coerce others. Sometimes the constraints are more explicit, such as the imposition of a price ceiling, a minimum wage rate, and the minimum use of some material input for a product. We consider here how a price ceiling and a minimum wage influence the optimal decisions of our model firm.

If the firm's demand curve is a market price, without any slope, a price ceiling is easy to handle. If the price ceiling is above the market price, the price ceiling would not affect the P,Q opportunity set (it would not be an "effective" constraint), and the firm's decisions would not be affected. If the price ceiling is set below the market price, the price ceiling, as viewed by the firm, becomes the same as the market price. The effect of this price ceiling on output (and by extension on the use of the inputs) can be ascertained by finding the optimal values for Q at the market price and ceiling price. If the production function is composed of a large number of processes, such as the Cobb-Douglas or classical, the lower ceiling price will tend to lead to a reduction in output. But if the production function consists of only one or a small number of processes, the price ceiling, if not too low, may have no effect upon output. Figure 5.36 shows the effect of the price ceiling when the production function is classical, and Figure 5.37 shows the effect when the production function consists of a single process. In these graphs, P_m is the free market price, and P_c is the ceiling price.

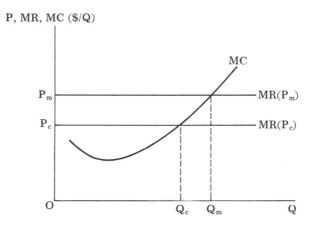

FIGURE 5.36   Effect of price ceiling on output: classical production function

When the demand curve slopes, it is possible, perhaps even likely, that a price ceiling will lead to increased output. We have found the optimal Q for the Cobb-Douglas production function by using the programming method, where we did not incorporate the demand curve constraint in the objective function. (See Figure 5.18.) When we used the output cost function for the expenditure terms and neglected the fixed costs, the cash-flow objective function was

$$Z = PQ - C(Q), \qquad (5.107)$$

P, MR, MC ($/Q)

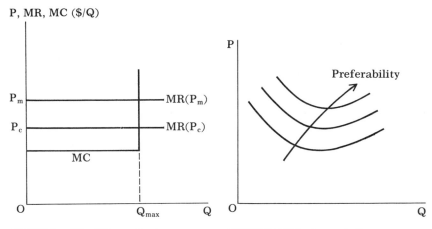

FIGURE 5.37   Effect of price
ceiling on output: single-process
production function

FIGURE 5.38   Isocash-flow map
in terms of P and Q

where $C(Q)$ is the total variable cost function. A cash-flow function
such as equation 5.107 would generate an isocash-flow map as shown
in Figure 5.38.

Let us say that the demand curve slopes and that the government
imposes a price ceiling at P_c. If there were no price ceiling, the demand curve would be the boundary of the P,Q opportunity set. With
the ceiling, both constraints would determine the P,Q opportunity
set, as in Figure 5.39.

We can now superimpose the isocash-flow map on the P,Q opportunity set to determine the quantity without the price ceiling and the
quantity with the price ceiling. This is done in Figure 5.40. As the

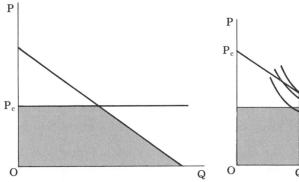

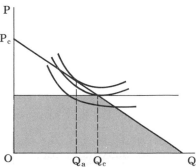

FIGURE 5.39 P,Q opportunity set
as determined by demand curve
and price ceiling

FIGURE 5.40   Optimum value of
Q with and without price ceiling

diagram shows, the firm's profit-maximizing output is Q_a without the price ceiling and Q_c, a higher value, with the price ceiling.[13]

Let us now consider the effect on output of a minimum wage rate on input x_1, which we take to be labor. If this minimum is below the market price for labor, it is clearly an ineffective constraint, and nothing will be affected. If, however, the minimum wage is above the market price, clearly the marginal, average variable, and average total cost curves will be higher at all levels of output. Whether there will be some effect of the higher wage on output (and employment) depends mostly on whether the production curve is classical or Cobb-Douglas or whether it is single process.

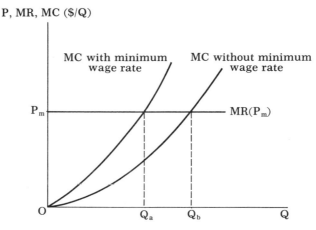

FIGURE 5.41   Effect of minimum wage rate on output: Cobb-Douglas production function

Figure 5.41 shows the Cobb-Douglas *MC* curves with and without an effective minimum wage rate. At the lower wage rate, the optimal output is Q_b, and at the higher wage rate it is Q_a.[14] Figure 5.42 shows the same curves for the single-process production function. As the diagram shows, the higher *MC* resulting from the minimum wage rate has no effect on output. However, if the wage rate were raised to the point where *MC* is greater than *MR*, there would be no output. The effect of the minimum wage rate on unemployment in both cases can be much greater in the long run, when the firm has time to alter its stock of fixed assets.

Selling in Different Markets at Different Prices. Sometimes the market for a given product or service can be segmented by geographic

---

[13]This analysis shows that there is a good case for government price ceilings when the firm's demand curve slopes – that is, if it has some monopoly power.

[14]We can see in this analysis a case against a minimum wage rate on the grounds that it reduces employment. Minimum wage rates, however, may redistribute income in a favorable direction.

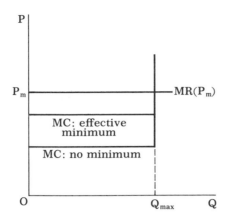

FIGURE 5.42   Effect of minimum wage rate on output: single-process production function

area, type of customer, income level. The firm would then face two different demand curves – one for each segment. In this section we consider the case in which the firm can sell in two market segments and develop a model for optimal decision-making.

When the demand curve for each segment is completely horizontal, so that the firm can sell as much as it wants in each segment without affecting the price in either, the problem is trivial. The firm simply sells only in the market segment with the higher price, assuming the cost of serving each segment is the same. The interesting question arises when the firm faces sloping, but independent, demand curves. Suppose that $P_1 = a_1 - b_1 Q_1$ in market segment 1 and $P_2 = a_2 - b_2 Q_2$ in market segment 2.

The optimization problem is to find how much to produce and how to allocate that output between the two markets. Because we are assuming that costs are the same no matter which market the output is sold in, profit will be maximized by allocating output to make marginal revenue for each market the same as it is for the other. Otherwise, without affecting costs we could raise revenue and profit by shifting a unit of output to the market segment with the highest marginal revenue. Such a shift would lower marginal revenue in the segment in which it is higher and raise marginal revenue in the other segment.

An allocation of any given output between the two market segments so that $MR_1 = MR_2$ would give the highest possible profit for that output level. But we must then ask whether the total output level is optimal. The answer can be found by combining the two MR curves and finding that level of total output at which the combined MR is equal to the marginal cost (MC) curve.

This can be done graphically. Figure 5.43 consists of three panels. Panels 1 and 2 show the two demand curves and their corresponding

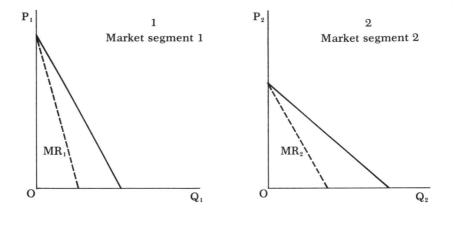

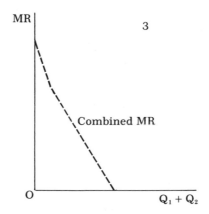

FIGURE 5.43   Market segment demand curves and combined marginal
revenue curve

marginal revenue curves. Panel 3 combines the two marginal revenue
curves by adding them horizontally and shows the total marginal
revenue for each level of output allocated between the market segments such that $MR_1 = MR_2$.

Figure 5.44 is identical to Figure 5.43, except that in panel 3 the
marginal cost curve is superimposed on the combined marginal
revenue curve. The intersection of the two curves gives the optimal
output, $\hat{Q}$, and the optimal value of the combined marginal revenue,
$\hat{MR}$. Panels 1 and 2 show the values of $\hat{Q}_1$ and $\hat{Q}_2$ that correspond to
the optimal $\hat{MR}_1 = \hat{MR}_2$. The demand curve in each market segment
shows the prices, $\hat{P}_1$ and $\hat{P}_2$, that can be charged for the optimal
quantities.

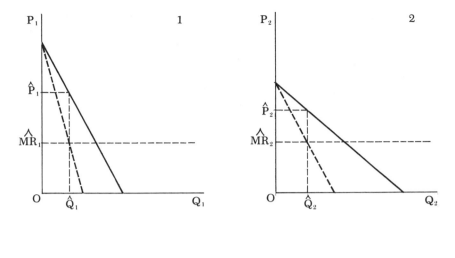

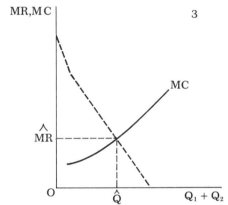

FIGURE 5.44   Optimal outputs and prices in market segments

Discussion Questions

1. Explain why, when the firm's demand curve slopes, the marginal revenue per unit of output declines more rapidly than the price as output is expanded. What is the marginal revenue when the price is not affected by the firm's output? In general, if we assume identical cost curves, which firm would produce at a higher rate, one with a horizontal demand curve or one with a sloping demand curve?

2. What are the advantages of using cash flow rather than profit as the criterion variable in optimization procedures?

3. What are some of the advantages of not incorporating some of the constraints into the objective function in the optimization procedure?

4. If we assume a horizontal demand curve, would a firm with a high proportion of fixed to variable costs produce more, or less, than a firm with a lower proportion of fixed to variable costs? Might this be relevant to differences in price and output observed in different industries in recessions?

5. What is the relation between the number of production processes in a production function and the responsiveness of a profit-maximizing firm's output to changes in the market prices?

6. A candy-bar manufacturer produces two products: an almond bar and a coconut bar. The almond bar sells for $4 per hundred, and the coconut bar sells for $5 per hundred. It is estimated that all materials and labor cost $2 per hundred for the almond bar and $2.50 per hundred for the coconut bar. The manufacturing processes for both products require the use of mixing, cooking, and packaging equipment, each of which can provide 24 hours of its services per day. A hundred almond bars require 1/2 hour of mixing equipment, 1/3 hour of cooking equipment, and 3/8 hour of packaging equipment. A hundred coconut bars require 1/3 hour of mixing equipment, 1/2 hour of cooking equipment, and 3/8 hour of packaging equipment. Using linear programming, determine the optimal output mix of the two products if the plant is run on a 24-hour basis. How might this optimal output mix change if the variable costs per 100 coconut bars rise from $2.50 per hundred to $4 per hundred?

7. What is linear about linear programming? What must be the nature of the production functions, the demand functions, and the supply curves of variable inputs if this popular technique is to be used?

6 Long-Run Decision Models: The Firm as Owner

The role of the firm as owner of assets, rather than its role as producer, is our focus of attention in this chapter. In Chapter 2, we considered briefly the role of the firm as owner, stressing changes in fixed assets. In the light of the concepts developed in Chapters 3, 4, and 5, we are now able to consider a broad range of questions having to do with the worthwhileness to the firm of efforts and expenditures directed toward changing the constraints under which it operates as producer in future short-run planning periods. The ability and value to the firm of changing these constraints provide the link between the short run and long run.

We assumed that the constraints in the short-run models were not subject to change by the firm. A change in the constraints that enlarges the opportunity set, however, might permit the selection of a superior set of values for the decision variables. New alternatives might yield higher profit or cash flow, or a beneficial change in any short-run criterion variable. The question arises whether the firm must accept short-run constraints as "given," or whether it can do something to change them. The answer to this question is partly yes and partly no. Some constraints are completely determined by events and the actions of others over which the firm has no control. The parameters of other constraints, however, may be amenable to actions consciously taken by the firm. Often the parameters are subject to the influence of both "outside" events and the firm's conscious actions. If subject to the firm's influence, in effect the short-run constraint parameters can be thought to be variables to be changed by long-run decisions.

In this chapter we formulate and evaluate the actions that the firm can take to influence its constraint parameters. Such actions will influence short-run choices in future time periods and the obtainable values of criterion variables such as profit and cash flow. Choice among alternative possible changes in constraints requires a comparison of consequences at several points in time. Long-run decision models, therefore, must be formulated to take time explicitly into account. Both the costs and the benefits to the firm of constraint-changing actions must be considered and compared as dollar magnitudes expended, foregone, or received during specified periods of time.

Ideally, long-run decision models would be formulated, like short-run models, with explicit and precise assumptions about the firm's objective, the constraints on its ability to choose that cannot be changed even in the long run, the short-run constraint parameters that can be treated as decision variables when time for change is allowed, and the optimization technique that relates the decision variables to the long-run objective. Unfortunately, economic theory is not sufficiently developed to allow such a high degree of neatness and elegance in long-run models if they are to be realistic enough to be useful. Instead of such well-defined optimization models, we work with models designed to show the conditions under which a constraint change is a move in the right direction.

THE MEANINGS OF LONG RUN AND INVESTMENT

The concept of investment is a part of the vocabulary of almost any "man in the street." We need, however, to give this commonly used term more specific content before considering the investment behavior of business firms. First, we present examples of changes in the types of constraints assumed in the short-run models of Chapters 4 and 5 and the effects of such changes on the opportunity sets of the short-run models. Then we define investment in terms of the long-run consequences of such changes in short-run models.

Constraint Changes and Short-Run Choices. A firm may take many different kinds of action to influence constraint parameters and the opportunity set. Consider the demand curve. In a large number of instances the firm can do nothing to change the demand curve for its output, for this constraint results from the freedom of others to refuse to deal. In some cases, however, a firm can favorably influence its demand curve by promotional efforts or changes in the quality of its product. Advertising, changing the product by styling, selecting different marketing channels, or perhaps broadening the product line, if successful, may "shift" the demand curve to the right, thus enabling the firm to sell a larger quantity at each possible price – or, alternatively, to obtain a higher price for each possible output level. Such a shift, in effect, enables an increase in the set of possible P, Q

combinations available to the firm in the short run, as shown in panel 1 of Figure 6.1. Quality changes, including reductions in durability, or planned obsolescence, may also pivot the demand curve, as in panel 2 of Figure 6.1. Such a rotation would add some P, Q combinations and eliminate others.

The other "freedom to deal" constraint is the supply curve of inputs to the firm, which limits the p, x combinations from which the firm may choose in the short run. Although economists have given much more attention to the power of the firm to change the demand curve, many firms can and do change the supply curve as well. Developing alternative sources of supply may be one way a firm can influence a particular supply curve. Political support for or against various governmental programs – such as education, agricultural price supports, and depleting stockpiles – can influence the supply curve. These activities generally increase the p, x combinations available in the short run by lowering the price at which various quantities of the input can be purchased. Vertical backward integration can change the inputs acquired from others by including production of inputs in the firm's activities.

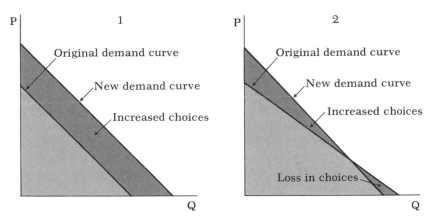

FIGURE 6.1   Impact of activity to change demand curve on available *P,Q* combinations

We have labeled as "technology" the relations between inputs and output that we sum up in the production function. Viewed purely as a short-run constraint, the production function limits the input combinations from among which the firm can choose for any given level of output. Technology, however, is not constant. Often the firm, through experience, research, or by the acquisition of patents, can find ways of improving production methods. Sometimes the new production methods use different inputs; at other times the same inputs are used, but they are employed more efficiently. When an improvement of the latter type is made, additional combinations of the same inputs become possible in the short run for any particular level of output. These additions can be depicted as a shift in an isoquant. Figure 6.2 graphically portrays what the firm's input choices might be for some given level of output before and after the improvement of technology.

If a technological improvement enables the firm to consider new inputs rather than only a better use of the same inputs, then the short-run "live options" with regard to inputs are expanded. Although the increase in these options can be considered under the constraint category "technology," we will think of them as new knowledge — thus assigning them to the constraint category that we have called knowledge or, more nearly accurately, lack of knowledge.

Perhaps the most obvious type of constraint that can be changed is "fixity" — the limitation on the availability of an input. This limitation can be altered when the firm acquires more of the agent that provides the input service — generally, building new plant or purchasing additional machinery — or sometimes by renegotiating a contract that had imposed an upper limit on the availability to the firm of a particular input. Figure 6.3 provides an example of how more of the fixed input — here x_2 — could change the input choices. Obviously, the increase in the availability of x_2 could change the expansion path and the short-run cost curve.

Sometimes the divisibility constraint can be changed. A change in technology might enable the firm to use less than the full quantity of its fixed plant. A change in contractual arrangements, such as time-sharing of a large computer facility, might also eliminate indivisibility of an input. We have seen in Chapter 4 how such a change in divisibility can lead to changes in expansion paths and cost curves.

The legally imposed constraints are generally fairly difficult to

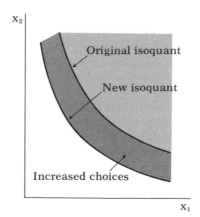

FIGURE 6.2   Isoquant shift
from improvement in technology

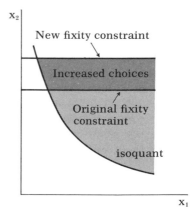

FIGURE 6.3   Effect of more
"fixed" input on short-run choice

change. A large firm, however, or a trade association can affect the formulation of public policy by legislative, judicial, and executive branches of state, federal, and foreign governments. Legal constraints are changed by lobbying, litigation, public relations efforts, and political activity. Figure 6.4 provides an illustration of how a change in a regulation that at least some minimum quantity of, say, x_2 be employed in the production process can increase the firm's short-run options.

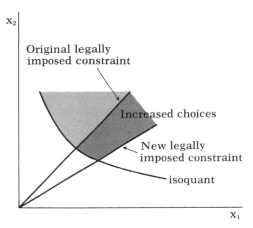

FIGURE 6.4   Effect of change in legally imposed constraint on input choices

In Chapter 3, we introduced the notion of self-imposed constraints and showed how they could limit the firm's short-run choices for the decision variables. Some of these constraints result from the firm's efforts to reconcile conflicting objectives—most importantly short-run and long-run profits. Others arise because of attempts to maintain the "organizational viability" of the firm, and still others arise when one part of the firm imposes constraints (budgets or fixed targets) on another part or parts. Any of these constraints can be changed, for example, by giving greater weight to one goal or another, by altering conceptions of viability, or by changing budgets. When the firm changes a self-imposed constraint, it might want either to increase or to decrease the short-run opportunity set. Figure 6.5 provides an example of an increase in this set: The firm increases the maximum price it is willing to consider charging, which then expands the P, Q opportunity set.

We may ask why the firm will not *always* want to change its self-imposed constraints to increase the opportunity set, for such changes will generally make it possible to increase short-run profits. The answer is that such changes may hamper the attainment of other goals or change other constraints in later periods. Raising the "limit" price, as in our example, may lead to higher short-run profits but, by

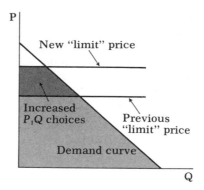

FIGURE 6.5   Increase in P,Q opportunity set with change in self-imposed "limit" price

making the market more attractive to potential entrants and by creating some ill will, the higher limit price could lead to lower profits in the longer run.

The knowledge constraint is a little ambiguous. In our view, the lack of knowledge plays a part in every constraint. Thus, the demand curve may limit the P,Q options because the firm may not be quite sure what to do to change it. Or the firm may impose a constraint upon itself, as in the foregoing example of a limit price, because it is uncertain of future developments. We, however, use the knowledge constraint in a more restricted sense of limiting the set of inputs and outputs that the firm could consider in the short run. The firm is typically limited in this sense, not because it does not know that it is possible to use a certain input or produce a certain product, but because it does not have detailed knowledge of the technology and markets for these inputs and outputs.

The firm, of course, can often obtain such knowledge. When it does, then it can actively consider the use of additional inputs and the production of additional products. This knowledge will not change the opportunity set as did the other constraint changes by adding new possible combinations to the existing decision variables. Instead, the opportunity set is increased by adding new decision variables. If, for example, it is learned how to use x_3 in the production process, where before the firm only used x_1 and x_2, the technological constraint for some given amount of output is expanded to include all possible x_1, x_2, x_3 combinations rather than just the x_1, x_2 combinations.

The "compound" constraints, discussed in Chapter 3, can be changed with a change in one or more of the simple constraints. Contracts to buy or sell can obviously be altered and will as obviously affect the available choices in the short run. Changes in technology or the acquisition of more of the "fixed" inputs will have an influence upon the production possibility frontier.

From these examples, it should be clear that the results of changes in the constraints will usually be an increased number of alternative possible values for the short-run decision variables. In fact, we can say that the efforts and expenditures involved in "expanding" a constraint results in a "purchase" of additional short-run choices. Generally, the increases in alternatives are desirable by themselves because they can be expected to enable more profitable short-run choices. There are times, however, when the firm may consciously change its constraints in a way that decreases the short-run opportunity set. One example of such a change is the sale of some of the firm's fixed assets. Another example is the discontinuation or reduction of an advertising program. The self-imposed constraints are particularly interesting from this viewpoint. A firm, by entering into an agreement about prices with its rivals (which may be illegal), may purposefully eliminate part of its P,Q set—the part having low prices. Sometimes action is taken to keep a constraint from changing in a way that decreases the opportunity set—as by replacing a machine that has worn out.

It is informative to contrast these possible methods of changing the constraints with the possible changes usually treated in neoclassical economics. The type of constraint changes emphasized in traditional economics have dealt with the short-run fixities of a particular input. All other constraint changes are assumed to be caused by "outside" forces or by the firm adopting something, such as new technology, that was developed outside the model firm. The ability to change its constraints can be thought of as a measure of a firm's economic and, sometimes, political power. The notion of the firm presented here is one with a great deal more power than the firm in neoclassical theory. Firms will vary greatly, however, in their power to change all the constraints; generally, though, the larger the firm, the more control it will have over its constraints.

The Long Run and Investment. In the short-run decision models of Chapter 5, the firm made choices among alternative values of controllable decision variables subject to constraints assumed to be fixed for the planning period for which each choice would be effective. We here define as long-run decisions all choices among alternative sets of constraint parameters. The analyst, however, must not be too mechanical in the way he handles these concepts. The short-run decision model might be reformulated to include as decision variables some of the parameters we are treating here as subject only to long-run decision. Advertising, for example, is often treated as a short-run decision variable: We have chosen to view it as a means of changing a short-run parameter.[1] Whether a decision can most usefully be treated in a short-run model or in the long-run context depends primarily on

[1]Economists and others have been split over how to treat advertising. We have chosen to consider it an investment, mainly on the grounds that it can influence a firm's earnings over a number of short-run periods.

the time element. A decision that affects cash flow over more than one short-run planning period and cannot be costlessly reversed needs to be treated as a long-run decision so that comparisons can be made with the alternative uses the firm can make of its money.

A long-run decision may or may not take a long time to implement. Activities designed to change constraints in subsequent short-run periods may or may not require large sums of money. But in all cases a long-run — that is, constraint-changing — decision requires evaluation of costs and benefits in more than one short-run planning period and comparison of values in one time period with those in another. In the classic case of investment in new plant in order to expand an input fixity constraint, the firm must compare the present and future costs of acquiring the plant with the additional cash flow from its activity as producer in future short-run periods. But, more broadly any expenditure or effort, or even foregone revenues in the present, that leads to higher future cash flows can be viewed as an investment.

An asset addition can be defined as something that will give rise to higher cash flows, or profits, in the future. A change in the constraints, therefore, can be classified as an asset addition if, as is usually the case, the change in the short-run opportunity set enables higher profits or cash flow than would otherwise have been the case. But the action to change the opportunity set may not always result in a *marketable* asset.

The concepts of assets and investments may not seem readily to apply to our self-imposed category of constraints. But consider a self-imposed constraint that limits short-run profits but which, by influencing future behavior of rivals, potential and actual, leads to higher future profits than would be the case in the absence of this constraint. This involves a sacrifice of profit in some periods in exchange for increased profit in other periods. Thus a change in this constraint should be considered both an asset addition and an investment. Other things being equal, it would show up as such in greater market value of the firm's common stock.

The long-run decision models that we will develop in the remainder of this chapter are concerned with two problems. The first is the formulation of alternative investment programs or constraint changes. The second is the evaluation of alternative investment programs and, as a result, the solution of the optimization problem of choosing among them. Unlike the short-run case, in which the constraints place well-defined limits on the choices of the short-run decision variables, it is generally impossible to formulate all the possible investment alternatives. There can literally be an infinite number of ways that the constraint parameters could be changed. All that we can generally hope to do, therefore, is to formulate the investment programs that appear to promise the highest payoffs and then evaluate them to select the best.

THE FORMULATION OF INVESTMENT PROGRAMS

In our simple examples, changes in the constraint parameters all led to changes (generally increases) in the opportunity set. If, however, there are a number of constraints, it is possible that a change in one of them will not actually change the opportunity set because the *other* constraints will effectively limit the choices for the short-run decision variables. Furthermore, even if a change in a constraint changes the opportunity set, it may work out that it does not enable a higher level of short-run profits or cash flow. Again this can come about because of other constraints. We need, therefore, to consider the circumstances under which a particular constraint is or is not "binding" on the solution to the short-run optimization problem—that is, whether a change in that constraint enables a higher, or leads to a lower, cash flow. Having done so, we can then ask how the benefits from a constraint change can be determined. After illustrating those conceptual problems with a specific short-run model, we can develop some generalizations about the formulation of investment programs.

Binding and Nonbinding Constraints. For our purposes, we can divide the short-run constraints into two categories, binding and nonbinding. The binding constraints are those whose "expansion" would both increase the opportunity set and enable a better selection of values for the short-run decision variables. Conversely, if binding constraints are shifted back—that is, if the opportunity set is contracted—there will be a poorer selection of values for the decision variables. Better and poorer are measured by the effect of the selections on profit, cash flow, or some other short-run criterion variable, depending on the objective of the firm. Other terms in use to designate binding constraints are "bottlenecks" and "critical constraints." Nonbinding constraints, on the other hand, are those for which either an expansion or a small contraction will not affect the optimal selection of values for the short-run decision variables and, hence, the short-run criterion variable. Obviously, when a firm is considering actions to change the parameters of the constraints, it would be helpful to identify the binding and nonbinding constraints in order to know whether long-run planning should aim for expansion or contraction. As we shall see, however, this identification is not a cut-and-dried matter, for the classification of a constraint into binding or nonbinding will change with changes in other constraints.

To see some of the problems, let us consider a simple example. The production department of a firm uses two machines, M_1 and M_2, in the production of a single product. Each unit of output requires an hour of M_1 and an hour of M_2. Let us say that the firm now has 20 hours of M_1 available per day and 30 hours of M_2 available per day and that the objective is to maximize output. The maximum amount of output that could be produced per day is obviously 20 units. Clearly M_1 is the binding constraint, because an expansion or contraction of M_1 will lead to a change in the possible output level. The limitation of M_2, on the other hand, is as obviously a nonbinding constraint. If the firm were to acquire more M_2, the maximum output level would remain at 20. A firm with such short-run constraints should consider only whether to expand M_1 capacity or contract M_2 capacity.

Let us now say that the firm decides to acquire a second machine yielding 20 more hours of M_1, so that 40 hours of M_1 are available per day. Now it is clear that M_2 is the binding constraint and that M_1 is nonbinding. Whether the two capacities should be brought into balance depends on the cost of change and the effect of such changes on the future stream of cash flow. But such analysis must start with identification of binding and nonbinding constraints. An alternative to fixity changes might be changes in production methods such that only 1/2 hour of M_1 is required per unit of output. Once again the effect would be to make the limited availability of M_2 the binding constraint and M_1 the nonbinding constraint. From this example we should see that the relative scarcity of the machines governs the classification of the constraints into binding or nonbinding.

Consider next a firm whose P,Q opportunity set is subject to two constraints – a demand curve and a legally imposed price ceiling. Let us say that the price ceiling is $75 and that the profit-maximizing price, lying on the demand curve, is $50. If the demand curve is such that the firm does not want to charge more than $50, then the price ceiling is not a binding constraint, for an increase in the price ceiling will not by itself lead to a higher price and higher profits. But now let us say that forces the firm has nothing to do with "shift" the demand curve to the right, so that the profit-maximizing price becomes $100. Under these new conditions, the price ceiling becomes a binding constraint, and the firm would have incentive to join in a campaign to have the ceiling raised.

Benefits from a Constraint Change. The formulation of investment programs requires not only identification of the binding constraints but also estimation of the benefits in each short-run period from changing a particular constraint. What are the benefits of a constraint change? Very simply they are the changes in the short-run criterion variable that can be attributed to that constraint change – for example, the change in the maximum attainable cash flow. Thus the benefit from a constraint change – its value to the firm – is different from the market value of whatever causes the change. Another hour of M_2, in our example where the limited availability of M_2 was nonbinding, may cost $100 or may be sold for $100 but in its use to the firm would have no value.

Let us return to our simple example to illustrate this valuation process. Let us say that we are at our "initial position," where M_1 is limited at 20 hours per day and M_2 is limited at 30 hours per day. Let us say that a unit of output sells for $10 and that the variable costs per unit are $8. What would happen if an additional hour of M_1 were available? If we assume the firm wishes to maximize its profit, it would raise its output from 20 to 21 units per day, and its cash flow would increase by $2. We could then say that that additional hour of M_1 is worth $2 per day to the firm, if we assume that all conditions remain as they are into the future. If, on the other hand, M_2 were expanded by one unit per day, neither output nor cash flow would rise and we would infer that the thirty-first hour of M_2 is not worth anything to the firm.

The benefit from a particular change in a constraint could vary with changes in other constraints, even when these changes are brought about by forces over which the firm can exercise no control. Consider, for example, the value of the twenty-first hour of M_1 if the price of the output rises to, say, $12 while the variable costs remain at $8. Now, clearly, the value of that twenty-first hour is $4 per day. If, alternatively, the variable costs drop to $6 with the selling price remaining at $10 per unit of output, the twenty-first hour of M_1 would also be worth $4 per day. From this simple illustration, it should be clear that the valuation of a change in a constraint, as well as the classification of a constraint as binding or nonbinding, depends on the other constraints.

An Example from Linear Programming. The linear programming model as applied to the allocation problem of the output mix provides an excellent opportunity to clarify still further the notions of binding and nonbinding constraints and their valuations.

Consider a firm making two products, whose outputs are Q_1 and Q_2. It uses four machines in the productive processes, M_1, M_2, M_3, M_4, whose capacities are limited. The quantities of services of these machines available per day, in hours, are designated $\bar{x}_1, \bar{x}_2, \bar{x}_3, \bar{x}_4$. We can add a second subscript to these inputs to designate the product to which these input services are assigned. Thus, x_{11} is the quantity of M_1 devoted to product 1; x_{12} is the quantity M_1 devoted to product 2. Let x_5 be the variable inputs (materials, labor) used in the production of product 1 and x_6 the variable inputs used in the production of product 2. Further, let p_5 be the price of a "package" of x_5, p_6 the price of a package of x_6, P_1 the selling price of product 1, and P_2 the selling price of product 2.

Let us say the production functions are

$$
\left.
\begin{aligned}
x_{11} &\geq 0.5\,Q_1 \\
x_{21} &\geq Q_1 \\
x_{31} &\geq Q_1 \\
x_{41} &\geq 0\,Q_1 \\
x_5 &\geq 3\,Q_1
\end{aligned}
\right\} \text{Production function for product 1}
\qquad
\begin{aligned}
&(6.1) \\
&(6.2) \\
&(6.3) \\
&(6.4) \\
&(6.5)
\end{aligned}
$$

$$x_{12} \geq 0.5\,Q_2 \tag{6.6}$$
$$x_{22} \geq 0.5\,Q_2 \tag{6.7}$$
$$x_{32} \geq 0\,Q_2 \quad\left.\right\} \text{Production function for product 2} \tag{6.8}$$
$$x_{42} \geq 0.5\,Q_2 \tag{6.9}$$
$$x_6 \geq 2\,Q_2 \tag{6.10}$$

These inequalities can be interpreted in this way. In inequation 6.1, at least 1/2 hour of M_1 is needed per unit of product 1. In inequation 6.2, at least 1 unit of M_2 is required per unit of product 1. In 6.4, no M_3 is needed in the production of a unit of product 2. In 6.5, 3 units of x_5 are required for a unit of product 1. In inequation 6.10, 2 units of x_6 are needed per unit of product 2.

Let us now say that 80 hours of M_1 are available per day, 100 hours of M_2, 80 hours of M_3, and 100 hours of M_4. The four "fixity" constraints place limits on the quantities that can be assigned to the different outputs:

$$x_{11} + x_{12} \leq 80 \quad M_1 \text{ constraint} \tag{6.11}$$
$$x_{21} + x_{22} \leq 100 \quad M_2 \text{ constraint} \tag{6.12}$$
$$x_{31} \leq 80 \quad M_3 \text{ constraint} \tag{6.13}$$
$$x_{42} \leq 100 \quad M_4 \text{ constraint} \tag{6.14}$$

We do not bother with x_{32} and x_{41}, because M_3 is not required for product 1 and M_4 is not required for product 2.

Next we have the "freedom of others" constraints. Let us say that the firm's demand curves and the supply curves to that firm do not depend on its outputs or purchases of variable inputs. The demand and supply curves, with the prices assumed for this example, are:

$$P_1 \leq 18 \tag{6.15}$$
$$P_2 \leq 14 \tag{6.16}$$
$$p_5 \geq 3 \tag{6.17}$$
$$p_6 \geq 4 \tag{6.18}$$

We turn now to the construction of the production possibility frontier, which limits the Q_1, Q_2 feasible combinations. These limitations arise, of course, because of the fixed capacities of M_1, M_2, M_3, M_4. The frontier is easily found by assuming that no inputs will be wasted— that is, that inequalities 6.1 through 6.10 are all equalities, which enables us to use 6.1 through 6.4, and 6.6 through 6.9 to substitute the outputs for the inputs in 6.11 through 6.14. Making these substitutions gives us the following set of inequations:

$$0.5\,Q_1 + 0.5\,Q_2 \leq 80 \quad M_1 \text{ constraint} \tag{6.19}$$
$$Q_1 + 0.5\,Q_2 \leq 100 \quad M_2 \text{ constraint} \tag{6.20}$$
$$Q_1 \leq 80 \quad M_3 \text{ constraint} \tag{6.21}$$
$$0.5\,Q_2 \leq 100 \quad M_4 \text{ constraint} \tag{6.22}$$

These four inequations determine the feasible Q_1, Q_2 set. When they are treated as equalities, they become the boundary. They are shown graphically in Figure 6.6.

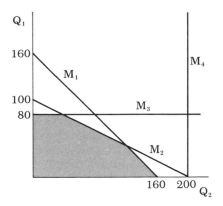

FIGURE 6.6   Feasible set of Q_1, Q_2 combinations

We next turn to the objective function. Let us take cash flow (or contribution to profits and overhead), designated by Z, as the criterion variable. This cash flow is equal to the revenues minus the payments for the variable inputs. Using our symbols, this is

$$Z = P_1 Q_1 + P_2 Q_2 - p_5 x_5 - p_6 x_6. \tag{6.23}$$

The constraints not entering the construction of the feasible (opportunity) set can all be incorporated into this objective function if we assume the firm will sell for the maximum price, buy at the minimum price, and not waste any of the variable inputs. Thus inequations 6.5 and 6.10 can be incorporated into equation 6.23 by substituting for x_5 and x_6. Inequations 6.15 through 6.18 can be incorporated by substituting for P_1, P_2, p_5, and p_6. These substitutions yield the following objective function:

$$\begin{aligned}
Z &= 18Q_1 + 14Q_2 - 3(3Q_1) - 4(2Q_2) \tag{6.24}\\
Z &= 18Q_1 + 14Q_2 - 9Q_1 - 8Q_2\\
Z &= (18 - 9)Q_1 + (14 - 8)Q_2\\
Z &= 9Q_1 + 6Q_2.
\end{aligned}$$

From this equation, we can see that each unit of Q_1 contributes $9 to the cash flow, and each unit of Q_2 contributes $6.

The last version of equation 6.24 can be used to plot an isocash flow map. First, we solve for Q_1, which gives

$$Q_1 = \frac{Z}{9} - \frac{2}{3} Q_2. \tag{6.25}$$

Now, by assuming different values for Z, we can generate the isocash-flow map, as in Figure 6.7.

By superimposing the isocash flow map upon the feasible set, we can determine the optimal Q_1, Q_2 combination as in Figure 6.8. As the diagram shows, the optimal combination is $Q_1 = 40$, $Q_2 = 120$. By

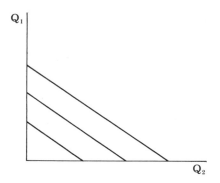

FIGURE 6.7   Isocash-flow (contribution) map

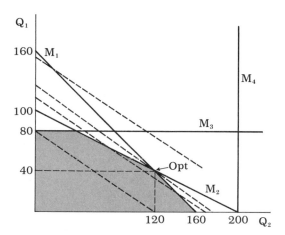

FIGURE 6.8   Graphic optimization

substituting these values for Q_1 and Q_2 in equation 6.24, we also see that the cash flow would be $1080 per day.

Which of the four capacity constraints are binding and which are nonbinding? Classification depends on whether a small increase in the capacity would lead to a better optimum and, consequently, a higher cash flow. The easiest constraint to classify is M_4. If we add an hour to M_4 capacity, the M_4 constraint would shift to the right. Such a shift would not even add to the feasible set, and our optimal Q_1, Q_2 and the associated cash flow would not change. It is somewhat less obvious that M_3 is also a nonbinding constraint. If M_3 were raised, new Q_1, Q_2 combinations would be added to the opportunity set, but the optimum would remain at $Q_1 = 40$, $Q_2 = 120$. Increases in M_1 or M_2, on the other hand, can be seen to lead to new optima and new cash flows. Hence, they are binding constraints.

To mathematically test the classifications of these constraints and to determine the short-run benefits from changes in them we take the following steps: (1) add an hour to a capacity, (2) calculate the new optimum combination of outputs, (3) calculate the new value of Z for the optimum combination, and (4) compare the new value of Z with the old value.[2]

Consider first an additional hour of M_1. The capacity constraint (6.11) now becomes $x_{11} + x_{12} \leq 81$, or, in terms of Q_1 and Q_2, inequation 6.19 becomes $0.5Q_1 + 0.5Q_2 \leq 81$. The only effect of this change on Figure 6.8 is to shift M_1 to the right. Figure 6.9 shows the new optimal values for Q_1 and Q_2 as the result of this shift.

The new optimal combination is $Q_1 = 38$ and $Q_2 = 124$, which yields a cash flow of \$1086. Because the cash flow before the expansion of M_1 was \$1080, we can conclude that M_1 is a binding constraint and that the eighty-first hour of M_1 is worth \$6 per day to the firm.

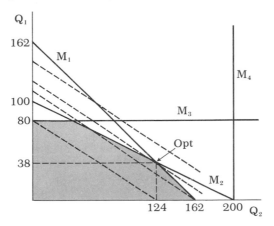

FIGURE 6.9   Graphic optimization

The same procedures can be used to determine the benefits from changing M_2, M_3, and M_4. To study M_2, we return to our initial condition and add an hour to M_2, so that inequation 6.20 becomes $Q_1 + 0.5Q_2 \leq 101$. With the change in this constraint, the optimal Q_1, Q_2 combination would be $Q_1 = 42$, $Q_2 = 118$, with Z again \$1086. We thus conclude that M_2 is a binding constraint and that the one hundred first hour of M_2 is also worth \$6 per day to the firm. (That an hour of M_1 and of M_2 are both worth \$6 is strictly coincidence. Generally they will differ.) If we changed the M_3 constraint so that inequation 6.21 becomes $Q_1 \leq 81$, or the M_4 constraint so that inequation 6.22 becomes $0.5Q_1 \leq 101$, we would find in both cases that the original optimum of

[2]In simplex solutions to linear programming problems a "dual" solution gives these short-run benefits of changes in the constraints.

$Q_1 = 40$, $Q_2 = 120$, would continue and that Z would remain at \$1080. Hence, M_3 and M_4 are nonbinding constraints and additional amounts of these machine hours are not worth anything to the firm.

The fact that an additional hour of a machine will lead to a different optimum and higher value of Z does not mean that all additional hours have the same value. Consider once more the expansion of M_1 to 81. This led to a new optimum of $Q_1 = 38$, $Q_2 = 124$, and a value of Z of \$1086, which is \$6 greater than the initial value of Z. If we add still another hour to M_1, the new optimum would be $Q_1 = 34$, $Q_2 = 132$, Z = \$1092, so that this hour too is worth \$6. Additional hours of M_1 would continue to be worth \$6 per day until the capacity of M_1 reaches 100 hours, in which event the solution would be as in Figure 6.10.

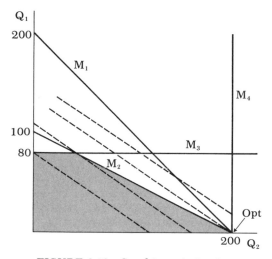

FIGURE 6.10   Graphic optimization

The optimal solution is now $Q_1 = 0$, $Q_2 = 200$, and Z is \$1200. Any further expansion of M_1 would not change the optimum solution or the value of Z. Consequently, M_1 is no longer a binding constraint, and the 101st hour of M_1 is not worth anything to the firm. In fact, M_2 is now the only binding constraint. However, if the capacity of M_2 were also increased, M_1 would once again be binding. A little experimentation would show that if the capacities of M_1 and M_2 were both expanded by very large amounts, M_4 would become a binding constraint.[3]

The constraints can be expanded or contracted in many different ways that change the classifications and the benefits from changing the constraints, and we urge the reader to experiment with the model.

---

[3]This confirms the notion that what is binding depends on relative scarcity. By extension, the marginal value-in-use of one of these machines depends on its relative scarcity. This is an important lesson in economics.

A particularly interesting case occurs if, instead of an expansion in capacity through the acquisition of a machine, the "expansion" takes place as the result of improved technology. With reference to our example, let us say that the firm has learned to use M_2 more efficiently in the production of both Q_1 and Q_2. Let us say that, instead of inequation 6.3, where one hour of M_2 is required, only half an hour becomes necessary. This technological constraint then changes to $x_{21} \geq 0.5Q_1$. And let us say that, instead of half an hour of M_2 required per unit of Q_2, only 0.3 hour is needed. Thus, the constraint of inequation 6.4 becomes $x_{22} \geq 0.3Q_2$. The M_2 constraint, which was inequation 6.20, now becomes $0.5Q_1 + 0.3Q_2 \leq 100$.

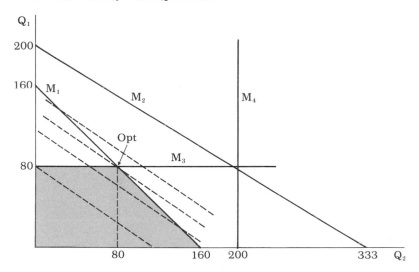

FIGURE 6.11   Graphic optimization

With this change in the M_2 constraint, let us once more find our optimal solution, shown in Figure 6.11. With this improvement in technology in the use of M_2, we see a number of important changes. M_2 and M_4 are now both nonbinding, and M_1 and M_3 are now binding. The optimal solution is $Q_1 = 80$, $Q_2 = 80$, which gives a Z of $1200. Because the original value of Z was $1080, we can infer that, in these circumstances, the technological improvement in the use of M_2 is worth $120 per day. If M_1 were now expanded by one unit, the new optimum would be $Q_1 = 80$, $Q_2 = 82$, Z = $1212, so that an additional hour of M_1 is now worth $12. If M_3 were expanded by one unit, the optimum would be $Q_1 = 81$, $Q_2 = 79$, Z = $1203, so that the additional hour of M_3 is worth $3. It is interesting to notice that an improvement in the technological use of M_2 increases the value to the firm of M_1 and M_3.[4]

[4]This is a very interesting finding. An improvement in the use of M_2 will increase the demand not for M_2 but for M_1 and M_3. The cooperating inputs are thus the beneficiaries of the improved use of one of the inputs.

Thus far we have illustrated only how changes in constraints initiated by the firm could alter the classifications of the constraints and the valuation of benefits from changes in these constraints. More serious from the viewpoint of formulating an investment program are changes in the constraints that come about as a result of forces beyond the firm's control. By far the most important of these externally caused constraint changes, at least in a market system where government regulation is not pervasive, are those affecting price-quantity relationships on both the buying and the selling sides. Externally caused constraint changes typically introduce important elements of uncertainty into the formulation of investment strategies.

To illustrate the impact of an externally caused change in a constraint, let us first return to the original constraints of inequations 6.1 through 6.18. Let us now say that P_2, the price of product 2, falls from \$14 to \$11, so that inequation 6.16 becomes $P_2 \leq 11$. Proceeding as in the construction of the objective function (see equations 6.23 and 6.24), we see that the new objective function becomes

$$Z = 9Q_1 + 3Q_2. \qquad (6.26)$$

Because the feasible set has not changed, we can proceed as before by using an isocash-flow map based on equation 6.26 to obtain the optimal solution, as shown in Figure 6.12.

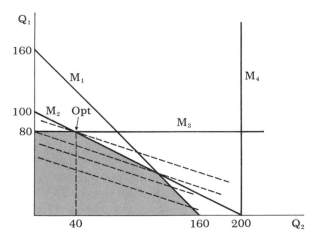

FIGURE 6.12   Graphic optimization

One result of this change in P_2 is that the optimal solution is now $Q_1 = 80$, $Q_2 = 40$, in contrast to the original optimal solution of $Q_1 = 40$, $Q_2 = 120$. As we should expect, a fall in P_2 should lead to a change in the optimal product mix in favor of Q_1. At this new optimal combination, Z is $9(80) + 3(40)$, or \$840. Because Z falls from \$1080 to \$840, the difference, a negative \$240, measures the loss per day of that lower price to the firm. It is worth noticing that the decrease in Z was not $3 times the original value of Q, 120, because the firm could shift its product mix.

Figure 6.12 makes clear that the binding constraints are now M_2 and M_3. If an additional hour of capacity were added to M_2, the optimal Q_1, Q_2 combination would be $Q_1 = 80$, $Q_2 = 42$. This yields a Z of $846, compared to the Z of $840 without this additional hour. We could say, therefore, that the additional hour is worth $6 per day to the firm—which fortuitously happens to be the amount this hour was worth before P_2 was changed. If another hour is added to M_3 capacity, the optimal Q_1, Q_2 combination is $Q_1 = 81$, $Q_2 = 38$, which yields a Z of $843. Thus an additional hour of M_3 is worth $3 per day to the firm, where before it was worth nothing. Additions in capacity to M_1 and M_4, now the nonbinding constraints, would change neither the optimal Q_1, Q_2 combinations nor the value of Z.

We have illustrated only a few of the things that can be learned from manipulating the constraint parameters of this model. We could think of simulations of interesting combinations of these parameters. What, for example, would be the effect if M_2 were raised, P_1 falls, and P_2 rises? These are precisely the kinds of problems that decision-makers in the real world have to deal with.

Investment Programs. The most important lesson to be learned from the preceding example is that the constraints, both those under the control of the firm and those influenced by external forces, are interrelated; a change in one of them could affect the "importance" of the others to the short-run cash flow. One implication of these interrelationships is that investments, or changes in particular constraints, should not be considered one at a time. Rather, the decision-maker should always think of investment *programs*, in which a number of constraints are changed.[5] A second implication is that the changes the firm can bring about in the constraints must always be evaluated in terms of forecasts of the changes brought about in constraints by outside forces.

Any particular firm might consider a large number of potential investment programs. In fact, each particular firm is a potential entrant to all possible economic activities unless it is constrained from entering by forces it cannot influence. Each firm can at all times consider expansion and contraction of the activities in which it already engages. Each firm can also consider investment in research and development activities in the hope of uncovering previously unknown opportunities for investment. Each firm can also consider merger with or acquisition of other going concerns. We must ask, therefore, what prevents each firm from at least considering engaging in all activi-

---

[5]This is why large firms seldom look at one investment project at a time. Instead, they are concerned with planning—that is, selecting a program of a number of projects.

ties. The answer is, first, each firm faces some constraints it cannot change, and second, each firm is limited in its ability to estimate and forecast changes in constraints with which it has little experience. Yet, even with these limitations, there may be an infinite number of investment programs that can be formulated. The firm can, however, use the procedures outlined here pertaining to binding and nonbinding constraints and the preliminary valuation of constraint changes to limit the formulation of investment programs to a reasonable number of promising alternative candidates.

Investment programs can be alternatives in two different senses. Programs may be mutually exclusive, or some unchangeable constraint may limit the number of investment programs that can be undertaken at one time. Expansion of the capacity of a machine by 50 hours per day is, for example, mutually exclusive with expansion of the same capacity by 100 hours per day. A limitation on financing or on the time of top management might force the firm to choose among investment programs that are not technically mutually exclusive. The passage of time, however, might allow removal of such nontechnical limitations to the formulation of many investment programs.

Three simple alternatives open to any corporation are important to keep in mind. A corporation with a positive cash-flow forecast for the future might simply accumulate cash balances. Such a program would amount to postponement of long-run decisions. In an uncertain world, at some points in time this extreme alternative may be desirable. Second, all activities could be continued without deliberate constraint changes and any accumulating funds from positive cash flow could be distributed to stockholders. Third, all activities could be continued and accumulating funds could be used to purchase and retire the outstanding securities of the corporation. Each of these extreme alternatives is a special case of what might be called a "do nothing" investment program. That is, the firm would be making no attempt to change the constraints under which it will operate in future periods. These three possibilities, or combinations of them, may be explicitly or implicitly included in the group of alternative investment programs from among which a firm chooses.

EVALUATION OF INVESTMENT PROGRAMS

Once alternative investment programs have been formulated, a way must be found to evaluate the desirability of each alternative so that it can be compared with each of the others. The evaluation procedure for any particular investment program is reasonably straightforward. One step consists of estimating the costs associated with the proposed constraint changes. A second step consists of estimating the benefits that can be attributed to that investment program. Because these costs and benefits generally occur in a number of periods into the future, we refer to them as "streams." A third step is then to compare the costs and returns in a way that the results are comparable for alternative investment programs. Complications in this third step generally arise from the fact that the costs, and especially the benefits, take place in the future and all investment decisions must be made and evaluated in the present.

Although the basic procedures are not conceptually very complicated, in practice many difficult questions have to be faced. How can we determine which future costs and benefits to attribute to the particular investment program? How can we tell how long into the future the returns, or benefits, will last? How do we measure the future costs and benefits from a particular investment when changes take place in the firm's future constraints that are not controlled by the firm? How do we handle the uncertainties inherent in having to forecast the future? What problems are encountered in comparing future costs and returns occurring in different time periods?

Identification of Consequences of an Investment Program. We have stressed that the constraint parameters can, to varying extents, be changed by the firm. These parameters are also subject to change as the result of forces "outside" the firm—that is, forces not subject to the firm's control. Because the benefits generally must be measured in the future, the problem has to be faced that the future constraints typically change because of the proposed investment program *and* forces beyond the firm's control. We must somehow select the portion of future cash flows to attribute to the particular investment program. Essentially, the attributable returns are calculated by comparing expected future cash flows of the firm with, and without, the particular investment program.

Often problems of interpretation arise when there is a connection between the "outside" forces and the particular investment program. Most frequently the external forces are independent of what the firm does. But sometimes a rival, a buyer or supplier, or a government may react to a firm's investment program. An investment program calling for a redesigned product and an advertising campaign may bring forth countermeasures from rivals. Or the building of a new plant may elicit the responses of a lower price by a rival. Reactions such as these should logically be taken into account when we estimate future cash flows *with* investment, although in practice it is often difficult to predict what another firm will do as a response to an investment program.

Another interesting problem in evaluation and attribution arises when a particular investment program, if adopted, provides the firm with future options for future investments. Say, for example, that the acquisition of a patent, by improving a firm's technological base, makes possible the creation of a number of new products in the future. The question is: In measuring the benefits from the patent acquisition, should we take into account the future options that the patent makes feasible? On conceptual grounds, the answer is yes, but in practice "valuing" these options is not easy.

Time Horizons. Virtually all investment programs are expected to change constraint parameters well into the future. Because the evaluation of an investment program requires an estimate of the returns in the future, it is obviously a crucial step to determine how long the effect of the investment program will last into the future. The last period in the future to which the investment applies is often known as its time horizon.

For many types of investments the time horizon could be estimated with a high degree of confidence. The life span of durable assets such as machinery and buildings is usually well known by engineers, although it could be prolonged or shortened by the degree of maintenance. For other types of investment, such as advertising and the acquisition of knowledge for a new product, the estimate of useful life may be subject to considerable error. Marketing experts are always trying to measure things such as the "life cycle" of a product and the cumulative effect of advertising. Difficult or not, the proper evaluation of investment programs requires that these time horizons be estimated.

A particularly interesting problem arises when the different parts of an investment program have different time horizons. As a simple example, an investment program consisting of the expansion of two machines would have a time horizon problem if one machine has an expected useful life of ten years, while the other is expected to last five years. The time horizon could be taken as ten years if, as part of the investment program, there is a provision and commitment to replace the five-year machine when it wears out. Or the time horizon might be five years with the investment program including a provision to dispose of the ten-year machine when the five-year machine wears out. We can see that the determination of the time horizon could require commitments of investment funds into the future.

The Cost Stream. One part of the evaluation process is to determine the costs that should be attributed to a particular investment program. To do this, it is necessary to maintain a distinction between the expenditures required to change and keep changed the constraint parameters and the expenditures required to exploit the new short-run opportunities made possible by the investment program. The first type are the costs that we want for the cost stream. The latter will enter into the calculation of the benefit stream.

The types of cost to include in the cost stream are those to which the firm is or will be committed as the result of the choice of the investment program. They would consist of all cash outlays that would take place, even if the investment were not exploited. Typically such costs would be acquisition payments, interest payments, maintenance expenditures, insurance, taxes that are not related to output levels or profits (but depend entirely on the investment), acquisition costs of patents, research, product development, and advertising. The costs entering the cost stream, in short, are all those expenditures that are necessary to change the short-run opportunity set and short-run choices.

The difference between the costs of changing the short-run choices and costs of exploiting the short-run choices can be seen from a simple example. Say a firm pays $100,000 for the right to use a patent, and in addition pays $1 royalty for every unit of output produced. The payment of the $100,000 for the right to use the patent provides the firm with new short-run choices: consequently this amount would be part of the cost stream. The payment of the royalty, on the other hand, is a cost of exploiting the patent, and in essence is a variable cost no different from the payment for labor or materials. The payment of the royalty would thus be included in the calculation of the short-run cash flow benefits.

Depreciation expenses are not included either in the cost stream or in the calculation of the benefit stream, because the asset costs are fully accounted for in the cash payments made for the assets. If depreciation expenses were included in either costs or benefits, this would amount to a double counting of the acquisition costs of the assets. The only way depreciation would affect the cost-benefit calculation is through the impact the depreciation might have upon the pattern of taxes. In general, to avoid problems of these types, the analyst need look only at actual cash flows. The costs of changing these opportunity sets were labeled ΔA in Chapter 2; we use that symbol here.

There are two identifiable categories of cash outflows to include in the cost stream for a particular investment program. One is the cash outflows required to pay for the asset acquisitions that change the constraints—which is generally the more important. The second is the cash outflows attributable to fixed commitments associated with changing the constraint parameters, which are generally such expenditures as interest payments, maintenance, and other contractual obligations. In Chapter 2, we used ΔA, as the cash outflow due to asset acquisitions. Since these outflows could take place in different time periods into the future, we attach "time" subscripts, so that the cash outflow is $\Delta A_0, \Delta A_1 \ldots \Delta A_t \ldots \Delta A_n$. In Chapter 2, we used F_t to represent fixed expenses. Since a particular investment program could change these fixed expenses, we can use ΔF_t to represent the changes. These outflows will also take place over different periods, so that we should again attach time subscripts to designate the periods in which these changes in cash outflow will take place. Sometimes, it should be noted, an asset acquisition might reduce fixed expenses, in which event the ΔFs could be negative.

The Benefit Stream. The main benefits of an investment program are
the short-run increments in the cash flows that can be attributed to
the particular investment program. These increments in the short-
run cash flows are known as the returns to the investment program
and are made possible by improvements in the short-run choices for
the short-run decision variables. That there will be returns at all
rests upon the assumption that the firm will take advantage of the
improved short-run opportunity set of the decision variables.

As a rule these returns will take place over a number of short-run
periods extending into the future, generally to the time horizon. As in
the case of the expenditures, we designate the returns according to
the period in which they are expected to occur. Thus, ΔZ_1 is the return in the period following the present, ΔZ_2 is the return two periods
from the present, ΔZ_t is the return t periods from the present, ΔZ_n
is the return in the time horizon period.

Unlike the cost stream, the only expenditures that enter the calculation of the ΔZs are those incurred through the exploitation of the
opportunities made available by the investment program. We would
thus include taxes, royalty payments, and others tied to the short-run
decision variables – the various P, Q, p, and x – but not those expenditures incurred in making the opportunities available. Cash generated
on capital account, such as through the sale of an asset, should be
included not in the returns stream but as a change in cash flow from
a constraint-changing action.

The simplest calculation of the returns stream occurs in the case
in which the investment program can be viewed as a subsystem –
that is, where it is not interdependent with other parts of the firm's
activities. In such cases, the returns are the short-run cash flows expected to take place in the present and future short-run, or accounting,
periods. The estimation of these cash flows initially requires a forecast of the constraints that determine the short-run opportunity sets.
This forecast can be quite difficult because some of the constraints,
most importantly the demand curves and supply curves facing the
firm, are typically not under the firm's control. Once the constraints
are forecast, the future benefits are determined as the cash flows associated with future optimal choices of the decision variables. For
the tth period, the return ΔZ_t to the firm would be the optimal cash
flow, Z_t, to the subsystem.

When the investment program is interdependent with other aspects
of the firm's activities, the calculations of the cash flows are somewhat more complicated. Two forecasts are needed – one in which the
constraints and associated short-run cash flows are estimated for
all future time periods on the assumption that the investment program is adopted; the second in which the constraints and associated
short-run cash flows are estimated on the assumption that the investment program is not adopted and nothing is done to change the constraints. The differences between these short-run cash flows is then
the "return" that can be attributed to the investment program. Sym-

bolically, if Z_t is the optimal short-run cash flow in year t without the investment program, and $Z_t{}^*$ is the optimal short-run cash flow for that year with the investment program, the return for that year is $\Delta Z_t = Z_t{}^* - Z_t$.

In practice the determination of the benefit stream is difficult and is by far the most crucial step in the evaluation of investment programs. The difficulty stems in part from the fact that forecasts are required of the constraints, and forecasting is a most delicate art, particularly of those constraints determined by the freedom of buyers and suppliers. Good forecasting rests on a thorough understanding of the forces that influence the constraints. Even with good understanding, the forecast of the benefit stream is usually subject to considerable uncertainty. Later we show how the firm can deal with this uncertainty, but we continue now under the assumption that all forecasts are made with a high degree of certainty.

Comparing the Cost and Benefit Streams. Once the cost and benefit streams have been estimated, we can evaluate the desirability of a particular investment project or program by comparing the present value of the cost stream with the present value of the benefit stream. With $\Delta A_0, \Delta A_1, \ldots \Delta A_t, \ldots \Delta A_n$ the cash outflows for acquiring the assets, and $\Delta F_0, F_1, \ldots \Delta F_t, \ldots \Delta F_n$ the changes in fixed cash outflows associated with the investment program, the present value of the cost stream would be

$$PV(C) = \sum_{t=0}^{t=n} \frac{\Delta A_t + \Delta F_t}{(1+r)^t}.$$

Similarly, the present value of the benefit stream is

$$PV(\Delta Z) = \sum_{t=0}^{t=n} \frac{\Delta Z_t}{(i+r)^t}.$$

The discount rate, r, should be that as suggested in Chapter 2: namely, the rate of interest at which the firm could loan out its money. We should point out, however, that many analysts prefer the cost of capital — the rate of payment for the use of cash — as the discount rate.

The extent to which $PV(\Delta Z)$ exceeds $PV(C)$ could then be used to determine the desirability of the investment. In this form, these present values could be calculated for alternative investments, so that they can be compared for desirability. Although many writers on investment analysis take these comparisons as the final criterion of an investment program, we are not completely satisfied with this criterion because investments frequently are linked to the issuing of debt securities and common stock, and can affect dividends, control of the firm, and its degree of liquidity. We therefore turn, in the next section, to assessing investment in new assets in the context of the whole financial management of the firm.

INVESTMENT AND FINANCIAL MANAGEMENT

Let us now reconsider the model of the firm as owner set forth in Chapter 2. If we assume that managers of a firm are able to forecast the state of short-run cash flows from operations in future periods, with and without the effects of each proposed investment program, what criterion should be used to pick among them? Let us assume that we have a forecast of Z and Z* for each future time period affected by the proposed program. Let us also assume that the costs associated with bringing about the constraint changes are also known. We can designate such cash inflows or outflows with the symbols ΔA_t and ΔF_t. (ΔA could be an inflow if the firm sells an asset.) How can we use such information to make appropriate investment decisions? We must first set forth more completely the objective function of the model firm and the long-run constraints on its ability to change short-run constraints. We can then examine the consequences of investment not only on the long-run objective function but also on such important financial policy considerations as liquidity and control.

A Long-Run Objective Function. Following the model set forth in Chapter 2, let us assume that the firm wishes to maximize, at each point in time at which decisions are made, the market value per share of its outstanding common stock. We will assume that per share market value is basically determined by the following factors: (1) the discounted present value of the firm's future stream of cash inflows and outflows, which we earlier called the going concern value of the firm, (2) the number of shares outstanding, and (3) the dividend policy of the firm. Cash flows in each time period include not only cash flow from operations — Z_t — and flows in and out to accomplish constraint changes — ΔA_t — but also several other categories. One other source of inflows of cash is interest received on money lent to others and rental from noncash assets used by others. As in Chapter 2, let us designate such nonoperating income as Y_t. Another cash-flow category includes the operating revenues and expenditures that are fixed in the short run but may vary from period to period. This category consists of interest payments to others for borrowed funds, rental payments for use of assets belonging to others, and contractually fixed payments for input services or materials. We shall designate such fixed cash flows as F_t. Their value will always be zero or negative. Funds may also flow in or out as a result of borrowing, lending, paying back, or being paid back for earlier loans. Such flows associated with changes in stocks of debt instruments shall be designated ΔL_t. Similarly, we will use ΔE_t to stand for cash flows in or out from sale or purchase of the firm's own equity securities. Cash may also flow into or out of the firm as a result of tax refunds and tax payments. These we can designate T_t.

We can think of the sum of all these cash flows in a particular period as the change in the firm's bank balance during that period. If it builds up, the firm can pay dividends. If it goes down, the account may be overdrawn unless the balance is large enough at the beginning of the period. If the sum of the cash flows is positive and a balance is building up, the firm must either pay dividends or consider lending the money out at interest, if no better alternatives are known to exist. Thus, the firm has reason to consider the rate of interest at which it can lend when evaluating the time value of its idle balances. We will use, therefore, the going rate of interest at which the firm can lend out its cash at each period in the future, r_t, as the discount rates in adding up cash flows from all future periods to find the discounted present value of the future stream of cash flows.[6] Letting V_0 stand for this present value, we have

$$V_0 = \sum_{t=0}^{t=\infty} \frac{Z_t + Y_t + F_t + \Delta A_t + \Delta L_t + \Delta E_t + T_t}{(1 + r_t)^t}. \tag{6.27}$$

The numerator consists of all the cash inflows and outflows, except for dividends. These arise from current operations, nonoperating income, fixed expenses that cannot be changed in the short run, asset acquisition or sales, borrowing, sales or retirement of equities, and taxes. These cash flows are for different periods and must be discounted and summed to obtain the "present value" of these cash flows.

To get the present value per share, we divide V_0 by S, the number of shares outstanding. Present value per share of future cash flows alone, however, does not determine the market value of common stock, for buyers and sellers also react to dividend yields. We can assume, therefore, that our model firm wishes to maximize some function of V_0/S and D_0, where D_0 stands for the present value of the expected dividend stream. The market value per share can be thought of as the simple sum of the two, but stock markets in the real world may not behave in so simple a fashion. In any event, management must weigh the effects of dividend policies against the effects of retaining earnings to be used in lieu of other sources of capital funds.

Financial Policy Considerations. It is well to ponder what might constrain the firm in making its long-run decisions to change the short-run constraints. The firm may not be able to change some constraints because of government policy or may not have enough experience to properly evaluate all investment programs. These limit

---

[6]In effect, the interest rate the firm could get is the opportunity cost of any investment using the firm's cash. In this formulation, the ts refer to years and the r_t to the annual rate of interest. We have assumed that interest is compounded only once a year. But if we wish to assume interest is compounded n times per year, we could divide r_t by n and multiply the t exponent in the denominator by n. Note that we should ideally discount not by the current rate of interest, but by the expected interest rate at which the firm could loan out money in all future years. It should also be noted that payments of interest is included in F_t.

the firm in its long-run decisions. But the firm may impose other constraints upon itself, limiting its desire, if not ability, to make new investments. These stem from considerations of avoiding liquidity crises, maintaining control of the firm by those currently in control, and maintaining dividends.

A primary concern of management in evaluating future plans is the danger of bankruptcy. Bankruptcy results from a lack of sufficient liquid assets to meet current obligations which, in turn, could occur if projected cash inflows fail to materialize. Liquidity problems can arise even in profitable companies unless care is taken to maintain adequate reserves and lines of credit. We can express the liquidity constraint for our model firm as a requirement that in each period the "bank account" not be allowed to be overdrawn. If it otherwise would be, borrowing must take place. If borrowing is impossible, nonliquid assets must be sold. If the liquidation value of the firm is insufficient, then bankruptcy proceedings become necessary so that all creditors get a fair share of the inadequate assets upon liquidation or reorganization of the business. There is some risk to most investments because the cash flows from the investments may not be sufficient to meet the obligations arising from the investments. Thus the firm would be constrained on the amount and form of investment to undertake.

A second important constraint has to do with the control of the corporation. Control may be lost by bankruptcy. But it also may be lost by issuing too much new common stock. Thus the firm's controlling stockholders are constrained from increasing ΔE_t as a means of increasing the inflow of cash. Borrowing, however, may be limited by the reluctance of lenders to lend too much relative to the amount of equity capital being raised by the firm. Lenders, too, may challenge the existing management for control. Thus a rapidly growing firm may be forced to supplement retained earnings with both new stock issues and borrowed funds. Control can be protected if new stock is bought by existing controlling stockholders and borrowing is not too large. Stock warrants are sometimes used to give existing stockholders prior rights to new issues.

A third constraint stems from the need to maintain dividends. We have already noticed that dividends as well as the going concern value of the firm influence the price of its common stock. In making its investment plans, therefore, the firm would not want to overextend itself to the point where its ability to maintain its dividends is impaired.

If a firm sees an opportunity to adopt an investment program that will increase Z_t in future periods, it must do more than merely compare the discounted increments in the stream of cash flows from operations — the ΔZ_ts — with the costs of changing the constraints — the ΔA_ts. Plans for managing the firm's assets and liabilities must also be evaluated. For example, suppose some stream of expenditures to change constraints requires certain ΔA_t outflows. The liquidity problem requires liquid funds in early periods before ΔZ_t begins to show up. Borrowing will effect F_t in future periods until the loan is repaid. Repayment will result in negative ΔL_t in the repayment periods. Use of retained earnings—that is, previously accumulated assets held in fairly liquid form such as U.S. Treasury bills—would reduce Y_t in future periods. Issuing new stock, on the other hand, would have no effect on F_t, ΔL_t, or Y_t. New stock would be best if the firm wished to maximize V_0. But if value per share is the goal, the firm must ask whether V_0 is raised enough to offset the increase in S. Even if it is, the firm must count in the effect of more shares on dividend requirements and on control.

Any proposed investment program can be evaluated by using equation 6.27 or, better still, V_0 divided by S, the number of common shares outstanding. The analyst must estimate the effect of the program on all the cash inflows and outflows in the numerator in equation 6.27. We have shown how the changes in Z_t and ΔA_t could be estimated, but in addition an evaluation of the program must consider the changes in the financial variables, ΔL_t and ΔE_t, taxes, nonoperating income Y_t, and contractual outflows F_t. Generally, investment programs that lead to a combination of cash inflows and outflows that give a higher value of V_0/S are the best. Exceptions to this rule would arise if the proposed investment program, including its financing, might lead to liquidity problems, a loss of control, or an inability to maintain a dividend policy.[7] Given our present state of knowledge, there are no formulas or techniques for choosing among alternative investment programs that are as cut and dried as the short-run decision models. The analyst simply estimates the effect of alternative programs on V_0/S, subject to the liquidity, control, and dividend policy constraints, and selects the programs most likely to lead to the highest increase in V_0/S.

Discussion Questions

1. We have formulated investment as the changing of constraint parameters. Could there be constraints on the ability to change constraints? Is there some carry-over of this concept to our legal system? The legal system imposes constraints on us. A legislative body, however, can change these constraints. But the ability of the legislative body is in turn constrained by a constitution or set of bylaws. Could there be still "higher" constraints?

2. Could a self-imposed constraint have an ethical basis? What do we mean when we say that somebody acts in a self-restrained manner? What distinguishes the scrupulous from the unscrupulous?

[7] These exceptions might be viewed as the firm's self-imposed constraints in long-run decision-making.

Long-Run Decision Models: The Firm as Owner

3. How does one value the use of an asset? Could this valuation-in-use of an asset differ from the market value of an asset? How can differences in method of valuation—in the market (in exchange) and in use—determine decisions to buy or sell?

4. Give some examples of binding and nonbinding constraints from everyday life? How does relative scarcity determine whether a constraint is binding?

5. What are the advantages of formulating and evaluating investment programs as opposed to investment projects?

6. Why is it so difficult to find an optimal investment program?

7. What advantages are there to considering a "do nothing" strategy as an alternative to investment programs?

8. Distinguish between the costs that should enter the cost stream and those that should enter the benefit stream in evaluating investment programs.

9. Why is it often necessary to compare alternative cash-flow streams in evaluating the benefits of an investment program?

10. What constrains the firm in its investment programs? Could a consideration of this question help us explain why some firms grow faster than other firms?

7 The Firm's Supply of Output to the Market and Its Demand for Inputs

In this chapter, we begin to investigate the determinants of market prices and, by extension, the parameters of the demand curves facing the model firm for its outputs and the supply curves facing the firm for its inputs. One step is to determine the quantity of a particular product (or service) that the firm would supply in the short run at every possible market price. The relationship between these market prices and the quantity the firm would supply is known as the firm's short-run supply curve to the market. If this supply curve is obtained for every supplying firm in the market, the individual supply curves could be added together, at least conceptually, to obtain the short-run market supply curve.

The position and shape of the model firm's supply curve to the market, and by extension the market supply curve, are not of course fixed for all time. The quantity the firm would supply at any particular market price depends on the various parameters of all the constraints facing the firm. Among the most important parameters influencing the supply curve are input prices, the amount of the firm's fixed assets, the prices of other products the firm can produce. For any set of values for these parameters, there will be a unique supply curve. But if the values of the parameters change, the position and sometimes the shape of the supply curve will shift. We thus have to ascertain how changes in the parameters of the constraints will change, or "shift," the firm's supply curve.

A second step in understanding market prices — specifically for the firm's inputs or factors of production as they are often called — is to determine the quantity of an input the firm would purchase at each possible price for that input. The relation between all the values of the input price and the quantities the firm would purchase is the firm's demand curve for that input. If such a demand curve is obtained for each firm that purchases that input in a market, the demand curves could be added, conceptually at least, to obtain the market demand curve for the input.

Like the firm's supply curve, the firm's demand curve for an input is not fixed for all time. Its position and shape will depend on the parameters of a number of the firm's constraints, such as the prices for outputs, the quantity of fixed asset services available, and technological relationships embodied in the parameters of the production function. For any set of values for these parameters, there will be a unique demand curve for the input. But, with changes in one or more of these parameters, the position of the demand curve could shift; sometimes the shape of the demand curve is altered as well. It is important that we be able to ascertain how changes in these parameters influence the shape and position of this demand curve.

In constructing the firm's supply curve, we limit ourselves to the important case in which the demand curve facing the firm for its output is horizontal. That is, we consider only the case in which the firm's output does not influence the price at which it can sell. The output price is therefore determined completely by the market.[1] Similarly, in constructing the firm's demand curve for an input, we consider only the case in which the supply curve of the input to the firm is horizontal; that is, the price of the input is independent of the quantity of the input the firm purchases. We will, however, study the demand curve for an input in which the demand curve for the firm's output slopes.

Although we will investigate many models and variations in deriving the supply and demand curves, the reader should be aware that we will not investigate all possible factors that influence these curves. As before, we urge that the reader concentrate on the techniques of model-building, so that he can go beyond our investigations.

SHORT-RUN SUPPLY TO THE MARKET

We shall study the firm's supply curve to the market in two stages. In the first stage, we assume that the parameters of all the constraints are constant values, except for the demand curve for its output facing the firm, which is completely determined by the market price. To calculate the quantity the firm would produce and supply to the market at some particular price, we use the short-run decision models of Chapter 5. The output that the firm would supply at one particular price gives us one point on the firm's supply curve. We then select

---

[1]The firm's supply curve when the demand curve for its output slopes is a difficult concept, and many economists believe there is no meaningful supply curve in such circumstances. We discuss these problems in Chapter 9.

another market price and again calculate the optimal (profit-maximizing) output the firm would supply at this second price. This combination of price and output provides a second point on the firm's supply curve. We can then repeat the procedure for every possible market price, obtaining the optimal output associated with each market price. All these combinations of market price and optimal output are points on the supply curve. The supply curve is then the locus of all the combinations of price and output. The curve tells us the quantity the firm would supply to the market at every market price. This supply curve rests on the assumption that the firm is a short-run profit maximizer.

In the first stage, we assume that all other constraint parameters do not change. In the second stage, we investigate how a change in one of the constraint parameters would change the position, and possibly the shape, of the short-run supply curve. We investigate changes in these parameters one at a time. The parameters of these other constraints can change either because of forces beyond the firm's control or because of long-run decisions taken by the firm.

We can outline the basic procedure to ascertain the way a change in a constraint parameter influences the firm's short-run supply curve. To be specific, let us assume that we are interested in the effect upon this supply curve of a change in the price of a variable input. First, we assume some value for the input price and derive the supply curve with the techniques described for the first stage. Next, we assume a different value for the input price and once again use the procedures for the first stage to derive the supply curve. This gives us two supply curves, each one corresponding to some value for the input price. By comparing the two curves, we can then ascertain how a change in the input price influences the supply curve. A change in the input price changes the relationship between the market price for the output and the quantity the firm would supply. In this context, the input price can be thought of as a "shift parameter," for a change in its value would shift the supply curve.

Supply Curve of the One-Product Firm. In this section, we derive the supply curve for a one-product firm (or a one-product division of a firm). We assume that all the constraint parameters are constant values, except for the market price. We shall show that the supply curve is obtained directly from the marginal cost curve. We explore only those cases in which the production function is classical, with an indivisible fixed input, and the two-process production function. The results would be similar for other types of production functions.

Let us look first at the case where the production function is classical (with indivisibility). Figure 7.1 depicts the marginal and average variable cost curves for such a production function. Also shown in this diagram are the marginal revenue curves associated with three alternative market prices, which we label $\bar{P}_a$, $\bar{P}_b$, $\bar{P}_c$. The profit-

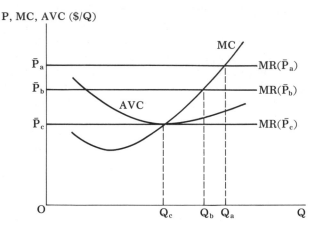

FIGURE 7.1   Optimal outputs at different prices: classical model

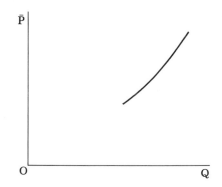

FIGURE 7.2   Firm's supply curve to market: classical model

maximizing firm will produce up to the level where MC is equal to MR, for that portion of the MC curve lying above the AVC curve. Thus, at price $\bar{P}_a$, the firm would produce Q_a. If the price were $\bar{P}_b$, the firm would produce Q_b; if the price were $\bar{P}_c$ the firm would produce Q_c. Nothing would be produced if the price were lower than $\bar{P}_c$.[2]

It should be clear that the position of the marginal cost curve above the AVC curve itself gives the quantity that the firm would supply to the market at any market price, $\bar{P}$. This is so because the firm produces to the point where $MC = \bar{P}$. Thus, using just $\bar{P}$ to label the ordinate axis, we see that the supply curve is nothing more than the replica of the MC curve above the AVC curve. This is shown in Figure 7.2.

---

[2]There is some ambiguity when the price is exactly $\bar{P}_c$, for the firm is indifferent to producing zero or Q_c. We can therefore think of $\bar{P}_c$ as the lowest limit of the price at which the firm would produce.

Let us next investigate the supply curve for a firm whose production function consists of two processes. We saw in Chapter 4 that the *MC* curve associated with such a production function is discontinuous, as shown in Figure 7.3. Also shown in this diagram is the *AVC* curve, which is never above the *MC* curve. (*MC* lies below *AVC* for some levels of output only in the classical case with indivisibility.)

Figure 7.3 also has the marginal revenue curves associated with a number of different market prices. If the market price were below $\bar{P}_a$, *MC* is always greater than *MR* and the firm would not produce. If the price were exactly $\bar{P}_a$, the firm would be indifferent to producing between 0 and Q_a units of output. At any market price between $\bar{P}_a$ and $\bar{P}_c$, such as $\bar{P}_b$, *MR* is greater than *MC* up to Q_a, and the firm would supply Q_a units. If the price were exactly $\bar{P}_c$, the firm is indifferent to any output between Q_a and Q_c. For all prices above $\bar{P}_c$, such as $\bar{P}_d$, *MR* is greater than *MC*, and the firm would produce Q_c units.

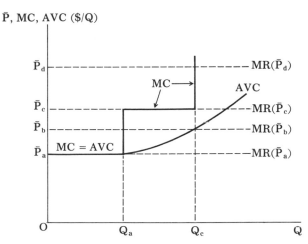

FIGURE 7.3 Optimal outputs at different prices: two-process production function

The *MC* curve can again be seen to give the relation between $\bar{P}$ and *Q* and is reproduced in Figure 7.4 as the supply curve. Notice that, in contrast to the classical case, the relation between the market price and output supplied is not a continuous curve. There are also some ambiguities in the quantities the firm would supply when the market price is exactly either $\bar{P}_a$ or $\bar{P}_c$.

Supply Curve of the Two-Product Firm. Let us now explore the relation between the market price for a particular product and the quantity of that product the firm would supply when the firm produces a second product that "competes" for an input in limited supply. Let us assume that the production function for each of the products consists of a single process.

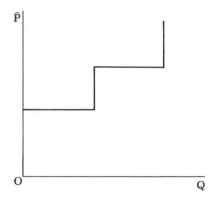

FIGURE 7.4   Firm's supply curve to market: two-process production
function

The construction of the supply curve for this case follows the techniques developed in Chapter 5 for finding the optimal output mix.
First, we determine the opportunity, or feasible, set of possible Q_1, Q_2
combinations. Figure 7.5 provides an illustration of such a feasible
set. The second step is to construct the cash-flow objective function,
part of which is $\bar{P}_1$, the market price for Q_1, which is the product
whose supply curve we are interested in. If we now assume some
value for $\bar{P}_1$, we can determine the optimal Q_1, Q_2 mix. The value of
Q_1 associated with that value of $\bar{P}_1$ provides one point on the firm's
supply curve of Q_1. If we now select a second value for $\bar{P}_1$, we can once
again calculate the optimum Q_1, Q_2 mix. This second $\bar{P}_1, Q_1$ combination gives a second point on the supply curve. By repeating this procedure for all values of $\bar{P}_1$, we can derive the whole supply curve for Q_1.

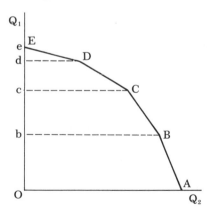

FIGURE 7.5 Q_1, Q_2 opportunity set: two-product firm

Let us investigate the objective function closely. If $\bar{P}_1$ and $\bar{P}_2$ are
the output prices, $\bar{p}_1$ and $\bar{p}_2$ are the prices of the variable inputs used

in products 1 and 2 respectively, and k_1 and k_2 are the technological coefficients that determine the quantities of the variable inputs required per unit of Q_1 and Q_2 respectively, then the cash-flow function is

$$Z = (\bar{P}_1 - \bar{p}_1 k_1)Q_1 + (\bar{P}_2 - \bar{p}_2 k_2)Q_2. \tag{7.1}$$

A solution of equation 7.1 for Q_1 gives

$$Q_1 = \frac{Z}{(\bar{P}_1 - \bar{p}_1 k_1)} - \frac{(\bar{P}_2 - \bar{p}_2 k_2)}{(\bar{P}_1 - \bar{p}_1 k_1)}Q_2. \tag{7.2}$$

The terms in parentheses are, of course, the cash flows associated with one unit of either Q_1 or Q_2.

The ratio of the two cash flows $-(\bar{P}_2 - \bar{p}_2 k_2)$ for product 2 and $(\bar{P}_1 - \bar{p}_1 k_1)$ for product 1 – can be seen to determine the slope of the isocash-flow lines. Notice what happens to the slope of these lines if $\bar{P}_1$ is changed, with all other parameters remaining the same. If $\bar{P}_1$ were made smaller, the cash flow from Q_1 would decrease and the slope of the cash-flow lines would become more steep. On the other hand, if $\bar{P}_1$ is made larger, the cash flow per unit of Q_1 is greater and the slope of the isocash-flow lines becomes gentler. Figure 7.6 provides two examples of the isocash-flow lines – when $\bar{P}_1$ is "low" (panel 1), and when $\bar{P}_1$ is "high" (panel 2).

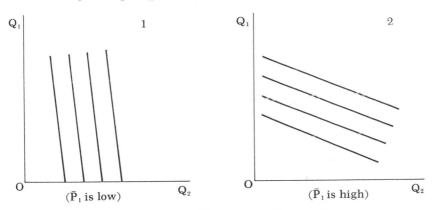

FIGURE 7.6   Influence of P_1 on slope of isocash-flow map

The optimal output mix is determined by superimposing the isocash-flow map on the feasible set and selecting the point from the set lying on the highest isocash-flow line. One of the corners of the feasible set will be an optimal Q_1, Q_2 combination – with point O optimal only when the cash flows from both products are negative.

Referring to Figure 7.5, we can now ask how much Q_1 the firm would produce at different market prices, $\bar{P}_1$. If $\bar{P}_1$ is very low, the isocash-flow map would be very steep, and the optimal output combination is at point A. Hence the firm does not produce any Q_1. A little thought would show that the firm would select the A output combination as long as the slope of the isocash-flow is steeper than the AB segment of the production possibility frontier. If $\bar{P}_1$ were now increased, the slope of the isocash-flow map would become gentler. There will be some value of $\bar{P}_1$ at which the slope of the isocash-flow lines would be the same as the slope of the AB segment. At this price any point on the AB segment is equally desirable to the firm. We can say that for all values of $\bar{P}_1$ below this price, the firm would not supply any Q_1.

Say now that the value of $\bar{P}_1$ is increased to the point where the slope of the isocash-flow lines is gentler than the AB segment but steeper than the BC segment. The optimal output mix would then be at point B, and the firm would supply b units of Q_1 to the market. If we continue to raise $\bar{P}_1$, the isocash-flow lines would continue to become gentler, and at some value for $\bar{P}_1$ the slope of the isocash flow lines will be the same as the slope of the BC segment. At that price the firm is indifferent between all output combinations on the BC segment.

There is a *range* of prices at which the firm will select the output mix designated by point B. The lower limit for these prices is the price at which the isocash-flow lines have the same slope as the AB segment. The upper limit for these prices is the price at which the slope of the isocash-flow lines is the same as the slope of the BC segment. We can say that the firm will supply b units of Q_1 for all values of $\bar{P}_1$ for which the slope of the isocash-flow lines is steeper than the slope of the BC segment but gentler than the slope of the AB segment.

We can obviously continue to increase the value of $\bar{P}_1$ to determine the effect on the amount of Q_1 supplied to the market. When the value of $\bar{P}_1$ is such that the slope of the isocash-flow lines is steeper than the CD segment but gentler than the BC segment, the firm will supply c units of Q_1. Similarly, for those prices in which the slope of the isocash-flow line is steeper than segment DE but gentler than the CD segment, the firm will supply d units. And, finally, when the value of $\bar{P}_1$ is so high that the slope of the isocash-flow lines is gentler than the DE segment, the firm will supply e units of Q_1 and will not produce any Q_2. The supply curve for product 1 would take the "stair-step" form as shown in Figure 7.7.[3]

Effect of the Price of a Variable Input on the Firm's Short-Run Supply Curve. We have been assuming that all the constraint parameters are constant values, except for the demand curve for the firm's output — that is, the market price. Let us now investigate what happens to the firm's supply curve to the market when the supply constraint of a variable input changes. We assume that the firm's purchases do not affect the price of the input, so that a change in an input price completely describes the change in this supply curve's parameters.

The procedure for deducing the effect of a change in a constraint

[3]For each value of $\bar{P}_1$, we also obtain the value of Q_2 the firm would supply. This relation could be interesting for some types of problems.

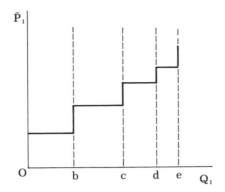

FIGURE 7.7   Supply curve to market of product 1 for two-product firm

parameter on the firm's supply curve to the market has already been described. In this case, we first assume one value for the input price and derive the supply curve. We then select another value for the input price and derive a second supply curve. A comparison of the two supply curves enables us to determine how the input price influences the whole supply curve.

Let us consider first the effect of an input price change when the firm's production function is classical with indivisibility of the fixed input. If the input price were to become smaller, both the *MC* and *AVC* curves would be lower for any level of output. Figure 7.8 depicts the *MC* and *AVC* curves for higher and lower prices of the variable input. The solid lines show the higher price of variable input; the dashed lines, the lower price. The same reasoning holds as before for obtaining the optimal output associated with each possible market price: It will still be the portion of the *MC* curve lying above the *AVC*

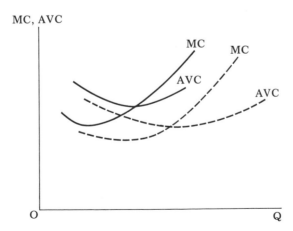

FIGURE 7.8   *MC* and *AVC* curves at two different price levels for variable input

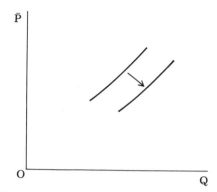

FIGURE 7.9   Shift in supply curve resulting from decrease in price of
variable input

curve. Figure 7.9 shows the supply curves corresponding to the two
input prices. It is clear that a decrease in the price of the variable
input "shifts" the supply curve in the SE direction. The firm would
be willing to supply more at the lower input price for any output
price and would also be willing to "start" supplying at a lower output
price. Conversely, an increase in the input price would shift the supply
curve in the NW direction.

The same procedure can be followed for any one-product firm with
any type of production function. We simply deduce the marginal cost
curves at the alternative values for the variable input price. These
MC curves provide the basis for the supply curves, and we can always
compare these supply curves to ascertain the effect of a change in
the price of the variable input on the supply curve. As a general
proposition, a lower input price shifts the supply curve in the SE
direction, and a higher input price shifts the supply curve in the
NW direction.

The procedure for determining the impact of a change in a variable
input price on the supply curve of an output for a two-product firm
is basically the same, but a little more complex.

Let us reproduce the cash-flow equation 7.2:

$$Q_1 = \frac{Z}{(\bar{P}_1 - \bar{p}_1 k_1)} - \frac{(\bar{P}_2 - \bar{p}_2 k_2)}{(\bar{P}_1 - \bar{p}_1 k_1)} Q_2. \qquad (7.3)$$

What would happen to the slope of the cash-flow lines if $\bar{p}_1$ were reduced? If we assume that all the other parameters remain the same,
the cash flow from product 1 would increase and the slope of the cash-
flow lines would become gentler. Put another way, for any value of $\bar{P}_1$,
the cash-flow lines are gentler for a lower value of $\bar{p}_1$. Because the slope
of the cash-flow lines determines the optimal output mix (see Figure
7.5), a lower price for $\bar{p}_1$ implies that a lower output price, $\bar{P}_1$, is necessary for the isocash-flow lines to have any given slope. Thus a lower
value for $\bar{P}_1$ (than with a higher value for $\bar{p}_1$) is needed for the optimal

output mix to "move" from A to B to C, etc., in Figure 7.5. As a consequence, b, c, d, and e units of Q_1 would be produced at smaller values for $\bar{P}_1$, and the supply curve for Q_1 would "shift" as in Figure 7.10. If $\bar{p}_1$ were to become larger, a similar analysis would show that the supply curve would shift in the NW direction.

What would happen to the supply curve for Q_1 if $\bar{p}_2$, the price of the variable input used in Q_2, were to increase? A glance at equation 7.3 shows that a higher value for $\bar{p}_2$, ceteris paribus, would decrease the cash flow from a unit of product 2. A decrease in this cash flow would by itself make the slope of the isocash-flow map gentler. The decrease in the cash flow from product 2 also means that a lower value of $\bar{P}_1$ is necessary than before for the optimal output mix to move, in Figure 7.5, from A to B to C, etc. Consequently, the firm would produce b, c, d, and e units of Q_1 at lower values for $\bar{P}_1$ than it would if $\bar{p}_2$ were lower. We can thus deduce that a higher value of $\bar{p}_2$ would shift the supply curve in the SE direction, in much the same manner as shown in Figure 7.10. Of course, a decrease in the value of $\bar{p}_2$ would shift the Q_1 supply curve in the NW direction.

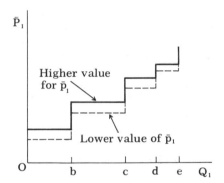

FIGURE 7.10 Effect of price of variable input used in product 1 in product 1 supply curve: two-product firm

Effect of a Price Change in a "Rival" Product. When a firm produces two or more products that use a common input in fixed supply, we should expect a change in the output price of one product to affect the supply curve of the other. To see this, let us consider once more equation 7.2 (reproduced as equation 7.4):

$$Q_1 = \frac{Z}{(\bar{P}_1 - \bar{p}_1 k_1)} - \frac{(\bar{P}_2 - \bar{p}_2 k_2)}{(\bar{P}_1 - \bar{p}_1 k_1)} Q_2. \tag{7.4}$$

Let us say that we continue to be interested in the supply curve of Q_1. Say $\bar{P}_2$ were to rise. Then, clearly, the cash flow per unit of product 2 increases and, ceteris paribus, the slope of the isocash-flow lines becomes steeper. For the slope of the isocash-flow lines to be such that, say, point B in Figure 7.5 is the optimal output mix, a higher value of $\bar{P}_1$ is required than would have been necessary had $\bar{P}_2$ been a lower value. Similarly, with a higher value of $\bar{P}_2$, a higher value of $\bar{P}_1$ is required for each of the other corner points in Figure 7.5 to be optimal. A higher value for $\bar{P}_2$ would therefore shift the $\bar{P}_1, Q_1$ supply curve to the NW direction much the same as the higher value for $\bar{p}_1$ in Figure 7.10. Conversely, a lower value for $\bar{P}_2$ would shift the $\bar{P}_1, Q_1$ supply curve in the SE direction.

An Improvement in Technology. The two-product model is also useful to explore the effect of changes in technology on the supply curve. Consider once more the cash-flow equation 7.2:

$$Q_1 = \frac{Z}{(\bar{P}_1 - \bar{p}_1 k_1)} - \frac{(\bar{P}_2 - \bar{p}_2 k_2)}{(\bar{P}_1 - \bar{p}_1 k_1)} Q_2. \qquad (7.5)$$

What if less of input 1 is required per unit of Q_1? This implies that k_1 in equation 7.5 becomes a smaller number. With k_1 smaller, ceteris paribus, the cash flow per unit of Q_1 increases, and the isocash-flow map has a gentler slope. For the isocash-flow map to have a slope so that point B in Figure 7.5 is the optimal output combination, the decrease in k_1 implies that $\bar{P}_1$ could be a smaller value. Thus, with a lower value of k_1, a lower value of $\bar{P}_1$ is required for the firm to supply b units of Q_1. By similar reasoning, lower values of $\bar{P}_1$ are needed for the firm to produce c, d, e units of Q_1. Consequently, an improvement in technology in the use of a variable input in the production of product 1 would shift the $\bar{P}_1, Q_1$ supply curve in the SE direction, in much the same manner as shown in Figure 7.10.

What if the improvement in technology is in the use of input 2 in the production of product 2? Such an improvement would reduce k_2 and, ceteris paribus, would increase the cash flow per unit of Q_2. This would mean that a higher value of $\bar{P}_1$ than before would be necessary for the slope of the isocash-flow line to be such that b, c, d, or e units of Q_1 are produced. As a consequence, the $\bar{P}_1, Q_1$ supply curve would shift in the NW direction. It would, of course, still maintain its "stair-step" shape.

An improvement in technology of the use of the fixed inputs would also affect the $\bar{P}_1, Q_1$ supply curve. If smaller amounts of the fixed inputs are required per unit of Q_1 or Q_2, the Q_1, Q_2 production possibility function would be "pushed out," as, for example, in Figure 7.11. The optimal solutions would be at the new corners, each of which consists of more $Q_1 Q_2$. Thus, for a value of $\bar{P}_1$ great enough to produce an output mix with some Q_1, the quantity of Q_1 would be greater. The shift in the $\bar{P}_1, Q_1$ supply curve would therefore be as in Figure 7.12. The shape as well as the position of the supply curve could also change, which would depend upon the new configuration of the production possibility frontier.

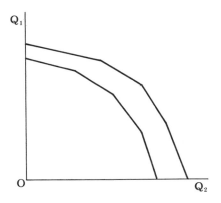

FIGURE 7.11   Effect of improved technology in use of fixed inputs on Q_1, Q_2 opportunity set

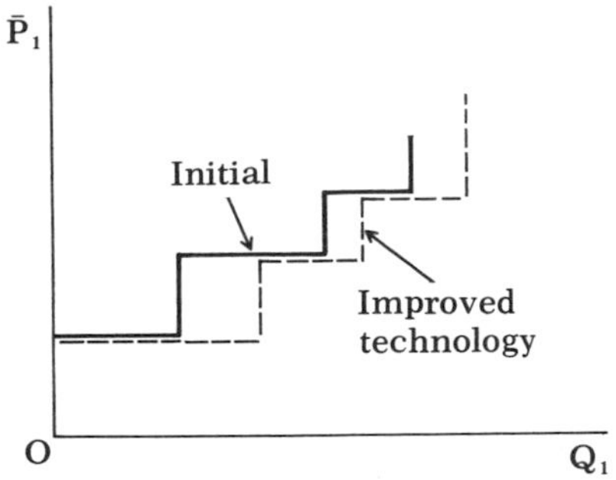

FIGURE 7.12   Effect of improved technology on supply curve of product 1: two-product case

Let us now turn to a one-product firm whose production function consists of a single process:

$$x_1 = 2Q \qquad (7.6)$$
$$x_2 = 3Q, \qquad (7.7)$$

which implies that

$$x_1 = \frac{2}{3} x_2.$$

Let us now say that x_2 is limited to 300 units, so that, according to equation 7.7, the maximum possible output is 100 units.

We first calculate the output cost function. In terms of inputs the cost function is

$$TC = \bar{p}_1 x_1 + \bar{p}_2 \bar{x}_2. \qquad (7.8)$$

Substituting for x_1 from equation 7.6 gives us the output cost function, which is shown with the condition that Q cannot be greater than 100:

$$TC = \bar{p}_1 2Q + \bar{p}_2 \bar{x}_2, \qquad Q \leq 100.$$

Marginal cost is then

$$MC = \frac{d(TC)}{dQ} = 2\bar{p}_1, \qquad Q \leq 100.$$

With the marginal cost curve as the supply curve, the supply curve would appear as in Figure 7.13.

Say now there is an improvement in technology such that the production function becomes

$$x_2 = 1Q$$
$$x_2 = 2Q.$$

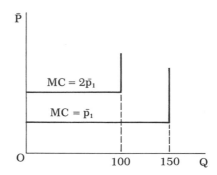

FIGURE 7.13   Effect of improved technology on supply curve: one-process
production function

With the decrease in k_2 from 3 to 2, the firm could now produce 150
units of Q. With 1Q now substituted for x_1 in equation 7.8, the MC
curve is now

$$MC = 1\bar{p}_1, \qquad Q \leq 150.$$

The result of both changes in the ks is that the supply curve shifts to
the SE direction as shown in Figure 7.13. The firm would be willing
to supply at a lower value for $\bar{P}$ and would supply a larger quantity
per period of time.

Effect of More Fixed Assets. In many ways an increase in the quantity
of the fixed assets should change the $\bar{P}_1, Q_1$ supply curve as does an
improvement in technology. Consider the two-product model. More
of the fixed assets would "push out" the production possibility frontier
as in Figure 7.11, although the exact nature of the new production
possibility frontier would depend on which fixed assets are expanded
and by how much. The same procedure as before is used to derive
the $\bar{P}_1, Q_1$ supply curve, which should shift in the SE direction in much
the same way as in Figure 7.12.

In our one-product one-process example in the preceding section,
the effect of more $\bar{x}_2$ would increase the maximum quantity the firm
could produce. If the technological coefficient relating x_1 to Q remained at 2, however, the only effect upon the MC curve would be
to change it from

$$MC = 2\bar{p}_1, \qquad Q \leq 100$$

to

$$MC = 2\bar{p}_1, \qquad Q \leq 150.$$

Then the corresponding supply curve in Figure 7.13 would have only
the vertical portion shift from Q = 100 to Q = 150.

Let us examine, finally, the classical case. More fixed assets would
raise the fixed costs. But diminishing returns would not set in till

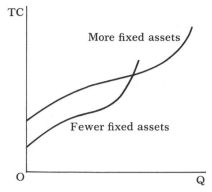

FIGURE 7.14 Effect of more fixed assets on *TC* curve: classical model with indivisibility

higher levels of output are reached, and the total cost curves could appear as in Figure 7.14. The *AVC* and *MC* curves corresponding to these *TC* curves are shown in Figure 7.15. With the *MC* curve farther to the right with the higher fixed assets, it is clear that the increase in assets has the effect of shifting the $\bar{P}, Q$ supply curve to the right; that is, the firm would supply more Q to the market at any value of $\bar{P}$.

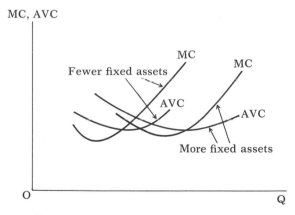

FIGURE 7.15 Effect of more fixed assets on *MC* and *AVC* curves: classical model with indivisibility

An Algebraic View of the Supply Curve. The mathematically tractable Cobb-Douglas production function enables us to see the whole picture of the supply curve. In Chapter 5, we were able to express the optimal value of Q in terms of a single equation 5.39, here reproduced:

$$Q_{\text{opt}} = \left[\frac{\bar{P}}{\frac{\bar{p}_1}{\alpha} \left(\frac{1}{a \bar{x}_2^\beta} \right)^{1/\alpha}} \right]^{\frac{1}{1/\alpha - 1}} \quad (7.9)$$

In this equation, $\bar{P}$ is the market price for the output, $\bar{p}_1$ is the price of the variable input, $\bar{x}_2$ is the quantity of the fixed input, and a, α, and β are the parameters of the production function

$$Q = ax_1^\alpha x_2^\beta. \tag{7.10}$$

Equation 7.9 is complicated, but it enables us to see many relationships.

If we have a set of values for the parameters $\bar{p}_1$, $\bar{x}_2$, a, α, and β, equation 7.9 tells us the quantity the firm would produce for any value of $\bar{P}$. This equation can, therefore, be viewed as that firm's supply curve.

We could examine, with the help of this equation, the effect of a change in the various parameters on the relation between $\bar{P}$, the market price, and the quantity the firm would produce and supply to the market, Q_{opt}. If, for example, $\bar{p}_1$ were to become a larger number, a careful examination of equation 7.9 shows that Q_{opt} would be smaller for any value of $\bar{P}$. Consequently, the supply curve would shift in the NW direction. On the other hand, a higher value for $\bar{x}_2$, the fixed assets, would result in a higher value for Q_{opt} for any value of $\bar{P}$. Thus, the supply curve shifts to the SE. Higher values for a, α, or β, all of which would reflect improvements in technology, would result in a SE shift of the supply curve.[4] Changes in these parameters, particularly α, could also change the shape of the supply curve.

Other Factors Influencing the Supply Curve. We have shown how the position and shape of the firm's short-run supply curve, defined as the relationship between the market price and the output supplied to the market, is influenced by the following factors—the prices of variable inputs, the price of rival goods in production, the amount of fixed assets, the various technological coefficients. Other factors can influence the supply curve. Price expectations in the future are often an important determinant of the position and shape of the firm's supply curve. If a higher price is expected in the future, the firm may not offer for sale all its output but may instead build up its inventory. Expectations of higher prices could therefore shift the supply curve in the NW direction. Conversely, an expectation of a lower price could lead the firm to offer goods for sale from its inventories as well as from its current production. Sometimes the supply curve of the firm is not completely under the control of the firm but may depend on the weather, strikes, wars, and so forth. Real-world firms have to take these into consideration. Sometimes, the short-run supply curve depends on former prices. Farmers, for example, have to make commitments in planting before they know what the output price will be and

---

[4]We must be careful when discussing the technological coefficients α and β, because α and β are often expected to add to unity. Thus, a technological change that raises one of these exponents would often reduce the other.

are often guided by the most recent prices. Various public policy measures such as taxes, controls on output (such as in agriculture), minimum wage laws, and the disallowance of the use of certain types of production processes could also influence the supply curve. Indeed, an important use of this type of analysis is to test the effect of various public policy measures on the supply curve.

The Short-Run Market Supply Curve. The short-run market supply curve is the relation between market prices and the quantities that all sellers are willing to supply to that market. It is conceptually obtained by "adding together" the supply curves of all the firms selling in that market. To get one point on the market supply curve, a market price is selected and the quantities all sellers are willing to sell at that price are added together. This market price and the sum of these quantities provide one point on the market supply curve. All other points on the market supply curve can be similarly obtained by repeating this procedure for different market prices.

Because the market supply curve is the sum of the supply curves of the selling firms, it will tend to shift and change its shape for the same reasons the firm's supply curve shifts or changes shape. There is one additional reason why the market supply curve could shift. It can shift to the SE if new selling firms enter the market or to the NW if existing sellers leave the market.

From our analysis, then, the market supply curve would shift to the right (or the SE)—that is, the sellers would be willing to sell more at each alternative output market price—for the following reasons: a fall in the price of a variable input used in producing that product; a fall in the prices of other products the firms could produce; a rise in the price of a variable input used in rival products; an increase in the firms' fixed assets; improvements in technology; the entry of new firms; expectations of lower prices in the future; and good weather (sometimes). Shifts of the market supply curve to the left would be for the opposite reasons.

There is one more important attribute of the market supply curve — the "elasticity" of the quantity supplied with respect to the price. If an increase in the price leads to a relatively large increase in the quantity supplied, we say the supply curve is elastic. If, on the other hand, an increase in the price leads to a relatively small increase in quantity supplied, we say the supply curve is inelastic.

THE FIRM'S DEMAND FOR A VARIABLE INPUT

In demand analysis, products and services are divided into two categories—(1) consumer products and services that directly satisfy consumer wants and (2) intermediate products and services that firms require for production. The demand for intermediate products and services is "derived": The firm's demand for them ultimately depends upon the demand for consumer goods and services. These intermediate products and services are often called factors of production and are generally divided into variable and fixed – depending on whether they are purchased by the firm as the result of short-run or long-run decisions.

The relationship between the input price and the quantity demanded is the firm's demand curve for an input. Like the supply curve of an output, the demand curves of all the buying firms in a market for an input can be added together to obtain the market demand curve. Also like the supply curve, "shift parameters" of the demand curves determine the position and shape of these curves.

This section is divided into a number of subsections. First, we discuss the general approach the firm would take toward the purchase of a variable input service – with an emphasis on labor services. Next we discuss the demand curve for a variable input for a firm with a Cobb-Douglas production function. We then examine the effect of some of the "shift parameters" on such a demand curve. After that, we turn to the demand curve for a variable input by a firm with a one-process production function. We also examine the effect on this demand curve of the various shift parameters. We emphasize these two production functions because of their convenient mathematical properties, and also because they are probably the most common in the real world. In all this work, we assume at first that the firm's output price is completely determined by the market. In a later subsection, we investigate the demand curve for a variable input when the demand curve facing the firm for its output slopes. We conclude this section with a subsection on the market demand curve for the input.

General Approach. Marginal reasoning can provide immediate insight into the basic procedure for deriving the firm's demand for a variable factor of production. Consider, for example, a firm, whose plant is fixed, in its search for the optimal amount of labor services to purchase. Let us say it weighs the purchase of one hour of labor. This unit of labor will produce some amount of output, which we call the marginal product of labor. If we multiply the marginal product by the price of the output, we obtain the value of the marginal product, which we label VMP. What should determine whether the firm should purchase this unit of labor? The answer will depend on whether the VMP is greater or smaller than the price of the unit of labor, which is the wage rate. If VMP is greater than $\bar{p}_1$, where $\bar{p}_1$ is the wage rate, then the purchase and use of the unit of labor produces more revenue to the firm than the associated expenditure, cash flow is positive, and marginal reasoning dictates that it should be purchased. Precisely the same reasoning would be applied to the second unit of labor, and it too should be purchased if its VMP is greater than $\bar{p}_1$. Extending this reasoning, the firm should continue to increase its purchases of labor so long as the VMP of each additional unit of labor exceeds $\bar{p}_1$. What will limit the firm's purchase of labor? The answer depends on whether the production function consists of a very large number of processes, such as the Cobb-Douglas and classical functions, or whether the production function consists of only one or a small number of processes.

When the production function is Cobb-Douglas, increasing amounts of labor lead to smaller and smaller increments in output when one or more of the other inputs is in fixed supply. These diminishing returns to labor occur because with increases in the variable input (labor), the firm uses production processes that have a continuously smaller ratio of the fixed to the variable input. Thus, the marginal product of each additional unit of labor, and the value of this marginal product as well, continuously fall as more labor is employed. At some level of labor input, the VMP should fall to the point where it just equals $\bar{p}_1$, the wage rate. Before this point is reached, VMP is greater than $\bar{p}_1$, cash flow from hiring labor is positive, and the firm should expand its use of labor. Beyond this point, VMP is less than $\bar{p}_1$, and cash flow is negative. Evidently, labor should be hired to just the level where VMP is equal to $\bar{p}_1$. This is an optimizing condition for the purchase of a variable output in much the same way that $MR = MC$ is an optimizing condition for the level of output. Indeed, the VMP can be considered the MR from hiring an additional unit of labor, and $\bar{p}_1$ can be considered the MC.

When the production function is classical with an indivisible fixed input, the problem is not so straightforward. This is because the MP at first increases with increases in the use of labor – in the uneconomic range of production processes. Thus, the VMP takes the shape shown in panel 2 of Figure 7.16 in contrast to the continuously falling VMP for the Cobb-Douglas shown in panel 1. We should apply the optimization rule that $VMP = \bar{p}_1$ not in the rising portion of the classical VMP curve but only in the portion that falls. The firm would never actually produce in the range where VMP rises (or MC falls).

When the production function consists of a single process, the limit on the amount of labor that should be hired will depend mainly on the amount of the fixed asset services. Consider a case in which 100

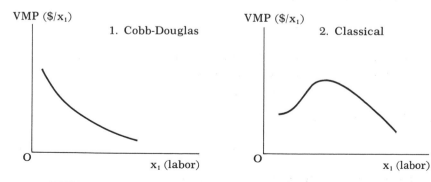

FIGURE 7.16 Value of marginal product of each unit of labor: Cobb-Douglas and classical production functions

hours of a machine is available per day and one hour of labor is used with one hour of machine time. If the value of the output of the first man-hour working with one hour of machine time is greater than the wage rate, marginal reasoning leads to the conclusion this man-hour should be hired. With a one-process production function, every additional man-hour will produce the same marginal output – and hence VMP – so long as there is a corresponding hour of machine time. Unlike the Cobb-Douglas and classical production functions, in which the proportion between labor and the fixed asset varies, the fixed proportions in the one-process production function imply that VMP will not fall as labor is expanded – if we assume that the output price is constant. Hence, there need be no amount of labor input for which $VMP = \bar{p}_1$. Instead, in our example the firm would purchase 100 man-hours of labor but would not purchase the one hundred first hour. For this last man-hour, the marginal product falls to zero, because there is no unit of machine time to combine with it.

Demand for a Variable Input: Cobb-Douglas Production Function. We first derive the demand curve for a variable input when the production function is Cobb-Douglas:

$$Q = a x_1^\alpha \bar{x}_2^\beta,$$

where x_1 is the variable input, labor, $\bar{x}_2$ is the fixed input, and a, α, and β are the parameters. The marginal product of labor is

$$MP_{x_1} = \frac{\Delta Q}{\Delta x_1},$$

that is, it is the ratio of the change in output to a change in the labor input. If we think of Δx_1 as being very small, we can use the calculus and define MP_{x_1} as

$$MP_{x_1} = \frac{\partial Q}{\partial x_1}.$$

Working this out gives us

$$MP_{x_1} = \frac{\partial(a x_1^\alpha \bar{x}_2^\beta)}{\partial x_1} = a\alpha x_1^{\alpha-1} \bar{x}_2^\beta.$$

The value of the marginal product is obtained by multiplying the marginal product by the output price. Thus,

$$VMP = \bar{P} a\alpha x_1^{\alpha-1} \bar{x}_2^\beta,$$

which can also be written

$$VMP = \frac{\bar{P} a\alpha \bar{x}_2^\beta}{x_1^{1-\alpha}}. \tag{7.11}$$

In equation 7.11 there is only one variable in the right-hand term, x_1; all the other symbols are constant parameters in this context.

Because α is generally a positive number that varies between zero and 1, the exponent of x_1 is a positive number. Thus, we can see that higher values of x_1 result in lower values for *VMP*. The general shape of the relation between *VMP* and x_1 is shown in Figure 7.17 ($\bar{p}_1$ designates the wage rate).

We can now turn to the firm's optimum purchase of x_1 for any value of $\bar{p}_1$, which we argued should be the value of x_1 for which $VMP = \bar{p}_1$. Figure 7.17 has in it three alternative wage rates, $\bar{p}_{1a}$, $\bar{p}_{1b}$, and $\bar{p}_{1c}$. Consider the optimal value for x_1 when the wage rate is $\bar{p}_{1a}$. For purchases less than a units of x_1, an expansion of x_1 results in $VMP > \bar{p}_{1a}$. Hence x_1 should be expanded. If the firm uses labor beyond a, the VMP produced by an additional unit of labor is less than the cost of this unit. Clearly the firm should not purchase more than a units of labor at that price. The amount of labor that should be purchased, therefore, is a units, which is where $VMP = \bar{p}_{1a}$. With precisely the same reasoning, b units of labor should be purchased when the price is $\bar{p}_{1b}$, and c units should be purchased when the price is $\bar{p}_{1c}$. It is quite obvious that, for any wage rate, the optimal purchase of labor is where the corresponding wage rate line intersects the *VMP* curve. Thus, the *VMP* curve itself, with $\bar{p}_1$ the axis, is the demand curve for labor. It is shown as Figure 7.18.

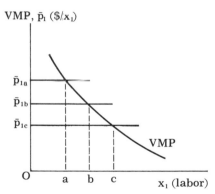

FIGURE 7.17   Optimal purchases of labor at different wage rates

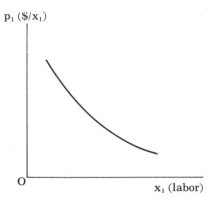

FIGURE 7.18   Firm's demand curve for labor: Cobb-Douglas

Because we know that the optimal use of labor is that at which $VMP = \bar{p}_1$, we can algebraically determine the demand curve — that is, the relation between $\bar{p}_1$ and x_1 — by substituting $\bar{p}_1$ for *VMP* in equation 7.11. Thus the demand curve can be written as

$$\bar{p}_1 = \frac{\bar{P}a\alpha\bar{x}_2^{\beta}}{x_1^{1-\alpha}}$$

or, alternatively,

$$x_1 = \left(\frac{\bar{P}a\alpha\bar{x}_2^{\beta}}{\bar{p}_1}\right)^{\frac{1}{1-\alpha}}. \tag{7.12}$$

In the latter form, with $\bar{P}$, a, α, β, and $\bar{x}_2$ all constant parameters, we can tell how much x_1 would be hired for any wage rate, $\bar{p}_1$. The parameters will determine the position and shape of this relationship.

Let us illustrate the derivation of this demand curve with some numbers. Say that the production function is

$$Q = 2x_1^{0.5}x_2^{0.5},$$

that x_2 is fixed at 400 units, and that the price of the output is \$5 per unit. We substitute 400 for x_2 to get

$$Q = 2x_1^{0.5}400^{0.5} = 40x_1^{0.5}.$$

The marginal product of labor is

$$MP_{x_1} = \frac{dQ}{dx_1} = \frac{d(40x_1^{0.5})}{dx_1} = \frac{20}{x_1^{0.5}}.$$

The value of the marginal product is the price of the output times the marginal product:

$$VMP = 5\left(\frac{20}{x_1^{0.5}}\right) = \frac{100}{x_1^{0.5}}.$$

Since $VMP = \bar{p}_1$ for an optimal value for x_1, we get the demand equation

$$\bar{p}_1 = \frac{100}{x_1^{0.5}}$$

or, alternatively,

$$x_1 = \left(\frac{100}{\bar{p}_1}\right)^2.$$

From this equation we can easily determine the amount of x_1 the firm would purchase for any value of $\bar{p}_1$.

Shifts in the Demand Curve: Cobb-Douglas. From equation 7.12 (reproduced as equation 7.13), we can determine how all the various parameters would shift the demand curve:

$$x_1 = \left(\frac{\bar{P}a\alpha\bar{x}_2^{\beta}}{\bar{p}_1}\right)^{\frac{1}{1-\alpha}}. \tag{7.13}$$

What if $\bar{P}$, the output price, were to become larger? An analysis of equation 7.13 shows that, if everything else remains the same, more x_1 would be purchased at each value of $\bar{p}_1$ than before the rise in $\bar{P}$. We can therefore say that a rise in the price of the output would shift the demand curve for labor to the right. Conversely, a lower output price would shift this demand curve to the left.

What if $\bar{x}_2$, the amount of the fixed asset services, were to be increased? A similar analysis of equation 7.13 shows that more x_1 would be purchased at any level of $\bar{p}_1$. Thus, a greater investment in fixed assets leads to a greater demand for labor at each possible wage rate.

The other three parameters that influence the position and shape of the demand curve for labor are a, α, and β, which are also the parameters of the Cobb-Douglas production function shown as $Q = ax_1^\alpha x_2^\beta$. From this production function it can be seen that increases in the value of a, α, or β, ceteris paribus, increase the quantity of Q that can be obtained for any quantity of the input services, x_1 and x_2. Hence, these parameters reflect productivity. From equation 7.13, it can be seen that an increase in either a or β would lead to a larger amount of labor hired at each wage rate. The effect of an increase in α, which directly reflects labor productivity, is more complex. Because α is in the exponent of 7.13 an increase in α would change the shape of the demand curve, making it more "steep" as in Figure 7.19. This steepness implies that with an increase in labor productivity the demand for labor is less responsive to changes in the wage rate, a very interesting deduction indeed. We can infer that the higher the productivity of labor, the smaller will be the loss in employment if the wage rate rises.

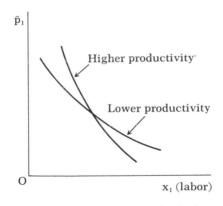

FIGURE 7.19   Effect of labor productivity on firm's demand curve for labor

Demand for a Variable Input: One-Process Production Function. Let us investigate the firm's demand for x_1, labor, when the production function consists of a single process, designated as

$$x_1 = k_1 Q \qquad (7.14)$$
$$x_2 = k_2 Q$$

where, by using equalities, we assume neither of these inputs will be wasted.

By solving one of these equations for Q and substituting for Q in the other equation, we obtain the relation

$$x_1 = \frac{k_1}{k_2} x_2. \tag{7.15}$$

This equation implies that x_1 and x_2 are used in fixed proportion, which is determined by the ratio of the technological coefficients. If x_2, which is, say, the services of the fixed asset, is limited to $\bar{x}_2$, equation 7.15 implies that the maximum amount of labor that can be efficiently employed is $(k_1/k_2)\bar{x}_2$.

Let us now apply our procedures to obtain the firm's demand curve for labor. First, solve equation 7.14 for Q, which gives

$$Q = \frac{1}{k_1} x_1.$$

Now we find the marginal product of labor:

$$MP_{x_1} = \frac{dQ}{dx_1} = \frac{d\left(\frac{1}{k_1} x_1\right)}{dx_1} = \frac{1}{k_1}.$$

The marginal product is constant; each unit of labor produces the same increment in output. This is in sharp contrast to the Cobb-Douglas case, where we found that each additional unit of labor leads to a smaller increment in output than the previous unit of labor; the marginal product of labor fell as we increased the labor input.

In the one-process case, labor can be used only up to the point where the full amount of the fixed services is used. If labor is expanded beyond that point, there are no fixed assets to combine with the additional labor, and the marginal product of the labor drops to zero. Equation 7.15 shows us the maximum amount of labor that can be efficiently used, which, when x_2 is fixed at $\bar{x}_2$, is $(k_1/k_2)\bar{x}_2$. Thus, we can say that the marginal product of labor is $1/k_1$ only in the range in which x_1 varies between 0 and $(k_1/k_2)\bar{x}_2$. Using this side condition, the formula for the marginal product of labor should therefore be

$$MP_{x_1} = \frac{1}{k_1}, \qquad 0 \le x_1 \le \frac{k_1}{k_2} \bar{x}_2.$$

The value of the marginal product of labor is obtained by multiplying the marginal product by the output price, $\bar{P}$. The side condition still holds, so

$$VMP_{x_1} = \bar{P} \frac{1}{k_1}, \qquad 0 \le x_1 \le \frac{k_1}{k_2} \bar{x}_2.$$

Clearly, the VMP is still a constant amount that does not depend on the amount of labor employed. However, the VMP will also drop to zero if the firm tries to expand labor beyond $(k_1/k_2)\bar{x}_2$. The *VMP* "curve"

VMP, $\bar{p}_1$ ($/x_1$)

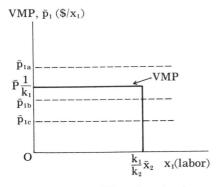

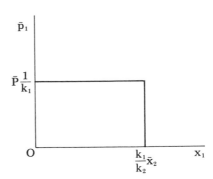

FIGURE 7.20 *VMP* and optimal
labor purchases: single-process
production function

FIGURE 7.21   Demand curve for
labor: single-process production
function

for this one-process case is shown in Figure 7.20. It is a horizontal
line up to the maximum amount of labor that can be efficiently used,
at which point it drops to zero.

According to our marginal reasoning, the firm should hire labor so
long as $VMP_{x_1} > \bar{p}_1$, where $\bar{p}_1$ is the wage rate. If, as in Figure 7.20,
the wage rate is $\bar{p}_{1a}$, the firm should hire no labor. But if the wage
rate is either p_{1b} or p_{1c}, as in Figure 7.20, the firm should hire the maximum amount of labor that can be efficiently used. To generalize, we
can say the firm will hire either zero or $(k_1/k_2)\bar{x}_2$ units of labor. It will
not hire any labor if $VMP_{x_1} < \bar{p}_1$ but will hire the maximum efficient
amount of labor, $(k_1/k_2)\bar{x}_2$, if $VMP_{x_1} > \bar{p}_1$. The *VMP* "curve" is therefore
the firm's demand curve for labor. This demand curve is shown in
Figure 7.21.

It is worth contrasting the demand curves in the Cobb-Douglas and
one-process cases. When there is continuous substitutability of labor
for capital, as in the Cobb-Douglas production function, the quantity
of labor the firm will hire is responsive to the wage rate. But when
capital and labor are used in fixed proportions, the demand for labor
is an all-or-nothing affair. If the wage rate is above the VMP of labor,
no labor would be demanded. But if the wage rate is below the VMP,
the firm would hire the full amount of labor that can be used, given
the limitation on the fixed assets. These differences hold true, however, only when all prices are determined by the market and are not
influenced by the firm's output level or purchases of labor.

A numerical example might help in understanding the construction of the demand curve for labor (or any variable input) when there
is a single-process production function. Let us say the production
function is

$$x_1 = 2Q \qquad\qquad (7.16)$$
$$x_2 = 3Q$$

so that x_1 and x_2 are used in the following fixed proportions:

$$x_1 = \frac{2}{3}x_2.$$

Let us also say that x_2 is limited to 300 units per time period. Thus, the maximum amount of labor that can be efficiently used is

$$x_{1\max} = \frac{2}{3}\,300 = 200.$$

Let us also say the price of the output, $\bar{P}$, is \$5.

First, we solve equation 7.16 for Q, to obtain

$$Q = \frac{1}{2}x_1.$$

The marginal product of labor is then

$$MP_{x_1} = \frac{dQ}{dx_1} = \frac{d\left(\frac{1}{2}x_1\right)}{dx_1} = \frac{1}{2}.$$

That is, every unit of labor produces 1/2 unit of output so long as there is sufficient x_2. The value of the marginal product is

$$VMP_{x_1} = \$5(1/2) = \$2.50.$$

The demand curve for labor is then as shown in Figure 7.22. The firm would not hire any labor if the wage rate is above \$2.50 but would hire 200 units of labor if the wage rate is below \$2.50. If the wage rate is exactly \$2.50, the firm is indifferent; it may or may not hire labor.

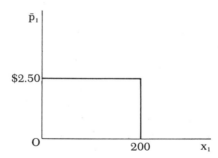

FIGURE 7.22   Demand curve for labor: single-process production function (numerical example)

Changes in the Demand for a Variable Input: One-Process Production Function. What would change the firm's demand curve for a variable input such as labor? This question can be answered by analyzing the various parameters that determine the demand curve, as in Figure 7.21.

Let us say that the output price, $\bar{P}$, rises. Then the horizontal portion of the demand curve rises. The firm would be willing to hire labor at a higher wage rate than before, because the higher value of $\bar{P}$ raises the VMP. However, the firm would hire the same amount of labor, if it hires at all. Thus, the higher price of the output raises the threshold wage rate at which the firm hires labor but not the quantity that would be hired below the threshold wage rate.

Let us now say that $\bar{x}_2$, the amount of fixed asset services, is expanded. Such a change shifts the vertical portion of the demand curve to the right. This shift would not affect the threshold wage rate at which the firm would hire but would increase the amount of labor the firm would hire at any wage rate below the VMP.

What if there is an improvement in the technological use of x_2? This implies that less x_2 is required per unit of Q; that is, k_2 becomes smaller. Such a change in k_2 would also shift the vertical portion of the demand curve to the right. (See Figure 7.21.) Its effect on the demand for labor is similar to that of an increase in $\bar{x}_2$.

The analysis of an improvement in the technological use of labor is more complex. Such an improvement would be reflected in a smaller value for the coefficient k_1; that is, less labor is required per unit of output. Because the marginal product of labor was shown to be $1/k_1$, a decrease in k_1 raises the marginal product of labor. The VMP is also increased, so that the horizontal part of the demand curve in Figure 7.21 is raised. Thus, the threshold wage rate at which the firm would hire is raised.

The decrease in k_1 will also affect the vertical portion of the demand curve; this portion would move to the left. This implies the firm would hire less labor than before for wage rates below the threshold. Our numerical example used in the preceding section could make this clear. If $k_1 = 2$, $k_2 = 3$, and $\bar{x}_2 = 300$, it was shown that the firm would hire 200 units of labor if the wage rate were below VMP. But if k_1 falls to, say, 1, one unit of labor is used with 3 units of the fixed asset service, and, with $\bar{x}_2$ limited to 300, only 100 units of labor are required.

An improvement in labor efficiency thus has a dual effect in the one-process case: It raises the maximum wage rate at which the firm is willing to hire labor, but it decreases the amount of labor the firm will hire. These are the immediate results. In the long run, the improved labor productivity could lead to a large expansion in $\bar{x}_2$ and an increase in the quantity of labor the firm would hire at appropriate wage rates.

A Sloping Demand Curve for the Output. Thus far, we have been working under the assumption that the price of the output is determined by the market and therefore does not vary with the firm's output. Thus the value of the marginal product of using an additional unit of x_1, the variable input, is obtained by multiplying the marginal product by a constant output price. However, it is frequently the case that the demand curve for the firm's output slopes, so that additional output can be sold only if the firm's selling price is reduced. Such an output demand curve complicates the construction of the *VMP* curve, because the use of more of the input increases the output, which in turn leads to a lower price on *all* the output, which in turn decreases the additional cash inflow from the use of each additional unit of the variable input.

It might be helpful to construct a simple example to illustrate the problems. Say a firm can sell 1 unit of output at $10; 2 units of output at $9; 3 units of output at $8; etc. Let us also say that a one-process production function exists and, as long as there are sufficient amounts of the fixed input, x_2, each unit of the variable unit, x_1 (labor), results in one additional unit of output.

Consider now the value of the marginal product of the first unit of labor. It produces one unit of output, which is worth $10. Say now we consider the *VMP* of the second unit of labor. It too produces one unit. But, if we assume the firm sells at a single price, the first and second units of output, which now sell at $9 per unit, result in a revenue of $18. Thus the additional revenue to the firm from using the second unit of labor is not $9, the value of the second unit of output, but $8, the difference between the $18 from selling two units and the $10 in revenue from one unit. The additional revenue associated with the second unit of labor is not $9, the value of the second unit of output, because the price has been lowered by $1 on the first unit. Consider now the hiring of the third unit of labor. The third unit of output could be sold only if the price on all three units drops to $8. Thus the total revenue from the three units is $24, and the additional revenue from using the third unit of labor is $6. The fourth unit of labor is used to produce the fourth unit of output. The price of all four units of output falls to $7; the total revenue becomes $28; and the additional revenue from using the fourth unit of labor is $4.

The additional revenue associated with each additional unit of labor when the output demand curve slopes is known as the marginal revenue product (*MRP*). The following table shows, for this simple illustration, the calculation of the *MRP* for each unit of labor:

x_1	Q	P	Total Revenue	MRP
1	1	$10	$10	$10
2	2	9	18	8
3	3	8	24	6
4	4	7	28	4
5	5	6	30	2

The same marginal reasoning holds as before in the purchase of labor. The firm would increase the amount of labor it would hire as long as the MRP is greater than $\bar{p}_1$, the wage rate. It would hire labor up to the point where MRP is equal to $\bar{p}_1$ as long as there are sufficient amounts of x_2 to combine with the labor. Thus, the MRP curve is the firm's demand curve for labor in exactly the same way as was the VMP curve.

The MRP curve can always be calculated as in the table. Another method exists for calculating the MRP curve if the production function is mathematically tractable, as are the Cobb-Douglas and one-process production functions. We would first express total revenue in terms of output. Next we would use the production function to express total revenue in terms of the variable input, which we call the revenue product curve. Then we could get the MRP curve by taking the first derivative of the revenue product curve with respect to the variable input.

Let us illustrate the procedure with the one-process production function:

$$x_1 = k_1 Q \qquad (7.17)$$
$$x_2 = k_2 Q.$$

From these equations we have, as before,

$$x_1 = \frac{k_1}{k_2} x_2,$$

and, if x_2 is limited to $\bar{x}_2$, the maximum quantity of x_1 that can be efficiently employed is $(k_1/k_2)\bar{x}_2$. Notice that equation 7.17 can also be written as

$$Q = \frac{x_1}{k_1}. \qquad (7.18)$$

Let us now say the demand curve can be expressed as

$$P = b - cQ.$$

Then total revenue in terms of output is

$$TR = PQ = (b - cQ)Q = bQ - cQ^2. \qquad (7.19)$$

We can express the TR curve in terms of x_1 by using equation 7.18 to substitute for Q in equation 7.19. The RP (revenue product) curve, is:

$$RP = b\left(\frac{x_1}{k_1}\right) - c\left(\frac{x_1}{k_1}\right)^2, \qquad x_1 \le \frac{k_1}{k_2}\bar{x}_2.$$

The side condition denotes the maximum value x_1 can take.

The first derivative of RP with respect to x_1 is the MRP curve. It tells us the additional revenue associated with each unit of x_1. Thus,

$$MRP = \frac{d(RP)}{dx_1} = \frac{b}{k_1} - \frac{2c}{k_1^2} x_1, \qquad x_1 \le \frac{k_1}{k_2}\bar{x}_2.$$

It can be seen that, for the single process case, the MRP depends on the parameters of the demand curve, here b and c, and k_1, the technological coefficient that relates x_1 to Q. The side condition showing the maximum value x_1 can take still holds. Because we would use x_1 up to the point that $MRP = \bar{p}_1$, the demand curve for x_1 for this case is[5]

$$\bar{p}_1 = \frac{b}{k_1} - \frac{2c}{k_1^2} x_1. \qquad (7.20)$$

We can readily calculate the MRP curve with these methods if the production function is Cobb-Douglas, such as

$$Q = a x_1^\alpha \bar{x}_2^\beta. \qquad (7.21)$$

We would substitute the right-hand term of equation 7.21 for Q in equation 7.19 and proceed in the same way.

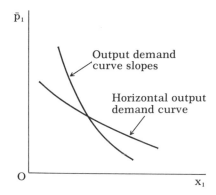

FIGURE 7.23   Demand curves for labor when output demand curve does and does not slope

Because we hire a variable input up to the point where MRP is equal to $\bar{p}_1$, the MRP becomes the demand curve for x_1 when we label the ordinate axis $\bar{p}_1$. Such a demand curve is shown in Figure 7.23, along with one in which the firm's demand curve does not slope (the VMP curve). The demand curve for the variable input, when the demand curve for the output slopes, will always have a steeper slope than when the output demand curve does not slope. The differences in slope imply that a change in the price of the variable input (the wage rate for labor) will have a greater impact on the quantity of the variable input demanded (employment) when the output demand curve does not slope.

Other Influences upon the Demand Curve for a Variable Input. We have shown how changes in various parameters can influence

[5]Notice that now, with a single-process production function, there should be a level of x_1 at which $MRP = \bar{p}_1$. This is because, with the sloping demand curve for the output, MRP always falls.

the position and shape of the demand curve for a variable input. In the sections dealing with cases in which the output demand curve has no slope (a given market price, $\bar{P}$), we illustrated the effect of a change in the output price, the quantity of the fixed assets, and the parameters of the production function on the p_1, x_1 demand curve. A look at equation 7.20 shows that when the output demand curve slopes, the parameters of the output demand curve also have an effect on the p_1, x_1 demand curve.

Other factors can affect the p_1, x_1 demand curve, but unfortunately we cannot explore them here. When the firm produces two or more products, other parameters will influence the demand curve for a variable input. If, for example, x_1 is used in product 1 but not in product 2, changes in the output price of product 2, by changing the output mix, will influence the demand for x_1. Changes in the prices of the variable inputs used in product 2 could also influence the demand for x_1. When the production function has more than the two inputs we have been using, changes in the prices of other variable inputs could also affect the firm's demand for x_1.

The Market Demand for a Variable Input. The market demand for a variable input is obtained conceptually by adding up all the demand curves for that input of the buying firms in that market. To find one point on the market demand curve, we select a price for the input and then sum the quantities that all the firms would purchase at that price. By repeating this procedure for all the alternative prices for that input, we obtain all the points on the market demand curve.

The market demand curve – the relation between p and x – would shift for the same reasons that the demand curves of the firms shift. Thus, the position and sometimes the shape of the market demand curve would shift with increases or decreases in output price, increases or decreases in the amount of fixed assets, changes in the technological parameters. It could also shift because of the entry or exit of firms into that market.

THE FIRM'S DEMAND FOR FIXED ASSETS

The demand of firms for capital assets has not been as well developed by economic theory as that for variable inputs. Yet it is possible to point out the general relationship between the cost of a capital asset and the demand for this asset by a firm and a market, and some of the forces that will influence this demand relationship.

Consider the "going concern" value of a firm:

$$V_0 = \sum_{t=0}^{t=\infty} \frac{Z_t + F_t + Y_t + \Delta A_t + \Delta L_t + \Delta E_t + T_t}{(1 + r_t)^t},$$

where V_0 is the going value, Z_t is short-run cash flow from productive activities, F_t is fixed costs, Y_t is nonoperating income, ΔA_t is the cash outlay for assets, ΔL_t is the change in cash flows due to loans, ΔE_t is the change in cash flows due to issuing or redeeming equities, and T_t is taxes. Any investment project or program can be evaluated by estimating the impact of the investment on these various cash inflows and outflows.

Let us say that the price of a capital asset that the firm is considering purchasing rises. Then, ΔA_t, the cash payment, will be a larger negative number. If nothing else changes, it is less likely that the firm will undertake the purchase of the asset. On the other hand, if the price of the capital asset is lower, ΔA_t will be a smaller negative number and the firm would be more likely to make the investment. If all other projected cash inflows and outflows are unrelated to the price of the asset, there should therefore be a negative relation between the price of the asset and the amount of investment that the model firm, and all other firms, will undertake.

What other forces would affect this relationship between the demand for and price of the capital assets? Let us say that r, the discount rate, falls. Then if the cash inflows from operations, Z_t, are further in the future than the cash outlay for the asset, the going concern value will rise as the result of this investment, and it would more likely be undertaken. F_t, the fixed payments, which include payments for interest, would also be lower (this is negative), thus further increasing the going concern value of the investment. In general, lower interest rates, which influence r and F_t, would lead to an increase in assets purchased at any asset price. Conversely, higher interest rates would reduce the demand for these assets. This is a very important proposition for macroeconomics.

Let us look next at the effect of optimism. The firm has to forecast Z_t (short-run cash flows), and optimism for higher future cash flows would raise the estimates of Z_t. Optimism would therefore tend to increase the demand for the assets at any price; that is, the whole demand curve for the assets would shift to the right. An expectation of lower taxes would have a similar effect. The main determinants of the demand for assets will therefore generally be the asset prices, interest rates, expectations of future short-run cash flows, and expectations of taxes. With the relation between the quantity of assets and the asset prices taken to be the demand curve for assets, this demand curve would "shift" with change in interest rates, expectations of cash flow from operations, and taxes.

MULTI-PRODUCT ALLOCATION:
COBB-DOUGLAS AND CLASSICAL PRODUCTION FUNCTIONS[6]

In Chapter 5, we developed optimization techniques to determine the optimal output mix for a firm producing two or more products. An

---

[6]We present here a technique for solving the optimal mix that is generally not part of the economic theory literature. In Chapter 5, it will be recalled, we

important step in these techniques was the construction of a Q_1, Q_2 opportunity set (for the two-product case) in which the outer boundary of this set was called the production possibility frontier. We restricted ourselves, however, only to the cases in which the production function consisted of either a single process or a small number of processes. We postponed until now two-product optimization for cases in which the production function is either Cobb-Douglas or classical.

The construction of a production possibility frontier in these cases presents special problems. Let us say that the firm produces two outputs with Cobb-Douglas production functions:

$$Q_1 = 2x_1^{0.4} x_2^{0.6}$$
$$Q_2 = 3x_1^{0.5} x_2^{0.5}.$$

Let us say that there is some upper limit to x_2, say $\bar{x}_2$. What are the maximum amounts of Q_1 and Q_2 that can be produced? In this case there are no maxima because the firm can always use more of the variable input to produce more output. Thus, there is no production possibility frontier.

If the production functions are classical, there is a production possibility frontier. This frontier exists because a continuous increase in the variable input will at some point lead to a decrease in output. But the construction of this production possibility curve implies that the firm would purchase a variable input up to the point at which its marginal product is zero. This would not occur if the input has a price. Hence, although a production possibility frontier can be constructed when the production functions are classical, the firm would normally not want to select a point on that frontier for its output mix.

Because the output mix problem has not been solved when the production functions are either Cobb-Douglas or classical, we present here a new technique for dealing with this problem. The method focuses upon the allocation of the common fixed input.

Let us say that x_2 is limited to $\bar{x}_2$ and that x_{21} is the amount of input 2 allocated to product 1 and x_{22} is the amount of x_2 allocated to product 2. Let us say that the production functions are Cobb-Douglas or classical but leave them unspecified as

$$Q_1 = f_1(x_1, x_{21}) \qquad (7.22)$$
$$Q_2 = f_2(x_3, x_{22})$$

where x_1 is the variable input used in product 1 and x_3 is the variable input used in product 2.

Let us now work out the basic procedure. Say we use some x_2 in the production of product 1. What is the payoff to the firm? With some

---

presented output mix solutions only for single (or few) process production functions. This technique should logically be in Chapter 5, but could not be presented until we learned the optimum use of a variable input. The technique may require more mathematics than we have generally assumed. Nothing, however, that follows in this book depends upon a knowledge of the technique.

value of x_{21} (the x_2 allocated to product 1) and some "appropriate" amount of the variable input x_1, there will be some level of output that, when multiplied by the output price, gives the value of the output. The payoff to the firm from devoting x_2 to product 1, however, is not this value of the output, because it has to pay for the x_1 that it uses with the x_2. The difference between the value of the output and the expenditures on x_1, however, could be viewed as the net revenues (NR) obtained by using x_2 in the production of product 1. Symbolically, we can write this net revenue as

$$NR_1 = \bar{P}_1 Q_1 - \bar{p}_1 x_1.$$

Substituting for Q_1 from equation 7.22, we can also write this net revenue function as

$$NR_1 = \bar{P}_1 f_1(x_1, x_{21}) - \bar{p}_1 x_1. \tag{7.23}$$

The net revenue apparently depends on the amount of x_{21} and x_1, for we are taking prices as given. If we can now express x_1 in terms of x_{21}, we can find this net revenue in terms only of x_{21} and the parameters. How much x_1 should be used? The profit-maximizing firm should use the variable input up to the point that the value of its marginal product equals the price of the variable input. By making use of this optimizing condition, we can find the optimal amount of x_1 to use for any given amount of x_{21}.

The marginal product of x_1 used in product 1 can be found from the production function, equation 7.22, as

$$MP_{x_1} = \frac{\partial f_1(x_1, x_{21})}{\partial x_1}.$$

The value of this marginal product is

$$VMP_{x_1} = \bar{P}_1 \frac{\partial f_1(x_1, x_{21})}{\partial x_1}.$$

If the price of input 1 is $\bar{p}_1$, we can get the optimal use of x_1 by setting $VMP_{x_1} = \bar{p}_1$:

$$\bar{P}_1 \frac{\partial f_1(x_1, x_{21})}{\partial x_1} = \bar{p}_1.$$

This equation can, in principle, be solved for x_1, where x_1 in an unspecified equation will be

$$x_1 = g_1(x_{21}).$$

We now substitute for x_1 in equation 7.23 to get the net revenue attributable to x_{21} on the assumption the optimal amount of x_1 is used. Symbolically, this is

$$NR_1 = \bar{P}_1 f_1[g_1(x_{21}), x_{21}] - \bar{p}_1 g_1(x_{21}).$$

With exactly the same procedures, we can find NR_2 as a function of x_{22}, the amount of the fixed input devoted to product 2. Let us write this relation in general symbols:

$$NR_2 = f_2(x_{22}).$$

Using

$$NR_1 = f_1(x_{21})$$

as a general relationship between NR_1 and x_{21}, we can set up the cash-flow equation to the firm, which is the net revenue from both products.[7] Thus,

$$Z = NR_1 + NR_2 = f_1(x_{21}) + f_2(x_{22}). \tag{7.24}$$

This equation is our objective function. Because there is a limited amount of input 2, at $\bar{x}_2$, we have the constraint

$$x_{21} + x_{22} \le \bar{x}_2. \tag{7.25}$$

With inequation 7.24 defining the opportunity set, and equation 7.25 the objective function, our optimization techniques can be used to determine how much of input 2 to devote to product 1 and how much to product 2. With this determination, we can readily find the associated values of Q_1 and Q_2.

Basically, the procedure we have just given is not difficult. The important steps are (1) seeing the problem as the allocation of the fixed input, (2) constructing the net revenue equations, (3) determining an optimal amount of the variable inputs corresponding to any allocation of the fixed inputs.

Discussion Questions

1. In deducing the short-run supply curve, what do we assume to be constant and what do we assume to be variable?

2. If the price of labor rises when all firms in an industry expand their outputs, what kinds of adjustments might we have to make when calculating the market supply curve?

3. How would the degree of mobility of resources into or out of the industry affect the market supply curve? How would ease of entry or exit of firms from a market affect the shifting of the market supply curve?

4. Does it seem true, as our analysis seems to show, that increased productivity of labor increases the demand for labor? Which countries have the highest demand for labor, those in which productivity is high or those in which it is low?

---

[7] Notice that the f_1 and f_2 are not the same here as in the production functions.

5. If a labor union pressing for higher wages had to concern itself with the effect of these wages on employment, would it prefer the production functions to be single process or Cobb-Douglas? Why?

6. What factors can increase the demand for labor at all alternative wage rates? What would decrease this demand?

7. In what ways could a sloping demand curve for a firm's output adversely affect its demand for labor?

8. What would be the likely effect of an expectation of a wage increase on the demand for labor in the short run? What would be the likely effect if this expectation concerned a type of material? How might we explain the differences, if any?

9. Enumerate and evaluate the various events and expectations that could increase the firm's demand for fixed assets.

8 Consumer Demand and Market Demand Curves

In this chapter we take another step toward our objective of estimating the demand curves facing firms for their outputs. We turn to the market demand for "final" products, those sold to consumers. The focus of attention is no longer the firm; instead we try to understand what influences consumers' purchasing.

Although economists have a well-established theory of consumer demand, in practice empirical work and introspection are the keys to the study of it. Thus by using our common sense and intuition, we can identify variables that influence demand for a particular product or service. We then discuss some concepts crucial to an understanding of demand, present established theories of consumer demand, and suggest ways to empirically estimate market demand curves for consumption goods.

VARIABLES THAT INFLUENCE CONSUMER DEMAND

What determines the quantity of a good or service that an individual consumer or all the consumers in the market will purchase during some period of time? Many variables influence the quantity demanded; but they can be combined into a fairly small number of categories. One is price. Generally speaking, with everything else remaining the same, we expect an inverse relation between the price of a product and the quantity demanded; a low price usually produces more demand for a product than a higher price does. The general notion that price and quantity demanded have an inverse relation is not, however, sufficient for most purposes. We want to know the magnitude of the relationship—that is, whether a rise in price leads to a large or a small decrease in the quantity demanded or whether a fall in price leads to a large or a small increase in the quantity demanded. The current price is not the only price that can influence the current quantitative demand. Past prices and expectations of future prices can also help determine the quantitative demand in any time period.

A second variable that, ceteris paribus, will generally influence the quantity demanded is the income of consumers. "Income" may be too narrow a term, because consumers could supplement their current income for the purchase of goods and services with past savings or by borrowing. Perhaps "budget of consumers" is preferable, although we will often say "income" because it is in such wide use. We generally expect a positive relation between income (budget) and quantitative demand; that is, the higher the income, the greater is the demand. However, for many types of goods and services higher income results in a lower demand. When income rises, for example, consumers may purchase more steak but less hamburger. As in the case of price, we want to know how "elastic" the quantity demanded is with respect to income: Will a change in income lead to a comparatively large or small change in the quantity demanded? Also, as in the case of price, expectations of future income sometimes influence the current quantity demanded.

Although we treat income and price separately, we should be aware that income and prices are connected. When a price or prices in general rise, the real (as opposed to monetary) income of consumers fall. Conversely, a fall in prices results in a rise of real income. Later, we will have to separate the "price effect" from the "income effect" when we investigate the impact of a price change on a consumer's demand for a product.

A third variable that influences the quantitative demand for a product is the price of substitute products. We generally expect a positive relation between the price of a substitute and the quantity demanded of a particular product. As the price of the substitute rises, ceteris paribus, consumers can be expected to switch their demand—at least partly—from the substitute to the product whose demand is being studied. Conversely, a reduction in the price of the substitute should lead to a decrease in the demand for our product. It is of great interest to be able to estimate the extent to which the demand for one product changes with a change in the prices of substitutes.

A fourth variable is the price of complementary products—products used with the product of interest. We expect a negative relation between the price of a complement and that of the product being analyzed. Because complements are used together as a "package," a rise in the price of one of the complements, by raising the price of the total package, would normally lead to a reduction in demand of the whole package, including the complement whose price does not change. We are interested in the magnitude of the response in the demand for one product to a change in the prices of its complements.

The demand for a particular product is also determined partly by "tastes" or "preference." Taste itself is influenced by many factors — the general culture, habits, advertising, product design, whether the product is purchased by others. The first four variables can be measured, but there is no well-established way to measure tastes. We can, however, measure the *effect* of tastes by marketing surveys, consumer panels, and statistical analysis.

These five variables influence the demand of a particular consumer for the product. Because the market demand is nothing more than the sum of individual demands, market demand also depends upon the number of consumers in the market for that product.

To get some insight into the relationships of the variables, let us first ask how an econometrician approaches the problem of estimating the demand for a product. First, he would set up an equation relating the quantitative demand to the price of the product, income of consumers, prices of substitutes, and prices of complements.[1] The equation might be

$$Q = b_0 + b_1 P + b_2 Y + b_3 P_s + b_4 P_c,$$

where Q is the quantity purchased (per period of time), P is the price of the product, Y is the income of consumers, P_s is the prices of substitutes, and P_c is the prices of complements. The bs are the parameters: They are the constants that relate the variables in the equation.

The econometrician's task would then be to estimate the values for the parameters through the use of statistical analysis. The procedure for doing this will be explained later in this chapter. For the time being, let us assume that the estimates of the parameters have been made and that the equation is

$$Q = 100 - 0.3P + 0.4Y + 0.2P_s - 0.1P_c.$$

Taste, it will be noticed, is not explicit in this equation, though in a way it is reflected in all the parameters.

With such an equation, we can explicitly determine the relation between Q and any of the four "explanatory" variables, if the other three explanatory variables are given constant values. Say, for example, that we want to determine the relation only between Q and P, which is *the* demand curve. If $Y = \$1000$, $P_s = \$50$, and $P_c = \$100$, the Q, P relation is

$$Q = 100 - 0.3P + 0.4(1,000) + 0.2(50) - 0.1(100) \tag{8.1}$$
$$Q = 500 - 0.3P.$$

If we wish to follow the convention of expressing P in terms of Q, equation 8.1 can be solved for P to get

$$P = 1,666.66 - 3.33Q. \tag{8.2}$$

[1]Econometrics is primarily concerned with the empirical estimation of the parameters of the different types of economic relationships.

This demand curve—that is, the P, Q relation—depends on the values of the other three explanatory variables. These values, in fact, help to determine the parameters of the demand curve. To write this demand curve more completely, we would say that equation 8.2 is the P, Q relation when $Y = 1,000$, $P_s = 50$, and $P_c = 100$. If the value of one of these three variables changes, we would expect the demand curve to change, or shift. Say, for example, that Y, the income, rises to \$1500. Then the P, Q demand curve would become

$$Q = 100 - 0.3P + 0.4(1,500) + 0.2(50) - 0.1(100)$$
$$Q = 700 - 0.3P$$

or, in terms of Q,

$$P = 2,333.33 - 3.33Q. \tag{8.3}$$

Figure 8.1 shows the demand curves described by equations 8.2 and 8.3, with one corresponding to $Y = 1,000$ and the other to $Y = 1,500$. Clearly, the higher value of Y has shifted the demand curve to the NE; that is, more Q would be purchased at any price with the higher value of Y. A lower value for Y would clearly shift the demand curve in the SW direction. With a similar analysis, it is easily shown that a higher value for P_s or a lower value for P_c also favorably shifts the demand curve to the NE. And, of course, a lower value for P_s or a higher value for P_c shifts the P, Q demand curve in the SW direction.

Using much the same procedures, we can explicitly study the relation between Q and any explanatory variable. Say, for example, we are interested in the relation between Q and Y. It can be determined for some given set of values for P, P_s, and P_c. Thus, if $P = 60$, $P_s = 50$, and $P_c = 100$, the Q, Y relationship is

$$Q = 100 - 0.3(60) + 0.4Y + 0.2(50) - 0.1(100)$$
$$Q = 82 + 0.4Y.$$

This equation tells us the quantity that would be demanded at each income level, when the three prices are as given above. If one of the prices would change, so would the Q, Y relationship. If, for example, $P = 30$, the Q, Y relationship would be

$$Q = 100 - 0.3(30) + 0.4Y + 0.2(50) - 0.1(100)$$
$$Q = 91 + 0.4Y.$$

As Figure 8.2 shows, lowering the product's price shifts the Q, Y relationship in the NW direction; that is, more Q would be demanded for each possible value of Y at the lower value for P.

KEY CONCEPTS IN DEMAND ANALYSIS

Elasticity. Elasticity is an important concept in economics. It measures the extent to which a percentage change in one variable leads

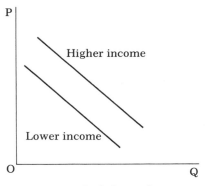

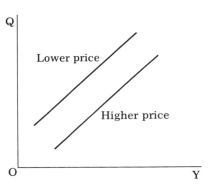

FIGURE 8.1 *P, Q* demand curve
at two different income levels

FIGURE 8.2 Relation of income
and quantity at different prices

to a percentage change in another variable. If Y and X are any two
economic variables related so that Y is a function of X, then η (eta),
the symbol used for elasticity, is defined as

$$\eta_{Y/X} = \frac{\% \text{ change in Y}}{\% \text{ change in X}}. \tag{8.4}$$

Because the numerator and the denominator of this equation are both
percentages, the units in which Y and X are expressed cancel out and
η is an abstract number directly comparable from one situation to
the next.

   Elasticity measures the responsiveness of the change in one variable (here Y) with respect to a change in the other variable (here X).
If η is greater than 1, we say that the relation between Y and X is
elastic; that is, a percentage change in X leads to a larger percentage
change, or response, in Y. In the extreme, it is possible for the response
in Y to a change in X to be so great that elasticity is infinite, in which
case we have perfect elasticity. If the value of η is less than 1 (but still
positive), we say the relation is inelastic; that is, a percentage change
in X leads to a relatively smaller percentage change or response in Y.
If Y does not change at all with a change in X, then η is zero and we
have a perfectly inelastic relation between Y and X. When η is exactly
1, we say there is unitary elasticity; that is, a given percentage change
in X results in the same percentage change in Y.

   The η can have either positive or negative values. It will be positive
if Y changes in the same direction as the change in X and negative
if a change in X leads to a change in Y in the opposite direction. When
η is negative, the same definition of elastic and inelastic relations
still holds. Thus if η is a greater negative number than -1, we call
the relation elastic. And if η lies between 0 and -1, we say the relation is inelastic.

Equation 8.4 can also be written

$$\eta_{Y/X} = \frac{\Delta Y/Y}{\Delta X/X} = \frac{\Delta Y}{\Delta X} \cdot \frac{X}{Y}. \tag{8.5}$$

If X and Y is some *particular* point on the function that relates Y to X, then the elasticity could be found approximately at that point by increasing X by some small amount, ΔX, and then finding the resulting increase in Y, which is ΔY.[2]

Let us use a simple function to demonstrate how we would calculate η. Say we have the relationship

$$Y = 100 + 0.5X. \tag{8.6}$$

And we want to know the elasticity where $X = 50$, in which event $Y = 125$. If we make $\Delta X = 1$, so that X becomes 51, the new value of Y is 125.5. Thus, ΔY, the change in Y, is 0.5. We now insert these values in equation 8.5 to calculate the elasticity:

$$\eta_{Y/X} = \frac{0.5}{1} \cdot \frac{50}{125} = \frac{25}{125} = 0.2.$$

This is interpreted in this way: A 1 percent increase in X results in a 0.2 percent increase in Y. Some experimentation would show that a 1 percent decrease in X also leads to a 0.2 percent decrease in Y. The measure of elasticity holds for both increases and decreases in X. Figure 8.3 shows how X, Y, ΔX, and ΔY are determined.

We noted that the elasticity was "approximately" 0.2, because we are really measuring the elasticity over the *range* of X varying between 50 and 51. If we want to find the elasticity precisely at $X = 50$, we can do this by making ΔX very small. If we think of ΔX approaching zero in the limit, we can use the calculus, and equation 8.5 becomes

$$\eta_{Y/X} = \frac{dY/Y}{dX/X} = \frac{dY}{dX} \cdot \frac{X}{Y}, \tag{8.7}$$

where dX is an infinitely small ΔX.

Let us use the calculus to find the elasticity at $X = 50$ for equation 8.6, where Y is still 125. The first derivative of Y with respect to X — that is, dY/dX — is calculated in this way:

$$\frac{dY}{dX} = \frac{d(100 + 0.5X)}{dX} = 0.5.$$

Using 0.5 for dY/dX is equation 8.7 and $X = 50$ and $Y = 125$ gives us the elasticity as

$$\eta_{X/Y} = 0.5\left(\frac{50}{125}\right) = 0.2.$$

---

[2]Notice that $\Delta Y/Y$ is the percentage change in Y. Similarly, $\Delta X/X$ is the percentage change in X.

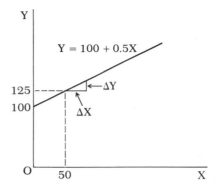

FIGURE 8.3   Graphic calculation of elasticity

We see that the elasticity is the same as before. But this is so only because the function (equation 8.6) is a straight line. If this function were curved, the elasticities calculated by the two methods might differ by a small amount.

Elasticity need not be the same at all points on a function. Say we want to know the elasticity where $X = 100$. We see from equation 8.6 that $Y = 150$. The first derivative, dY/dX, remains the same, but if the new values for X and Y are inserted into equation 8.7, we get the elasticity as

$$\eta_{X/Y} = 0.5\left(\frac{100}{150}\right) = 0.33.$$

Clearly, the elasticity at $X = 100$ differs from that at $X = 50$.

One equation form gives the same elasticity for all values of X. This is the "exponential" form

$$Y = aX^{\beta}. \tag{8.8}$$

The β term gives the same elasticity at all values of X. Let us prove this with the use of equation 8.7. The first derivative of equation 8.8 is

$$\frac{dY}{dX} = \beta aX^{\beta-1}. \tag{8.9}$$

Using equation 8.9 for dY/dX in equation 8.7 and equation 8.8 for Y, we get elasticity as

$$\eta_{Y/X} = \frac{\beta aX^{\beta-1}X}{aX^{\beta}} = \frac{\beta aX^{\beta}}{aX^{\beta}} = \beta.$$

This "constant elasticity" exponential equation has proved useful in empirical estimates of elasticity.

Price Elasticity of Demand. One use of the concept of elasticity in demand analysis is to ascertain price elasticity. Price elasticity of demand is defined as the percentage response in the quantity demanded of a particular product (or group of products) with respect to a percentage change in the price of that product (or prices, if a group of products), with all other variables that can influence Q held constant. Symbolically, price elasticity is defined as

$$\eta_{Q/P} = \frac{\% \text{ change in } Q}{\% \text{ change in } P} = \frac{\Delta Q}{\Delta P} \cdot \frac{P}{Q} = \frac{dQ}{dP} \cdot \frac{P}{Q}. \tag{8.10}$$

Price elasticity is almost always negative because we expect a change in P in one direction to result in a change in Q in the other direction, ceteris paribus. When $\eta_{Q/P}$ is a larger negative number than -1, we say that demand is price elastic; when $\eta_{Q/P}$ is a smaller negative number than -1, we say demand is price inelastic.

It is useful to examine how elasticity varies at different points on a demand curve. Consider the linear demand curve

$$P = 100 - 0.5Q,$$

which can also be written

$$Q = 200 - 2P, \tag{8.11}$$

shown in Figure 8.4. How does price elasticity change for different values of P? Consider the "calculus" version of equation 8.10, in which elasticity is

$$\eta_{Q/P} = \frac{dQ}{dP} \cdot \frac{P}{Q}. \tag{8.12}$$

The dQ/dP can be readily calculated from equation 8.11 and is a constant value of -2. What happens to $\eta_{Q/P}$ as we, say, raise P? A higher value of P, according to equation 8.11, results in a lower value for Q. Thus, according to equation 8.12, elasticity rises as P is increased (and Q is decreased). Conversely, a decrease in P (and a corresponding increase in Q) can be seen from equation 8.12 to result in a lower elasticity. The change in elasticity with movements along the demand curve is shown in Figure 8.4.

We could find the P,Q combination at which elasticity is exactly -1 from equation 8.12 by substituting -1 for $\eta_{Q/P}$, substituting -2 for dQ/dP, substituting for Q from equation 8.11. Equation 8.12 is now in terms only of P; a solution for P gives the value of P for which elasticity is -1. By the same procedure, we can find the P,Q combination for any selected value for $\eta_{Q/P}$.

Our finding that price elasticity increases as the price is increased is of considerable importance to an understanding of demand. But it was based only on a linear demand curve. If the demand curve is of the exponential type, such as

$$Q = 2P^{-0.6},$$

which would have the shape shown in Figure 8.5, price elasticity is

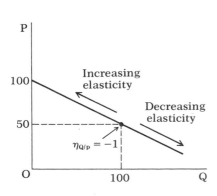

FIGURE 8.4 Changes in elasticity when demand curve is linear

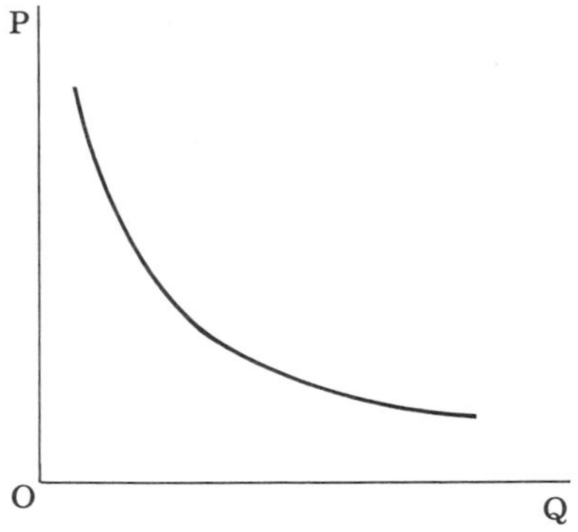

FIGURE 8.5 Demand curve with constant elasticity

−0.6 for all values of P. In some equation forms a higher price may not result in higher elasticity.

The degree of price elasticity at some particular price determines whether an increase or a decrease in the price raises or reduces total revenue. To see this effect, let us symbolize revenue as

$$R = PQ. \tag{8.13}$$

If we change the price of P by ΔP, Q would change by ΔQ. The new revenue would therefore be

$$R' = (P + \Delta P)(Q + \Delta Q).$$

If we multiply these terms out, ignoring the term $\Delta P \Delta Q$, we get

$$R' = PQ + (\Delta P)Q + (\Delta Q)P. \tag{8.14}$$

Recall from equation 8.10 that the elasticity (neglecting the subscripts) is

$$\eta = \frac{\Delta Q}{\Delta P} \cdot \frac{P}{Q},$$

which, when solved for ΔQ, becomes

$$\Delta Q = \frac{\eta(\Delta P)Q}{P}. \tag{8.15}$$

Now we substitute the right-hand term of equation 8.15 for ΔQ in equation 8.14:

$$R' = PQ + \Delta PQ + \left(\frac{\eta(\Delta P)Q}{P}\right)P.$$

Collecting terms gives us

$$R' = PQ + (1 + \eta)(\Delta P)Q. \tag{8.16}$$

We can now ask if R', the revenue after the price change, is greater than R, the revenue before the price change. The difference in revenue, ΔR, will be

$$\Delta R = R' - R,$$

which, on substituting equation 8.16 for R' and equation 8.13 for R, gives us

$$\Delta R = (1 + \eta)(\Delta P)Q.$$

Recall that η is negative. What happens to ΔR if η is a negative number smaller than -1 (inelasticity) and ΔP is positive — that is, the price is raised? The term $(1 + \eta)$ will be positive, and ΔR is positive. What if η is inelastic and ΔP is negative — that is, the price is lowered? Then ΔR is negative. We can conclude that when price elasticity is low, an increase in price increases revenue, while a decrease in price decreases revenue. Now say that η is a negative number larger than -1. The term $(1 + \eta)$ will now be negative. If ΔP rises (ΔP is positive), it should be clear that ΔR is negative. Conversely, if ΔP is lowered (ΔP is negative), ΔR is positive. We can therefore conclude that when price elasticity is high, an increase in price reduces revenue but a decrease in price raises revenue. Finally, when η is equal to -1, a small change in the price will not change revenue.

What are the main determinants of whether the demand for a product will be price elastic or price inelastic? The availability of substitutes for the product and the substitutability of the product for other products are important factors. If there are good substitutes for the product, we should expect a rise in its price to result in a large switch by consumers from the purchase of the product to the purchase of the substitutes — if the prices of the substitutes do not also rise. On the other hand, if the product is a good substitute for other products, a decrease in its price can lead to a large switch from the other products to the product of interest. In interpreting degrees of elasticity because of substitutes, we must be careful in assessing how broadly or narrowly the product has been defined. A narrowly defined product, such as apples, will have better substitutes than a broadly defined product such as fruit. In general, the more narrowly defined the product, the higher will be the price elasticity.

The availability of substitutes is not by itself sufficient to influence price elasticity. In addition the prices of the substitutes must be reasonably similar to the price of the product. Champagne, for example, may be a more than adequate substitute for inexpensive wine. But because of large price differences, a small increase in the price of the wine is not likely to lead to a large switch by consumers from wine to champagne. If, however, the price of the wine were raised by a very large amount, many consumers would probably switch to champagne. The demand for wine would then be price inelastic at the lower prices and price elastic as the price of wine became high.

Of course, if the price of the champagne were to become much lower, the demand for wine could become price elastic in the lower price ranges.

The availability and prices of substitutes may not be the only reason that demand for a product may be highly price elastic at high prices. Because consumers cannot spend much more than their income, a high enough price can drastically reduce demand even if there are no substitutes for the product. Even when the product is essential, none or very little may be demanded at very high prices. People have been known to starve or go without medical care when prices go out of their reach.

A number of important conclusions follow from this discussion. Most importantly, measures of price elasticity could be meaningless without reference to the price range of the demand curve at which elasticity is being measured. The existence of close substitutes may affect only the elasticity of the demand curve for those prices in which the prices of the substitutes are comparable to the price of the product. Finally, price elasticity could be high at very high prices because the price of the product is high relative to the income of potential buyers.[3]

Are there any conditions in which the quantity demanded of a product rises with a rise in its price?[4] Three possibilities come to mind. First, if buyers obtain the product mainly for status or prestige, they may gain satisfaction from paying more. When this is so, it is conceivable that the quantity demanded may increase with an increase in price—at least over a limited range of price increases. A second possibility arises when consumers cannot make an independent evaluation of a product and as a result tend to judge the quality of the product by its price. A third possibility arises when the product takes such a large proportion of consumer expenditures that a change in the price of the product appreciably changes the real income of consumers. Consider a poor country that subsists mainly on grain products because they are the cheapest way for consumers to meet their essential food needs. If the price of the grain product drops, the real income of consumers could rise to the point where they might buy fewer grain products and increase their consumption of meats, fruits, and vegetables. On the other hand, a rise in the prices of the grain products may compel consumers to buy more of them. A positive relation between price and quantity demanded was found for bread by a statistician, R. Giffen, in the nineteenth century. It is known in economics as Giffen's paradox.

[3]Our argument that price elasticity should increase with higher values of the price should make us careful in the use of the "exponential" equation, such as 8.12 because this type of equation assumes elasticity is the same at all prices. Thus, the exponential form has some theoretical weaknesses. It could still be used in empirical work, but we should interpret the measured elasticity to hold true only over the range of values of the observations.

[4]Such a relation would be every seller's dream.

Income Elasticity. Another important application of elasticity in demand analysis is in ascertaining the relationship between a change in the income of consumers and the quantity demanded, ceteris paribus. Income elasticity is measured as the ratio of the percentage change in the quantity demanded for a product to the percentage change in the income of consumers. With Q designating quantity demanded and Y income, income elasticity is defined as

$$\eta_{Q/Y} = \frac{\%\ \text{change in Q}}{\%\ \text{change in Y}} = \frac{\Delta Q/Q}{\Delta Y/Y} = \frac{dQ}{dY} \cdot \frac{Y}{Q}.$$

As before, we can use the first derivative of the quantity-income function to obtain elasticity precisely at some income point.

Income elasticity could be either positive or negative for any particular product. It will be positive when a rise in income leads to a rise in the demand for the product or when a fall in income leads to a reduction in demand. Products with positive income elasticities are known as normal products. For some products a rise in income could lead to a reduction in demand. Hence $\eta_{Q/Y}$ could be negative. Such products are known as inferior, not because they do not perform their functions properly but because they are not preferred by consumers when their income rises.

What tends to make income elasticity high or low? Generally, consumer tastes and views on whether a product is a necessity or a luxury. But whether a product is a necessity or a luxury depends on the income level of consumers as well as on their tastes. Consider staples such as bread, milk, and electricity. With a rise in income, middle-class American consumers do not usually increase their consumption of these items appreciably: neither do they consume much less of them when their income falls. The quantity demanded for such products by middle-class consumers is therefore income inelastic. For poor people, however, the income elasticity for such "staples" may be much greater. Income elasticity for grain products in a low-income country like India, for example, has been estimated at about 0.7; in the United States it is probably about 0.2. Rises in income for middle-class Americans usually result in commensurately larger rises in the purchase of comparative luxuries such as steak, fine wines, and vacations abroad. The demand for these items is therefore income elastic for these consumers. But for wealthy consumers, the income elasticity for such "luxuries" would be much smaller. As a general rule, we may conclude that the income elasticity for any product tends to become smaller with increases in consumer income.

Expenditure Elasticity. Another measure of elasticity, in many ways similar to income elasticity, is expenditure elasticity. Expenditure elasticity is the ratio of a percentage change in expenditures (rather than quantity) for a product to a percentage change in income. With *E* designated as expenditures, expenditure elasticity is

$$\eta_{E/Y} = \frac{\% \text{ change in } E}{\% \text{ change in } Y} = \frac{\Delta E/E}{\Delta Y/Y} = \frac{dE}{dY} \cdot \frac{Y}{E}.$$

Expenditure elasticities are not often discussed in theoretical analysis, but are important in empirical work. They are much easier to calculate than income elasticities. In the latter we have to empirically hold prices "constant," but prices are already included in expenditures. Expenditure elasticities are especially useful when a product is heterogeneous, like furniture or clothing. For heterogeneous products, it is often difficult to devise a measure of quantity. Expenditure data are also more readily available than data on quantities. Expenditure elasticities tend to be high or low for the same reasons that income elasticities are.

Cross-Price Elasticity. Another useful measure in demand analysis is cross-price elasticity, often simply called the cross elasticity. In cross elasticity, the relationship of interest is the percentage change in the quantity demanded of one product to a percentage change in the price of a second product. If product 1 is taken as the one whose price changes and product 2 is that whose quantity demanded responds to the price change, the cross elasticity of these products is defined as

$$\eta_{Q_2/P_1} = \frac{\% \text{ change in } Q_2}{\% \text{ change in } P_1} = \frac{\Delta Q_2/Q_2}{\Delta P_1/P_1} = \frac{dQ_2}{dP_1} \cdot \frac{P_1}{Q_2}.$$

The concept and measurement of cross elasticities is useful for determining whether any pair of products is closely related as substitutes or complements in a relative price neighborhood. If products 1 and 2 are close substitutes, then we would expect an increase in the price of product 1, ceteris paribus, to result in many buyers shifting their demand to product 2. Conversely, a decrease in the price of product 1 should result in many buyers shifting from product 2 to product 1. Thus, a statistically determined high positive value for η_{Q_2/P_1} provides evidence that buyers view these products as close substitutes in the range of prices observed. If, on the other hand, the two products are used together as a jointly consumed package, an increase in P_1, by raising the price of the whole package, would lead to a reduction in Q_2. Thus, a large negative value for η_{Q_2/P_1} provides evidence that the products are complements. If the cross elasticity is close to zero, the products are neither substitutes nor complements.

We must resist the temptation to infer that the cross elasticity of Q_1 to P_2 would be the same as that between Q_2 and P_1. Consider the case where the products are complements and product 1 contributes 90 percent to the cost of the jointly consumed package, while product 2 contributes only 10 percent. A rise in the price of product 1 would have a large impact on the joint cost and would therefore lead to a large reduction in the demand for product 2. But a similar rise in the price of product 2 would not raise the joint cost greatly, and as a consequence the reduction in demand for product 1 would not be large. (If these two products are always used together, the price elasticity of product 2 would tend to be smaller than the price elasticity of product 1.) When the two products are substitutes, the cross elasticities will tend to be the same "both ways" if there are no other substitutes. But if there are other substitutes, it is not likely that the two cross elasticities will be the same.

The Product. The concept of a product presents a number of theoretical and empirical problems to economic analysis. Up to this point we have used the term "product" without carefully defining it. Intuitive understanding of a product may suffice in each particular context, but we must be more precise before going on to examine the interrelationship of firms and consumers. The notion of a product as that which a firm produces with a particular technology may not correspond to the notion of a product as that which a household consumes to obtain a specific satisfaction. A consumer may treat as perfect substitutes two things that are produced by different firms with different technologies and inputs. Conversely, two things produced identically may, if branded, packaged, and advertised differently, be treated by the consumer as different products.

From the producer's viewpoint, products can be defined and classified in a flexible way that depends mainly on the context of a particular problem. The question may be posed for example, in demand forecasting, in the form of asking whether two distinguishable items such as red Chevrolets and blue Chevrolets can be considered the same product. For purposes of ordering metals and headlights, they can be classified together. But for purposes of ordering paint, they cannot.

From the buyer's viewpoint, two distinguishable items can be considered the same, or different, according to the uses to which they are put. Milk may be close enough to Coca-Cola to be considered the same product in the quenching of thirst but not when the use of the product is to deliver protein. Whether products are substitutes in use is a question frequently brought up in antitrust cases in which there is litigation to establish whether competition would be lessened, for example, by a merger. In one such case, it was determined that aluminum and copper wire and cable were separate products when used near salt water but were interchangeable when used inland.[5]

Because products are interchangeable in use, however, does not necessarily make them effective substitutes. In addition, the prices of the products must make substitution feasible. Platinum wire and cable are good technical substitutes for copper and aluminum wire and cable, but the price of platinum is so high that it was not considered a substitute in defining the product in the antitrust case just mentioned.

[5]*U.S.* v. *Aluminum Co. of America*, 377 U.S. 271 (1964).

An understanding of the classification and relation of products is aided by distinguishing between the product itself and the various services it performs for the buyer, be he a consumer or a purchasing agent for a firm. A bottle of milk, for example, delivers vitamin A services, vitamin D services, calcium services, protein services, taste, among others.[6] It also provides certain services manifested only when used with other products—mixing services, for example, such as when used with a cake mix to produce a cake.

On the basis of these services, we can show different kinds of relations between any pair of products. If two products yield precisely the same set of services, with the units of the services the same per unit of the products, then clearly the products are perfect substitutes in use and will be considered the same products by buyers. If they yield the same services but in different proportions and different amounts of services per unit of product, then they are close substitutes in use. Whether they will be close substitutes on the market—that is, whether their cross elasticities will be high—will depend on whether their prices are in a range that makes them feasible substitutes. If two products yield services that can only be manifested with their joint use, we can call them perfectly complementary. Automobiles and gasoline are good examples of such complementarity. If two products provide services that need not be jointly consumed but together provide the mix of services needed by the buyer, they are also complements. But they are not such strong complements as products that must be jointly used.

Perhaps the most general relation arises when two products provide some common services and some unique services. In such cases the products are both complements and substitutes—although obviously not perfect in either respect. Depending on the mixes of these services, the degree of complementarity could be greater or smaller than the degree of substitutability. Whether complementarity or substitutability is more important to a consumer depends on the alternative combinations of the products. If he is using the products in approximately equal proportions and receives more than sufficient amounts of the unique services, the element of substitutability would predominate. But if he is faced with such proportions of the products that his minimum requirements for some of the unique services are just barely met, complementarity would dominate.

The Market. Anybody familiar with antitrust, marketing, industrial organization, or economic data classification systems cannot be unaware that "the market" is both a difficult and a crucial concept. The market can be somewhat naively defined as a place where trans-

---

[6]Kelvin Lancaster has made the case for viewing products in terms of the different types of services they deliver. See Kelvin Lancaster, "A New Approach to Consumer Theory," *Journal of Political Economy*, vol. 74 (April 1966).

actions are made, but in economic analysis the term "market" is used to denote a broad set of interrelations of buyers and sellers.

The key to defining and understanding the concept of a market is interdependence. We can say that buyers and sellers, and goods and services, are in the same market if the terms on which offers to buy and sell for some of the buyers and sellers for some of the goods and services have a "substantial" influence on the transaction terms of other buyers and sellers for the same or other goods and services. For a high degree of interdependence to exist, the products or services must be reasonably close substitutes for each other, they must have relative prices that make substitution feasible, the buyers and sellers must be in contact with each other, barriers must not prohibit buyers and sellers from trading with each other, and information must be reasonably available. The greater the degree to which these conditions are met, the greater the degree of interdependence and the sharper the definition of a market.

A crucial concept in understanding markets is their "broadness" or "narrowness." In a sense all the products and services sold in the United States, or even in the whole world, can be considered in the same market, because they are all, to an extent, interdependent. But the degree of interdependence of some products and some buyers and sellers could be much greater than their interdependence with other products and buyers and sellers. Thus, products, buyers, and sellers with a high degree of interdependence could be grouped together as a narrow market within a broader market. And within a narrow market, there can still be subgroups of products, buyers, and sellers that are sufficiently more strongly interdependent to be considered still a narrower market. We must think, then, of markets within markets within markets. Sometimes these markets can overlap in a kind of chainlike fashion. For example, copper competes with aluminum as an electrical conductor, aluminum competes with steel for use in conduits for wires, steel competes with fiber glass in automobile bodies. Although copper does not compete with fiber glass, it is possible that through these overlaps a change in the price of fiber glass could affect the price of copper.

There is no sure formula with which we can define precisely a narrow market, so ultimately we must use judgment. There are, however, a number of factors that we must be aware of when determining whether any group of products (or services) and buyers and sellers should be grouped together in the same narrow market. First, there is the product dimension. Products grouped together in a market should be reasonably close substitutes in use. Second, there is a price dimension. Not only should the products be substitutes; they should also be priced to make substitution feasible. A third factor is transportation costs. High transportation costs relative to the value of the product or service could effectively separate one group of products, buyers, and sellers from another. Thus, products with high values relative to transport costs, such as jewelry, have wide geographic markets, and commodities such as cement and gravel have small geographic markets. A geographic dimension to markets depends on product values and transport costs.

Time can be another dimension defining a market. The market for strawberries in December is not the same as that in July. The market for public transportation services in a city differs during rush hours from the rest of the day. Markets can also be defined on the basis of the functions of buyers and sellers. Thus, there are wholesale and retail markets. Finally, markets are often delimited by artificial barriers. Professional licenses issued by the various states tend to separate markets for professional services. Import quotas effectively separate markets within a country from the world market.

Perhaps the best test of whether products, buyers, and sellers are in the same market or in different narrow markets is based on the cross elasticity of demand. When there is a strong positive relation between the price of one product and the quantity demanded of another, these products are in the same narrow market. Or if the price of a product in one geographic area strongly influences the price of the same product in another area, the buyers and sellers in these areas are in the same market.

The distinction between narrow markets could change as the factors that determine markets change. Narrow markets could be combined into broader markets or further subdivided into narrower markets with changes in the nature and use of products, transport costs, prices, artificial barriers, technology, and information. Generally, the broadening of markets tends to increase competition.

The extent to which markets are broadened or narrowed can be studied in the antitrust literature. A monopolist controlling a narrow market could raise his price just to the point where his market begins to merge into other markets. We might then incorrectly conclude that the monopolist has competition. This problem was clearly analyzed by Judge William Howard Taft in the Addyston Pipe and Steel Case in 1898.[7] An association of six producers of cast iron in Alabama, Tennessee, Ohio, and Kentucky agreed not to compete in the thirty-six states west of the Alleghenies. Because of transportation costs, the East Coast states had been a separate market from the states west of the Alleghenies. The association of cast-iron producers raised the price to the point where it paid East Coast producers to absorb the freight costs and sell in the states west of the Alleghenies. The question arose whether the six producers were monopolizing the market. If Taft looked at the narrow market west of the Alleghenies the answer was yes, but if he looked at the broad market—the whole country—the answer was no. Taft saw that the competition from the East Coast was brought on by the high prices west of the Alleghenies and reasoned that the narrow market was the relevant one. The narrow market within the broad market was monopolized.

[7]85 Fed. Rep. 271.

This case reveals that prices and other transaction terms in one narrow market are bounded by other surrounding narrow markets. Thus, there is an upper limit to prices in one narrow market before it becomes merged into surrounding markets. On the other hand, other narrow markets could be merged with a particular narrow market if the price in the latter becomes low enough.

Time Lags and Long-Run Demand. One of the most difficult problems in demand analysis to deal with empirically and theoretically is the time lag between a price change and a related change in the quantity demanded. For technological reasons or simply inertia, buyers do not always react immediately to price changes. Consider what would happen if electricity rates went up sharply. At first, there would not be a great fall in demand because buyers of electricity are "locked in" by their investment in electricity-using appliances. Thus, at first the fall in demand would be small, mainly because buyers become careful about wasting electricity. With the passage of time, however, with appliances wearing out, users of electricity are more free to reduce their demand for electricity. Some users might elect to do without some appliances; others might switch to appliances using alternative sources of energy, such as natural gas; still others may opt for electric appliances that economize on electricity consumption.

Economists have handled this problem with the concepts of short-run and long-run demand. The short-run demand curve gives the relation between price in a particular period and the quantity demanded in the same period. The long-run demand curve gives the relation between the price, assumed constant over several periods, and the quantity demanded in a future period after buyers have had time to change the quantities demanded. If we designate O as the period when the price might first be changed and t as some future period when buyers are free to make all adjustments, the two demand curves might appear as in Figure 8.6. The long-run demand curve is more price elastic than the short-run demand curve for each price. This will generally be the case, but there may be exceptions.

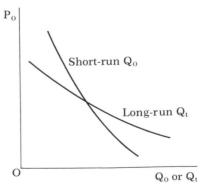

FIGURE 8.6   Short-run and long-run demand curves

There is a second way to view the lagged effect of a price in one period on the quantity demanded in a later period. We could think of the price in the earlier period as one of the determinants of the position and perhaps shape of future short-run demand curves. Thus, if the rise in electricity prices in initial period O prompted buyers to shift away from the use of electricity in later period t, the demand curve in period t would be further to the left than if the price in period O had not been increased. Figure 8.7 depicts what the alternative demand curves could be in future period t with and without the price increase in earlier period O.

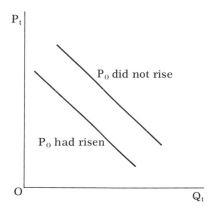

FIGURE 8.7   Effect of price in earlier period on demand curve in future period

CONSUMER DEMAND: UTILITY ANALYSIS

In this and the following sections, we present two interrelated models of the variables that determine the consumer's choice of purchases. Although these models have not been completely satisfactory, mainly because of conceptual difficulties in measuring "satisfactions" and "preferences" and comparing them among different consumers, they nevertheless provide us with a useful language and framework.

One of the models rests on the proposition that it is at least conceptually possible to cardinally measure the "utility" or "satisfaction" that a consumer derives from consuming any particular product or service or combinations of products and services. This proposition, which is closely associated with Jeremy Bentham and the aptly named utilitarian school of thought, dominated a good part of nineteenth-century economic theory in England and is also part of the American heritage in economic thought. But, essentially because of inability to measure utility, a model known as "indifference" analysis was developed. It did not depend on the cardinal measurement of utility. The pioneering work on the "indifference" model was done by the Italian economist Vilfredo Pareto and was developed in more modern times by the English economist J. R. Hicks.[8] Pareto did most of his work in the late nineteenth century; the work by Hicks in this area was done (or at least published) in the 1930s. Although for the most part indifference analysis has carried the day, utility analysis still has a variety of uses – mainly in the formulation of theoretical problems.

Let us assume for simplicity that there are only two products, 1 and 2 (we can also think of alternative bundles of goods). Then the total utility that a consumer would receive per period of time would depend on the quantities he consumes of these goods per period of time. With U the measure of utility and Q_1 and Q_2 the quantities consumed of the two goods, we can write the utility function as an unspecified function:

$$U = f(Q_1, Q_2). \qquad (8.17)$$

Although it may not be possible to measure utility, the analysis could proceed by making plausible assumptions about how utility changes as the consumption of either of the products changes. The change in utility with an increase in the consumption of either of the products is known as the marginal utility (MU), defined in general terms as

$$MU_1 = \frac{\partial U}{\partial Q_1} = \frac{\partial f(Q_1, Q_2)}{\partial Q_1} \qquad (8.18)$$

$$MU_2 = \frac{\partial U}{\partial Q_2} = \frac{\partial f(Q_1, Q_2)}{\partial Q_2}.$$

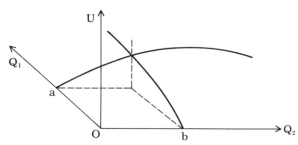

FIGURE 8.8   Utility surface

Figure 8.8 displays the type of utility surface generally assumed. As the consumption of either product increases, total utility increases, but at a decreasing rate. The decreasing rate of increase in utility is known as the law of diminishing marginal utility. In plain English, this means that an increase in consumption of one unit of a product yields a smaller increment in utility than the consumption of the previous unit yields. The notion of diminishing marginal utility also applies to money and is the theoretical basis for progressive taxation.

[8] John R. Hicks, *Value and Capital* (New York: Oxford University Press, 1939).

If the marginal utility of money decreases, then some amount of money taxed away from a rich man causes less loss of utility to him than a similar amount taxed away from a poor man. Thus, if we accept the ethical proposition that both the poor man and the rich man should make equal sacrifices of utility in paying taxes, the rich man should be taxed at a higher rate than the poor man.

The notion of diminishing marginal utility can be seen more clearly by taking cross-sections of the utility surface at, say, points a and b of Figure 8.8. The resulting cross-sections appear in Figure 8.9. Marginal utility at any level of consumption for either of the products is the slope, or first derivative, of the cross-sections. Notice that such a slope decreases as consumption of a product increases. There is a level of consumption for each product at which utility is at a maximum, beyond which utility actually falls (or marginal utility is negative). These levels are meant to convey the possibility that a consumer can consume so much of a product that he wants no more of it. These levels could be called the satiation points.[9]

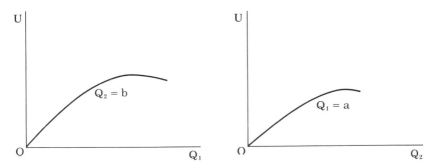

FIGURE 8.9   Cross-sections of the utility surface

How much of each of the products would the consumer want? If possible, he would consume up to the satiation levels for both products. But, though he may want to consume these levels, he may not be able to do so if he has a limited budget to spend and if the products have positive prices. His choice is subject to a budget constraint. If B is the size of his budget and if the prices of the two products are P_1 and P_2, the budget constraint can be expressed as

$$B = P_1 Q_1 + P_2 Q_2. \tag{8.19}$$

That is, he cannot spend more on the two products than his budget. By showing this constraint as an equation rather than as an inequation, we are assuming the whole budget will be spent.

[9]Satiation levels are real enough. For almost any product we can think of, there is an upper limit to the satisfaction we could obtain from increasing the quantities consumed. Perhaps the main exceptions might be when the product or service connotes some status or prestige.

If we assume the consumer will want to maximize his utility, we have a standard optimization problem. The decision variables are Q_1 and Q_2. Equation 8.17 is the preference function, with U the preference variable. Equation 8.19 is the constraint on the Q_1, Q_2 choices. Notice that Q_1 and Q_2 are the only variables in the equation: B, P_1, and P_2 are all parameters in this context.

Given the unspecified nature of the utility function, we can find the optimum Q_1, Q_2 combination with the use of the LaGrangian multiplier. We first set up the LaGrange equation:

$$U' = f(Q_1, Q_2) + \lambda(B - P_1 Q_1 - P_2 Q_2).$$

Notice that we have incorporated the constraint into the objective function by this step. Next we take the first derivative of U' with respect to Q_1, Q_2, and λ, and set them equal to zero. This is the way to find the value of Q_1, Q_2, and λ that maximizes U'. Thus, we have

$$\frac{\partial U'}{\partial Q_1} = \frac{\partial f(Q_1, Q_2)}{\partial f Q_1} - \lambda P_1 = 0 \qquad (8.20)$$

$$\frac{\partial U'}{\partial Q_2} = \frac{\partial f(Q_1, Q_2)}{\partial Q_2} - \lambda P_2 = 0 \qquad (8.21)$$

$$\frac{\partial U'}{\partial \lambda} = B - P_1 Q_1 - P_2 Q_2 = 0.$$

With these three equations in terms of three variables, a solution could, in principle, be found.[10] The resulting values for Q_1 and Q_2 are those that maximize U subject to the budget constraint.[11]

Even though we may not actually be able to measure utility, we can obtain some insights through some algebraic manipulations. Notice that $\partial f(Q_1, Q_2)/\partial Q_1$ is the marginal utility of product 1 (see equation 8.18) and that $\partial f(Q_1, Q_2)/\partial Q_2$ is the marginal utility of product 2. Thus, we can rewrite equation 8.20 and 8.21 in this way:

$$MU_1 - \lambda P_1 = 0$$
$$MU_2 - \lambda P_2 = 0.$$

Solving these equations for λ gives us

$$\lambda = \frac{MU_1}{P_1}$$

$$\lambda = \frac{MU_2}{P_2}.$$

[10]"Second order" conditions must be met for utility to be maximized rather than minimized. These are that the second derivatives of these equations must be negative.

[11]The lambda has an interesting interpretation. It signifies the increase in total utility that would come about with an increase in the budget. It is in many ways analogous to the value of a change in a constraint to the firm that we investigated in Chapter 6.

From these equations, we have the following relationships:

$$\frac{MU_1}{P_1} = \frac{MU_2}{P_2} \tag{8.22}$$

$$\frac{MU_1}{MU_2} = \frac{P_1}{P_2}. \tag{8.23}$$

These last two equations give us the optimizing conditions for the consumer. From equation 8.22, we can say the consumer allocates his budget between the two products so that the marginal utilities of the two products are proportional to their prices. Or, alternatively, we see from equation 8.23 that, for an optimum allocation, the marginal utilities should have the same ratio to each other as the prices of the products.

CONSUMER DEMAND: INDIFFERENCE CURVE ANALYSIS

The "indifference curve" model of the consumer is in much wider use than "utility" analysis. Indifference curve analysis avoids the assumption that consumers can measure utility cardinally. Instead this approach assumes only that the consumer is able to *rank* alternative combinations of goods; that is, he can measure utility ordinally.

The model of the consumer is similar to the basic decision model of the firm. The decision variables are the quantities to purchase of each of the goods. A preference map displays the consumer's preference for various combinations of goods. An opportunity set limits the combination of goods from among which the consumer can choose. This opportunity set is determined by the budget constraint, which depends on the consumer's budget (income, borrowing, past savings) and the prices of the goods. There is an optimization procedure in which we assume the consumer would select the optimal combination of goods. With this model, the analyst can generate a number of useful relationships. For example, by changing the price of one of the goods, it is possible to determine the quantity of that good that would be purchased at all alternative prices. This relation is, of course, the consumer's demand curve for that product.

To make maximum use of graphic analysis, where each product can be thought of as bundles of goods, we will limit ourselves to situations in which the consumer chooses between only two products. There will be three variations on the two-product model. In one there will be no money, so that all trade takes place through barter. This model is not, of course, realistic, but it does give some insights into what we mean by "price," "income," and "trade." The second variation consists of the choices between one product and money. In such a choice, it is well to realize that money represents all other products, including savings, which is all other future goods that can be consumed. Thus, the choice between a particular product and money is really the choice between that product and all other products. In the third variation, we assume the consumer has a sum of money, his budget, which is to be allocated to two products.

The Preference Map.

THE INDIFFERENCE CURVE AND INDIFFERENCE MAP. It is conceptually possible to develop a preference map for a consumer by considering some combinations of goods and then asking the consumer to name alternative combinations that yield him the same level of total satisfaction, or utility, as the first combination. All alternatives, when plotted on a diagram, indicate an indifference curve—so named because the consumer is indifferent to the various alternatives. By starting at other combinations and repeating this procedure, we can generate a large number of indifference curves. All the curves together constitute an indifference map, which enables us to readily ascertain the consumer's preference for any alternative combinations.

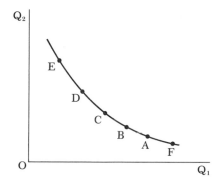

FIGURE 8.10   Construction of an indifference curve

Referring to Figure 8.10, let us say that we start with point A, which represents a combination of Q_1 and Q_2, the quantities of the two goods. We can now ask the consumer this question: If we take a certain number of units of product 1 away, how much more of product 2 would be required for the consumer to be at the same level of satisfaction as at point A? If some units of product 2 can compensate for the loss of product 1, there will be another point that gives the same total satisfaction as point A. Let us say this alternative combination is at point B, which represents less of product 1 than point A does but has more of product 2. At point B, the same question can be asked, and another alternative combination might be represented by point C. By the same procedure we can find points D and E. Starting at point A, we can also work the "other way." We can ask: If some of product 2 were taken away, how much of product 1 would be needed to give the same total satisfaction? This might be point F. In principle, by making very small changes in the amount of one of the products we "take away," we can determine all the points that give "equal" satisfaction. The line connecting the "equal satisfaction" points is an indifference curve.

Given such a curve, we can determine the rate at which the consumer is willing to trade one product for another at any point on the curve. This rate could be viewed as $\Delta Q_2/\Delta Q_1$. Thus if three units of product 2 are needed to compensate for the loss of one unit of product 1, the trade-off is three for one. If we think of ΔQ_1 as a small change, we call this trade-off the marginal rate of substitution (*MRS*). We can find the *MRS* at any point on the curve by drawing a tangent to the curve at that point. The slope of the tangent measures the *MRS*.

The *MRS* is not the same at any two points on the curve in Figure 8.10. If we take away a unit of product 1 at point *A*, less of product 2 is needed as compensation than if we take away a unit of product 1 at point *E*. Why should this be so? At point *A*, the consumer has a great deal of product 1 and not much of product 2. If the law of diminishing marginal utility holds true, he does not lose much utility by giving up a unit of product 1, and he gains a great deal of utility from more of product 2. Thus, he does not require much more of product 2 to make up for the loss in product 1. At point *E*, however, the relative scarcities of the two products are reversed. He loses a "high" amount of utility by giving up a unit of product 1 and does not gain a great deal of utility from an additional unit of product 2. Thus, he requires a much larger amount of product 2 to compensate for the loss of a unit of product 1 at point *E* than at point *A*.

Transferring the curve in Figure 8.10 to Figure 8.11, let us consider the combination represented by point *G*. Point *G* is drawn to be superior to point *A*; point *G* has more of both goods. If *G* is superior to *A*, it must also be preferred to all other combinations on the indifference curve through point *A*, because these other combinations are as good as *A*. Proceeding as before, we can again query our consumer about other combinations that are as good as the *G* combination. All these combinations, of which point *H* is one, then define a second indifference curve. Next we select point *J*, which is superior to *G*, and use the same procedure to derive a third indifference curve. We can start at any point and draw an indifference curve, and we can draw as many as we wish. All the curves taken together constitute an indifference curve map.

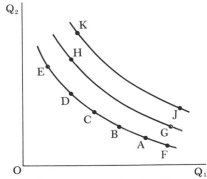

FIGURE 8.11   Construction of an indifference curve map

The resulting indifference curves can be thought to be the contours of a hill, defining a surface much as in Figure 8.8. But, unlike Figure 8.8, we do not know how high the hill is because we are not assuming that we can measure utility. All we know is that if we assume no satiation of either product, a combination in the NE direction is preferable to a combination that is SW of it.

We might wonder whether two indifference curves might cross — that is, have a point in common. The answer is no, if we assume that our model consumer's preferences are transitive. (By transitive, we mean that if a first combination of goods is preferred to a second combination and if the second combination is preferred to a third combination, then the first combination must be preferred to the third combination.) Consider the possibility that points H and E are the same in Figure 8.11, implying they give equal preferences. If G is preferred over A, and E is equally as good as A, and H is equally as good as G, then H must be preferred over E. The first and second indifference curves cannot have a point in common; they cannot cross or touch.

PRODUCTS AS PERFECT SUBSTITUTES. What if the two products are perfect substitutes; that is, a unit of product 1 delivers the same services in the same quantities as a unit of product 2? This condition implies that the consumer, starting at some Q_1, Q_2 combination, is always willing to give up one unit of product 2 for one unit of product 1 and vice versa. The indifference map would then appear as in Figure 8.12. Notice that the marginal rate of substitution, which is -1, is the same at all points on a particular indifference curve.

What if products 2 and 1 yield the same services, but twice as many of these services are yielded by each unit of product 2 than by each unit of product 1? This case implies that the consumer has a marginal rate of substitution of two units of product 1 for one unit of product 2 at all points on an indifference curve. The indifference map would then appear as in Figure 8.13.

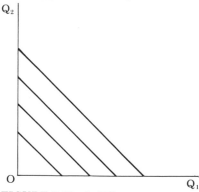

FIGURE 8.12   Indifference map: products are perfect substitutes

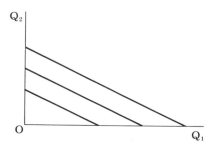

FIGURE 8.13   Indifference map: two units of product 1 are perfect substitutes for one unit of product 2

PRODUCTS AS PERFECT COMPLEMENTS. Two products are perfect complements in the technical sense when the services yielded by one are of use to the consumer only when they are combined with the services yielded by the other. Obvious examples are left and right shoes and nuts and bolts. To see what the indifference curve looks like, let us assume that the consumer starts with equal proportions between these products, at point A in Figure 8.14. We now ask the consumer whether he would be willing to give some Q_1 in exchange for more Q_2 in order to stay at the same level of satisfaction. He would not be willing to make this trade because he would have fewer useful Q_1, Q_2 combinations and would thus be at a lower level of satisfaction. If we gave him more Q_2 without any additional Q_1, he would not be any better off, if we assume that he does not sell any of the excess Q_2. The indifference map therefore has the shape shown in Figure 8.14. The *MRS* is zero at all points on a curve because the consumer cannot trade one product for another and still remain at the same level of satisfaction.

A COMBINATION OF SUBSTITUTABILITY AND COMPLEMENTARITY. Let us now assume that each of the products yields two services. One service from each of the products is the same, so that the products are substitutes for that service. The other service is unique. If the consumer needs some of the unique services, the products are also complements. Let us further say that with some combinations the consumer has so much of the common service that he is not willing to give up any of the unique services for the common service.

Figure 8.15 depicts the nature of the indifference curves under these conditions. Points A and B represent combinations in which the consumer is not willing to trade either of the unique services for the common service. For combinations of Q_1 and Q_2 on segment AB, the products are substitutes and the consumer is willing to give up some units of one of the products for some units of the other prod-

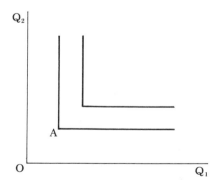

FIGURE 8.14 Indifference map: products are perfect complements

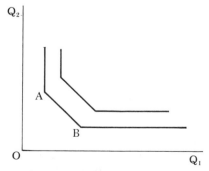

FIGURE 8.15 Indifference map: products deliver one service in common and unique services

uct. At points *A* and *B*, however, the consumer is not willing to give up more of the scarcer product for the other. There is a constant nonzero *MRS* within the *AB* segment, and a zero *MRS* beyond points *A* and *B*.

ALL SERVICES DELIVERED BY EACH PRODUCT. Let us consider the case in which both products deliver all the services needed by the consumer but the services are in different proportions in the two products. It is now possible to have combinations in which there are zero amounts of one of the products on the same indifference curve, as at points *B* and *C* in Figure 8.16. Why is more and more Q_2 needed to compensate for the loss of a unit of Q_1 if we move from *A* to *B*, or more and more Q_1 needed to compensate for a unit of Q_2 as we move from *A* to *C*? The answer lies in the differing proportions of the services in each of the products. Say that product 2 has a lot of service 4 and that product 1 does not have much of service 4. Say also that product 1 delivers a great deal of service 5 and that product 2 does not have much of this service. Then as we move from *A* toward *B*, we require increasing amounts of product 2 to compensate for the large loss of service 5 from giving up product 1. Similarly, as we move from *A* toward *C*, by giving up product 2 we give up a lot of service 4 and need increasing amounts of product 1 as compensation.

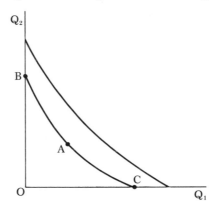

FIGURE 8.16   Indifference map: both products deliver all services

UNIQUE SERVICES IN EACH PRODUCT. Let us say that both products have many services in common that vary in proportion. But let us also say that each of the products has some unique services of which some minimum is required for survival. Then substitution between the two products is possible only in the range where the minimum requirements for the unique services from both products are satisfied. The indifference map would then appear as in Figure 8.17, where each indifference curve approaches the minimum requirement of each product.

SATIATION POSSIBILITIES. Thus far, we have assumed that the consumer cannot have too much of either of the products. But actually a

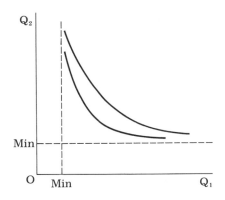

FIGURE 8.17 Indifference map: each product delivers some unique services, some minimum of which are required

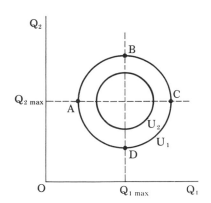

FIGURE 8.18 Indifference map: satiation possibilities

consumer can have too much of one or both of them. It is of some interest to explore the indifference curve map under conditions of satiation. Figure 8.18 depicts what the indifference curves might look like with satiation. On the axes of this graph we have denoted the maximum for both products the consumer may want. Beyond these maxima, the products are undesirable; that is, they are nuisances.

Consider first the curve denoted by U_1. In the AD segment both products are desirable, and we can trade one for the other and remain at the same level of satisfaction. In the AB segment, product 2 is undesirable but product 1 is not. If we asked the consumer what would be necessary in the way of product 1 if we were to give him more of product 2, he would require *more* of product 1 as compensation for *more* of product 2. In the DC segment, product 1 is undesirable. If the consumer gets more of product 1, he therefore requires more of product 2 as compensation to keep him at the same level of satisfaction. In the highly unlikely case where the consumer has too much of both products, he would be somewhere on the BC segment. As in segment AD, we can again compensate the consumer for (this time) a gain in one product with a loss in the other product. But, whereas starting from D we need increasing amounts of Q_2 to compensate for a loss in Q_1 (as we move toward A), from C we need decreasing amounts of Q_2 to compensate for a loss in Q_1 as we move toward B. Notice that U_2 is a higher indifference curve than U_1. It has greater amounts of Q_1 and Q_2 when they are desirable and less of Q_1 or Q_2 when they are undesirable.

INFLUENCING THE INDIFFERENCE MAP. Some of the services delivered by the two products are tastes or status. The indifference curves for any consumer are thus subject to influence by others. Advertising, for example, can convince the consumer that one product is not an adequate substitute for another or that one product provides more taste or status. Consumers can also be influenced by the consumption of others. Sometimes high consumption of a product, particularly by those in a higher social class, will increase preference for the product.[12] But, if a product is consumed heavily by lower social classes, preference can be decreased. Preferences could also be increased or decreased for a product with changes in income or in the overall standard of living. We can show the general nature of such influences on the consumer's indifference map.

Let us investigate first an advertising campaign by the producers of product 1 to convince consumers that product 2 is not an adequate substitute for product 1. If the campaign is successful, the indifference curves would have sharper curvatures, as in panel 2 of Figure 8.19, as compared to panel 1. In panel 1, the products are better substitutes; that is, a comparatively small amount of Q_2 is required for compensation for a loss of product 1.

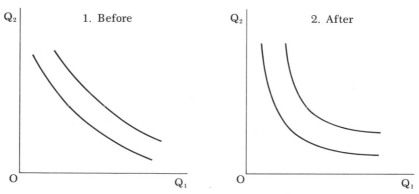

FIGURE 8.19   Indifference map: effect of successful advertising campaign stressing differences in products

Advertising and perhaps the consumption patterns of others could convince the consumer that somehow product 1 is superior to product 2. In terms of our indifference maps, the superiority of product 1 implies that a larger amount of product 2 is needed to compensate for the loss of a unit of product 1. The indifference map would then change from that in panel 1 of Figure 8.20 to that in panel 2.

Preferences for the two products could also change with increasing standards of living, represented by movements from lower to higher indifference curves. If product 1 is considered inferior to product 2 as the standard of living rises, the quantity of product 2 needed

[12]See Harvey Leibenstein, "Bandwagon, Snob and Veblen Effects in the Theory of Consumers' Demand," *Quarterly Journal of Economics*, vol. LXIV (May 1950).

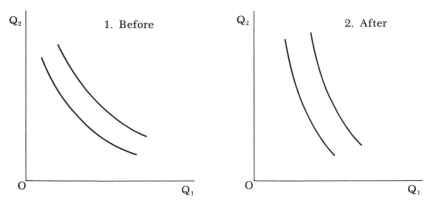

FIGURE 8.20   Indifference map: effect of successful advertising campaign to promote superiority of product 1

to compensate for the loss of a unit of product 1 becomes smaller as we move to successively higher indifference curves. The satiation point for product 1 could also be at lower levels for higher indifference curves. The "inferiority" of product 1 with improvements in the standard of living would be depicted in an indifference map as in Figure 8.21. Such a map lies behind the Giffen paradox.

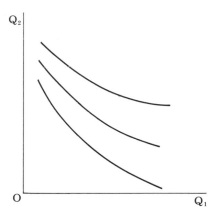

FIGURE 8.21   Decreasing desirability of product 1 at higher living standards

MONEY AS THE OTHER GOOD.   In all the indifference maps we have presented, we can show the trade-offs between product 1 and all other goods by the simple expedient of using money in place of Q_2 on the Q_2-axis. The same analysis of the shapes of the indifference curves holds, except they are determined by comparisons of Q_1 and all other good for substitutability, complementary, superiority, and inferiority.

The Budget Constraint. The indifference maps are our models of the consumer's preferences. If unconstrained, the consumer would select a consumption combination on the highest indifference curve. But of course he is constrained by his budget and by the positive prices of the goods.

We can examine the budget constraint in several ways. One is to assume the consumer has a budget of B dollars, which he divides between the amount spent on one product, Q_1, and the amount available for all other goods. If M is the money available for all other goods and P_1 is the price of product 1, and if we assume the whole budget is spent on either Q_1 or on all other goods (M), the budget constraint is

$$B = M + P_1 Q_1. \qquad (8.24)$$

M, the money spent on all other goods, and $P_1 Q_1$, the amount spent on product 1, evidently together must be equal to the budget B.

Another way to look at the budget constraint is to think of a consumer having a budget, B, which is to be devoted to the two products, 1 and 2. This budget can be thought of as the money allocated for both of these goods. If the entire budget is spent on the two products, the budget constraint is

$$B = P_1 Q_1 + P_2 Q_2. \qquad (8.25)$$

We can also consider the pure barter case. Let us say that the consumer is a producer of product 2 and that his production is Q_2' units. He consumes part of this (Q_2), and the rest he trades for product 1, so that his consumption of product 1 is Q_1. What is the price of product 1? Consider the trade of some amount of money M for some amount of Q_1. The price is then M/Q_1. By analogy, if the trade is Q_2 per Q_1, the price of a unit of product 1 is Q_2/Q_1 – that is, the number of units of product 2 required to obtain a unit of product 1. The budget equation, then, is

$$Q_2' = Q_2 + \left(\frac{Q_2}{Q_1}\right) Q_1. \qquad (8.26)$$

If, for example, the consumer produces 20 units of Q_2' (his budget), and if two units of product 2 trade for one unit of product 1, $Q_2/Q_1 = 2$, and the budget constraint is

$$20 = Q_2 + 2Q_1.$$

Notice that the greater the number of units of product 2 that must be traded to obtain a unit of product 1, the higher is the price of product 1.

If we know the budget and the prices in any of these three cases, we can readily determine the *possible* combinations of the products that can be consumed. Consider, for example, the case where the two products are product 1 and "all other" products (represented by money). If the budget is $100 per week and the price of a unit of product 1 is $4, the budget constraint, according to equation 8.24 is

$$100 = M + 4Q_1$$

or

$$M = 100 - 4Q_1.$$

Figure 8.22 shows graphically all the combinations of M and Q_1 that the consumer could purchase. Notice that the slope of this line is determined by the trade of money for Q_1, which is 4, the price of Q_1.

Consider next equation 8.25 and solve it for Q_2 to get

$$Q_2 = \frac{B}{P_2} - \frac{P_1}{P_2}Q_1.$$

The slope of this line is the ratio of the two prices. The ratio of these two prices, although expressed in dollars, is really the exchange rate between Q_1 and Q_2. If, for example, $Q_1 = \$4$, and $Q_2 = \$2$, we can say that one unit of Q_1 exchanges for two units of Q_2. If we again assume that $B = 100$, and that $P_1 = 4$, and $P_2 = \$2$, the budget constraint is

$$Q_2 = \frac{100}{2} - \frac{4}{2}Q_1.$$

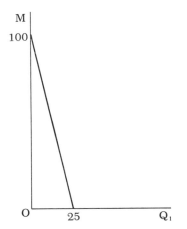

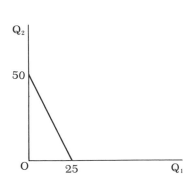

FIGURE 8.22 Budget constraint: one product and all other products (money)

FIGURE 8.23 Budget constraint: two products

Figure 8.23 shows all the combinations of Q_1 and Q_2 the consumer can obtain.

Let us now consider the barter case. If Q'_2, the amount produced by the consumer is, say 50, and the ratio Q_2/Q_1 is 2, the budget constraint from equation 8.26 is

$$50 = Q_2 + 2Q_1$$

or

$$Q_2 = 50 - 2Q_1.$$

The last equation is shown as Figure 8.24, which graphically gives the Q_1, Q_2 choices.

The budget constraint will change with changes either in the budget or in the prices – which are, of course, the parameters. Changes in the parameters, in turn, will change the possible combinations of products the consumer can obtain.

To show these changes, let us consider equation 8.24, product 1, and all other products, written as

$$M = B - P_1 Q_1.$$

If we assume some fixed amount of money for the budget, say \$100, we can investigate the effect of P_1 on the possible M, Q_1 combinations. Consider the alternative prices of P_1: \$1, \$2, \$3, \$4, \$5. The corresponding budget constraints are

$$M = 100 - 1Q_1$$
$$M = 100 - 2Q_1$$
$$M = 100 - 3Q_1$$
$$M = 100 - 4Q_1$$
$$M = 100 - 5Q_1.$$

Figure 8.25 graphically depicts the constraints corresponding to each of these five prices. The lower the value of P_1, the greater are the combinations of Q_1 and M that can be obtained by the consumer.

If we use the second case, where a given budget is available to be spent on two products, Q_1 and Q_2, we can study the effect of either P_1 or P_2 on the budget constraint. Consider this budget equation:

$$Q_2 = \frac{B}{P_2} - \frac{P_1}{P_2} Q_1. \tag{8.27}$$

Say we want to study the effect of different values of P_1 on the Q_1, Q_2 combinations possible to the consumer. If the budget is \$100, and $P_2 = \$2$, equation 8.27 becomes

$$Q_2 = 50 - \frac{P_1}{2} Q_1.$$

By inserting different values for P_1, we can obtain the constraints that correspond to alternative values of P_1. Figure 8.26 shows a sample of these constraints for different values of P_1.

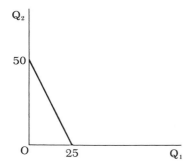

FIGURE 8.24   Budget constraint: pure barter case

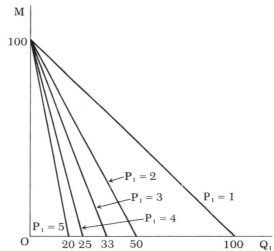

FIGURE 8.25   Alternative budget constraints with different values of P_1

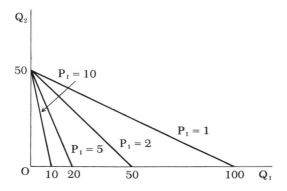

FIGURE 8.26   Alternative budget constraints at different values of P_1

With equation 8.27, we can also investigate the effects of different values of P_2 on the budget constraint. We must assume values for B and P_1. If we assume $B = 100$, and $P_1 = \$4$, the budget constraint is

$$Q_2 = \frac{100}{P_2} - \frac{4}{P_2}Q_1.$$

By taking different values for P_2, we can see how the value of P_2 affects the budget constraint. These are shown in Figure 8.27.

We can also investigate the effect on the constraint of changes in the budget. Consider equation 8.27 again. If the value of P_1 is \$4 and the value of P_2 is \$2, the budget equation becomes

$$Q_2 = \frac{B}{2} - \frac{4}{2}Q_1.$$

From this equation, we should be able to see that a change in B "shifts" the budget constraint parallel to itself. If, for example, $B = \$100$, the budget constraint would be

$$Q_2 = 50 - 2Q_1,$$

but if B were \$200, the constraint would be

$$Q_2 = 100 - 2Q_1.$$

Figure 8.28 shows the effect of changes in the budget on the budget constraint.

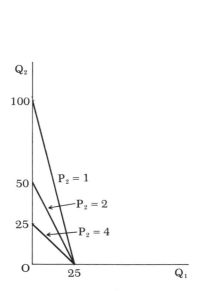

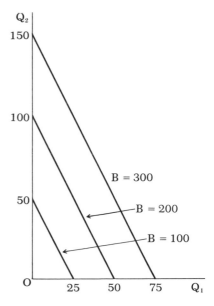

FIGURE 8.27   Effect on budget constraint of changes in P_2

FIGURE 8.28   Effect of changes in budget size on budget constraint

The Optimum Consumption Pattern. With the indifference curve map showing preferences for consumption patterns and the budget constraint showing the possible combinations of goods that can be obtained (the budget constraint can be thought to define the opportunity set), we can use our familiar techniques to obtain the optimum consumption pattern for our model consumer. Let us consider first the barter case. In Figure 8.29, we show the consumer's indifference curve map for two products, together with his budget constraint. Notice that the budget constraint is determined by his production of Q_2, designated Q_2', and the price of Q_1 – that is, the number of units of Q_2 needed to obtain a unit of Q_1. The point on the budget constraint lying on the highest indifference curve is then the optimal Q_1, Q_2 consumption pattern.

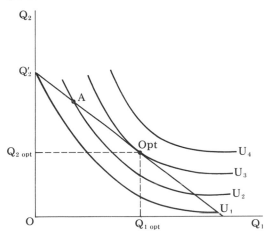

FIGURE 8.29   Optimum consumption pattern: barter case

At this optimum, the marginal rate of substitution is equal to the exchange rate at which the products trade on the market. The *MRS* measures the trade the consumer is *willing* to make; the market exchange rate measures the trade he is *able* to make. Whenever these two exchange rates differ, the consumer can improve his position. Say that at point A, he is willing to trade two units of product 2 for one unit of product 1 (the *MRS*) and that the market exchange rate is 1:1. The consumer can then trade one unit of product 2 for one unit of product 1 on the market. Because he is willing to trade two units of product 2 for one unit of product 1, he comes out one unit of product 2 ahead – thereby moving to a higher indifference curve. Only when the two exchange rates are equal is he not able to improve his position.

This consumer, starting with Q_2', would actually trade $(Q_2' - Q_{2_{opt}})$ units of Q_2 for $Q_{1_{opt}}$ units of Q_1. If there were no market, we would have to consume his whole production and would be on the indifference curve U_1. By being able to trade, however, he could get to U_3. In this example, we see the importance of trade. It enables this producer to specialize in the production of Q_2, yet obtain a more desirable combination of Q_1 and Q_2 for consumption. This is what Adam Smith was getting at when he argued that markets enable specialization of production.[13]

Deducing Relationships. We can now deduce how changes in price and the budget (or income) influence the quantity of a particular product the consumer would purchase. This is done by changing the appropriate parameter (for example, the price of the product), finding the optimal consumption at each value of the parameter, and then determining the relation between the parameter and the quantity purchased.

THE DEMAND CURVE. Let us consider first the relation between the price of a product and the quantity purchased. We use here as the two products Q_1 and M, where the latter, money, represents all other products. Figure 8.30 shows an indifference map between Q_1 and M and different budget constraints, each corresponding to a different value for $P_1 - P_{1a}$, P_{1b}, P_{1c}, P_{1d}. The tangencies of each of the budget constraints with the indifference curves show, for each budget constraint (which corresponds to different prices), the optimal M, Q_1 consumption pattern. The line connecting all these optima is known as the price-consumption curve, for it shows how consumption changes as the price of Q_1 changes.

For each value of P_1, which is represented by the slope of a budget line, there is a corresponding optimal value for Q_1. Thus, when the price is P_{1a}, the consumer would purchase a units of Q_1; when the price is P_{1b}, the consumer would purchase b units of Q_1; etc. If we plot the purchase of Q_1 corresponding to each price as in Figure 8.31, we have a number of points on that consumer's demand curve for product 1. Because we can draw in as many budget lines as we wish (each one corresponding to a value of P_1) and as many indifference curves as we wish, we can get all the P_1, Q_1 combinations on the demand curve. The demand curve itself is the locus of all these points.

THE EFFECT OF OTHER FACTORS ON THE DEMAND CURVE. By changing other parameters and the nature of the indifference curve, we can learn how various factors influence the position and shape of the demand curve. Say, for example, we want to know how a change in B, the budget, would influence the demand curve. We simply start with a higher value of B, say B' in Figure 8.30, draw in another set

---

[13]Adam Smith, *The Wealth of Nations* (New York: Random House, 1937); originally published in 1776. Smith was impressed with the way specialization in production increases productivity. Yet people prefer to consume a variety of products and services. Markets and the possibilities of exchange enable specialization in production and variety in consumption. This is one of the main reasons that most economists have advocated free trade.

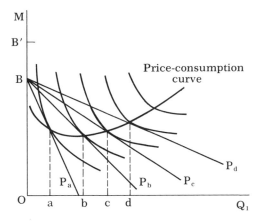

FIGURE 8.30   Derivation of price-consumption curve

of budget lines corresponding to different values for P_1, and derive a new demand curve. The P_1, Q_1 demand curves for B and B' can be shown on the same diagram, as in Figure 8.32, to deduce the effect of an increase in the budget on the demand curve. As we would normally expect, a rise in the budget from B to B' should shift the demand curve to the right; that is, with the higher budget, more Q_1 would be purchased at each price.

We could also experiment with the model by assuming different shapes for the indifference curves. If, for example, we assume that "all other" products contain many good substitutes for Q_1, the indifference curves would have a gentle curvature and the demand curve would have a gentle slope – indicating that a change in P_1 has a large effect on the demand for Q_1. On the other hand, if Q_1 tends to be unique, the indifference curves would have a sharper curvature and

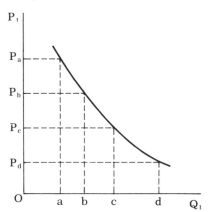

FIGURE 8.31   Derivation of
demand curve

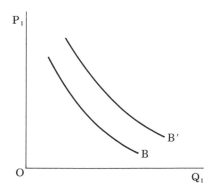

FIGURE 8.32   Effect of budget
level on position of demand curve

the demand curve would have a steeper slope—indicating that the quantity demanded does not respond greatly to a change in price. Figure 8.33 depicts two such demand curves to show the contrast.

THE EFFECT OF INCOME ON DEMAND. Using similar techniques, we can investigate the relationship between changes in the budget and quantity demanded when prices are held constant. Figure 8.28 depicts the manner in which a change in the budget affects the budget constraints. Using M (all other goods) for Q_2, we can superimpose these budget constraints on the indifference curve map, as in Figure 8.34, to obtain the quantity of Q_1 that would be purchased at each value of B. Thus, when the budget is B_a, a units of Q_1 will be purchased, and so forth. The line connecting the optimal M, Q_1 combinations corresponding to the different values for B is known as the income-consumption curve. Because we have the amount of Q_1 that would be purchased for every value of B, these B, Q_1 combinations can be used to show the relationship between B and Q_1, as in Figure 8.35. This curve is known as an Engel curve, named for a nineteenth-century statistician who investigated these types of relationships.

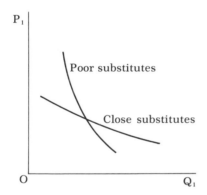

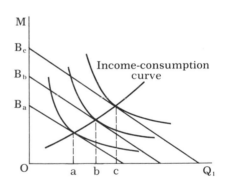

FIGURE 8.33   Effect of closeness
of substitutes on shape of demand
curve

FIGURE 8.34   Derivation of
income-consumption curve

Just as we investigated the effect of a change in the budget or the nature of the indifference curve map on the demand curve, we can investigate the effect of a different price or different indifference curves upon the Engel curve. Say, for example, we wanted to know how a lower value for P_1 would affect the Engel curve. We simply assume a lower value for P_1, which will lead to a set of budget constraints (see Figure 8.28) with gentler slopes. We then repeat the analysis carried on in Figure 8.34 for these new budget constraints and derive a second Engel curve. The new Engel curve and the first Engel curve are then placed on the same graph, as in Figure 8.36, to show the effect of the change in P_1 on the Engel curve. As we can see, the Engel curve shifts to the NW, implying that, at a lower value for P_1, more Q_1 would be purchased at any value of B.

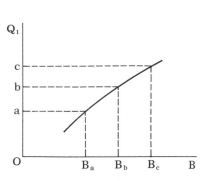

FIGURE 8.35 Engel curve

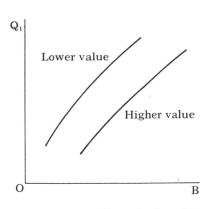

FIGURE 8.36 Effect of value of P_1 on the Engel curve

The Engel curve is particularly interesting when Q_1 is viewed as inferior at higher living standards, in which event the indifference map could appear as in Figure 8.20. When the budget lines corresponding to different values of B are superimposed on such an indifference map (using M instead of Q_2), the income-consumption line would appear as in Figure 8.37. Notice that it "bends back" at higher levels of B. The corresponding Engel curve is shown in Figure 8.38.

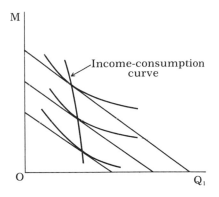

FIGURE 8.37 Income-consumption curve when product 1 is inferior

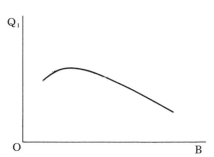

FIGURE 8.38 Engel curve for an inferior good

THE EFFECT OF THE PRICE OF ONE GOOD ON THE DEMAND FOR ANOTHER GOOD. In our final exploration, we can consider the relation between the price of product 2, P_2, and the demand for product 1. Figure 8.27 shows how changes in the value of P_2 affect the budget constraint. In Figures 8.39 and 8.40, we show how the different values for P_2 could influence the demand for Q_1. In Figure 8.39, the two products are taken to be strong complements, and a reduction in P_2 leads to an increase in the consumption of Q_1. But, when the two products are

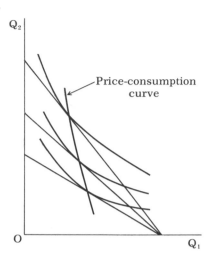

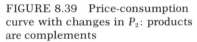

FIGURE 8.39   Price-consumption
curve with changes in P_2: products
are complements

FIGURE 8.40   Price-consumption
curve with changes in P_2: products
are good substitutes

good substitutes, as in Figure 8.40, a reduction in the price, P_2, results
in smaller values for Q_1. The Q_1, P_2 relations for both cases are shown
in Figure 8.41.

The Income Element in a Price Change. In deducing the demand
curve – that is, the relation between the price of a product and the
quantity of that product demanded – we were careful to hold income
(or budget) constant. But we are not really able to hold income constant, because a change in a price also changes a consumer's real
income, as opposed to his monetary income. It is of some interest to
ask what change in monetary income would be equivalent to a change
in price. It is also of interest to ask to what extent we can attribute a
change in consumption to the change in real income and to what
extent we can attribute this consumption change to the change in
price.
   Figure 8.42 shows two indifference curves, labeled U_1 and U_2. Assume at first that the individual has a budget B_a and that the price of
product 1 is P_a, so that the consumer selects the M, Q_1 combination
represented by point A. Now assume that the price drops to P_b, so
that the consumer can now select the M, Q_1 combination represented
by point D, which clearly lies on a higher indifference curve.
   We can now ask the following question: How much additional
monetary income would be equivalent to this consumer to the reduction in the price? If the price remained at P_a, a rise in income from
B_a to B_b would allow the consumer to move from U_1 to U_2, as did the

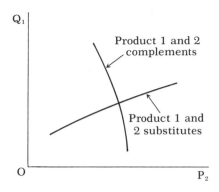

FIGURE 8.41   Relations between
P_2 and Q_1

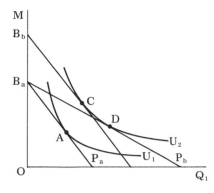

FIGURE 8.42   Income equivalent
of a price change

fall in the price. Thus, we can say that the change in money income
from B_a to B_b is *equivalent* to the fall in price from P_a to P_b, for both
bring the same higher level of satisfaction. This equivalence between
a price change and a change in monetary income has many useful
applications in the study of costs of living.

A rise in income from B_a to B_b, however, would change the consumption pattern from point A to point C, rather than from point A to point
D. We can therefore think of the observed change in consumption
from A to D to be comprised of two parts. The movement from A to C
can be designated the "income effect," for it is the change that
would have come about if income rose from B_a to B_b. But the lowering
of the price does not change only income; in addition it changes the
price of product 1 relative to all other prices. This change in relative
prices can be thought to be responsible for the movement from C to D.
It is known as the substitution, or price, effect. Thus, we can conceptually partition the observed change from A to D into two parts:
(1) change due to a rise in real income and (2) change due to a change
in relative prices.

The Concept of the Market Demand Curve. The market demand
curve is, conceptually, the "adding up" of all the demand curves of
the individual consumers in a given market. If we know the individual
demand curves, we can obtain one point on the market demand curve
by selecting a price and adding together the quantities that all the
consumers would purchase at that price. By repeating this procedure
for all different prices, we obtain all the points on the market demand
curve.

The market demand curve would shift or change its shape for the
same reasons that individual demand curves shift or change their
shape. In addition, the market demand curve could shift as the
result of a change in the number of consumers in the market.

EMPIRICAL ESTIMATES OF MARKET DEMAND

Although our theories of consumer demand are useful for identifying the variables that influence consumption and the types of relationships expected, in the real world demand functions are obtained empirically from the analysis of data. Sometimes the data are obtained from observing real-world prices, quantities purchased, incomes, and so forth. At other times, the data are obtained from experimentation, in which firms purposefully charge different prices in different areas to ascertain the extent to which price affects the quantity demanded. The actual estimation of the demand function falls within the province of the part of economics known as econometrics. Although econometrics works partly through "art" and "trial and error," the theory we have developed is crucial to the econometrician. It enables him to select the relevant variables, to formulate their relations, to make the necessary simplifying assumptions, and to check the reasonableness of his findings. Unfortunately, empirical demand functions are not always readily available in published form. Although many studies are made all the time by private firms, they are expensive and valuable and the firms try to keep the results confidential.

Estimating a Market Demand Equation. The first step in the estimation procedure is simply to identify the variables that could be expected to "explain" the level of purchases of the product being studied. Let us say that four important variables are selected: P, the price of the product; Y, the level of income of buyers; P_s, the prices of substitutes; and P_c, the prices of complements. This simple identification step is shown as a nonspecified equation:

$$Q = f(P, Y, P_s, P_c, u).$$

It will be noticed that we have included the variable u in this equation along with the other four variables. The variable u is known as the "stochastic" variable and is meant to represent all other forces that can influence Q other than P, Y, P_s, and P_c. In statistical analysis, we seldom expect a small number of variables to "explain" all the changes in the dependent variable — Q in this case. The u attempts to capture the effect of all other forces that are not explicitly specified in the model. Through the assumption of the distribution of u (it is usually assumed to be "normally" distributed), the statistician can make his estimates.[14]

Sometimes it is also desirable to include still one more variable, time. This is usually desirable (and necessary) when the data are

[14]For some leading works in econometrics and statistical demand analysis, see J. Johnston, *Econometric Methods* (New York: McGraw-Hill, 1963); and H. Wold and L. Jureen, *Demand Analysis* (New York: Wiley, 1958).

time series—that is, a sequential set of data for different periods of time. The time variable, usually designated t, is necessary to avoid spurious relations that could occur simply because the time series for the different variables have trends. If these variables have trends, they are related to time and would show a statistical relationship to each other, even though there may be no theoretical basis for such a relationship. (If, for example, we had two time series—the price of rice in India and the number of college students in the United States— they would have a statistical relationship because they would both have had upward trends. Yet there is no basis for logically expecting any kind of *causal* relationship between these two variables.) By putting the variable "time" into the model, we can guard against such spurious relationships.

The second step consists of formulating a relationship between the dependent variable, Q, and the other variables. One simple type of formulation is the "linear" model:

$$Q = b_0 + b_1 P + b_2 Y + b_3 P_s + b_x P_c + u.$$

A second type of formulation is the "exponential" model:

$$Q = b_0 P^{b_1} Y^{b_2} P_s^{b_3} P_c^{b_4} u. \tag{8.28}$$

The bs in these formulations are the parameters, and the job of statistical analysis is to estimate values for them. There is no explicit parameter for u, the stochastic variable, because, as part of the statistical techniques, u has an expected (average) value of zero in the linear formulation and an expected value of 1 in the exponential formulation. The constant terms in these equations—the b_0—are sometimes difficult to interpret. In such a demand equation, they probably reflect "taste."

The third step consists of gathering the data for the variables. An observation is a set of values for Q, P, Y, P_s, and P_c in our example. The observations could either be "time series" or "cross-sectional." An example of time-series observations could be a set of annual observations. Each year would then be the basis for an observation, which would consist of a value for each variable in that year. In cross-sectional analysis, the observations take place at some point in time. For example, each of the fifty states in the United States could provide the basis for an observation. For each state we would obtain a set of values for the variables.

Gathering the data and putting them into a useful form is not a cut-and-dried operation. If the observations are time series, we would have to adjust all the data on prices and incomes by a price index (deflating them) if there was any kind of inflation, so that these data are comparable among the various time periods. Sometimes the product is not homogeneous; there are a number of different prices for the product (we call the different prices a price structure); and there may be a number of different substitutes or complements. We then have to use index numbers to combine the products and prices into single numbers. Sometimes a variable cannot be measured directly. Consider, for example, the problem of measuring an expectation of a price increase. With some ingenuity, it is often possible to develop "proxy" variables to represent the variables that cannot be directly measured.

With the formulated model and the data, the next step is to estimate the values for the parameters. Estimation is done with some variant of multiple regression analysis in which the formulated model of the second step is "fit" to the data. We cannot go into this operation here, for to do so would take us too far afield.

The next step is to evaluate the results. One aspect of evaluation is to compare the parameters against what theory leads us to expect. When the parameters are not reasonable in light of the theory, either the theory or the statistical analysis may be incorrect. Usually, the statistical analysis is in error, although in many instances statistical analysis shows the theory to be wrong. In any event, we must have a strong case if theory does not support the statistical results, and in the absence of such a case, it is highly desirable to reevaluate the data and the statistical techniques. Many subsidiary statistics other than the parameter estimates—the coefficient of correlation, the standard errors of the regression coefficients (the parameters), the standard error of estimate, the residuals—enable the experienced econometrician to evaluate the quality and dependability of his results.

If evaluation shows the results to be unsatisfactory, the model can be reformulated and "refit" any number of times. Evaluation may show, for example, that some variables may not be necessary or that excluded variables should be included or that the exponential form would be better than the linear form or that more data are needed. Econometricians seldom stop after obtaining the first round of estimates for the parameters. With computers taking care of the computational work, it is generally not too difficult to tinker with the model and bring about improvements.

An important attribute of the multiple regression technique makes it a tool to the economist in much the same way that the laboratory is to the chemist. This attribute is the ability to hold the effect of other variables constant when the relationship between a pair of variables is being studied.

To see the importance of this attribute, let us say that we are interested in obtaining a relation between the price of gasoline and the quantity of gasoline consumed. Say we obtain data for each of the last ten years on the amount of gasoline purchased and the average price for each year. Let us say that we then adjust the price by a price index to account for inflation.

Would we obtain a demand curve if we "fit" a line to these data? No, we would not. The reason we would not get a demand curve — which is the relation between the quantity demanded and price for the gasoline with *everything else held constant* – is that many variables other than price could have influenced the quantity of gasoline purchased. Among these other variables could be increases in incomes of consumers, number of automobiles on the road, airplane fares.

Somehow the effect of these other variables on quantity and on price have to be held constant. The important attribute of multiple regression analysis is that when the other variables are included in the model, their effect is held constant.

To see this better, let us say that we have fit equation 8.28 to a set of data and have estimated the parameters to yield the following equation:

$$Q = 1.2P^{-0.5}Y^{0.3}P_s^{0.4}P_c^{-0.2}.$$

The parameters of the variables are technically known as *partial regression coefficients* that indicate the relation between Q and the particular variable when the effect of the other variables in the equation is removed or held constant. The parameter of P, for example, which is -0.5, gives the relation between Q and P with the effect of Y, P_s, and P_c held constant. Similarly, the parameter of Y, which is 0.3, gives the relationship between Q and Y with the effect of P, P_s, and P_c held constant.

Because the chemist in his laboratory generally arranges a controlled experiment in which only two variables are allowed to vary, we can see why multiple regression is used in much the same way by social scientists as physical scientists use the controlled experiment in a laboratory. The major difference, however, is that the social scientist cannot keep the "other" variables from varying. Instead, he statistically accounts for them.

Some Empirical Studies. Let us look at the result of a study of the demand for cars, originally published in the *U.S. Survey of Current Business* (June 1950). On the basis of annual observations from 1925 to 1940, the demand function was estimated as

$$Y = 0.00028X_1^{2.5}X_2^{2.1}X_3^{-1.3}(0.985)^t,$$

where Y is new car registrations per 1,000 households, X_1 is disposable income per household in 1939 dollars, X_2 is current income as a percentage of the preceding year's income per household, X_3 is a ratio of an automobile price index to the Consumer Price Index, and t is the year minus 1933 (1925 = -8; 1926 = -7; etc.).

We turn first to the variables: X_1, disposable income per household (in *real* terms, obtained by dividing by a price index) is certainly a variable that we should expect. The next independent variable, X_2, should be interpreted as a "proxy" for income expectations. We should generally expect purchases of expensive consumer durables to be guided by the consumer's expectation of future income. The difficulty usually lies in finding some way of measuring these expectations.

ɔnsists of an index of automobile prices (a price structure)
by the Consumer Price Index, where the latter would have
1.00. This procedure enables us to specify prices in terms of
ne kinds of dollars (1939). The time variable is treated here
as aɪɪ ᴇxponent to a parameter estimated by the regression techniques.
In this form, the parameter (here 0.985) is comparable to the rate of
interest in a compound interest formula.

Because this equation is in exponential form, the exponents (the
parameters) directly measure the elasticities. Thus, income elasticity
averaged 2.5 for that period, which we interpret in this way: If everything else remained the same, each 1 percent change in income
would result in a 2.5 percent change in quantitative demand, where
these changes were in the same direction. The 2.1 exponent for X_2 is
also a measure of elasticity: For every 1 percent change in the percentage of income in one year to the previous year, there would have
been a 2.1 percent change in quantitative demand, ceteris paribus.
These two measures of income elasticity, especially when taken together, show how sensitive automobile sales were to income in the
1925–1940 period.

Price elasticity was −1.3, indicating that, ceteris paribus, for each
1 percent increase (decrease) in price, a 1.3 percent decrease (increase) in quantity would occur.[15] In the observation period automobile sales were fairly price elastic. The parameter 0.985, which is
taken to the t power, can be interpreted as all the long-term "steady"
factors affecting automobile demand *other* than the variables treated
explicitly in the equation. If this parameter were 1, then these long-
term factors would have balanced out, with no effect on automobile
sales. With the actual parameter less than 1 (by 0.015), we can make
the following interpretation: If incomes and automobile prices did
not change over this period, auto sales would have declined by 1.5
percent per annum.

What if, knowing this equation in 1950, we wanted to forecast the
price-quantity demand curve for, say, 1960? Our first job would be to
forecast values for X_1 and X_2. To do this, of course, we would have to
have studied income changes and what could be expected in ten
years. We would also have to forecast a value for t, but this requires
nothing more than an ability to count. Let us work this out, using as

[15]A later study of automobile demand, based on more recent data, by Gregory
Chow, showed both price and income elasticities smaller than those in the
earlier study. With the automobile becoming more of a necessity, income elasticity should fall. With the breakdown in public transportation, the substitutes
for automobiles became poorer. Hence the decrease in price elasticity. See
Gregory Chow, "Statistical Demand Functions for Automobiles and Their Use
for Forecasting," in Arnold C. Harberger, ed., *The Demand for Durable Goods*
(Chicago: University of Chicago Press, 1960).

rough estimates $X_1 = \$3000$, $X_2 = 102.5$, and $t = 27$. The demand equation (price-quantity) is then

$$Y = 0.00028(3{,}000)^{2.5}(102.5)^{2.1}X_3^{-1.3}(0.985)^{27}$$

$$Y = \frac{1{,}535{,}000}{X^{1.3}}. \tag{8.29}$$

Actually, if we had used this equation to make a forecast for 1960, we would have been fairly close. The price of cars in 1960, in 1939 dollars, was roughly \$1200. At that price the demand should have been about 152 cars per 1,000 households. Because there were about 53 million households in 1960, sales in that year should have been about 8 million cars. The actual sales in 1960 were about 7 million cars. This error may have been due to the fact that 1960 was a recession year. If 1960 had been normal, the forecast would have been quite accurate.

Another demand study reported in the *U.S. Survey of Current Business* (May 1950), on furniture sales in the United States, yielded the following equation:

$$F = 0.0036Y^{1.08}R^{0.16}P^{-0.48}. \tag{8.30}$$

The model was fit to annual data on furniture sales, from 1923 through 1940, and the symbols have the following meanings: F is furniture expenditures per household (1939 dollars), Y is disposable personal income per household (1939 dollars), R is the value of private residential construction per household (1939 dollars), and P is the ratio of the furniture price index to the Consumer Price Index (1939 dollars).

In this case, expenditure is the dependent variable. Given the heterogeneous nature of furniture, expenditures makes sense. This avoids the complicated job of constructing an index of quantity.

As equation 8.30 indicates, the expenditure elasticity with respect to income is 1.08. R, the value of private residential construction, is a measure of a complementary product, which here affects expenditure. Notice that more residential construction results in an increased expenditure on furniture. The price elasticity is -0.48, but we must be careful in our interpretation because expenditure, not quantity, is our dependent variable.

If we are willing to think of an index of quantity for furniture, then we can substitute PQ for F in equation 8.30, where Q is this index of quantity and P is the price index. Then,

$$PQ = 0.0036Y^{1.08}R^{0.16}P^{-0.48}.$$

Dividing both sides by P yields

$$Q = 0.0036Y^{1.08}R^{0.16}P^{-1.48}. \tag{8.31}$$

This is the usual form of the demand equation. By comparing equation 8.31 with equation 8.29, it can be seen that income and "residential construction" elasticities for expenditures are the same as for quantities. The price elasticities differ, however. Equation 8.31 gives the price elasticity of −1.48, in the form we generally think of price elasticity — the response of quantity (rather than expenditure) to price.

An old study of steel by Theodore Yntema is of particular interest because it is for an intermediate, rather than a consumer, product.[16] His equation was

$$y = 1.49 - 1.27p + 6.27(dp/dt) + 4.64I - 0.03^t,$$

where y is the index of monthly sales of steel (millions of dollars), p is the price of steel (cents per pound, corrected for trend), dp/dt is the rate of change of the price of steel over time, approximated by $(p_t - p_{t-1})$, I is the index of industrial production, and t is time (January 1921 = 1). Observations were made monthly, from 1921 through 1930.

Because this equation is in linear rather than exponential form, the elasticities are not so readily seen. The coefficient of p, the price, is negative as expected. We should also expect, as found, a positive relation between I, the index of industrial production, and the demand for steel. In many respects, this index of industrial production plays the role income would play for a study of a consumer product. The fact that dp/dt was found to influence steel sales is especially interesting. Rising prices apparently had some influence on expectations of future prices. Thus, if a price rise is expected to lead to additional price rises, it could result in increases in demand. Those familiar with pricing in the steel industry would probably agree that this lesson has not been lost on the steel industry.

Perhaps the most important empirical work in demand analysis has been done by Richard Stone and his colleagues at Cambridge University in England.[17] Models of the exponential type, such as equation 8.28, were fit to data on virtually all food items. Table 8.1 presents the income elasticities, price elasticities, and cross-price elasticities with respect to particular products. These are given for the most important food items in England. The exponential form yields these elasticities directly from the exponent coefficients. The "standard errors" of these coefficients are given in parentheses. To have a great deal of confidence in a coefficient (which here also measures elasticity), the coefficient should be at least twice as large as its standard error. When this is not so, we can say the coefficient does not differ significantly from zero.

[16]Hearings before the Temporary National Economic Committee, Part 26, *Iron and Steel Industry*, 1940.

[17]Richard Stone, *Measurement of Consumers' Behavior in the United Kingdom, 1920–1938* (Cambridge: Cambridge University Press, 1954). The data were from the 1920s and 1930s.

TABLE 8.1   Elasticities for specified food commodities in
            Great Britain

Stone's equation number	Commodity	Income elasticity	Price elasticity	Cross elasticity to price of specified product
1	Flour	−0.15 (0.11)	−0.79 (0.21)	
2	Bread	−0.15 (0.04)	−0.08 (0.07)	
3	Cakes and biscuits	0.73 (0.13)	−0.74 (0.20)	
7	Other cereals	0.49 (0.13)	−0.09 (0.01)	Condensed milk: 0.52 (0.18); bread: 0.22 (0.13)
9	Home-produced beef and veal	0.34 (0.06)	−0.41 (0.18)	Imported lamb and mutton: 0.50 (0.15)
13	Imported beef and veal	0.34 (0.06)	−0.55 (0.45)	Home-produced beef and veal: 1.57 (0.41); fresh fish: 0.33 (0.30)
25	Bacon and ham	0.55 (0.09)	−0.88 (0.12)	Carcass meat: 1.45 (0.43)
33	Eggs	0.54 (0.07)	−0.43 (0.12)	Home-produced mutton and lamb: 0.86 (0.35)
35	Fish, fresh and cured	0.88 (0.07)	−0.74 (0.15)	Carcass meat: 0.85 (0.24)
37	Fresh fish	0.92 (0.07)	−0.57 (0.14)	Carcass meat: 0.85 (0.24)
39	Cured fish	0.76 (0.15)	−0.65 (0.37)	Fresh fish: −0.89 (0.31); home-produced beef and veal: 0.73 (0.15)
51	Fresh milk	0.50 (0.18)	−0.49 (0.13)	Cream: −0.23 (0.07)
67	Condensed milk	−0.53 (0.18)	−1.23 (0.82)	Fresh milk: 2.25 (0.53); margarine: 0.80 (0.23); tea: 1.06 (0.35); cheese: 0.43 (0.19)
69	Cream	1.71 (0.29)	−0.69 (0.36)	Imported eggs: −1.06 (0.25)
81	Butter	0.37 (0.08)	−0.41 (0.13)	Fresh milk: −0.21 (0.11), cakes and biscuits: 0.56 (0.26); tea: 0.63 (0.30)
97	Margarine	−0.16 (0.11)	0.01 (0.17)	Butter: 1.01 (0.17); chocolate: 1.02 (0.26); cakes and biscuits: −0.46 (0.31)
101	Home-produced potatoes	0.21 (0.06)	−0.56 (0.06)	Imported potatoes: 0.09 (0.06)
103	Imported potatoes	0.21 (0.06)	−1.32 (0.21)	Home-produced potatoes: 1.67 (0.22)
125	Home-produced apples	1.33 (0.21)	−1.67 (0.20)	Other fresh fruits: 2.77 (0.66)
141	Oranges	0.92 (0.17)	−0.97 (0.24)	Dried fruit: 0.63 (0.32); fresh green vegetables: 0.37 (0.26); bananas: 0.32 (0.27)
145	Bananas	0.95 (0.18)	−0.89 (0.23)	Canned and bottled fruit: −0.54 (0.25); oranges: −0.26 (0.18)
183	Tea	0.04 (0.04)	−0.26 (0.09)	Coffee: 0.14 (0.08); beer: 0.08 (0.05)

Source: Richard Stone, *Measurement of Consumers' Behavior in the United Kingdom, 1920–1938* (Cambridge: Cambridge University Press, 1954), table 106.

Even though Stone is an acknowledged authority on statistics and demand analysis, we should not accept his results blindly. Instead, we should ask whether they are reasonable in the light of what is known about the consumption habits of the English and the nature of the product. If the results were not reasonable, we should obviously be extremely cautious about using them.

A few questions could illustrate how we might evaluate the results. Could the *negative* income elasticities for flour, condensed milk, and margarine be explained? Why does neither income nor price have any appreciable affect upon the demand for bread? Is such a low income elasticity for tea to be expected in the United Kingdom? What about in the United States? Are the high income elasticities for fruit to be expected? Is there any way to rationalize a negative cross elasticity between the prices of imported apples and the demand for home-grown apples? Or between the price of fresh fish and the demand for cured fish? Should we be a little surprised that the price elasticity for fish, fresh and cured, is greater than the price elasticity for either fresh fish or cured fish? Why do the prices of home-produced potatoes have a very large effect upon the demand for imported potatoes while the price of imported potatoes has a negligible effect upon the demand for home-grown potatoes?

To some of these questions reasonable explanations would support Stone's statistical findings. Other of his findings appear difficult to rationalize – and should not be accepted for any decision-making purpose. Stone should not, of course, be criticized for presenting questionable results. Instead he should be applauded for his honesty and adherence to the best in the scientific tradition: only by presenting the bad with the good can any reader be in a position to evaluate Mr. Stone's work and techniques.

When interpreting the elasticities in Stone's study, and those in the automobile and furniture studies, we should be aware of problems that arise because the exponential form of the relationships assumed in these cases yields constant elasticities. Earlier, however, we suggested that as the price of a product became very high or low, the price and cross-price elasticities should be expected to change. Thus, the elasticities of these statistically tractable exponential models should be thought to be valid not for the whole possible demand curve but for the portion of the demand curve for which the observations were collected.

Another large-scale study, that of expenditure elasticities, was published in the *U.S. Survey of Current Business* in 1950. Based on United States annual data for 1929–1940, the *expenditure*-to-income elasticities were estimated for a large number of products and services. These elasticities are shown for selected products and services in Table 8.2.

These figures also raise many interesting questions. Why are the durables so much more income elastic than services and nondu-

TABLE 8.2 Expenditure-to-income elasticities for selected products and services for the United States

Product or service	Expenditure elasticity with respect to income
Boats and pleasure aircraft	3.1
Radios, phonographs, records	2.5
Pianos and other musical instruments	2.3
New cars and net purchase of old cars	2.0
Luggage	1.9
Jewelry, watches	1.8
Furniture	1.6
Floor coverings	1.4
Books and maps	1.2
Refrigerators, washing machines, sewing machines	1.0
Stationary and writing supplies	1.4
Clothing and accessories (not footwear)	1.1
Admissions, legitimate theater and opera	1.9
Admission – professional baseball	.9
Dentist service	.9
Beauty parlor service	.8
Drug preparations and services	.6
Gasoline and oil	.5
Magazines, newspapers, sheet music	.5
Barber shop services	.7
Owner-occupied dwellings	.5
Telephones	.4
Legal services	.3
Water, gas, electricity	.2

Source: From *Survey of Current Business*, January 1950.

rables? Why are cars and gasoline, two complementary products, so different in their expenditure elasticities? Can we understand why public utility stocks are considered good hedges against depressions? Do these elasticities look reasonable for the 1970's, and in what way could they be changing? Is it better to be in a business with high or with low expenditure elasticities?

SUGGESTIONS FOR EMPIRICAL ESTIMATES OF DEMAND FUNCTIONS

We would like to close this chapter by suggesting an approach to empirical demand curves. Its value lies in working with data on expenditures rather than quantities. Data on expenditures are usually much more available than data on quantities, and the use of expenditures avoids some difficult problems that arise when a product is heterogeneous.

Let us say that E is the expenditure on the product of interest, and ΣE is the expenditures on all consumer goods and services. Then the ratio $E/\Sigma E$ gives the proportion of all expenditures made on the product. This proportion could generally be easily determined. It could be influenced by the price of the product, income, and the prices of substitutes and complements. One way to formulate the relationship is:

$$\frac{E}{\Sigma E} = b_0 P^{b_1} Y^{b_2} P_s^{b_3} P_c^{b_4}. \tag{8.32}$$

If data were gathered, the parameters of such a model could be readily estimated. The parameters b_1, b_2, b_3, and b_4 would still be elasticities, but instead of quantity, the elasticity would refer to the proportion of total expenditures made on the product. Thus, if b_2, say, was 0.5, we would interpret it as a 1 percent increase in income leads to a 0.5 percent increase in the proportion of all expenditures devoted to that product.

Equation 8.32, whose parameters should be fairly easy to estimate, can be converted into a more usual demand equation. If we know the average price for the product and the number of units sold, we can say that $E = PQ$ and write equation 8.32 as

$$\frac{PQ}{\Sigma E} = b_0 P^{b_1} Y^{b_2} P_s^{b_3} P_c^{b_4}. \tag{8.33}$$

We can also replace ΣE. From macroeconomic theory we know that consumption expenditures generally have a fixed relation to national income (or GNP), which is Y. We can write this relation as $\Sigma E = aY$, where a is the proportion of GNP devoted to all consumer goods. We can now write equation 8.33 as

$$\frac{PQ}{aY} = b_0 P^{b_1} Y^{b_2} P_s^{b_3} P_c^{b_4}.$$

Now, by solving this equation for Q, we get the more usual form of the demand function:

$$Q = ab_0 P^{b_1-1} Y^{b_2+1} P_s^{b_3} P_c^{b_4}.$$

The exponent of P, $(b_1 - 1)$, is now the usual price elasticity, and the exponent of Y, $(b_2 + 1)$, is the usual income elasticity. (Notice that Y could be alternatively specified as GNP or disposable household income.)

Discussion Questions

1. It was argued that the quantity demanded of a product depends on variables in addition to the product's price. If we define the price-quantity relationships as the demand curve, in what sense should the other variables be viewed as "shift" variables?

2. What would we expect to influence the degree of price elasticity of a product? Might we expect price elasticities in general to increase or decrease as an economy becomes richer? How might the availability of information, the willingness to search by buyers, and habit influence the degrees of price elasticity?

3. What happens to the revenue to sellers when price is increased for a product when the price is in a range where price elasticity is low? Is it in the buyer's interest for demands to be price elastic or price inelastic?

4. What relationship is there between income elasticity for a particular product and whether it is more of a necessity or a luxury?

5. Provide some examples of products that we considered "inferior."

6. If data were available on average housing expenditures for different income groups, how might we calculate expenditure elasticities?

7. How might an analyst use income or expenditure elasticities to forecast the demand for a particular product?

8. How might the concept of cross elasticity of demand be useful for determining how "close" markets might be to each other? How might this concept be helpful in defining a market?

9. Should we expect the cross elasticity of demand of one product with respect to another product to be about the same going both ways? Why or why not?

10. What are some of the factors that determine whether goods are complementary to each other? Give examples of complementary and substitute products.

11. What effects do tariffs and trade restrictions have on market definitions? Who might benefit from the broadening of markets? Who might be hurt? Is there any relation between the reduction of trade barriers between countries and the specialization of production in the various countries?

12. In an antitrust case resolved by the Supreme Court in 1956, the issue was whether the DuPont Company, which produced almost all the cellophane in the United States, had monopolized "the market." What do you think was the government's definition of the market? What would DuPont have argued is the market? How might the Supreme Court have tested these contradictory definitions? Similarly, in 1945 Alcoa was charged with having monopolized the aluminum market. What might Alcoa's defense have been on the grounds of market definition?

13. How might we test whether two products are in the same market?

14. Why might there be a time lag between a change in the price of a product and the quantity demanded of that product? How might this time lag lead to a miscalculation of price elasticity?

15. What evidence might there be for the proposition that marginal utility decreases with an increase in the consumption of a product? Would marginal utility decrease more rapidly for a product that satisfies basic biological needs or for a product whose consumption gives a great deal of status and enjoyment to the consumer? Why?

16. In what way is the assumption that indifference curves are convex to the the origin consistent with the notion of diminishing marginal utility?

17. Explain the equivalence of a change in prices and a change in monetary income.

18. Consider the following procedure for estimating the demand curve for gasoline: First, obtain the average price and quantity sold for each of the last ten years. Second, plot the price-quantity observations for each of these years on a scatter diagram where price is one axis and quantity the other. Third, find the curve that best fits these observations. Would this curve then be a demand curve? Why or why not? What might have to be done to get the demand curve?

19. What are some of the pitfalls we should be aware of when using a demand function estimated from historical data to forecast a future demand curve?

9 Market Models and the Firm's Demand Constraint

Of all the constraints facing the firm, the parameters of the demand curve constraint are typically the most difficult to estimate and forecast. In this chapter we consider the problem of estimating these parameters, and we develop a methodology that holds great practical promise for this purpose. The firm's demand curve is intimately linked with the structure and behavior of markets, so a study of market models is included here. We discuss a general demand function in terms of some market structures—namely, pure competition, pure monopoly, monopolistic competition, and oligopoly—and examine the problems of determining the firm's demand curve for them.

GENERAL MODEL OF THE FIRM'S DEMAND CONSTRAINT

In Chapter 8, we considered both theoretical and empirical studies of market demand functions. The demand functions related the quantity demanded of a product (or group of similar products) by all buyers from all sellers in the market to the price of the product, the incomes of buyers, prices of substitutes and complements, and so forth. In this chapter we assume that the market demand function has been estimated for the product, one of whose suppliers is our model firm. We should recall from the last chapter that, in the real world, we have to define a market in terms of its narrowness or broadness. Here we will assume that the market has not been so narrowly defined that it consists of only one firm's product but instead is defined broadly enough to include products that are close substitutes. However, even in a

311

fairly broadly defined market, the products of the sellers may be perfect substitutes. Furthermore, there may still be just one seller in even a broadly defined market.

Our problem in this chapter is to make the transition from the market demand curve for all sellers to the demand curve facing a particular firm. We can begin by asking what influences an individual firm's share of the market, where the share is symbolized by Q/Q_m, in which Q is the number of units demanded from the firm and Q_m is the total number of units demanded by the market. Surely we would expect the firm's price relative to the prices asked by all sellers to be one of the determinants of the firm's market share. Another determinant is the ability of the firm to deliver its product or service as compared to the delivery ability of all firms selling in the market.[1] Still another factor would be the preference of buyers for the firm's product (or service) relative to their preference for all products sold by all sellers. Other factors could determine a firm's market share, but we think relative price, relative delivery ability, and relative preferability are the most important determinants.

Several equation forms could relate the firm's market share to prices, delivery ability, and preferability. However, we have chosen one that has the virtue of simplicity and holds great promise for enabling firms to empirically estimate their demand curves:

$$\frac{Q}{Q_m} = a + b(P_m - P) + c(D_m - D). \tag{9.1}$$

In this equation, a, b, and c are parameters, reflecting the degree and intensity of preferability for the firm's product and the sensitivity of market share to price and delivery time differentials. Q is the quantity demanded of the firm; Q_m is the quantity demanded from all sellers. The value of Q/Q_m, of course, can vary only between 0 and 1. P is the firm's price, and P_m is the average market price. If the products of all sellers are exactly alike, there will generally be only a single value for P_m. However, if the products of the sellers are not homogeneous, there will not be a single market price. Instead, there would be a "structure" of prices, and P_m could be interpreted as an average of all prices asked by all sellers.[2]

---

[1]Economists have generally neglected the role of delivery ability on the firm's demand curve. It is a crucial factor in explaining why firms of different sizes that produce identical products could have different demand curves.

[2]When a market consists of a number of products that are differentiated, although they compete with one another, there need not be a single price for all products. Instead there would be different prices for the various products. All the prices together could be defined as a price structure. In a structure of prices, individual prices should bear a fairly stable relationship to each other if the products are substitutes. There is, for example, no single automobile price. Rather different brands and styles have different prices, and these prices are a structure of prices. We generally expect the price of one type of car to maintain a stable relation to the prices of other types of car.

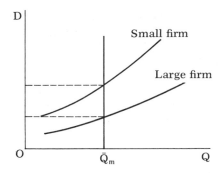

FIGURE 9.1   Hypothetical relation between volume of business and delivery time for small and large firms

The variable D is the firm's delivery time, which could be the length of time between the placing of an order and its delivery, the length of time it takes a customer to be serviced, and so forth. Delivery time is meant to reflect the limitation on the capacity of firms to take business from each other in the short run. D_m is the average delivery time of all suppliers in the market. The measurement of D and D_m is not simple. The value of D for any firm is best thought of as the length of time it would take that particular firm to deliver *if* the total quantity demanded by the market – that is, Q_m – were divided equally among all the selling firms. Thus, firms with small capacities would have a high value for D, while firms with larger capacities would have a lower value for D.

The delivery time in the short run could be expected to vary with the firm's level of orders. Figure 9.1 depicts what the relation between D (delivery time for orders) and Q (the amount of orders) might be for two firms – one with a low capacity and the other with a high capacity. $\bar{Q}_m$ is the amount of business each firm would have if Q_m were divided equally among all firms. With $\bar{Q}_m$, we can conceptually estimate the value of D for each firm.

Even though D could vary with Q (and by implication D_m could vary with Q_m), the *difference* between D and D_m could remain reasonably stable in the short run. Notice in Figure 9.1 that a rise in $\bar{Q}_m$, although it may affect the value of D, may not greatly influence the *difference* in delivery times between a small firm and large firm. Thus, in the short run, although D and D_m are variable, in many cases it would be reasonable to treat the *difference* between D_m and D as a constant.[3]

[3]It is crucial that D be measured as the delivery time for a particular firm if the market output were divided up equally among all sellers. We cannot obtain D by observing the actual delivery times of different firms because buyers will tend to apportion themselves among the sellers in such a way that delivery times would be observed to be approximately equal. If we are to *explain* market shares, the values of D must be obtained in the way described in the text rather than by observation of actual delivery ability.

The parameters a, b, and c require some detailed discussion. Parameter a represents the market share the firm would have if its price and delivery ability were the same as the average market price and delivery time. When this is so, $P_m = P$, $D_m = D$, and the second and third right-hand terms of equation 9.1 are zero. Parameter a can vary between 0 and 1 and depends on the relative preference for the firm's product when its price and delivery time are the same as those of the average of all firms in the market. The value of a could also be affected by the number of firms in the market.

If a firm's product or service were viewed as exactly the same as that of all other supplying firms in the market, buyers would have no preference for dealing with any particular firm. It is thus reasonable to expect in such a case that buyers would apportion their purchases equally among all sellers. If, then, there are n supplying firms in the market, the value of a should be $1/n$. If, however, the firm's product is differentiated, the value of a could be anywhere between 0 and 1. If the firm's product is considered inferior to all other products supplied in the market (remember that $P_m = P$, $D_m = D$), then a would be zero. But if the firm's product is considered superior to all other products supplied in the market, the value of a would be 1. If the firm's product is neither completely inferior nor superior to other such products, a would reflect the proportion of the buyers (weighted by their purchases) that prefer the firm's product, given the equality of prices and delivery times.

The firm should be able to influence the value of a. If it successfully styles its product to appeal to buyers, advertises, or otherwise convinces buyers of the superiority of its product, the firm can increase the value of a. The effect of such a campaign on the consumer's indifference map was shown in Chapter 8. The value of a, however, is also susceptible to similar activities by the firm's rival suppliers. The value of a could therefore decline if rivals mount successful advertising or product styling (or improvement) campaigns. Because we have taken advertising and product change to be long-run decisions, we can consider the value of a stable in the short run but susceptible to change in the long run.

The coefficient b reflects the sensitivity of the firm's market share to differences between the firm's price and market prices. This sensitivity in turn depends on the degree of substitutability between the

---

We should note that there may be alternative methods of handling delivery times. Instead of D_m, we might use D_r, which reflects the delivery time of rivals. It is also possible to express D as a function of Q, the firm's output, and D_r as a function of Q_r, the output of all rivals. In the latter event, it would make sense to view D_r not as the average delivery time of rivals, but as the delivery time of all rivals taken as a group. Because this treatment of delivery time is rather novel, and we do not wish to make our models too complicated, we make the simplifying assumption that D_m is an average and that $D_m - D$ tends to be constant in the short run. Other interpretations are of course possible.

firm's product and the products of all others. If the products are poor substitutes, the value of b will tend to be low. On the other hand, if the product of the firm is a close substitute for the products of rivals, b will be large. In the case of perfect substitutability, b can be so high that it approaches infinity. Whereas the a parameter reflects preferability, parameter b could be thought to reflect the *intensity* of the preferability of the firm's product relative to the products of rival firms. The intensity of the preference for a product relative to preference for all products ultimately depends on the degree to which price differentials influence a firm's share of the market. If, for example, the firm's product were intensity preferred, the parameter a would be high, but the parameter b would be low.

Parameter c reflects the sensitivity of the firm's market share to differences in the firm's delivery time and average delivery time. Parameter c will tend to be high or low for the same reasons that b will be high or low. If the firm's product is highly substitutable for products of rivals, the value of c will tend to be high. If, on the other hand, the firm's product tends to be more unique, the value of c could be low. In other words, buyers would be unwilling to wait a long time for a firm's delivery if its product is no different from that of rivals, but they might be willing to wait if the product is more unique and preferred by some buyers.

The firm, through some of its long-run policies, could influence the values of the b and c parameters. If it differentiates its product, it can reduce the values of b and c; if it makes its product like those of its rivals, it can raise the values of b and c. All other things remaining the same, the firm should prefer low values for b and c, because they mean that the firm's market share is less sensitive to its price and delivery capability. But all other things are not the same. A change in the product influences not only b and c but also the parameter a, which reflects preferability. Thus a more unique product, although it may reduce b and c, may also reduce a if the uniqueness is not well thought of by many buyers. On the other hand, a product that is not unique, if viewed as more preferable by buyers, may raise parameter a along with increases in the values of b and c. In the real world, we do not observe firms always trying to make their products more unique. More frequently, perhaps, they tend to copy successful products of other firms. Ideally, of course, the firm would want to design its product and slant its advertising to simultaneously increase a and reduce b and c.

The value of D is susceptible to the firm's policies. Sufficient production capacity, the maintenance of inventory, delivery facilities, locating warehouses close to buyers, are all means by which the individual firm could influence D. Although a lowering of D relative to D_m would increase the firm's market share, there are costs involved and the firm must weigh them against the benefits of a higher market share. Sometimes a firm could increase its market share by influencing D_m—by acting to deny materials to rivals or by interfering in any other way with their ability to produce. It is mainly because of differences between D and D_m that large multi-locational firms face demand curves "farther to the right" than those of smaller firms.

We should point out that P_m and Q_m in equation 9.1 are not independent of each other. They are related as in the market demand functions discussed in Chapter 8. Thus, a substantial change in P_m could affect Q_m, and therefore the firm's demand curve, even though the firm's market share does not change.

The firm would, of course, face problems in estimating values for the parameters a, b, and c. If data were available on Q, Q_m, P, P_m, D, and D_m, the parameters could be estimated with multiple regression analysis. They could also be estimated with the use of consumer panels, test marketing, and other tools of market research.

MARKET STRUCTURE

The structure of a market can influence the firm's demand curve (based on equation 9.1). The structure of a market consists of all characteristics that affect the decisions of buyers and sellers. If the product is homogeneous and is traded among a well-defined set of buyers and sellers, the two basic structural characteristics that will affect the demand curve of a particular firm are the number of independent buyers and sellers and the conditions of entry of new sources of supply of the product. The number of independent buyers and sellers would be the crucial characteristic in the short run; the conditions of entry would become important only in the long run. If, in addition, the product is not homogeneous—that is, if it can be differentiated—we need to consider also the degree of substitutability of the various products when we estimate the firm's demand curve.

The possibility of some uniqueness in a firm's product creates a number of difficulties in the definition of a market and its structural characteristics. Let us say that a firm produces a unique product sold to a particular group of customers. If we define the product, the firm, and the customers to constitute a market, then the firm would be classified as a monopolist. If, however, we define the unique product of the firm as a reasonably close substitute for similar items produced by other firms, then the firm is not a monopolist but shares the market with other firms. The number of sellers in the market, then, clearly depends on how narrowly or broadly the product is defined. Individual firms with their unique products can all be thought to monopolize their narrowly defined submarkets, yet be competitive with other firms in a more broadly defined market. Throughout this chapter, we assume a broadly defined market.

Bearing in mind some of the difficulties in defining markets, economists have used four basic market structures – pure competition, pure monopoly, monopolistic competition, and oligopoly.

The purely competitive market is defined as one in which there are large numbers of independent buyers and sellers, none of whom is large relative to the size of the market; the products of all producers are homogeneous (nondifferentiated); and there is comparative ease of entry and exit for buyers and sellers.[4] The term "perfect competition" is sometimes used to denote complete ease of entry and exit and perfect information. What is a "large number" of sellers? It is such that even the largest firm considers the effect of its own output on the price to be negligible. Furthermore, no firm reacts to the decisions of particular rivals.

We can interpret the purely competitive case in terms of equation 9.1 (reproduced as equation 9.2):

$$\frac{Q}{Q_m} = a + b(P_m - P) + c(D_m - D). \qquad (9.2)$$

If a particular firm's product is identical to the products of all other sellers in the market, the firm's market share would be extremely sensitive to differences in price and delivery capability. Thus, the coefficients b and c approach infinity in the limiting case. This implies that if P is greater than P_m and the firm's ability to deliver is no better than the ability of other firms, its market share would be zero. On the other hand, if P is less than P_m, the firm could have the whole market if (a very big if) its delivery time were the same as that of the others; that is, if $D = D_m$. With completely homogeneous products, the coefficient a would be $1/n$, where n is the number of sellers in the market. Because the purely competitive market is characterized by a large number of sellers, the parameter a would be very small.

Pure monopoly is the market structure in which there is only one seller but a substantial number of buyers. It is also characterized as the market structure in which entry by new suppliers is either completely barred or difficult. Whether a firm is a pure monopolist depends very much on how the market is defined. Here we use a reasonably broad definition.

In equation 9.2, the parameter a for the pure monopolist would be 1. Because the firm is the only seller, its price, P, is the same as the market price, P_m, and its delivery time, D, is the same as D_m. Thus, the two right-hand terms, $b(P_m - P)$ and $c(D_m - D)$, are zero, and the values of b and c are immaterial. The firm's market share is therefore $Q/Q_m = 1$.

The monopolistically competitive market structure is characterized by a large number of independent buyers and sellers, comparative

---

[4]Notice the term "independent." If there are large numbers of buyers and sellers but their prices and output are somehow coordinated, we do not have pure competition. The independence is more crucial to pure competition than the number of sellers or buyers is.

ease of entry into the broad market, and nonhomogeneous (differentiated) products. Each firm can be thought to have a monopoly of a market defined narrowly enough to consist only of its own product, while at the same time its product is competitive (although not perfectly so) with other products in the more broadly defined market. This strange combination of monopoly in the narrow market and competition in the broad market accounts for the term "monopolistic competition."[5] New entry may be barred from the narrow market but not from the broad market.

In monopolistically competitive markets, the parameters a, b, and c of equation 9.2 can take on a wide range of values for a particular firm. The more unique the firm's product, the lower will be the values of b and c. To the extent the firm's product is unique, b and c are small and the firm's market share is less sensitive to differences between its price and delivery capacity and "market" prices and delivery capabilities. The value of parameter a can vary anywhere between 0 and 1, and a depends on the preferability for that firm's product, given $P = P_m$, and $D = D_m$. The firm will not automatically always want to make its product unique because, although uniqueness is desirable because it lowers b and c, it might also lower a. Conversely, a product policy of similarity, although it may raise b and c, might also raise a.

The oligopoly is the market model used to describe a structure in which there are a large number of buyers but only a "few" sellers. The products may be homogeneous or nonhomogeneous; we often divide oligopolies into differentiated and nondifferentiated. When the products are differentiated, the oligopolist has a monopoly on his narrow market, but his product competes with other products in the broader market.

The parameters a, b, and c in equation 9.2 for any particular firm depend largely on the degree of differentiation. The greater the degree of differentiation, the lower are the values of b and c and the wider is the range of values of a. The less the degree of differentiation, the greater are the values of b and c and the closer the value of a approaches $1/n$, where n is the number of selling firms. We could see that when products are not differentiated—that is, when b and c are very high—the market share of the individual firm is greatly influenced by differences between P and P_m and between D and D_m.

The key element that distinguishes the oligopoly from monopolistic competition is the recognized interdependence of the firms in

[5]The term "monopolistic competition" was coined by Edward Chamberlin. See E. H. Chamberlin, *The Theory of Monopolistic Competition* (Cambridge, Mass.: Harvard University Press, 1933). Similar concepts were developed by Joan Robinson in *The Economics of Imperfect Competition* (London: Macmillan, 1933). Before these books, markets were generally viewed by economists as either purely competitive or purely monopolistic, although some economists had explored oligopoly.

the oligopolistic market. This interdependence comes about because when there are just a few firms, each firm through its policies has a large impact on the fortunes of the other firms. Furthermore, with a small number of firms, coordination of the policies of the oligopolists becomes feasible. In terms of our equation, this interdependence is depicted in an expected relation between P_m, the price of all firms, and P, the firm's own price. In monopolistic competition, the individual can take the prices of others—that is, P_m—as stable; in oligopolies, the individual firm must expect some change in P_m if it changes P. Similarly, in the long run, where the firm could influence D, its delivery capabilities, it might expect other firms to react; that is, D_m could change as the result of a change in D.

Market structures are also defined in terms of the number of buyers. When there is one buyer and many sellers, we have what is known as pure monopsony. When there is a small number of buyers and many sellers, we have an oligopsony. The case of a single buyer and single seller is known as bilateral monopoly. We will study these market structures in Chapter 10, where we view the firm in its role as a buyer.

THE FIRM'S DEMAND CURVE
UNDER PURE COMPETITION

The purely competitive model provides the best explanation of how markets are supposed to work. In this market model we derive the concept that market prices are determined by the "law" of supply and demand. We approach the firm's demand curve under pure competition with our general equation, 9.2, after which we explore the determinants of the market price.

The Firm's Demand Curve. Consider once more this equation:

$$\frac{Q}{Q_m} = a + b(P_m - P) + c(D_m - D). \tag{9.3}$$

To simplify matters somewhat, let us first assume that all firms deliver with the same time lag between order and delivery. Thus, $D_m = D$, and the equation becomes

$$\frac{Q}{Q_m} = a + b(P_m - P).$$

Let us now solve for P:

$$\frac{Q}{Q_m} = a + bP_m - bP$$

$$bP = a + bP_m - \frac{Q}{Q_m}$$

$$P = \frac{a}{b} + P_m - \frac{1}{b} \cdot \frac{Q}{Q_m}. \tag{9.4}$$

When the products of all the firms are homogeneous, parameter b tends to become very large. Parameter a also tends to equal $1/n$, where n is the number of selling firms. Thus, with a large number of selling firms, an important characteristic of the purely competitive market, parameter a becomes a very small number. With a very small and b very large, the first and third right-hand terms of equation 9.4 approach values of zero. Thus, the demand curve becomes

$$P = P_m. \tag{9.5}$$

Such a demand curve plots as a straight horizontal line as in Figure 9.2. It implies that the firm's own output does not *perceptibly* influence the price at which it can sell, so that the firm need not take into account its own output in calculating the price at which it can sell. However, we must not view the independence of the firm's output and the price too mechanically. If one firm were to grow very large relative to the size of the market, it would learn that its output would have a perceptible effect on the market price. The horizontal demand curve depicted in Figure 9.2 should therefore be considered valid only over the range of the firm's output in which its output can be thought to have only a negligible effect on the market price.

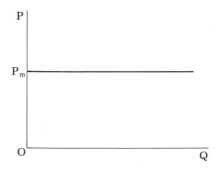

FIGURE 9.2   Firm's demand curve in purely competitive market

Equation 9.5 and Figure 9.2 clearly show that the only information the firm requires to know the demand curve facing it is P_m, the market price. In any immediate period, the market price can generally be easily found, usually in a newspaper or by a telephone call. But the firm for many types of problems would typically want to know what the market price is likely to be in the future. It is therefore necessary to understand how competitive markets work to determine market prices. Of course, to an economist, the workings of such markets are of great interest aside from the problem of forecasting prices.

What can we say about the firm's demand curve if its delivery time is smaller or greater than the average market delivery time – that is, if D is not equal to D_m? If we solve equation 9.3 for P, we get

$$P = \frac{a}{b} + P_m - \frac{1}{b} \cdot \frac{Q}{Q_m} + \frac{c}{b}(D_m - D).$$

With a very small and b very large, the first and third right-hand terms still approach zero, as before. But the coefficient c is also a large number, so that we cannot assume that the fourth right-hand term approaches zero. Thus, the firm's demand curve would be

$$P = P_m + \frac{c}{b}(D_m - D).$$

How do we interpret such a demand curve? If D is less than D_m, this demand curve implies that the firm can obtain a higher price than the market price. We could think of this higher price as a premium for rapid delivery. Conversely, if D is greater than D_m, the firm would have to take a price below the market price. The difference between P and P_m would then be the penalty for poor delivery.

We should note that either b or c could approach infinity. However, both cannot be infinitely high: this leads to the illogical conclusion that a firm's market share is completely sensitive to both price and delivery time differentials. Traditional economic analysis takes b to be very high—infinitely high. However, there is no reason to expect that b is necessarily always higher than c. If the product or service is of a crucial nature—medical services or weapons during a war—c could be higher than b. From our analysis, it is obvious that the extent of price premiums and penalties would depend on how high c is compared to b—that is, on the relative importance to buyers of rapid delivery and low prices.

The Market Supply Curve. The market price is determined by the interaction of the market supply and demand curves. In Chapter 8, we provided the theoretical basis of the demand curve for a consumer good, showing that the position of the price, quantity demand curve is influenced by incomes, prices of substitutes, prices of complements, and tastes. In Chapter 7, we laid the theoretical basis for the demand curve for a factor of production (or an intermediate good). In Chapter 8, we also gave a number of examples of empirically determined demand functions.

Chapter 7 was also partly devoted to the short-run market supply curve—the summation of the supply curves of the individual sellers in a market. The market supply curve, which is the relation between the market price and the quantity that all firms are willing to sell, was shown to be influenced by the prices of inputs, the nature of the production function, and the prices of alternative goods the firms could produce. In the longer run, the short-run supply curve could also be influenced by the acquisition or disposal of fixed assets, the exit or entry of new selling firms, and possibly by changes in technology. Figure 9.3 depicts the general relationship that we expect the short-run supply curve to show.

There is a concept of supply elasticity that is in many ways analogous to price elasticity of demand. Supply elasticity is defined as the percentage increase (decrease) in quantity supplied with respect to a percentage increase (decrease) in the market price. We say that supply is elastic if the response in quantity supplied is large relative to a change in the market price. The degree of supply elasticity is largely determined by how fast costs rise as output is expanded and, in the case of multi-product firms, the degree of ease with which fixed assets could be shifted to the production of different products. If costs do not rise rapidly, and if fixed assets are easily shiftable, the supply curve would tend to be price elastic. On the other hand, if costs rise rapidly with output expansions, or if assets are highly specialized to the production of the product of interest, the supply curve would tend to be inelastic. Figure 9.4 provides examples of elastic and inelastic supply curves.

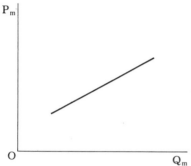

FIGURE 9.3   General nature of short-run market supply curve

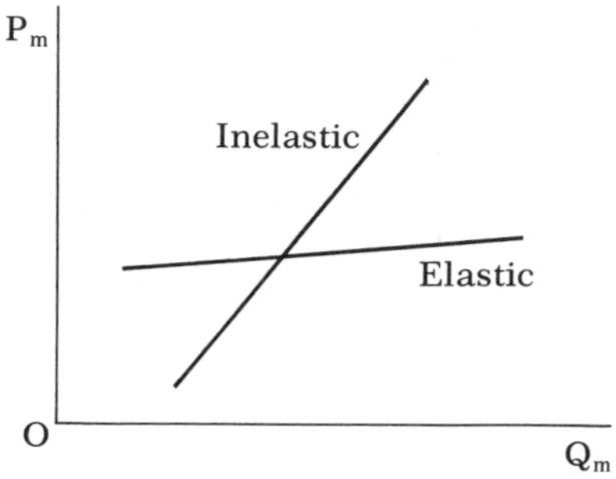

FIGURE 9.4   Examples of price elastic and price inelastic market supply curves

There have been numerous empirical studies of supply curves for agricultural products. As one example, we present the results of a study of milk that would be supplied by fifty-one farms in New Hampshire and Maine, shown in Table 9.1. The investigators did not actually observe the output of these farms. Instead, they worked out the optimal output for each farm, given the price of milk and assuming other factors (such as the price of feed) remained constant. From such a sample study, they could estimate the total supply of all farms in these two states by "blowing up" the sample to the universe.

Let us turn next to a more formal econometric study by Griliches.[6] In this study, among other results he estimated the following supply function for all crops in the United States:

$$Q = \left(\frac{P_o}{P_i}\right)^{0.152} W^{0.428}(1.0062)^t,$$

[6]Zvi Griliches, "Estimates of the Aggregate U.S. Farm Supply Function," *Journal of Farm Economics*, vol. 42 (May 1960).

TABLE 9.1 Optimal supplies of milk
from 51 farms

Price of milk (per 100 pounds)	Millions of pounds of milk supplied per year
$3.40	13.7
3.80	15.1
4.20	17.6
4.60	18.7
5.00	20.0
5.40	20.7
5.80	21.0
6.20	21.4

Source: George E. Frick and Richard A. Andrews, "Aggregation Bias and Four Methods of Summing Farm Supply Functions," *Journal of Farm Economics*, vol. 47 (August 1965).

where Q is the index of output of all crops, P_o is the index of prices of output, P_i is the index of prices of input, W is Stallings weather index, and t is time (1935 = 1, 1936 = 2 . . .).

According to this equation, crop output is rather inelastic with respect to price. A 1 percent rise in the price of outputs, ceteris paribus, leads to only a 0.152 percent increase in quantity supplied. This low elasticity is due partly to the broad definition of the product; with more narrowly defined products, we should expect to find higher elasticities, for farmers have increased options on whether to produce particular crops. The high elasticity for weather suggests that, in the short-run at least, weather is some three times as important as price in determining the supply of crops. If we wanted to use this equation to forecast the supply function for all crops, we would have to first forecast what we think P_i and W will be for the forecast year. To do this, we would have to study price trends for P_i and would probably use some average for W.

In a study sponsored by the Bureau of Mines of the U.S. Department of the Interior, investigators were interested in the willingness of owners of automobile junkyards to supply scrap metal.[7] Their statistical analysis showed this supply equation, $y = -83256.3 + 31261.56x$, where y is the number of "number 2" bundles supplied in a given month and x is the "real" price (actual price deflated by the GNP implicit deflator) in the previous month.

The Market-clearing, Equilibrium Price. Armed with our market demand curve, which shows the quantities buyers are willing to buy

---

[7]U.S. Department of the Interior, *Automobile Disposal: A National Problem* (1967).

at different prices, ceteris paribus, and the market supply curve, which gives the schedule of quantities sellers are willing to supply at different prices, ceteris paribus, we can now turn our attention to the market price. Figure 9.5 depicts a market demand curve and a market supply curve. The market price, P_m, is shown to be determined by the intersection of the supply and demand curves. The quantity both supplied and purchased is shown to be Q_m. Because the market price, P_m, is such that the quantity demanded just equals the quantity supplied, this price is known as the market-clearing price. It is also known as the equilibrium price because if there are no forces to shift the supply or demand curve, the price would remain at P_m.

The best way to demonstrate why the equilibrium price will take place at the intersection of the supply and demand curves is to inquire about what would happen if there were some other price. Assume, for example, that the price is initially above P_m, at P_1. At P_1, Figure 9.5 shows that sellers would want to sell more than buyers are willing to buy. The suppliers, perhaps burdened with excess inventories or unused productive assets, would tend to induce buyers to purchase from them by lowering their prices. This "higgling and jiggling" of the market should cause the price to fall. When the price falls to P_m, there are no longer incentives for sellers to reduce their prices. Conversely, if P_2 were to prevail, buyers would want to buy more than suppliers are willing to sell. Sellers would find they cannot supply the quantities buyers want to buy at that price, and they would there-fore tend to raise their prices. As prices rise, sellers are willing to sup-ply more, while buyers reduce the quantities they demand. The price should rise until the point where P_m is reached, at which price the quantity supplied would equal the quantity demanded.

Put another way, any price other than P_m is unstable in a free, com-petitive market, and the forces of self-interest would tend to move

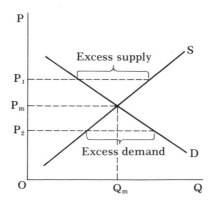

FIGURE 9.5 Determination of equilibrium price and quantity in a competitive market

the price toward P_m. One function of the market price can be seen to be the equalization of the quantity demanded and supplied.

It is interesting to ask what would happen if, say, the government tried to set a price other than the market-clearing price. Say, for example, the government set the price at P_2, which is below the market-clearing price. Then the quantity demanded would be greater than the quantity supplied. If the government did not institute a rationing scheme, the early buyers might be the ones to get the goods, and late buyers would find empty shelves. In countries that do try to set prices below the market-clearing price, long lines outside retail establishments are common. Another possibility is that the sellers would favor their friends and relatives. Still a third possibility is that the sellers would receive secret kickbacks from buyers or otherwise operate in the black market. These are all undesirable consequences of a controlled price, and in fact governments usually accompany price controls with a direct rationing scheme in which goods are directly allotted to various buyers.

If the government tries to set the price above the market-clearing price, say at P_1, other problems will arise. At such a price, the supply will be greater than the demand. One result would be an accumulation of excess stock, which would have to be kept off the market if the price at P_1 is to be maintained. The government would be tempted to somehow control the supply to avoid excess stocks. This has been the experience in the United States in the government's efforts to maintain agricultural prices above the market-clearing prices.

Exogenous and Endogenous Variables. Given the market supply and demand curves, the interactions on the market, reflecting competition and self-interest, *jointly* determine three variables — P_m, the market price; $Q_m^{(D)}$, the quantity demanded; and $Q_m^{(S)}$, the quantity supplied. When the market is allowed to clear, we learned that $Q_m^{(D)} = Q_m^{(S)}$; that is, the quantity supplied equals the quantity demanded. The next question is: What can cause the values of P_m, $Q_m^{(D)}$, and $Q_m^{(S)}$ to change? The answer is whatever causes the demand and supply curves to shift their positions.

The quantity demanded, we have shown in the last chapter, depends on a number of variables in addition to the product's price. Among them are incomes, prices of substitutes, and prices of complements. When we try to empirically estimate a demand function, it will be recalled, we first set up an unspecified equation such as

$$Q_m^{(D)} = f(P_m, Y, P_s, P_c),$$

where Y is income, P_s is the price of substitutes, and P_c is the price of complements. If we have determined the demand *function*, then the demand *curve* — that is, the relation between just $Q_m^{(D)}$ and P_m — depends on the values of the variables Y, P_s, and P_c. We showed in the last chapter that a change in the value of these variables leads to a shift in the demand curve.

It was similarly shown in Chapter 7 that the supply curve – that is, the relation between P_m and $Q_m^{(S)}$ – is influenced by a number of factors. Among them are the prices of inputs, the quantity of fixed assets, and the prices of rival goods. The full supply function for the market could therefore be written

$$Q_m^{(S)} = f(P_m, p_1, \bar{x}_2, P_r),$$

where P_m is the market price of the product, p_1 is the price(s) of variable inputs, $\bar{x}_2$ is the amount of fixed assets, P_r is the price(s) of rival products the firms could produce. If we have statistically determined the supply *function*, then the supply *curve* – that is, the relation between $Q_m^{(S)}$ and P_m – depends on the values of $p_1, \bar{x}_2, P_r$. Changes in the values of these variables lead to shifts in the supply curve.

If we assume the market is allowed to clear – that is, if there is no interference with the price – the model of the market can be expressed in three simultaneous equations:

$$Q_m^{(D)} = f(P_m, Y, P_s, P_c)$$
$$Q_m^{(S)} = f(P_m, p_1, \bar{x}_2, P_r)$$
$$Q_m^{(D)} = Q_m^{(S)}.$$

The first two equations are, of course, the demand and supply functions; the last equation expresses the market-clearing phenomenon.

The variables in these equations can be divided into two groups, exogenous and endogenous. The exogenous (outside) variables are $Y, P_s, P_c, p_1, \bar{x}_2, P_r$. They are called exogenous because the values for them are not determined by the particular market for the product. Rather their values are determined by the operations of other markets, long-run decisions made by the firms, policies to determine the national level of income, and so forth. As far as this particular market is concerned, the values of the exogenous variables are *given*. The endogenous (inside) variables, on the other hand, are those whose values are determined in this particular market. These variables are $P_m, Q_m^{(S)}, Q_m^{(D)}$. Notice that there are three endogenous variables and three equations. When the number of endogenous variables equals the number of equations, it is an important mathematical proposition that the values of the endogenous variables can be determined.

If the parameters of the demand and supply functions are stable, the values of the exogenous variables ultimately determine the values of the endogenous variables. In other words, for any set of values for the exogenous variables, a corresponding set of values for the endogenous variables will be determined by the working of the market. It follows that all changes in the values of the endogenous variables come about because of changes in the values of the exogenous variables.

Determining the Impact of the Exogenous Variables on the Endogenous Variables. Let us work through the impact of changes in the values of the exogenous variables on the values of the endogenous variables. First, let us assume that income rises. If the product is not inferior, the effect of an increase in income would be to shift the demand curve to the right. Figure 9.6 depicts the demand curves at the initial value of income, labeled D, and the demand curve after the rise in income, labeled D'. Panel 1 has a highly elastic supply curve; panel 2 has an inelastic supply curve. The initial values of the endogenous variables are P_m and Q_m (where the latter is $Q_m^{(D)}$ and $Q_m^{(S)}$), and the new values of the endogenous variables are P_m' and Q_m'. By comparing P_m with P_m', and Q_m with Q_m', we can measure the effect of the change in income on the values of the endogenous variables. When the supply curve is highly elastic (panel 1), most of the impact of the rise in income is on changes in Q_m rather than on changes in P_m. On the other hand, when the supply curve is inelastic (panel 2), most of the impact of the income increase is on higher prices rather than on higher quantities produced and sold. We can see from this example that the elasticity of supply determines the extent to which an increase in income will lead to higher prices or higher output.

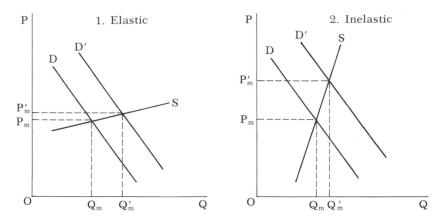

FIGURE 9.6   Effect of a rise in income on equilibrium price and quantity supplied and demanded: elastic and inelastic supply curves

Let us now assume that the price of a rival product in production increases. We should expect suppliers who produce both products to produce more of the rival product and less of the product of interest for any value of P_m. Thus, the supply curve shifts to the left. Figure 9.7 shows the impact of the rise in the price of the rival product on P_m and Q_m, which become P_m' and Q_m' after the shift in the supply curve. As we might expect, the rise in the price of the rival product results in a higher market price and a lower level of output and purchases of the product of interest. It can be seen from the two panels of Figure 9.7 that the impact on the market price will be much greater if the demand curve is inelastic.

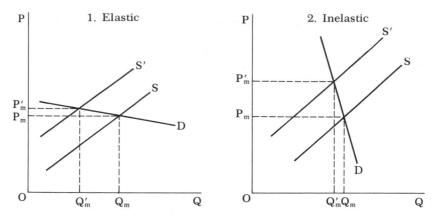

FIGURE 9.7   Effect of a rise in price of a rival good in production on
equilibrium price and quantity supplied and demanded: elastic and
inelastic demand curves

Assume now that the price of a complementary product in consumption rises. Because this raises the "package" price to consumers, the demand curve for the product of interest should shift to the left. Figure 9.8 shows the effect of the rise in the price of the complement on the market price and on the quantity supplied and demanded. Once again, we can see that the extent of the impacts on P_m and Q_m depend on the elasticity of the supply curve.

For our final exercise, let us assume that new firms enter the market as suppliers and that the existing firms in the industry expand their fixed assets. Thus, more will be supplied at the different values of P_m; that is, the supply curve shifts to the right. Figure 9.9 shows the impact of the new entry and increased assets on P_m and Q_m. As

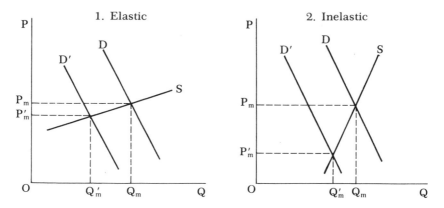

FIGURE 9.8   Effect of a rise in price of a complementary product on
equilibrium price and quantity supplied and demanded: elastic and
inelastic supply curves

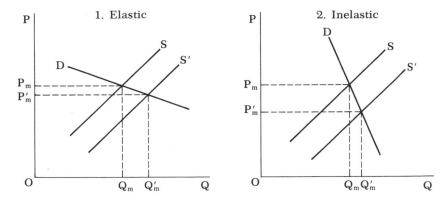

FIGURE 9.9   Effect of new entry and expansion on equilibrium price
and quantity supplied and demanded: elastic and inelastic demand curves

we might expect, P_m should fall and Q_m should rise. The extent to
which the impact is greater on P_m or Q_m again depends on the elasticity of the demand curve.

Many other changes in the values of the exogenous variables will
influence the position and sometimes the shape of the supply curve
or demand curve—changes such as tastes, prices of substitutes, price
expectations, technology. Unfortunately, we cannot go through all
the possible combinations of changes in the exogenous variables
and their impact on the endogenous variables. However, it should be
clear that any forecast of market prices and quantities supplied and
demanded requires an understanding of how the exogenous variables
influence the supply and demand curves and a forecast of the values
of the exogenous variables.

Some of the exogenous variables are prices in other markets. These
prices provide the linkages between different markets. Thus, the price
of a rival good in production, determined in a different market, by
shifting the supply curve in the market of interest, influences price
and quantity in the latter market. The prices of substitutes and
complements, determined in different markets, influence price and
quantity in our market of interest through the mechanism of shifting
the demand curve in this market. Also, an increase in demand in one
market, by increasing the income of producers, could increase the
demand in a second market if these producers are customers in the
second market. Markets are linked by income as well as prices.

The Notion of Long-Run Equilibrium. One of the most important
attributes claimed for the purely competitive market is that, in the
long run, when supplying firms have had the time to enter or leave
a market or expand or reduce their fixed assets, the market price tends
to approach a level where the firm covers its costs of production and

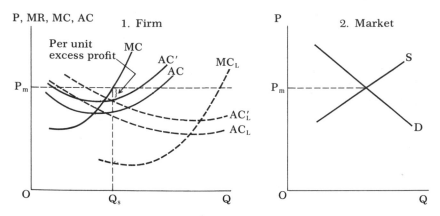

FIGURE 9.10   Short-run equilibrium of firm and market in which firm makes excess profits (Quantity axes have different scales)

makes a "normal" profit. For this to occur, it must be comparatively easy for firms to enter or leave an industry or expand or reduce their fixed assets.

Figure 9.10 consists of two panels, one showing the determinants of the firm's output and the other showing the model of a competitive market. Two sets of AC and MC curves are shown for the firm. One set, depicted by the solid lines, shows the existing AC and MC curves. The other set, depicted by the dashed lines, and with an L subscript, are assumed to represent a plant of optimal size – that is, one in which the minimum point on the AC curve is lower than for any other size of plant. The firm is not operating with the optimal-sized plant in the current period but could expand the plant to the optimal size in the long run. Added to the AC curves to get the AC' curves are "normal" profits – that is, such profits that existing firms would neither want to leave the industry nor expand or reduce their fixed assets.[8] In addition, firms not in the industry would not wish to enter.

Let us consider first the short-run situation. Let us say that the market-determined price is P_m, in which event the firm will produce Q_s units of output. Because AC' includes normal profits, the difference between AC' and P_m at output Q_s measures the "excess" profits per unit of output.

With these excess profits to be made, two things should happen in the long run: The firm should be willing to expand its fixed capacity, perhaps to the AC_L level.[9] Clearly, this expansion, by shifting the

---

[8]The level of normal profits can vary from industry to industry. The level is widely thought to depend on the degree of risk. Because businessmen and investors in general prefer to avoid risk, the normal profits would have to be higher in risky industries to attract and keep firms.

[9]The firm under these conditions should be willing to expand its fixed assets even if the average cost curve does not have a lower minimum. The profits

MC curve to the right, means that the firm would be willing to supply more output at any market price. Second, new firms should enter the industry, also increasing the quantity that would be supplied at any price. The effect of the expansions of existing firms and the new entrants would be to shift the market supply curve to the right. If the demand curve remains the same, the rightward shifting of the supply curve will reduce the value of P_m. Expansion and new entry should continue to the point where the market price is reduced so that the firm makes normal profits. Figure 9.11 shows the final long-run equilibrium price. This mechanism works the other way if short-run profits are less than normal. In that case, existing firms will either reduce their fixed assets or leave the industry, the supply curve shifts to the left, and the market price rises to the level at which firms make normal profits.

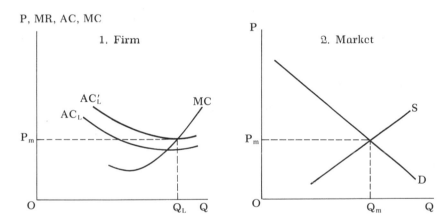

FIGURE 9.11   Long-run equilibrium of firm and market in pure competition (Quantity axes have different scales)

Does this long-run model imply that all the selling firms in the industry will just make normal profits? Not necessarily. Very inefficient firms can still be driven out of business, while the highly efficient firms would make above-normal profits. The firms making just normal profits might be called marginally efficient; they are the least efficient firms that are still capable of remaining in the industry.

There is a sharp contrast between the determinants of price in the short run and in the long run for the purely competitive market. In

per unit may not increase in the latter case, but the firm could produce more output, so that total profit is expanded. On the other hand, if the *AC* curve falls as the result of an expansion of fixed assets, an existing firm would be willing to expand, even if there were no excess profits. This expansion could still increase profits.

the short run, the period in which the fixed assets committed to the industry can be neither expanded nor (easily) reduced, both supply and demand determine the price. But in the long run, when the stock of fixed (in the short run) assets could be adjusted, the price tends to be determined by the cost of production plus a normal profit. This suggests that long-run forecasts of market prices in competitive markets might well begin with estimates of costs.

In long-run equilibrium, the marginally efficient firm would produce at the output level at which the average total cost curve is at a minimum. This is considered a very attractive feature of the purely competitive market.[10]

Consumer and Producer Surplus. Economists trying to develop conceptual measures of how well the economic system is working use two related notions – consumer surplus and producer surplus. To see the meaning of these terms, let us assume that the market price of a product is $5 and that some individuals are *willing* to pay $12 but have to pay only $5. It seems reasonable to call the difference between these amounts, $7, a measure of the extent to which the value of the product to the consumer exceeds the price he has to pay. This could be thought of as a surplus, something extra provided by the economic system. Individuals willing to pay $9 would have a surplus of $4; individuals willing to pay $6 would have a surplus of $1; etc.

Consider now the producers who are willing to supply some of the product at $3. They are receiving $2 more than they are willing to accept. We call this a producer surplus. The concepts also hold for the same producer willing to sell some units at $2, some at $3, some at $4. The differences between these supply prices and the market price are all part of producer surplus.

These surpluses are shown quite readily on a graph, as in Figure 9.12. The area between the demand curve and the market price is the geometric representation of consumer surplus; the area between the supply curve and the price is the representation of producer surplus. These concepts are very important in welfare economics.

A Simple Dynamic Model. So far we have not taken into account explicitly the effect of past prices on the shape and position of the supply and demand curves in the current market period. But past prices sometimes influence these curves, particularly the supply curves, to a very large extent. A particularly important area where past prices have a large effect on current supply curves, and thus on the

---

[10]The deduction that the long-run price is determined by the minimum average cost plus a "normal" profit has played an important role in the ideological defense of the free competitive market system. Before the market system became dominant in Europe, economists and theologians were very concerned with the notion of a "just" price. We could defend the free market system on the ground that, in the long run, the price tends to be "just"; it reflects cost plus a "fair" profit.

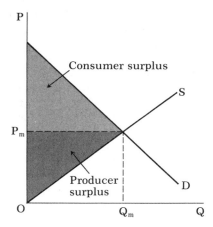

FIGURE 9.12   Consumer and producer surplus

current market price, is in agricultural products. Economists have been intrigued with the way these prices fluctuate.

Farmers often must determine their crop plantings in the spring — about half a year before they know the prices the crops will fetch at harvest time. Thus, when harvest time comes, they have already made their commitments and do not have many options about how much of a particular crop to sell. If the price turns out to be low, they might somewhat reduce their supply to the market by building up inventories or feeding the crops to animals. Or, if the price is high, they might increase their supply to the market, perhaps from past inventory holdings or by feeding fewer cattle. But for the most part the supply will be fairly insensitive to the market price at harvest time, so that the supply curve is steep (and inelastic) as in Figure 9.13.

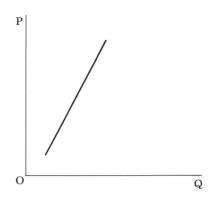

FIGURE 9.13   Short-run inelastic supply curve

What influences the planting of a certain crop? Farmers seem to be heavily influenced by the price the crop brought in the *previous* harvest time. Thus, the supply in any particular harvest market period is determined by last year's price more than by the current price. Symbolically, we can write that Q supplied is

$$Q_m = f(P_m, P_{m-1}),$$

where P_{m-1} is last year's price.

Let us now see how the influence of last year's prices will lead to price fluctuations. If last year's price was high, farmers will plant a great deal, and, as a result, in the current harvest period the supply curve shifts to the right and price is low, as in Figure 9.14. Next year, however, because of the low price in this year, farmers plant less. Thus next year's supply curve shifts to the left, and the price rises as in Figure 9.15.

This cycle could continue with prices fluctuating from one year to the next indefinitely.[11] However, some experimentation with this model would show that the year-to-year price fluctuations tend to become smaller if the demand curve is elastic over the range of price fluctuations.

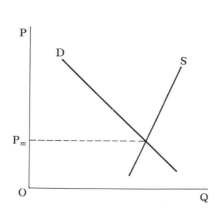

FIGURE 9.14   Effect of high previous price on current supply curve and equilibrium price

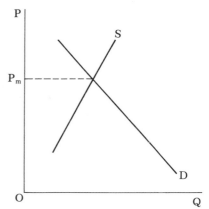

FIGURE 9.15   Effect of low previous price on current supply curve and equilibrium price

PURE MONOPOLY

Monopoly means, literally, a single seller of a product for which there are no substitutes. The discussion of product and market definition in Chapter 8 should raise the question of whether the concept of monopoly has meaning in the real world, because at a sufficiently high price consumers will find substitutes for any product. When we

[11]This is sometimes known as the cobweb theorem.

apply the monopoly concept in economic analysis and in the antitrust law, however, having a monopoly is only the power to enhance the price of a product substantially above its cost of production without attracting competitors. Just as the delimitation of products and of markets is a matter of degree, so is monopoly power. Complete freedom to raise price without limit without losing sales can never exist. Pure monopoly, however, does not imply such infinite power. It means simply that for a reasonably broad definition of a market, one firm is the supplier of all that is bought and can determine the price without regard to close, existing rivals. In this section we consider the demand curve for such a firm, how a firm becomes a monopolist, limits on its willingness to price as high as its power warrants, and the relation of monopoly power to price discrimination.

The Monopolist's Demand Curve. Because a monopolist is the single seller in a market, the demand curve facing him is the market demand curve. To see this in terms of our "general" equation, let us reproduce equation 9.1:

$$\frac{Q}{Q_m} = a + b(P_m - P) + c(D_m - D). \tag{9.6}$$

Because there are no rivals, the price of "all" firms, P_m, is the same as the monopolist's price, P, and the delivery time of "all" firms, D_m, is similarly equal to D. Thus, the second and third right-hand terms of the equation are equal to zero. The monopolist is the only seller; therefore all buyers "prefer" his product, so that $a = 1$. Thus, the equation becomes

$$\frac{Q}{Q_m} = 1$$

and

$$Q = Q_m.$$

Q_m can be determined from the market demand function, shown in general terms as

$$Q_m = f(P_m, Y, P_s, P_c),$$

where P_m is the market price, Y is income, P_s is the price of substitutes (in "adjoining" markets), and P_c is the price of complements. Because $Q = Q_m$, and $P = P_m$, the market demand curve is itself the monopolist's demand curve.

The market power of the monopolist, as for any firm, can be thought to be the power to raise the price without losing much business. The monopolist's product has poorer substitutes than would the product of a firm sharing the broad market with others; thus the monopolist's demand curve is less price elastic at any given price than the demand curves of firms with rivals producing similar products. As a result, the profits of a monopolist should be higher than those of firms with competitors. It is conceivable, however, that the demand curve facing a monopolist may be so "small" relative to its costs that no profit could be made. Figure 9.16, in panel 1, shows a monopolist who makes high profits; panel 2 depicts a monopolist with a small demand curve.

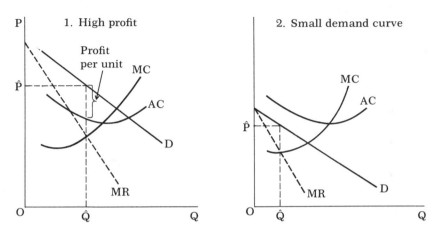

FIGURE 9.16   Profit-maximizing price and output by a monopolist

Monopolists who produce durable goods can often influence the position of their future demand curves. Because a good portion of the sales of durable goods are for replacement, the monopolist could influence future demand by how durable he makes his product or by planning for the products to become obsolete.[12]

How a Firm Becomes a Monopolist. Firms can become monopolists in a number of ways. In many cases, legal authorities grant exclusive privilege to sell a product. Obtaining patents is an obvious way for a firm to become a monopolist. Sometimes because of the nature of production there is room for only one efficient-sized plant in a market. Such firms are called natural monopolies and are prevalent in public utility industries in which production and consumption require physical connection by wires or pipes. The government allows only one such firm in the market but almost always regulates it.

Often monopolies are obtained by means that, if not illegal, border on illegality. Among them are predatory practices such as cutting prices in specific areas to drive weaker competitors out of business. Sometimes the monopolist achieves his position by gaining control of key resources, particularly raw materials. Sometimes monopolies are formed through a merger of formerly competing companies. Often

[12]See David D. Martin, "Monopoly and the Durability of Durable Goods," *Southern Economic Journal*, vol. XXVII (1961).

a firm has a monopoly in a particular market through an agreement with others that the parties to the agreement will not sell in each other's markets.

Not all monopolies are illegal; in the United States exceptions have been made to the general policy against monopoly embodied in the antitrust statutes. Every time a firm develops a new product, it necessarily has a monopoly on that product until other firms come up with competing products, and such competition may be legally barred by patents.

Limit Pricing. We think it is a mistake to view a monopolist simply as a short-run profit-maximizer. Unlike the firm in pure competition, which cannot perceptibly influence its future demand curve, the monopolist's policies may have an influence on its future demand curves. Too high a price, for example, might lead to antitrust action by the government or, more likely, might provide incentives for others to enter the monopolist's market or develop closer substitutes. Entry could take place by the monopolist's large customers becoming his competitors.[13] As a result of having to take into account in his short-run decision-making the influence of price, and perhaps the quality of the product and associated services, on his future demand curves, the monopolist is believed by many economists to place self-imposed constraints on his short-run activity. The most important of these is an upper "limit price." It would logically be calculated as the highest price the monopolist could charge without making new entry very likely. It follows that the more difficult the monopolist can make new entry into the market the higher the limit price can be. The choice of the limit price is an investment problem: The firm foregoes profits or cash flows in the immediate periods in the expectation of higher cash flows in the future.

Price Discrimination. As a general rule, individual firms can increase their profits if they can segment their markets and charge each customer or, more usually, each group of customers "what the traffic will bear." Consider, for example, a seller dealing with two buyers, one of whom is willing to pay $10 per unit, while the other is willing to pay only $5. If the firm can make profits on both sales, what should its price be? If it charges $10, it loses the $5 sale. If it charges $5, it loses the $5 it could have made by charging $10 to the buyer willing to pay that amount. If it charges a price between $5 and $10, it loses the $5 sale and does not make all it could from the $10 customer. Evidently, rather than charge a single price, the firm makes higher profits if it charges $10 to one customer and $5 to the other. This is price discrimination.

[13]This is an example of Galbraith's "countervailing power" thesis. Large powerful firms that are buyers could inhibit a monopolist from fully exploiting his monopoly power because they present an entry threat. See John K. Galbraith, *American Capitalism* (Boston: Houghton Mifflin, 1952).

Although to any seller price discrimination is usually desirable, it may not always be possible. The firm may not have the information that enables it to know which prices to charge particular buyers. If the firm has competitors charging the lower price, it will not be able to sell at the higher price. Buyers at the lower price may be able to buy and resell the product to the buyers willing to pay the higher price. Such resale is known as arbitrage.

Monopolists are usually in a good position to overcome these difficulties. Because they deal with all the buyers, they are likely to know their markets better than firms who have to compete. The monopolist obviously does not have to concern himself with competitors undercutting his ability to sell to buyers willing to pay a higher price. The monopolist can counter the resale problem by threatening to cut off sales to those engaging in resales. When the monopolist provides a direct service, such as transportation, the resale problem is virtually nonexistent.

The limiting case of price discrimination occurs when the monopolist charges a separate price to every buyer. We call this perfect discrimination. The consumer surplus discussed previously disappears, for each buyer is charged the maximum he is willing to pay. Hence, there is no difference between the market price and the price a buyer would pay. Indeed, there is no single market price. More often, however, perfect price discrimination is not possible. Instead, the monopolist segments his market on a number of different bases — geographic area, class of customer (retailer, wholesaler, jobber), product design and advertising, time period (off-season prices), age of customer (special air fares for students). He then charges different prices to these different segments, depending on the demand curves in these segments. The larger the number of market segmentations, the closer the monopolist comes to perfect discrimination, which is the ultimate in profit maximization. Under some circumstances, however — particularly if price differences tend to lessen competition — price discrimination can be illegal.

The Case Against Monopoly. Economists as well as others have for hundreds of years been concerned with monopolies. Their main objection to them is that the monopolist charges a higher price and produces less than would a large number of small firms in a competitive market with comparable capacity. Thus, there is a loss of welfare to consumers, which can be measured by the change in consumer surplus.

Figure 9.17 measures this loss in consumer surplus. The curve labeled *MC* can be thought of as both the monopolist's marginal cost curve and the supply curve to the market if there were a large number of firms. If there were pure competition, the price would be P_m, the consumer surplus would be the area ACP_m, and the producer surplus would be the area BCP_m. The profit-maximizing monopolist, selling at a single price, however, would equate his *MR* and *MC* curves

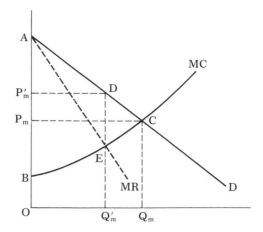

FIGURE 9.17 Effect of monopoly on consumer and producer surplus compared to purely competitive market

to determine his output, Q'_m, and would set the price at P'_m. Now the consumer surplus is reduced to the area ADP'_m, while the producer surplus expands to the area $BEDP'_m$. The total producer and consumer surplus is also less under monopoly than under competition. Whereas the total surplus under competition is the area BCA, under monopoly it becomes $BEDA$. The area ECD measures the complete loss to society.

Monopoly may cost society in other ways. Monopolists may waste resources by investing in barriers to entry, by producing too much of less durable products, by withholding technical advances, by designing goods to require costly repairs, or by limiting desirable variety and proliferating superficial variety in product design. Monopoly also affects the distribution of income and wealth. Furthermore, economic power gives a few persons political power out of proportion to their numbers, and enables monopolists to use governments to improve the firm's constraints. It has also been argued that, if too many markets are characterized by monopoly power, fiscal and monetary policies by the government will fail to accomplish full employment without inflation. Perhaps the greatest cost of monopoly is the lost production that results from unemployment under such conditions.[14]

MONOPOLISTIC COMPETITION

The monopolistically competitive market is characterized by a large number of sellers in a broadly defined market producing differentiated products. Each seller has a monopoly of a market defined so narrowly that it includes only his own product but competes with the other

[14]See *Control or Competition*, Hearings, U.S. Senate Subcommittee on Antitrust and Monopoly, January 1972.

sellers who produce close, but not perfect, substitutes. We can assume that entry to the very narrow markets is either impossible or difficult but that entry into the broader market is unrestricted and comparatively easy.

The Demand Curve Facing the Firm. The demand curve facing the firm in a monopolistically competitive market is considerably more complicated than the demand curves facing firms in the purely competitive and purely monopolistic markets.

Let us begin by reproducing our general demand function:

$$\frac{Q}{Q_m} = a + b(P_m - P) + c(D_m - D').$$ (9.7)

When we solve this equation for P, we get the demand function:

$$P = \left[\frac{a}{b} + P_m + \frac{c}{b}(D_m - D)\right] - \left(\frac{1}{bQ_m}\right)Q.$$ (9.8)

The term in brackets is a constant, so the demand curve – that is, the relation between P and Q – is a straight line. The coefficient of Q – that is, $1/bQ_m$ – determines the *slope* of the demand curve, and the constant term in brackets determines the *position* of the demand curve.

Let us look first at the slope. The higher the value of b (which measures the sensitivity of market share to price differences) or the higher the value of Q_m, the lower is the coefficient of Q and the more gentle is the slope of the demand curve. We can infer then that the higher the values of b or Q_m, the smaller will be the effect of a change in Q (the firm's output) on the price it can obtain. As a corollary, the higher the value of b and Q_m, the greater would be the impact of a change in P on Q. This could be seen more clearly if equation 9.7 were solved for Q.

The analysis of the constant term in the brackets is more complicated. Clearly, the higher the market price, P_m, the farther to the right will be the demand curve. It is also clear that a higher value for parameter a, which measures preferability for the firm's product, also shifts the demand curve to the right. The difference between D_m and D, which can be assumed to be constant in the short run, also affects the position of the demand curve. If D_m is greater than D, the demand curve is more to the right, but if D_m is less than D, the demand curve is farther to the left. The individual firm can influence D by building more capacity, a long-run decision. Parameters b and c can also be seen to influence the magnitude of shifts in the demand curve due to differences between D_m and D. The higher the value of c relative to b, the greater will be the effect of differences in delivery time on the demand curve's position. The higher the value of b, the less important is the effect of parameter a on the position of the demand curve.

Estimating the Demand Curve. Let us assume that the firm has estimated values for parameters a, b, and c in equation 9.8. Let us also assume that the difference in delivery time—that is, $D_m - D$—is fixed in the short run. Then all that is needed to obtain the P, Q demand curve are estimates for P_m and Q_m. The market model for the pure competition case, with the market demand and supply curves determining P_m and Q_m, can roughly serve our purpose. There are, however, a number of problems in using market supply and demand curves for monopolistically competitive industries. These problems stem almost entirely from the heterogeneous nature of the products of the different sellers.

First, there are empirical problems of measurement. Because the products of the firms differ somewhat, their prices are not likely to be the same. Therefore, P_m, the market "price," must be thought of as a price structure—that is, as a set of different prices that tend to have a fixed relation to each other. This requires the use of either a representative price or some sort of price index—problems easily handled by economic statisticians. More serious is the fact that the products are somewhat different. We have no problems in adding prices, for they are expressed in dollars. But there are conceptual problems in adding different products. How do we add apples, oranges, and pears? We have to go to a higher level of abstraction and call them fruit; then they can be added. We can see that difficulties in measuring Q_m can be partly overcome through the use of abstraction and quantity indexes.

The more difficult problem lies in the theoretical concept of a market supply curve when, because of the uniqueness of each firm's product, the individual demand curves all slope. The theoretical difficulty has as its root the reaction of the firm with a sloping demand curve to P_m, the market price. A firm in a purely competitive market, whose demand curve does not slope, can be assumed to sell only at the market price. Thus, a change in P_m will change this firm's output. But a firm in a monopolistically competitive market, whose demand curve shifts with a change in P_m, may respond to this shift with a *combination* of a change in output *and* price. Because the prices of the individual firms determine P_m, we have the rather intractable problem that a change in P_m itself brings about further changes in P_m. It is therefore not easy with elementary techniques to work out the equilibrium values for P_m and Q_m. Many economists would contend there is no meaningful supply curve under these conditions.

Despite these theoretical problems, in the real world we do estimate supply and demand curves for heterogeneous groups of products, and we use the same type of analysis to estimate P_m and Q_m as in the purely competitive model. We must sometimes compromise theory in empirical work. The good analyst understands the compromises and hence the weaknesses in his empirical work.

Short-Run and Long-Run Equilibrium. With estimates for parameters a, b, c in equation 9.8, estimates for P_m and Q_m, and a fixed value for the differences between D_m and D, we would have all the information with which to obtain a numerical relation between P and Q – the firm's demand curve. The firm can then select the optimal values for P and Q with the tools we developed in Chapter 5. Diagrammatically, if we assume a classical production function, the resulting optima appear in Figure 9.18. We call these optimal values of P and Q the short-run equilibrium position of the firm. At these optimal values the firm would not wish to change the values of either P or Q unless something happened to change either the demand curve or the cost curve. We should be aware that the selection of these optimal values depends on estimates of a, b, c, Q_m, P_m, and $D_m - D$, any of which may turn out to be incorrect. If there are such errors, the firm may find that its price is too high or that it has not produced enough or other inconsistencies.

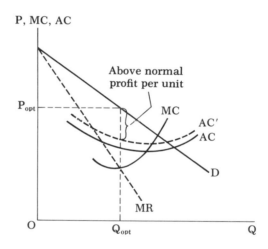

FIGURE 9.18   Optimal price and output: firm in monopolistically competitive market

In Figure 9.18, the firm is making excess profits; this is the difference per unit of output between the optimal price and AC', where the AC' curve includes normal profits. If our model firm is typical of firms in the market, what should happen in the long run? In the long run, firms in the market would tend to expand, and new firms would enter. These expansions and entries should lead to a rightward shift of the supply curve (see Figure 9.9) and as a consequence a lower value for P_m but a higher value for Q_m. It is also possible that with expansion and new entry D_m will fall relative to D. We should also expect changes in the parameters. To the extent that new firms produce products that are more similar to the product of the model firm than those of firms already in the market, there would be closer substitutes for the firm's products. As a consequence, parameter a should fall, but b and c should become larger.

To see the full long-run impact, we reproduce equation 9.8:

$$P = \left[\frac{a}{b} + P_m + \frac{c}{b}(D_m - D)\right] - \left(\frac{1}{bQ_m}\right)Q. \qquad (9.9)$$

A fall in P_m and a would clearly tend to make the "constant" term, which is in brackets, smaller. Thus on these grounds the demand curve should shift to the left. A fall in D_m relative to D would also make the constant term smaller. Whether D_m will in fact fall relative to D would, however, depend on the model firm's expansion of capacity. If we look next at the coefficient of Q, which is $1/bQ_m$, we see this coefficient becomes smaller because both b and Q_m should increase with new entry and expansion of existing firms. Thus, the effect of the new entry and general expansion should be both to shift the P,Q demand curve to the left and to make it flatter. Figure 9.19 shows what the demand curves in the short run and long run might look like. We should be aware that the model firm can partly counteract these effects on the demand curve by its choice of new capacity (which will show up in D) and by changes it might make in its product (which would show up in changes in the a, b, and c parameters).

How long would this expansion and new entry continue? It is reasonable to suppose that it would continue till the marginally efficient firm is making no excess profits. If we assume our model firm to be marginally efficient, Figure 9.20 depicts where the model firm's demand curve would be in the long run after expansion and new entry. It also shows the firm's output and price. Notice that the firm is

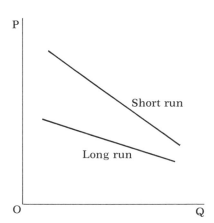

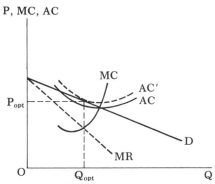

FIGURE 9.19 Short-run and long-run demand curve facing firm in monopolistically competitive market

FIGURE 9.20 Long-run equilibrium price and output: firm in monopolistically competitive market

making only normal profits, so new firms would not want to enter and existing firms would not want to expand, contract, or leave. We call this the long-run equilibrium of the firm.

Contrasting the long-run equilibrium position of the firm under monopolistic competition with the same position in pure competition is worthwhile. Because the demand curve is completely horizontal in pure competition, the firm in a purely competitive market produces up to the point at which its average total cost curve is a minimum. The firm in the monopolistically competitive market, in contrast, produces to the left of this minimum *ATC* output level. Thus, the theory leads to the conclusion that if the cost curves are the same, output would be smaller and price higher under monopolistic competition than under pure competition. This conclusion has provided a basis for attacks on any form of monopoly.

We must stress that long-run equilibrium is a highly abstract concept and that in a dynamic world we seldom can observe such equilibria. The notion of long-run equilibrium is the economist's way of working out the directions in which firms and markets adjust when there is sufficient time for the full adjustment to take place.

OLIGOPOLY

A market structure in which there is only a small number of sellers in the broad market is known as an oligopoly. Usually, an oligopoly is characterized as a market in which new entrants are either completely barred or can break in only with great difficulty. Oligopolies are generally divided into two groups—those in which the products of the sellers are undifferentiated, or very close substitutes, and those in which the products of the sellers are differentiated, or are poorer substitutes for each other. Prominent examples in the United States of undifferentiated oligopolies are the steel, aluminum, glass, copper, and electrical equipment industries—generally those in which products are sold to expert buyers, namely other firms. Most of the differentiated oligopolies are in consumer goods; automobiles, cigarettes, soap, toothpaste, and cereal are some prominent examples. Perhaps the main difference between the two types of oligopoly is the greater sensitivity to price of the undifferentiated oligopolies and the greater scope of the differentiated oligopolies for the firms to influence their market shares and demand curves by product styling, advertising, and other techniques of promotion.

The oligopoly has been a difficult market structure for economists to analyze, and no completely established theory of oligopoly is in general acceptance. The main source of the difficulty is the recognized interdependence of the oligopolists. This results from the small number of firms in the market and the great impact that the policies of one oligopolist can have on its rivals. The individual oligopolist, when making his decisions, has to take into account the likelihood that his decisions will influence his rivals' decisions. The existence of a small number of sellers also makes likely the possibility of some kind of collusion.

This section contains a number of subsections. We first review some suggestions that the oligopoly be viewed in the context of warfare. We next look at the types of information required by the firm to estimate its demand curve. We then present various models of interaction between duopolists, the two-firm case, in order to understand the options available to oligopolists. We then turn to the forces making for cooperation among oligopolists, and the reasons why cooperation may break down. Next, we discuss the tendency toward rigid prices in oligopolies, and how this has been explained. We close this section with suggestions for the individual oligopolist in estimating his demand curve. Given the difficulty of the subject, it is well to stress the insights one can obtain from our analysis.

The Need to Go Beyond Traditional Economic Analysis. The recognized interdependence of the oligopolists and the interactions of their decisions have been difficult to analyze with traditional tools of economic theory. A number of factors account for this general failure. Economic theory developed in England and the United States has centered about the individualism of the household and the firm. Indeed, one of the main arguments for the free competitive market system is that it maximizes the scope for individual choice. Thus, except for a few early exceptions, only in the last thirty years or so have economists studied interactions within small groups. Perhaps another reason for the lack of progress in oligopoly theory has been the emphasis on quantity rather than on price as the variable with which the firm was concerned. The preoccupation with quantity stems from the purely competitive model, in which the market determines the price. Until the 1930s, the purely competitive market structure was considered the only important market structure. Another drawback of traditional economic theory in its analysis of oligopolies can be attributed to the assumption that all firms are short-run profit-maximizers. This might well be a reasonable assumption for other types of market structure, but, as we shall see, simple short-run profit maximization can be inconsistent with longer-run profit maximization for an oligopolist. (We found it might be for a monopolist in our discussion of limit pricing.)

Shortly after World War II, more sophisticated tools of analysis began to be applied to the theory of oligopolies. Von Neumann and Morganstern published their important book on game theory, which developed tools with which to analyze conflict.[15] K. Rothschild, in a

---

[15]John von Neumann and Oskar Morganstern, *Theory of Games and Economic Behavior* (Princeton: Princeton University Press, 1953).

well-known article, suggested that economists who want to understand oligopoly would do well to study international diplomacy and the writings on warfare of Clausewitz.[16]

We can immediately get some insight into the oligopoly problem by starting with Rothschild and seeing some analogies between countries in their relations with each other and the interrelations of oligopolists. Countries compete for land, power, and trade in much the same way that the firms in an oligopoly compete for market shares and profits. The main difference is that countries at times use physical force to attain their objectives, while the means by which firms can attain theirs are circumscribed by law, mainly the antitrust laws, and rules against coercion. Yet, although firms do not use physical force, they can take strong action to purposefully harm or discipline rivals, notably through the "price war." The physical wars of countries may thus serve as an analogy to the price wars of oligopolists.

Physical wars among countries and price wars among firms are generally costly to the participants. Thus, countries try to work out certain peaceful "rules of the game" by which they may attain their ends. The United States and the Soviet Union, for example, talk about "peaceful competition" to advance their competing systems. By analogy, a small group of firms would use only certain means to compete for market shares. Firms may have a tacit agreement to compete for market shares by advertising, by product styling, by offering various services, but they may rule out lower prices as an undesirable (from their point of view) means of competing for market shares in much the same way that major nations may try to avoid nuclear war.

Although countries may try to compete by peaceful means, they are aware that wars may break out. This can happen if one of the countries learns it may not do very well by peaceful competition. Or it may happen if one of the countries becomes militarily stronger than its rivals. As a result, countries maintain some physical force, concern themselves with the balance of power and deterrence, and try to maintain a credible threat that they are prepared to use force if necessary.

This analogy holds for the firms in an oligopoly. Any firm may be tempted to go beyond the "acceptable" means of competition and decide to compete by lowering its price. If this happens, the other firms must be prepared for a price war. Thus, according to Rothschild, oligopolists, even while tacitly agreeing on rules of acceptable means of competition, must be prepared for the "test of strength" of a price war, in which all the rivals may suffer. They thus try to establish "impregnable positions," such as gaining control of marketing channels, and diversify and maintain sufficient liquidity so that they can "hold out" in a price war. By doing this, they hope to deter aggressive price-cutters.

[16]K. Rothschild, "Price Theory and Oligopoly," *Economic Journal*, vol. LVII (1947).

The leading countries, although in competition with each other, also have a concert of interest in limiting the power of other countries. Thus, spheres of influence and recognized hegemony in certain areas of the world are often agreed upon by major rivals. Similarly, a group of oligopolists has a concert of interest in keeping other firms out of their market. They can do this by patent pooling, joint control of scarce resources, and in other ways.

Alliances are another aspect of international diplomacy that may also characterize oligopolies. Oligopolists become allies when they deal with labor or lobby for their common interest before governments. They may also sometimes band together against a "maverick."

The Problem in Demand Curve Estimation. We can see some of the individual firm's problems in estimating its demand curve by analyzing some of the special relationships in the oligopoly in terms of our general demand function:

$$\frac{Q}{Q_m} = a + b(P_m - P) + c(D_m - D).$$

When solved for P, it becomes

$$P = \left[\frac{a}{b} + P_m + \frac{c}{b}(D_m - D)\right] - \left(\frac{1}{bQ_m}\right)Q.$$

We have seen that the problem faced by the firm in the monopolistic competition market was the estimation of the parameters a, b, c, the difference between D_m and D, and the values of P_m and Q_m. Once the firm has estimated these values, it can then select any values it wishes for P and Q in the short run and try to influence a, b, c, and D in the long run. It could make these decisions under the assumption that its own decisions will have only minor effects upon P_m, Q_m, and D_m and that any efforts to change a, b, and c will not *by themselves* cause other firms to adopt policies that will influence the values of a, b, and c.

The oligopolist is faced with problems that stem from the likelihood that rivals will react to what it does. Consider, most importantly, the price of all firms, P_m. The monopolistically competitive firm can select a value for P with the expectation that P_m will change by only a small amount, for P_m also includes the firm's price. But the oligopolist must expect other firms to change their prices in response to his price. Put symbolically, the oligopolist should be aware that $P_m = f(P)$; that is, the prices charged by all firms will be influenced by his own price. Not only will P_m be influenced by his price; in addition, the market demand, Q_m, which depends on P_m, is substantially influenced by the value the firm selects for P.

The oligopolist's selection of a value for Q can also influence the variables in the demand function that would have constant values to the monopolistically competitive firm. If the firm selects a high value for Q, it could substantially affect the total supply on the market and depress the value of P_m. Or, other firms may react to a "too high" value of Q by lowering their prices, thereby also leading to a lower value for P_m.

Oligopolists cannot always assume they are completely free to select any value they want for D. An aggressive firm – one that selects low values for P or high values for Q – may find its rivals have ways of physically interfering with its ability to produce. This can be accomplished if rivals control some of the materials required by the firm. Or the rivals may pressure suppliers to limit their sales to an aggressive firm or even to engage in a boycott. Such actions would influence the value of D.

Finally, even efforts by the firm to change the values of the *a*, *b*, and *c* parameters may lead to countermeasures by rivals. An advertising campaign by one firm, for example, frequently results in advertising campaigns by rivals that are designed to counter the claims of the initiator. But, in all likelihood, efforts to influence *a*, *b*, and *c* are usually considered within the tacit rules of competition and do not elicit a response as immediate and strong as would a price reduction.

The Various Possibilities of Strategies, Interactions, and Payoffs. We will now analyze a special case of oligopoly, namely the duopoly, in order to assess the various strategies and interactions and their payoffs open to duopolists. We will assume that the two firms produce an identical product and, to simplify matters, that production costs are zero. We will examine what the cash flows (or profits) would be when (1) the two firms act completely independently of each other, (2) one firm uses "conjectural variation" – that is, it takes into account the other firm's actions when it forms its own policies, (3) one firm uses "defensive strategies" to counteract aggressive behavior by its rival, (4) the two firms form a cartel that agrees on the output, (5) after the promotion of the cartel, one firm double-crosses the other.

With identical products, there is not a great deal of scope for price rivalry because the whole market would go to the firm with the lower price and the other firm will always match a price decrease. Thus, we will assume that the firms compete by varying their output levels. Most of the insights we obtain from studying competition by output will be applicable to competition by price. We will pay more attention to price in the following section.

INDEPENDENT ACTION BY DUOPOLISTS. A French economist, Augustus Cournot, is generally given credit for first analyzing the behavior of a pair of duopolists.[17] He assumed that both duopolists were in the business of bottling mineral water from a stream, in this way allowing costs to be either zero or negligible. He assumed a market demand

---

[17]A. Cournot, *Researches into the Mathematical Principles of the Theory of Wealth* (Homewood, Ill.: Irwin, 1963); originally published in 1838.

curve known to both duopolists. He also assumed that both were somewhat naive, in that they took each other's output as given datum and then selected their profit-maximizing output.

To study Cournot's results, let us designate P the market price at which both duopolists sell, Q_1 the output of duopolist 1 and Q_2 the output of duopolist 2. Using numbers for the parameters, let us assume the demand curve for some period of time to be

$$P = 100 - 0.5(Q_1 + Q_2). \tag{9.10}$$

Consider now the profit-maximizing output of duopolist 1. Because there are no costs, his profits equal his revenue, which is the market price times his own output. Thus, we have $\pi_1 = PQ_1$. We can now substitute for P from equation 9.10 to get profit as

$$\pi_1 = [100 - 0.5(Q_1 + Q_2)]Q_1 \tag{9.11}$$
$$\pi_1 = 100Q_1 - 0.5Q_1^2 - 0.5Q_1Q_2.$$

To find the output that maximizes π_1, the duopolist takes the first derivative of π_1 with respect to his own output, sets this equal to zero, and solves for Q_1. (We assume our duopolist knows differential calculus.) Thus we have

$$\frac{\partial \pi_1}{\partial Q_1} = 100 - Q_1 - 0.5Q_2 = 0$$

and

$$Q_1 = 100 - 0.5Q_2. \tag{9.12}$$

The optimum value of Q_1 evidently depends on the output of the second duopolist. For any value of output selected by the second duopolist, equation 9.12 can be used by the first duopolist to calculate the output that would maximize his profits.

By very much the same reasoning process, the second duopolist could calculate his profit-maximizing output. It could be found from

$$Q_2 = 100 - 0.5Q_1. \tag{9.13}$$

Clearly the second duopolist's profit-maximizing output depends on the output of the first duopolist. The two equations, 9.12 and 9.13, are known as reaction curves, for each duopolist in effect reacts to the output of his rival when selecting his profit-maximizing output.

If both duopolists continually adjust their output in response to the output of their rivals, both firms will reach an output level at which neither would wish to change: This is the equilibrium. Say, for example, that the first duopolist decides to produce 100 units. The second duopolist substitutes 100 for Q_1 in his reaction curve (equation 9.13) and produces 50 units. The first duopolist, when the second duopolist produces 50, finds from his reaction curve that 75 units maximizes his profits. The second duopolist restudies his reaction curve and produces 62.5 units. These changes in output will continue until both duopolists produce 66 2/3 units. When they each produce this quantity, neither would want to change his output.

With each producer producing 66 2/3 units, we can also find the final equilibrium price from equation 9.10. Thus,

$$P = 100 - 0.5(66.66 + 66.66) = \$33.25.$$

With the price and the output, we can find each firm's profit:

$$\pi_1 = \pi_2 = (33.25)(66.66) \approx \$2222.$$

These outputs, price, and profits are known as the Cournot solution.

THE USE OF CONJECTURAL VARIATIONS. Cournot's duopolists are somewhat naive; they do not take into account the effect of their own output on their rival's output. When one or both of the duopolists takes his rival's output pattern into account when planning his own output, we call this conjectural variation.

Let us say that duopolist 1 is sophisticated and notices that the second duopolist behaves in accordance with equation 9.13. Thus, because the second duopolist's output depends on the first duopolist's output, the first duopolist would take this into account when determining his own output. This can be done by duopolist 1 by using equation 9.13 to substitute for Q_2 in his profit equation. Thus, equation 9.11 becomes

$$\pi_1 = \{100 - 0.5[Q_1 + (100 - 0.5Q_1)]\} Q_1$$

or

$$\pi_1 = 100Q_1 - 0.5Q_1^2 - 50Q_1 + 0.25Q_1^2$$
$$\pi_1 = 50Q_1 - 0.25Q_1^2.$$

The profit of duopolist 1 now depends only on his own output. The profit-maximizing output by duopolist 1 is then

$$\frac{d\pi_1}{dQ_1} = 50 - 0.5Q_1 = 0$$

$$Q_1 = 100.$$

If the second duopolist continues to be a short-run profit-maximizer, he substitutes 100 for Q_1 in equation 9.13 and produces only 50 units. From the market demand curve (equation 9.10), the market price becomes

$$P = 100 - 0.5(100 + 50) = \$25.$$

The profit of the first duopolist is now

$$\pi_1 = PQ_1 = (25)(100) = \$2500,$$

while the profit of the second duopolist is

$$\pi_2 = PQ_2 = (25)(50) = \$1250. \tag{9.14}$$

A comparison of these profits with the Cournot solution, in which each duopolist had profits of $2222, shows that conjectural variation pays for the first duopolist, while the profit of the second duopolist is substantially reduced. The key element in the conjectural variation solution is that the first duopolist is able to discern the second duopolist's behavioral pattern – simple profit maximization – and take advantage of this information. Clearly, the second duopolist comes out second best if he is a profit-maximizer. From this analysis we should conclude that simple short-run profit maximization may not be a desirable behavioral pattern for a duopolist because it enables the other duopolist to "manipulate" him.

DEFENSIVE STRATEGIES AND DETERRENCE. What can the second duopolist do if faced with an aggressive rival who uses conjectural variation?[18] If he does not want to be permanently consigned to the lower profit figure, he must act in a way that would punish the first duopolist, with the hope that the first duopolist will give up his aggressively high output. To do this, the second duopolist must be prepared to sacrifice some of his *immediate* profit to deter the first duopolist from his aggressive behavior (in this case a high output level). In this way, he hopes to make higher profits in the *future*.

One possible strategy the second duopolist can adopt is to produce the same level of output as the first duopolist. However, duopolist 2 would want to produce the same level of output as duopolist 1 only when the latter produces "too high" an output. If duopolist 1 is not aggressive, duopolist 2 would be best off by simply maximizing short-run profits. If the second duopolist calculates that whenever the first duopolist's output is greater than or equal to 66 2/3 (the Cournot output), he should produce the same, we can express this strategy as

$$Q_2 = Q_1, \qquad Q_1 \geq 66\,2/3. \tag{9.15}$$

But if the first duopolist does not produce more than 66 2/3, in which case the second duopolist has no reason to deter him, the second duopolist could produce his profit-maximizing output in accordance with equation 9.13. Thus, his output when Q_1 is less than or equal to 66 2/3 is

$$Q_2 = 100 - 0.5Q_1, \qquad Q_1 < 66\,2/3. \tag{9.16}$$

With the second duopolist switching his tactics in accordance with the first duopolist's output, we can obtain a picture of the first duopolist's demand curve. Notice that equation 9.10 can be viewed as the first duopolist's demand curve for any given value of Q_2. Let us write it as

$$P = (100 - 0.5Q_2) - 0.5Q_1. \tag{9.17}$$

[18]See I. M. Grossack, "Duopoly, Defensive Strategies, and the Kinked Demand Curve," *Southern Economic Journal*, vol. 32 (1966).

If the second duopolist uses equation 9.16 to select his output level whenever Q_1 is less than 66 2/3, the first duopolist's demand curve would be

$$P = [100 - 0.5(100 - 0.5Q_1)] - 0.5Q_1, \qquad Q_1 < 66\,2/3 \qquad (9.18)$$
$$P = 50 - 0.25Q_1, \qquad Q_1 < 66\,2/3.$$

But if the second duopolist uses equation 9.15 to select his output whenever Q_1 is greater than or equal to 66 2/3, the first duopolist's demand curve is

$$P = [100 - 0.5Q_1)] - 0.5Q_1, \qquad Q_1 \geq 66\,2/3 \qquad (9.19)$$
$$P = 100 - Q_1, \qquad Q_1 \geq 66\,2/3.$$

As a result, the first duopolist's demand curve is equation 9.18 when Q_1 is less than 66 2/3 and equation 9.19 when Q_1 is greater than or equal to 66 2/3. The resulting demand curve is shown in Figure 9.21. Notice that it has a kink at $Q_1 = 66\,2/3$. This kink comes about because the strategy of duopolist 2 changes in accordance with the output level of duopolist 1.

If the first duopolist persists in his aggressive output level of 100 and duopolist 2 acts to deter him by also producing 100 units, an insertion of these values of Q_1 and Q_2 into equation 9.10 shows that the price will drop to zero. In that event, neither duopolist will make any profit. The ability and willingness of either firm to accept zero profits will determine how long the first duopolist will persist in his aggressive output level and the second duopolist will persist in his rather strong deterrence. Here we have an example of warfare.

Somewhat less drastic deterrence strategies are available to the second duopolist if he cannot afford to be without profits for a substantial period of time. One possibility is to select an output of 66 2/3 and stay there whenever the first duopolist's output is greater than 66 2/3. Then equation 9.18 will continue to be the first duopolist's demand curve when Q_1 is less than 66 2/3, but when Q_1 is greater than or equal to 66 2/3, the demand curve for the first duopolist can be obtained by substituting 66 2/3 for Q_2 in equation 9.17 to get

$$P = [100 - 0.5(66.66)] - 0.5Q_1, \qquad Q_1 \geq 66\,2/3 \qquad (9.20)$$
$$P = 66.66 - 0.5Q_1, \qquad Q_1 \geq 66\,2/3.$$

Thus, equations 9.18 and 9.20 would be the first duopolist's demand curve. This is shown in Figure 9.22. It will be noticed that the demand curve also has a kink in it at $Q_1 = 66\,2/3$. This kink also comes about because at that output level the second duopolist switches his output strategy.

The selection of 66 2/3 by the second duopolist to counteract an aggressive strategy by the first duopolist ($Q_1 = 100$) in effect penalizes the first duopolist's short-run profits more than it does the second's.[19]

[19]Ibid.

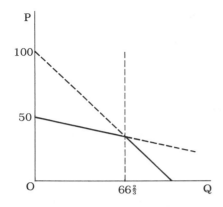

FIGURE 9.21   Duopolist's demand curve when rival matches output beyond his output of 66 2/3

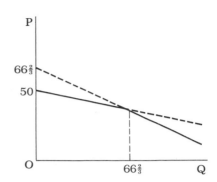

FIGURE 9.22   Duopolist's demand curve when rival maintains output of 66 2/3 when he produces beyond 66 2/3

If $Q_1 = 100$, and $Q_2 = 66\,2/3$, the price would be $16\,2/3$. The profit of the first duopolist would then be about $1667, and that of the second duopolist would be about $1111. It is true the first duopolist makes higher profits. But there is a high opportunity cost to him. If he was not aggressive, he could make the profit of $2222 found in the Cournot model. Thus, the "cost" to him of this strategy is $2222 − $1667, or about $565. The second duopolist, on the other hand, has a much smaller opportunity cost for his deterrent strategy. If he were simply a short-run profit-maximizer, when faced with the first duopolist's aggressive output he could make a profit of $1250. (See equation 9.14.) Thus the opportunity cost to him of not maximizing profits is $1250 − $1111, or $139. As a result, the strategy of duopolist 2 of producing 66 2/3 units when duopolist 1 produces 100 units costs the first duopolist $565 per period, but it costs the second duopolist only $139 per period. The second duopolist is in a better position to "hold out."

COLLUSION. Another possibility is that the duopolists will collude and jointly determine the output levels that maximize their joint profits. They would then view the demand curve, equation 9.10, with their total output Q replacing the individual outputs, Q_1 and Q_2. Thus, the demand curve is

$$P = 100 - 0.5Q.$$

The joint profit is then

$$\pi = PQ = (100 - 0.5Q)Q = 100Q - 0.5Q^2.$$

The profit-maximizing joint output is then

$$\frac{d\pi}{dQ} = 100 - Q = 0$$
$$Q = 100.$$

The market price with this output is

$$P = 100 - 0.5(100) = \$50.$$

If we assume the output is divided equally between the two duopolists, their profits are

$$\pi_1 = \pi_2 = (50)(50) = \$2500.$$

Compared to the profits of $2222 for each duopolist when they behave in accordance with Cournot's assumptions, collusion is obviously desirable for the duopolists. The collusion profit of $2500 is no higher for the duopolist who successfully uses conjectural variation, but with collusion, the potentially aggressive duopolist does not have to concern himself with counterstrategies by this rival. There is little question that, so far as the joint profits of the duopolists are concerned, collusion is highly desirable.

INCENTIVE TO "CHEAT" ON A COLLUSIVE ARRANGEMENT. If the duopolists agree on their output level (collusion), but one of them secretly breaks his part of the bargain, the "cheating" duopolist can make still higher profits. Let us assume the duopolists agree that each will produce only 50 units of output. Let us further assume that the first duopolist breaks the agreement and the second duopolist maintains his part of the bargain. Then, starting with equation 9.17 as his demand curve, the first duopolist's demand curve, with $Q_2 = 50$, is

$$P = [100 - 0.5(50)] - 0.5Q_1 = 75 - 0.5Q_1.$$

The profit-maximizing output for the first duopolist is

$$\pi_1 = PQ_1 = (75 - 0.5Q_1)Q_1 = 75Q_1 - 0.5Q_1^2$$
$$\frac{d\pi_1}{dQ_1} = 75 - Q_1 = 0$$
$$Q_1 = 75.$$

With this output by the first duopolist, and $Q_2 = 50$ for the second duopolist, the market price would be

$$P = 100 - 0.5(75 + 50) = \$37.50.$$

The profit of the "cheating" duopolist is now

$$\pi_1 = PQ_1 = (37.50)(75) = \$2712.50.$$

For the second duopolist it is

$$\pi_2 = PQ_2 = (37.50)(50) = \$1875.00.$$

Clearly, there is incentive for the first duopolist to cheat, for his profits would be considerably higher than if he abided by the collusive agreement. However, this kind of cheating can be effective only if somehow it can be done secretly; otherwise, the second duopolist would retaliate. We can infer from this analysis that there is an incentive toward secret cheating in oligopolies, given collusion. It is worth noting that in this case buyers benefit from the cheating. With collusion adhered to, the price was $50, but with cheating the price falls to $37.50.

There is, of course, a good chance that duopolist 2 will learn of the cheating by the first duopolist. The second duopolist would presumably try to punish the first duopolist. He might raise his output by a very large amount, forcing profits down for both firms. Or he may produce the same output as the cheater. If the latter strategy is adopted, both firms produce 75 units each, and the price becomes

$$P = 100 - 0.5(75 + 75) = \$25.$$

The profits of each duopolist are then

$$\pi_1 = \pi_2 = (25)(75) = \$1875.$$

COMPARISON WITH MONOPOLY. Of course the best that either duopolist can do for himself is to drive the other duopolist out of business or perhaps persuade the government to give him a monopoly. Then, the profit-maximizing output is the same as in perfect collusion. But the whole profit, now $5000, goes to the remaining duopolist. Pure monopoly clearly is the ultimate in desirability to the oligopolist.

SUMMARY AND COMPARISON. It would be instructive to compare all the profits for the duopolists that correspond to the different types of behavior and strategies that they adopt. Table 9.2 displays the profits for each duopolist for the eight cases we have discussed.

TABLE 9.2   Profits for duopolists 1 and 2 that correspond to different types of behavior

Strategy combinations	π_1	π_2
1. Each duopolist acts independently and adjusts to the other's output (Cournot).	2,222	2,222
2. Duopolist 1 uses conjectural variation (C.V.) to produce 100 units. Duopolist 2 is a simple profit-maximizer.	2,500	1,250
3. Duopolist 1 uses C.V. to produce 100. Duopolist 2 deters by producing the same amount.	0	0
4. Duopolist 1 uses C.V. to produce 100. Duopolist 2 deters by producing 66 2/3, which makes duopolist 1's opportunity cost higher than duopolist 2's opportunity cost.	1,667	1,111
5. Full collusion with exact split of market.	2,500	2,500
6. Duopolists collude, but duopolist 1 cheats.	2,712	1,875
7. Duopolists collude, duopolist 1 cheats, and duopolist 2 retaliates by producing the same as duopolist 1.	1,875	1,875
8. Duopolist 1 forces duopolist 2 out of business.	5,000	0

We can now consider the courses of action that are desirable, say, to the first duopolist.[20] Of course, his profits are highest if he can monopolize the market by forcing duopolist 2 out of business. His next best option is to collude and cheat, but this runs the risk of retaliation. His third best option is to collude and remain honest, thus getting $2500 profit. This does not yield a higher profit than the use of conjectural variation, if duopolist 2 is a simple profit-maximizer. But collusion, if duopolist 2 is "honest," is preferable because duopolist 2 may turn out not to be a simple profit-maximizer but may instead use one of his defensive strategies. Behavior according to Cournot's assumptions would give lower profits than some of the other strategies but is less risky if both firms behave that way.

Given all these possibilities but ruling out that in which the first duopolist becomes a monopolist, most economists, we think, would conclude that full collusion is the most likely pattern. But, as we shall show, collusion in practice may not be so simple as it seems. Furthermore, the incentives to cheat may be very strong in many cases.

Cooperation and Breakdowns in Cooperation among Oligopolists. Having shown the major types of interactions in our theoretical models, we now turn to one of the major debates among specialists in the area of oligopolies. On one side of this debate are those who stress the ability of oligopolists to collude, or "cooperate," in their determination of prices and output levels. They propose what is known as the joint profit maximization thesis; that is, that oligopolists collude in such a way that the profits of all sellers, taken as a group are maximized.[21] On the other side of the debate are those who emphasize the tendency toward breakdowns in agreements and noncollusive actions of firms.[22]

The basis for the disagreement can be found in some of the models discussed in the preceding section. It was shown that collusion maximizes the joint profit of the duopolists. But it was also shown that there are incentives for the duopolists to cheat on a collusive arrangement.

---

[20]For extensions of these types of analysis, see Martin Shubik, *Strategy and Market Structure* (New York: Wiley, 1959).

[21]This thesis is developed in William Fellner, *Competition Among the Few* (New York: Knopf, 1947). Fellner qualified this thesis in a number of ways. It is also well presented in W. J. Baumol, *Business Behavior, Value and Growth* (New York: Macmillan, 1959).

[22]G. Stigler has investigated breakdowns in collusion. See George Stigler, "A Theory of Oligopoly," *Journal of Political Economy,* vol. 72 (1964). Two writers who also have investigated the conditions for collusion and breakdowns in collusion are O. E. Williamson and A. Phillips. See Oliver Williamson, "A Dynamic Theory of Interfirm Behavior," *Quarterly Journal of Economics,* vol. 79 (1965); and Almarin Phillips, *Market Structure, Organization and Performance* (Cambridge, Mass.: Harvard University Press, 1962).

INCENTIVES TO COLLUDE AND CHEAT. We can illustrate the incentives to collude and cheat with the help of a payoff matrix that shows the cash flows (or profits) to two firms from various types of actions they may take. Table 9.3 provides a payoff matrix in which the only actions taken by the firms are with regard to prices. Each element shows the payoffs to the firms for a pair of strategies (or actions), the SW number referring to duopolist 1's payoff and the NE number to duopolist 2's payoff.

TABLE 9.3   Hypothetical payoff matrix

		DUOPOLIST 2 STRATEGIES		
		Lower price by 5%	*Price unchanged*	*Raise price by 5%*
DUOPOLIST 1 STRATEGIES	*Lower price by 5%*	50 50	25 175	0 250
	Price unchanged	125 25	100 100	50 200
	Raise price by 5%	250 0	200 50	150 150

Table 9.3 is meant to illustrate that oligopolists are playing what game theorists call a non-zero-sum game. A non-zero-sum game is one in which there are actions by both participants (players) in the game in which they *both* can be better off compared to other possible pairs of strategies. Thus, both players are better off if they both raise prices (their joint payoff is $300) than if they both lower prices or leave them unchanged.

From our hypothetical payoff matrix, the firms, if they wanted to maximize their total joint payoff, would both raise their prices. That this gives the maximum payoff to both firms provides the basis for the thesis that firms collude in some form to find the combination of actions that maximizes the joint profits. But, as we try to demonstrate in Table 9.3, an individual firm could be still better off if it somehow gets its rival to raise prices, perhaps by an agreement, while it secretly lowers or keeps unchanged its prices. Thus, if the two duopolists agree to raise their prices, but the first duopolist instead lowers his price, the first duopolist has a higher profit than if he abides by the agreement. On this basis we have the incentive to cheat on an agreement, which in turn is the basis for the breakdown of price-fixing agreements.

Faced with the incentive to cheat, those defending the high likelihood of joint action by the firms would argue that cheating may not be profitable when the other firm learns about it. Thus if duopolist 1 reduces his price despite an agreement to raise prices, the second duopolist, when he learns of the "double-cross," will also reduce his price. In that event, both duopolists will be making only $50 apiece, and it is likely they will both learn that there is more to be gained by collusion and abiding by the agreement.

In our very simple example, collusion might well be the expected pattern of behavior. But if there are, say, six or seven oligopolists whose products differ somewhat, they compete on a number of levels in addition to price, and there is uncertainty about what the payoffs will be for different strategy pairs, double-crosses may not be so readily detected and may thus be a more attractive option than in the simple example of Table 9.3.

METHODS OF COOPERATION. Oligopolists can agree about a number of joint patterns of behavior. Foremost, perhaps, is price. If the market demand curve is inelastic with respect to price, which is widely although perhaps erroneously believed to be the case, higher prices are of benefit to all sellers. The higher prices produce more revenues and, with smaller outputs, costs are reduced. Higher prices, if charged by all sellers, are then frequently in the interest of all the oligopolists. There are, however, limits to just how high a price is in the interest of the oligopolists. Too high a price could lead to a switch to substitutes and could induce efforts to develop new substitutes. Too high a price could also result in new entry by sellers. Thus, oligopolists acting jointly have to concern themselves with making entry difficult and perhaps using a limit price. Sometimes the oligopolists might be better served if they lower prices. Demand in the long run could be more price elastic than the oligopolists believe it to be.

Another subject of agreement could be output. The smaller the output placed on the market, the greater is the likelihood that prices will be more satisfactory. Restrictions on output are also needed as part of a price agreement. If all the firms agree on price but do not restrict output and the building of new capacity, pressures are engendered that would lead to a breakdown in the agreement on price. However, an agreement on output is generally more difficult to reach than one on price, and disagreement on output levels could undermine agreements on prices.

The oligopolists can also reach agreements on transaction terms other than the price. For example, it may be common policy to sell only at delivered prices (the buyer pays the price delivered at his site), rather than F.O.B. (the buyer obtains the goods at the production site). Other agreements could concern discounts for payment within a given period, credit terms, discounts to wholesalers or jobbers, returns of defective or unsold merchandise, and various types of tied services such as repair facilities.

Oligopolists can also coordinate policies regarding their products. They may agree on a planned obsolescence strategy, which is of course designed to stimulate future sales. They may agree to not adopt various design or manufacturing innovations because such innovations could upset their relationships. They may try to develop standards for variations of a product, which can be helpful in coming to an agreement on prices when products are differentiated. There may be codes on advertising. For example, stressing prices or blatantly pointing out the shortcomings of a competitor's product may be unacceptable.

Oligopolists have also been known to coordinate their purchases of the factors of production. Sometimes they set standards for what they pay for different types of labor or materials. Sometimes they jointly try to control sources of raw materials; this practice could bar entry and limit the output of any particular firm. Sometimes they pressure suppliers not to sell to price-cutters. That such actions are taken by oligopolists has been attested to in many antitrust cases.

Finally, oligopolists can agree to not compete at all and simply share the market. This could be done by the oligopolists' agreeing not to sell to customers in each other's territories and to confine themselves to limited submarkets. There is a wide range of possible market-sharing agreements.

In the real world there can be innumerable combinations of agreements on price, output, quality, and so forth. Often, we suspect, agreements may pertain only to price, with the understanding that the oligopolists may compete by other means such as product styling, tied services, and advertising. The oligopolists, in short, could agree on the types of competition that are not to be permitted and the types that are to be allowed. We should point out, however, that failure to agree on some methods of competition could undermine the agreements reached on other methods of competition. The lack of an agreement on product quality, for example, may make it difficult to maintain an agreement on price. A firm losing its market share because of what it thinks is an unwarranted improvement in the services or products of rivals may be tempted to retaliate or defend its market position with a price reduction.

How can oligopolists agree to coordinate their policies when the Sherman Act clearly makes such agreements illegal?[23] The penalties of the law may not always be an adequate deterrent. Since the Sherman Act was enacted in 1890, there have been about a thousand cases in which direct collusion among firms was at issue. These cases, of course, have been brought to court only when collusion has been detected and the antitrust authorities have taken action. Much direct collusion certainly has been either undetected or not bolstered with sufficient evidence.

There are, however, more subtle means of reaching agreements among oligopolists than meeting in a hotel room and sitting down with competitors to discuss the industry's "problems." One of the most common methods of coordinating policies, especially with

[23] For some of the methods of collusion, see Richard Caves, *American Industry: Structure, Conduct, Performance* (Englewood Cliffs, N.J.: Prentice-Hall, 1967).

regard to price, is through price leadership. In price leadership, one firm is recognized as the price leader, and there is an understanding that all sellers will charge the same price as the leader.

A second method is by the common use of formulas. In many industries it is widely understood that prices "should" be set by some kind of standard markup on costs. Trade associations may be obliging enough to calculate what costs should be the basis for the markup. A widely used pricing formula for many years was the basing price system. In this system, all sellers quote only delivered prices, which are calculated on the basis of the price in some city plus the freight from that city to the consuming point.[24] This system had been common in industries where freight costs are important. It has been declared illegal.

A third method of coordinating policies is through experimentation. It may be the "talk" in an industry that the price is "too low." One firm may then "test the market" by raising its price to see if others will follow suit. The other firms then "assess" the significance of the price increase and follow the increase, refuse to follow, or select different price increases. Through this kind of experimentation, or trial and error, oligopolists can effectively coordinate their pricing.

With such subtle means of reaching agreements among oligopolists, we may ask whether the Sherman Act is effective in stopping collusion. It has, in fact, been difficult for the courts to determine just what constitutes collusion and conspiracy. At times, some courts have been willing to infer conspiracy on the basis of evidence showing there was a "meeting of the minds" of the oligopolists or that there was a "conscious parallelism" of their actions.[25] The issue of inferring conspiracy is, however, still not resolved and is one of the gray areas in antitrust laws. Those who argue for a breakup of large firms contend that oligopolists virtually must engage in subtle collusion simply because of the fact that, with a small number of sellers, they have to recognize their interdependencies.

We do not wish to suggest that all oligopolists reach agreements on a purely voluntary basis. Many things can be done to force a recalcitrant oligopolist into an agreement. Large firms could threaten to reduce their prices on products or in geographical areas where the noncooperating oligopolist has most of his sales. Pressures can be exerted on suppliers not to deal with a maverick. Influence can be exerted by large firms on financial interests, unions, transport companies, and so forth to make life difficult for noncooperating firms.

---

[24]The best-known system along these lines has been in the steel industry, widely known as the Pittsburgh-plus system.

[25]For a good picture of the workings of the antitrust laws in this and other areas, see A. D. Neale, *The Antitrust Laws of the USA* (Cambridge: Cambridge University Press, 1966).

BREAKDOWNS IN AGREEMENTS. One of the greatest difficulties in maintaining an agreement on prices is obtaining an agreement on output or market shares. Although it may seem to be clearly in the interest of all sellers to charge a high price, it is not at all clear how an agreement can be reached on the output levels of individual firms. Such an agreement on output is necessary to the maintenance of a high price. When it comes to agreeing on output levels for individual firms, the interests of the firms clash. The simplest solution may seem to be apportioning the output equally among all sellers. This, however, may not appeal to the larger firms. Another solution may be to apportion market shares and output on the basis of past output levels. This may not be appreciated by the smaller firms, who might well be dynamic and aggressive and have big plans for themselves.

If firms cannot agree on how to divide the restricted output among themselves, the larger firms may decide to limit their output in order to maintain a high price, even when the smaller firms are free to produce as much as they want. The large firms are then said to maintain a "price umbrella" for the industry. However, reductions in output by the larger firms can undermine their positions, for the smaller firms may continue to expand their output. Unilateral output restrictions by the large firms may then not be a desirable way to limit output. At any rate, agreements on output could be difficult to attain, and there is little doubt that many cartels have broken down over the problem of apportioning output.

Price and output agreements could prove difficult to reach because of cost differences among the various sellers. The level of price and output in a potential agreement that would be desirable to one firm may not be desirable to another because of the nature of their costs and the various contractual commitments they may have.

Price agreements may be particularly difficult to reach in dynamic, fast-growing industries. The market is generally unsettled in them, and there is likely to be a great deal of product development. With rapidly changing situations, it is difficult to reach agreements, especially when the law inhibits direct contact between the sellers. It is widely recognized that price and output agreements are more common in settled, mature industries than in the newer, more dynamic ones. Business journals are fond of pointing out when discussing a new industry that there must be a "shake out" before prices can be stabilized.

Even with an agreement on price, there are ample incentives for individual firms to secretly cut prices, especially when business is slow. Such price cuts usually begin with the seller offering discounts off the "list price" to selected, usually large, buyers. It is difficult, however, to keep these price concessions secret. The favored buyers, in particular, are tempted to use the lower price quotes of some sellers as leverage to get even larger price concessions from other sellers. (Shrewd buyers, incidentally, may confuse the price-fixing sellers by falsely telling some sellers that other sellers have offered them a lower price.) Prices probably fall in an oligopoly in just this way: There is at least a quasi-agreement on prices among the sellers; some sellers secretly cut prices; the news of the price cuts spreads to the remaining sellers, who then cut their prices. The prices charged by competitors are especially crucial in undifferentiated oligopolies in which price is one of the few determinants of market shares.

There is, of course, some danger to the firm that breaks an agreement on price, or on any other subject of an agreement. If rivals find out about the price cuts in a short period of time, the advantage of the original price-cutter may be short-lived. There is also the danger of a price war, in which the larger firms, which generally are most likely to abide by the agreement, attempt to punish the price-cutters.

After this review of the arguments favoring the wide existence of cooperation and those that emphasize the difficulties of attaining and maintaining agreements, we are back at Rothschild's thesis that the oligopoly is best seen in terms of war and international diplomacy. There is sometimes agreement on the methods of competition. There is much to be gained by the double-cross and secrecy. Occasionally wars that test the strength of the oligopolists break out.

Rigid Prices and the Kinked Demand Curve. It has long been recognized that the prices of oligopolists tend to be rigid, or "sticky." There are a number of explanations for these observations. First, prices may not be so rigid as they seem to outsiders. An agreement between the oligopolists with regard to prices may result in a nominal list price that all firms ostensibly adhere to; yet various oligopolists might be secretly giving discounts off the list price. Another explanation of rigid prices is that there is a quasi-agreement among oligopolists to compete by nonprice means. Thus, instead of lowering prices, they may choose to compete on the basis of product improvement, promotion, rapid delivery. Often, especially for consumer goods, oligopolists are convinced that price is immaterial and that all meaningful competition takes place in product design changes and in various types of sales promotion.

The observation that prices tend to be rigid in oligopolies played an important role in the 1930s, beset by the great depression. One economist, Gardiner Means, made a comparative study of prices from 1929, the beginning of the depression, to 1933, the trough of the depression.[26] He divided products into those for which prices are market determined (competitive industries) and those for which prices are "administered" (oligopolies and monopolies). He found that prices fell to a much greater extent in the competitive industries. Output

---

[26]See Gardiner C. Means, *Industrial Prices and Their Relative Inflexibility,* Senate Document No. 13, 74th Congress, 1st Session (January 1935).

and employment, however, fell to a much greater extent in the industries in which prices were administered. It was only a short step to the charge that large firms caused the severity of the depression, stronger enforcement of the antitrust laws, and congressional investigations of big business.[27]

One theory of rigid prices, first proposed by Paul Sweezy in the 1930s, rested on the asymmetry in the response of rivals to an individual firm's change in price.[28] If a firm lowers price, it is almost certain that its rivals, once they learn about the price reduction, will also lower their prices. Hence, the decrease in a firm's price will not lead to a large increase in sales volume. But if a firm raises price, it might be unlikely that rivals will also raise their price. Hence, an increase in price can lead to a large loss in sales volume to the price-raiser. If a firm does not gain sales by lowering price but loses sales by raising price, it is clear that the firm should stay at its current price. The demand curve thus has a kink in it, appearing as in Figure 9.23. The marginal revenue curve has a discontinuity at the kink and could be negative beyond the kink as in the diagram. The profit-maximizing firm would adhere to this price as long as the marginal cost curve intersects the *MR* curve in the wide range of the discontinuity.

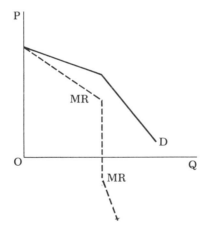

FIGURE 9.23 Kinked demand curve and discontinuous marginal revenue curve to explain rigid prices in oligopolies

The kinked demand curve theory still has a great deal of support, but it has also been attacked. Stigler, in a famous article, claimed that Sweezy underestimated the ability of businessmen to come to

[27]These investigations led to a large number of hearings on monopolies and oligopolies, known as the TNEC (Temporary National Economic Committee) reports, which provide a comprehensive picture of the operations of big business before World War II.

[28]Paul Sweezy, "Demand Under Conditions of Oligopoly," *Journal of Political Economy*, vol. XLVII (1939).

an understanding about raising prices.[29] The kinked demand curve as proposed by Sweezy is also somewhat unsatisfactory because, although it provides a reasonable explanation of why prices tend to be rigid, it says little about how the price got to any level or how it changes.

Estimating the Demand Curve. Having obtained some insights into the types of behavior expected in oligopolies, we can once again return to the problem of estimating the individual firm's demand curve, which can be obtained from the function

$$\frac{Q}{Q_m} = a + b(P_m - P) + c(D_m - D).$$

Because price is so crucial and price policies are so interdependent, the oligopolist must concern himself with the relation between all prices and his own price, depicted in the following function:

$$P_m = f(P). \tag{9.21}$$

Also, because an oligopolist typically has a substantial share of the market, he must concern himself with the size of whole market. That is, he is also concerned with the function

$$Q_m = f(P_m).$$

In the short run, the parameters a, b, and c can be considered stable, as can the difference between D_m and D. The oligopolist's main job is therefore to estimate P_m, which in turn influences Q_m. More importantly, he should attempt to evaluate the function, equation 9.21, which can be put in the form of a question: What will rivals do if I select a given value for P?

The answer to this question could be simple if there is any agreement or understanding among the oligopolists, or if an oligopolist has a great deal of experience in forecasting the behavior of rivals. In such cases there might be a fixed relation between P_m and P, in which event the oligopolist would know P_m as soon as he has determined a value for P.

If there is no understanding or if there is uncertainty of any type, the oligopolist may have to assume different possible values for P_m and for the relationship embodied in equation 9.21. In that case he would have to face the fact that there might be one of a number of different demand curves, each one depending on the price policies of his rivals. Not knowing which demand curve will actually materialize, he has to make his decisions under risk and uncertainty, a topic we study in Chapter 13.

---

[29]George Stigler, "The Kinky Oligopoly Demand Curve and Rigid Prices," *Journal of Political Economy*, vol. LV (1947).

It is very possible that the function, equation 9.21, may take on different values depending on whether the oligopolist raises or lowers *P*. If, for example, he lowers *P*, others may also lower prices, so that we may have $P_m = P$ when *P* is lowered. But if *P* is raised, others may not raise their prices and P_m would stay at approximately the same level. (P_m would change somewhat because the firm's own price is part of P_m.) This asymmetry in the behavior of rivals lies behind the kinked demand curve.

The firm, of course, may be able to substantially influence the parameters *a*, *b*, and *c* and the value of *D* in the long run. If the products produced by the oligopolist are not differentiated, increases in productive capacity and better methods of distribution by lowering *D* may be the only feasible ways of shifting the demand curve to the right. However, if product differentiation is feasible, the firm can engage in activities that might change the *a*, *b*, and *c* parameters.

Exact knowledge of his demand curve may not be quite as important to the oligopolist as it is to firms in other types of market structures. The reasoning behind this statement is that the oligopolist should not be considered a simple short-run profit-maximizer. Whereas firms in, say, a monopolistically competitive market use the demand curve to select their profit-maximizing prices and outputs, the oligopolist has to select his price and output mainly with an eye to how his decisions affect those of his rivals.[30] He has to use the self-imposed constraints to restrict his price choices, in particular, perhaps giving up some possible short-run profits, in order to either discipline or "get along" with his rivals.

Unlike the market structures characterized as purely competitive and monopolistically competitive, there is no established concept of long-run equilibrium in the oligopoly. The reason for this is that it is characterized by great difficulty of entry. Without ease of entry, above-normal profits could persist indefinitely in the oligopoly. There may, therefore, be little relation between long-run costs and prices.

Discussion Questions

1. For what kinds of products or services might the market share of a particular firm be more sensitive to differences in delivery times than to differences in prices?

2. What kinds of problems might measuring the average price of all the sellers in a market present? Should we include in that average the price

---

[30]An important large-scale empirical investigation of pricing behavior by large firms found that short-run profit maximization was not the major objective of these firms. This is what we should expect on the basis of our theories. See A. D. H. Kaplan, J. B. Dirlam, and R. F. Lanzillotti, *Pricing in Big Business* (Washington, D.C.: Brookings Institution, 1958).

of a seller who is unable to deliver the goods? Consider a seller whose price is so high that nobody buys from him. Should his price be included in the average?

3. Discuss how the definition of a market might affect our views on the structure of that market.

4. Is it conceivable that a firm producing a product that is identical to the products of rivals might obtain a price higher than that of rivals? What must be the relation between sensitivities to price and delivery time differentials for the firm to be able to command a price premium?

5. Explain clearly the distinction between exogenous and endogenous variables.

6. To what extent do the elasticities of demand and supply curves affect the degree to which quantities purchased and supplied respond to price changes?

7. If incomes rise, is inflation more, or less, likely if supply curves are elastic rather than inelastic? What affect would the rapidity with which supply curves could shift have upon inflation? How could a policy to increase the mobility of resources into and out of industries affect inflation?

8. How can the concept of economic surplus be used to measure how well an economy or an industry is performing in the public interest?

9. Explain how the need to plan production before the market price is completely known can lead to large fluctuations in prices.

10. What deters a firm from raising its price? Why is a firm facing a less elastic demand curve more likely to charge a higher price than one facing a more elastic demand curve?

11. What incentives are there for a monopolist to bar entry into his market? How might this be done?

12. How might price discrimination by a monopolist lead to higher output, in comparison with selling at a single price? How might price discrimination be abused?

13. What key elements distinguish monopolistic competition from oligopoly?

14. What special difficulties must the oligopolist estimating his demand curve face?

15. There appears to be much greater price collusion in the steel industry than in the automobile industry. How can oligopoly theory explain this difference?

16. There appears to be much greater price stability in oligopolies than in other types of market. How could this be explained?

10 Factor Markets and Income Distribution

In this chapter we concern ourselves with the supply curve of inputs —
or factors of production — that faces the firm. To a considerable extent,
the problems of estimating such a supply curve have much in common with those of estimating the demand curve, and some of the
concepts in Chapter 9 will be applicable here.

We can distinguish three basic arrangements under which the
firm can obtain inputs. One of these is through purchase in the open
market. When we say the firm purchases in the open market, we imply that it is free to deal with any supplier and has no obligations to
any supplier beyond a single transaction. A second arrangement for
obtaining inputs is through contracts that extend over a time period
and can encompass a large number of transactions. In the real
world, contractual arrangements are perhaps more common than
open market transactions, especially in the important purchases of
labor. A third method of obtaining inputs is for the firm to actually
gain control of sources of supply. Of course a firm can simultaneously
obtain inputs under all three arrangements.

In Chapter 9, in which we viewed the firm as a seller, we considered
only its sales on the open market. But the firm can also sell under
contract and can gain control of outlets as well. Therefore, much of
what we have to say on contracts and control in this chapter, in
studying the firm's role as a buyer, would also apply to the firm in its
role as seller.

We organize this chapter by the three types of arrangements for
obtaining inputs: open market, contract, and control. We then go into
a related topic, the distribution of income. It is through the firm's
purchases of labor, money, entrepreneurial services, and "land,"
that wages, interest, profit, and rent are determined.

PURCHASE ON THE OPEN MARKET

When the firm purchases on the open market, we can distinguish two relationships between the quantity it purchases and the price it pays. In one, the price at which it can purchase is completely independent of the quantity purchased. The buying price is somehow set by the market, and the firm's only option concerns how much it wishes to purchase at that price. In this case, the purchase price is not a decision variable to the firm; rather, it is a given parameter.

In the second relationship, the purchase price is influenced by the quantity the firm purchases. The price can vary in either direction with the quantity. In one instance the price of the input would rise with an increase in quantity purchased, or, put another way, the price could be lowered by reducing purchases. This relation between price and quantity can take place when the buying firm is such a dominant purchaser in a market that its own purchases affect the price. Such a purchaser is said to be a monopsonist. Higher average prices with increased input purchase may also occur if the firm has to go further distances to obtain inputs as it expands its purchases; this would, of course, raise transport costs. Perhaps more commonly, a firm's price is reduced when it purchases large amounts from particular suppliers; discounts for large purchases are common phenomena. When the firm's purchases can influence its purchase price, that price is no longer a parameter. Rather, it becomes a decision variable to the firm, and the firm will take into account its affect on the input price when planning its purchases.

Supply Price as "Given." The problem the firm faces in estimating its supply curve constraints – that is, the constraint for a product that determines the price and quantity choices – comes down essentially to knowing the open market purchase price for the particular product. In the short run, it is usually a simple matter to learn what this price is – by contacting suppliers, reading trade journals, and so on. However, when the firm assesses long-run plans, it is usually necessary to estimate what prices will be in the future.

Some of the models developed in Chapter 9 are completely applicable here. Whereas a seller is interested in forecasting P_m, the market price, in order to determine this future demand curve, a buyer is just as interested in the same price, for it will determine the supply curve facing him. When the market structure is either purely or monopolistically competitive, the analysis of supply and demand curves as the determinant of P_m can also be used by buyers. When, however, the market structure is monopolistic or oligopolistic, forecasting the price is generally difficult because prices are determined more by the individual firms – that is, they tend to be administered – rather than by the impersonal, better-understood interplay of the market. All a buyer could do is try to understand how the monopolist or oligopolists will behave. These difficulties help explain the tendencies toward long-term contracts rather than open market sales in monopolistic and oligopolistic industries.

When the supply price is known or forecast, the supply curve constraint on the firm is nothing more than a straight line as in Figure 10.1, where p is the purchase price for a particular input, x is the quantity of that input, and p_m is the market price. Later in this chapter we investigate the determinants of the price of that most important input, labor.

Supply Price as a Function of a Firm's Purchases. In many markets, the buying firm is faced not with a single price for an input but with a schedule of prices that depends on the quantity it purchases. Sometimes the buying firm has to pay more as it increases the quantity of its purchases; at other times it can receive lower supply prices as it expands its level of purchases.

MONOPSONY. Monopsony is the market structure in which the buying firm pays higher prices as it expands its purchase of a particular input. A monopsonistic market structure is characterized by a single or dominant buyer facing a large number of sellers of identical or similar products or services. Perhaps the most common example of a monopsony occurs in company towns, where a single large firm is the main purchaser of labor services. Colonial powers were generally monopsonists in their colonies; they set up a single trading company to purchase exportables and would not allow the colonials to sell to anybody else. Very large firms are often monopsonists, or come close to being monopsonists, for a variety of specialized types of labor, materials, and components. Monopsonies are common for some agricultural products in local geographic areas where farmers have to sell to a single buyer.[1]

Whereas the market demand curve is the monopolists' demand constraint, the market supply curve is the monopsonists' supply constraint and might appear as in Figure 10.2. When the monopsonist increases its purchase of this input, it raises the price. Therefore it has an interest in calculating the effect of its purchases on the price.

It is an important proposition that a monopsonist paying a single price will employ less labor (or buy less of any variable input) when the supply curve slopes as in Figure 10.2 than when the price is given by the market, as in Figure 10.1. In Chapter 7, we saw that when the supply curve is a horizontal line, the firm will purchase input up to the point where the supply curve intersects the value of the marginal product curve. (If the firm's demand curve slopes, the intersection would be with the marginal revenue product curve.) We used marginal reasoning to deduce that this intersection determines the

---

[1] For the last hundred years, farmers have complained that they are often forced to sell to monopsonists and buy from monopolists.

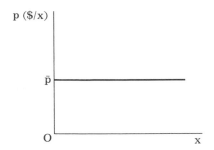

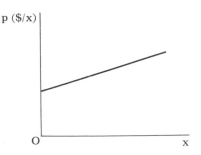

FIGURE 10.1   Supply curve facing
firm: price is independent of firm's
purchases

FIGURE 10.2   Supply curve
facing a monopsonist

optimal purchase of the input. The *VMP* (or *RMP*) measures the increase in revenue per additional unit of input; the supply curve measures the marginal expenditure per unit of input; the firm would purchase input up to the point the increase in revenue is no longer greater
than the increase in expenditure – that is, up to the point where the
marginal expenditure (*ME*) is just equal to the *VMP* (or *RMP*). Figure
10.3 shows the optimal purchase of that input.

When, however, the supply curve of the input (let us refer to labor)
rises, as in Figure 10.2, the intersection of the supply curve with the
VMP curve no longer gives the optimal amount of labor to purchase.
This is because, if we assume a single price, the sloping supply curve
does not give the marginal expenditure per unit of input. Rather the
ME is higher than the supply curve because the firm, in hiring another
worker at a higher wage rate, pays a higher wage to workers who were
willing to work for lower wage rates.

To see this, let us assume one worker could be hired at $3.00 per
hour and the hiring of a second worker costs $3.10 per hour. What is

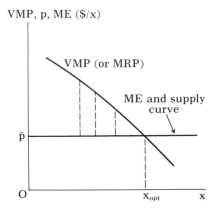

FIGURE 10.3   Optimum purchase of input when supply curve does not slope

the *ME* of hiring this second worker for one hour? It is not the $3.10 wage rate for this worker. Rather, the *ME* is the $3.10 for this worker plus the extra 10 cents the firm has to pay the first worker. Thus, the *ME* for the second worker is $3.20. Say now that a third worker can be hired only at a wage rate of $3.20. The *ME* of hiring that third worker is $3.40 – the $3.20 to the third worker plus the additional 10 cents paid to each of the first two workers. We can see that the *ME* rises to a greater extent than the supply curve as more of the input is purchased.

Given the supply curve, we can derive the marginal expenditure curve in much the same way that the marginal revenue curve was obtained from the demand curve. Say the supply curve is

$$p_1 = a + bx_1, \tag{10.1}$$

where p_1 is the wage rate and x_1 is the amount of labor hired. Then the total expenditure, E, on this input is

$$E = p_1 x_1 = (a + bx_1)x_1 = ax_1 + bx_1^2. \tag{10.2}$$

The marginal expenditure for any unit of input is the increment in total expenditure that occurs as the result of purchasing that unit, or

$$ME = \frac{\Delta E}{\Delta x_1}.$$

If we think of Δx_1 as very small, the *ME* is the first derivative of E with respect to x_1. With E given in equation 10.2, the *ME* is then

$$ME = \frac{dE}{dx_1} = a + 2bx_1. \tag{10.3}$$

A comparison of equation 10.3 with equation 10.1 shows that the *ME* per unit of labor rises twice as fast as the supply curve. These two curves are shown in Figure 10.4.

Using marginal reasoning, we can deduce that the monopsonist would hire labor up to the point where the *ME* is just equal to the *VMP* (or *MRP*), because up to that point cash flow is positive from hiring more labor while beyond that point the marginal cash flow is negative. Figure 10.5 depicts the amount of labor that would be hired, x_{1n}, and the wage rate, $\bar{p}_{1a}$. It should be clear that, if the wage rates are comparable, the monopsonist would hire less labor than would a firm whose supply curve of labor facing it does not slope.

In the preceding analysis, we have assumed that the firm pays the same wage rate to all its workers. However, if the firm could make a separate wage deal with each worker, paying only the minimum each particular worker is willing to accept – perfect wage discrimination – the supply curve itself becomes the marginal expenditure curve, and the firm would hire more workers.

Say the first worker is paid $3.00 per hour. If the second worker gets $3.10 per hour, while the first worker continues to get only

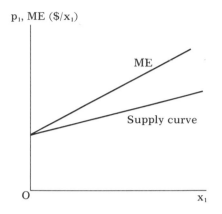

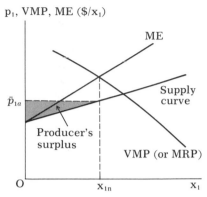

FIGURE 10.4   Marginal expendi-   FIGURE 10.5   Purchase of labor
ture when supply curve slopes   by a monopsonist: no
                                     discrimination

$3.00 per hour, the marginal expense of the second worker is $3.10.
The ME is now smaller compared to the nondiscriminatory case in
which the ME of the second worker was $3.20. Similarly, with dis-
crimination, the ME of the third worker is only $3.20 compared to
the higher figure of $3.40 when there is no discrimination. Evidently,
the supply curve itself is also the ME curve, and in Figure 10.6 we
see that the firm would hire x_{1d} units of labor, which is greater than
the x_{1n} units hired in Figure 10.5, which depicts the nondiscriminatory case. There is no single wage rate in the perfectly discriminating
case; rather, the firm pays a different wage rate to each worker.

In Chapter 9, we introduced the notion of a consumer and producer
surplus. Consumer surplus can be defined as the differences between
the prices consumers are willing to pay and the market price. Producer surplus is defined as the differences between the prices producers are willing to supply at and the actual market price. These
are shown in Figure 10.7. The notion of producer's surplus also holds
for workers and the wage rates workers would be willing to take.

When the monopsonist does not discriminate, all workers except
the last one hired obtain producer's surplus. Thus, if we have three
workers, the first one willing to work for $3.00 per hour, the second
for $3.10, and the third for $3.20, and if the firm pays $3.20 to all
workers in order to hire the third worker, the first worker gets a
surplus of 20 cents per hour and the second worker gets a surplus of
10 cents per hour. The third worker does not receive any surplus because his wage rate is just enough to get him to work for the firm. The
total producer surplus could be measured as the area between the
supply curve and the wage rate, as shown in Figure 10.5.

When the perfectly discriminating monopsonist makes a separate
wage deal with each worker, paying only the minimum each worker
is willing to work for, the monopsonist is able to appropriate the

p_1, VMP, ME ($/x_1$)

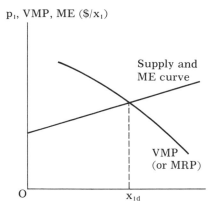

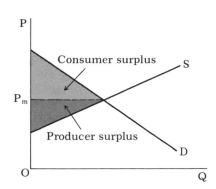

FIGURE 10.6   Purchase of labor
by a perfectly discriminating
monopsonist

FIGURE 10.7   Producer and
consumer surplus

surplus to himself. Thus perfect discrimination leads to a loss of the
surplus to the workers. But there might be some advantages to such
discrimination. As we have seen, the discriminating monopsonist
will hire more workers than will the nondiscriminating monopsonist.

More usually, the monopsonist would not be able to discriminate
perfectly. Instead, the suppliers (or workers) would be broken down
into a number of groups and a separate price (or wage rate) would be
paid to each group. The labor market is frequently divided into groups
so that discrimination is possible. Thus, there could be different
wage rates for women and men, or for blacks and nonblacks, or for
union and nonunion workers. When the monopsonist subdivides the
labor markets, with a separate wage rate for each group, he is prac-
ticing imperfect discrimination.

DISCOUNTS. When markets are not purely competitive, there may be
opportunities for buyers to obtain lower prices for some types of
inputs as they increase their purchases from particular sellers. For
a number of reasons sellers may be willing to give discounts for large-
volume purchases, especially when business is slack. Sometimes,
costs are lower to the seller: "Set-up" costs per unit fall with longer
production runs; transportation costs are lower for high-volume
shipments; selling and administrative costs are lower per unit of
sale. Perhaps more often, discounts are offered for large orders because the buyer is large and in a position to use various bargaining
levers; large buyers have a number of options open to them not
readily available to smaller firms.

When buyers are in a position to obtain discounts from a variety of
sellers, their *p,x* supply constraint is negatively sloped and might
appear as in Figure 10.8. (Sometimes this curve may take a stairstep
shape, if discounts are given over precise ranges of input purchases.

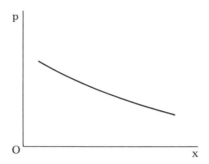

FIGURE 10.8   Supply curve to firm when discounts are available

If discounts are available from a number of suppliers, the supply curve could be approximated with a smooth curve as shown.) Such a constraint would lower the buying firm's cost curves and tend to lead to higher output levels and lower selling prices. From some points of view, the discounts are socially desirable, especially if the large-volume sales enable lower unit costs of production and marketing. But lower prices are also weapons with which large buyers can drive their smaller competitors out of business. If the lower buying prices are not justified by lower costs, or if the seller has not lowered his price to meet a competitor's price "in good faith," such discounts may be illegal under the Robinson-Patman Act.

When the supply curve of an input to the firm falls, as in Figure 10.8, the marginal expense of a unit of input lies below the supply curve. Say if the firm buys one unit of an input, the price is $2.00, but if it buys two units, the price of *each* unit is $1.90. Then the marginal expense of the second unit is not $1.90. It is, instead, $1.80 – the total expenditure on the two units ($3.80) minus the total expenditure on one unit ($2.00). Figure 10.9 depicts the quantity of the input the firm would purchase; the firm would have positive cash flows for each

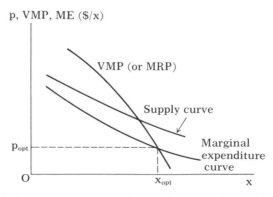

FIGURE 10.9   Purchase of an input when price falls with increase in quantity demanded

unit of input up to the point where the ME curve intersects the VMP (or MRP) curve. Such falling supply curves are rare for labor markets, although quite common for other types of input.

Futures Markets and Hedging. In many types of business, the price of a raw material may fluctuate by large amounts. If the firm has to purchase the raw material substantially before it will be delivered or used, the firm takes a risk. If the price of the raw material falls after the firm makes its purchase and the fall in price is accompanied by a fall in the output price, the firm can lose a great deal of money. On the other hand, if the prices of the raw material and the output rise, the firm can come out ahead. Risks of this type are common in agricultural raw materials, which tend to have wide price movements.

Some businessmen are willing to make speculative activity part of their routine and to accept the risks of changing prices. Other businessmen, however, would rather hedge their risks. The institution of "futures markets" enables the firm to hedge against such risks. In a futures market, a buyer and seller could agree in the present for the seller to deliver a certain amount of a commodity in the future at a price determined in the present. When purchases and sales are made for immediate delivery, in contrast, the price is known as the spot price.

Say now that the firm buys 2,000 bushels of wheat for its own use at \$1.75 per bushel. It may not actually receive or use the wheat for a month. To completely hedge, it will also make a futures sale of 2,000 bushels to be delivered one month hence. Say the future price is also \$1.75, although it could be higher or lower than the spot price. Now if the spot price of the wheat falls to \$1.50 a month from the present, the firm will lose money on the wheat it owns. But it will buy another 2,000 bushels at \$1.50, deliver it to the buyer who signed the futures contract at \$1.75, and thereby make up its loss. If the future spot price rises say to \$2.00, the firm comes out ahead on the wheat it purchased but loses on the futures contract because it has to pay \$2.00 per bushel for the wheat it had agreed to sell at \$1.75.

LONG-TERM CONTRACTS

In the open market, buyers and sellers are completely free to transact business with whomever they wish. Very often, however, specific buyers and sellers enter into long-term contracts that bind them to deal with each other for a number of transactions or for a specified time period. These contracts could have a vast variety of terms— price, conditions under which price could be changed, maximum and minimum quantities that must be purchased or sold, whether the parties to the contract may deal with others, when the contract can be renegotiated. In this section we discuss motivations and types of long-term contracts, how they are evaluated and enter into decision models, and negotiating and bargaining.

Motivations and Types. Every contract limits to some extent the freedom to deal with others and therefore amounts to a self-imposed constraint on opportunity sets. Thus we must inquire about the forces that motivate the parties to a contract. There appear to be two main motives – to avoid uncertainty and to exclude or forestall competitors. Another "motive" might be the lack of an effective open market as an alternative.

In the real world, there is often a great deal of uncertainty about future prices, whether buyers will even be able to obtain some inputs, and whether markets will be available to sellers. To businessmen who have to make investments whose payoff would be in an uncertain future and who are concerned with keeping their profits and organizations on an "even plane," too much uncertainty is undesirable. Given the choice between buying and selling in an uncertain open market, and signing long-term contracts that provide some guarantees, many would opt for the long-term contract, even if they *may* do better in the less certain open market. In effect the parties to the contract are willing to give up some of their future options in return for a smaller degree of uncertainty regarding their profits.

Long-term contracts to avoid uncertainty are common in many types of businesses. Large expensive facilities that process a great deal of raw material, such as power plants, usually sign long-term contracts to assure themselves of supplies. Such contracts are also desirable to the suppliers, who often are not willing to undertake some types of investment, such as in a mine, unless there is some kind of an assured off-take. Canners of fresh fruit, vegetables, and fish, who must be assured of a supply of cans during the canning season, frequently sign at least season-long contracts with can-makers. Apparel manufacturers frequently sign season-long contracts with textile manufacturers for much the same reason.

A second motive for signing long-term contracts is to exclude or forestall competitors from selling to or buying from a particular firm. All long-term contracts are not necessarily completely exclusionary. A firm can make any number of contracts and can even still deal in the open market. However, even with a nonexclusionary long-term contract, part of the market is preempted and therefore not available to competitors.

Many long-term contracts are, and are meant to be, exclusionary. Franchise operations such as dealerships frequently have contracts— though sometimes only an understanding – that all purchases will be made from the franchiser. There are some benefits to society from such arrangements. Dealers learn to properly service the product, and they have a stake in its success. But they also can restrict competition. A second type of exclusionary contract is the tie-in, in which a buyer, in order to obtain some products that he may want, is forced to buy other products or services that he may prefer to obtain elsewhere. Thus IBM, which held patents on the precomputer data processing equipment, used to compel buyers to buy punchcards from IBM as a condition for renting the equipment.[2] Perhaps the exclusionary contract in widest use is that of a firm with a labor union in which the firm signs a contract to hire only union members.

Sometimes firms sign long-term contracts because there are no effective open markets as alternatives. This is frequently the case in the purchase of energy — natural gas, electricity — where it is usually necessary to make some kind of special investment in pipelines or cables. Of all inputs, labor perhaps depends least on the open market. Firms of course sign contracts with labor unions specifying prices, seniority. But even for nonunion labor, there is an understanding that the firm will not hire and fire new people every week, and we can view these understandings as kinds of contracts. Firms do not have these understandings out of sentimental feelings. Rather, good personnel policy requires that employees be given some security in exchange for loyalty and effectiveness. Such informal or formal contracts with workers do not usually mean that the labor is no longer a variable input; the firm usually retains the option to lay workers off. Rather it means only that the firm will rehire the same individuals instead of searching the open market.

Short-Run and Long-Run Aspects. After a long-term contract consisting of terms such as price, minimum purchases, and maximum purchases has been negotiated, the purchaser has constrained part of his opportunity set — the part concerning input price and quantities. How the contract constrains these decision variables was described in Chapter 3, where we also suggested that a contract is a compound constraint consisting of elements of "freedom to deal" and self-imposed and government-imposed constraints. If the firm is obligated to take a minimum quantity, that minimum times the negotiated price becomes a fixed cost to the firm in the short run. If the buyer is also limited to a maximum quantity, and if no other sources are available, the contract also leads to a fixity constraint.

When the firm has long-term contracts with one or more suppliers and can perhaps also purchase on the open market, we can handle such complications in our optimizing models by treating each contract source and the open market as separate market segments. To illustrate, let us say that the firm uses two inputs, 1 and 2, and that part of input 1 is purchased under contract while input 2 is all purchased on the open market. Let us call the contracted portion market segment 1 and the open market portion market segment 2. Then x_{11} is the quantity of input 1 purchased in segment 1, and x_{12} is the quantity of input 1 purchased in segment 2. Similarly, $\bar{p}_{11}$ is the contract price in market segment 1, and $\bar{p}_{12}$ is the open market price. Also, let $\bar{p}_2$ be the price of input 2 and x_2 the quantity of input 2. Let us also say that the firm must take a minimum of $\bar{x}_{11}$ from the contract source. Then the input cost function is

$$C = \bar{p}_{11} x_{11} + \bar{p}_{12} x_{12} + \bar{p}_2 x_2.$$

Under these conditions, we can derive the least-cost expansion path and the associated cost curve, although not without a little ingenuity. The x_{11} that must be paid for as part of the contractual terms would have a price of zero in use; that is, because it must be paid for, it costs nothing to use. Thus, all x_{11} up to $\bar{x}_{11}$ would surely be used. Beyond this level of output, expansion might take place by using the contracted x_{11} more intensively by combining it with more x_2 or by purchasing x_{12} in the open market.

At the point of negotiation, an assessment of the signing of a long-term contract is similar to the assessment of the purchase of any asset. Assuming an alternative exists of purchasing in the open market, the evaluation of the contract can be made with the techniques discussed in Chapter 6. The cash flows are projected with and without the contract, and the alternative V_0, the "going concern" values, are calculated. The contract, to the extent it compels the firm to take certain minimum quantities, would raise F_t, the cash outflows due to fixed costs. But it will also raise Z_t, the current cash inflows of operating revenues less variable costs. We would normally take the contract if it leads to a higher value of V_0, but to the extent the firm is concerned about reducing risk, it may opt for the contract even with a lower value of V_0.

Negotiation and Bargaining. We turn now to some of the elements of negotiation and bargaining, where we consider the "one-shot" as well as the long-term contract. Because bargaining and negotiation have developed into full-scale fields of their own, with a sophisticated literature, we will be able to touch on only some of the basic elements in bargaining.[3]

It is well to realize that a "bargaining situation" arises between a buyer and a seller only when a *range* of terms is acceptable to both parties. The extent of the range will be bounded by the availability of alternatives to the buyer and to the seller. If, say, a market is perfectly competitive, and a market price of \$5 exists at which the buyer can buy and the seller can sell, there will be no effective range over which to bargain. The buyer will not pay more than \$5, the seller will not sell for less than \$5, and there is no room for bargaining.

But let us say that there is no "ruling" market price and that the best alternative open to the buyer is a purchase at \$6 and that the best

[3]See John Cross, *The Economics of Bargaining* (New York: Basic Books), 1970; and Thomas Schelling, *The Strategy of Conflict* (New York: Oxford University Press, 1963).

alternative open to the seller is a sale at $4. Now, clearly, the transaction price can be anywhere from $4 to $6, and bargaining will be over the precise price within this range. For such a range to exist, there must be various types of market imperfection – a small number of buyers and sellers, lack of information, sellers tied to buyers by contracts. As a rule, the more perfect the market, the smaller will be the bargaining range.

The ultimate in market imperfections occurs when there is a single seller and buyer of a product or service. This is known as bilateral monopoly. A labor union dealing with a firm or an industry is perhaps the most common example of a bilateral monopoly. The range of mutually acceptable terms could be quite wide in such conditions, but not infinite. There are bounds to the range because some terms can be so extreme that they are completely unacceptable to either party to the bargain.

The extent to which the buyer and seller find their interests in direct conflict depends largely on whether there is one term or many terms to the contract. When there is only one, say the price, the conflict will tend to be most intense. It is true that the buyer and seller are both ahead if they can agree to a term within the bargaining range, but any improvement in that term from the viewpoint of one party results in an equal deterioration of the term from the viewpoint of the other party.

When, however, a contract has a number of terms – price, minimum quantity, quality standards, penalty for nonfulfillment, conditions for renegotiation – there is more scope for negotiation and accommodation and less direct conflict of interests of the parties. Increased scope for accommodation arises because the various terms may lead to different kinds of impacts on the assessment of the burdens and benefits to the buyer and seller. Say, for example, high-quality standards are more important to the buyer than a low price, while high-quality standards can be assured by the seller without a great deal of cost on his part. Then a mutually advantageous "trade" can be made of these terms, and both buyer and seller may come out ahead with a higher price and higher quality. We might say that the skilled negotiator knows how to find mutually advantageous trades of contract terms.

Much of the literature on bargaining has focused on the bilateral monopoly, in which one term of the contract is of dominant importance. Under these conditions, we have direct opposition of the buyer and seller and the seeds for conflict. The literature is often quite sophisticated and considers factors such as toughness or flexibility in negotiating postures, bluffs, communicating false information (it is advantageous to both parties not to let the other know their least acceptable terms), changing expectations, "focal points" for agreements. We will not survey the literature here but will concentrate on two strategies used to influence the terms of the bargain.

One strategy for "winning" the bargain (that is, to get the most advantageous terms) is to be in a position where one can "hold out" longer than the opponent. A lack of an agreement between the parties will usually entail some costs to both sides. In the case of a labor negotiation that may lead to a strike, the cost to the workers is their lost wages and the loss to the firm is its fixed costs, its lack of revenue, and possibly a loss of customers. The party better able to withstand these losses can "outwait" the other side and thereby force terms favorable to it. This is why labor unions have strike funds and agreements with other unions to help each other financially during strikes. Companies entering negotiations may build up their finished inventory and stock their customers heavily. The diversified company is usually in a better position than the specialized company to outwait the union because the part of its operations not struck can be used to keep the firm solvent. This advantage of diversification helps explain the strong movement of American companies toward diversifying their activities, although labor unions are learning how to coalesce when dealing with a diversified company. Sometimes, companies emulate unions by making agreements with their "competitors" for those who are not struck to pay those who are. This happened in the late 1960s, when a group of airlines not struck turned over part of their receipts from their "extra" business to the airlines that were struck.

A second strategy, not necessarily mutually exclusive from the first, is for one of the parties to place itself in a position from which it cannot back down. In effect, this party purposefully gives up its negotiating options and offers the opponent a take-it-or-leave-it option. Labor union leaders pursue this strategy when they purposefully build up the wage expectations of the union members to the point where anything less than very favorable terms is not acceptable to the membership; the union negotiator has in effect limited his options to accept a lower wage settlement. A prominent American company has invoked this strategy by making a single public wage offer and refusing thereafter to discuss any other figure.[4] Although giving up negotiating options might work, it is a dangerous game and the courts have ruled that this strategy violates the part of the law that says the parties to a labor contract have to negotiate in good faith.

Forecasting Contract Terms. There is no foolproof method for forecasting contract terms. However, some writers studying collective bargaining results have shown that profits, price levels, degree of monopoly, wages of others, can influence the wage rate settlement terms.[5] For very long-run forecasting, the models of markets de-

---

[4]General Electric has been accused of using this strategy, which is sometimes called Boulwarism, after a former vice-president in charge of labor negotiations. This practice can be in violation of the National Labor Relations Act. Its use has been denied by the company.

[5]See, for example, D. Q. Mills, "Wage Determination in Contract Construction," *Industrial Relations*, vol. 10 (February 1971).

veloped in Chapter 9 – specifically the supply and demand relationships that determine price in purely competitive industries – can
give tolerably good estimates of what the terms of bargains are likely
to be. Even with the types of market imperfections that underlie bargaining, the forces of supply and demand associated with the competitive model still have some impact on at least the range within
which the bargaining process takes place. Thus, if we have the supply
and demand curves for an input as in Figure 10.10, the intersection
of these curves gives at least the approximate price for the bargain.
In forecasting the price, it is crucial to understand how changes in
the exogenous variables "shift" the curves.

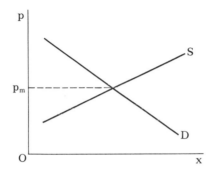

FIGURE 10.10   Supply and demand for an input

INVESTMENT AS A MEANS OF OBTAINING INPUTS

As an alternative to the purchase of inputs from others, many firms
have the option of gaining control over facilities and raw materials.
There are two ways such control can be obtained – by developing new
sources of supply through building new facilities and by acquiring
control of existing suppliers, which is known as merging. Gaining
control of supply sources is known as backward vertical integration.
In this section, we look at some of the advantages and disadvantages
of it from the firm's point of view by comparing the integration with
the option of purchasing the inputs directly.

One advantage of backward vertical integration is that the firm
can reap the profits that are made by its suppliers. However, this
would be a true advantage only if the suppliers are making profits
that are above "normal." If the supplier markets are truly competitive, it probably would not be wise to acquire such facilities. Thus, we
find petroleum companies integrating backward because extra-high
profits are to be made in crude oil. We do not find many food-process-
ing companies purchasing farms, where profits tend to be lower.

A second possible advantage of backward vertical integration is
that the firm would have better control over the production of its supplies and might be better able to coordinate the activities of the
supplying and using units. Through proper location of the facilities,

freight and inventory costs might be minimized. There can also be savings in transactions costs because salesmen and purchasing agents are no longer needed.

Sometimes there are possibilities of tax savings. Different states and different countries have different tax rates on profits. When one unit of a vertically integrated firm "sells" to another unit, the price at which the sale is made is an administratively determined transfer price. Through its determination of these prices, the firm can reduce the profits of units in high-tax jurisdictions and shift them to units in which taxes are not so great.

Backward vertical integration through merger, especially of raw materials, can be a means by which a firm can obtain some control over its competitors. This control is most readily exercised when the firm acquires more raw materials than it needs and becomes a supplier to its competitors. The acquiring firm is then in a position to "squeeze" its competitors by raising the price of the raw materials and to discipline price-cutters by denying them these materials. Of course backward vertical integration by some firms in an industry will tend to induce the same kind of integration by the other firms, for defensive if for no other reasons. Backward vertical integrations can be seen to have the effect of making entry to an industry difficult. The new firm may not be able to get raw materials, or, if it is possible to develop new sources of supply, the cost of entry to the new firm is increased.

Many firms acquire some supplying facilities to give them some bargaining leverage with other suppliers. Supermarkets, for example, control some supplying facilities partly to mount a credible threat that they can supply themselves when negotiating prices with independent suppliers.

There are also several disadvantages to backward vertical integration. It is possible that prices of inputs may fall on the open market, in which event the firm will be locked in to its now high-cost facilities. The acquired unit, selling through administrative action rather than facing the rigors of the free market, may lack incentives to be efficient. The using unit may also tend to slacken its search for new materials, components, and so forth.

Perhaps the main disadvantage of integrating backward is the conversion of what had been variable costs to the firm at least partly into fixed costs. The firm purchasing on the market has to pay for only what it wishes to purchase, but once it acquires a supplier, some costs will be incurred even when the firm does not need all the output of the supplying unit. The conversion of variable into fixed costs tends to limit the firm's flexibility and increase its risks.

There is some evidence that vertical disintegration tends to take place in new industries. When new products are developed, supplies of components and materials often are not available, and the firms making these products have to set up diverse and often uneconomic facilities to produce a wide range of components and materials. As the industry develops, it is frequently in the interest of firms to divest themselves of some of their activities, which they allow specialists to take over. This was the pattern in the development of the automobile industry.[6] The desire to vertically disintegrate has been voiced by firms operating in less-developed countries.[7]

A proposal to purchase a supplying facility as an alternative to purchasing inputs on the open market can be evaluated with our investment criterion cash-flow equation of Chapter 6:

$$V_0 = \sum_{t=0}^{t=\infty} \frac{Z_t + Y_t + F_t + \Delta A_t + \Delta L_t + \Delta E_t + T_t}{(1 + r_t)^t}$$

where Z_t is the cash flow from operations in period t, Y_t is nonoperating income (also in period t), F_t is fixed costs, including finance charges, ΔA_t is the outflow (or inflow) of cash from the purchase (or sale) of an asset, ΔL_t is receipts or payments of borrowed cash, ΔE_t is receipts (or payments) from sale (or purchase) of equities, T_t is taxes, and r_t is the discount rate, which we have taken as the rate at which the firm can lend out its cash. V_0 is, of course, the "going concern" value of the firm, which, together with dividends, has an influence on the firm's stock price, the maximization of which the firm as owner is assumed to take as its long-run goal.

Any investment can be evaluated by estimating the impact of that investment on the various cash inflows and outflows and then calculating whether V_0 would rise or fall. The acquisition of a supplying facility is virtually certain to reduce the firm's payments for variable inputs, so that Z_t, the cash flow from current operations, is likely to rise. There can also be a favorable effect on Z_t if the acquisition gives the firm a bargaining lever that could reduce the price of inputs purchased from others or raise the price of its final outputs. Fixed costs, F_t, which is an outflow, will increase because the fixed costs of the acquired facility will have to be borne by the firm. The F_t will also rise if the firm has to pay financing charges. The ΔA_t, the cash payment for assets, will be a larger negative number in the period in which the payment of cash, if any, is made. The ΔL_t will rise or fall in future periods, depending on whether the firm has to borrow to finance the new facility: The rises and falls will depend on when the proceeds of the loan are obtained and the terms of repayment. If financing is made by sales of equities, ΔE_t will rise, but S, the number of shares outstanding, will also increase, so that V_0/S could conceivably be reduced. Taxes, T_t, could either rise or fall with the purchase of the facility. In the final analysis, the decision should depend on

---

[6]See George Stigler, "The Division of Labor Is Limited by the Extent of the Market," *Journal of Political Economy* (1951).

[7]Jack Baranson found this in a study of Cummins Engine in India. See Jack Baranson, *Manufacturing Problem in India — The Cummins Engine Experience* (Syracuse: Syracuse University Press, 1967).

the estimation of all these cash inflows and outflows, with and without the investment, and the calculations of V_0, again with and without the investment.

There are many interesting complications when the acquisition of the supplying facility takes the form of a joint venture with other firms. In assessing such a project, much would depend on the contractual terms that would specify terms such as the transfer prices, the ability of individual firms to expand their off-takes, the arrangements for financing the venture. Joint ventures are usually a legitimate form of business arrangement but could be abused if the venture becomes a means of jointly restricting the output of the individual owners by centralizing control of a vital raw material, or if the control of such a raw material raises barriers to the entry of new capacity.

INCOME DETERMINATION

We now turn to the principles of income determination in a predominantly capitalist market system. All income is obtained by households, although sometimes the income, such as the retained earnings of a corporation, which legally belongs to the stockholder households, is held in their name. We distinguish two basic sources of income — that earned by households contributing to the productive activity of the economic system and "transfer income," not directly related to the recipients' productive activity in a particular period of time. Income from the contribution to productive activity is generally divided into wages, interest, profit, and rent, though these categories overlap in some ways. Transfer income consists of categories such as social security, welfare payments, gifts, and veterans' bonuses. The income from productive activity concerns us here; transfer income falls under the part of economics known as public finance.

Households can be thought to sell various services to the productive enterprises in the economic system, where these enterprises are generally either private and profit oriented or public. Productive enterprises sell intermediate goods and services to each other and final goods and services to the households. Some households, as an exception, sell their services directly to other households. Physicians are examples, yet we can generalize our model by classifying a physician or any other direct seller as an enterprise. Some households receive wages from these enterprises in return for their labor. Some households receive interest payments in return for lending money. Some households receive profits, although only from private enterprises, in return for their risks and entrepreneurship. Still other households receive "economic rent," which is not necessarily the same as the commonly used definition of rent as a payment for the use of real estate. Any particular household could receive any combination of these four types of income.

We will not have too much to say about income determination from services rendered to public enterprises. Instead we concentrate on the income generated by sales of household services to profit-seeking private enterprise. Perhaps the most striking feature of the capitalist market system is that the prices and quantities of household services sold to private enterprises are determined by markets in which there is an interplay of supply and demand. We organize our discussion about the market determination of wages, interest, profit, and rent. Although we are less sure about these income determinations when households sell to public enterprises, there is some carry-over from the analysis of income determination from private enterprises to public enterprises.

Wages. Conservative economists like to stress the notion that a wage rate is just another price determined by the law of supply and demand in a particular labor market. There is a demand curve for a particular kind of labor in a particular market, a supply curve, and an equilibrium market-clearing wage rate. Even though labor is seldom sold in the *open* market, and, with labor unions and monopsonies, many labor markets cannot be viewed as purely competitive markets, the traditional supply and demand analysis provides at least a starting point for understanding wage determination and in many instances provides all the information we need.

In Chapter 7, we developed the demand curve by a model firm for a variable input, among which we included labor services. It was shown that this demand curve was normal, in that the demand for labor varies inversely with the wage rate. It was also shown that the demand for labor tends to be more elastic if the production function enables substitutability among inputs compared to production functions with fixed proportions among inputs. Furthermore, it was shown that this demand curve shifts if the price of the final output changes or if the firm acquires additional fixed assets. (The firm could also, of course, sell or liquidate fixed assets.) The market demand curve for labor is nothing more than the addition of the demand curves of all the firms in the market, and the market demand curve will shift for the same reasons that the firm's demands shift.

Let us consider now the supply curve of labor into that particular market. If everything else remains the same, we should expect more workers to be willing to supply their labor, the higher the wage rate is. Hence, the supply curve to that market should have the usual shape; there should be a positive relation between the wage rate and the amount of labor services that will be available. This supply curve could be more, or less, elastic, depending on how great the response in supply would be to a change in the market wage rate. If the type of labor is highly specialized to that market, the supply curve will tend to be inelastic. An increase in the wages of brain surgeons, for example, is not likely to lead to a large increase in the supply of brain

surgeons, at least not in the short run. Nor would a decrease in that
wage reduce by large amounts the supply of brain surgeons. On the
other hand, if the type of labor is not highly specialized, a comparatively small increase in wages in one market could draw many workers from other markets. Given the supply and demand curves for
labor in a particular labor market, competition should lead to a wage
rate that clears the market, as shown in Figure 10.11.

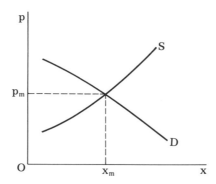

FIGURE 10.11   Wage and employment determinations in open,
competitive market

Having investigated how the demand curve for labor shifts, we can
now ask what shifts the labor supply curve in a particular market. In
the short run, wages in other markets will be the main factor in shifting the supply curve in a particular market, if labor is comparatively
willing and able to move from one market to the next and if artificial
barriers do not exist. If wage rates rise elsewhere, for example, fewer
workers would offer their services in this particular labor market at
any wage rate, and the supply curve would shift to the left. From
Figure 10.11, it can be seen that such a leftward shift in the supply
curve would lead to higher wages in the particular market. Conversely, lower wage rates elsewhere would induce more workers to
offer their services at any wage rate in this particular market. Thus,
the supply curve shifts to the right and wages fall. Through the supply curve mechanism, wages tend to be "in balance" in different
labor markets, which, again, assumes some degree of mobility and
lack of entry barriers. The extent to which changes in wage rates in
other labor markets would shift the supply curve in the market of
interest would depend on labor mobility and degree to which workers
can transfer their skills from one market to another.

In the longer run the supply curves would shift also as the result of
training and education that qualify workers for particular labor markets. Generally, of course, training and education are taken to qualify
workers for the high-wage markets instead of for the low-wage markets they would otherwise be qualified for. The effect of training and
education, then, is to shift the supply curves to the right in the high-

wage markets and to either shift the supply curves to the left in low-wage markets or at least to hinder their shifts to the right. Because rightward shifts of the supply curves tend to lower wages and leftward shifts tend to raise incomes, we see that mass education and training tend to equalize wage income among different types of labor.

In the last fifteen years or so, economists have become increasingly interested in the education and training of workers; this is known as human capital formation.[8] What economic factors determine whether an individual will seek an education? The individual is faced with much the same analytical problem in making such a decision as the firm in assessing an investment. He would project the cash inflows and outflows into the future on the assumption that he obtained the education. The inflows would be his expected life-time earnings; the outflows would be the monetary costs of obtaining the education. The cash inflows and outflows could then be discounted to find their "present value" – which is equivalent to our having determined the "going concern" value of the firm. The same procedure could be followed for the earnings stream without the education.

We could write these techniques in terms of symbols. Let E_t^* be the earnings with education in year t; $C_1, C_2, \ldots$, the cost of the education; n the year of retirement; r the discount rate. Then $PV(W)$ the present value of cash flows with the education, is

$$PV(W) = \frac{-C_1}{1+r} + \frac{-C_2}{(1+r)^2} + \frac{-C_3}{(1+r)^3} + \frac{-C_4}{(1+r)^4} + \frac{E_5^*}{(1+r)^5}$$
$$+ \ldots + \frac{E_t^*}{(1+r)^t} + \ldots + \frac{E_n^*}{(1+r)^n}$$

if the education takes four years.

The present value of the cash flow without education, where earnings in year t is E_t, is

$$PV(N) = \frac{E_1}{1+r} + \frac{E_2}{(1+r)^2} + \ldots + \frac{E_t}{(1+r)^t} + \ldots + \frac{E_n}{(1+r)^n}.$$

To the extent monetary factors alone dominate the decision, the education is worthwhile if $PV(W)$ is greater than $PV(N)$.

The rate at which the individual discounts future income – that is, the value of r – will have large effects on the calculation of the present values. If the individual uses a high value of r – implying that he has a high regard for income in the near future (in economics we call this a high time preference) – the no-education option is more likely to be selected, although expected earnings also affect the decision. If, on the other hand, a low value of r is selected, the individual places a relatively high value on future income, and he is likely to

---

[8] The leading work in this field is Gary S. Becker, *Human Capital* (New York: National Bureau of Economic Research, 1964).

select the education option. As economists, we cannot say what the discount rate should be. All we can do is point out that it affects the decision.

We do not include the opportunity costs of education in the calculation of $PV(W)$; this would be the income the individual could have earned if he had entered the labor force instead of seeking education. This is because these opportunity costs are already included in the calculation of $PV(N)$. Since we compare these two PVs, inclusion of the opportunity costs in the calculation of $PV(W)$ would amount to double-counting them.

When the human capital formation consists of on-the-job training, the analysis is more complicated because both the worker and the firm are making investment decisions. The firm's interest in the on-the-job training is that workers become more productive. But if the training is so general that the worker could apply it anywhere and, once trained, may not stay with the firm, on-the-job training is not likely to pay for the firm, unless the worker receives a very low wage during training or the firm is somehow compensated. On the other hand, if the training results in the worker's acquiring skills that are specific to the firm, the firm is more likely to consider the training a good investment. This is why firms are more willing to train managerial personnel than, say, machinists; the training of the former tends to be more specific to the firm.

In the very long run, labor supply curves are susceptible to the growth of population and the labor force. If, as a result, the supply curves shift to the right over time to a greater extent than do the demand curves for labor, wage rates tend to fall. Long-run wage rates thus tend to depend on the relative changes in investment, the main long-run determinant of the demand curves, and the growth of the labor force. If the labor force grows more rapidly, wages tend to fall, a point that generations of economists have tried to get across by advocating a limit to population growth.

Another useful notion concerning the labor supply curve is that wage rates can reach such a high point that wages above this point lead to a smaller supply. The supply curve is then said to be backward bending and could appear as in Figure 10.12. The reasoning behind such a curve is that when wages and income are high enough, workers increasingly prefer leisure to still higher incomes. Also, with their husbands' wages high, housewives may tend to leave the labor force.

As a conceptual device with which to view the extent of participation in the labor force and the relation of this participation to wage rates, we can employ indifference analysis of the type used in Chapter 8. The household can then be thought to have two consumption goods—leisure and all other goods. The notion of the backward-bending labor supply curve is based on the proposition that "all other goods" become inferior to leisure at higher living standards and incomes. The indifference curve map would then appear as in Figure

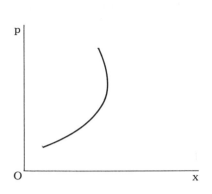

FIGURE 10.12 Backward-bending supply curve of labor

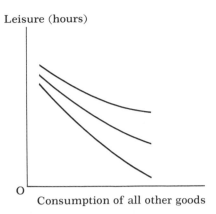

FIGURE 10.13 Indifference map: household's preferences for leisure and consumption of all other goods

10.13. The budget constraint would be determined by the number of hours the household has available and the wage rate, which measures the terms of trade between leisure and all other goods. Figure 10.14 shows what the budget constraint might look like at different wage rates. If Figure 10.14 is superimposed on Figure 10.13, we could see why the supply curve might bend backward as in Figure 10.12.

How do labor unions affect wages? Through collective bargaining, a union could obtain a wage rate, p_u, above the market-clearing wage rate p_e, which is shown in Figure 10.15. At this higher wage rate,

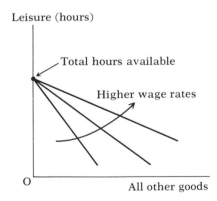

FIGURE 10.14 Effect of higher wage rates on budget constraint of household hours

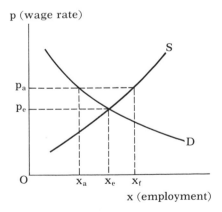

FIGURE 10.15 Effect of new market-clearing wage rate on employment

firms would hire only x_u workers rather than x_e, the amount that would clear the market at the equilibrium wage rate, p_e. Furthermore, at p_u the number of workers who want to work is x_f. The difference between x_f and x_u would then be the number of unemployed workers as the result of the higher wage, p_u. The same effect on unemployment can come about if the government imposes a minimum wage rate above the market-clearing wage.

Many, therefore, blame unemployment on unions and minimum wage laws. Unions also get blamed for inflation because it can be argued that the government must continuously stimulate the economy, through "easy money" and budgetary deficits, to counteract the union-caused tendency toward unemployment. Unions, on the other hand, argue that higher wages stimulate the demand for consumer goods, thereby shifting the demand curve for labor to the right. They also argue that very large firms have monopsony power and that the market-clearing wage rate is not brought about by competition.

A second way in which wages can be raised by a union or by a professional licensing group is through restrictions on the supply. Many unions limit their membership, as do medical associations, bar associations, and other professional groups. The effect of entry barriers is to either shift the supply curve to the left or keep it from shifting too rapidly to the right. These policies tend to raise wage rates. But they also tend to reduce wage rates in labor markets in which there are no restrictions to entry, because those not able to enter the restricted markets are forced to offer their services in the unrestricted markets.

Interest Rates. Households can lend money to business firms either directly by purchasing debt securities of corporations or indirectly through banks. Money can also be loaned to governments by purchase of government securities and to other households; this is done almost exclusively through the banking system. The interest rate at which money is loaned is the price of money, and the interest received provides income to the lending households. Corporations also loan money, but the interest received belongs to the stockholder households who own the corporation. There is no single interest rate but a structure of rates where the individual rates vary according to the terms of the loan, the degree of risk of nonrepayment, and the length of the loan.

From the earliest days of the market system, some have questioned the moral right to receive interest, for interest-receivers do not seem to contribute anything to the productive activity of a nation. This theme was prominent in the middle ages; theologians attacked interest, especially when loans were made for consumption. It was later taken up by Karl Marx in his criticism of the capitalist system. There are two main defenses of interest receipts, both based on the notion that the lender, who is also a saver, makes a sacrifice. Economists beginning with Nassau Senior and extending through Irving Fisher, argued that households acquire the money to lend by saving — that is, by not consuming — part of their income.[9] People generally prefer to consume rather than to save; thus their saving entails a sacrifice of current consumption, which would not be made without some sort of reward. John Maynard Keynes saw the sacrifice of lenders in terms of their giving up some of their liquidity when they exchange their cash for a debt security. He argued that individuals prefer to hold cash, because cash enables them to transact business more easily, protects them against adverse circumstances, and enables them to take advantage of favorable opportunities to purchase. Hence, the interest paid is necessary to compensate for the loss of liquidity.[10]

Although interest-receivers make a sacrifice according to these views, their contribution to the economy must still be clarified. The body of economics known as "neoclassical" saw interest rates as nothing less than the key element in the growth of the economy. The mechanism works in this way. Interest rates induce saving by households, thereby making funds available to businessmen for investment. The savings mean that households do not spend their whole income on consumption goods, thereby releasing the factors of production — land, labor, and capital assets — from the production of consumer goods. Businessmen use the borrowed funds to employ the released resources in the production of investment goods, such as structures and machinery, thereby increasing productivity and making the economy grow. If households become more thrifty, thereby saving more at any interest rate, more funds are made available at lower interest rates to businessmen, consumption is decreased, more resources are released from the production of consumer goods, investment activity is increased, and the national economy grows more rapidly. No wonder that thrift was considered the cornerstone of the Protestant ethic!

If money markets are purely competitive, the forces of supply and demand will set the price of money — that is, the interest rate — and the quantity of borrowing and saving. Let us consider the simplified model in which all the funds are borrowed by businessmen for investment. All other things held constant, businessmen would borrow more investment funds at lower interest rates. Thus, there is a demand curve for money (investment funds) that has the usual inverse relation between price and quantity demanded. Again all other things remaining the same, households are willing to save and loan larger amounts of money at higher interest rates. Thus, there is a supply

[9]The classic work in this field is Irving Fisher, *The Theory of Interest* (New York: Kelly, 1930).

[10]The great book here is John Maynard Keynes, *The General Theory of Employment, Interest, and Money* (London: Macmillan, 1936).

curve of investment funds that has the usual positive relation between price and quantity offered. The intersection of these two curves,
shown in Figure 10.16, determines the market-clearing interest rate
and also the quantity of saving and investment, which must be equal.
The interest rate serves as a rationing device of the investment funds.

What exogenous variables shift these curves? If, for some reason,
households become more thrifty, more money would be saved at any
interest rate, the supply curve shifts to the right, the interest rate is
lowered, and there is more investment and economic growth. Un-
equal income distributions, incidentally, have been defended on the
grounds that they lead to more savings and, consequently, more economic growth. If, on the other hand, households save less at any interest rate, the supply curve moves to the left, interest rates increase,
and investment falls. An inflationary period always presents special
problems along these lines because expectations of higher future
prices have the effect of inducing households to save less, thus shifting the supply curve to the left. The demand curve shifts mainly as a
result of businessmen's expectations of the future. If they think business is going to be good in the future, or if they expect prices to rise,
they are willing to borrow more at any given rate of interest. These
expectations shift the demand curve to the right. A leftward shift in
the supply curve for money and a rightward shift in the demand curve
will raise the interest rate, as in Figure 10.17. Whether saving and
investment rises or falls depends on the relative magnitude of the
shifts in the two curves.

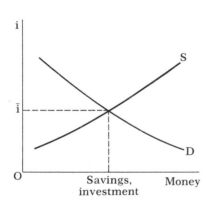

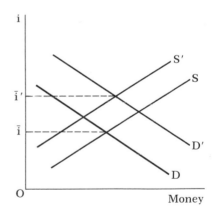

FIGURE 10.16   Market determination of interest rate, savings,
and investment

FIGURE 10.17   Effect of inflation
expectations on interest rates

We must make clear that the neoclassical model of interest rates,
savings, and investment determination, although still useful, no
longer holds the center of the stage. The Keynesian revolution of the
last three decades has devised new ways of analyzing the interaction

of interest rates, savings, and investment. There is, moreover, a whole panoply of government actions that can be taken to influence these key aspects of the economy. Through the workings of the Federal Reserve System, the U.S. government can influence the supply curve of money by altering the lendable funds of banks. The government can also influence the demand for investable funds in a number of ways. But these techniques are part of macroeconomics and are beyond the scope of this book.

Profits. Profit is the difference between revenue and outlays for a firm and is therefore a "residual" that could be either positive or negative (losses). Profits legally belong to the owners of a firm and are therefore sources of income for the households owning firms. Like interest, profits have been attacked as a payment for which there has been no contribution to an economy's productive activity. The defense of the legitimacy of profits has as its core the proposition that risk-taking and entrepreneurship are productive activities. Investors have to make commitments for capital assets without being sure that they will be able to realize a return on these assets. The owners of an enterprise also agree to pay all suppliers of labor, materials, and money, whether or not the output can be sold at prices that cover their outlays. They have, in effect, pledged their assets to make up any shortfalls in revenue. The organization of firms unquestionably requires effort, and profits could be defended as the payment for such effort. As we shall see, profit also performs the task of allocating assets to different economic activities.

There is no accepted theory of profits as a market-clearing price in the short run. We do, however, have a theory of "normal" long-run profits for any particular industry. These normal long-run profits are defined as the rate of return on assets at which the quantity of assets committed to the industry is in "equilibrium"; that is, normal profits are such that firms on balance wish neither to commit additional assets nor to withdraw assets from that industry. Normal profits for an industry generally depend mainly on the riskiness of the industry. The higher the risk, the greater are the possibilities of liquidity problems and, as a consequence, the higher profits must be to attract capital. Nothing in the theory says all firms must earn "normal" profit in the long run, because there could be differences in efficiency among firms. However, some economists prefer to label above-normal profits "economic rent."

If firms are free to leave or enter an industry or to expand or contract their commitments to that industry, there should be a tendency for short-run profits to approach the long-run normal profit. If profit rates are above normal, we should expect new entry and expansion, which would tend to reduce the prices of outputs, raise the prices of inputs, and therefore reduce profits. On the other hand, if profit rates are below normal, firms would either leave or contract; prices of outputs should rise, prices of inputs should fall, and profits should increase. A normal profit is more than one that is fair. It is the mechanism by which capital assets are allocated to different industries. If barriers to entry are strong, the mechanism does not work.

The concept of long-run normal profits is useful for explaining the movement of capital funds from one industry to another. But there is no generally accepted theory of the determinants of the general level of normal profits. We can conceive of a supply function: The higher the general rate of profits, the greater should be the level of investment commitment.

But it is not easy to specify a demand function for investment. Who demands the investment commitments? What relation is there to profit rates? These questions have not been fully answered. We could, however, think of the general level of business activity "demanding" investment commitments. This "demand" would not vary with the profit rate but would depend only on the level of business activity. Thus, we can think of a supply curve between investment commitments and profits and a demand curve for investment commitments as shown in Figure 10.18. This demand curve would move to the right with higher levels of general business activity. The supply curve could shift to the right with a greater willingness of businessmen to commit investment funds at any profit rate. The position of the supply curve would depend on the "entrepreneurial spirit" of the population. The intersection of these two curves would determine the general level of profit, although there is no neat mechanism to show how it would come about.

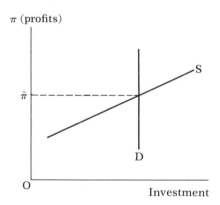

FIGURE 10.18   Determination of normal profit rates

Economic Rent. The concept of economic rent has gradually changed from payment for the use of land and natural resources to any payment to a factor of production greater than is necessary to get it to participate in productive activity. From society's viewpoint, economic rent is therefore an "unearned surplus."

David Ricardo is generally considered the first economist to systematically explore the meaning of rent and why it arises, although his analysis applied only to land rent.[11] His theory of land rent was based on quality differences in land for the production of food and on the premise that a community first puts its best land to use. Assume now that the population is small and that only the best land is used. Assume also that only normal profits are made. Let us then say that the population increases and that food prices rise. With higher food prices it becomes profitable to use poorer land. The owners of the best land, who have lower costs of production than owners of poorer land, are now able to make extra profits, which could not be made if production of food could be expanded on high-quality land. This question arises: What have the owners of the better land done to deserve the extra profits? Very little. They are the beneficiaries of the relative scarcity of good land. Because they would presumably produce at the lower prices for food, they are paid more than is necessary by society. England in Ricardo's time was experiencing a fight for supremacy between the old landed interests and the newly emerging commercial and manufacturing interests; thus Ricardo's theory of rent as unearned played a part in the victory of the "new" classes, which culminated in the removal of tariffs on food imported to England. Later, in the United States, Ricardo's theory of land rent played a role in Henry George's advocacy of a single tax all on the increment in value of land.[12]

The concept of economic rent has been broadened to include any payment to a factor of production that is above the amount necessary to bring forth that factor to productive activity. Thus, if the "normal" profit rate in an industry is 10 percent, any rate above that can be considered economic rent. Any payments to workers of any type above that necessary to get them to perform is regarded as economic rent. If, for example, an athlete receives $100,000 a year and his next best job is as a truck driver at $15,000 per year, he is being paid $85,000 beyond that necessary to obtain his services as an athlete. These surplus payments arise because of shortages — investment in an industry or athletes of high caliber. But from society's viewpoint, they are payments beyond what is necessary.

The main defense of economic rent is that it helps to allocate factors of production to buyers who can best use them and to whom they have higher value. If, for example, the star athlete is allowed to receive only $15,000, all teams would want him. But if the price of his services were bid up, the team that wanted him the most would hire him. If the government taxed away the economic rent, there would be no incentive for the athlete to sign with the team that can make

[11]David Ricardo, *The Principles of Political Economy and Taxation* (Homewood, Ill.: Irwin, 1963); originally published in 1817.
[12]Henry George, *Progress and Poverty* (New York: Random House, 1929); originally published in 1879.

the best use of his services. There is, however, an argument for taxing the economic rent at a high (though not 100 percent) rate.

Some economists have preferred to label above-normal profits as economic rent.[13] Their argument rests on the answer to the following question: Why are some firms able to make above-normal profits? Assuming no barriers to entry, the above-normal profit may be due to very good management. If this were so, it could be argued that the firm is not paying enough for its managers. But if the proper payment were made, then the profits would no longer be above normal. Nevertheless, the question of why the managers do not receive their full value remains.

Discussion Questions

1. Distinguish between purchases on the open market and purchases under contract. What are the advantages and disadvantages to buyers and sellers of these alternative arrangements? To new firms and potential entrants?

2. In the old days of colonialism, a company from the "mother" country was usually given exclusive rights to purchase a particular product from the colony. Could monopsony theory help explain such a policy?

3. Can we see, from our theory of bargaining, why competing leagues in professional sports often merge?

4. How might we define the act of negotiation? How does the availability of alternatives affect the bargain? What can be some of the dangers to society of bilateral monopoly?

5. What are the advantages and disadvantages of vertical integration, both backward and forward, to the firm? In what ways could vertical integration interfere with the operations of markets in society's interest?

6. How are changes in wage rates in one labor market transmitted to other labor markets? What determines the degree to which such transmission takes place?

7. In what ways do wage rates in the long run depend on population growth and investment?

8. Does it necessarily follow from our analysis that workers doing more "important" work get paid more than workers doing less "important" work?

9. Given our analysis of the effect of mass education on relative wage rates, does it follow that those who go to college are the only beneficiaries of their education?

10. Assess the assertion that labor unions are responsible for unemployment and inflation.

[13]See Milton Friedman, "Comment," in *Business Concentration and Price Policy* (Princeton: Princeton University Press, 1955).

11. What effect does an expectation of future inflation have on interest rates? What is the mechanism?

12. It has been observed that when interest rates are low, houses, plants, and other types of fixed investment tend to be built to last for a long time. Why should this be true?

13. Describe the role of profits as an allocating device for fixed investment. If there were no substantial entry barriers to different industries, how should rates of return in different industries behave?

14. Give some examples of economic rent.

15. What effect does a "reserve clause" have on the distribution of rent arising from the scarcity of good athletes?

11 Topics in Production and Cost

In Chapter 4, we considered some of the elementary aspects of production theory and output cost functions. In this chapter, we present a variety of problems and concepts that are somewhat more advanced, and we also review some empirical work.

VARIETIES OF PRODUCTION FUNCTIONS

Some Inputs as Substitutes and Some Inputs Used in Fixed Proportion. In Chapter 4, we limited ourselves to production functions in which there were only two inputs. Some consisted of only a single process in which the inputs were in fixed proportion to each other. Others consisted of an infinite number of processes, enabling continuous substitutability. Still other production functions consisted of a small number of processes in which some, but not continuous, substitution was possible.

When three or more inputs are in a production function, there may be mixtures in the relation between the inputs and outputs with regard to substitutability and fixed proportions. Some of the inputs may be substitutable for each other; some may be in fixed proportions to the inputs for which substitution possibilities exist; others may be in fixed proportion to the output.

Consider, for example, a case in which there are four inputs—labor, capital asset services, energy, and materials. Labor and asset services might be substitutable; energy may be in fixed proportion to the capital services; and materials may be in fixed proportion to the output. If the labor and asset services are related to output as a Cobb-Douglas production function, the whole production function could be expressed in these inequations:

$$Q \le a x_1^\alpha x_2^\beta$$
$$x_3 \ge k_1 Q$$
$$x_4 \ge k_2 x_2. \tag{11.1}$$

Here x_1 is the amount of labor services, x_2 is the quantity of asset services, x_3 is materials, and x_4 is the energy services. The coefficients a, α, and β specify the relations between labor, asset services and output; k_1 is the technological coefficient showing the amount of materials required per unit of output; k_2 is the technological coefficient showing the amount of energy required per unit of capital services. By using a number of equations or inequations, we can evidently express a production function in which some of the inputs are substitutable and others are in fixed proportion to each other and to output.

The computation of the output cost function in such cases requires a bit of ingenuity. One approach would be to concentrate first on the selection of inputs that are substitutable for each other. Figure 11.1 thus draws in the x_1, x_2 isoquant map, with x_2, the asset services, assumed to be in limited supply at $\bar{x}_2$.

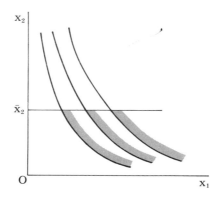

FIGURE 11.1 Cobb-Douglas isoquant map

When using an isocost map to derive the least-cost expansion path, we must be careful to account for the fact that other inputs may be in fixed proportion to x_1 and x_2. Thus, in our example, even if x_2 is paid for and "free" in use, costs will be associated with the use of the energy, x_4, in the use of x_2.

Let us neglect for the moment the materials, x_3. The cost equation in terms of the inputs is

$$C = \bar{p}_1 x_1 + \bar{p}_2 x_2 + \bar{p}_4 x_4,$$

where $\bar{p}_1$ is the wage rate, $\bar{p}_2$ is the price of a unit of capital services, and $\bar{p}_4$ is the price of a unit of energy. Now, using inequation 11.1 and assuming no energy is wasted, we can substitute for x_4 to get the cost equation:

$$C = \bar{p}_1 x_1 + \bar{p}_2 x_2 + \bar{p}_4 k_2 x_2. \tag{11.2}$$

If x_2 is paid for and thus costs nothing to use, $\bar{p}_2 = 0$, and the cost equation is

$$C = \bar{p}_1 x_1 + \bar{p}_4 k_2 x_2.$$

From this we derive the isocost map by solving for x_1:

$$x_1 = \frac{C}{\bar{p}_1} - \frac{\bar{p}_4 k_2}{\bar{p}_1} x_2. \tag{11.3}$$

If, on the other hand, the firm is making a long-run decision, where x_2 is not fixed and paid for, equation 11.2 is the cost equation. This can be written

$$x_1 = \frac{C}{\bar{p}_1} - \frac{(\bar{p}_2 + \bar{p}_4 k_2)}{\bar{p}_1} x_2$$

in the isocost form.

When, say, $\bar{x}_2$ is fixed and paid for, the isocost map based on equation 11.3 can be used to determine the least-cost expansion path in the use of x_1 and x_2 as in Figure 11.2. The expenditures on x_1 are one component of the variable cost. To these expenditures we must add the expenditures on the materials, x_3, and the energy, x_4.

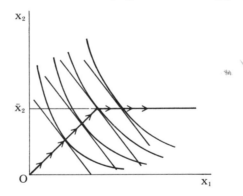

FIGURE 11.2   Derivation of expansion path

Table 11.1 shows how we could calculate the total cost curve. The first column gives different output levels. The next two columns give the least-cost combinations of x_1 and x_2 that correspond to each level. The x_1 and x_2 values are obtained from the least-cost expansion path. The fourth column gives the amounts of materials, in fixed proportion to the level of output. The fifth column gives the quantity of energy used for each level of output; this energy is in fixed proportion to x_2 in column 3. The sixth column gives the total variable costs corresponding to each output level. Total variable cost is obtained by multiplying the quantity of each of the variable inputs by its price and then summing the results. The total fixed cost is constant – the fixed expenditure on the fixed assets. The last column is the addition of *TVC* and *TFC* for each level of Q. When columns 1 and 8 are plotted on the same graph, the result is the total cost function.

TABLE 11.1   Calculation of total cost functions

Q	Optimal x_1	Optimal x_2	$x_3 = k_1 Q$	$x_4 = k_2 x_2$	TVC $\bar{p}_1 x_1 + \bar{p}_3 x_3 + p_4 x_4$	TFC $\bar{p}_2 \bar{x}_2$	TC $TVC + TFC$
(1)	(2)	(3)	(4)	(5)	(6)	(7)	(8)
1							
2							
3							
$\vdots$							

Sequential. In the real world, firms often have one production operation followed by a second production operation. When operations are so sequenced, the output of the first operation becomes the input of the second operation.

Let us say that the second operation, which produces the final product, uses inputs x_1 and x_2. In an unspecified form the production function would then be

$$Q = f(x_1, x_2). \tag{11.4}$$

If x_2 is produced by the firm with the use of x_5 and x_6, the first production function would be

$$x_2 = f(x_5, x_6). \tag{11.5}$$

By viewing the output of one production operation as the input to another production operation, we can depict complex sequences of productive operations.

When we have a number of sequential production functions, the total cost function in terms of the output has to be "built-up" from the cost functions in terms of the input produced by the "earlier" operations. Thus, using our example, we would first have to obtain a cost function in which x_2 is the output. This would be done in the usual way. Equation 11.5 is the basis for the isoquants, and the iso-cost map would be based on the equation $C = \bar{p}_5 x_5 + \bar{p}_6 x_6$. By deriving the least-cost expansion path, we can get the cost function of x_2, expressed symbolically as $C_{x_2} = f(x_2)$.

With this cost function for x_2, we can then go on to get the cost function in terms of Q. Equation 11.4 can provide the isoquants. The isocost lines would come from the following equation: $C = \bar{p}_1 x_1 + C_{x_2}$. Notice that C_{x_2} is the expenditures on x_2 – although the actual expenditures are made for x_5 and x_6. We can then proceed to obtain the least-cost expansion path for the x_1, x_2 combinations and derive the total cost curve in terms of Q.

Partial. In some instances quantifying one or more of the inputs in a production function may not be feasible. Say, for example, we want to understand the relation between the milk output of cows and the different types of feed they eat – such as alfalfa and corn mash. The cow itself is one of the inputs to the production of milk, but it is not an easy matter to quantify this input. Thus, a relationship established only between milk and the two types of feed will be a partial production function because we have not included the cow.

EMPIRICAL PRODUCTION FUNCTIONS

The economist's knowledge of empirical, as opposed to theoretical, production functions comes from several sources. Many are provided by engineers. Other production functions are obtained by purposeful statistical experimentation, particularly in agriculture. Still others can be statistically derived from data gathered and analyzed from particular firms on their various inputs and outputs.

Engineering. Economists with good engineering backgrounds have derived production functions from physical engineering relationships. Vernon L. Smith provides a substantial number of such production functions, many of which should be designated partial production functions.[1] Smith concentrates on the substitution possibilities of different capital assets, although some of his examples include "variable" inputs. In one example, that of the production of timber from trees, he shows the trade-off possibilities between the number of saplings planted and the amount of land under cultivation. To produce some level of timber, we can cut the trees down early and use more saplings and less land, or we can allow the trees to grow to maturity, thereby using more land (and time) but fewer saplings over a period of time. In the production of electricity consumed at points some distance from the point of generation, substitution possibilities exist between the size of the generator and the weight (and diameter) of the transmission cable. The amount of electricity lost in transmission increases with a decrease in the weight of the cable; thus equal amounts of electricity can be delivered at the consuming points with thicker cables and smaller generators and with thinner cables and larger generators. Similar substitution possibilities between inputs

[1] Vernon L. Smith, *Investment and Production* (Cambridge, Mass.: Harvard University Press, 1961).

exist in the transmission of heat or gas. In the transmission of heat through a pipe, the output is the heat at the consuming end of the pipe. The inputs are the heat from the boiler and the insulation of the pipe, and substitution possibilities exist between the size of the boiler and the amount of insulation. In the transmission of gas, the same amount of gas can be delivered with a wide variety of combinations of pipe diameters and compressor sizes. A particularly interesting production function has as its output the number of trucks to be kept operative during some period of time. Using notions of queuing theory from operations research, Smith derives the trade-off possibilities between the inventory of trucks and the amount of repair labor. Figures 11.3 and 11.4 show some of the isoquants for the production of electricity and trucking services.

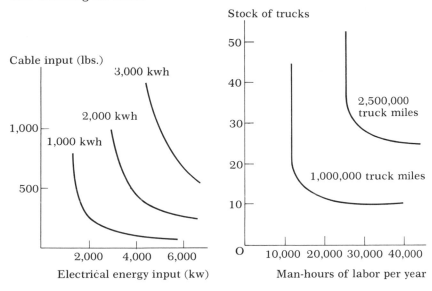

FIGURE 11.3 Isoquant map for transmission of electricity

FIGURE 11.4 Isoquant map for trucking process

During the last twenty-five years or so, there have been a large number of engineering studies of production functions, many in connection with W. Leontief's work in constructing input-output matrices that show the relationships between various producing sectors in the economy. For the most part these production functions are of the single-process type in which all the inputs are in fixed proportion to the various outputs. In all likelihood, most manufacturing production functions are single process, although only for the short run, where some technology has already been adopted. They should be considered short run because they show not all the technically possible production possibilities but only the dominant single-process function.

Production functions consisting of a single process are readily depicted as a set of equations showing the fixed relation of each input to the output. Thus, n inputs in a particular process would be depicted in this way:

$$x_1 = k_1 Q$$
$$x_2 = k_2 Q$$
$$\vdots$$
$$x_n = k_n Q$$

We can find many such production functions.[2]

Statistical Experimentation. E. Heady and J. Dillon report a large number of agricultural production functions based on experiments.[3] In a typical experiment, plots of land are treated with various combinations of fertilizer. Each plot provides an observation giving the quantities of the fertilizers applied and the output. We can then statistically fit, say, a Cobb-Douglas function,

$$Q = a x_1^\alpha x_2^\beta,$$

where the inputs are the quantities of the two fertilizers, to the data, to estimate the parameters a, α, β.

One study reported by Heady and Dillon concerns the use of phosphate and nitrogen fertilizer in the production of corn. The result was the production function

$$Y = 0.442 P^{0.409} N^{0.2877},$$

where Y is bushels of corn per acre, P is pounds of phosphates per acre, and N is pounds of nitrogen per acre. Another study concerned the effect of feeding corn and soybeans to broilers. The production function was statistically estimated to be

$$G = 0.9922 C^{0.5537} S^{0.3371},$$

where G is the weight gain of the broilers and C and S are corn and soybeans, everything measured in pounds.

The exponents in both of these production functions do not add to 1. Consequently, they are not homogeneous to degree 1, and a doubling of inputs in both cases would lead to less than a doubling of output. This is so because some of the inputs are not included in the functions; thus they are partial production functions. Nevertheless, they are obviously very useful.

---

[2] See, for example, W. W. Leontief, *Studies in the Structure of the American Economy* (New York: Oxford University Press, 1958); and Alan Manne and H. Markowitz, *Studies in Process Analysis* (New York: Wiley, 1963).

[3] E. Heady and J. Dillon, *Agricultural Production Functions* (Ames: Iowa State University Press, 1961).

Inter-Firm. It is often possible to statistically estimate the parameters of a production function by using the firms in an industry as observations. The inputs and outputs of each firm are the basic data. The inputs are usually aggregated into labor, capital, and materials, and, being heterogeneous, various types of price indexes are needed to adequately express the inputs in physical quantities. Similar problems must be solved when the outputs of the firms are heterogeneous.

Most of the work along these lines has assumed Cobb-Douglas functions, expressed as

$$Q = aL^\alpha K^\beta M^\gamma,$$

where Q is output, L is labor, K is capital, and M is materials. The statistical task is to estimate the parameters of the function – that is, a, α, β, and γ.

As a variation on these production functions, materials are sometimes left out of the equation. When this is done, "value added" is used instead of quantitative output. Value added is defined as the value of the output minus the value of the material inputs. Then the equation is

$$V = aL^\alpha K^\beta,$$

where V is value added.

In a review article A. A. Walters presented the results of a number of such studies, although he did not give the values of the coefficient a.[4] In one study, the production function for coal in the United Kingdom was estimated as

$$V = aL^{0.79}K^{0.29}.$$

Notice that the exponents add to 1.08, which, given errors in statistical estimation, is close enough to unity to conclude that the production function is homogeneous to degree 1; that is, there are constant returns to scale.

A study of milk production in Australia yielded the production function

$$Q = aL^{0.23}F^{0.13}C^{0.62},$$

where Q is the output of milk, L is labor input, F is feed, and C is the number of units of livestock. It can again be seen that the function is homogeneous to degree 1.

A study of the railroad industry in the United States by Lawrence Klein is also given in the Walters article. The production function was estimated as

$$Q = aL^{0.89}K^{0.12}M^{0.28},$$

[4]A. A. Walters, "Production and Cost Functions: An Econometric Survey," *Econometrica*, vol. 31 (1963).

where Q is ton-miles, L is labor, K is capital, and M is materials. With the exponents adding to more than 1, to 1.3, the production function is homogeneous to degree 1.3. Thus there are increasing returns to scale: A doubling of all inputs increases output by 2.6 times.

Most of these aggregative studies are of limited use in models of the firm and decision-making. Their main purpose is to try to understand labor-capital ratios and to explain the distribution of the income generated to labor and capital. They have done a credible job in this respect.[5]

ECONOMIES OF SCALE AND ECONOMIES OF SIZE

A question of great interest in business, economics, engineering, and public policy is whether economies are to be gained or perhaps lost as a business operation becomes larger. Inquiries into this question have been hampered partly by a failure to maintain a sharp enough distinction between economies of scale and economies of size.

When we discussed returns to scale in Chapter 4, we were concerned with the relation between inputs and outputs when everything is expressed in terms of physical units. When a given percentage increase in all the inputs leads to a larger percentage increase in output, we said there were increasing returns to scale. We could also say that, with such increasing returns to scale, there are "economies of scale." In most of our work in Chapter 4, however, we assumed there were constant returns to scale. Economists, in their theoretical work, have generally assumed production functions that give constant returns to scale.

We define economies of size as a relation between average costs and output. When we say there are economies of size, we mean that the short-run average minimum cost per unit of output falls as the size of a plant is expanded. Although the expression "economies of scale" is used by many to express such a relationship between average cost and output, we think it best to reserve this phrase for the relationship between physical units of inputs and outputs.

It is important to realize that economies or diseconomies of size are completely compatible with constant returns to scale. Say a firm requires one unit of labor, one unit of capital services, and one unit of materials per unit of output. This is clearly a production function with constant returns to scale. Now let us also say that the firm can

---

[5]Many studies of this type have been done in recent years. They give the production functions for a whole industry or sector of the economy. See, for example, G. Hildebrand and T. C. Liu, *Manufacturing Production Functions in the United States, 1957* (Ithaca: Cornell University Press, 1965). Robert Solow reports that almost all new advances in production theory in the last few decades have been of this type. See Solow's article and other articles in Murray Brown, *The Theory and Empirical Analysis of Production* (New York: Columbia University Press, 1967).

pay lower prices for the materials if it buys larger quantities of them. Then clearly the average cost of the output can fall even though there are still constant returns to scale. Or say a big machine delivers twice as many asset services as a smaller machine but has not cost the firm twice as much to purchase. Then a plant using the big machine would show lower average costs for comparable output levels than a plant using the smaller machine. This too is not incompatible with constant returns to scale.[6]

Perhaps the main source of size economies is geometrical relationships between the capacities of various assets and the cost of providing these capacities. Consider a pipe that carries liquids or gases. A large pipe with twice the carrying capacity of a smaller pipe does not require twice the amount of materials or, probably, twice the amount of construction labor. If we double the length and width of a warehouse, thus requiring twice as much wall construction, we quadruple the amount of floor space. The capacity of any kind of a vat or boiler can be made larger without a corresponding increase in the use of materials and labor. A 200,000-ton oil tanker does not cost twice as much to build as a 100,000-ton oil tanker. Such reductions in cost with size, however, may not go on indefinitely. As the boiler, vat, pipe, or ship is made larger, problems with weight and pressures may require the use of stronger materials or other means of reinforcement.[7]

We see, then, that large pieces of capital equipment can often result in lower costs per unit of capacity of the equipment. Lower costs by themselves, however, do not always mean that a plant with large equipment will have lower average costs in the short run than a plant with small equipment. The plant with larger pieces of equipment will still have higher fixed costs and, at low levels of output, could have higher average total costs than the firm with smaller pieces of equipment. However, as output is expanded, the plant with the larger (but cheaper per unit of input services) equipment should at some point have the lower average total costs. Figure 11.5 shows what the short-run *ATC* curves might look like for these two plants.

When a firm uses a number of pieces of capital equipment and some give low costs per unit of capacity when very large, the need to fully utilize the large pieces will often dictate the optimal efficient size of the plant. Sometimes there must be multiples of the large pieces of equipment to keep them in balance and fully utilized. If one large machine can perform its operation on 100 units per day and another large machine can process 75 units per day, then we would need three of the first machine and four of the second machine if both are to be completely utilized.

[6]These points are well explained in W. David Maxwell, *Price Theory and Applications in Business Administration* (Pacific Palisades: Goodyear, 1970).
[7]These relations were studied quite some time ago by J. M. Clark. See John M. Clark, *The Economics of Overhead Costs* (Chicago: University of Chicago Press, 1923).

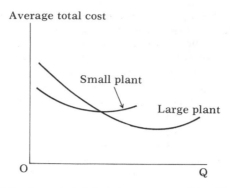

FIGURE 11.5   Average total cost curves: small and large plants

Some economists have examined the relationship between size of plant and costs when the plant works at high capacity. They have used the formula $C = aX^\beta$ to give the relation, where X is a measure of capacity output and C is a measure of costs, and a and β are parameters that can be determined either by statistical analysis or from engineering data. One study, by Moore, reports that engineers use a rule-of-thumb that $\beta = 0.6$. A value for β of 0.6 implies that a 1 percent increase in output capacity leads to only a 0.6 percent increase in cost.[8] In another study, Haldi and Whitcomb found that the value of β varied widely among industries but was almost always less than 1.[9] Whenever β is less than 1, cost rises less rapidly than output at capacity. We can therefore infer that economies of size are quite common.

There may be other sources of size economies. Large operations may enable greater specialization, including the use of highly specialized personnel. Large firms typically do not have to carry as much inventory in proportion to sales as small firms do. Large firms may have various advantages in advertising, which tends to be most effective when repetitive. Large firms may also have greater bargaining power vis-à-vis their suppliers than do smaller firms, therefore being able to buy at lower prices. Many would argue, however, that these are "pecuniary" economies and that society does not gain: Income is transferred from the sellers to the buyers, but there is no real overall reduction in costs.

Despite this impressive array of advantages for the large firm, there can also be diseconomies of size. A large operation needs increasing layers of management, with the well-known problem of bureaucracy this can bring. In large operations, the top managers are far removed

---

[8]Frederic T. Moore, "Economies of Scale: Some Statistical Evidence," *Quarterly Journal of Economics* (1959).

[9]John Haldi and David Whitcomb, "Economies of Scale in Industrial Plants," *Journal of Political Economy* (1967).

from day-to-day activities and may therefore not always have a complete grasp of the information needed for good decisions. As firms (especially plants) expand in size, they often have to go greater distances to acquire inputs and to market their products, thereby raising transport costs. Large firms, by investing in highly specialized equipment, may have less flexibility than smaller firms to cope with changes in demand. In short, in many industries, small firms do as well or better than larger firms.[10]

Much of the empirical work on economies of size suggests that in a given industry there is a minimum efficient size for a plant or firm. For plants smaller than that size, increasing sizes lead to average total cost curves that have lower minimums; but beyond that size, all plants have average total cost curves with the same minimums. A well-known work by Joe Bain provides a number of studies of the minimum efficient size for various industries.[11]

LONG-RUN COST FUNCTIONS

Virtually all the output cost functions we have discussed have been of a short-run nature, in which at least one of the inputs is subject to a fixity constraint. There is of course interest in long-run cost functions as well. One way to obtain the long-run cost function is to treat all the inputs as completely variable. The cost function can then be calculated first by the construction of isoquant and isocost maps and then by superimposition of the latter on the former to get the least-cost expansion path. From this expansion path, we can readily obtain the total cost curve, from which the long-run marginal and average cost curves can be derived. If the production function gives constant returns to scale, and if there are no economies of size so that the price per unit of each input remains the same for all levels of output, the expansion path will be along a process ray. The long-run total cost curve will then be a straight line through the origin, and the long-run marginal and average cost curves will be the same horizontal line. Figure 11.6 illustrates these curves.

A second way of viewing the long-run cost functions is generally more useful. This way is to look at the long run as a set of alternative short-run choices. Consider a firm planning to build a new plant. It usually has a number of choices about how large to make the plant, where the size of the plant could be measured by the quantity of limited input services it would provide during short-run periods. For each alternative-sized plant, we could derive a short-run average

[10]For a good review of the advantages and disadvantages of size, see Frederic Scherer, *Industrial Market Structure and Economic Performance* (Chicago: Rand McNally, 1970).

[11]See Joe Bain, *Barriers to New Competition* (Cambridge, Mass.: Harvard University Press, 1956). Also see Leonard Weiss, *Economics of American Industry* (New York: Wiley, 1961).

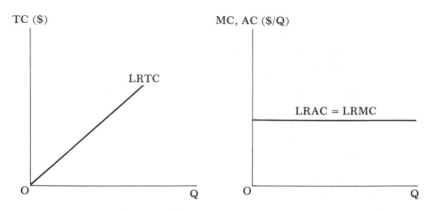

FIGURE 11.6   Long-run total, average, and marginal cost curves

total cost curve. The long-run average total cost curve could be viewed as the range of choices of the short-run average total cost curves.

To illustrate the construction of the long-run average total cost curve, let us say that the firm has a choice of three different-sized plants and let us assume the production function is either classical (with indivisibility) or Cobb-Douglas. The larger the size of the plant, the higher will be the short-run fixed costs, so that the short-run average total cost curve is higher for the larger plants at low levels of output. However, because the larger plants have more of the fixed input services, the short-run average total costs will fall over a larger range of output for the larger plants. Two phenomena explain the tendency for these average total costs to fall over a large range of output. First, the larger plants have higher fixed costs; hence the average fixed cost (AFC) curve decreases to a greater extent as output is expanded, thereby causing the ATC curve to fall. Second, because the larger plants provide more of the fixed input services, diminishing returns to the variable inputs are stronger to the smaller plants at any level of output than they are to the larger plants. Hence the average variable cost (AVC) curve rises more rapidly for the smaller plants, thereby increasing the ATC curve at lower levels of output. If there are also economies of size – that is, if the prices of input services fall for the larger plants – the average total cost curves will not only fall over a larger range for the larger plants; they will also have lower minimum costs. Figure 11.7 illustrates what the short-run average total cost curves ($SRAC$) may look like when there are economies of size. The long-run average total cost curve ($LRAC$) can be viewed as the "envelope" of the various short-run average total cost curves, as shown in the diagram.

The $LRAC$ curve can take on a variety of shapes, depending on whether there are economies or diseconomies of scale or size. If the production function is homogeneous to degree 1 (constant returns to scale) and there are neither economies nor diseconomies of size,

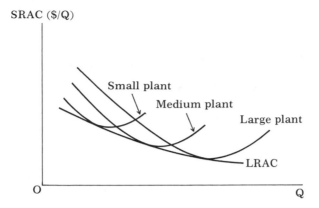

FIGURE 11.7 Short-run average total cost curves for plants of different size

the *SRAC* curves all have the same minimums (although at different levels of output), and the *LRAC* curve will be a straight horizontal line as in Figure 11.8. (That under these conditions all *SRAC*s have the same minimum cost can be proven mathematically, but unfortunately not without some complicated algebra and calculus.)

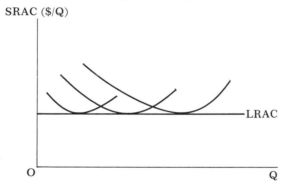

FIGURE 11.8 Shape of LRAC curve with constant returns to scale and no economies of size

What evidence there is on the subject suggests that the *LRAC* curve often declines with size of plant until some minimum optimal plant size is reached; then it becomes a horizontal straight line. This is shown in Figure 11.9. Although we cannot be sure on the basis of empirical evidence, the declining portion is probably attributable to economies of size. Once a firm can acquire assets that provide input services at the lowest costs, large plants do not exhibit further economies of size.[12]

[12]Bain and others have generally found this to be the shape, implying some minimum efficient size rather than continuous decreases in cost with size.

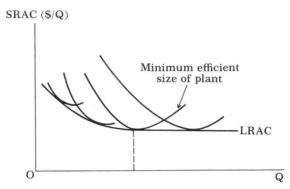

FIGURE 11.9   Shape of LRAC curve most consistent with empirical evidence

Traditional economic theory assumes that the *LRAC* falls at first as plant sizes are increased but, after plants reach an optimal size, begins to rise with still larger plants. Behind this assumption are the further assumptions that economies of size are to be gained by increasing the size of operation and that as plants become very large diseconomies of size begin to set in. That the empirical evidence does not suggest this type of *LRAC* curve does not necessarily mean that it cannot exist. Instead, it could mean that plants in the real world are simply not built in the range in which there are diseconomies of size. Figure 11.10 illustrates such a "traditional" *LRAC*. Once the *LRAC* curve has been determined, we can deduce the long-run total cost and long-run marginal cost curves.

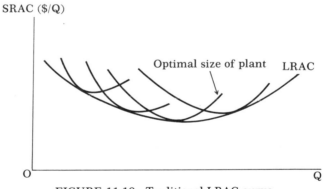

FIGURE 11.10   Traditional LRAC curve

In some industries, the long-run average cost curve continues to fall over the whole range of plant sizes and output needed to supply the whole market. These declining *LRAC* curves typically appear in highly capital intensive industries, such as the production of electric power, where great economies of size are to be reaped from the use of large units of capital assets. When *LRAC* falls over a wide range of output, society is best served if there is only one producing firm in a particular market. But if there is only one firm in a market, it is a monopoly and the forces of competition cannot be relied on to assure reasonable prices. For this reason, direct regulation of such firms by public authorities is generally deemed necessary.

ESTIMATING COST FUNCTIONS

In Chapter 4, we showed how output cost functions can be deduced from production functions and data on prices. In the real world, however, it is frequently easier to obtain cost curves by observing output and costs and obtaining a cost-output relationship. Most standard cost accounting textbooks show how, with observations on output and different cost categories, statistical analysis can be employed to estimate cost curves. Much of the empirical work done by accountants and economists shows the total cost curves to be linear – although we must be aware that empirical work is always limited by the range of the observations.

J. Johnston discusses various procedures for obtaining cost functions statistically and reviews much of the empirical work in this area.[13] In a study of a silk-hosiery mill, Joel Dean determined the relationship between output and cost to be

$$X_1 = 2,935 + 1.998X_2,$$

where X_2 is output (pairs of hose) and X_1 is total cost, both measured on a monthly basis.

A study of costs for United States Steel, by T. O. Yntema, yielded a total cost function of

$$X_t = 182,100,000 + 55.73X_2,$$

where X_t is annual dollar costs and X_2 is a weighted composite of steel output, measured in tons. The years 1927 to 1938 provided the observations.

An interesting "joint cost" study of British railroads gave the following total cost function:

$$E = 54,250,000 + 0.1000M_p + 0.3680M_f,$$

where E is annual pounds sterling, M_p is coach train miles, and M_f is freight train miles.

THE USE OF LINEAR PROGRAMMING
FOR INPUT MIX DETERMINATION

One of the most common problems faced by business is the determination of the best (least-cost) combinations of inputs of materials. Given a prespecified product, feed manufacturers may be able to use

[13] J. Johnston, *Statistical Cost Analysis* (New York: McGraw-Hill, 1960).

different combinations of grains. Refiners of petroleum can use different grades of the raw petroleum. Manufacturers of frankfurters can vary the proportions of beef, pork, chicken, and dried milk. Packagers of mixed nuts can vary the percentages of cashews, filberts, almonds, and peanuts.

With the specification of the product, it is usually possible to determine the isoquant of the various inputs that can be used for a unit of the product. Say, for example, that a candy bar manufacturer produces a product that consists only of nuts and chocolate. Say a one-pound bar must contain at least 25 percent nuts and at least 50 percent by weight must be chocolate. Then, if x_1 is nuts and x_2 is chocolate, the possible combinations of nuts and chocolate (which together must equal at least a pound) are

$$x_1 + x_2 \geq 16$$
$$x_1 \geq (0.25)(16)$$
$$x_2 \geq (0.50)(16).$$

These form an isoquant (where x_1 and x_2 are in ounces) as shown in Figure 11.11. With the prices on chocolate and nut inputs, we can select the least-cost combinations of inputs with the help of an isocost map.

A particularly interesting variation on this problem occurs when the manufacturer promises that some unit of output will contain certain nutritional elements, such as various amounts of vitamins, calcium, phosphate. If the nutrients are embodied in the inputs, we can formulate the problem as selecting the least-cost combination of the inputs that will deliver the nutrients. To illustrate the procedure, let us assume that a chicken-feed manufacturer mixes wheat and corn and sells the product in sacks weighing at least 100 pounds. The manufacturer guarantees at least 800 units of vitamin B and 1,200 units of calcium in a sack. Each pound of wheat contains 5 units of vitamin B and 20 units of calcium, and each pound of corn contains 10 units of vitamin B and 6 units of calcium. This information can be arrayed as in Table 11.1.

TABLE 11.1   Units of nutrients per unit
of input

| Nutrients | Units of nutrients | | Requirements (guarantees) |
	Wheat	Corn	
Vitamin B	5	10	800
Calcium	20	6	1,200

If we now allow W and C to represent the quantities of wheat and corn in pounds, then the combination of wheat and corn necessary for vitamin B is $5W + 10C \geq 800$. Similarly, the combination necessary to provide the calcium is $20W + 6C \geq 1,200$. These two inequations constrain the W,C combinations. Another constraint, implicit in the 100 pounds weight of the sack, is $W + C \geq 100$.

These three constraints, when plotted as a graph, can be seen to form an isoquant, as in Figure 11.12. Because we are allowed to "overfulfill" the nutrients and weight, the isoquant is the boundary of all possible W,C combinations. With the prices of W and C, an iso-cost map can be used to select the least-cost combination. If the prices of wheat and corn are completely determined by the market — that is, if these prices do not vary with the firm's purchases – the isocost map will consist of straight lines. Hence, one of the "corners" of the isoquant will provide an input combination that has at least as small a cost as any other point on the isoquant. Thus, with such isoquants and isocost maps, the simplex method of linear programming can be used to solve complex problems of the optimal input mix. Notice that in our example the prices of W and C can be such that the firm may find it cheapest to use either just wheat or just corn, in which event each sack may contain more than 100 pounds.

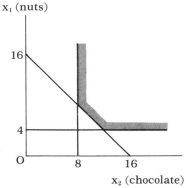

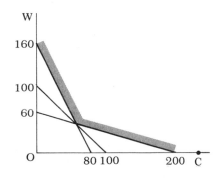

FIGURE 11.11 Isoquant map for one-pound chocolate nut bar

FIGURE 11.12 Isoquant map for chicken-feed mix

PRODUCTIVITY

When we speak of productivity, we mean the relationship between physical quantities of inputs and outputs. There are two types of productivity – factor productivity and total factor productivity.

Factor productivity is the relationship between a single input, generally labor, and output. We say that labor has become more productive if the output per unit of labor input rises. There can be increasing productivity of labor for any given production function if the quantity of the fixed asset services has increased. Say the production function is Cobb-Douglas,

$$Q = ax_1^\alpha x_2^\beta, \tag{11.6}$$

where x_1 is labor and x_2 is the capital services. If x_2 is increased, a little experimentation with this equation would show that any given amount of labor used would produce a higher quantity of output than when x_2 is lower. Thus, the productivity of labor is increased by having a larger amount of capital assets to combine with it.

In total factor productivity we have an improvement only if the same quantity of both labor and capital produces a higher output.[14] This can happen only if the production function itself changes. If the exponents of the inputs, x_1 and x_2, remain the same, then any increase in total factor productivity would be reflected in parameter a. If, for example, twice as much output could be produced with the same quantities of the two inputs, then a would double.

Changes in production could also entail changes in the exponents of the inputs. If, for example, with new technology, α in equation 11.6 is enlarged (β would have to fall if the production function remains homogeneous to degree 1), the marginal productivity of labor is increased and the marginal productivity of capital is decreased. On the other hand, if β is increased (with α falling), the marginal productivity of capital is increased. When the exponents remain the same and a rises, we call this a neutral productivity gain. When the increase in a is accompanied by an increase in α, we call such an increase in productivity labor biased. Finally, if β is increased, the increase in productivity is known as capital biased.

Increases in productivity are even more easily seen in the single-process production function. Say this function is

$$x_1 \geq k_1 Q$$
$$x_2 \geq k_2 Q.$$

A decrease in either k_1 or k_2 implies that less of the designated input is required per unit of output; hence, it is an increase in productivity. If k_1 falls by more than k_2, the productivity gain can be said to be labor biased. On the other hand, if k_2 falls by more than k_1, the productivity gain is capital biased.

PRODUCTION EXTERNALITIES
AND ENVIRONMENTAL QUALITY

In recent years human beings have become increasingly aware of the ecological consequences of their economic activity. Particularly in economically developed countries, pollution of air and water has required growing investment in control equipment or a switch to more costly but less polluting methods of production. Part, but of course not all, of the environmental protection problem stems from the fact that many of the costs and benefits to society of the produc-

[14]The seminal work in total factor productivity is John Kendrick, *Productivity Trends in the United States* (Princeton: Princeton University Press, 1961).

tion of economic goods do not show up as costs and revenues to firms making production decisions. Such costs and benefits are called "externalities" because they occur to others outside the firm. Our theory has, to this point, dealt only with the internal costs and benefits taken into account by firms making decisions. For example, a firm producing chemical products in a plant on a river typically considers as costless the dumping of zero-valued by-products into the river or into the atmosphere. Production that results in such dumping, how-ever, is costing something to the users of the water downstream and to the breathers of the air downwind.

Many of the public policy measures already adopted or now being considered to cope with pollution can be viewed as measures de-signed to force internalization of such external social costs. One such suggestion would be to force any firm or municipality that both uses water from and dumps sewage into the same river to place its water intake downstream from its sewer outlets. More subtle mea-sures may have similar effects.

Without attempting a thorough economic analysis of the environ-mental quality problem, we will consider here several ways in which conscious consideration of the problem might be incorporated into our models of the firm. First we deal with the simple technique of treating the dumping of waste as an input of the scarce resource called "sink capacity." We also consider the dumping of waste as the "sale" of one of the "products" of a multi-product firm. Finally, we consider the interrelationship of a number of separate pollutants and sources of pollutants by adapting production theory to the work-ings of an ecological system such as a river with inputs and outputs.

Effluent Charges and the Idea of the Commons. If we start with the assumption that people wish to maintain and insist on maintaining a certain level of water quality or air quality, then we can think of the watershed or atmosphere in the neighborhood of a plant as a scarce resource. If population and the total amount of production and consumption of goods grow large enough to produce a pollution problem, then the right to dump wastes must be constrained. Volun-tary action cannot be counted on to yield desirable results even if everyone wishes to have a decent environment. Each decision-maker knows his own voluntary restraint will be negligible, and he has no power alone to insist that everyone exercise restraint. In other words, individuals' changing their objective functions will not solve the problem. Constraint changes are needed on all who dump into the same common sink.

The problem of the "commons" is not new. Many years ago when grazing land was treated as a free good, each farmer could graze as many animals as he wished without interfering with the quality of the common pasture. But as the population of farmers and there-fore of animals grew larger, the common pasture was overgrazed.

Each farmer had incentive to add animals up to the point at which the marginal revenue to himself was just offset by the marginal cost to himself. But his marginal animal also cost all other farmers something in lowered productivity. Out of such problems came the enclosing of common pasture lands. That is, private property in pasture land internalized the external costs. If a farmer's animals are fenced into his own plot of ground, any loss of productivity from overgrazing falls on his own output and revenue and not on his neighbors'.

Perhaps some pollution problems could be solved by dividing the common capacity of the environment to absorb wastes. We might force the smokestacks to be inside factories. But such a solution is not likely to be practical in most cases. An alternative way of internalizing external costs of production is to charge firms a price for the use of the common dump. Use of the dump can then be treated as one of the necessary inputs in the firm's production process. Consider, for example, a firm whose production process has heretofore required one ton of coal to be burned for every unit of output. The firm has used the cheapest coal that serves its needs. Suppose cheap coal contains a high amount of sulfur. The firm has been dumping sulfur dioxide into the atmosphere free of charge. Because the firm had free use of the common dump, it would have given no consideration to the amount of sulfur in its coal or to the amount of sulfur dioxide coming out of its smokestack. Environmentally they were part of its production process, but economically sulfur and sulfur dioxide were not part of the firm's production function and were not consciously managed by management.

Suppose the government began to charge everyone for the privilege of dumping sulfur dioxide into the atmosphere. Suppose the price is fixed at $\bar{p}_3$ per unit. What would be the effect on the behavior of a profit-maximizing firm?

Let x_3 be the quantity of sulfur dioxide dumped by the firm. Before the government acted, the firm viewed its production function as

$$Q \le f(x_1, x_2).$$

If x_2 is the amount of coal used, the firm would have a cost function into which $\bar{p}_2$, the price of coal, entered. As a result of the government action, the firm now must view its production function as including x_3, the amount of sulfur dioxide dumped. The firm must take this new view of its production function not because its technology has changed but because its costs are now affected by the price of polluting. If the government sets the price, $\bar{p}_3$, just right, then the external costs of dumping sulfur dioxide in the air will be internalized. The reaction of the firm will depend on the technical characteristics of its process. In most general terms, its production function becomes

$$Q \le f(x_1, x_2, x_3).$$

Perhaps, however, the production function will be similar to those discussed earlier in this chapter. The dumping of sulfur dioxide, that is, x_3, may occur in fixed proportion to the burning of coal, x_2. If so, then the government's effluent charges for dumping sulfur dioxide will have exactly the same effect on the firm in the short run as a rise in the price of coal. What would that effect be?

The short-run effect of an effluent charge depends on the firm's cost function and the size of the charge. If the isoquants have the same general form as in Figures 11.11 and 11.12, we would see that the government's charge would have no effect at all until the charge is raised high enough to switch the firm to an optimum solution at a "corner" for which less dumping is required. That point would come at a different price of dumping for different firms. The government could raise the charge until enough firms cut their dumping to achieve any desired level of cleanness of air.

The long-run consequences of government charges for dumping may be somewhat different from the short-run effects. One obvious consequence will be to induce in each firm a search for alternative technologies to by-pass the charge. Such alternatives are not limited to new discoveries. Older methods not previously optimal from the viewpoint of least cost may become so in the light of the new cost of dumping. With some investment in new equipment, the firm might be able to switch from high-sulfur coal to some other fuel such as natural gas. The effluent charge may make the investment worthwhile. But if all firms switch to natural gas, its price may rise or its availability may be affected. Technology may be readily available, but only at some cost, for removing the sulfur dioxide from the smoke. The charge for pollution may make such investment profitable.

Presumably, the ultimate cost of the cleanup of the smoke from the stacks will fall on the consumers of the final products. In the process of charging, however, incentives will have been provided for a switch to alternative methods of production that yield less pollution.

Two related public policy problems exist with the effluent charge approach to environmental quality: (1) The next-best solution from the firm's point of view may be an alternative technology that gives rise to different but perhaps equally damaging pollution. (2) The "appropriate" price to achieve socially optimal changes in economic activity is not specified in this analysis. Our society has no mechanism for resolving the conflicts of interest inherent in weighing social costs and social benefits of pollution and its remedies. Finding appropriate charges would require weighing not only the interest of diverse parts of the citizenry but also weighing one form of pollution against another. Most technical "solutions" to one problem give rise to other problems. We may not gain much from cleaning up the smokestacks by "washing" the smoke and dumping the sulfur dioxide into the nearest stream or by burning the residuals collected in the sewage treatment plant.

Residual Materials as Outputs with Negative Prices. The pollution problem can be thought of in terms of output rather than input. We can, for example, think of mercury being dumped into the Great Lakes as the disposal of a product with a price of zero. Several of the models in Chapter 5 included the assumption that the firm is a multi-product firm. If a firm produces several products but produces them with completely separate production processes, the value of its output of any one product would be zero if the market price were zero. Let us consider, however, a case in which the firm's production function involves a technical interdependence of two outputs. Suppose that

$$Q_1 \leq f(x_1, x_2, \ldots)$$

and

$$Q_2 = kQ_1.$$

That is, the inputs result in the production of the first product and also some amount of a second by-product, Q_2. The ratio of Q_1 to Q_2 is here assumed to be a constant, k. Mercury may be this second product. Suppose that mercury is produced in a form and at a place such that it can be dumped "free" but that no one will pay anything for it. Therefore, the price of the second output is zero. Thus the firm can ignore this output in its decisions.

One approach to the effluent charge problem is to view the charge as a negative price for an output. The firm's objective function would then be

$$Z = P_1 Q_1 - P_2 Q_2 - (p_1 x_1 + p_2 x_2 + \ldots).$$

With no government policy, the price, P_2, is zero. Therefore, the quantity of mercury dumped, Q_2, is irrelevant to the firm. A negative price imposed by government for the privilege of dumping mercury would reduce the short-run cash flow of the firm and give it incentive to seek alternatives. These alternatives might include either ways to produce Q_1 with less Q_2 or ways to dispose of Q_2 without dumping. Even if the firm finds a use for the previously dumped mercury, the problem may be merely passed on to the user of the mercury who later dumps it.

The Production Function for an Ecological System. The production concepts developed to understand firms can also be used to gain insight into the workings of a nonhuman ecological system. Many of the most vexing environmental quality problems stem from the inter-relationships of the things dumped by humans and the organisms with whom humans share the environment. We "manage" only a small part of the transformations of matter and energy caused by man's economic activity. It may be useful to conceive of production in the larger context. Already we have introduced the notion of se-quential and partial production functions. In a sense all production functions are sequential in that the things dumped – unwanted outputs – from one process become inputs into another. So far, in considering pollution, we have assumed the thing dumped to be a pollutant automatically and instantaneously. But much pollution results from combinations of things happening over time after the dumping.

Let us first consider a simple case of chainlike interrelationships. Unwanted mercury for several decades has been dumped into the Great Lakes watershed. Let us view this mercury as an input to an unmanaged production process. The "natural" or "ecological" system of life in the Great Lakes produces, among other things, edible fish. The production function can be written as

$$f(Q_1, Q_2, Q_3, \ldots, x_1, x_2, x_3, \ldots) = 0. \text{ [15]}$$

This production process contains many inputs, but no mercury, and many outputs including edible fish. The introduction of mercury as an additional input changes the quality of the outputs. The fish become inedible. Much about the nature of this production process may be known to scientists. But such knowledge is not the normal, routine, result of the management of economic activity. The firm that dumps the mercury looses concern with mercury's role as an input into the lake. The fishermen who catch the edible fish are not required to know much about the ecology of the lake to catch fish. Yet inputs and outputs are taking place in such an environment. As a result of concern about mercury poisoning, scientists have now discovered that the heavy metal does not simply sink harmlessly to the mud on the bottom. It enters the "life chain" of a multitude of organisms that are inputs and outputs of the ecosystem. One problem with effluent charges is the time lag between the dumping of wastes and our discovery that pollution has taken place.

The concept of a production function is also useful for considering pollution problems that stem from interactions of pollutants. We can think of clean water, for example, as an output of a river basin. Its cleanness depends on the input of many distinguishable polluting inputs. Let Q be the quantity of clean water per day available at some point on a stream. Let $x_1, x_2, \ldots, x_i, \ldots, x_n$ be the quantities of things being dumped in the river upstream and inputs of nature and efforts to clean the water. Thus

$$Q \le f(x_1, x_2, \ldots, x_i, \ldots, x_n).$$

The mathematical properties of such a function might be investigated as a way of conceptualizing the water pollution problem. Suppose that some of the inputs enter with positive coefficients in that they increase outputs, while some inputs – chlorine and phosphates,

[15]This is the most general form of a production function, showing that the various outputs and inputs are functionally related.

for example – have negative coefficients in that they decrease output. The function also contains some variables such as runoff of rain water that are subject to only a small degree of control. Some variables are inputs of services of equipment such as sewage disposal plants. No single firm or other decision-maker is managing all the inputs. Anyone who controls some must treat the uncontrolled ones as parameters to be forecast.

Such a concept of the problem is not a complete model, but it may suggest some of the problems of environmental quality. For example, we cannot expect rainfall in the Mississippi valley to change very much. If the population continues to grow, and if economic activity per capita continues to increase, we can see that clean water will be more and more difficult to obtain. The "inputs" that enter this production function with negative coefficients – for example, detergents and sewage – must be offset by increases at an increasing rate over time of inputs such as the services of sewage disposal plants. In addition, with fixed rainfall (the fixed input), diminishing returns to the inputs with positive coefficients can be expected to occur. Therefore, the cost per unit of clean water will rise as population grows, and it is likely that the rise in cost will be nonlinear. More than proportional increases in the cost of water will occur with population growth unless technological advance is rapid enough to offset it.

Discussion Questions

1. Let us consider the fencing problem once more. The area encloser wishes to enclose 100 square yards. One pair of parallel sides is to consist of wood fencing, and the other pair of sides is to consist of steel fencing. Let us say that two hours of labor are needed to install a yard of wood fencing and three hours of labor are needed to install a yard of steel fencing. Say the price of wood fencing is $3 per yard, and the price of steel fencing is $5 per yard. The labor to install the wood fencing cost $4 per hour; the labor to install the steel fencing only costs $3 per hour. Given this information, express the production function. Then determine the least-cost combination of inputs to enclose 100 square yards.

2. Explain how it is possible to have economies of size even though there are constant returns to scale.

3. If you were in a debate, taking the position that competition can regulate prices and that government regulation is unnecessary, what kind of long-run average cost curve would support your position?

4. A manufacturer of frankfurters uses different combinations of beef, pork, and chicken in his product. Assume that government law states that a pound of franks must contain at least 50 units of protein and 40 units of amino acids. Let us say the units of these nutrients per ounce are as given in the following table:

	Protein	Amino acids
Beef	6	3
Pork	4	4
Chicken	3	5

Let us further say that the prices of these meats per ounce are: beef, 10 cents, pork, 8 cents, and chicken, 4 cents.

Formulate, up to the optimization stage, the problem of finding the least-cost combinations of meats to use per pound of frankfurters.

5. Assume that as the result of a change in technology, a firm's production function changes from $Q = 2x_1^{0.5} x_2^{0.5}$ to $Q = 2x_1^{0.2} x_2^{0.8}$, where x_1 is labor and x_2 is machinery services. Assuming in both cases that the value of a unit of output is \$10 and that 100 units of machinery services are available per day, analyze the effect of the change in technology on the firm's demand curve for labor.

12 Legally Imposed, Self-Imposed, and Knowledge Constraints

In Chapter 3, we briefly discussed seven constraints on the firm's short-run choices of values for its decision variables. In Chapter 6, we discussed many of the steps that the firm could take to influence the parameter of these constraints. In Chapters 7 through 11, we concentrated on understanding and measuring four of these constraints. Now we turn our attention to the remaining three. We have, to a considerable extent, woven them into all the chapters, so there will be some repetition. There is something to be gained, however, by organizing an explicit discussion of these constraints, since they have not received a great deal of attention in textbooks on price theory. Moreover, they are likely to assume important roles in the future, as governments become more active and as business organizations become more complex.

LEGALLY IMPOSED CONSTRAINTS

Governments impose a variety of constraints on business firms, and the future is likely to see more as concern mounts about pollution and the economic power of very large firms and labor unions. These constraints can be divided into two types, general and specific. We define general constraints as those that limit the power of the firm to influence the parameters of all the constraints that limit its short-run choices—the types of activities we designated long run, discussed in Chapter 6. The most important limitation imposed by general constraints is on the power of the firm to influence the demand and supply curves that face it. General constraints consist mainly of the rules of the marketplace—the antitrust laws, laws of contract, and fair bargaining techniques.

Specific constraints are those in which governments directly limit the firm's opportunity set—that is, the short-run choices of values for the firm's decision variables. Examples of specific constraints are price ceilings and floors, minimum wages, stipulations requiring the use or nonuse of certain inputs, and the prohibition of certain outputs.

Governments do not rely completely on general and specific constraints to influence business behavior. In addition, they use taxes and subsidies meant to alter incentives rather than available choices.[1]

General Constraints. The primary purpose of the general constraints is to limit the methods that can be used by a firm to influence its demand and supply curves.

ANTITRUST LAWS. The basic rationale for the free market system is the belief that self-interest and competition will lead to an allocation of productive resources that will produce products and services that best match up resource limitations and consumers wants, with minimal state supervision. Prices, in this view, are the signals that induce firms to produce more, or less, of certain goods and to use inputs in a way that reflects their relative scarcities. Prices not only have an allocative purpose; in addition, when the system works well, they should tend to reflect long-run costs.[2]

The main mechanism inducing the firm to act in the social interest is the supply and demand curves facing it. When prices are set on the free competitive market, the demand curve brings about socially desirable behavior in two ways. It provides signals and incentives to the firm that consumers want more, or less, of a particular output. It also limits the ability of the firm to make high profits by charging high prices. True, there is usually no legal upper limit to a firm's asking price, but the demand curve constraint, by reducing the amounts the firm can sell if it sets its prices "too high," forces the firm in its own self-interest to ask lower prices as a condition for selling its goods.[3] The supply curve also influences behavior. It provides signals on the relative scarcities of inputs and induces the firm to use more of those that are relatively plentiful. It also constrains the firm from paying "too low" a price for its inputs.

Because demand and supply curves limit the ability of firms to make profits, it is in their interest to take action that would "shift" the curves in a favorable way. When the market structure is purely

---

[1]There are many good books on the government regulation of private enterprises. See especially Clair Wilcox, *Public Policies Towards Business*, 4th ed. (Homewood, Ill.: Irwin, 1971).

[2]We saw in Chapter 9 that price in a purely competitive market should approach the cost of production plus a normal profit in the long run. These costs are at the minimum point of the long-run average total cost curve.

[3]The more price elastic the firm's demand curve, the more the firm has to lose by raising its price and the more it has to gain by lowering its price. When the demand curve is perfectly price elastic, the price is effectively determined by the market.

competitive — that is, when there are many small buyers and sellers, entry is not restricted, firms act independently, products are homogeneous — the individual firm by itself can do little to change the demand curve or supply curve that faces it. But if there is a small number of sellers or buyers, if they do not act independently, if they use political influence, if they can persuade buyers that their product is superior (or make it superior), or if they can interfere with the activities of their competitors, the individual firm acting either alone or with other firms can favorably influence its demand curve or its supply curves. By so doing, the firm can enhance its profits and, although firms do not generally have this as an objective, can interfere with the allocative efficiency of the price-market system.

Many of the efforts a firm can make to influence the demand or supply curves that face it are legitimate under our legal system, although some would argue that those efforts sometimes hinder the workings of the economic system. Product improvement is one way to influence a demand curve that few would condemn. Better service and faster delivery are other ways for firms to favorably influence their demand curves. Advertising and the use of other promotional devices, if not overtly deceptive, can favorably change a firm's demand curve. The offer of better working conditions or more security may influence the supply curve facing the firm. Political action may also be legitimate, though controversial.

Other activities of firms to influence the demand and supply curves facing them are not considered legitimate. One class of such activities are those taken by firms in collusion with other firms to influence the individual firm's demand and supply curves by coordinating their policies on prices asked, output, prices offered, and inputs purchased. A second class of activities are those taken either by individual firms or by firms acting jointly to hinder or restrict the activities of actual or potential competitors or to eliminate them from the market.

Collusion can take a number of forms. Selling firms may make an agreement on the prices they will charge; this is usually accompanied by an agreement on output. Higher prices by rivals (and the "market") will favorably influence the individual firm's demand curve, although as its part of the agreement the firm may not have complete freedom to pick any point on the demand curve; that is, it will select higher prices and lower output rather than the opposite. A market-sharing agreement is another collusive form. When firms agree not to sell in each other's narrow markets, buyers cannot find good substitutes for a firm's products, and that firm's demand curve becomes price inelastic. These market-sharing agreements can also work on the buying side. If some firms refuse to buy in some input markets, the effect can enhance the bargaining power of the group and therefore also lead to favorable prices.

A firm can also favorably influence the demand and supply curves it faces by either reducing the number of competitors or by making them less effective. One way to reduce the number of competitors is through horizontal mergers. By acquiring competitors, the number of competitors is obviously reduced, thereby, all other things remaining the same, expanding the acquiring firm's demand curve and possibly reducing supply prices. A second way of reducing the number of competitors is to take some kind of predatory action to drive them out of business. This may be done by cutting prices in particular markets served by smaller competitors, thereby either forcing them out of business or into submission, or by gaining control over some resource needed by them. Individual firms acting alone or with others may also make entry of new firms difficult. The "inside" firms may tie up sources of supply and markets, build "patent pools" that are not available to new firms, and sometimes pressure suppliers not to deal with new entrants.

There are other ways in which firms can make it more difficult for competitors to effectively compete with them. By obtaining control over key inputs, powerful firms can force smaller competitors to not be too aggressive on price cuts or on output expansion. This can be done by threats to cut off supplies of these key inputs. Long-term requirements contracts, in which firms require that suppliers sell them a large share of their output or that customers guarantee to make purchases from them, have the effect of foreclosing markets to competitors. Exclusive-dealing arrangements, in which a customer or supplier can deal only with a particular firm, are common and also have the effect of foreclosing competitors from markets. Often powerful firms have tie-in arrangements, in which a customer, in order to obtain one product from a firm, is compelled to purchase products it may not want. American Can, for example, which had a patent on can-closing machinery, would allow customers to use its machines only on the condition that they purchased their cans from American Can. Such a tie-in contract obviously limited the effectiveness of competitors in tin cans. A large buyer, by forcing its suppliers to sell to it at prices lower than others, can make it difficult for other firms to compete with it.

Barriers to entry of new competitors as well as barriers to expansion of capacity by existing competitors take many forms. A common method by which firms bar entry and maintain market power is by bottling up crucial inputs, especially raw materials.[4] In its role as owner of assets a firm may gain control of agents of production far in excess of its foreseeable needs in order to adversely affect the supply curves facing other actual and potential competitors. Sometimes existing firms may work together through joint ventures to discover and control high-grade deposits of minerals essential for the production of their products. The iron and steel industry and the

---

[4]See, for example, David D. Martin, "Resource Control and Market Power," in Mason Gaffney, ed., *Extractive Resources and Taxation* (Madison: University of Wisconsin Press, 1967).

petroleum industry are good examples of the use of such techniques of maintaining market control in the hands of established firms.

There is, of course, a limit to the profitability of investing in unneeded assets merely to forestall potential competitors. Such action can indeed be pushed too far. The profits from market control might be required to maintain that control. For this reason, among others, the existence of market power is not always evidenced by high profits.

The federal antitrust laws are designed to prohibit collusion and all the various things a firm can do to eliminate or forestall competitors or make them less effective.[5] The statutes are the Sherman Act (1890), parts of the Clayton Act (1914), and part of the Federal Trade Commission Act (1914), which spell out the activities that are illegal. These basic statutes have been amended to strengthen them, most importantly by the Robinson-Patman Act (1936), which applies to price discrimination, and the Celler-Kefauver Act (1950), which applies to mergers. These statutes are written in broad language, and their precise meaning and application are determined by the interpretation of specific cases by the federal courts. Various groups are exempt from these laws. Labor unions, professional associations, farm cooperatives, export groups, sports such as baseball, regulated industries such as railroads, banking, and insurance all have been given at least partial exemptions.

OTHER INDIRECT LEGAL CONSTRAINTS. Other legal constraints indirectly influence the firm's ability to sell or buy. "Consumer" legislation prohibits deceptive advertising and other forms of misrepresentation and forces disclosure of ingredients. Some laws prohibit fraud, and others are making it feasible for buyers to sue under the general laws of "warranty." All these laws limit the firm's ability to influence its supply or demand curve. Laws also pertain to the enforcement of contracts, which can result in penalties to firms that break or do not fulfill their contracts. Penalties inhibit the firm from changing constraints placed on them by their signing of contracts.

Specific Government Constraints. Governments impose many types of direct constraint both on the short-run opportunity sets of firms and on their opportunity-changing decisions. Government constraints can be classified in many ways. For simplicity, we will discuss briefly a few categories – namely, regulation of "natural monopolies," regu-

---

[5]There are many good books on the antitrust laws: A. D. Neale, *The Antitrust Laws of the U.S.* (Cambridge: Cambridge University Press, 1966); Richard Caves, *American Industry: Structure, Conduct, Performance* (Englewood Cliffs, N.J.: Prentice-Hall, 1967); David D. Martin, *Mergers and the Clayton Act* (Berkeley: University of California Press, 1959); Hans Thorelli, *The Federal Antitrust Policy* (Baltimore: Johns Hopkins Press, 1955), H. L. Fugilier and J. C. Darnell, *Competition and Public Policy: Cases in Antitrust* (Englewood Cliffs, N.J.: Prentice-Hall, 1971).

lation of firms generally to protect the public health and safety, and intervention in markets to alter the distribution of income.

"Natural monopolies" are firms with technical constraints that make competition wasteful to society. These businesses have one essential characteristic — concomitance of production and consumption. In other words, the nature of the product is such that equipment used in consumption must be physically connected with the equipment used in production. All the businesses we normally think of as a "regulated industry" or as a "public utility" have wires, pipes, rails, or some other physical connection between the "plant" and the "consumer." For more than one firm to stand ready to supply the service to each consumer would require more than one set of distribution equipment. Thus, to divide the total plant capacity of the industry among several competing suppliers would multiply the amount of plant required. Society benefits, therefore, from a legal constraint limiting entry to such businesses. As a result, exclusive franchises are given by governments. A private firm that takes advantage of such an exclusive privilege is devoting its property to a public purpose. In exchange, the public receives an interest in the manner in which the property is used; the utility becomes a "business affected with a public interest," to use the legal description. A public regulatory body — local, state, or federal — will exercise veto power over management decisions to invest in extensions of the system or to abandon part of it, as well as veto power over decisions affecting price and product quality. Such a regulated firm is usually treated as a "common carrier," which means that it must stand ready to serve all consumers in whatever quantities they wish to buy at the regulated price.

Regulatory authorities make their decisions on the basis of a principle easy to state but difficult to implement: The industry should function with regard to resource use and income distribution as it would if the industry were perfectly competitive. For example, the profits of a regulated company should be just enough to provide the going competitive rate of return on investment in capital used and useful in the business.

Most firms, even though they are not natural monopolies, are regulated to some degree, depending on the business, in order to protect public health and safety. We might suppose that it would be "good business" for any firm to behave in a manner consistent with the public health and safety; yet history shows that this is not the case. A million and a half Americans have been killed and many more injured in automobile accidents in the past four decades. As early as the 1830s the federal government was regulating the design of steam engines to lessen the danger to steamboat passengers from explosions. Society, through the political process, has chosen to protect the technically ignorant consumer or the innocent passerby from product design decisions made by firms that are assumed to maximize profits.

Society has been unwilling to rely on the indirect negative effect of dangerous design on the firm's future demand curve. One reason is that the optimum amount of consumer deaths and injuries for the firm may not be zero. How high would the highway or emphysema death toll have to go before automobile companies would voluntarily install seat belts or devices to control exhaust emission in order to improve its demand curve? The answer is not unrelated to the degree of competition, but whether there is perfect competition or monopoly, profit-maximizing behavior does not necessarily correspond to the public interest. Therefore, the public uses the government mechanism to impose direct constraints on product qualities. Only recently have such constraints become a popular issue of "consumerism," but we have had them for many years in many areas of economic activity. Not only in food, drugs, and cosmetics, but in buildings such codes are well established.

In addition to direct controls on product design, governments impose direct controls on production processes in order to protect the public health and safety. Some issues are related to pollution from production. In addition, governments regulate production processes to provide for the safety of workers. In an economy with unemployed workers, the profit motive does not ensure that firms will share society's interest in protecting the health and life of workers. Therefore, we have, for example, mine safety laws.

Governments also directly intervene in the market system in order to affect the distribution of income. Some analysts argue that even in a perfectly competitive economy the distribution of income resulting from the sale of the services of labor and property at market prices is not necessarily an equitable basis for distributing the goods and services produced, although this is a controversial topic indeed. Many economists would argue that income ought to be redistributed through taxation and subsidies of a sort that do not interfere with decisions affecting resource use. But such taxes and subsidies are difficult, if not impossible, to enact and administer in a democracy. Therefore, many government constraints are imposed to directly affect prices and incomes. Minimum wage laws and agricultural price supports are obvious examples, but there are many others. Programs to enhance agricultural prices generally specify maximum output for individual producers or, more often, the maximum use of an input, most importantly land. Quotas are common in many industries. Oil producers in Texas have uppper limits imposed on their output by the Texas Railroad Commission. These quotas are ostensibly made to limit the exploitation of oil resources but really attempt to keep prices "firm" by reducing supply. Quotas are also common in foreign trade, where the quantities of products that could be imported by individual producers are limited by the government.

Subsidies and Taxes. Subsidies and taxes, especially the latter, are quite common. These enter the firm's calculations not as constraints on the short-run opportunity set but rather as part of the objective function. Say, for example, a one-product two-input firm has to pay a tax, T, on every unit of output it sells. Its profit function, instead of being

$$\pi = PQ - p_1 x_1 - p_2 x_2$$

would become

$$\pi = (P - T)Q - p_1 x_1 - p_2 x_2.$$

Such a tax would reduce the firm's marginal revenue, which would tend to reduce its output level, which in turn would "shift" the market supply curve to the left, which would tend to raise the market price. Public finance is concerned with such types of analysis. A subsidy on the use of input 2, which we symbolize by S, would cause the objective function to be

$$\pi = (P - T)Q - p_1 x_1 - (p_2 - S)x_2.$$

This would have the effect of making it more profitable for the firm to use more of input 2.

SELF-IMPOSED CONSTRAINTS

We have been using the notion of a self-imposed constraint, in which the firm purposefully limits its short-run opportunity set and, as a result, its short-run profit. For a variety of reasons a firm may want to take a step of this kind, which at first may seem irrational. One reason is that a selection of values for the short-run decision variables that maximizes short-run profits may hamper long-run profit. Another is that the firm may wish to avoid too much uncertainty and may be concerned with its "viability"—that is, with its ability to adapt to new situations. A third reason for the imposition of self-imposed constraint is the reconciliation of conflicting goals. A fourth type of self-imposed constraint takes place within the firm and is designed to coordinate the various divisions of a firm.

Inconsistency of Short-Run and Long-Run Profits. In many instances a naive selection of values for the decision in the short run may have an undesirable effect on the firm's *future* short-run constraints and thus on future profits. The monopolist, for example, by charging a profit-maximizing price in the short run, may induce new entries and thereby face an unfavorable demand curve in the future. Thus, we introduced the notion of a self-imposed "limit" price designed to deter potential entrants. The oligopolist, in particular, must be sensitive to the behavior of rivals, which affects his own demand curve. Naive short-run profit-maximizing could result in lower profits; consequently, the firm must sometimes select prices and quantities that would deter its rivals from becoming too aggressive. The firm must be prepared to forgo short-run profits in order to have higher profits in later periods.

There are other examples in which a purposeful sacrifice of profits in the short run may lead to longer-run profits. An introductory price is one example. New firms or new products are often at a disadvantage because trade connections have not been developed or buyers are accustomed to using competitive products. A low price may be the best way to overcome these handicaps. The firm charging this price may not maximize profit in the short run, but the price may have a favorable impact on its demand curves in future periods. Paradoxically, the firm may sometimes introduce a new product at a high price – perhaps sacrificing short-run sales and profits. The high price may lead buyers to believe the product is in some way superior, and a reduction of the price in later periods could raise sales and profits by large amounts.

Avoidance of Uncertainty and Maintenance of Viability. In the real world the firm often does not perfectly know some of its constraint parameters, especially, as in the case with its demand curve, when the constraint depends on the behavior of acknowledged rivals. Sometimes the firm may know its demand curve, or other constraints, with a tolerable degree of certainty only over certain ranges of its variables. For example, on the basis of past experience it may be reasonably confident of its demand curve within a given price range, but beyond that range it may be much less certain. Faced with these uncertainties, the firm may choose values for its decision variables only within the ranges of high confidence. To do this it would constrain itself during the optimization process from selecting values for the decision variables that may have too much risk.

The firm could also view itself as an organization capable of adapting to new conditions and taking advantage of new opportunities as they arise. We can think of this attitude as one of keeping the organization viable. Viability is usually best achieved when the firm keeps some of its options open, even though a policy of open options may interfere with short-run profits. Perhaps the most important way of preserving these options is to keep stakes in various markets. Thus, in the short run the firm may wish to produce some minimum amount of a given product, even though not profitably, if there are possibilities that in the future the product might become highly profitable. This strategy would be especially desirable if it is difficult to establish connections with buyers and with suppliers of inputs for the product or to assemble an organization within the firm concerned with the product.

Reconciliation of Multiple Goals. In the early stages of what we think of as modern economic analysis, economic theory was greatly influenced by the concept of man as a hedonist. Man was viewed as a pleasure-seeker and a pain-avoider. Because most economic activities have both pleasure and pain connected with them, economic man was viewed as selecting activities and their levels that would maximize the *difference* between the pleasure and the pain. We might call this difference "net happiness." When a man organized and managed a business enterprise, the pleasure-pain principle was extended to his decision-making for his firm. The revenue he received for his output became the measure of his pleasure; the costs incurred in producing the output were his pain. The difference between revenues and costs, which are profits, was analogous to "net happiness." Thus, the traditional assumption that the firm seeks to maximize profits was based on the view of a man as a hedonist and the firm as an extension of a particular individual, the entrepreneur.

With the growth of the modern corporation, which is legally recognized as a person, what we mean by the "entrepreneur" and even who belongs to the firm have become less clear. Are the common stockholders the firm? They bear some of the risks and are the residual claimant to profits and assets, but stockholders do not usually manage the firm, generally do not have any particular loyalty to the firm, and can easily dissolve their role by a telephone call to a stockbroker. Are the managers the firm? As a rule they probably have a larger personal stake in the firm than the stockholders, although they too are free to change jobs. Should the workers, lenders, suppliers, customers, or public be considered part of the firm? Organization theorists are debating these issues.

With less certainty about what groups constitute the firm, there has been considerable controversy over what the goals of the firm are and should be. Within the last forty years, there has been a strong current of thought that managers are the dominant group within the firm. It follows from this that we can best understand the goals of the firm by understanding the goals of management. Thus, it is argued, the prime goal of the firm is not profits but rather sales growth, power, economic security—all goals that are conducive to the well-being of management.[6] Critics of the large corporations are thus inclined to view the firm as catering to the desires of a self-perpetuating oligarchy of managers rather than to profits or needs of the public.[7] However, the experience of the last decade should have led to a reassessment of our views of the management-dominated firm. The power of management to pursue its own goals is ultimately based on the dispersion of common stockholders and their inability to threaten managers with loss of jobs if they do not maximize profit. But with the growth of mutual funds and new techniques for taking over a firm against the will of its managers, we could argue that power is swinging away from the managers to the stockholders.[8]

[6]See Oliver Williamson, *The Economics of Discretionary Behavior* (Englewood Cliffs, N.J.: Prentice-Hall, 1964).

[7]This is one of Galbraith's main themes. See John K. Galbraith, *The New Industrial State* (Boston: Houghton Mifflin, 1967).

[8]See Editors of *Fortune*, *The Conglomerate Commotion* (New York: Viking Press, 1970).

With many not sure where ultimate power lies in corporations and consequently with much debate about the firm's objectives, some organization theorists are inclined to view the firm as a coalition. Stockholders, different categories of management, lenders, and to some extent workers, suppliers, customers, and even the public are viewed as coalescing to achieve their diverse objectives. In effect these groups "bargain," as a condition of being part of the coalition, about how the firm will meet their different objectives. The concept of a coalition with bargaining among the members is valuable, but there is still much to be learned about how the bargaining takes place and what factors determine the conditions of the coalition.

One useful development in studies of coalitions has been the notion of organizational slack. If we think of each party to the coalition requiring some minimum objective met by the coalition as a condition of its joining the coalition, then the slack can be thought of as some kind of "payment" to the various parties above the minimum amount necessary to keep them part of the coalition. Slack induces loyalty to the firm and enables the coalition to survive when the firm runs into difficulties.[9]

If every group insists that its own objective be maximized to the detriment of the objectives of others, there can be great difficulty in forming a coalition; in fact it may be impossible. Instead, we could think of each group as having a minimum requirement – a rate of growth of profits (stockholders), a rate of growth of sales (sales managers), a maximum degree of risk (lenders), a minimum expenditure on research (research managers), a minimum wage rate (workers), a minimum degree of service to customers (service managers). As we showed in Chapter 3, it is possible to have these minimum target goals and still have one open-ended goal to be maximized. We can argue that this goal should be the maximization of the growth of the "going concern" value of the corporation: Profit maximization in the short run is generally consistent with this long-run goal. The argument for this open-ended goal is that it is the one most likely to lead to the payments of "slack" to the members of the coalition, which in turn keeps the coalition together as a viable entity. In our decision models, the minimum target goals of the various members of the coalition can enter the models as self-imposed constraints on the prime goal(s) of short-run profit maximization and long-run maximization of the "going concern" value of the firm.

"Within Organization" Constraints. Most organizations are managed by setting up subsystems within the organization and assigning them goals consistent with the goals of the organization. However, there is almost always a problem of coordinating the subsystems so

[9]The notion of "slack" is developed in R. Cyert and J. March, *A Behavioral Theory of the Firm* (Englewood Cliffs, N.J.: Prentice-Hall, 1963).

that one, in pursuing its goal, does not unduly interfere with the goal pursuits of others. This coordination effort can be made by the top managers (the peak coordinators) placing constraints on the various subsystems.[10] The budget is one means of imposing these constraints; a related method is the allocation of fixed inputs to the various subsystems. A fixed target goal determined by one subsystem of a firm can become a constraint on another part of the firm. The setting and monitoring of goals and the imposition of these constraints are the essence of management and the development of systems and organizations.

BARRIERS TO ENTRY AND KNOWLEDGE CONSTRAINTS

We may ask why a firm, at least in the long run, does not consider going into every market. Its considerations of markets and products may be limited for two main reasons—entry barriers and lack of knowledge.

Even in a predominantly market system, entry barriers are widespread. Sometimes government imposes these barriers to entry, either directly or indirectly. A firm is barred from many activities without government sanction—broadcasting, transportation, the provision of medical services, various phases of agriculture. Sometimes entry is barred by governments giving monopolies to others, most often by patents and by the granting of direct licenses. But perhaps the main source of entry barriers is the activities of firms, sometimes in collusion with labor unions. Many large firms try to gain control of raw materials in particular and to preempt markets by tying customers to long-term contracts or by merging with them. Sometimes groups of firms restrict entry through joint action, by cross-licensing patent pools, by placing pressure on suppliers not to sell to new entrants. Even when direct barriers are not imposed, firms within an industry purposefully make it very costly for new entrants. The requirements of U.S. automobile manufacturers that dealers not handle any other makes, for example, placed the additional burden on a prospective entrant into the automobile manufacturing business of developing a network of dealers.

Lack of knowledge can also inhibit firms' entry to new markets. The production of most products and the structure and mode of operation of most markets have their peculiar individual quirks, and it is in fact difficult for firms outside an industry to accurately know what its production function or demand curve will be. However, a firm can obtain this special knowledge, by hiring away key personnel from other firms or, an increasingly common phenomenon, by gain-

[10]See Herbert A. Simon, *Administrative Behavior* (New York: Macmillan, 1957).

ing control of an established firm in the market it wishes to enter. Knowledge becomes more critical as the economy moves toward the production of sophisticated products. But with education and free labor markets, knowledge is more easily transmitted to firms that want to enter new markets.

Discussion Questions

1. Enumerate and discuss the different actions a firm can take to reduce the effectiveness of competitors and to eliminate them. Might some of these actions appear to be normal business practice? How might the courts distinguish between normal business practice and a positive attempt to monopolize and control a market?

2. Why is government regulation of natural monopolies a universal practice?

3. Using the models developed in previous chapters, demonstrate how subsidies to firms in purely competitive markets, where the subsidies are proportional to output, might reduce market prices.

4. Evaluate "slack" as a way to keep an organization viable.

5. In what ways do education, information, and the diffusion of technology make markets more competitive?

13 A Framework for Dealing with Risk and Uncertainty

In Chapters 5 and 6, we assumed that the model firm knew its constraint parameters with a high degree of certainty, although we pointed out in various chapters that the firm faces difficulties when estimating these parameters. Some of the constraint parameters—particularly the production functions, fixity constraints, self-imposed constraints, and current legally imposed constraints—are generally readily known to the firm. Other constraint parameters, though at times known with a high degree of certainty in an immediate period, are often difficult to forecast. Perhaps the most difficult constraint parameters to forecast are those for the demand curves facing the firm for its outputs and those for the supply curves facing the firm for its inputs.

In this chapter we consider the problems of decision-making when decisions have to be made before it is clear what the constraint parameters will be. Decision-making under risk and uncertainty is a complex, specialized field with a vast, recent literature. We will therefore be able to give no more than an introduction to this subject.[1]

FORMULATION OF THE PROBLEM

We have learned enough about constraints on the firm, particularly the demand curves facing it for its outputs and the supply curves

---

[1]Several textbooks are devoted entirely to decision-making under uncertainty. See, for example, Ira Horowitz, *Introduction to Quantitative Business Analysis* (New York: McGraw-Hill, 1965).

facing it for its inputs, to know that the parameters of these constraints can be influenced by many forces over which the firm can
exercise no or little control. Among these forces are levels of income
of buyers, prices of rivals, tastes, government policies, new technologies. If the firm does not know what these forces—or events, as
we shall call them—will be, and if the firm must determine its various
short-run and long-run decisions before the manifestation of these
events, it must make decisions and commitments without complete
knowledge of the parameters of its constraints.

The firm can take two basic approaches to its problem of making
decisions when faced with an uncertain future. One is to estimate the
set of events most likely to occur, translate the events into the constraint parameters, and then take action. A second approach is to
survey alternative sets of events, translating each alternative set
into constraint parameters, formulating alternative actions (strategies), and assessing the consequences of all combinations of events
and strategies. By then analyzing the consequences associated with
each particular strategy under all sets of events, the firm can devise
some rule with which to select one of the strategies.

For two good reasons the second approach is to be preferred. One
reason is based on the asymmetry of the penalties associated with
being wrong on the choice of a strategy. The firm can be said to be
wrong if it bases its decisions on one set of events and another set of
events materializes. Various penalties can be attached to being
wrong. If, for example, the firm expects its demand curve to be more
favorable than it turns out to be, its price may turn out to be too high
to sell all the firm thought could be sold, inventories could pile up, too
many inputs would have been purchased, and so on. These errors
have costs attached to them, which would reduce profits and cash
flow or lead to losses. If, on the other hand, the firm underestimates
the favorability of its demand curve, it asks too low a price, loses sales
because it has not produced enough, has dissatisfied customers. The
penalty in this case is not a direct decrease in cash flow but a loss of
cash flow that the firm could have had.

Because the penalties of being wrong in the "overage" case may
differ substantially from the penalties of being wrong in the "under-
age" case, we may not want to base a decision on the most likely set of
events. Say that an automobile dealer, on the basis of past experience,
estimates that he can sell five cars in a given month about 25 percent
of the time, six cars about 50 percent of the time, and seven cars
about 25 percent of the time. If he based his decision of how many
cars to order from the factory on the most likely number he could
sell, he would order six. But let us add some further information. The
carrying cost of an unsold car is $50 per month, and the profit from a
sale is $500. The penalty of having too many cars is then $50 per car,
and the penalty of not having enough cars is $500 for every car
that he could have sold if he had had it in stock. It is not clear at all
now that he should order six cars; seven would seem to be the right
amount.

A second reason for assessing all the penalties of being wrong has to do with the flexibility of the firm's decisions. A firm may make a contract with a supplier regarding how much it may be required to take. If the firm is willing to commit itself to a large quantity during an upcoming period of time, it may be able to get a low price. On the other hand, at the cost of a higher price, the firm may have more options and flexibility on the quantity it can obtain. Flexibility can have an important bearing on the magnitude of the penalties of selecting the wrong set of decisions. If the penalties of being wrong are great with the inflexible contract, the firm would be well advised to opt for the more flexible contract.

In light of these arguments, in this chapter we will follow the second approach. The basic procedure of this method is to determine the alternative sets of events that can occur, estimate the relative likelihood of the occurrence of these alternative sets of events, devise alternative strategies, estimate the payoff or penalty that would result from each combination of a strategy and set of events, and select the best strategy by applying some "decision rule."

There is a clear distinction between decision-making subject to risk and decision-making subject to uncertainty.[2] The term "risk" refers to situations in which the firm is able to estimate tolerably well the probabilities of the occurrence of alternative events. Probabilities can be deductively worked out for various games of chance. But for most business problems, probabilities have to be inductively determined by the study of past data. If the firm's sales depend on the weather, for example, an analysis of past data on rainfall in a particular month enables an assignment of probabilities to the alternative numbers of rainy days in a particular month. An analysis of monthly changes in prices in the past enables us to assign probabilities to various percentage price changes from one month to the next. The probabilities of machine breakdowns, defective products, fires, and so forth are readily determined by an analysis of historical data.

We say that the firm's decisions are subject to uncertainty when assigning a probability to an event is very difficult. A new invention, an earthquake, discovery of a new natural resource, can occur with no pattern that is discernible from past data. Perhaps the most common source of uncertainty to the firm is actions taken by recognized rivals—especially in an oligopolistic market structure. A change in a price by a rival, its styling of a product, its decision to merge with another company, are all events that could affect the model firm. Yet assessing the likelihood of such events may be difficult, especially if they are taken to consciously affect the model firm.

Events that may have been uncertain in the past—that is, not amenable to a probability assessment—could become subject to

[2]Economists have tended to follow this distinction since the publication of Frank Knight, *Risk, Uncertainty, and Profit* (Chicago: University of Chicago Press, Phoenix Books, 1971); originally published in 1921.

probability assessment. As we learn more about the world through research and experience and as we accumulate data, we increase our ability to make tolerably good assessments of probabilities of the occurrence of events. With this expansion of knowledge, we suspect that to an increasing extent most business decision-making is subject to risk rather than to uncertainty.

THE PAYOFF MATRIX
AND DECISION RULES

All information necessary for decision-making, under either risk or uncertainty, can be assembled in what is known as a payoff matrix, which is a two-way classification of all the different payoffs that can occur with every combination of a "state-of-the-world" and a strategy. The states-of-the-world represent different sets of events that might occur. The events might be a price on the market, the change in income of buyers or of the price of a rival, a war, an action by a government. The strategies are the various sets of decisions the firm could make. They could be short-run decisions pertaining to prices or outputs or long-run decisions pertaining to the acquisition or sale of assets. The payoffs are the criterion variables we have been using in our various decision models. For short-run decisions, the payoffs would be either the cash flow or profit; for long-run decisions, the payoffs could be the expected change in the "going concern" value of the firm. Although not technically a part of the payoff matrix, part of the format consists of the likelihood, or probability, of the occurrence of the alternative states-of-the-world.

	States-of-the-world				
	θ_1	θ_2	$\cdots$	θ_j $\cdots$	θ_n
S_1	Z_{11}	Z_{12}		Z_{ij}	Z_{1n}
S_2	Z_{21}	Z_{22}		Z_{2j}	Z_{2n}
$\vdots$					
S_i	Z_{i1}	Z_{i2}		Z_{ij}	Z_{in}
$\vdots$					
S_m	Z_{m1}	Z_{m2}		Z_{mj}	Z_{mn}
Probabilities	$\Pr(\theta_1)$	$\Pr(\theta_2)$		$\Pr(\theta_j)$	$\Pr(\theta_n)$

Strategies

FIGURE 13.1   Format of the payoff matrix

Figure 13.1 provides the general form of the payoff matrix. With $\theta_1, \theta_2, \ldots, \theta_j, \ldots, \theta_n$ representing alternative states of the world, we have each column of the matrix headed by a particular theta. The $S_1, S_2, \ldots, S_j, \ldots, S_m$ represent the alternative strategies, each one heading a row of the matrix. We have written m strategies and n states-of-the-world to emphasize the fact that there need not be the same number of strategies as states-of-the-world. The columns and rows form the elements, or cells, of the matrix, and for m strategies and n states-of-the-world, there will be m times n elements. Each cell represents, of course, the combination of a particular S and θ. Within each cell we have the payoff associated with a particular S,θ combination. Thus, with Z representing cash flow, Z_{11} would be the cash flow if S_1 were chosen and θ_1 occurred, Z_{12} would be the cash flow if S_1 were chosen and θ_2 occurred, and, to generalize, Z_{ij} would be the cash flow if S_i were chosen and θ_j occurred. Although we use cash flows here, in long-run decision-making instead of Z we would have ΔV_0, the change in the "going concern" value of the firm. The bottom row – which is not part of the matrix – gives the probabilities of the various θs occurring. Thus, the symbol $Pr(\theta_j)$ represents the probability of the occurrence of the jth state-of-the-world.

Events and States-of-the-World. The firm must identify all the major events that can substantially influence its constraint parameters. Combinations of these events then define the various states-of-the-world.

GENERAL AND SPECIFIC EVENTS. In the English language there is no term to distinguish a class of events from the individual events that constitute that class. We will therefore have to use the expression "general events" to mean the class of events and the expression "specific events" to represent the individual events.

The best way to discuss the difference between general and specific events is with examples. Consider the economic activity of the country, which is measured by GNP. The level of GNP may be the general event that influences the firm's demand curve. The number of alternative GNPs that could occur are the specific events. These specific events could be given in great detail – for example GNP = $1150 billion, $1151 billion, etc. But in the real world we often cannot work with this much detail, and we might instead define the specific events as $1150 billion–$1160 billion, $1160 billion–$1170 billion, etc., or even "boom," "steady growth," "recession."

Another type of general event could be the prices of other firms. Again the specific events could be the actual alternative prices ($10, $11, $12, etc.), ranges of prices ($10–$15, $15–$20, etc.), or even the direction of movement (up 5 percent, no change, down 5 percent). Sometimes the specific events could be a "yes" or "no." Say, for example, the government *may* take some action that will affect the firm's demand curve. The *type* of action is the general event; "yes" or "no" is the specific event.

We can use symbols to designate the different events: E is an event; the first subscript designates the general type of event, and the second subscript designates the specific event:

General and specific events	Symbol
State of the economy	E_1
Recession	E_{11}
Steady growth	E_{12}
Boom	E_{13}
Prices of competitor's product	E_2
Up 5 percent	E_{21}
No change	E_{22}
Down 5 percent	E_{23}
Passage of law	E_3
Yes	E_{31}
No	E_{32}

NATURE AND OPPONENTS. Events can also be divided on the basis of whether they are independent of, or interdependent with, the firm's policies. Independent events have little or nothing to do with the firm and are in no way aimed at the firm. Examples might be level of GNP, the price in another market, new inventions. Other events could be aimed at the firm, most importantly the price behavior of a recognized rival in an oligopolistic market structure.

When the events are not particularly aimed at the firm, we can call them "nature," but when they are aimed at the firm we can call them "opponents." Decision-making varies greatly, depending on whether the events are of nature or opponents. Nature is not out to make life difficult for our model firm, so nature's events can be assessed for their likelihood and will not change as the result of our model firm's policies. However, when the events are those of opponents, it is difficult to assign probabilities to them, for opponents are trying to outguess the model firm and have much to gain through misinformation about what they will do. Moreover, probabilities of the events of opponents cannot be considered to be stable, because opponents could react to our model firm's decisions.

MUTUAL EXCLUSIVENESS AND INDEPENDENCE OF EVENTS. It is important that the specific events within a general event class be defined as mutually exclusive of each other, in the sense that only one of the specific events could occur. We have done this with our three examples. We can, for example, have a boom, steady growth, or recession in the state-of-the-economy general event, but we cannot have any two occurring simultaneously. We could, however, make an error of this type if, along with the "yes" and "no" specific events in the passage of the law, we add a "maybe."

Specific events in different general event classes may or may not be independent of each other. If, for example, the passage of a law has nothing to do with the state of the economy or price of competitors, we would say these different events are independent. Sometimes, however, a specific event in one general event class may influence the likelihood of the specific events in another general event class. It may, for example, be more likely that competitors will raise prices if the state of the economy is "boom" than if there is steady growth or recession.

STATES-OF-THE-WORLD AS COMBINATIONS OF EVENTS. Assume that the firm has identified the three general events in our earlier example and that the specific events that have been identified for each general event class exhaust the possibilities of things that can happen. Under this assumption a state-of-the-world can be defined as the joint occurrence of a specific event from each general event class. With three specific events in "state of the economy" and "price of competitor's product," and two specific events in "passage of law," there will be $3 \times 3 \times 2$, or 18, states-of-the-world. These states-of-the-world can be defined in this way:

$$\theta_1 = E_{11}, E_{21}, E_{31}$$
$$\theta_2 = E_{11}, E_{22}, E_{31}$$
$$\theta_3 = E_{11}, E_{23}, E_{31}$$
$$\theta_4 = E_{12}, E_{21}, E_{31}$$

.
.
.

$$\theta_{18} = E_{13}, E_{23}, E_{32}$$

The Likelihoods of the States-of-the-World. The probability, or likelihood, of any particular θ depends on the joint probability of the specific events that constitute that θ. There are two variations on the calculations of the θ probability, which depends on whether the specific events are independent, or interdependent.

Let us consider first the case where the events are independent. For any event class determined by nature, it is necessary to our methodology to assign a probability of the occurrence of each specific event. A probability is the percent, or proportion, of the time that we expect a specific event to occur. The simplest probabilities occur in games of chance, which can be mathematically worked out. What, for example, is the probability of drawing a club from a regular deck of fifty-two cards? Obviously it is 0.25. The probabilities for the specific events in economics are not so easily obtained. They could involve analysis of past events, sampling of opinion, judgment.

If the specific events exhaust all the possibilities of a given general event class, then the probabilities assigned to the specific events must total 1. In the card example, if we define the specific events as the drawing of a spade, heart, diamond, or club, then it is obvious that the probabilities of all these events total 1. In our earlier example of the three general events, the specific events in each general event class must equal 1. Thus we have

$$Pr(E_{11}) + Pr(E_{12}) + Pr(E_{13}) = 1$$
$$Pr(E_{21}) + Pr(E_{22}) + Pr(E_{23}) = 1$$
$$Pr(E_{31}) + Pr(E_{32}) = 1$$

In probability theory, the joint probability of the occurrence of two or more independent events is obtained through the multiplication of the probabilities for the individual events. Thus, the joint probability of drawing a club from a deck of cards and tossing heads in the flip of a coin is $(1/4)(1/2) = 1/8$. To get the joint probabilities of the various states-of-the world, we multiply the probabilities of the specific events that constitute that state-of-the-world. Thus, for example, if we define θ_1 as the occurrence of E_{11}, E_{21}, and E_{31}, the probability of θ_1 occurring is

$$Pr(\theta_1) = Pr(E_{11})Pr(E_{21})Pr(E_{31}).$$

The probabilities of all other states-of-the-world are similarly obtained. The probabilities of all the states-of-the-world, when added together, total 1. This can be written as

$$Pr(\theta_1) + Pr(\theta_2) + \ldots + Pr(\theta_{18}) = 1.$$

When the probability of the occurrence of one event depends on the occurrence of another event, we have what is known as conditional probability. If, in our example, the occurrence of a competitor's price decrease, E_{23}, depends on the state of the economy, we would have three different conditional probabilities for E_{23}, depending on whether E_{11}, E_{12}, or E_{13} occurred. We write these conditional probabilities as $Pr(E_{23}|E_{11})$, $Pr(E_{23}|E_{12})$, $Pr(E_{23}|E_{13})$. These are read in this way: $Pr(E_{23}|E_{11})$ is the probability that E_{23} will occur if E_{11} occurs, etc.

The conditional probabilities of the "conditioned" events for any "conditioning" event must add to $1 -$ if we assume the conditioned events exhaust all the possibilities. Thus we have

$$Pr(E_{21}|E_{11}) + Pr(E_{22}|E_{11}) + Pr(E_{23}|E_{11}) = 1$$
$$Pr(E_{21}|E_{12}) + Pr(E_{22}|E_{12}) + Pr(E_{23}|E_{12}) = 1$$
$$Pr(E_{21}|E_{13}) + Pr(E_{22}|E_{13}) + Pr(E_{23}|E_{13}) = 1$$

The probability of any θ is obtained as before, except that we use the conditional probability for the conditioned event, which depends on which conditioning event is in that θ. Thus, if $\theta_1 = E_{11}$, E_{21}, E_{31}, the probability of θ_1 is

$$Pr(\theta_1) = Pr(E_{11})Pr(E_{21}|E_{11})Pr(E_{31}).$$

Similarly the probability of θ_4, if it is comprised of E_{12}, E_{21}, and E_{31}, is

$$Pr(\theta_4) = Pr(E_{12})Pr(E_{21}|E_{12})Pr(E_{31}).$$

The probabilities of all θs will still add to 1.

The States-of-the-World and the Constraint Parameters. For any state-of-the-world, which consists of a set of events, there will be a unique set of values for the firm's constraint parameters. The firm should know enough about the constraints to be able to estimate these parameters once it has postulated the occurrence of a set of events. In the real world this is a difficult task, but good decision-making requires the firm to be able to make tolerably good estimates. The techniques we have developed in Chapters 8 through 10 should prove helpful in this task.

Formulation of the Strategies. Having identified and formulated the various states-of-the-world, after which they are translated into the constraint parameters, our next step is to formulate the strategies.

SHORT-RUN STRATEGIES. Given a state-of-the-world, there should be an optimal corresponding strategy. The techniques developed in Chapter 5 are applicable to the calculation of optimal strategies, which would consist of a set of optimal values for the short-run decision variables. There would be a different optimal strategy for every state-of-the-world. For convenience we could designate S_1 as the optimal strategy for θ_1, S_2 as the optimal strategy for θ_2, etc.

If a firm were simply a profit-maximizer, then one of these optimal strategies could be shown to be the best under the main decision rule to be developed for decision-making under risk. Thus, we would have to formulate only optimal strategies for the various θs, so that the number of strategies would equal the number of θs.

However, if we introduce the possibility that the firm may want to stabilize earnings or avoid a loss or very low profits, the firm may be willing to consider strategies in which the risks are not too great. Consider, for example, the simple case where there are two θs and where S_1 gives a Z of \$1000 if θ_1 materializes and a Z of \$0 if θ_2 materializes, while S_2 gives a Z of \$0 if θ_1 materializes and a Z of \$1000 if θ_2 materializes. In both strategies, the "expected values" of the strategies are \$500 if θ_1 and θ_2 have the same probability of occurrence. If, now, it is possible to devise a strategy somewhere "between" S_1 and S_2 that yields a Z of \$400 if *either* θ occurs, the firm may prefer the less risky (though on the average less profitable) strategy. Because of this possibility, it is desirable to add to the optimal strategies (one for each θ) a number of nonoptimal strategies that lie "between" the optimal strategies. If, for example, the S_1 strategy is $P = 50$, $Q = 100$, and the S_2 strategy is $P = 30$, $Q = 150$, a possibly desirable nonoptimal strategy might be $P = 40$, $Q = 120$.

LONG-RUN STRATEGIES. In Chapter 6, we pointed out that because there can be a virtually infinite number of choices, there can be no single optimal long-run strategy—even if everything were known with certainty. We therefore suggested that the firm should consider a substantial number of "good candidate" long-run investment programs. With uncertainty, we would still devise as many long-run investment strategies as possible. Although there is no optimal strategy for any particular θ, it is nevertheless useful to survey the alternative θs when formulating the different long-run strategies. Such a survey can narrow the list of "promising" investment programs.

The Payoffs. The payoffs for this decision-making technique must be calculated for each S,θ combination. It will be helpful to consider the short run and long run separately, though we will devote most of our attention to a short-run problem.

THE SHORT RUN. The short-run payoffs are most conveniently calculated in terms of Z, the cash flows. They are comparatively simple to calculate for the elements in the matrix where an optimal strategy corresponds to a particular θ. But when the "wrong" theta occurs for some given strategy, it is necessary to assess what the firm could do.

Let us say that there are only two θs and that the demand curve for θ_1 is $P = 100 - 0.5Q$, while for θ_2 it is only $P = 50 - 0.5Q$. Let us assume that the marginal cost of a unit of output is \$10. Then, for θ_1, the optimal strategy is to equate marginal revenue with marginal cost and calculate the optimum price and quantity. The MR of the θ_1 demand curve is calculated in this way:

$$R = Q(100 - 0.5Q) = 100Q - 0.5Q^2$$
$$MR = \frac{dR}{dQ} = 100 - Q.$$

Setting this equal to MC of \$10, gives

$$100 - Q = 10$$
$$Q = 90.$$

Inserting this value of Q in the θ_1 demand curve gives a price of $P = 100 - 0.5(90) = \$55$. Thus the optimal strategy for θ_1, the S_1, is $P = 55$, $Q = 90$. The cash flow is clearly

$$Z = PQ - 10(Q) = (55)(90) - (10)(90) = \$4050.$$

Let us now determine what Z would be if the θ_2 demand curve materialized after the firm had selected the S_1 strategy. The firm may be able to do a number of different things when the wrong θ occurs. As one possible option (option 1), it may decide to lower the price to the level that would "move" the full 90 units. As a second option, it may keep the S_1 price and sell the unsold output in the next period, perhaps at a "distress" price. This would involve some carrying costs. As a third possibility, it may pick some price that would sell more of the Q than could be sold at the S_1 price and sell the remainder in the later period at the distress price.

If option 1 were selected, the firm would use the θ_2 demand curve to pick a new price. Thus, with this demand curve,

$$P = 50 - 0.5Q,$$

with $Q = 90$, the price would be \$5. The cash flow from option 1 is then

$$Z = (5)(90) - (10)(90) = -\$450.$$

Let us say that in option 2 the distress price is \$10 for the unsold merchandise. Then, with the initial price set at \$55, the θ_2 demand curve tells us that nothing can be sold. The full 90 units will then have to be sold at \$10, so that the total cash inflow is \$900. One part of the cash outflow is still the \$900 in production costs. If, say, there are \$2 carrying costs per unit of output (storage and interest payments), there is an additional cash outflow of \$180. Thus, the net cash flow from this option is

$$Z = 900 - 900 - 180 = -\$180.$$

Let us consider a third possibility. Say the firm lowers the price to \$30, sells all it can at that price, and then dumps whatever is left at the \$10 distress price. Then with the θ_2 demand curve, the quantity that can be sold at $P = 30$ is

$$30 = 50 - 0.5Q$$
$$Q = 40.$$

The cash inflow from regular sales is then $(30)(40) = \$1,200$. The cash inflow from the distress sales is $(10)(50) = \$500$. The cash outflow from production is still \$900, while the cash outflow from the carrying costs is $(2)(50) = \$100$. The net cash flow from this third option is then

$$Z = 1,200 + 500 - 900 - 100 = \$700.$$

Obviously, the third option is best.

It is possible to devise an optimal strategy after it is clear that the wrong θ has occurred. Say the firm selects $P = \$55$ and $Q = 90$ on the expectation that the demand curve will be $P = 100 - 0.5Q$. But say that the demand curve turns out to be $P = 50 - 0.5Q$. If the firm is locked in to the 90-unit output but has some flexibility with regard to price, it can decide the best price and quantity in the immediate period and the quantity to be sold in the later period at the distress price.

Following our example, let Q_r be the quantity to be sold in the immediate period and Q_d the quantity sold in the later period. The price to be charged in the immediate period is P, and the distress price continues to be \$10. Let us continue to assume that production costs are \$900 and that the carrying cost of the unsold units is \$2 per unit. Then the cash-flow equation can be written as

$$Z = PQ_r + 10Q_d - 900 - 2Q_d.$$

The first right-hand term is the cash inflow from goods sold in the immediate period; the second right-hand term is the cash inflow from the distress sales; the third right-hand term is the production costs (which are fixed in this context); and the last right-hand term is the cash outflow from the carrying costs.

Noticing that $P = 50 - 0.5Q_r$, and that $Q_r + Q_d = 90$, we can use these relations to express Z in terms only of Q_r. Thus, we have

$$Z = (50 - 0.5Q_r)Q_r + 10(90 - Q_r) - 900 - 2(90 - Q_r),$$

which can be multiplied out as

$$Z = 500Q_r - 0.5Q_r^2 + 900 - 10Q_r - 900 - 180 + 2Q_r.$$

We can now optimize the value of Z with respect to Q_r by taking the first derivative of Z, setting this equal to zero, and solving for Q_r:

$$\frac{dZ}{dQ} = 50 - Q_r - 10 + 2 = 0$$

$$Q_r = 42.$$

Thus, 42 is the optimum quantity to be sold in the immediate period, with 48 the quantity to be sold at the distress price. By placing 42 for Q in the θ_2 demand curve, $P = 50 - 0.5(Q)$, we find the optimal price to ask is $29. The cash flow in this case would be

$$Z = (29)(42) + (10)(48) - 900 - 2(48) = \$702.$$

This is the best that can be done.

This rather long exercise is designed to stress one point: The payoff to the firm when the wrong θ occurs for a particular strategy depends very much on the firm's options and flexibility. When S_1 is selected and θ_2 occurs, the $S_1\theta_2$ payoff is $702 – under the assumption the firm does the best it can with its options. We can go even further and measure the value to the firm of a flexible price policy. If it has to stick to the S_1 price of $55, it has a negative cash flow of $450; but with full flexibility, the cash flow is positive at $702. We can thus say that in this situation the price flexibility is worth $1152 to the firm.

Let us now consider the optimal S_2 strategy. With the θ_2 demand curve $P = 50 - 0.5Q$, and MC still $10, we have Z as

$$Z = (50 - 0.5Q)Q - 10Q.$$

The optimal value of Q is found in this way:

$$Z = 50Q - 0.5Q^2 - 10Q$$

$$\frac{dZ}{dQ} = 50 - Q - 10 = 0$$

$$Q = 40$$

Substituting $Q = 40$ in $P = 50 - 0.5Q$, we see that the optimal P is 30. Thus the optimal S_2 for θ_2 is $P = 30$, $Q = 40$, and the cash flow is

$$Z = (30)(40) - (10)(40) = \$800.$$

What if S_2 were selected but the θ_1 demand curve, $P = 100 - 0.5Q$, materializes? Then if the firm keeps the price at $30, it could sell

$$30 = 100 - 0.5Q$$
$$Q = 140.$$

But it only has 40 units to sell, so its cash inflow remains at $800. On the other hand, if the firm changes its price to get the highest possible price for its 40 units of output, it will charge

$$P = 100 - 0.5Q = 100 - 0.5(40) = \$80.$$

Its net cash flow is now

$$Z = (80)(40) - (10)(40) = \$2800.$$

If it selects its best option, the $S_2\theta_1$ payoff is then $2800.

We now have enough information on the payoffs to construct the payoff matrix for this simple illustration. It is shown in Figure 13.2.

An important lesson in this example stems from the flexibility the firm has when the wrong θ occurs. In calculating the $S_1\theta_2$ payoff, we had assumed a distress price of $10 for the output not sold during the regular period. If, however, we had assumed a higher distress price, say $15 or $20, the $S_1\theta_2$ payoff would have been greater than the $S_2\theta_2$ payoff. This brings up the question of whether S_2 is really the optimal strategy for θ_2. It may or may not be, depending on the flexibility the firm has in adjusting to the "wrong" parameters.

THE LONG RUN. The long-run payoffs are much more difficult to calculate than those of the short run. The events constituting the states-of-the-world for the long run would generally consist of various trends. Thus as alternative specific events for "state of the economy," we might have GNP growth at 3 percent per year or 4 percent per year, etc., or the output price rises by various percentages over long periods of time. The payoffs would be calculated as the expected changes in the "going concern" values of the firm. The payoffs must consider the range of flexibility the firm may have when the wrong θ materializes. In the long run, the penalties for too high a level of investment are the fixed costs for assets that are not fully utilized. The penalties for too low a level of investment are high variable costs and lost sales.

		States-of-the-world	
		θ_2	θ_1
Strategies	$S_1(P = 55, Q = 90)$	4,050	702
	$S_2(P = 30, Q = 42)$	2,800	800

FIGURE 13.2   Illustrative payoff matrix

The Regret Matrix. In our construction of the payoff matrix, we have thus far used cash flows for the short-run payoffs and changes in "going concern" value for the long-run payoffs. In calculating the short-run cash flows we are not able to take into account one "cost of being wrong" in the calculations of the payoffs—namely, the "missed opportunity" of not selling all that could have been sold. Missed opportunities do not show up in a payoff matrix, but we can capture them in what is known as a regret matrix.

Ths missed opportunity can be calculated as the difference between the payoff for a "wrong" strategy for a given θ and the payoff for the "correct" optimal strategy for that same θ. If an automobile dealer ordered only five cars (his strategy) but could have sold seven, then he loses whatever profit he could have made on the two cars he could have sold but did not have in stock. The cash-flow matrix does not show such lost opportunities.

To illustrate the construction of the regret matrix, which is derived from the payoff matrix, let us construct a simple example based on the car dealer. Say he knows that he could sell either five, six, or seven cars. The five, six, or seven that could be sold would then constitute the alternative states-of-the-world, and ordering five, six, or seven could constitute the dealer's strategies. Let us say his net cash inflow per sold car is $500 and his carrying cost on an unsold car is $50. Then the payoff matrix in Figure 13.3 shows the cash flows associated with the various S,θ combinations.

What are the complete costs of being wrong—that is, of selecting the wrong strategy for a given θ? If the dealer orders six but can sell only five, his cost of error is $50. These costs are adequately reflected in the payoff matrix because there are actual cash outflows to measure the cost of being wrong. Consider now the possibility that he orders five but could sell seven. Now there is no cash outflow, but the dealer has lost the opportunity to make an additional $1000 in cash flow. This loss can be called an opportunity cost.

The regret matrix, which reflects the opportunity costs as well as the costs measured by cash outflow, is easily derived from the payoff matrix. What is the cost of being wrong if a particular θ materializes? It is the difference between the payoffs of selecting a "wrong" rather

		States-of-the-world		
		θ_1 (sell 5)	θ_2 (sell 6)	θ_3 (sell 7)
	S_1 (order 5)	2,500	2,500	2,500
Strategies	S_2 (order 6)	2,450	3,000	3,000
	S_3 (order 7)	2,400	2,950	3,500

FIGURE 13.3   Hypothetical payoff matrix

than "right" strategy. Thus, in Figure 13.3, if θ_1 occurs, the right strategy is S_1, in which event the payoff is $2500. But if the firm selects S_3, the payoff is only $2400. The difference, or $100, is the "cost of being wrong" – that is, selecting S_3 instead of S_1. To calculate the cost of being wrong for all S,θ combinations, we work with each θ, which represents a column. The cost of being wrong is calculated for each element in that column as the difference between the maximum payoff in the column and the payoff for a particular element in the same column. Figure 13.4 gives the regret matrix based on the payoff matrix of Figure 13.3. Notice that in the regret matrix the "regret" is zero when the "right" strategy has been selected for a given θ. Also notice that both types of "costs of being wrong" are captured in this regret matrix – the carrying costs of the overage (ordering too many cars) and the opportunity costs of the underage (ordering too few cars).

		States-of-the-world		
		θ_1	θ_2	θ_3
	S_1	0	500	1,000
Strategies	S_2	50	0	500
	S_3	100	50	0

FIGURE 13.4   Hypothetical regret matrix

Decision Rules. A decision rule can be defined as some basis on which to select a strategy after the payoff and regret matrices have been completed. The selection of decision rules is governed largely by whether the θs are determined by nature or by active opponents. When nature determines the θs, the firm can estimate the probabilities of the different thetas without concerning itself that nature will react in any way to the firm's decisions. But when the θs are determined by recognized rivals, the firm may not be tolerably able to estimate the probabilities because the rivals may be trying to out-guess, bluff, and misinform our model firm. In this section, we treat only the case in which nature determines the θs.

The main, but not exclusive, decision rules are to select the strategy that maximizes the "expected value" of the payoffs or minimizes the expected value of the regrets. The expected payoff value of a strategy is obtained by multiplying each possible payoff by the probability of that payoff (obtained from the probability of the associated θ) and then adding the results. This tells what the payoff would be "on the average" if that strategy were selected. The expected regret value of a strategy is similarly determined.

Let us use the payoff matrix in Figure 13.3 and the regret matrix in Figure 13.4 to illustrate the calculation of the expected values of the various strategies. Assume that the probabilities of θ_1, θ_2, and θ_3 are, respectively, 0.4, 0.5, and 0.1. Then the expected values of S_1, S_2, and S_3 from Figure 13.3 are

$$E(S_1) = (0.4)(2,500) + (0.5)(2,500) + (0.1)(2,500) = \$2500$$
$$E(S_2) = (0.4)(2,450) + (0.5)(3,000) + (0.1)(3,000) = \$2780$$
$$E(S_3) = (0.4)(2,400) + (0.5)(2,950) + (0.1)(3,500) = \$2785$$

The expected values of the strategies from the regret matrix are

$$E(S_1) = (0.4)(0) + (0.5)(500) + (0.1)(1,000) = 350$$
$$E(S_2) = (0.4)(50) + (0.5)(0) + (0.1)(500) = 70$$
$$E(S_3) = (0.4)(100) + (0.5)(50) + (0.1)(0) = 65$$

It can be seen that S_3 is optimal according to both the payoffs and regrets: the expected values are maximized and minimized respectively. Actually, it can be shown that, when the decision rule is simply to maximize the expected value of the regrets, the use of either criterion always yields the same optimal strategy. But when other criteria are used in the decision rule, the two matrices may yield different optimal strategies.

In some instances we might not want to choose the strategy that gives either the lowest expected value of regrets or the highest expected value of the payoff. These instances arise when some of the possible payoffs for the best strategy from the expected value criterion give either very low or negative cash flows. If the firm's financial position is such that a possible loss may be catastrophic, it may be better for the firm to select a safer strategy, which, though having a lower expected cash flow, may promise that the cash flow will be at least positive under all alternative θs. This is clearly a second-best solution. The strategies that maximize expected values of payoffs or minimize expected values of regrets will, if consistently applied, lead to higher profits on the average. It seems valid to point out that if the firm is to maximize its profits under uncertainty and risk, its financial position must be such that it can withstand occasional losses.

EVENTS AND THEIR LIKELIHOODS

This section considers some of the problems involved in determining the various events. We subdivide this section by considering first the events, and then their likelihoods.

Selecting Events. How should the analyst go about determining which of all the possible events that might occur to select as the bases for the firm's states-of-the-world? The analyst must first know enough about the forces that directly affect the parameters of the constraints – the income of the firm's customers, the actions of rivals, the prices of complementary goods, wage rates.

Sometimes the analyst could or should stop after enumerating the events that directly affect the parameters and then proceed to the problem of assigning probabilities to these events. At other times, it may be more advantageous to "trace back" along what we call "event chains" in order to select events that are somewhat removed from the direct events. Consider, for example, the general event "income of customer." It is largely determined by another event, the level of GNP, which is in turn at least partly determined by the monetary and fiscal policies of the federal government. These policies might in turn depend on whether the Republicans or Democrats control the government.

Usually a chain of events leads to the event that directly affects the parameter; thus the question arises as to whether the firm should "move back" along the chain to select the events on which to base the θs. Take, for example, the income of customers. There is a choice of using this as the "event" or instead using GNP or government policy or the political party expected to be in office.

We know of no definitive answer to the question of how far back in the "event chain" to look to select the event. Generally, the "closer" the event is to the parameters, the better. However, there may be advantages in tracing back along the chain. One major advantage stems from the possibility that many of the "direct events," when traced back, are at least partly caused by common events. Thus, the direct events "income of customers" and "prices of competitive goods" may both, in turn, at least partly depend on GNP levels. One advantage of using GNP rather than the two direct events is that the number of events to consider can be reduced. This could lead to important savings in analytical work. Another advantage may be that the interdependence of events may be more clearly seen, so that we may better know if the probability of one event is conditional on the occurrence of another event.

There is one more advantage to selecting events "back" in the event chain. Generally, the further back we go, the more likely it is that information and expert opinion will be available on the particular events. Although the firm may be most directly interested in the income of its customers, there is greater general interest in GNP, because the latter becomes the basis for so many other decisions. There are also likely to be better data and more experts working on GNP forecasting. By pushing back along the event chain, the firm can take advantage of these data and opinions. Of course, once GNP, say, is selected as the event to be used in determining the θs, the firm will still have to move from GNP to income of customers before it can estimate the impact of some level of GNP on the parameters.

Assigning Probabilities to the Events. How do we assign probabilities to the events? Unfortunately, there is no standard procedure for doing this. In practice, the assignment of probabilities is made by studies of historical data, forecasts, sampling of opinion and intentions, experimentation, and intuition. It almost goes without saying that the better the analyst understands the events and their underlying causes and the better he is informed, the better is his position for making reasonably good estimates of the probabilities.

THE USE OF HISTORICAL DATA. Historical data provide perhaps the most important basis for determining probabilities. By studying, for example, historical time series on incomes, prices, and production, it is possible to uncover seasonal patterns, cyclical movements, trends, and irregularities in the behavior of the data. We could array such data into frequency distributions and assign probabilities on the basis of the relative frequencies. For example, the year-to-year changes in GNP could be grouped into percentage classes – −2–0, 0–2, 2–4, etc. – and the number of changes counted for each class. Then, if there were, say, twenty observed changes and nine were in the class of 2–4 percent, we might conclude that the probability of a 2–4 percent GNP increase from the current year to the next is 9/20. Very much of the same type of analysis could be performed for any event for which there is a historical record. We should not rely completely on such analyses of historical data, but they yield at least credible "first order" magnitudes of the probabilities.

Generally, we would want to go further in using historical data than a simple counting of what happened in the past. Whenever past events are used to determine the probabilities of future events, there is an implicit assumption that the forces that determined events in the past will operate in the future. Thus, we would want to understand past events in terms of these underlying forces, for only if the forces can be expected to continue is it valid to use the history of past events to assign probabilities to future events. If the underlying forces are expected to change in the future, we would of course want to modify the probabilities based on past data.

TREND PROJECTIONS. Projections of trends offer another means of assigning probabilities to future events. Such projections are generally made by "fitting" some mathematical function to past data and then continuing the function into the future to give the single most likely estimate. It is usually not necessary to rely completely on the single estimate obtained from the function. Statisticians have worked out the probabilities that future events will vary from the trend line, and this information can be used to define alternative events and their probabilities.

To see some of these principles, consider Figure 13.5. In this graph a line is "fit" to the historical data and then "projected" into the future. The most likely specific event would be point *A*, which lies on the trend line. Other specific events are, however, possible, although their likelihoods will be smaller than that of *A*. A good way to proceed would be to consider *A*, *B*, and *C* the alternative specific

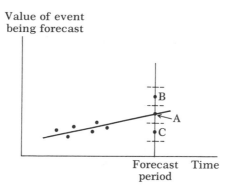

FIGURE 13.5   Estimating events by trend forecast

events, using each of these points as representative of ranges. Statisticians have devised ways of assessing the probabilities for events (here points) that depend on how far these points are from the trend-value; so it is generally not too difficult to assign probabilities to the alternative events.

We should not use these trend projections too mechanically and should be aware of the assumptions underlying this technique. There are problems in selecting the form of the curve to fit: Should it be a straight line, a second or third degree polynomial, logarithmic, exponential, asymptotic? In making such projections, there is always the assumption that the future will continue the broad patterns established in the past. This is summed up in Alfred Marshall's famous phrase, "Natura non facit saltum." "Nature does not make leaps."[3] Although we generally have to assume the truth of Marshall's dictum if we are to do much forecasting, we should realize that nature is not always obliging.

SURVEYS. Often surveys can help the analyst assign probabilities to events. Sometimes they are designed precisely for that reason. Surveys are conducted by business magazines, academic institutions, and other organizations interested in phenomena such as buying intentions and production plans. Many firms conduct their own surveys, using panels of consumers or experts, test marketing techniques, and informal polling of knowledgeable people.

Many informal sources of information are helpful for assessing the likelihood of events. Among them are contacts with political experts, economists, experts in various industries, plus simply keeping up with the news and comments of news analysts. There are no neat ways of using such informal bits of information in mathematical models to estimate probabilities. Nevertheless, the intelligent analyst takes them into account. It is important to be able to assess the

---

[3]Alfred Marshall, *Principles of Economics* (New York: Macmillan, 1961); originally published in 1890.

validity of such information and to understand how it bears on the events whose probabilities we wish to estimate.

INTUITION AND INFORMED JUDGMENT. Intuition and informed judgment also have roles to play. Executives usually have wide ranges of personal contact who together with themselves are attuned to what makes their industry prosper. Often they have a "feel" for the likelihood of many of the events that affect their firm. Indeed, to assess the probabilities of actions of rivals, executives can make a good start by asking themselves what they would do if they were in their rivals' positions.

Many scientists are naturally wary of the use of intuition and personal judgment, for there is no sure way to assess somebody else's ability to make judgments. Nevertheless, we do not hesitate to advise that the intuition and judgment of informed people be used freely in conjunction with available "objective" data to arrive at probabilities. In a world of imperfect knowledge and models, where the facts bearing on any event are generally limited and often suspect, we simply cannot afford to ignore informed judgment. There is a danger, however, that because the use of intuition and judgment is much simpler than hunting down the objective data, analysts and decision-makers may be tempted to rely completely on them.

The use of intuition in the assessment of probabilities is the subject of a lively debate among statisticians, specialists in scientific methodology, and others concerned with decision-making under uncertainty. On the one hand we have the "classicists," who have little use for intuition and who argue that we should rely only on objective data and scientific experiments (including surveys) to assess the likelihood of future events. Until the 1950s and since the pioneering days of eminent statisticians such as Gauss, Fisher, and Pearson, the classicists have dominated statistics and our notions of how to act when faced with uncertainty.

Since the 1950s there has been a wide interest in the use of intuition in conjunction with objective data to assess probabilities that in many respects is revolutionizing our ideas of knowledge and decision-making. The use of intuition with data has become known as Bayesian statistics, named for an eighteenth-century statistician and clergyman, Thomas Bayes, who did some germinal thinking on this subject. Bayesians argue that models in our minds reflect a deep familiarity with a subject and can provide an initial basis for assigning probabilities. When objective data become available, the Bayesians argue, intuitive models should not be discarded. Rather, the data should be used to *modify* the intuitive model, after which the model should be used to assign probabilities. The Bayesians suggest this approach on grounds that all objective data are subject to various errors and that informed judgment rests on many facts that cannot be formally analyzed, yet are real nevertheless.

To see how the approaches of the classicists and Bayesians differ, let us construct a problem in which a firm wishes to assess the proportion of a market that is interested in a new product under consideration. The classicists would devise a sample of, say, a hundred individuals in the market and ask whether they are interested in the product. On the basis of the percentage answering affirmatively, the classicists would infer a similar percentage for the whole market. A good statistician would not say flatly that the percentage of the whole market will be the same as that of the sample because he is aware of "sampling" errors (the sample may not be perfectly representative of the whole market, or "universe") and "observation" errors.

The Bayesian analyst would conduct the same type of survey. But he would also ask an executive familiar with the market the percentage of the market that *he thinks* would be interested in the new product. The Bayesian would then use the objective sample data in combination with the intuitive probabilities to arrive at the probabilities to assign to the various possible percentages of the market interested in the product. We do not show the formula for combining these two sources of information, not because it is complex in a mathematical sense but because a good understanding requires concepts in probability theory that we have not provided.

CONFLICT SITUATIONS

When a firm's states-of-the-world are determined not by nature but by the activities of opponents who are aware of their interdependence with the firm, we can say the firm is in a conflict situation. Because the opponent could be out to make life difficult for our firm and because "bluff," misleading information, outguessing, and subterfuge are elements in a "game" of conflict, two course of action are generally advocated; they make the game against opponents different from the game against nature. One of the action courses—really, part of the methodology—is to work on the assumption that probabilities should not be assigned to the action of rivals. The other difference lies in the decision rule: When faced with hostile opponents, the first priority of the firm should be to safeguard its minimum interests. Thus, if losses are possible, the firm should "minimax"—that is, select the strategy that minimizes its maximum loss. The corollary of the minimax decision rule, when all the payoffs are "positive," is to maximize the minimum profit. This can be called the maximin decision rule. Minimax and maximin can be viewed as conservative defensive decision rules. They are defensive in the sense that they seek to avoid catastrophe rather than maximize cash flow.

These attitudes toward the assigning of probabilities and the selection of decision rules have been advocated by students of conflict theory who have devised models of what may be called "pure" conflict. In pure conflict, we have a situation where "one man's meat is another man's poison"; any gain made by one "player" must be matched by losses to the other players. We usually apply a model known as the zero-sum game to analyze such pure conflict situations.[4] However, there can also be situations in which the conflict between rivals is not pure but partial. Partial conflict can occur when strategy combinations are possible in which all the rivals could be better off. Such cases are known as non-zero-sum games. In addition, some partial conflict situations have been somewhat neglected by students of conflict theory. The most important of these occurs when the states-of-the-world are determined by a combination of nature and the activities of recognized and interdependent rivals. Finally, some conflict situations are characterized not by the opponents simultaneously selecting their strategies but by some firms *reacting* to the strategy selected by the other firm or firms.

In the remainder of this section, we will deal with the case of pure conflict and two cases of partial conflict. We will be somewhat critical of the pure conflict model, particularly as it pertains to business problems. We will also show that some of the dicta associated with pure conflict do not readily apply to partial conflict situations.

The Zero-Sum Game. The zero-sum game, which is the pure conflict model, received its name mainly from considerations of the game of poker, which is an example par excellence of pure conflict. If, after a game of poker, the winnings are added to the losses (the latter being treated as negatives), the total is zero — hence the notion of a zero-sum game. The expression "zero-sum game" has been extended to include all conflict situations in which the "prize," or "pie," is fixed. Thus the gains and losses of the players add to zero only if we consider "not winning the prize" as a loss. Although some players do not have to actually lose whatever is gained by other players, all games in which the "pie" is fixed are characterized by "one man's meat is another man's poison," and the zero-sum game model applies.

The zero-sum game model uses the payoff matrix format, with its derivative, the regret matrix, that we have been using all along. The states-of-the-world are determined by the strategies of the opponents, and we can continue to use θ to represent these states, which by implication represent the opponent's strategies. The major difference in the format of the zero-sum game payoff matrix from the format of the other matrices is that it is not desirable to assign probabilities to the θs in the zero-sum game. This is not done because in conflict misinformation can be important; we could be misled into making the wrong probability estimates. However, after our review of the zero-

[4]The seminal work in game theory is John von Neumann and Oskar Morganstern, *Theory of Games and Economic Behavior* (Princeton: Princeton University Press, 1953). A perhaps more accessible book is D. Luce and H. Raiffa, *Games and Decisions* (New York: Wiley, 1957).

sum game model, largely in terms of an example, we will find that the nonassignment of probabilities places the zero-sum game model on a rather shaky foundation.

How do we handle the problem of the firm having more than one opponent? This is equivalent to extending what we call a two-player game to a three- (or more) player game. Actually, students of game theory have not met with much success in trying to analyze these games when there are three or more players. Instead, game theorists work on the proposition that if more than two players are in a game, the players will coalesce into two groups and the two-player game becomes the model. This view stems from the old adage of war and diplomacy: "My enemy's enemy is my friend." The terms on which the coalitions are made are called side payments; this is a specialized subject for study.

In business conflict situations, coalitions do not always form. When they do, we get the two-player game with side payments. The model firm has to concern itself with the terms of the coalition, which can be a game of its own, and the coalition's selection of a coordinated strategy. In the United States, the scope of coalitions among firms is limited, largely because the antitrust laws that govern competitive behavior prohibit the collusion necessary for forming coalitions.

How do we then proceed when there are a number of opponents, the three-or-more player game is too difficult to analyze, and coalitions are not allowed? The best approach appears to be to define the states-of-the-world as combinations of the strategies of the opponents. Thus, a company such as Ford, concerned with General Motors' and Chrysler's activities, should list GM's strategies (they could be called events and labeled E_{11}, E_{12}, etc.), Chrysler's strategies (E_{21}, E_{22}, E_{23}, etc.), and define its θs as combinations of GM and Chrysler strategies. Ford can then view itself as playing against GM and Chrysler strategy combinations. Whether Ford should consider some combinations more likely than others—in contradiction to one of the basic notions of the zero-sum game that no probabilities should be assigned—is a question that has not received adequate consideration.

We turn now to an example with which to illustrate some of the aspects of the two-player zero-sum game. Let us stipulate that two automobile dealers in a town both sell the same brand. In some particular month, both know that the number of sales will be exactly twenty. If we assume that no price competition is allowed and that each dealer has to purchase from the factory (not from inventory) all the cars he thinks he can sell that month, then the number of cars that each dealer can sell will depend on the number of cars purchased by his rival.

Let us say that the factory permits purchases only in lots of five, so that each dealer's strategies consist of buying zero, five, ten, fifteen, or twenty cars. Let us also stipulate that our firm makes $300 per car sold (the contribution to overhead and profits) but takes a loss of $200 on every car that it purchases but does not sell. (These could reflect carrying costs and having to sell the unsold cars at discount in the following month.)

How can we tell how many cars our dealer will sell? If the two dealers together purchase twenty or fewer cars, both dealers will sell all their cars. When, however, they together purchase more than twenty, there will be some unsold cars and we have to determine how the unsold cars will be distributed between the dealers. A number of assumptions can be made about this overage. One can be that the unsold cars will be divided equally. Let us adopt, however, what appears to be a more reasonable assumption: Each dealer captures a share of the market (the twenty cars) in proportion to the ratio of his purchases of cars to the purchases of both dealers. Thus if dealer 1 orders ten cars and dealer 2 orders fifteen, dealer 1's portion of the market becomes $10/25 \times 20$, or 8, and dealer 2's sales are 12. Then dealer 1 is left with two unsold cars, and dealer 2 is left with three. This assumption regarding each dealer's sales is reasonable if there is some variety in the car models, for the dealer with the larger stock (and variety) would presumably attract more customers and make more sales.

Let us now designate S_1, S_2, S_3, S_4, and S_5 the strategies for our firm, which consists, respectively, of buying 0, 5, 10, 15, or 20 cars. Let us designate θ_1, θ_2, θ_3, θ_4, and θ_5 as the similar strategies for the rival. Allowing for the possibility that the application of our assumption on the "market share" of the two dealers may sometimes lead to a fractional sale of a car (we do not make adjustment for this possibility), we can calculate the payoffs for our firm for all the possible S, θ combinations. Figure 13.6 shows the resulting payoff matrix.

This payoff matrix can be readily converted into a regret matrix, which measures the lost opportunities of not having enough cars as well as the losses of having too many, and it is shown as Figure 13.7.

We can now apply our conservative minimax and maximin decision rules to selecting a strategy on the grounds that the opponent is try-

Firm's strategies	*Opponent's strategies*				
	θ_1 (0)	θ_2 (5)	θ_3 (10)	θ_4 (15)	θ_5 (20)
S_1 (0)	0	0	0	0	0
S_2 (5)	1,500	1,500	1,500	1,500	1,000
S_3 (10)	3,000	3,000	3,000	2,000	1,333
S_4 (15)	4,500	4,500	3,000	2,000	1,300
S_5 (20)	6,000	4,000	2,667	1,700	1,000

FIGURE 13.6   Payoff matrix for zero-sum example

Firm's strategies	Opponent's strategies				
	θ_1 (0)	θ_2 (5)	θ_3 (10)	θ_4 (15)	θ_5 (20)
S_1 (0)	6,000	4,500	3,000	2,000	1,333
S_2 (5)	4,500	3,000	1,500	550	333
S_3 (10)	3,000	1,500	0	0	0
S_4 (15)	1,500	0	0	0	33
S_5 (20)	0	500	333	300	333

FIGURE 13.7 Regret matrix for zero-sum example

ing to outguess our firm and that it is not safe to assign probabilities to the opponent's actions. Thus, turning to Figure 13.6 first, we would select the strategy that maximizes the minimum profit. This is S_3, because the minimum possible profit ($1333) is higher for this strategy than the minimum possible profit for any of the other strategies. Thus, by the selection of S_3, the firm assures itself that the worst that could happen will not be too bad.

If we instead use the regret matrix, which reflects all the costs of being wrong, the conservative decision rule is to select the strategy that minimizes the maximum "loss" or "cost of being wrong." Because the maximum loss for S_5, at $500, is smaller than the maximum loss for the other strategies, we would select S_5 by this minimax rule.

Several aspects of this zero-sum game model are disturbing. The S_5 strategy that would be selected on the basis of the regret matrix does not seem to be intuitively correct. Notice what would happen if we somehow decided that θ_1, where the opponent does not order any cars, is so unlikely that it should be ignored and thus disregarded the θ_1 column. Then, by the minimax rule, S_4 would be the best strategy. Now consider what might happen if we added another strategy, S_6, in which the opponent purchases twenty-five cars. This would probably result in different strategies being selected by the minimax rule. We can of course argue that S_6 is so unlikely that it should not be considered. But then does this argument not contradict one of the cardinal principles of the zero-sum game—namely that we should not assign probabilities to the opponent's strategies? Does not the analyst implicitly assign a probability of zero to *possible* strategies that are left out of the analysis?

Evidently, the zero-sum game model has some major logical problems. The strategy selected by the minimax rule depends heavily on the definition of the opponent's strategies. Here the dilemma begins. If the analyst includes every conceivable strategy of the opponent in the model, then the selection of the firm's strategy could be influenced by the inclusion of opponent strategies that are virtually impossible of selection by the opponent. Yet, if the analyst is to decide which opponent strategies are possible, he has begun to assign probabilities, and it is hard to see why he should not continue. Because of these contradictions, it is important that the zero-sum game be strictly limited to conflict situations in which all the opponent's strategies could be defined and all are feasible of being undertaken by the opponent.

The Non-Zero-Sum Game. We are said to have a non-zero-sum game when the pie, or whatever the payoff is that is to be split between the players, is not constant. Instead, the size of the total pie would depend on the strategy combination selected by the players. The illustration in the preceding section would be converted into a non-zero-sum game if we stipulated that the number of cars that could be sold by both dealers is not constant but depends on the number of cars they stock. (Presumably, if it is known that these dealers carry large stocks, buyers from outlying areas would come to the town to shop.) Price strategies frequently are part of a non-zero-sum game. The total profit of the players is likely to be higher if all raise their prices than if one or some lower prices. However, this mutuality of interest need not guarantee that all firms would necessarily raise prices. Although the *total* payoff may be smaller if all do not raise prices, an individual's payoff could be enlarged if he does not raise his price. Firm A and firm B, for example, may make higher profits *in toto* if they both raised prices by 5 percent. However, if firm A cuts prices while firm B raises prices, firm A's profit could be higher than in the case where they both raise prices, despite a decline in the joint profit of firms A and B. (Recall the discussion on the non-zero sum game in the section on oligopoly in Chapter 9.)

Because we have both the total joint profits and the split of the profits among the players varying with the strategy combinations, the non-zero-sum game is characterized by a curious mixture of conflict and concert of interest on the part of the players. Most business situations are probably described by the non-zero-sum model. The firms find some combinations of policies that are better than others for the group of firms as a whole. Yet, there is temptation for the individual firm to adopt a strategy that gives it a better split of a lower total. Some students of conflict argue that many games thought to be zero-sum are really non-zero-sum games – diplomacy between major antagonistic powers being the most important example. Once we are convinced we are playing a non-zero-sum game, we are prepared to at least consider joint strategies in which the total payoff to the players is enhanced.

Whether a game is zero-sum or non-zero-sum frequently depends on how the players are defined. The automobile companies are in a non-zero-sum game if an increase in prices leads to higher joint profits. But if the auto-buying public is included as one of the players, the game is transformed into the zero-sum type, with the companies becoming, in effect, a coalition.

The analysis of non-zero-sum games can be complex, and there is much that we do not understand about these conflict and concert situations. As a topic the non-zero-sum game belongs in the study of oligopoly and bargaining as much as it does in the study of decision-making under risk and uncertainty.

Nature-Opponent Combinations. Perhaps the most common states-of-the-world the firm faces occur when the θs are determined by a combination of "nature's" events and activities by opponents in which the interdependence is recognized. This mixed case, where nature and opponents both determine the firm's parameters, has not received a great deal of attention in the literature dealing with conflict and decision-making under risk and uncertainty. Yet, in many ways, these mixed θ situations are easier to analyze, and decision rules easier to formulate, than the cases in which the opponent's strategies alone determine the states-of-the-world.

The mixed case is more "tractable" primarily because it is usually feasible to assign probabilities to the opponent's strategies. This is because the firm, when contemplating its rival's strategies, must consider not only the element of conflict but also the strong likelihood that nature also plays a part in inducing the adoption of certain strategies by the rivals. Consider once more the θs faced by Ford. In devising its price policy, it has to take into account both the state of the economy and the price policies of GM and Chrysler. Ford should be able to assign probabilities to the alternative states of the economy. But should it also assign probabilities to the alternative strategies of GM and Chrysler?

There is a good case for an affirmative answer to this question. Ford knows that GM and Chrysler must also formulate and adopt their strategies in the light of the events of opponents and nature. Although they may be hostile to Ford, it is unlikely that GM and Chrysler would completely aim their strategies at Ford, because the strategies aimed at making life difficult for Ford may not be very good in the light of nature's events. Knowing this, Ford could attach conditional probabilities to its rivals' activities, where these probabilities are conditioned on the occurrence of nature's events. Thus Ford might be able to make a reasonably good estimate that the probability of its rivals' raising prices in the event of a recession is very low and the probability of a price increase in the event of a boom should be much higher.

Discussion Questions

1. Compare the advantages of assessing the benefits and costs for different states-of-the world as the basis for making decisions with basing decisions on the most likely state-of-the-world.

2. What advantages does the regret matrix have over the payoff matrix as the basis of decisions?

3. How would we measure the benefits of flexibility when faced with uncertain demand?

4. Under what conditions might we want to modify the general decision rule that the best strategy maximizes the expected payoff or, alternatively, minimizes the expected regret?

5. Discuss possible pitfalls of trend projection.

6. Provide some examples of zero-sum and non-zero-sum games.

7. How should playing against "opponents" rather than against "nature" alter the firm's decision rule?

Index